AF724889

Law and Regulation of Tax Professionals

Law and Regulation of Tax Professionals

General Editors

Julian Hickey

Adrian Shipwright

Barristers of Addington Tax Chambers

With contributions by
David Bloom, Sonn Macmillan Walker solicitors
Hartley Foster, Partner, Fieldfisher LLP
George Gillham, Partner, Fieldfisher LLP
Christopher Kientzler, Barrister, Fieldfisher LLP
Mark McLaughlin CTA (Fellow), ATT (Fellow), TEP, Chartered Tax Adviser
Arun Srivastava, Partner, Paul Hastings (Europe) LLP

Bloomsbury Professional

LONDON • DUBLIN • EDINBURGH • NEW YORK • NEW DELHI • SYDNEY

BLOOMSBURY PROFESSIONAL
Bloomsbury Publishing Plc
50 Bedford Square, London, WC1B 3DP, UK
1385 Broadway, New York, NY 10018, USA
29 Earlsfort Terrace, Dublin 2, Ireland

BLOOMSBURY and the Diana logo are trademarks of Bloomsbury Publishing Plc

© Bloomsbury Professional 2021

All rights reserved. No part of this publication may be reproduced or transmitted in any form or by any means, electronic or mechanical, including photocopying, recording, or any information storage or retrieval system, without prior permission in writing from the publishers.

While every care has been taken to ensure the accuracy of this work, no responsibility for loss or damage occasioned to any person acting or refraining from action as a result of any statement in it can be accepted by the authors, editors or publishers.

All UK Government legislation and other public sector information used in the work is Crown Copyright ©. All House of Lords and House of Commons information used in the work is Parliamentary Copyright ©. This information is reused under the terms of the Open Government Licence v3.0 (http://www.nationalarchives.gov.uk/doc/open-government-licence/version/3) except where otherwise stated.

All Eur-lex material used in the work is © European Union, http://eur-lex.europa.eu/, 1998-2021.

British Library Cataloguing-in-Publication Data

A catalogue record for this book is available from the British Library.

ISBN: PB 978 1 52650 620 7
Epub 978 1 52650 621 4
EPDF 978 1 52650 622 1

Typeset by Evolution Design & Digital Ltd (Kent)
Printed and bound by CPI Group (UK) Ltd, Croydon, CR0 4YY

MIX
Paper from responsible sources
FSC® C013604

To find out more about our authors and books visit www.bloomsburyprofessional.com. Here you will find extracts, author information, details of forthcoming events and the option to sign up for our newsletters

Foreword

When I was first asked to write this foreword for the Law and Regulation of Tax Professionals my immediate thought was that the authors have been extremely clever in filling a much needed gap in the tax advisers 'bookshelf'.

To the best of my knowledge, this is the first book to bring together the many strands of the law and current guidance for UK tax professionals and agents. It is a massive team effort. The general editors are Julian Hickey and Adrian Shipwright – both hugely eminent and experienced tax barristers from Addington Chambers – ably assisted by renowned tax experts and authors David Bloom, Hartley Foster, George Gillham, Christopher Kientzler, Mark McLaughlin and Arun Srivastava.

All reputable tax advisers and agents will recognise the increasing importance of high standards of professional conduct in relation to dealing with their clients' tax affairs and providing robust advice. It is generally accepted that tax advice that purports to offer substantial and unrealistic tax savings usually turns out to be 'too good to be true'. The unfortunate consequences of this 'improbable' type of advice are only realised many years after – often involving expensive litigation, stress and sometimes heartache. Even as I write this foreword, we hear anecdotal stories of (invariably) unregulated promoters still peddling tax schemes that would not stand up to scrutiny.

Management of tax and reputational risk is now a key priority for tax advisers. Reputable tax practitioners must have a firm understanding of their professional obligations and the potential risks arising from a combination of many different facets of law. These include contract law, the law of tort (professional negligence), regulatory guidance, government directives and so on. This book offers comprehensive and practical insight on all these areas. Among its vast array of subjects, this work covers terms of engagement, professional negligence issues, specific tax reporting obligations (including DOTAS and POTAS), tax evasion, criminal investigations, anti-money laundering and general fiduciary duties.

An entire chapter is devoted to the important regulatory guidance on 'Professional Conduct In Relation to Taxation' or PCRT – which includes practical benchmarks for providing 'acceptable' tax mitigation advice. The regulation of tax lawyers and barristers is also covered here.

This impressive work brings together all these many strands of tax law and guidance which underpin the provision of tax advice and tax compliance services. Well done to Julian Hickey and Adrian Shipwright and their expert team of authors for putting together this comprehensive and highly practical book on the law and regulations covering the tax practitioner's work. I am sure that it will quickly become the 'Go To' book on all these matters.

In conclusion, I recommend that every reputable tax professional should have a copy of this book close at hand as it will deliver increasingly invaluable guidance in the current environment in which they operate.

Peter Rayney FCA CTA (Fellow) TEP
Independent Tax Consultant
March 2021

Preface

Arthur Vanderbilt[1] said:

> 'Taxes are the lifeblood of government and no taxpayer should be permitted to escape the payment of his just share of the burden of contributing thereto.'

This has become more the accepted norm in the UK with the move away from the *Duke of Westminster* approach[2] that every taxpayer can minimise their tax liabilities, and the emphasis on fairness and morality in the general tax debate and what is expected of professionals in advising on tax planning (particularly, by ensuring that it reflects the intention of Parliament).

As our tax code grows ever more complex and longer[3] issues arise for the taxpayer as to how to navigate it and to know what is the 'just share of the burden'. This has increased the need for, and reliance on, tax advisers. This is particularly the case in a self-assessment system when a view on the law may have to be taken when making a return which can raise many issues when statutes are drafted using words that are not always as clear as their meaning as might be wished[4]. This is not always an easy task for the adviser, particularly where the facts of a transaction or circumstances of a client are not always settled, if at all, until immediately prior to their implementation.

There is now a cadre of professional tax advisers and tax officials. It could be described as a profession. We have discussed in Chapter 1 how we have used the nomenclature 'tax professional', which embraces those individuals subject to the PCRT and others who also lawfully advise on tax matters. The question arises '*quis custodiet ipsos custodes*'[5], ie who regulates the tax professionals and tax advisers.

1 Arthur T Vanderbilt was an American judge and judicial reformer: see https://hyperleap.com/topic/Arthur_T._Vanderbilt.

2 *Inland Revenue Commissioners v Duke of Westminster* [1936] AC 1, 19 TC 490.

3 See www.telegraph.co.uk/finance/newsbysector/banksandfinance/6146911/UK-has-longest-tax-code-handbook-in-the-world.html.

4 See HLA Hart, Definition and Theory in Jurisprudence 70 LQR 37 (1954).

5 Juvenal, Satire VI (lines 347–348), sometimes translated as 'Who watches the watchers'. See https://en.wikipedia.org/wiki/Juvenal.

The UK does not have one tax profession (as in, say, the Netherlands[6]) but members of various professions and none[7]. It is the none that can cause issues as they are not regulated *ex hypothesis* by a professional body. In the UK, a person can set up as a tax adviser with no formal qualifications and no professional indemnity insurance. Many promoters of tax scams in the past have operated in this way through short-lived companies.

Sir Amyas Morse's independent review into the Loan Charge prompted the further consideration of the issue of the regulation of tax advisers. This has elicited further action on the part of HMRC to raise standards in the Tax Advice Market. It is likely that there will be developments in the near future. We would hope to cover these in future editions, and possibly as an e-bulletin to address these specific changes.

This prompted the logical prior question what is the current position as regards the regulation of tax advisers? A simple question but, as ever with such questions, not an easy one to answer. Julian Hickey has experience of the TDB in his practice and appeals to and from it and related matters. However, we are not aware of any publication that has sought to bring together the learning and practice as to the regulation of UK tax professionals from the perspective of English Law. This book seeks to do that on the basis of our experience and that of others together with the material available to us and consulted by us as at 1 January 2021. Chapters 1 and 2 set out the nature of the regulation, both direct and indirect, applicable to tax professionals (which is then examined throughout the book).

We are grateful to David Wright and the Publishers for undertaking this project. We are particularly grateful to our various contributors for their erudition and time in producing their particular chapters (in order of their contributions):

Mark McLaughlin CTA (Fellow), ATT (Fellow), TEP, Chartered Tax Adviser (Chapter 3: PCRT)

Hartley Foster, Partner, Fieldfisher LLP (Chapter 4: Disclosure of tax avoidance schemes)

George Gillham, Partner, and Christopher Kientzler, Barrister, Fieldfisher LLP (Chapter 7: Privilege in tax disputes)

David Bloom, Sonn Macmillan Walker solicitors (Chapter 8: Criminal investigations and prosecution)

Arun Srivastava, Partner, Paul Hastings (Europe) LLP (Chapter 10: Anti-Money Laundering)

6 Belastungadviseur. See Victor Thuronyi and Frans Vanistendael, 'Regulation of Tax Professionals', Ch 5, *Tax Law Design and Drafting* (1996), which is an interesting chapter on the various models in various countries and the need for tax advisors in a well-functioning tax system (at www.imf.org/external/pubs/nft/1998/tlaw/eng/ch5.pdf).

7 This is not to decry the CIOT and its good works of which the authors are both members.

Finally, we should thank our respective long-suffering spouses and families for their support which has enabled us to complete this edition.

We have sought to iron out as many inconsistencies, infelicities, and errors as we can, but such as remain are our own unaided work.

Use of the masculine pronoun shall be deemed to include usage of the feminine pronoun where appropriate.

We hope this work will prove to be of utility and commend itself to its users. Obviously, if in doubt, then please do feel free to contact us to discuss any problems in the area addressed by this book and beyond.

The book is dedicated to Katherine and Diana.

JJBH
AJS
General Editors
Addington Chambers, 1 January 2021
www.addingtonchambers.com

Contents

Glossary and abbreviations

AAT	Association of Accounting Technicians
ACCA	Association of Chartered Certified Accountants
AML	Anti-money laundering
ASPs	Accountancy Service Providers
ATT	Association of Tax Technicians
BSB	Bar Standards Board
CA (Crim Div)	Court of Appeal Criminal Division
CCAB	Consultative Committee of Accounting Bodies
CCO	Corporate Criminal Offence
CFA 20017	Criminal Finances Act 2017
CIOT	Chartered Institute of Taxation
CPIA 1996	Criminal Procedure and Investigations Act 1996 CPIA 1996
Client Money	Money that a firm holds or receives for or from a client
Contempt of Court	When someone risks unfairly influencing a court case
CN	Contributory negligence
CPD	Criminal Practice Directions
CPS	Crown Prosecution Service
CRA 2015	Consumer Rights Act 2015
CrimPR	Criminal Procedure Rules
Cross Border Arrangement	An arrangement concerning either more than one EU Member State or a Member State and a third country
CRS	Common Reporting Standard
DAC	EU Directive on Administrative Cooperation
DAC6	The EU Council Directive 2011/16
DOTAS	Disclosure of Tax Avoidance Schemes
DVATS	Disclosure of VAT Avoidance Schemes
EDD	Enhanced due diligence
EU	European Union
EU Member State	Member of the European Union

FA	Finance Act
FATCA	Foreign Account Tax Compliance Act
Fiduciary Duties	Responsibility to act in the best interests of another person
Fisc	The relevant Revenue authority, eg HMRC
FTT	First-tier Tribunal (Tax Chamber)
Help Sheet B	Provides guidance on the application of the PCRT
HMRC	Her Majesty's Revenue & Customs
HRA 1998	Human Rights Act 1998
ICA	Institute of Chartered Accountants
ICAEW	Institute of Chartered Accountants in England and Wales
IDPC	Initial details of the prosecution case
Implementation Period	*See* transition period
LOE	Letter of engagement
Member State	Member State of the EU
MLD	Money Laundering Directive
MLR 2017	Money Laundering, Terrorist Financing and Transfer of Funds (Information on the Payer) Regulations 2017
MLRO	Money Laundering Reporting Office
NCA	National Crime Agency
NoR	Notice of Requirement
OPBAS	Office for Professional Body Anti-Money laundering Supervision
PACE	Police and Criminal Evidence Act 1984
PCRT	Professional Conduct in Relation to Tax
PEP	Politically exposed person
POCA 2002	Proceeds of Crime Act 2002
SAR	Suspicious activity report
Services Regulation 2009	Provision of Services Regulations 2009
SGC	Sentencing Council Guidelines
SI	Statutory Instrument
SOCPA 2005	Serious and Organised Crime and Police Act 2005
SRA	Solicitors Regulation Authority
STC	Simon's Tax Cases
STEP	The Society of Trust and Estate Practitioners
TACT 2000	Terrorism Act 2000
TDB	Tax Disciplinary Board

TIN	Tax Identification Number
Transition period	The Brexit transition is the period agreed in the UK–EU Withdrawal Agreement. The transition period started immediately after the UK left the EU on 31 January 2020 and ended on 31 December 2020. The UK Government does not use the term 'transition', preferring to refer to this period as an 'implementation period'.
UCTA 1977	Unfair Contract Terms Act 1977
UTT	Upper-tier Tribunal (Chancery and Tax)
UWOs	Unexplained Wealth Orders
VAT	Value Added Tax
VATA 1994	Value Added Tax Act 1994

Table of Statutes

[*All references are to paragraph numbers*]

Table of Statutory Instruments

[*All references are to paragraph numbers*]

M

Table of Cases

[*All references are to paragraph numbers*]

J

K

N

O

P

R

S

T

Z

Chapter 1

Introduction

SIGNPOSTS

- Tax professionals and tax agents are subject to direct and indirect regulation (see **1.8–1.13** and **1.17–1.20**).
- Who is a tax professional and professional bodies imposing specific standards (ICAEW, CIOT, ATT, STEP, BSB, SRA) (see **1.10**).
- Forms of regulation (see **1.18**):
  - Tax legislation and courts imposing limits of acceptable tax planning
  - Contract law: terms of engagement
  - Tort law: professional negligence
  - Privilege: absolute obligation not to disclose unless waiver by client
  - Reporting obligations: DOTAS, DAC 6
  - AML
  - Tax offences and facilitation of tax evasion
  - Fiduciary duties, handling client money, restitution, misfeasance in public office.
- Future regulation: Raising standards in the tax advice market and next steps (see **1.21–1.29**).

OVERVIEW

1.1 The purpose of this book is to provide a detailed overview of the law and associated matters concerning the regulation of tax professionals and tax agents; and to seek to draw some practical lessons as to how tax advisers (ie those regulated by a professional body such as the Chartered Institute of Taxation (CIOT) and those who are not members of such a body) and the business they work in can organise themselves to comply with what is required by regulation, best practice and to eliminate so far as possible the consequences of errors, mistakes and unforeseen occurrences. A tax adviser will usually provide their client with tax advice on planning and/or tax services, such as preparation and filing of tax returns and associated material (referred to as tax compliance).

1.2 In the current regulatory environment and the ever-increasing scrutiny of individual, corporate and trust tax affairs, planning arrangements and investigations into possible unacceptable tax avoidance and evasion is of fundamental importance for tax advisers to understand and appreciate fully the scope of their obligations and potential liabilities arising from contract law, professional negligence (tort law), professional regulators and the government. The aim of this book is to assist in this and so assist in better compliance and risk management.

1.3 The tax adviser must be particularly vigilant to ensure that tax advice is given which correctly falls within the ambit of the applicable legislation as to the scope of any tax liability, any exception to such a liability, including the availability of any applicable relief. The regulation of tax professionals is in essence designed to ensure that only tax mitigation is adopted by clients and not tax avoidance (to the extent it is regarded as not being within the spirit of the tax legislation).

1.4 In *IRC v Willoughby and Another* [1997] STC 995 (HL), Lord Nolan drew the following distinction between tax mitigation and tax avoidance:

> 'The hallmark of tax avoidance is that the taxpayer reduces his liability to tax without incurring the economic consequences that Parliament intended to be suffered by any taxpayer qualifying for such reduction in his tax liability … Where the taxpayer's chosen course is seen upon examination to involve tax avoidance (as opposed to tax mitigation), it follows that tax avoidance must be at least one of the taxpayer's purposes in adopting that course, whether or not the taxpayer has formed the subjective motive of avoiding tax.
>
> My Lords, I am content for my part to adopt these propositions as a generally helpful approach to the elusive concept of "tax avoidance", the more so since they owe much to the speeches of Lord Templeman and Lord Goff of Chieveley in *Ensign Tankers (Leasing) Ltd v Stokes (Inspector of Taxes)* … respectively …'

1.5 If a tax adviser provides advice on matters which trespass into the category of tax avoidance, then it is necessary for the adviser to ensure that their advice is clear as to why the tax rules operate in the way which is being advised on the particular facts, and to identify why, as a matter of statutory interpretation, the rules apply to give the tax result which is being advised on. It is well established that there is no requirement for anyone to organise their commercial affairs so as to maximise his tax burden. It is therefore perfectly legitimate to organise commercial transactions in a way which minimises the tax burden. This was made clear by the House of Lords in *IRC v Brebner* [1967] 2 WLR 1001 where Lord Upjohn said:

> 'My Lords, I would only conclude my judgment by saying, when the question of carrying out a genuine commercial transaction, as this was, is considered, the fact that there are two ways of carrying it out – one by paying the maximum amount of tax, the other by paying no, or much less, tax – it would be quite wrong as a necessary consequence to draw the inference that in adopting the latter course one of the main objects is, for the purposes of the section, avoidance of tax. No commercial man in his senses is going to carry out commercial transactions except upon the footing of paying the smallest amount of tax involved.'

1.6 More recently, in the Supreme Court, Lord Neuberger stated in *Secret Hotels 2 Ltd v HMRC* [2014] STC 937 at [57]:

> '… one must be careful before stigmatising the contractual documentation as being "artificial", bearing in mind that EU law, like English law, treats parties as free to arrange or structure their relationship so as to maximise its commercial attraction, including the incidence of taxation …'

1.7 Ultimately, the crucial question for a tax adviser is to determine whether all that is proposed to be done by the taxpayer (in reliance on the adviser) in structuring his affairs to minimise the incident of taxation is permitted in a way that Parliament had intended. Often a tax adviser will be reliant on his client (or another adviser, eg a valuer or transfer pricing specialist) in determining whether the proposed transactions are commercial and/or entered into on an arm's length basis. For any tax adviser it is of fundamental importance that they understand the underlying facts (ie transactions, entities involved, etc) before advising on the tax issues (and in doing so the adviser must have up-to-date knowledge of the law). If the tax consequence from any proposed planning is not intended by Parliament and/or the transactions have been structured on an uncommercial basis, then the tax adviser and his or her client can expect the close scrutiny of those transactions and tax planning advice by the tax authorities. Such forms of planning are likely to require detailed analysis by a tax adviser, among other things, as to the scope and application of the applicable statutory provisions, what Parliament intended, anti-avoidance case law, the Disclosure of Tax Avoidance Scheme (DOTAS), Promoters of Tax Avoidance Scheme (POTAS) and DAC 6.

'TAX PROFESSIONAL' AND 'TAX AGENT'

1.8 'Tax professional' is not a term of art but is used here to cover those who provide tax advice, tax compliance and other tax-related services in the United Kingdom on UK tax and related matters. Accordingly, for the purposes of this book, references to a tax professional or tax agent includes an individual regulated by a body such as the CIOT, but the discussion in this book will also extend in most circumstances to an individual who is not regulated by such a professional body. The main point of distinction is that a professional body will impose the standards of the Professional Conduct in Relation to Taxation (PCRT) (see **Chapter 3**), which, from a client protection perspective, imposes the gold standard of what is expected from any individual advising a client on tax matters.

1.9 'Tax'[1] here is used in the ordinary sense and includes income tax, capital gains tax, corporation tax, stamp duty, stamp duty land tax, VAT, inheritance tax, customs duties, etc. Other related matters are considered where thought appropriate.

1.10 Tax professionals will include members of the CIOT, the Association of Tax Technicians (ATT), the Society of Trust and Estate Practitioners (STEP), the Institute of Chartered Accountants in England and Wales (ICAEW), the Association of Chartered Certified Accountants (ACCA), solicitors and barristers. This list is not exhaustive and intends no slight to others, including those who are not members of such organisations. It is in that sense that the phrase 'tax professional' is used here. Individuals who are members of such organisations will be subject to the PCRT (see **Chapter 3**) and HMRC's Standard for Tax Agents. Legislation relevant to tax professionals refers to 'tax agent' and 'tax adviser', and in this regard:

- *Finance Act 2012, Sch 38, Pt 1, para 2(1)–(6)* defines a tax agent as an individual who in the course of business assists other persons with their tax affairs. *FA 2012* relates to dishonest conduct by a tax agent and the imposition of penalties (see *FA 2012* at www.legislation.gov.uk);
- the *Money Laundering, Terrorist Financing and Transfer of Funds (Information on the Payer) Regulations 2017, SI 2017/692* ('the *Money Laundering Regulations*'), state that: 'a tax adviser means a firm or sole practitioner who by way of business provides material aid, or assistance or advice, in connection with the tax affairs of other persons, whether provided directly or through a third party, when providing such services' (www.legislation.gov.uk/uksi/2017/692/contents);
- the Fifth Anti-Money Laundering Directive defines a 'tax adviser' as a firm or sole practitioner who by way of business provides material aid, or assistance or advice, in connection with the tax affairs of other persons, whether provided directly or through a third party, when providing such services[2].

1.11 HMRC has published in relation to 'tax agents' the standards which such individuals are expected to meet in advising clients and in their dealing with

1 Tax is notoriously difficult to define. The legislation contains no helpful definitions. See also *Institute of Patent Agents v Lockwood* [1899] AC 347; *AG v Wilts United Dairies* (1921) 37 TLR 884; and compare *China Navigation Co v AG* [1932] 2 KB 197.

2 There is a Sixth Anti-money Laundering Directive (6AMLD). EU Member States have until 3 December 2020 to transpose 6AMLD into national law, which regulated entities must implement by 3 June 2021.

HMRC ('HMRC: the standard for agents') (referred to here as 'the Standard'). The Standard is set out at **Appendix 2**. HMRC states at para 1.1 that:

> 'These are HMRC's expectations of all individuals and businesses involved in professionally representing or advising taxpayers. The standard applies to all tax agents who transact with HMRC and to any professional who advises or acts on behalf of others in relation to their tax affairs.'

1.12 In essence, the Standard sets the following minimum expectations:

- Integrity.
- Professional competence and due care.
- Professional behaviour (comply fully with tax law and regulations);
- Standards for tax planning:
  - agents must act lawfully and with integrity at all times and expect the same from their clients;
  - tax planning should be based on a realistic assessment of the facts and a credible view of the law;
  - agents should advise their clients where there is a material uncertainty in the law, for example, if it is known that HMRC's view differs or is unknown. The risk and costs of challenge by HMRC, and any resultant court case, should be made clear to clients.
- Disclosure and transparency (any disclosure by agents to represent all relevant facts fairly).
- Advising on tax planning arrangements:
  - agents must not create, encourage or promote tax planning arrangements or structures that:
    - set out to achieve results that are contrary to the clear intention of Parliament in enacting relevant legislation;
    - are highly artificial or highly contrived and seek to exploit shortcomings in the relevant legislation.
- Professional judgement and appropriate documentation (ie keep timely notes of the rationale for judgements exercised in seeking to keep to the Standard).

1.13 'Regulation' is a wide-ranging word. The Shorter Oxford Dictionary includes in its definition 'the act of regulating or the state of being regulated'. It is the second of these alternatives that this book is mainly concerned with. This is discussed further in **Chapter 2**.

1.14 Although written with the intention of it being a continuous whole it is accepted and expected that the book will be used as a starting point in dealing with a particular issue (eg what are the duties of the adviser under his or her professional rules, what are the rights and obligations under the terms of the contract of engagement; does the individual have a disclosure obligation under DOTAS?). To help with this there is much cross reference and, to some extent, necessary repetition. This is for the convenience of the reader.

1.15 At the start of each chapter there are 'Signposts' to provide an overview for each chapter, and a summary of the important principles covered.

1.16 The structure of this book is as follows:

Chapter	*Title etc*
1	Introduction
2	Regulatory framework
3	Professional conduct in relation to taxation (PCRT)
4	Disclosure of tax avoidance schemes
5	Contract: terms of engagement
6	Negligence and the tax professional
7	Privilege in tax disputes
8	Criminal investigations and prosecution
9	Tax evasion and tax facilitation offences
10	Anti-money laundering
11	DAC 6
12	Miscellaneous forms of regulation
Appendix 1	Checklist of matters to be considered on any engagement
Appendix 2	HMRC: The standard for tax agents
Appendix 3	Solicitors Regulation Authority – Warning notice
Appendix 4	The Law Society – Guidance for solicitors advising on tax
Appendix 5	Illustrative assumptions to incorporate into a tax professional's terms of engagement

REGULATION

1.17 In general, advisers must comply with the following principles:

- meet the standards required by their governing professional body (eg the PCRT);
- adhere to the requirements of the law both as:

- to the efficacy of the tax advice given to a client; and
- to ensure that it is not negligent advice.

1.18 Broadly, the regulation of tax professionals has developed across each of the following areas:

- *Legislative regulation of tax schemes or planning* thereby controlling the scope of what any tax professional can advise a client to consider in order to mitigate tax. Tax statutes have constantly evolved to reflects changes in government policies, to remove loopholes in the tax code and to respond to the behaviour of taxpayers. In *RFC 2012 Plc (in liquidation) (formerly The Rangers Football Club Plc) v Advocate General for Scotland* [2017] UKSC 45, Lord Hodge (at para 10) commented:

  > '10. The legislative code for the taxation of income has developed over time to reflect changing governmental policies in relation to taxation, to remove loopholes in the tax regime and to respond to the behaviour of taxpayers. Such responses include the enactment of provisions to nullify the effects of otherwise successful tax avoidance schemes (or schemes which were apparently successful pending a definitive judicial determination). As a result, the legislative code is not a seamless garment but is in certain respects a patchwork of provisions. Over time, judicial decisions on the interpretation of sections of the tax legislation have assisted in clarifying the boundaries of those provisions. …'

  Parliament introduced legislation in the *Finance Act 2004* to require disclosure of tax schemes under the Disclosure of Tax Avoidance Scheme (DOTAS) rules which enables HMRC to identify and then target appropriate responses to unacceptable forms of tax planning. This has been further supplemented and amplified by the General Anti Avoidance Rule introduced by the *Finance Act 2013* (see generally: Tax avoidance: General Anti-Abuse Rule – GOV.UK, available at www.gov.uk).

- *Court regulation of 'tax schemes'* through the interpretation of tax legislation have effectively determined the limits of what a tax professional can advise a client to implement when advising on the scope of tax legislation and the interaction of tax reliefs and liabilities. However, the approach by the courts to the interpretation of tax statutes was to initially adopt a formulaic and literalist interpretation which over a period of time has moved to a purposive construction. In *RFC 2012 Plc (in liquidation) (formerly The Rangers Football Club Plc) v Advocate General for Scotland* [2017] UKSC 45, Lord Hodge (at paras 12–15) commented:

  > '12. Another, more recent, judicial development in the interpretation of taxing statutes is the definitive move from a generally literalist interpretation to a more purposive approach. This can be

traced to the speech which Lord Nicholls of Birkenhead delivered in the House of Lords in *Barclays Mercantile Business Finance Ltd v Mawson* [2005] 1 AC 684, in which he explained the true principle established in *W T Ramsay Ltd v Inland Revenue Comrs* [1982] AC 300 and the cases which followed it. As he explained (para 28), the modern approach to statutory construction is to have regard to the purpose of a particular provision and interpret its language, so far as possible, in a way which best gives effect to that purpose. In the past, the courts had interpreted taxing statutes in a literalist and formalistic way when applying the legislation to a composite scheme by treating every transaction which had an individual legal identity as having its own tax consequences. Lord Nicholls described this approach as "blinkered" (para 29). Instead, he removed the interpretation of taxing statutes from its literalist enclave and incorporated it into the modern approach to statutory interpretation which the court otherwise adopts. He stated (para 32):

> "The essence of the new approach was to give the statutory provision a purposive construction in order to determine the nature of the transaction to which it was intended to apply and then to decide whether the actual transaction (which might involve considering the overall effect of a number of elements intended to operate together) answered to the statutory description. … [T]he question is always whether the relevant provision of the statute, upon its true construction, applies to the facts as found. As Lord Nicholls of Birkenhead said in *MacNiven v Westmoreland Investments Ltd* [2003] 1 AC 311, Page 7 320, para 8: 'The paramount question always is one of interpretation of the particular statutory provision and its application to the facts of the case'."

13. Lord Nicholls (para 34) recognised two features which were characteristic of tax law. First, tax is generally imposed by reference to economic activities or transactions which exist, as Lord Wilberforce said (in *W T Ramsay*, 326) "in the real world". In the Court of Appeal in *Barclays Mercantile* [2003] STC 66, para 66, Carnwath LJ made the same point: taxing statutes generally "draw their life-blood from real world transactions with real world economic effects". Secondly, the prodigious intellectual effort in support of tax avoidance results in transactions being structured "in a form which will have the same or nearly the same economic effect as a taxable transaction but which it is hoped will fall outside the terms of the taxing statute". He continued: "It is characteristic of these composite transactions that they will include elements which have been inserted without any business or commercial purpose but are intended to have the effect of removing the transaction from the scope of the charge". The correct response of the courts was not to disregard elements of transactions which had

no commercial value. That, he said, was going too far. Instead the court had, first, to decide, on a purposive construction, exactly what transaction would answer to the statutory description and secondly, to decide whether the transaction in question did so (para 36).

14. Lord Reed in *UBS AG v Revenue and Customs Comrs* [2016] 1 WLR 1005, para 62, has helpfully summarised the significance of the new approach, which *W T Ramsay*, as explained in *Barclays Mercantile*, has brought about, in these terms:

> "First, it extended to tax cases the purposive approach to statutory construction which was orthodox in other areas of the law. Secondly, and equally significantly, it established that the analysis of the facts depended on that purposive construction of the statute."

15. In summary, three aspects of statutory interpretation are important in determining this appeal. First, the tax code is not a seamless garment. As a result provisions imposing specific tax charges do not necessarily militate against the existence of a more general charge to tax which may have priority over and supersede or qualify the specific charge. I return to this point towards the end of this judgment (paras 68–72 below). Secondly, it is necessary to pay close attention to the statutory wording and not be distracted by judicial glosses which have enabled the courts properly to apply the statutory words in other factual contexts. Thirdly, the courts must now adopt a purposive approach to the interpretation of the taxing provisions and identify and analyse the relevant facts accordingly.'

- *General law, such as contract and tort law*: each tax professional is subject to their contractual terms of engagement with a client as to the nature, content and quality of the advice to be provided, which generally ensures that a competent level of service is provided which does not fall below professional standards. If there is a breach of these terms, the client will be compensated under the law of contract. If there is no contractual protection, then the laws of negligence will compensate the person who has suffered damage in consequence of relying on the defective advice. Clearly the level of compensation will depend on the adviser being insured (and to what amount).

- *Professional standards*: each regulated tax professional referred to in this book is the subject of minimum professional standards imposed by their governing body. Failure to comply with such rules may result in financial penalties, public admonishment or even expulsion (eg see the powers of the Taxation Disciplinary Board (https://tax-board.org.uk) over tax professionals regulated by CIOT and ATT).

1.19 Further, the tax professional must also be vigilant to ensure that their services are not being exploited by a client or third party for the purposes of tax evasion (particularly, in light of recent legislation which has been introduced by the *Criminal Finances Act 2017*, which creates offences relating to the facilitation of the evasion of UK tax or, in the case of businesses with a UK connection, the facilitation of evasion of non-UK tax). A business will be liable if an employee or other associated person criminally facilitates tax evasion while acting in that capacity for the business, even if the senior management of the business was not involved or aware of what was going on. Under this legislation, advisers face the possibility of substantial financial penalties, reputational damage and possibly prison.

1.20 Further key areas of concern to advisers include the scope and application of POTAS legislation and the DOTAS legislation; as well as the impact of the *Money Laundering Regulations 2017*, and the codes of conduct of the various professional bodies.

FUTURE REGULATION: RAISING STANDARDS IN THE TAX ADVICE MARKET

1.21 The absence of a single comprehensive code regulating tax professionals and unregulated advisers in respect of devising and marketing tax schemes and/or unacceptable forms of tax planning has been the subject of criticism, and the government has consulted on whether to introduce further regulation. The criticism was made by Sir Amyas Morse in the 'Independent Loan Charge Review: report on the policy and its implementation' (December 2019) where it stated:

> 'The Loan Charge is a one-off with no prospective effect. The factors which led the government to tackle the use of loan schemes remain, including significant usage of schemes. Evidence shows that usage of loan schemes continues, with there being more first-time users in 2017–18 (over 6,000) than in any year dating back to 1998–99. To address this, and wider issues that have been raised during the Review, we are recommending the following:
>
> 16 given the one-off nature of the Loan Charge, government should explain how it will tackle loan scheme usage in the future;
>
> 17 *the government must improve the market in tax advice and tackle the people who continue to promote the use of loan schemes, including by clarifying how taxpayers can challenge promoters and advisers that may be misselling loan schemes. There should be a new strategy published within 6 months, addressing how the government will establish a more effective system of oversight, which may include formal regulation, for tax advisers;*
>
> 18 the strategy for communicating what is considered tax avoidance must be improved to reflect the "mass market2" nature of loan schemes. In

particular, HMRC should continue enhancing its usage of Pay As You Earn (PAYE) Real Time Information to communicate with taxpayers who they suspect may be engaging in tax avoidance, and proactively put taxpayers directly on notice of its view.' [Emphasis added].

1.22 In response to the *Independent Loan Charge Review*, HMRC issued *Raising standards in the tax advice market: call for evidence* (19 March 2020)[3] in which they emphasise the piecemeal nature of the regulation of tax advisers (paras 4 and 5):

'4. A partial regulatory regime operates in this market. Tax advisers who belong to a professional body are required to maintain professional competency and sign up to codes of conduct, most notably the Professional Conduct in Relation to Taxation (PCRT), although not all professional bodies incorporate the PCRT in their standards. Similarly, HMRC expects agents to adhere to the standards set out in its Standard for Agents[4] and is taking steps to ensure compliance.

5. However, anyone can set up as a tax adviser. And while they must be supervised for anti-money laundering purposes, there is no market-wide competence requirement or code of ethics except the HMRC Standard for Agents. HMRC has been discussing ways to raise standards with the profession for some time, but the issues that arise from not meeting those standards have been highlighted recently by the findings of the independent review into the loan charge.'

1.23 At paragraphs 8 and 9, HMRC set out the range of possible actions that might be taken in the area of tax adviser regulation:

'8. Given that the market is diverse and any action has the potential to impact customers and the wider economy, this call for evidence seeks evidence on the case for intervention and on potential steps that could be taken to raise standards in both the tax advice and wider tax services market and give taxpayers confidence in the quality of the advice they receive.

9. The government is asking for views on a range of potential approaches to tackling issues of poor performance in the tax advice and wider tax services market. These approaches vary from improving HMRC interventions to full regulation of the market as shown in figure 1[5].'

---

3 See https://assets.publishing.service.gov.uk/government/uploads/system/uploads/attachment_data/file/873540/Call_for_evidence_-_raising_standards_in_the_tax_advice_market.pdf.

4 See **Appendix 2**.

5 Figure 1 is illustrative only and does not represent the full range of approaches: these could be implemented singly or in conjunction.

Figure 1: the spectrum of potential approaches[5]

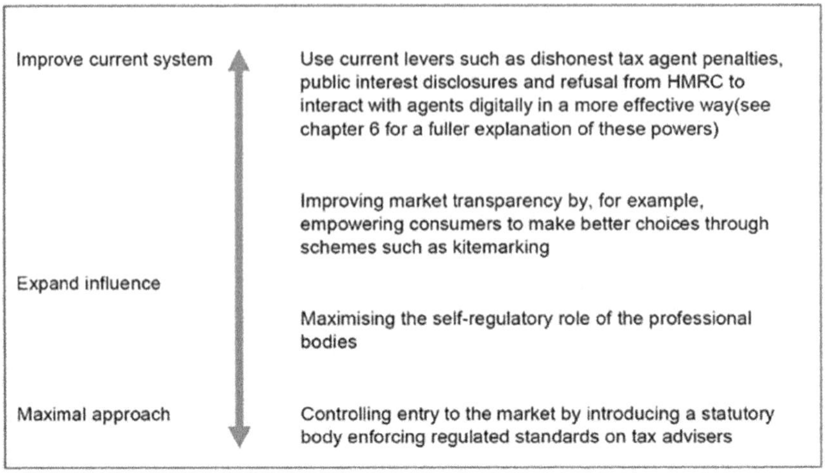

1.24 The approach adopted by HMRC in their review is as follows:

Stage 1	–	Setting out objectives and identifying options.
Stage 2	–	Determining the best option and developing a framework for implementation including detailed policy design.
Stage 3	–	Drafting legislation to effect the proposed change.
Stage 4	–	Implementing and monitoring the change.
Stage 5	–	Reviewing and evaluating the change.

1.25 At the time of publication of the document 'Raising standards in the tax advice market: call for evidence', HMRC stated they were exploring a range of future options which might be implemented on their own or in conjunction with any of the others, namely[6]:

- **Option A: Better use of HMRC's or government's current powers.** HMRC summarises its interventions in the regulation of tax advisers as follows:

  (1) HMRC has published its *Standard for Agents* (first published February 2016 and updated in January 2018), which sets out HMRC's expectations of agents to include requirements for providing advice on tax planning and make clear that HMRC expects agents to comply fully with anti-money laundering

6 See https://assets.publishing.service.gov.uk/government/uploads/system/uploads/attachment_data/file/873540/Call_for_evidence_-_raising_standards_in_the_tax_advice_market.pdf.

regulations. The Standard applies to all individuals and businesses involved in professionally representing or advising taxpayers, both those who transact with HMRC and any professional who advises or acts on behalf of others in relation to their tax affairs, located both onshore and offshore.[7]

(2) HMRC carries out direct compliance interventions that target poor adviser behaviour and competence. In HMRC's 'Raising standards in the tax advice market: call for evidence' (at para 53) it states:

'53 For example:

(a) (i) Since working with the accountancy profession to strengthen their code of conduct (Professional Conduct in Relation to Taxation) and the banking sector, the vast majority of major accountancy, legal and banking firms and others who are members of the professional bodies no longer design or sell mass marketed avoidance schemes. This leaves a smaller pool of promoters who are mainly unregulated, unlike other providers of financial services and advice.

(ii) HMRC is always looking for opportunities to disrupt promotors business model and dissuade customers from buying their schemes. Its strategy is to stop promoters from selling tax avoidance. Activity includes:

- the proportionate use of our powers (such as DOTAS and POTAS) to penalise those who enable avoidance;
- the disruption of the supply channels that promoters use to sell their products;
- proactive interventions and contact with promoters and their intermediaries;
- collaborative work with agents and intermediaries so that they help their clients to not fall into the avoidance trap;
- the mounting of criminal prosecutions where appropriate.

(b) HMRC works with tax advisers to address taxes at risk by providing educational support to help ensure the agent and their clients get their taxation affairs right

7 See HMRC: the standard for agents – GOV.UK (www.gov.uk/government/publications/hmrc-the-standard-for-agents/hmrc-the-standard-for-agents).

first time. Where errors are identified, HMRC works with the adviser to amend clients' previous returns thereby reducing the burden on the agent's customers, the agent and HMRC.

(c) Where HMRC identifies poor adviser behaviour, it aims to work in partnership with the adviser to improve standards. As part of this process, where necessary HMRC will consider a range of available powers and sanctions including Schedule 38 of the Finance Act 2012 (Tax Agents: dishonest conduct) and Section 20 of the Commissioners of Revenue and Customs Act 2005 (public interest disclosures for members of professional bodies).

(d) Where HMRC has engaged with advisers to improve standards and those standards do not improve, it will consider removal or suspension of the agent code (this allows the adviser access to HMRC online services).

(e) Compliance with the Money Laundering, Terrorist Finance and Transfer of Funds Regulations is one of the standards HMRC expects tax agents to meet. These regulations require tax advisers (among others) to carry out risk assessments of their business, identity checks on their customers (included ultimate beneficial owners of corporate entities) and ongoing reviews of transactions in order to spot suspicious activity. Any suspicious activity should be reported to the National Crime Agency.

(f) HMRC is one of 14 UK anti-money laundering supervisors whose supervised population includes paid tax agents. Its role is to ensure that all the businesses it regulates are complying with this legislation. HMRC does this by carrying out a range of interventions to test compliance. Where HMRC finds non-compliance it draws on a wide range of enforcement options to either encourage better compliance standards or hold rule-breakers to account. These options include fines, suspensions, prohibitions and prosecution. HMRC also works to ensure that all tax agents are registered for supervision with either HMRC or a professional body supervisor, and with professional body supervisors of tax agents to share best practice, align standards and ensure there is a joined-up approach to UK anti-money laundering.

(g) HMRC has identified a number of tax advisers who submit high levels of claims that have no merit. It is working closely with them to reduce the levels of these claims through education and the review of claim forms and advertising.

(h) From 1 October 2019 HMRC launched its Business Risk Review+ (BRR+) which requires the HMRC customer compliance manager (CCM) of a large tax adviser to monitor and assess whether HMRC's Standard for Agents is being met.

(i) HMRC carries out activity to look at charity agents and representatives suspected of abusing the Gift Aid repayment scheme. These activities have identified a range of inaccuracies with some relating to the agent acting dishonestly and some due to lack of due diligence or professionalism. HMRC provides education to agents on the standards it expects. HMRC works with the Charity Commission to inform charity trustees of HMRC's agent standard so that the trustees can be better informed when choosing an agent.

(j) HMRC has introduced new procedures for agents making research and development claims in amended returns with the aim of protecting companies from costly errors by low quality agents. This has restricted the ability of 'specialist' agents, often working on a 'no win no fee' basis, to submit poor claims without the knowledge of the company or authorised corporation tax agent.

(k) Access to HMRC digital systems is only permitted for agents who can demonstrate that they fulfil certain criteria such as that they are supervised for anti-money laundering purposes, have a UK address, and an HMRC agent reference number.

(l) Other interventions that HMRC has available include:

- for the most extreme cases, usually when a criminal prosecution has taken place, the power to refuse to deal with an adviser at all. The agent will have engaged in persistent unacceptable behaviour, or behaviour which is a significant threat to the Exchequer

- dishonest tax agent penalties, imposed on an agent who has engaged in dishonest behaviour. This can mean a penalty of up to £50,000
- where an agent is a member of a professional body and their behaviour breaches professional body misconduct rules, HMRC can make a public interest disclosure to the professional body for that body to carry out its disciplinary process as appropriate
- promoters of tax avoidance schemes legislation, which allows HMRC to deal with promoters by firstly issuing a conduct notice. If that is breached HMRC can apply to a tribunal for a monitoring notice. This means the adviser is monitored and is subject to extra reporting requirements, penalties and their name may be made public
- the use of existing criminal offences such as being knowingly involved in fraud or evasion of tax, including aiding and abetting, as well as the use of money laundering offences, against both individuals and companies where there is evidence to do so.

54. Other parts of government and local authorities also play a role in maintaining and improving standards. For example:

- Advertising Standards Authority (ASA). HMRC will refer tax advisers to the ASA who are suspected of false advertising
- Trading Standards. Consumers are able to refer poor advisers to their local trading standards authority in certain circumstances, such as if there are unfair trading practices
- Some accountancy professional bodies have agreed to be overseen for accountancy by the Financial Reporting Council. If a consumer is unhappy with one of these professional body's handling of a complaint they can complain to the FRC who can review the handling of the complaint. The FRC cannot overturn the result, however in circumstances which meet a high public interest and misconduct threshold the FRC can undertake its own investigation. The FRC is due to be replaced by a new regulator the Audit, Reporting and Governance Authority (ARGA).'

- **Option B: improve rights of recourse for consumers** (paras 75 to 78). HMRC state consideration could be given to setting up an independent complaints or arbitration process such as a tax advice ombudsman, which would be an independent body to which a person can complain and seek redress. HMRC also comment that another way of ensuring consumers have access to redress would be to require all tax advisers to have professional indemnity insurance before they could operate.
- **Option C: Improving transparency – helping consumers to make better choices** (paras 79 and 80). HMRC comment that standards would be raised through consumer choice facilitated by providing consumers with information so that they can choose a trustworthy adviser (such as by a government-endorsed scheme such as Trustmark, or a method of 'kitemarking' good agents could be developed as is carried out in Australia and New Zealand).
- **Option D: Penalties for tax advisers** (paras 81 to 83). HMRC comment that the tax system is designed so that accountability lies with the taxpayer, whether or not an adviser has been used. HMRC comment that one option may be the levying of penalties on the adviser instead or, or in addition to, the client.
- **Option E: maximising the regulatory/supervisory role of current professional bodies** (paras 84 to 86). HMRC comment that one option which could meet the objectives for reform would be to introduce a legal requirement for anyone who wants to provide tax advice on a commercial basis to belong to a recognised professional body. In this regard, legislation could set out the criteria by which a professional body would be recognised as providing the necessary high standards for inclusion. Criteria for recognition could include:
  - the organisation has an independent regulatory disciplinary process;
  - the organisation has a public interest function;
  - the organisation carries out assurance of the fitness to practise of its members;
  - there is appropriate governance, so that regulatory functions and representative functions are separate;
  - members must be required to demonstrate professional competence either through a relevant qualification or through many years' experience;
  - all members in practice must have professional indemnity insurance;
  - all members in practice are required to undergo continuing professional development (CPD);
  - the professional body is an anti-money laundering supervisor.

- **Option F: External regulation** (paras 87 to 90). HMRC comment that a further option would be to require anyone who wanted to provide tax advice by way of business to register with a government regulator before they could operate in the market. HMRC set out some of the criteria that might be imposed, such as advisers could be required to satisfy a fit and proper person test in order to register, and this test could include provisions such as:
  - possessing relevant qualifications or length of professional practice;
  - having professional indemnity insurance;
  - being registered for AML supervision;
  - not having been subject to a penalty for promoting or enabling tax avoidance;
  - up to date with their own tax affairs;
  - up to date with responsibilities as a company director, ie was not an undischarged bankrupt or a disqualified director;
  - not having been expelled by a professional body for misconduct.

HMRC comment that advisers who were admitted to the register could be subject to regular reviews of their continuing fitness and propriety, with appropriate enforcement action taken against those that breach standards.

1.26 The following submissions by various professional bodies in response to HMRC's 'Call for evidence on Raising standards in the tax advice market' can be accessed as follows:

- **CIOT**: www.tax.org.uk/sites/default/files/200825%20Raising%20standards%20in%20the%20tax%20advice%20market%20-%20CIOT%20response.pdf
- **ICAEW:** www.icaew.com/-/media/corporate/files/technical/icaew-representations/2020/icaew-rep-45-20-response-to-the-call-for-evidence-on-the-tax-services-market.ashx?la=en
- **ATT:** www.att.org.uk/sites/default/files/file_uploads/200806-ATT-Response-to-Call-for-evidence-on-Raising-standards-in-the-tax-advice-market.pdf
- **STEP:** www.step.org/sites/default/files/2020-08/STEP_response_to_HMRC_Call_for_Evidence_Raising_standards_in_the_tax_advice_market.pdf
- **TDB:** https://tax-board.org.uk/wp-content/uploads/2020/06/Raising-Standards-TDB-response-final-270520.pdf

- **Law Society of England & Wales:** www.lawsociety.org.uk/campaigns/consultation-responses/raising-standards-in-the-tax-advice-market-call-for-evidence
- **PCRT Group of Professional Bodies:** www.step.org/sites/default/files/media/files/2020-08/STEP_PCRT_Group_joint_response_to_standards_call_for_evidence_27082020.pdf

1.27 In November 2020, HMRC published 'Raising standards in the tax advice market – Summary of responses and next steps'[8] where they set out their view on the current position and next steps for the regulation of tax advisers. The nature of the current problem in the regulation of tax advisers is identified as follows (at p 8):

> 'The government wants to ensure that tax advice is competent, professional and trustworthy. The call for evidence into raising standards in the tax advice market has opened a conversation about how to tackle the problem, highlighted in the independent review of the loan charge, that the tax advice market is not working as well as it should be. Taxpayers are in many cases receiving advice that subsequently leaves them open to substantial tax bills and while responsibility for their tax affairs remains with the individual taxpayer, the government recognises that it can be hard for a taxpayer, faced with a complex and fragmented tax advice market, to know what advice to trust.'

1.28 In order to raise standards, the following steps will be taken by the government:

(1) Raise awareness of the Standard[9] and review HMRC powers to enforce the Standard.

(2) Consult on a requirement for professional indemnity insurance to be held by advisers. In this regard, HMRC comment (at p 9):

> 'HMRC believes that there are many potential benefits to this:
>
> - it would allow market forces to drive up standards including potentially removing from the market those advisers who were unable, as a result of riskier practices, to get insurance;
> - it would enable clients of unaffiliated advisers to have a method of redress should things go wrong and therefore improve taxpayer protection;

8 See HMRC's 'Raising standards in the tax advice market: Summary of responses and next steps', November 2020: available at https://assets.publishing.service.gov.uk/government/uploads/system/uploads/attachment_data/file/934614/Raising_standards_in_the_tax_advice_market_-_summary_of_responses_and_next_steps.pdf.

9 HMRC: the standard for agents – GOV.UK (www.gov.uk/government/publications/hmrc-the-standard-for-agents/hmrc-the-standard-for-agents.

- initial costs to those already subject to some form of oversight, such as professional body members, and members of other regulated professions, such as financial advisers, are likely to be minimal.'

(3) Work collaboratively with Professional Bodies. In this regard, HMRC will work in partnership with adviser professional bodies to understand the role they play in supervising and supporting their members and raising standards in the profession.

(4) Tackle high costs to consumers of claiming tax refunds. In this regard, the government states it is concerned about the cost to taxpayers of advisers who are claiming tax refunds on their behalf.

The government comments (at pp 9 and 10) that these next steps:

> '… will significantly move the market towards the desired outcomes as outlined in the call for evidence:
>
> - market transparency, so that taxpayers have the information they need to choose an adviser that meets their need, and are able to steer clear of unsuitable providers;
> - that taxpayers who want to engage a tax adviser are able to access reliable advice from an appropriately competent professional who maintains high ethical standards;
> - that market access is preserved so that taxpayers can continue to get reliable advice should they wish to;
> - enhanced tax compliance.'

1.29 It is beyond the scope of this book to comment on HMRC's 'call for evidence' and next steps at this point in the consultation process. Any proposals by government in this area will be included in subsequent printed editions. An electronic update specific to HMRC's next steps in the form of proposed and final legation once available can be accessed at: tinyurl.com/HMRC-RSTAMO. See also **3.16** below.

Chapter 2

Regulatory framework: an outline

SIGNPOSTS

- Introduction: tax agent and tax professional (see **2.1**).
- Forms of regulation: direct and indirect regulation (see **2.2–2.14**).
- Regulation and the law of obligations (see **2.15–2.20**).
- Limits of regulation: 'Statute of Limitations' (see **2.21–2.23**).
- Contract: rights and obligations under terms of engagement (see **2.24–2.27**).
- Tort: professional negligence and competence (see **2.28–2.30**).
- Other claims: breach of fiduciary duties, misfeasance in public office (see **2.31**).
- *Criminal Finances Act 2017* (see **2.33**).
- Risk management (see **2.49–2.62**).
- Checklist (see **2.109**).

INTRODUCTION

2.1 This chapter provides a broad outline of how tax professionals are regulated. This is intended to provide an overview at a high level of the regulatory framework and give a setting for what follows in the rest of this book. Where appropriate, cross-references are made to other chapters of this book where particular matters are dealt with in more detail.

2.2 Regulation in this context includes control of activities (tax services), imposition on a tax professional of duties and obligations and liability to others, whether to an individual, business or tax authority.

2.3 Profession and Professional are words that are commonly used but depend on the context in which they are used for their meaning. This meaning can change over time. Even in tax this is true. The case law illustrates this point[1].

2.4 For example, the Special Commissioners (the predecessor to the First-tier Tribunal (Tax Chamber)) held that the business of an income tax repayment agent was not a profession. The Court of Appeal unanimously upheld their decision in *Currie v CIR, CA 1921,* 12 TC 245, [1921] 2 KB 332. The Special Commissioners held that the business of an insurance broker was not a profession, and the Court of Appeal unanimously upheld their decision in *Durant v CIR, CA 1921,* 12 TC 245, [1921] 2 KB 332. It is an interesting question whether, on the current state of the authorities, a management consultant or an estate agent (both of whom can give tax-related advice) are professionals. The author has experience of HMRC accepting that they are. HMRC has published its own standard for Tax Agents (see 'HMRC: The standard for agents' at www.gov.uk and reproduced at **Appendix 2**), and as discussed in **Chapter 1**, a tax agent is identified as:

> '… all individuals and businesses involved in professionally representing or advising taxpayers. The standard applies to all tax agents who transact with HMRC and to any professional who advises or acts on behalf of others in relation to their tax affairs.
>
> HMRC's aim is to clarify what is expected of agents, particularly those who are not members of professional bodies.'

Any tax agent who is not a professional adviser will be subject to the general law as it applies to a professional tax adviser (such as the laws of contract relating to terms of engagement, and professional negligence as to the standard of service to be provided). Obviously, there is a material difference between the non-professional and professional tax adviser because the latter is subject to the ethical rules and regulation of the PCRT (as discussed in **Chapter 3**).

2.5 Tax Professionals also need to be aware of the impact of the *Consumer Rights Act 2015* and the *Provision of Services Regulations 2009, SI 2009/2999,* which impose obligations on professionals and limit the ways in which they can conduct themselves. These are discussed in **Chapter 5**.

2.6 HMRC Officers, as tax professionals, are also subject to regulation both within the Civil Service and as individuals where, for example, they are members of a Professional Organisation such as the CIOT. Misfeasance in Public Office is an old common law offence and tort that has come back into fashion. The Law Commission has published a background paper and has concluded a final report[2]. It can also be a tort or civil wrong, see

1 Compare *IRC v Maxse* (1919) 12 TC 41; *Carr v IRC* [1944] 2 All ER 163; *Davies v Braithwaite* [1931] 2 KB 628.

2 See the final report at www.lawcom.gov.uk/project/misconduct-in-public-office.

https://s3-eu-west-2.amazonaws.com/lawcom-prod-storage-11jsxou24uy7q/uploads/2016/01/apb_tort.pdf. This is not considered further in this book.

2.7 Fiduciary duties (ie a duty to act in the interests of another person), particularly for solicitors, can also impose a form of regulation – see *Nocton v Lord Ashburton* [1914] AC 932 (see also **Chapter 12**). It was used to claim damages for a solicitor's negligence before the development of the general tort of negligence. It is sometimes cited and used in more recent cases, see, eg *Target Holdings Ltd v Redferns* [1995] UKHL 10.

TYPES OF REGULATION

2.8 The regulation in question here can be direct or indirect. In both cases it can lead to a change in a tax professional's behaviour so as to minimise the risk of the tax system being exploited, and also to protect the tax professional from the unrealistic expectations of some clients as to what can be achieved by tax planning. This is discussed below under 'Risk management' at **2.49**.

2.9 Direct regulation tends to be enforced by specific regulators (eg The Law Society, CIOT, STEP) whereas indirect regulation tends to be enforced by the client or other persons affected by the advice and associated matters provided by the professional.

As to direct regulation, this is discussed in depth in **Chapter 3** (particularly in the context of the PCRT) and, as to indirect regulation, this is discussed in **Chapter 5** (contract), **Chapter 6** (professional negligence) and **Chapter 12** (miscellaneous matters). Direct regulation imposed by Parliament is discussed in **Chapter 4** (DOTAS/POTAS), **Chapter 9** (facilitation of tax evasion), **Chapter 10** (AML), **Chapter 11** (DAC 6).

Direct regulation

2.10 Direct regulation is often prior to any provision of services and preventative. As discussed in **Chapter 1**, direct regulation in the provision of tax services takes the form of legislation which imposes the liability to a particular tax, together with any exceptions and reliefs to tax. The tax legislation sets out the scope and limitations of what a tax adviser can legitimately advise their clients on in order to structure their personal and business interests to minimise tax. The courts then interpret the legislation which itself imposes boundaries on what is acceptable tax planning. It is beyond the scope of this book to comment in detail on the scope of direct regulation arising under all the different forms of taxation. However, the following sections set out a number of core principles arising from the tax legislation and how it is to be interpreted since every tax professional must ensure they are correctly interpreting the tax legislation and how it applies in the particular circumstances of their clients. Direct regulation can take the form of legislation, eg as to who, and on what basis legal services can be provided – the *Legal Services Act 2007, s 1* sets out the regulatory objectives[3].

2.11 Direct regulation includes:

- professional qualification;
- continuing professional development (CPD) (ie having up-to-date knowledge);
- insurance requirements;
- information disclosure (LoE);
- reserved and regulated activities (LSA FiSMA);
- anti-money laundering (AML);
- the *Criminal Finances Act 2017*;
- EU General Data Protection Regulation (GDPR);
- legislation (General Anti-Abuse Rule (GAAR), DOTAS, POTAS), the tax regime and court cases determining the limits of acceptable planning;
- privilege (which limits the information that an adviser can disclose to a third party outside of the client/adviser relationship)[4].

2.12 The general criminal law also provides some regulation of behaviour, particularly by way of deterrence. A solicitor running away to Brazil with client funds would commit several criminal offences. The regulation of client accounts is to some extent a preventative measure against this. The 1907 amendment to the *Larceny Act* illustrates this (see the American Bar Association's History of Client Protection Rules). This Criminal Law Regulation includes the *Criminal Finances Act 2017* outlined below and discussed in depth in **Chapter 9**.

---

3 The regulatory objectives (1) In this Act a reference to 'the regulatory objectives' is a reference to the objectives of:
(a) protecting and promoting the public interest;
(b) supporting the constitutional principle of the rule of law;
(c) improving access to justice;
(d) protecting and promoting the interests of consumers;
(e) promoting competition in the provision of services within subsection (2);
(f) encouraging an independent, strong, diverse and effective legal profession;
(g) increasing public understanding of the citizen's legal rights and duties;
(h) promoting and maintaining adherence to the professional principles.

4 Privilege is a common law protection for a client to ensure that legal advice is obtained without fear of disclosure (ie to facilitate access to justice) and an obligation that is imposed on a lawyer preventing disclosure of such advice to ensure that full and frank communications are made between client and lawyer. The different forms of privilege, Legal Advice Privilege and Litigation Privilege are discussed in **Chapter 7**.

Indirect regulation

2.13 Indirect regulation is often after the event and tends to be compensatory where things have gone wrong and standards have not been met. This potential liability can have a deterrent effect and regulate a professional's behaviour partly because of the desire to be compliant and partly because of the reputational risk and impact on the professional's business if found non-compliant.

2.14 Indirect regulation includes:

- reputational risk (**Chapter 3**);
- contractual liability (**Chapter 5**);
- law of negligence (**Chapter 6**);
- *Criminal Finances Act 2017* (**Chapter 9**);
- anti-money laundering (**Chapter 10**);
- restitution (**Chapter 12**).

REGULATION AND THE LAW OF OBLIGATIONS

General

2.15 In England, Obligations Law commonly refers to the study of the laws of contract, torts and restitution – the principal (but not sole) sources of civil liability[5]. These are essentially private law matters governing relationships between persons. This approach is derived from Gaius and Justinian, the great Roman Law jurists. Tort is called 'delict' in Scottish usage, a Roman Law term.

2.16 The law of contract and of tort developed mainly under the Common law in England and was essentially a 'cash' system giving its remedy in damages. This is reflected in the different objectives Contract and Tort law seek to achieve[6].

2.17 Contract law seeks to put the consumer (ie the claimant) in the position the claimant would have been in had the contract (ie that formed by the letter and acceptance of engagement, etc) been properly performed. For authority on this, see eg *Addis v Gramophone* [1909] AC 488 and *The Liesbosch* [1933] AC 449, and *Morris-Garner and Another v One Step (Support) Ltd* [2018] UKSC 20 (at 31).

2.18 Tort damages (eg for professional negligence) seek to put the claimant in the position the clamant would have been in had the tort not been committed

5 See https://libguides.bodleian.ox.ac.uk/law-oblig.

6 For a case illustrating the difference between recovery in tort and contract, see *Wemyss v Karim* [2016] EWCA Civ 27. See also *Wellesley Partners LLP v Withers LLP* [2015] EWCA Civ 1146.

(see *Morris-Garner and Another v One Step (Support) Ltd* [2018] UKSC 20 at 25–31). In other words, the claimant is compensated by being put in the position he would have been in if the advice had not been negligent.

2.19 Damages are something in a successful claim the defendant professional has to pay. This is the is the reason many professionals carry professional indemnity insurance. The insurer's requirements can also regulate the behaviour of the professional, eg acting or not for US clients (ie because the award for damages in the US may be high and punitive).

2.20 The legal burden of proving the case for breach of contract and/or tort is usually on the claimant (to the civil standard of proof, which is on the balance of probabilities). Evidence is then a crucial matter, and particularly contemporaneous evidence of events. Third party written objective evidence, which is corroborated, is usually the best but can often be hard to find several years after the event. The practice of producing and retaining a 'Bible' of documents has much to commend it; together with ensuring that an electronic archive is maintained (obviously, in accordance with the requirements of GDPR). Reliance on witness evidence has its limitations, particularly where there has been a material passage of time, such as those identified by Leggatt J (as he then was) in *Gestmin SGPS SA v Credit Suisse* [2013] EWHC 3560 (Comm), in particular, the following:

> '18. Memory is especially unreliable when it comes to recalling past beliefs. Our memories of past beliefs are revised to make them more consistent with our present beliefs. Studies have also shown that memory is particularly vulnerable to interference and alteration when a person is presented with new information or suggestions about an event in circumstances where his or her memory of it is already weak due to the passage of time.
>
> 19. The process of civil litigation itself subjects the memories of witnesses to powerful biases. The nature of litigation is such that witnesses often have a stake in a particular version of events. This is obvious where the witness is a party or has a tie of loyalty (such as an employment relationship) to a party to the proceedings. Other more subtle influences include allegiances created by the process of preparing a witness statement and of coming to court to give evidence for one side of the dispute. A desire to assist, or at least not to prejudice, the party who has called the witness or that party's lawyers, as well as a natural desire to give a good impression in a public forum, can be significant motivating forces.
>
> …
>
> 22. In the light of these considerations, the best approach for a judge to adopt in the trial of a commercial case is, in my view, to place little if any reliance at all on witnesses' recollections of what was said in meetings and conversations, and to base factual findings on inferences drawn from the documentary evidence and known or probable facts. This does not mean that oral testimony serves no useful purpose – though its utility is often

disproportionate to its length. But its value lies largely, as I see it, in the opportunity which cross-examination affords to subject the documentary record to critical scrutiny and to gauge the personality, motivations and working practices of a witness, rather than in testimony of what the witness recalls of particular conversations and events. Above all, it is important to avoid the fallacy of supposing that, because a witness has confidence in his or her recollection and is honest, evidence based on that recollection provides any reliable guide to the truth.'

'STATUTE OF LIMITATION'

2.21 There are time limits within which claims must be brought provided by the Statute of Limitation – which is now the *Limitation Act 1980*.

2.22 For contract claims the time limit is generally six years from 'the date on which the cause of action accrued'[7].

2.23 For tort claims, generally, a claim must be issued within six years of the date on which the negligence occurred. However, if the claimant did not know about the loss (known as latent damage), then the time limit is three years from the date that knowledge was acquired. There is a 15-year long stop date[8].

CONTRACT

2.24 A contract is broadly an agreement between two or more parties that a court will enforce. Thus, there may be a letter of engagement between a tax professional and the client. The Professional Body may make recommendations as to this, particularly as regards content[9].

2.25 A contract is usually enforceable only by the parties to the contract or, as it is sometimes said, by those who are 'privy' to it. This seems to follow from the idea that in English law terms the contract was a bargain that only those who were a party to the bargain could enforce it. Bargain Theory is not so prominent these days but had considerable influence on English Contract law. Civilian systems are more concerned with the promises or 'causa' but reach a similar outcome.

7 See *Limitation Act 1980, s 5.*

8 See *Limitation Act 1980, ss 14A, 14B.*

9 See, for example: SRA – www.sra.org.uk/solicitors/guidance/ethics-guidance/client-care-letters; BSB (public access) – www.barstandardsboard.org.uk/uploads/assets/20f0db2a-a40c-4af9-95b1b9557ad748e9/Public-Access-Guidance-for-Lay-Clients.pdf) and as to the regulaton of a barrister, see the BSB Handbook (Version 4.5) –www.barstandardsboard.org.uk/uploads/assets/de77ead9-9400-4c9d-bef91353ca9e5345/5e4e495f-84b7-4655-b95a729980c5346c/second-edition-test31072019104713.pdf; CIOT ATT – www.tax.org.uk/professional-standards/professional-standards-%E2%80%93-full-listing/engagement-letters.

2.26 The position on privity has been modified by the *Contracts (Rights of Third Parties) Act 1999*[10]. The Act is regularly excluded in written contracts. In these circumstances, a third party will only be able to claim loss under the tort of negligence provided that a duty of care is imposed between the person who has given advice and the third party (which turns on whether loss to such a third party was reasonably foreseeable).

2.27 For there to be an enforceable contract, writing is not usually required in the context under consideration here, although it can be for some contracts, eg contracts for the sale of land in England. However, a written contract provides proof of the terms of the contract and is common usage for professionals and is a way in which the Law of Obligations affects the behaviour of professionals. Any tax professional who is a member of a professional body will be expected to have written terms of engagement with their client. Any provider of tax services should ensure, as a matter of good practice, that they have a contract with their client which precisely sets out the terms, and the parties respective rights and obligations (and reflects the requirements/guidance of their professional body)[11]. This is discussed in depth in **Chapter 5**.

TORT

Introductory

2.28 Tort law can provide compensation for professional negligence.

2.29 Professional negligence takes place broadly when a professional does not perform his or her professional duties to the level required of a reasonably competent practitioner in that profession. This kind of claim can be made against professionals, such as financial advisers and financiers, accountants, auditors, solicitors, independent financial advisers, tax advisers or agents, surveyors, and insurance brokers. This is discussed in depth in **Chapter 6**.

Elements in professional negligence

2.30 To establish professional negligence there are four necessary elements which usually have to be established. These are as follows:

(1) *A Duty of care*

Normally, a professional owes a duty of care to the client engaging them. The issue then is how much wider the duty goes. Does it cover the position of a person not privy to the contract? At one time, following *Anns v Merton* [1978] AC 728, a wide foreseeability test seemed to

10 See **Chapter 5** at **5.123**.

11 For example, the CIOT guidance is available at www.tax.org.uk/professional-standards/professional-standards-%E2%80%93-full-listing/engagement-letters.

be emerging. However, the House of Lords moved away from this in cases such as *Murphy v Brentwood DC* [1991] 1 AC 398, particularly for economic loss. Generally, economic loss (ie having to pay tax, interest and penalties) is likely to be the matter claimed for against a tax professional.

An approach often adopted these days is that of Lord Bridge in *Caparo Industries Plc v Dickman* [1990] 2 AC 605. This is a three-stage test for imposing a duty of care broadly under which the claimant must establish that:

(i) harm was reasonably foreseeable;

(ii) there was a relationship of proximity; and

(iii) it is fair, just and reasonable to impose a duty of care.

(2) *Breach of duty*

It is necessary to show that there was a breach of the duty of care where the duty has been established.

This requires it to be shown that the professional fell below the standards of a reasonably competent professional, having regard to the usual standards of that particular profession. Error is not necessarily enough to amount to negligence (eg *Thomas and Another v Triodos Bank NV* [2017] EWHC 314 (QB), cf HL).

(3) *Causation*

To be recoverable, the loss must be shown to have been caused by the breach of duty. In other words, the loss must have been caused by the negligence. Thus, a claim would not succeed if the loss would have occurred regardless of the negligence. Often the rule of thumb is to ask whether the loss would have occurred 'but for' the negligence? However, although this is a useful approach, it is too simplistic for many cases.

(4) *Loss*

The loss must be proved by the claimant on the civil standard of proof (ie on the balance of probabilities). As noted above, Tort damages seek to put the claimant back into the position he or she would have been in but for the negligence. The cases illustrate that the loss must have been reasonably foreseeable. This can be difficult as the cases conflict, eg as to whether furnace oil on seawater was combustible (see *The Wagon Mound* case)[12]. Much depends on the particular circumstances of the case, especially if there is a claim for a lost opportunity. Claimants have a

12 The full name of this landmark case is *Overseas Tankship (UK) Ltd v Morts Dock and Engineering Co Ltd (Wagon Mound No 1)* [1961] UKPC 2, [1961] AC 388; *Overseas Tankship (UK) Ltd v The Miller Steamship Co (Wagon Mound No 2)* [1966] UKPC 10, [1967] AC 617.

duty to mitigate their losses and to take reasonable steps to do so, where possible. This needs careful consideration.

There are also a number of defences including 'contributory negligence' by the claimant, which will limit or possibly extinguish any liability to pay damages.

OTHER CLAIMS

2.31 **Chapter 12** explains in overview other possible claims which may be relevant to tax professionals, their client and third parties. The miscellaneous matters covered are:

- restitution;
- breach of statutory duty;
- HMRC Officers: misfeasance in public office;
- HMRC negligence: *Neil Martin v Commissioners for HMRC* [2007] EWCA Civ 1041; and
- vicarious liability for employees.

REGULATION AND PRIVILEGE

2.32 Any tax professional who is a lawyer will be subject to their client's privilege that all legal advice and associated communications with the client cannot be disclosed (see **Chapter 7**). Legal professional privilege is a fundamental right of the client whose privilege it is. Generally, privileged documents cannot be ordered to be provided in respect of an HMRC enquiry or litigation by the party whose privilege it is, unless this is as a result of a waiver. The fact that such documents might be highly relevant does not entail their production. Accordingly, a tax professional who is a legal adviser is under an absolute obligation not to disclose any privileged communications without waiver of privilege (see *DAC Beachcroft LLP v HMRC* [2018] UKFTT 502 (TC) where HMRC were refused access to certain documents in respect of a third-party information notice issued under the *Finance Act 2008, Sch 36*).

Legal privilege does not apply to non-lawyers (ie accountants and tax advisers who are not lawyers acting as such).

CRIMINAL FINANCES ACT 2017

2.33 The *Criminal Finances Act 2017* is wide-ranging legislation which received Royal Assent on 27 April 2017. It introduced criminal offences in respect of the criminal facilitation of tax evasion, which came into force on 30 September 2017. The Act also introduced Unexplained Wealth Orders. The Act is in addition to existing legislation such as POCA.

This is discussed in depth in **Chapter 9**.

2.34 The 2017 Act, which is in four parts, broadly applies to the whole of the UK[13].

2.35 Part 3 of the Act creates two new corporate offences of failure to prevent facilitation of tax evasion. This is discussed in depth in **Chapter 9**.

2.36 These offences apply to a 'relevant body'[14]. This is any corporation or partnership.

Only relevant bodies can commit the new offences. They cannot be committed by an individual.

2.37 The Act provides[15] that a person 'acts in the capacity of a person associated with a relevant body' where the person is:

- an employee acting in that capacity;
- an agent acting in that capacity; or
- any other person who performs services for or on behalf of that relevant body and acts in the capacity of a person performing such services.

FAILURE TO PREVENT FACILITATION OF UK TAX EVASION OFFENCES

2.38 *Section 45* of *CFA 2017*, 'Failure to prevent facilitation of UK tax evasion offences' creates the offence of corporate failure to prevent the facilitation of tax evasion in relation to UK taxes:

> '(1) A relevant body (B) is guilty of an offence if a person commits a UK tax evasion facilitation offence when acting in the capacity of a person associated with B.
>
> (2) It is a defence for B to prove that, when the UK tax evasion facilitation offence was committed:
>
> (a) B had in place such prevention procedures as it was reasonable in all the circumstances to expect B to have in place, or
>
> (b) it was not reasonable in all the circumstances to expect B to have any prevention procedures in place.
>
> (3) In subsection (2) "prevention procedures" means procedures designed to prevent persons acting in the capacity of a person associated with B from committing UK tax evasion facilitation offences.

---

13 Annex C to the Explanatory Notes provides a summary of the position regarding territorial extent and application in the UK.

14 Defined in the *Criminal Finances Act 2017, s 44(2)*.

15 See *Criminal Finances Act 2017, s 44(4)*.

(4) In this Part "UK tax evasion offence" means:

(a) an offence of cheating the public revenue, or

(b) an offence under the law of any part of the United Kingdom consisting of being knowingly concerned in, or in taking steps with a view to, the fraudulent evasion of a tax.

(5) In this Part "UK tax evasion facilitation offence" means an offence under the law of any part of the United Kingdom consisting of:

(a) being knowingly concerned in, or in taking steps with a view to, the fraudulent evasion of a tax by another person,

(b) aiding, abetting, counselling or procuring the commission of a UK tax evasion offence, or

(c) being involved art and part in the commission of an offence consisting of being knowingly concerned in, or in taking steps with a view to, the fraudulent evasion of a tax.

(6) Conduct carried out with a view to the fraudulent evasion of tax by another person is not to be regarded as a UK tax evasion facilitation offence by virtue of subsection (5)(a) unless the other person has committed a UK tax evasion offence facilitated by that conduct.

(7) For the purposes of this section "tax" means a tax imposed under the law of any part of the United Kingdom, including national insurance contributions under:

(a) Part 1 of the Social Security Contributions and Benefits Act 1992, or

(b) Part 1 of the Social Security Contributions and Benefits (Northern Ireland) Act 1992.

(8) A relevant body guilty of an offence under this section is liable:

(a) on conviction on indictment, to a fine;

(b) on summary conviction in England and Wales, to a fine;

(c) on summary conviction in Scotland or Northern Ireland, to a fine not exceeding the statutory maximum.'

2.39 The offence is committed by a relevant body where a person acting in the capacity of a person associated with it commits a tax evasion facilitation offence, broadly, criminally facilitating another person's offence of tax evasion (the *s 45(1)* offence)[16]. However, the associated person does not commit a tax

16 This is defined in *subsection (5)* as any offence under the law of any part of the UK committed by facilitating a UK tax evasion offence. It thus comprises being knowingly concerned in, or taking steps with a view to, the tax evasion of another, as well as aiding and abetting another person's offence of tax evasion.

evasion facilitation offence when he or she inadvertently, or even negligently, facilitates another's tax evasion. The facilitation by the associated person must be criminal under the existing law. Moreover, the associated person must commit the tax evasion facilitation offence in the capacity of a person associated with the relevant body.

2.40 Where an employee criminally facilitates his or her partner's tax evasion in the course of their private life and as a frolic of their own, they commit a tax evasion facilitation offence but not in the capacity of a person associated with their employer. Therefore, the employing relevant body does not commit the new offence. Likewise, a relevant body will not commit the new offence where it contracts with another relevant body that is evading its own tax.

2.41 Where a tax evasion offence[17] has been committed and a person acting in the capacity of a person associated with the relevant body has committed a tax evasion facilitation offence, the relevant body will be guilty of the *subsection (1)* offence (see **2.38**), unless it can raise the defence in *subsection (2)*. This provides a defence where the relevant body has in force reasonable prevention procedures, that is, procedures designed to prevent persons associated with it from committing tax-evasion facilitation offences (*subsection (3)*). The defence is also available where it is not reasonable to expect the relevant body to have such procedures. It is only reasonable or proportionate procedures, as opposed to foolproof or excessively burdensome procedures, that are required.

2.42 Guidance has been published to assist relevant bodies to devise reasonable prevention procedures[18].

FAILURE TO PREVENT FACILITATION OF FOREIGN TAX EVASION OFFENCES

2.43 *Section 46* of *CFA 2017*, is headed 'Failure to prevent facilitation of foreign tax evasion offences'[19]. It creates an offence of corporate failure to prevent the facilitation of foreign tax evasion offences.

---

17 Tax evasion offence is defined in *subsection (4)*, as an offence amounting to a cheat of the public revenue or any offence consisting of being knowingly concerned in or taking steps with a view to the fraudulent evasion of tax. It thus comprises conduct currently capable of being indicted as a cheat of the public revenue, or as a statutory fraudulent evasion offence, such as those found in the *Value Added Tax Act 1994, s 72* or of the *Taxes Management Act 1970, s 106A*. The new offence is only committed where such a UK tax evasion offence has been committed. Where the taxpayer is non-compliant or engaged in avoidance falling short of evasion the new offence will not be committed.

18 See *Criminal Finances Act 2017, s 47*.

19 **'46 Failure to prevent facilitation of foreign tax evasion offences**

(1) A relevant body (B) is guilty of an offence if at any time:

(a) a person commits a foreign tax evasion facilitation offence when acting in the capacity of a person associated with B, and

(b) any of the conditions in subsection (2) is satisfied.

2.44 This offence is broadly similar to the offence in relation to UK taxes. It is slightly narrower in scope, in that only certain relevant bodies can commit the foreign tax offence. Section 46(2) states that the offence can only be committed where the relevant body is incorporated under the law of the UK, the relevant body carries on part of its business from the UK, or where the associated person does the facilitating criminal act in the UK. Where a relevant body incorporated outside of the UK, that conducts no business from the UK, has an associated person carry out a criminal act abroad, the *section 46* foreign tax offence will not be committed.

2.45 *Subsection (5)* gives effect to the requirement that there be 'dual criminality'[20].

---

(2) The conditions are:
  (a) that B is a body incorporated, or a partnership formed, under the law of any part of the United Kingdom;
  (b) that B carries on business or part of a business in the United Kingdom;
  (c) that any conduct constituting part of the foreign tax evasion facilitation offence takes place in the United Kingdom;

  and in paragraph (b) "business" includes an undertaking.

(3) It is a defence for B to prove that, when the foreign tax evasion facilitation offence was committed:
  (a) B had in place such prevention procedures as it was reasonable in all the circumstances to expect B to have in place, or
  (b) it was not reasonable in all the circumstances to expect B to have any prevention procedures in place.

(4) In subsection (3) "prevention procedures" means procedures designed to prevent persons acting in the capacity of a person associated with B from committing foreign tax evasion facilitation offences under the law of the foreign country concerned.

(5) In this Part "foreign tax evasion offence" means conduct which:
  (a) amounts to an offence under the law of a foreign country,
  (b) relates to a breach of a duty relating to a tax imposed under the law of that country, and
  (c) would be regarded by the courts of any part of the United Kingdom as amounting to being knowingly concerned in, or in taking steps with a view to, the fraudulent evasion of that tax.

(6) In this Part "foreign tax evasion facilitation offence" means conduct which:
  (a) amounts to an offence under the law of a foreign country,
  (b) relates to the commission by another person of a foreign tax evasion offence under that law, and
  (c) would, if the foreign tax evasion offence were a UK tax evasion offence, amount to a UK tax evasion facilitation offence (see section 45(5) and (6)).

(7) A relevant body guilty of an offence under this section is liable:
  (a) on conviction on indictment, to a fine;
  (b) on summary conviction in England and Wales, to a fine;
  (c) on summary conviction in Scotland or Northern Ireland, to a fine not exceeding the statutory maximum.

20 A foreign tax evasion offence is defined as conduct that is criminal under the foreign law in question and would also be regarded by the UK courts as amounting to an offence of being knowingly concerned in, or taking steps with a view to, the fraudulent evasion of the tax. Thus, the *section 46* offence cannot be committed where the acts of the associated person would not be criminal if committed in the UK, regardless of what the foreign criminal law may be.

2.46 *Section 49* requires the consent of the Director of Public Prosecutions for Northern Ireland (DPPNI), or Director of the Serious Fraud Office (SFO) before any prosecution is brought for the foreign revenue offence. Such a prosecution may raise complex issues around the public interest and the relationship of the UK with other countries necessitating this safeguard.

GUIDANCE ABOUT PREVENTION PROCEDURES

2.47 *Section 47* is headed 'Guidance about preventing the facilitation of tax evasion offences'. It requires the Chancellor of the Exchequer to publish guidance about the procedures that relevant bodies might put in place. This requirement is similar to the requirement in the *Bribery Act 2010* to publish guidance on how to prevent bribery.

Subsection (7) enables the Chancellor to endorse guidance prepared and published by others.

2.48 Various bodies have issued guidance[21].

RISK MANAGEMENT

2.49 As can be seen from what has been discussed before, there are potentially considerable risks for tax professionals.

2.50 The simplest way to manage risk, of course, is to get everything right. Although that is ideal, it is not always what happens. Things do not always run smoothly, which may be due to matters under the control of the tax professional or outside their control due to reliance on a third party (eg the failure by a client to give full and proper disclosure on the nature of the transactions being entered into, failure to give access to the underlying transaction documents).

2.51 The areas of risk management which must be covered by a tax professional include:

- advising correctly on the law;

---

21 The Law Society has issued guidance approved by the Chancellor, see www.lawsociety.org.uk/support-services/advice/practice-notes/criminal-finances-act-2017.
ICAEW has published various documents online including 'Failure to Prevent Tax Evasion (The Criminal Finances Act 2017)' at www.icaew.com/-/media/corporate/files/technical/legal-and-regulatory/money-laundering/cfpta.ashx; ACCA, 'The Criminal Finances Act 2017' at www.accaglobal.com/gb/en/student/exam-support-resources/fundamentals-exams-study-resources/f4/technical-articles/cfa-2017.html; STEP, at www.step.org/sites/default/files/Policy/Briefing_Note_-_Failure_to_prevent.pdf (available to members); the CIOT Guidance which refers to the HMRC Guidance is at www.tax.org.uk/professional-standards/professional-standards-%E2%80%93-full-listing/criminal-finances-act-2017; and HMRC have also issued guidance 'Tackling tax evasion: Government guidance for the corporate offences of failure to prevent the criminal facilitation of tax evasion' at https://assets.publishing.service.gov.uk/government/uploads/system/uploads/attachment_data/file/672231/Tackling-tax-evasion-corporate-offences.pdf.

- liability to clients;
- liability to third parties;
- having proper insurance and complying with its terms;
- complying with a professional body and/or regulators requirements;
- complying with AML matters;
- complying with DOTAS and POTAS;
- complying with DAC6;
- dealing with risks under the *Criminal Finances Act 2017*;
- POCA, and other criminal matters;
- vicarious liability;
- miscellaneous matters.

2.52 The foregoing areas often involve having proper procedures and documentation and related matters in place.

2.53 It is essential that a good letter of engagement/terms of business (LOE) is in place for every client matter with appropriate AML checks performed and related matters being collected in a timely manner and retained. It is important to make sure the LOE is signed and the terms acknowledged by the client. Suitable matters relating to the terms of engagement between the professional and client may be provided on the adviser's website; but such terms need technical input, particularly from a legal perspective concerning their incorporation into the client terms of engagement. If terms of engagement on the website are to be included in the LOE, this needs to be made clear in the LOE and the material needs to be on the website. This must be checked.

2.54 A helpful checklist for some of the matters to include in a LOE are included in the Appendix at **2.109** below.

2.55 The relevant procedures concerning risk management need careful time and thought devoted to them. They need to be clearly explained to those working in the business and adhered to. The various professional websites can help with this. An Office Manual can be a useful tool for this and should be kept up to date. Having it available to employees online may help.

2.56 Retaining the appropriate documents is necessary in running a professional practice, and it will clearly help in avoiding any disputes. Checklists are often a useful adjunct for advisers.

2.57 Storage of these documents and case files needs care. The length of time to retain documents needs to be considered for each case.

2.58 Regular checks done within the business or by a third party in a cooperative way are also a useful process of reinforcing what is required and knowing the state of play and for continuously improving the standards of the adviser.

2.59 Ensuring everyone has the correct certificates and licences is essential to ensure that what is done is legal, that there have been no breaches of the applicable professional and regulatory rules and that the insurance has not been invalidated.

2.60 A useful starting point is to familiarise oneself with the guidance in 'Professional Conduct in Relation to Taxation' (PCRT). The Help Sheets on Tax Advice and Errors repay re-reading (eg see ICAEW Help Sheets: Help sheet B: Tax Advice, Help Sheet C 1: Dealing with errors at www.icaew.com/technical/tax/pcrt; and 'PCRT Help Sheet C: Dealing with errors' at aat.org.uk)

2.61 PCRT sets out the principles and standards of behaviour that all tax professionals should follow in their tax work. It is a good standard to try to live up to and assists in risk management including compliance with regulatory requirements.

2.62 The Law Society has published a 'Guidance for solicitors advising on tax'[22] which contains an appendix on 'Aspects of the tax environment to consider'. This Guidance is reproduced at **Appendix 4** since it succinctly emphasises a number of areas of risk for the tax professional.

LIABILITY TO CLIENTS

2.63 Liability to clients is usually a liability in contract and is discussed in **Chapter 5**.

As noted above, a suitably drafted LOE is important. This is because a contract, which an LOE is, is often essentially about risk allocation and the risk reward ratio.

2.64 The detailing of the services to be provided needs careful consideration and care in any event. This can help define the duty owed and the object to be attained which can assist greatly with dealing with potential claims. Clarity and precision are the watchwords.

2.65 In contractual claims, the object is generally to put the claimant in the position the claimant would have been in had the contract been properly performed. If the client has signed a LOE it can assist in determining the quantification of any claim for losses. Hence the need for careful drafting.

2.66 Limiting of liability should be in place in the LOE and carefully considered in each case. It is often helpful to discuss this with the client as it can go to the level of fee. Some clients may be willing to pay more for a higher

22 24 August 2020, see www.lawsociety.org.uk/topics/tax/guidance-for-solicitors-advising-on-tax#appendix.

level of insurance cover. It then needs to be checked for availability and, if wanted, put into place.

2.67 The rules on limitation of liability where consumers are involved can be different. *Part 2* of the *Consumer Rights Act 2015* deals with Unfair Terms. Unfair terms are not binding on a consumer.

2.68 By *section 2(3)* of the 2015 Act, 'Consumer' means an individual acting for purposes that are wholly or mainly outside that individual's trade, business, craft or profession. See further **Chapter 5.**

2.69 Thus, even a commercial lawyer may be a consumer in relation to inheritance tax (IHT) advice. It is important to know whether in the particular circumstances the client is a consumer and to act accordingly for risk management purposes. It can be part of the know-your-client (KYC) process to discover this. A suitable questionnaire for the client can assist in identifying and accurately documenting the client's objectives and the nature of the advice required.

2.70 The *Provision of Services Regulations 2009* must also be complied with (see generally: the Provision of Services Regulations 2009 at www.legislation.gov.uk). *Part 2* is important to comply with as to the provision of information and complaints. Information must be supplied in this context in a clear and unambiguous manner.

2.71 The Department of Business Energy and Industrial Strategy says in its December 2020 'UK Guidance on the provision of services regulations'[23] (at p 6):

> 'The Provision of Services Regulations were first introduced in 2009, in order to implement European Union (EU) Directive 2006/123/EC (hereafter the 'Services Directive') into UK law. The aim of the Services Directive was to make it easier for businesses to provide cross-border services with other European Economic Area (EEA) countries by lowering non-tariff barriers to trade. It specifically aimed to simplify administrative procedures and remove obstacles for services activities; enhance mutual trust between member states through effective administrative cooperation; and improve the quality of businesses and strengthen consumer rights in the Single Market. … the European Union (Withdrawal) Act 2018 preserved the Provision of Services Regulations 2009 (as amended in 2014) for UK nationals and businesses established in the UK and formed under UK law.'

These provisions continue after the end of the transition provision by virtue of the *European Union (Withdrawal) Act 2018, s 1, Sch 1.* Accordingly, these rules continue to be in force unless, and until, changed by the UK Parliament.

---

23 See https://assets.publishing.service.gov.uk/government/uploads/system/uploads/attachment_data/file/948983/provision-of-services-guidance-businesses-competent-authorities.pdf.

Liability to third parties

2.72 Liability to third parties is usually a liability in tort which is discussed in **Chapter 6**.

Having proper insurance and complying with its terms

2.73 To have, and to comply with, proper insurance is an important protection and often a professional requirement.

2.74 *Regulation 8(1)* of the *2009 Regulations* requires information on certain matters to be made available. It provides that this is the case (inter alia):

> '(n) where the provider is subject to a requirement to hold any professional liability insurance or guarantee, information about the insurance or guarantee and in particular—
>
> (i) the contact details of the insurer or guarantor, and
>
> (ii) the territorial coverage of the insurance or guarantee.'

This is the case for many professions, eg barristers and solicitors who are required to hold minimum levels of insurance. Many do carry higher levels, but this is not a professional requirement and so may not have to be disclosed. Many websites set out this and other information (eg see www.addingtonchambers.com).

Complying with professional body and/or regulators' requirements

2.75 Many professional bodies have useful websites that deal with such matters.

The Law Society – www.lawsociety.org.uk/support-services/advice/practice-notes/provision-of-services-regulations-2009.

2.76 The Solicitors Regulation Authority (SRA) has published a document headed 'Standards and Regulations' at www.sra.org.uk/solicitors/standards-regulations.

It is important to abide by such requirements as failure to do so may lead to disciplinary proceedings and could render insurance void.

Complying with AML matters

2.77 It is essential that AML matters are dealt with properly and efficiently and correct documents retained for the correct period. See, for example, the Financial Conduct Authority at www.fca.org.uk/firms/financial-crime/money-laundering-regulations.

2.78 Failure to comply with the AML regulations can lead to criminal sanctions. The highest maximum penalty is 14 years' imprisonment (for individuals) and/or an unlimited fine (applicable to both individuals and corporations). Other offences are punishable by up to two years' imprisonment (for individuals) and/or an unlimited fine (applicable to both individuals and corporations).

2.79 This is discussed in **Chapter 10**.

Complying with DOTAS and POTAS

2.80 This is discussed in **Chapter 4**.

Complying with DAC6

2.81 This is discussed in **Chapter 11**.

Dealing with risks under the Criminal Finances Act 2017

2.82 This is discussed at **2.51** et seq above and in **Chapter 9**.

POCA, and other criminal matters

2.83 This is discussed in **Chapter 10**.

Vicarious liability

2.84 An employer can be liable for the lapses of an employee. The leading cases on vicarious liability are: *Cox v MoJ* [2016] UKSC 10; *Mohamud v William Morris Supermarkets plc* [2016] UKSC 11; *Lister v Hesley Hall Ltd* [2001] UKHL 22; *Wilson v Exel UK Ltd* [2010] SLT 671; *Weddall v Barchester Health Ltd* [2012] EWCA Civ 25; and *Graham v Commercial Bodyworks Ltd* [2015] EWCA Civ 47.

GDPR

2.85 Any tax professional who collects information about individuals for any reason other than for their own personal, family or household purposes is required to comply with data protection laws under the *Data Protection Act 2018* (*DPA 2018*) (at www.legislation.gov.uk/ukpga/2018/12/contents/enacted), together with the General Data Protection Regulations (GDPR) (which also forms part of UK law). It is beyond the scope of this book to undertake a detailed examination of the laws on GDPR.

2.86 The Information Commissioners Office (ICO) regulates data protection in the UK, and the function of the ICO is to offer advice and guidance, promote good practice, carry out audits, consider complaints, monitor compliance and take enforcement action where appropriate.

2.87 Data protection under the GDPR concerns the fair and proper use of information about people and, in particular, the use of personal data. Businesses subject to GDPR must comply with the laws on the protection of an individual's personal data, and where necessary to provide an individual with a record of their relevant personal information which is being held. GDPR controls how personal data is processed by a data controller.

2.88 A data controller is the person that decides how and why to collect and use the data (an incorporated business or sole trader). An employee acting on behalf of an employer is not a controller, but the employer *would be* the controller. The controller must make sure that the processing of that data complies with GDPR.

2.89 GDPR allows for a request (the 'SAR') for copies of all information relating to an individual who is the data subject. The following provisions of the GDPR are of particular importance.

GDPR principles

2.90 The core GDPR principles are set out in *DPA 2018, ss 35–40*. There are six data protection principles:

(1) *section 35(1)* sets out the first data protection principle (requirement that processing be lawful and fair). *Section 35(2)* states:

> 'The processing of personal data for any of the law enforcement purposes is lawful only if and to the extent that it is based on law and either:
>
> (a) the data subject has given consent to the processing for that purpose, or
>
> (b) the processing is necessary for the performance of a task carried out for that purpose by a competent authority';

(2) *section 36(1)* sets out the second data protection principle (requirement that purposes of processing be specified, explicit and legitimate);

(3) *section 37* sets out the third data protection principle (requirement that personal data be adequate, relevant and not excessive);

(4) *section 38(1)* sets out the fourth data protection principle (requirement that personal data be accurate and kept up to date);

(5) *section 39(1)* sets out the fifth data protection principle (requirement that personal data be kept for no longer than is necessary);

(6) *section 40* sets out the sixth data protection principle (requirement that personal data be processed in a secure manner).

'Personal Data' (DPA 2018, s 3)

2.91 The GDPR applies to 'personal data':

'…

(2) "Personal data" means any information relating to an identified or identifiable living individual …

(3) "Identifiable living individual" means a living individual who can be identified, directly or indirectly, in particular by reference to—

(a) an identifier such as a name, an identification number, location data or an online identifier, or

(b) one or more factors specific to the physical, physiological, genetic, mental, economic, cultural or social identity of the individual.'

Right of access by the data subject (DPA 2018, s 45)

2.92

'(1) A data subject is entitled to obtain from the controller:

(a) confirmation as to whether or not personal data concerning him or her is being processed; and

(b) where that is the case, access to the personal data and the information set out in subsection (2).

(2) That information is:

(a) the purposes of and legal basis for the processing;

(b) the categories of personal data concerned;

(c) the recipients or categories of recipients to whom the personal data has been disclosed (including recipients or categories of recipients in third countries or international organisations);

(d) the period for which it is envisaged that the personal data will be stored or, where that is not possible, the criteria used to determine that period;

…

(g) communication of the personal data undergoing processing and of any available information as to its origin.

(3) Where a data subject makes a request under subsection (1), the information to which the data subject is entitled must be provided in writing:

(a) without undue delay; and

(b) in any event, before the end of the applicable time period (as to which see section 54).'

Other relevant GDPR provisions

2.93 Other relevant provisions to consider are:

- Article 12 (Transparent information, communication and modalities for the exercise of the rights of the Data Subject);
- Article 13 (Information to be provided where personal data are collected from the Data Subject);
- Article 14 (Information to be provided where personal data have not been obtained from the Data Subject);
- Article 15 (Right of access by the data subject);
- Article 20 (Right to data portability);
- Article 22 (Automated individual decision-making, including profiling).

2.94 HMRC is a data controller and itself has been subject to the issue of a Contravention Notice by the ICO[24], which arose from an ICO investigation into HMRC's use of voice authentication ('Voice ID') for customer verification on some of its helplines since January 2017. The Voice ID service authenticated customers through their voice when they called HMRC's helplines. The characteristics of a person's voice constitute biometric data. HMRC processed this biometric data for the purpose of uniquely identifying natural persons when they called its helplines. HMRC's automated recording did not inform customers that they did not have to sign up to the service. Customers were asked to repeat, 'my voice is my password', and there was no clear option for callers who did not wish to register. HMRC informed the Commissioner that it has deleted the biometric data of 156,360 customers who withheld consent as at 5 January 2019. HMRC has confirmed that it is able to identify the remaining data of roughly 5.5 million customers for which it does not have explicit consent. HMRC has also shown that it is able to delete this data. The ICO concluded (at para 20) that HMRC contravened DPP1 in that it had and continues to process personal data by collecting, retaining and using biometric data through their Voice ID service, without having a lawful basis for so doing. At para 24 of the Contravention Notice the ICO states:

> '24. The Commissioner considers that the contravention is a significant one which warrant enforcement action. Her reasons for this conclusion include that:

---

24 See https://ico.org.uk/media/action-weve-taken/enforcement-notices/2614924/hmrc-en-201905.pdf.

- An extremely large number of data subjects are affected.
- HMRC collected this personal data in circumstances where there was a significant imbalance of power between it and its customers. It did not explain to customers how they could decline to participate in the Voice ID system. It also did not explain that customers would not suffer a detrimental impact if it declined to participate.
- The imbalance of power may still be a factor in the number of customers who have not withheld consent, especially where customers rely on HMRC for benefit purposes.
- HMRC appears to have given little or no consideration to the data protection principles when rolling out the Voice ID service.'

In the particular circumstances the Contravention Notice required HMRC to take the steps set out below within 28 days:

- Delete all of the biometric data held under the Voice ID system for which it does not have explicit consent.
- Require its suppliers who operate, manage or are involved in the Voice ID system to delete all the biometric data they process under the Voice ID system for which it does not have explicit consent.

2.95 The ICO may serve a penalty notice on a person who has failed to comply with a Contravention Notice under *DPA 2018, s 155(1)(b)* requiring payment of an amount up to €20m or 4% of an undertaking's total annual worldwide turnover whichever is the higher.

MISCELLANEOUS MATTERS

2.96 Further matters which are relevant to the running of any business, and are not specific to tax practice include:

- staying in contact with former staff – alumni websites helps with tracing in the event that assistance is needed in the bringing or defence of a claim being made by a client; and
- confidentiality is crucial in the client relationship and it is necessary to ensure obligations are imposed on employees in their employment contracts.

DIRECT REGULATION: TAX LEGISLATION AND TAX COURTS

Tax planning

2.97 As a matter of general principle, any person is entitled to structure their personal and/or business activities to minimise the amount of tax that is paid (*IR Commrs v Duke of Westminster* [1935] All ER Rep 259, [1936] AC 1 (direct taxes) and *IRC v Pendragon* [2013] EWCA Civ 868 (VAT)). In the *Duke of Westminster*, the Duke covenanted with his employees to pay them an annuity. They remained contractually entitled to receive wages for the services they performed but it was explained to them by the Duke's solicitors that they were not expected to claim, and they did not in fact claim, those wages during the currency of the annuity. The Duke of Westminster was entitled to deduct the payments of the annuity for the purpose of calculating his taxable income thereby reducing his liability to surtax. The Crown challenged these arrangements contending that the payments made under the deed of covenant were in substance payments for services and were not annual payments which could properly be deducted from the Duke's assessment to surtax. The House of Lords rejected this argument. Lord Tomlin (at pp 19–21) stated:

> '… it is said that in revenue cases there is a doctrine that the Court may ignore the legal position and regard what is called "the substance of the matter," and that here the substance of the matter is that the annuitant was serving the Duke for something equal to his former salary or wages, and that therefore, while he is so serving, the annuity must be treated as salary or wages. This supposed doctrine (upon which the Commissioners apparently acted) seems to rest for its support upon a misunderstanding of language used in some earlier cases. The sooner this misunderstanding is dispelled, and the supposed doctrine given its quietus, the better it will be for all concerned, for the doctrine seems to involve substituting "the uncertain and crooked cord of discretion" for "the golden and straight metwand of the law".
>
> *Every man is entitled if he can to order his affairs so as that the tax attaching under the appropriate Acts is less than it otherwise would be. If he succeeds in ordering them so as to secure this result, then, however unappreciative the Commissioners of Inland Revenue or his fellow taxpayers may be of his ingenuity, he cannot be compelled to pay an increased tax.* This so-called doctrine of "the substance" seems to me to be nothing more than an attempt to make a man pay notwithstanding that he has so ordered his affairs that the amount of tax sought from him is not legally claimable.' [Emphasis added]

2.98 Lord Keith in the House of Lords in *Craven (HMIT) v White* [1989] AC 398 at 479 emphasised that tax planning is permitted:

> 'The [*Ramsay*] principle does not involve, in my opinion, that it is part of the judicial function to treat as nugatory any step whatever which a taxpayer may take with a view to the avoidance or mitigation of tax. It remains true in general that the taxpayer, where he is in a position to carry through a transaction in two alternative ways, one of which will result in liability to tax and the other of which will not, is at liberty to choose the latter and to do so effectively in the absence of any specific tax avoidance provision …'

2.99 Further, in the Supreme Court, Lord Neuberger stated in *Secret Hotels 2 Ltd v HMRC* [2014] STC 937 at [57]:

> '... one must be careful before stigmatising the contractual documentation as being "artificial", bearing in mind that EU law, like English law, treats parties as free to arrange or structure their relationship so as to maximise its commercial attraction, including the incidence of taxation ...'

However, as discussed below, any tax planning must be within the spirit of the legislation.

GAAR

2.100 Despite the general approach of the UK courts to tax planning, and the growth in specific targeted anti-avoidance rules in the UK tax legislation, there is also a general anti-abuse rule (GAAR) which has effect for the purpose of counteracting tax advantages arising from tax arrangements that are abusive (see, generally, the *Finance Act 2013* at www.legislation.gov.uk). Where the GAAR applies, it will prevent the tax advantages being available which are sought to be derived from 'abusive' tax arrangements. Broadly, there are four key conditions which are necessary for the GAAR to apply, namely:

- there must be tax arrangements;
- the tax arrangements must be abusive;
- there must be tax advantages which arise from such tax arrangements that are abusive; and
- the counteracting provisions of the GAAR have to apply to make adjustments so as to counteract the relevant tax advantages.

2.101 The GAAR applies to, inter alia, the following: income tax, corporation tax, capital gains tax, inheritance tax, stamp duty land tax and the annual tax on enveloped dwellings. To determine whether the GAAR applies, the tax professional must carefully consider the terms of the legislation.

2.102 In determining the scope of the GAAR, there is guidance available in the form of an HMRC GAAR Guidance (approved by the GAAR Advisory Panel with effect from 28 March 2018) and available at www.gov.uk/government/publications/tax-avoidance-general-anti-abuse-rules. The GAAR Guidance operates as an aid to the interpretation and application of the GAAR. It should be noted that Part D of the guidance gives examples of how the GAAR would be regarded as applying in specific circumstances. A review of these examples is outside the scope of this book but should be referred to by the reader where necessary.

2.103 Tax arrangements are regarded as 'abusive' if they are arrangements the entering into, or carrying out of, which 'cannot reasonably be regarded as a reasonable course of action' in relation to the relevant tax provisions, having regard to all the circumstances including:

(a) whether the substantive results of the arrangements are consistent with any principles on which those provisions are based (whether express or implied) and the policy objectives of those provisions;

(b) whether the means of achieving those results involves one or more contrived or abnormal steps; and

(c) whether the arrangements are intended to exploit any shortcomings in those provisions.

2.104 If the tax arrangements form part of other arrangements then regard must be had to those other arrangements. Key to the application of the GAAR is determining whether the relevant arrangements represented a reasonable course of action in relation to the relevant tax provisions. The GAAR Guidance emphasises that the 'double reasonableness' test is designed to operate as a safeguard for taxpayers. In this regard, it is emphasised (B12.1) as follows:

> 'Applying a "double reasonableness" test. This requires HMRC to show that the arrangements "cannot reasonably be regarded as a reasonable course of action". This recognises that there are some arrangements which some people would regard as a reasonable course of action while others would not. The "double reasonableness" test sets a high threshold by asking whether it would be reasonable to hold the view that the arrangement was a reasonable course of action. The arrangement falls to be treated as abusive only if it would not be reasonable to hold such a view.'

2.105 The *Finance Act 2013* (*FA 2013*) provides examples of arrangements which might indicate that tax arrangements are abusive, but with the important proviso in each case that only if it is reasonable to assume that such a result was not the anticipated result when the relevant tax provisions were enacted. The examples are where:

(a) the arrangements result in an amount of income, profits or gains for tax purposes that is significantly less than the amount for economic purposes;

(b) the arrangements result in deductions or losses of an amount for tax purposes that is significantly greater than the amount for economic purposes; and

(c) the arrangements result in a claim for the repayment or crediting of tax (including foreign tax) that has not been, and is unlikely to be, paid.

2.106 The examples given in (a)–(c) above are deemed not to be exhaustive under *FA 2013*. Additionally, the legislation deems that the fact that tax arrangements accord with established practice and HMRC had, at the time the arrangements were entered into, indicated its acceptance of that practice, is an example of something which might indicate that the arrangements are not abusive. In relation to the illustrations in (a)–(c) above, the features will not be indicators of abuse if it would be reasonable to assume that they were anticipated (or intended) when the tax provisions were enacted. For example, the capital allowance legislation may deliberately allow a taxpayer to claim a deduction for tax purposes in relation to capital expenditure on plant or equipment that is, in a particular period, substantially greater than the depreciation on those assets which is recognised for accounting purposes for that period. This result was clearly intended when the legislation was enacted, and HMRC's GAAR Guidance (C5.11.3) states:

> '… the capital allowance legislation may deliberately allow a taxpayer to claim a deduction for tax purposes in relation to capital expenditure on plant or equipment that is, in a particular period, substantially greater than the depreciation on those assets which is recognised for accounting purposes for that period. This result would clearly have been intended when the legislation was enacted.'

2.107 It is of crucial importance that the tax professional considers the potential application of the GAAR since it establishes the outer boundaries of acceptable tax planning. However, it is also of crucial importance to carefully consider the application of the relevant statutory provisions that are specific to the area being advised upon by the tax professional.

TAX STATUTORY INTERPRETATION

2.108 The courts have also imposed limits on the scope and application of tax legislation by reference to how a statute is interpretated (which obviously has the consequence of restricting the nature of a taxpayer's planning to limit tax liabilities). Accordingly, the Tax Professional must be particularly mindful of all relevant principles of statutory construction. In this regard, the following principles should always be considered:

- A purposive approach should be adopted to the construction of legislation. In *UBS AG v HMRC* [2016] STC 934 ('the *UBS* case'), Lord Reed outlined the approach to the interpretation of statutory provisions at [72]:

  > '… it seems to me to be preferable to begin with the interpretation of the legislation, and the fundamental question whether it can be given a purposive interpretation going beyond its literal terms: that is to say, whether a "Ramsay" approach is possible at all, and if so, the purposive construction on which it is to be based. … the question next arises how, on its proper interpretation, the legislation is to be applied to the facts.'

  Lord Reed then said at [73] that the statute under consideration in *UBS AG*, the *Income Tax (Earnings and Pensions) Act 2003*, contained no explanation of the purpose of the provision on which a purposive interpretation might be based and it was in that context that he examined the historical background to, and development of, the legislation by reference to budget notes, explanatory notes and case law. Accordingly, such an approach should be applied to all tax statutes where there is an ambiguity as to the scope and application of its provisions.

- Both the House of Lords (*Barclays Mercantile Business Finance Ltd v Mawson* [2005] 1 AC 684 per Lord Nicholls at [51]) and the Supreme Court (*Tower MCashback LLP 1 and Another v Revenue & Customs Commissioners* [2011] STC 1143 per Lord Walker at [47]) have endorsed Ribeiro PJ's succinct expression of the *Ramsay* principle of statutory interpretation in *Collector of Stamp Revenue v Arrowtown Assets Ltd* [2003] 6 ITLR 454, when he said:

  '… the driving principle in the *Ramsay* line of cases continues to involve a general rule of statutory construction and an unblinkered approach to the analysis of the facts. *The ultimate question is whether the relevant statutory provisions, construed purposively, were intended to apply to the transaction, viewed realistically.*' [Emphasis added]

- The long title to each Act will be relevant as an aid to interpretation of the provisions: see *Black-Clawson International Ltd v Papierwerke Waldhof-Aschaffenburg* [1975] AC 591, 647F. Further, the headings in an Act are aids to construction. See *Stephens v Cuckfield Rural District Council* [1960] 2 QB 373, 383 (Upjohn LJ for the Court of Appeal):

  'While the marginal note to a section cannot control the language used in the section, it is at least permissible to approach a consideration of its general purpose and the mischief at which it is aimed with the note in mind.'

- The principles identified by the Court of Appeal in *Pollen Estate Trustee Company Ltd v Revenue & Customs Commissioners* [2013] EWCA Civ 753 must be borne in mind. In that case, the CA took a broad purposive approach in circumstances where there was no policy reason for Parliament to have intended Stamp Duty Land Tax (SDLT) relief to be refused. The CA considered what policy reason there might be for denying relief to a charity under *FA 2003, Sch 8, para1(1)* where it purchased jointly with a non-charity. In applying a purposive approach to interpretation, the CA stated '… there is sufficient "policy imperative" to justify the reading … Not to afford a charity relief in such circumstances would, in my judgment, be capricious' [at 31]. The CA permitted the relief on a purposive construction of the legislation.

- Explanatory Notes to an Act of Parliament are relevant to aid the court's interpretation of the legislation as part of the contextual scene. In this regard, Lord Steyn, in *R (otao Westminster City Council) v National Asylum Support Service* [2002] UKHL 38, stated:

> '5. *The question is whether in aid of the interpretation of a statute the court may take into account the Explanatory Notes and, if so, to what extent. The starting point is that language in all legal texts conveys meaning according to the circumstances in which it was used. It follows that the context must always be identified and considered before the process of construction or during it. It is therefore wrong to say that the court may only resort to evidence of the contextual scene when an ambiguity has arisen…* [I]n his important judgment in *Investors Compensation Scheme Ltd v West Bromwich Building Society* [1998] 1 WLR 896, 912-913, *Lord Hoffmann made crystal clear that an ambiguity need not be established before the surrounding circumstances may be taken into account.* The same applies to statutory construction. In *River Wear Commissioners v Adamson* (1877) 2 App Cas 743, 763, Lord Blackburn explained the position as follows:
>
> I shall … state, as precisely as I can, what I understand from the decided cases to be the principles on which the courts of law act in construing instruments in writing; and a statute is an instrument in writing. *In all cases the object is to see what is the intention expressed by the words used. But, from the imperfection of language, it is impossible to know what that intention is without inquiring farther, and seeing what the circumstances were with reference to which the words were used, and what was the object, appearing from those circumstances, which the person using them had in view; for the meaning of words varies according to the circumstances with respect to which they were used.'*
>
> *Again, there is no need to establish an ambiguity before taking into account the objective circumstances to which the language relates. Applied to the subject under consideration the result is as follows. Insofar as the Explanatory Notes cast light on the objective setting or contextual scene of the statute, and the mischief at which it is aimed, such materials are therefore always admissible aids to construction. They may be admitted for what logical value they have…'* [Emphasis added]

- The predecessor legislation may be relevant to construing a later Act of Parliament since it may assist the court to place the provisions in the relevant context for the purposes of interpretation. In this regard, the House of Lords in *R v Environment Secretary (ex p Spath Holme Ltd)* [2001] 2 AC 349 at p 388 C–E, Lord Bingham stated:

> "From these authorities, it is plain that courts should not routinely investigate the statutory predecessors of provisions in a consolidation statute, particularly where (as in *Maunsell v Olins* and *Farrell v Alexander*) the issue concerns the construction of a single word or expression. Such a practice would reduce the benefit to be derived from the process of consolidation (although the advantage of gathering

scattered, and often amended and re-amended, provisions together in a coherent sequence in a single statute should not be underrated). But *the overriding aim of the court must always be to give effect to the intention of Parliament as expressed in the words used. If, even in the absence of overt ambiguity, the court finds itself unable, in construing the later provision in isolation, to place itself in the draftsman's chair and interpret the provision in the social and factual context which originally led to its enactment, it seems to me legitimate for the court – even, as Lord Simon said, incumbent on it – to consider the earlier, consolidated, provision in its social and factual context for such help as it may give, the assumption, of course, being (in the absence of amendment) that no change in the law was intended.* I agree with the Court of Appeal that it is, in the present case, appropriate to consider the statutory predecessor of section 31.' [Emphasis added]

See also *Mangin v Inland Revenue Commissioner* [1971] AC 739 at p 746E where Lord Donovan giving a majority judgment of the Privy Council set out various rules of statutory construction including: '... the history of an enactment and the reasons which led to it being passed may be used as an aid to its construction'. As to the limited use of background notes, see *Christianuyi v R & C Commrs* [2018] UKUT 10 (TCC) at para 25(1)–(5) (the decision of the Court of Appeal in *Christianuyi Ltd* [2019] EWCA Civ 474 does not detract from the statement of relevant principles).

- If the statute is a tax law rewrite statute (eg *Corporation Tax Act 2009, Corporation Tax Act 2010, Income Tax (Earnings and Pensions) Act 2003, Income Tax (Trading and Other Income) Act 2005* which consolidated prior law without making any change in the law (unless otherwise specified) then the prior law may be relevant. In this regard, it is important to apply the principles identified by the Upper Tribunal in *Scambler* [2017] UKUT 1 (TCC) (at 46–48) as to approach to be taken to the interpretation of a Tax Law Rewrite project consolidation Act:

'(1) We first examine the actual language used in the Act itself without reference to any of the statutes which it has replaced.

(2) In interpreting the language of the Act, we adopt the usual canons of statutory interpretation – giving consideration to the "clear words" of the legislation. What are "clear words" is to be ascertained upon normal principles; these do not confine us to literal interpretation. We must consider the context and scheme of the relevant Act as a whole, and its purpose.

(3) In undertaking this exercise, we are only permitted to adopt an interpretation that the statutory language is reasonably capable of bearing.

(4) Only when there is a real and substantial difficulty in interpreting the provisions, or there is an ambiguity which classical methods of

construction cannot resolve, can the recourse be had to the antecedent legislation.'

APPENDIX

CHECKLIST OF SOME MATTERS TO CONSIDER IN RESPECT OF ANY ENGAGEMENT

2.109 (This list is not exhaustive and is provided merely for illustrative purposes.)

1. What am I engaged to do?
2. What else could it include? Is it clear what is covered and what is not covered?
3. Who am I engaged by? Am I providing services to others? Could they reasonably think I am acting for them?
4. Who is the engagement with? Group companies etc?
5. How long is the engagement to last?
6. Has an engagement letter or terms of business been sent?
7. Has a duly signed copy of the engagement lateral terms of business being received back?
8. Does the letter clearly and accurately assess our services to be supplied? Does this fit in with questions 1 and 2?
9. Is it clear what the fee is? And how it is to be calculated? Is it VAT exclusive?
10. Basis of fees? Hourly rate? Hourly rate as default? What if rates change? Inflation link? Fixed fees? Basis? Additional work or services?
11. What is excluded? Is this sufficient?
12. Is there a cap on liability? Should there be? No responsibility for losses arising from the supply to the provider of incorrect or incomplete information, or to supply any appropriate information or to act on our advice provided or respond promptly to communications.
13. Indemnify against any misrepresentation, whether intentional or unintentional, and supplied orally or in writing in connection with this agreement.
14. Does the insurance cover available match this? Are there any relevant exclusions, restrictions, etc in the insurance documentation?
15. Should there be restriction to liability only for advice in writing? Should the letter provide that only advice in writing can be relied on?

16. Does the letter limit the scope of the duty as well as restricting the amount that can be recovered?
17. Is there an exclusion for changes in the law? Should it cover retrospective changes and changes arising from case law and practice?
18. Exclude reliance on advice where there is a different scenario even if it is only because of a healthy lapse of time?
19. Does it identify the client' obligations and responsibilities? Does it include notifying changes of circumstances?
20. Are there provisions as to the commencement and termination of the engagement? Does it cover work done before the return of the engagement letter? Are they clear?
21. Does it deal with confidentiality and retention of information?
22. Is GDPR covered? What about similar matters, eg DPA? Privacy Notice needed or desirable?
23. FATCA, CRS, DAC6, etc. Other exchange of information and reporting?
24. Who owns copyright in letters, reports and similar matters?
25. Client documents? What is the position to be in respect to these? Should there be a provision that only copies are provided?
26. Lien over documents for non-payment of fees?
27. Retention of papers? Copies? How long? Storage?
28. Health and safety?
29. Professional obligations?
30. Right to access for others who might be perceived as having different interests and/or as competitors?
31. Variation?
32. Other services?
33. Commissions?
34. Client monies
35. Time limit to query invoices?
36. Interest for late payment?
37. Guarantee of payment by other persons, eg personal investment company?
38. Right to request payment up front? Am I permitted to hold client monies?
39. Indemnity basis for all costs, expenses, etc?

40. No claims in respect of the engagement will be brought personally against any persons involved in performance of the engagement, whether actual or deemed servants or agents of the provider or not, including employees, office holders, consultants and third party contractors.

41. Liability in respect of breach of contract or breach of duty or fault or negligence or otherwise arising in connection with the engagement limited to the proportion ascribed to us by a court of competent jurisdiction and having regard to the contribution to the loss and damage in question of any other person (loss and damage having the same meaning as in the *Civil Liability (Contribution) Act 1978*). No application to any liability for death or personal injury or any other liability for which exclusion or restriction is prohibited by law or to liability arising as a result of fraud on the provider's part. No vicarious liability for fraud?

42. Any claim for breach of contract, breach of duty or fault or negligence or otherwise in connection with the engagement shall be brought within six years of the act or omission alleged to have caused the loss in question.

43. Quality control? By who?

44. Complaints? By who?

45. Conflicts of interest?

46. Termination?

47. Non-solicitation?

48. Email and internet communication?

49. *Contracts (Rights of Third Parties) Act 1999.* Also indemnity from client against third party liabilities?

50. *Proceeds of Crime Act 2002* and AML checks

51. Confirmation nothing involved which could fall within the *Criminal Finances Act 2017.*

52. Force majeure.

53. Severance etc.

54. Working with third parties.

55. Professional Indemnity Insurance.

56. Disputes – mediation and arbitration.

57. Governing or applicable law and jurisdiction.

58. Is the client a 'consumer'? Does the *Consumers Rights Act 2015* apply? Does *Part 2* on Unfair Terms apply? Include agreement terms that are fair, reasonable and appropriate. Include a checklist as to whether the client is a consumer.

59. Note also the *Consumer Contracts (Information Cancellation and Additional Charges) Regulations 2013, SI 2013/3134.*

60. *Provision of Professional Services Regulations 2009*? Is it (particularly *Part 2*) complied with?

61. Professional Rules? Is the PCRT relevant? Has reference been made to the recommended content for terms of engagement with a client?

62. What else?

Chapter 3

Professional conduct in relation to taxation

Mark McLaughlin CTA (Fellow), ATT (Fellow), TEP, Chartered Tax Adviser

SIGNPOSTS

- **Scope** – The commercial tax services market is largely self-regulated. For example, PCRT is produced by seven major professional bodies '... to assist and advise members on their professional conduct in relation to taxation, and particularly in the tripartite relationship between a member, client... and HMRC'. Those who are not members of professional bodies will still need to comply with standards expected of them. Solicitors and barristers are each subject to their own rules and regulations (see **3.1–3.16**).
- **Professional bodies and applicable standards** – PCRT sets out fundamental principles and standards for practising tax, including tax planning. Solicitors involved in tax are subject to SRA regulations, but may also be subject to PCRT if members of a relevant body. Barristers are regulated by the BSB. Tax barristers must not only adhere to the standards of conduct of the BSB (and PCRT, if they are also members of a relevant body), they also need to be aware of the professional standards of those instructing. Nothing in PCRT overrides legal professional privilege. In the event of any conflict between PCRT and the regulation of solicitors or barristers, the legal regulations prevail over PCRT (see **3.17–3.37**).
- **PCRT and tax planning** – PCRT sets out fundamental principles and standards for tax planning that are required to be followed. Failure to follow the fundamental principles and standards of PCRT can lead to a disciplinary process. PCRT features five fundamental principles and five standards for tax planning. The PCRT help sheet B on tax advice is useful (see **3.38–3.86**).

- **Regulation of tax lawyers** – Solicitors are regulated by the SRA and its 'Standards and Regulations' (effective 25 November 2019), which the SRA expects its regulated community to follow. In the event of any conflict between PCRT and the SRA, the SRA prevails (see **3.88–3.110**).
- **Regulation of tax barristers** – Barristers are regulated through the BSB. The standards of conduct it requires are set out in 'The BSB Handbook', which consists of six parts, including a code of conduct, 'core duties' and 'outcomes'. The BSB Handbook applies to barristers in general, so include those who advise on tax matters. Compliance with the core duties and rules is mandatory. In the event of any conflict between PCRT and the BSB, the BSB prevails over PCRT (see **3.111–3.134**).
- **Appendix** – The SRA's Standards and Regulations replaced the SRA Handbook with effect from 25 November 2019. This appendix outlines the SRA Handbook as it related to the law and regulation of those solicitors practising as tax professionals prior to that date (see **3.135–3.149**).

INTRODUCTION

3.1 The commercial tax services market is largely self-regulated. HMRC does not regulate tax professionals; although there has been a call for evidence as discussed in **Chapter 1** to identify whether there should be more regulation of tax professionals.

3.2 HMRC reported in September 2018 ('Role of professional bodies in in the regulation of tax agents') that 67% of tax agents are members of professional bodies that set standards for the behaviour expected of their members[1]. The research was undertaken to provide an understanding of (among other things) how professional bodies assess the adherence of members to the agreed standards, including the use of regulatory frameworks.

3.3 On the basis of the above statistic, it follows (rather worryingly) that one-third of tax agents are not affiliated to any professional body.

3.4 The principles and standards of behaviour that must be followed by those engaged in tax work who are members of professional bodies are generally set out in regulatory documents produced by those bodies.

3.5 For example, 'Professional Conduct in Relation to Taxation' (PCRT)[2] was produced by seven professional bodies, '…to assist and advise members

1 See tinyurl.com/HMRC-RPBRTA.
2 See tinyurl.com/CIOT-PCRT-2019.

on their professional conduct in relation to taxation, and particularly in the tripartite relationship between a member, client (including a former client) and HMRC' (see **3.21**).

3.6 Solicitors and barristers are each subject to their own rules and regulations (but solicitors have effectively adopted the PCRT).

3.7 Some professional bodies, who are not regulated by PCRT, have members engaged in tax work. Those professional bodies generally publish their own code or rules of conduct to which their members are expected to adhere (eg The Royal Chartered Institute of Surveyors).

3.8 As mentioned, a significant minority of individuals and firms who undertake tax work are not members of any professional bodies (see **3.9**). HMRC has been engaging with the tax profession to agree a single common standard for all agents, but this has not yet been achieved at the time of writing.

HMRC and the tax planner

3.9 Those individuals or firms who are not are members of professional bodies will nevertheless need to comply with standards expected of them by HMRC, if potential sanctions for breaches are to be avoided.

For example, HMRC can refuse to deal with a tax agent, pursue criminal cases, apply civil penalties where tax agents have been dishonest, or suspend access to certain online services for tax agents.

3.10 HMRC has produced a document called 'HMRC: the standard for agents'. The first standard was published in February 2016. The latest version published on 4 January 2018 includes standards for providing advice on tax planning (see **3.16**).

3.11 HMRC has incorporated three of the five PCRT fundamental principles into their own standard for tax agents, albeit that the principles are largely expressed in terms of the relationship between HMRC and agents. HMRC expects all agents (ie whether regulated by a professional body or not) to meet its standard.

3.12 The standard requires agents to maintain high standards in respect of the following:

- integrity;
- professional competence; and
- due care and professional behaviour.

3.13 The two PCRT fundamental principles not included in HMRC's standard are objectivity and confidentiality, as these are considered fundamental to the relationship between the adviser and client rather than that between the agent and HMRC.

3.14 In addition, HMRC has adopted the following PCRT standards[3] for those advising on tax planning (see **3.54**).

- lawful;
- disclosure and transparency;
- advising on tax planning arrangements; and
- professional judgement and appropriate documentation.

3.15 HMRC's standard is much briefer than PCRT and does not include further discussion on the standards for tax planning. As HMRC's standard is much briefer, it was not expected to impose further requirements on those who meet the PCRT standard.

3.16 The HMRC standard for tax agents can be downloaded from the gov.uk website (tinyurl.com/HMRC-SFTA). As discussed in **Chapter 1,** HMRC published a 'call for evidence' on raising standards for tax advice on 19 March 2020 (tinyurl.com/HMRC-RSTAM), which listed several issues for consideration, including:

- the scope of the market for tax advice and wider tax services;
- the characteristics of good and bad practice;
- current government interventions;
- international models; and
- possible approaches to raising standards.

The document also listed various potential approaches to raising standards and improving accountability in the tax adviser profession. The consultation closed on 28 August 2020. The outcome was published on 12 November 2020 (tinyurl.com/HMRC-RSTAMO), which listed the following 'next steps' intended by the government (these are awaited at the time of writing):

- raise awareness of the standard and review HMRC powers to enforce the standard;
- consult on requirement for professional indemnity insurance;
- work collaboratively with professional bodies; and
- tackle high costs to consumers of claiming tax refunds.

PROFESSIONAL BODIES AND APPLICABLE STANDARDS

Background

3.17 The largest accountancy and tax professional bodies share the standard 'Professional Conduct in Relation to Taxation' (PCRT) (see **3.21**).

3 The only standard not adopted is the 'client specific' standard.

3.18 Solicitors are regulated by the Solicitors Regulation Authority (SRA) (see **3.87**). Solicitors who are tax lawyers are therefore subject to SRA Standards and Regulations although they may additionally need to consider PCRT if they are also members of a relevant accountancy or tax professional body (but see **3.20** below).

3.19 Barristers are regulated by the Bar Standards Board (BSB) (see **3.111**). Tax barristers must not only adhere to the standards of conduct prescribed by the BSB but also need to be mindful of the professional standards applicable to the accountants and tax professionals they advise and who instruct them.

3.20 However, nothing in PCRT overrides legal professional privilege, and in the event of any conflict between PCRT and the above professional regulation of solicitors or barristers, the latter shall prevail over PCRT. Legal professional privilege is discussed in **Chapter 7**.

PCRT

3.21 PCRT is not a new publication. The first edition was published in November 1995. It is regularly updated to take account of evolving practices and circumstances.

3.22 The latest edition of PCRT (8th edition) is effective from 1 March 2019[4]. It sets out the fundamental principles and standards for members of the relevant professional bodies who practise in tax, including tax planning.

3.23 The eighth edition was produced in response to the government's challenge to professional bodies to take a greater lead in setting and enforcing clear professional standards around the facilitation and promotion of tax avoidance.

3.24 PCRT has been prepared jointly by seven professional bodies. These are:

- Association of Accounting Technicians (AAT);
- Association of Chartered Certified Accountants (ACCA);
- Association of Taxation Technicians (ATT);
- Chartered Institute of Taxation (CIOT);
- Institute of Chartered Accountants in England and Wales (ICAEW);
- Institute of Chartered Accountants of Scotland (ICAS); and
- Society of Trust and Estate Practitioners (STEP).

4 See tinyurl.com/CIOT-PCRT-2019.

3.25 PCRT has been acknowledged by HMRC as an acceptable basis for dealings between members of the above professional bodies and HMRC.

3.26 PCRT is supplemented by five help sheets. These are:

Help sheet A – Submission of tax information and tax filings;

Help sheet B – Tax advice (see **3.83**);

Help sheet C – Dealing with errors;

Help sheet D – Request for data by HM Revenue and Customs;

Help sheet E – Members' personal tax affairs.

3.27 The help sheet dealing with tax planning is help sheet B and repays careful reading.

3.28 The help sheets are not mandatory. However, a member of one of the participating professional bodies may, in a disciplinary case, be asked to explain why they did not follow the help sheet guidance.

3.29 The latest PCRT and help sheets can be downloaded from the websites of the above professional bodies. For example:

- ICAEW – www.icaew.com/technical/tax/pcrt; and
- CIOT – tinyurl.com/CIOT-PCRT-2019.

3.30 It should be noted that PCRT includes a legal disclaimer from any loss suffered or damage occasioned by reliance on PCRT.

SRA Standards and Regulations

3.31 As indicated at **3.88–3.90**, solicitors are subject to regulation by the SRA.

3.32 The SRA is not one of the sponsoring bodies of the PCRT.

3.33 The SRA has published 'SRA Standards and Regulations', which set out the standards and requirements that it expects its regulated community to achieve and observe, for the benefit of the clients they serve and in the public interest.

3.34 The SRA Standards and Regulations were introduced with effect from 25 November 2019. Prior to that date, the 'SRA Handbook' set out mandatory 'principles' that define the fundamental ethical and professional standards expected of all firms and individuals when providing legal services, and a 'code of conduct' setting out 'outcomes-focused' conduct requirements.

3.35 For commentary on the Standards and Regulations and the regulation of tax lawyers, see **3.91–3.93**.

BSB Handbook

3.36 As indicated at **3.111,** the professional conduct of barristers is regulated by the BSB.

3.37 The standards of conduct for barristers are set out in a handbook produced by the BSB ('The BSB Handbook')[5]. The handbook sets out to provide clarity about the regulatory regime with which barristers must comply.

For commentary on The BSB Handbook and the regulation of tax barristers, see **3.112**.

PCRT AND TAX PLANNING

General

3.38 As indicated at **3.24**, PCRT was produced jointly by seven major professional bodies for use by their members when providing advice on UK tax matters. It sets out the fundamental principles and standards for tax planning that all members of the relevant professional bodies are expected to follow.

3.39 The purpose of PCRT (and supporting help sheets) is to assist and advise members on their professional conduct in relation to taxation. The Foreword (March 2019 edition) states: 'PCRT is intended to guide members in their behaviour, to assist them and to ensure that they undertake work effectively and appropriately'.

3.40 However, it is not exhaustive; in cases of doubt, advice should be sought from the members' professional body (eg where there is a facility to raise questions on professional standards) and/or the member's legal advisers.

3.41 If a member of a relevant professional body fails to adhere to the fundamental principles and standards for tax planning under PCRT they are liable to be subject to a disciplinary process.

3.42 Furthermore, if a relevant professional body is notified of concerns about a member's behaviour involving tax matters, the body will take PCRT into consideration in determining whether disciplinary action is required. The potential disciplinary measures range from a reprimand to exclusion from the member's professional body.

3.43 However, PCRT is stated not to override legal professional privilege, or a member's professional duties. Nor should PCRT be interpreted as causing any conflict under general law, statutory regulation, or professional regulation of solicitors or barristers.

3.44 PCRT features five fundamental principles (see **3.47**) and five standards for tax planning (see **3.54**).

5 See tinyurl.com/BSB-BSBHB, latest version 4.6 (31 December 2020).

3.45 It is vitally important to distinguish between tax evasion and tax planning. It goes without saying that members of the relevant professional bodies (and tax advisers in general) must never be knowingly involved in tax evasion (unless acting for a client who is rectifying their affairs).

3.46 A tax advice help sheet ('PCRT help sheet B: Tax Advice') includes guidance on the standards for tax planning (see **3.83**).

Five fundamental principles

3.47 The five fundamental principles are as follows:

- **Integrity**

  To be straightforward and honest in all professional and business relationships.

- **Objectivity**

  To not allow bias, conflict of interest or undue influence of others to override professional or business judgements.

- **Professional competence and due care**

  To maintain professional knowledge and skill at the level required to ensure that a client or employer receives competent professional service based on current developments in practice, legislation and techniques and act diligently and in accordance with applicable technical and professional standards.

- **Confidentiality**

  To respect the confidentiality of information acquired as a result of professional and business relationships and, therefore, not disclose any such information to third parties without proper and specific authority, unless there is a legal or professional right or duty to disclose, nor use the information for the personal advantage of the member or third parties.

- **Professional behaviour**

  To comply with relevant laws and regulations and avoid any action that discredits the profession.

3.48 The PCRT document includes discussion of each fundamental principle. In the context of tax planning, the principles of most relevance in many cases will be integrity, professional competence and due care, and professional behaviour. Those three principles were the focus of the standards for tax planning.

3.49 The principle of integrity broadly involves honesty in all the relevant professional body member's dealings and ensuring that nothing is knowingly done to mislead others. The same applies to 'carelessly' misleading (ie either by commission or omission).

3.50 The PCRT commentary on the professional competence and due care principle points out that members should be careful not to stray beyond the original or revised agreed terms of their engagement and ensure that their professional indemnity insurance covers the work.

3.51 The commentary also states (among other things) that members must not undertake professional work which they are not competent to perform unless they obtain appropriate assistance from a suitably qualified specialist.

3.52 In relation to the professional behaviour principle, the PCRT commentary states that members should consider whether any tax arrangements with which they might be associated (ie on their own and/or a client's behalf) might bring the members and the profession into disrepute.

3.53 It follows that members will need to carefully consider whether (for example) becoming involved with a marketed tax avoidance scheme would breach this principle.

See also the standard for advising on tax planning arrangements (at **3.64**) and the help sheet on tax advice (at **3.83**).

Standards for tax planning

3.54 The relevant PCRT professional bodies have developed five standards for tax planning, which supplement the five fundamental principles set out at **3.47**.

3.55 The five standards for tax planning are:

- client specific (see **3.56**);
- lawful (see **3.59**);
- disclosure and transparency (see **3.62**);
- advising on tax planning arrangements (see **3.64**); and
- professional judgement and appropriate documentation (see **3.80**).

As indicated at **3.26**, PCRT is supplemented by help sheets. There is a help sheet on tax advice, which is relevant to tax planning (see **3.83**).

The 'client specific' standard

3.56 The client specific standard states:

> 'Tax planning must be specific to the particular client's facts and circumstances. Clients must be alerted to the wider risks and the implications of any courses of action.'

3.57 The PCRT commentary on this standard indicates that the 'risks' mentioned are those which are directly attributable to the planning, and which could be 'reasonably foreseeable' by the member. The latter risk is subjective and will therefore be a matter of judgement by the member.

3.58 Generic opinions or advice (ie where the taxpayer's specific circumstances are not taken into consideration) are regarded as presenting particular risks. If advice is generic, and/or it depends on certain assumptions, this should be highlighted, together with the need for specific advice to be taken before acting, with sufficient prominence to prevent any misunderstandings arising.

The 'lawful' standard

3.59 The lawful standard states:

> 'At all times members must act lawfully and with integrity and expect the same from their clients. Tax planning should be based on a realistic assessment of the facts and on a credible view of the law. Members should draw their clients' attention to where the law is materially uncertain, for example because HMRC is known to take a different view of the law. Members should consider taking further advice appropriate to the risks and circumstances of the particular case, for example where litigation is likely.'

3.60 The PCRT commentary on the lawful standard states that there is a requirement to advise clients on a material uncertainty in the law (including where HMRC take a different view) even if the likelihood of HMRC intervention is considered low.

3.61 If HMRC has a different view of the law the client should be alerted accordingly and advised of the risks and likely costs that might be incurred in order to determine any dispute.

The 'disclosure and transparency' standard

3.62 The disclosure and transparency standard states:

> 'Tax advice must not rely for its effectiveness on HMRC having less than the relevant facts. Any disclosure must fairly represent all relevant facts.'

3.63 Aside from any disclosure required by law, the extent of disclosure (eg in the 'white space' of an individual taxpayer's self-assessment return) will be a matter of professional judgement based on the relevant facts, specific law, and what the client consents should be disclosed. Advisers might feel they are in their client's hands when making white space entries on tax returns, but adequate disclosure is paramount.

The 'tax planning arrangements' standard

3.64 The tax planning arrangements standard states:

'Members must not create, encourage or promote tax planning arrangements or structures that:

(i) set out to achieve results that are contrary to the clear intention of Parliament in enacting relevant legislation; and/or

(ii) are highly artificial or highly contrived and seek to exploit shortcomings within the relevant legislation.'

3.65 The standard needs to be read very carefully for comprehension. For example, the terms 'create', 'encourage' and 'promote' are not defined in PCRT and have a potentially wide meaning. However, PCRT help sheet B on tax advice (at FAQ 1) offers some clarification on the rationale behind the tax planning standard:

'The concern is over advisers who create schemes to exploit loopholes and frustrate the will of Parliament, or who promote them to clients, or encourage clients into them.'

3.66 There is no definition of 'arrangements' or 'structures' for these purposes. Some assistance on the meaning of 'arrangements' may be derived from different parts of the tax legislation. For example, the term is defined in the *Corporation Tax Act 2010, s 464A* ('Charge to tax: arrangements conferring benefit on participator') as including 'any arrangements, scheme or understanding of any kind, whether or not legally enforceable, involving a single transaction or two or more transactions'[6].

3.67 It is important to note that the tax planning standard, and the adviser's compliance with it, is not concerned with whether the relevant planning arrangement is successful, but on the behaviour of the adviser in creating, encouraging or promoting it.

3.68 Thus (for example) an adviser may breach the PCRT tax planning arrangement standard in respect of an artificial tax planning arrangement even if it achieves the desired tax outcome.

3.69 The PCRT commentary on the tax planning arrangements standard offers some protection for advisers against misjudging whether tax planning arrangements breach the tax planning standard.

3.70 The commentary advocates the following course of action where a member has a 'genuine and reasonable uncertainty' about whether a planning arrangement breaches the standard (at para 3.9):

'• document the detailed reasoning and evidence sufficiently to be able to demonstrate why they took the view that any planning was not in breach of this Standard;

6 See www.bloomsburyprofessionalonline.com/view/uktaxlegislation/CTA2010-pt10-ch3A.xml.

- include in their client advice an assessment of uncertainties and risks involved in the planning…; and
- include in their client advice an assessment of the relevant disclosures that should be made to HMRC in order to enable it, should it wish to do so, to make any reasonable enquiries …'

3.71 It will be noted that there are two separate limbs ((i) and (ii)) to the tax planning arrangements standard.

(i) 'Contrary to the clear intention of Parliament'

3.72 An important question in relation to limb (i) is what steps a member should take to establish what was the 'clear intention of Parliament' in enacting relevant legislation. Helpfully, some guidance is provided in the PCRT help sheet B on tax advice (FAQ 3), which poses the question: 'How would I know if the planning is contrary to the clear intention of Parliament?' The response provided in the guidance states:

> 'Discerning the intention of Parliament at the time that the legislation was enacted is likely only to be an issue where more complex or ground-breaking planning is concerned. In such cases the legislation and any associated explanatory notes issued at the time of enactment should prove sufficient. Only rarely should it be necessary to consult Hansard. If the intention of Parliament was genuinely unclear at the time of enactment, then you would not be expected to second guess what was the clear intention of Parliament.'

3.73 A 'genuinely unclear' intention is such that this standard should not cause difficulties in most cases. However, the ambiguous drafting of tax legislation in some instances could require research to establish Parliament's intention, which may not necessarily prove conclusive.

3.74 The position is also presently unclear where a subsequent tax case provides clarification on the intention of Parliament; for example, if litigation proves necessary, could it be said that Parliament's intention was clear in the first place?

(ii) Highly artificial or highly contrived arrangements

3.75 The second limb to the tax planning arrangements standard contains two elements: (1) highly artificial or highly contrived; and (2) seek to exploit shortcomings within the relevant legislation.

3.76 It seems improbable that element (1) would present difficulties for practitioners undertaking mainstream tax planning for their clients. However, it is likely to affect (for example) the use of marketed tax avoidance schemes. The question therefore arises whether a practitioner could refer their client to a firm that designs and markets such schemes without contravening the tax planning standard. Care is also needed as 'highly' is a subjective word, which therefore requires a degree of judgement.

3.77 With regard to element (2), some assistance may be derived from HMRC's GAAR guidance, which states for those purposes (at C5.9.1):

> 'Whether arrangements are intended to exploit any shortcomings in the relevant tax provisions requires consideration because the drafting of particular tax rules may lead to unanticipated consequences.'

It goes on to point out (at C5.9.2):

> 'This may be because the tax rules have a defect that was not apparent to the drafter, or the drafter may not have contemplated that a particular type of transaction could be carried out (whether to come within the rules or to keep outside them).'

For further commentary on the GAAR, see **Chapter 2**.

3.78 The PCRT help sheet on tax advice includes the following (FAQ 11):

> 'Would it be acceptable under the 4th Standard to make a referral to another adviser whom I know offers planning which could be considered to be highly artificial or highly contrived and seeks to exploit the shortcomings within the relevant legislation?'

The response provided in the guidance states:

> 'Under the 4th Standard a member must not "create, encourage or promote tax planning arrangements or structures that are highly artificial or highly contrived and seek to exploit the shortcomings within the relevant legislation". If you refer clients to another adviser expressly so that they can benefit from such planning it is quite probable that this behaviour would be considered to be "encouraging" behaviour which is in contravention of the 4th Standard.
>
> If you are uncertain whether the planning being offered by the other adviser is highly artificial or highly contrived and still decide to refer it to them you should make the client aware of the risks associated with aggressive planning, including probable challenge by HMRC and potential damage to reputation. You should document your reasons for making the referral.'

3.79 The tax advice help sheet (at FAQ 5) contains a helpful list of points for PCRT members in considering whether to introduce a client to another adviser's planning arrangement, as well as points to consider when deciding whether a counsel's opinion which states that a tax planning arrangement is effective can be relied upon (FAQ 10) (see www.icaew.com/technical/tax/pcrt/2019/helpsheet-b-tax-advice).

The 'professional judgement and appropriate documentation' standard

3.80 The 'professional judgement and appropriate documentation' standard states:

> 'Applying these requirements to particular client advisory situations requires members to exercise professional judgement on a number of matters. Members should keep notes on a timely basis of the rationale for the judgements exercised in seeking to adhere to these requirements.'

3.81 Advisers may be required to defend the judgements they have made in applying PCRT requirements to their work. This could happen some years later, which underlines the importance of making and keeping contemporaneous notes and records to support any proposition that the judgements made were reasonable.

3.82 This standard may be particularly relevant in circumstances such as where a member's client wishes to engage in planning which the member does not consider to be appropriate and/or is not in accordance with the member's business principles and ethics; or where a client informs the member that they are proceeding with a tax planning arrangement without taking full advice from the member.

PCRT tax advice help sheet

3.83 As indicated at **3.46**, the PCRT document is supplemented by five help sheets, including help sheet B which deals with tax advice (tinyurl.com/PCRT-HS-B).

3.84 The tax advice help sheet reproduces the standards for tax planning from PCRT, and includes further discussion on the standards, which repeats the discussion in the PCRT document itself.

3.85 The help sheet also contains further discussion, which features the following helpful list of 'things to consider' for practitioners in relation to tax planning and advice:

- Have you checked that your engagement letter fully covers the scope of the planning advice?
- Have you taken the Standards for Tax Planning and the Fundamental Principles into account? Is it client specific? Is it lawful? Will all relevant facts be disclosed to HMRC? Is it creating, encouraging or promoting tax planning contrary to the 4th Standard for Tax Planning?
- How tax sophisticated is the client?
- Has the client made clear what they wish to achieve by the planning?
- What are the issues involved with the implementation of the planning?

- What are the risks associated with the planning and have you warned the client of them? For example:
  - The strength of the legal interpretation relied upon.
  - The potential application of the GAAR.
  - The implications for the client, including the obligations of the client in relation to their tax return, if the planning requires disclosure under DOTAS or DASVOIT and the potential for an accelerated payment notice or partner payment notice.
  - The reputational risk to the client and the member of the planning in the public arena.
  - The stress, cost and wider personal or business implications to the client in the event of a prolonged dispute with HMRC. This may involve unwelcomed publicity, costs, expenses and loss of management time over a significant period.
  - If the client tenders for government contracts, the potential impact of the proposed tax planning on tendering for and retaining public sector contracts.
  - The risk of counteraction. This may occur before the planning is completed or potentially there may be retrospective counteraction at a later date.
  - The risk of challenge by HMRC. Such challenge may relate to the legal interpretation relied upon but may alternatively relate to the construction of the facts, including the implementation of the planning.
  - The risk and inherent uncertainty of litigation. The probability of the planning being overturned by the courts if litigated and the potential ultimate downside should the client be unsuccessful.
  - Is a second opinion necessary/advisable?
- Are the arrangements in line with any applicable code of conduct or ethical guidelines or stances such as the Banking Code, and fit and proper tests for charity trustees and pension administrators?
- Are you satisfied that the client understands the planning proposed?
- Have you documented the advice given and the reasoning behind it?

3.86 The help sheet also includes responses to the following frequently asked questions (FAQs) on tax advice:

(1) My job is to advise clients on the law. Can I still do that under the Standards for Tax Planning?

(2) What if the situation is more borderline, don't I still have to advise my clients?

(3) How would I know if the planning was contrary to the clear intention of Parliament is?

(4) Do I need to have an engagement letter in place to cover tax planning advice?

(5) I am considering introducing my client to another adviser's planning arrangement. What should I consider?

(6) If I do introduce my client to the planning arrangement in FAQ (5) above I will receive commission. Do I have to tell my client about this?

(7) Can I receive commission if I am asked to give a second opinion on another adviser's tax planning arrangement?

(8) What is my responsibility if a client wishes to engage in planning which I do not consider to be appropriate or does not sit comfortably with my business principles and ethics?

(9) What is the position if my client tells me that they will go ahead with a tax planning arrangement without taking full advice from me?

(10) The tax planning arrangement my client is considering has Counsel's opinion which says the planning is effective. Can I/my client rely on that?

(11) Would it be acceptable under the 4th Standard to make a referral to another adviser whom I know offers planning which could be considered to be highly artificial or highly contrived and seeks to exploit the shortcomings within the relevant legislation?

(12) Unbeknown to me, my client has undertaken planning with another adviser and has now asked me to enter it on his tax return. What should I do if I am not sure whether the planning is effective or not?

(13) What is the position if the adviser responsible for the planning in FAQ (12) above is not a member of a professional body?

(14) What should I do if I believe the planning implemented by my client on the advice of another adviser constitutes evasion?

(15) What are the consequences if I create, encourage or promote tax planning which is contrary to the Standards for Tax Planning and the Fundamental Principles?

3.87 It should be noted that the help sheet commentary and FAQs are only intended to illustrate the practical application of the standards of tax planning and should not be taken to be comprehensive. Specific advice may be required from the relevant professional body and/or specialists in this area, depending on the particular circumstances.

REGULATION OF TAX LAWYERS

3.88 Solicitors (and barristers – see **3.111**) are subject to their own rules and regulations. As indicated elsewhere in this chapter, solicitors are subject to regulation by the SRA. The regulations focus on high professional standards and protecting the public.

3.89 Some solicitors may also be members of an accountancy or tax professional body, in which case they will also need to consider PCRT (if they are members of professional bodies that subscribe to it) and/or the standards and principles of any other participating body of which they are a member.

3.90 However, nothing in PCRT overrides legal professional privilege, and in the event of any conflict between PCRT and the above professional regulation of solicitors (or barristers), the latter shall prevail.

3.91 As indicated at **3.34**, the SRA Standards and Regulations at the time of writing came into effect on 25 November 2019, replacing the SRA Handbook.

3.92 The SRA Standards and Regulations were designed to be shorter and simpler than the SRA Handbook. The latter contains mandatory 'principles' that define the fundamental ethical and professional standards expected of all firms and individuals when providing legal services, and a code of conduct setting out 'outcomes-focused' conduct requirements. The handbook includes non-mandatory guidance and notes as an aid to compliance (see the Appendix at **3.135**).

3.93 Law firms must ensure that all employees (even if non-qualified and non-fee earners) receive appropriate training on the requirements in the SRA Standards and Regulations, albeit only to the extent necessary for the role they undertake in the firm (but, for example, all staff will need to understand that they should keep clients' affairs confidential and behave with integrity).

The SRA Standards and Regulations can be viewed or downloaded from the SRA website[7].

SRA Standards and Regulations: principles

3.94 There are the seven principles in the SRA Standards and Regulations, comprising the 'fundamental tenets of ethical behaviour' which are expected to be upheld by all those regulated by the SRA.

3.95 However, compliance with the principles is subject to any overriding legal and professional obligations.

3.96 The seven principles are reproduced below:

7 See www.sra.org.uk/solicitors/standards-regulations.

3.97 *Professional conduct in relation to taxation*

'You act:

1. in a way that upholds the constitutional principle of the rule of law, and the proper administration of justice.
2. in a way that upholds public trust and confidence in the solicitors' profession and in legal services provided by *authorised persons*.
3. with independence.
4. with honesty.
5. with integrity.
6. in a way that encourages equality, diversity and inclusion.
7. in the best interests of each *client*.'

In the context of tax planning advice, the principles of potential relevance in most cases are principles 1, 2, 5 and 7 (see below).

3.97 However, solicitors must (for example) meet the competencies set out in the SRA competent statement and should not go beyond their professional capabilities without obtaining expert assistance.

3.98 Acting in the best interests of each client (principle 7) requires solicitors to act in good faith and do their best for clients.

3.99 In the context of tax planning for clients, solicitors will need to consider (for example) whether recommending tax planning arrangements which are 'high risk' (including seeking to achieve results that are contrary to the clear intention of Parliament in enacting relevant legislation, and/or are highly artificial or contrived and seek to exploit shortcomings in the relevant legislation) and which are likely to be challenged by HMRC would breach this principle.

3.100 Principle 2 may be problematic for solicitors who (for example) design and/or implement tax planning arrangements for clients which are likely to be considered abusive and/or which seek to exploit loopholes in the tax legislation. The recent negative publicity surrounding tax avoidance 'schemes' is such that undertaking those activities might be regarded as a breach of principle 2, as it risks bringing the solicitor or the legal profession into disrepute.

3.101 The SRA has published a guidance note ('Public trust and confidence') explaining when a breach of principle 2 is likely to have taken place[8].

3.102 The SRA has also published a guidance note ('Acting with integrity'), to explain principle 5[9]. The guidance points out that it is possible to behave without integrity without necessarily being dishonest. The circumstances in which the SRA are likely to take disciplinary action for a lack of integrity

8 See www.sra.org.uk/solicitors/guidance/ethics-guidance/public-trust-and-confidence.

9 See www.sra.org.uk/solicitors/guidance/ethics-guidance/acting-with-integrity.

include 'Where there has been a wilful or reckless disregard of standards, rules, legal requirements and obligations or ethics, including an indifference to what the applicable provisions are or to the impacts or consequences of a breach'.

The SRA principles can be accessed via the Standards and Regulations section of the SRA website[10].

SRA warning notice: tax avoidance

3.103 The SRA's general guidance for law professionals includes a series of warning notices, one of which ('Tax avoidance – your duties') is aimed at regulated solicitors who are involved either directly or indirectly in advising clients about tax, handling client matters or transactions involving them in the design, implementation, organisation or management of tax affairs, schemes or arrangements. See Appendix C.

3.104 The SRA's tax avoidance warning notice highlights principles 1, 2, 5 and 7 (see **3.94–3.93**). The notice also states: 'We have concerns about anyone we regulate facilitating tax avoidance schemes that are aggressive in ways that go beyond the intentions of Parliament'. It also sets out the following SRA expectations for regulated solicitors:

(a) *Acting with integrity*

The SRA states: 'When advising a client on avoidance of tax schemes you should make clear that any avoidance arrangements the client enters into might deliver tax outcomes that were never envisaged or intended by Parliament and may be challenged. You should be clear as to the legal implications, the costs and penalties of non-compliance should the arrangement fail'.

The SRA also warns advisers to consider their own position in facilitating tax avoidance arrangements. It states: 'Should the arrangement be found to be abusive, your conduct may be called into question'.

(b) *HMRC and the wider context*

The SRA considers that it is important for advisers to be familiar with the underlying approach of HMRC, which is changing rapidly. It warns:

> 'The promotion or implementation of abusive arrangements (applying the definition set out in the GAAR, PCRT or otherwise) will lead both client and adviser into difficulties with HMRC and may leave you open to disciplinary action. The most common schemes we have seen in recent years have related to avoiding SDLT. We will continue to scrutinise any of these schemes carefully.'

10 See www.sra.org.uk/solicitors/standards-regulations/principles.

(c) *Legislation and the wider context*

The warning notice points out that advisers must be fully familiar with all changes in tax avoidance legislation to ensure compliance with SRA principles at all times, particularly the requirement to act with integrity.

Examples of recent anti-avoidance legislative changes include 'follower notices' and 'accelerated payment notices', as well as the serial tax avoidance regime.

(d) *Professional conduct in relation to taxation*

The SRA have welcomed PCRT and state: 'These standards reflect our own principles, particularly that solicitors must be honest and act with integrity, and uphold the rule of law'.

3.105 The SRA expects solicitors to be familiar with PCRT and adhere to its standards.

The warning notice on tax avoidance can be viewed and downloaded from the SRA website[11].

SRA Standards and Regulations: code of conduct

3.106 The SRA Handbook's Standards and Regulations include a code of conduct, which describes the standards and business controls that the SRA and the public expect of firms authorised by the SRA to provide legal services. A serious failure to meet the SRA's standards or a serious breach of its regulations could result in regulatory action.

3.107 The SRA's regulatory requirements are underpinned by its 'Enforcement Strategy', which explains in more detail the SRA's views about the issues considered to be serious, and its approach to taking regulatory action in the public interest. The Enforcement Strategy can also be viewed at the SRA website[12].

3.108 There are two separate codes of conduct. One code relates to firms, which is considered below. The other code applies to solicitors, registered European lawyers (RELs) and registered foreign lawyers (RFLs), which is not considered in this chapter but renders those to whom it applies personally accountable for compliance with it. The code of conduct for solicitors, RELs and RFLs is available from the SRA website[13].

3.109 The code of conduct for firms is divided into a number of sections as follows, with subsections setting out the requirement in detail:

11 See www.sra.org.uk/solicitors/guidance/tax-avoidance-duties.

12 See www.sra.org.uk/sra/corporate-strategy/sra-enforcement-strategy.

13 See www.sra.org.uk/solicitors/standards-regulations/code-conduct-solicitors.

(1) Maintaining trust and security.

(2) Compliance and business systems.

(3) Cooperation and accountability – the SRA states (at 3.5): 'You are honest and open with clients if things go wrong, and if a client suffers loss or harm as a result you put matters right (if possible) and explain fully and promptly what has happened and the likely impact'. This requirement will need to be followed carefully in the context of (for example) advice given to clients on tax planning arrangements, where those arrangements are successfully challenged by HMRC.

(4) Service and competence – the SRA states (at 4.3): 'You ensure that your managers and employees are competent to carry out their role, and keep their professional knowledge and skills, as well as understanding of their legal, ethical and regulatory obligations, up to date'. This requirement has particular relevance to solicitors who give tax advice to their clients, in view of the frequent changes to tax legislation, case law and HMRC practice.

(5) Client money and assets.

(6) This section is sub-divided: 6.1–6.2 covers conflict of interests; 6.3–6.5 deals with confidentiality and disclosure.

(7) Applicable standards in the SRA Code of Conduct for solicitors, RELs and RFLs.

(8) Managers in SRA authorised firms.

(9) Compliance officers.

3.110 Detailed commentary on the code of conduct is beyond the scope of this chapter. Reference should be made to the SRA website, which includes the full text of the current SRA code of conduct[14].

The SRA Standards and Regulations are also available in their entirety on the SRA website[15].

REGULATION OF TAX BARRISTERS

3.111 Barristers are regulated by the Bar Standards Board (BSB) (see **3.19**). Tax barristers must not only adhere to the standards of conduct prescribed by the BSB but also need to be mindful of the professional standards applicable to the accountants and tax professionals they advise.

14 See www.sra.org.uk/solicitors/standards-regulations/code-conduct-firms.

15 See www.sra.org.uk/solicitors/standards-regulations.

However, nothing in PCRT overrides legal professional privilege, and in the event of any conflict between PCRT and the above professional regulation of barristers (or solicitors) the latter shall prevail over PCRT.

BSB Handbook

3.112 As indicated at **3.36** above, the standards of conduct for barristers are set out in a handbook produced by the BSB ('The BSB Handbook'). The handbook sets out to provide clarity about the regulatory regime with which barristers must comply. It applies to barristers in general, so awareness and compliance is required by those barristers who advise on tax matters.

3.113 The Handbook consists of six parts:

(1) Introduction;

(2) Code of conduct;

(3) Scope of practice, authorisation and licensing rules;

(4) Qualification rules;

(5) Enforcement regulations; and

(6) Definitions.

The handbook includes 'core duties' (see **3.119**) and 'outcomes', as well as guidance, rules and regulations.

3.114 The latest version of the BSB Handbook at the time of writing (version 4.6) came into force on 31 December 2020.

BSB Handbook: Code of conduct

3.115 The BSB Handbook's code of conduct includes ten 'core duties', which underpin the BSB's entire regulatory framework, and the conduct rules which supplement those core duties. Compliance with both the core duties and the rules is mandatory.

3.116 The code of conduct includes rules applying to particular groups of regulated persons (eg self-employed barristers, barristers undertaking public access and licensed access work, etc).

3.117 In addition, the code of conduct contains 'outcomes', which explain the reasons for the regulatory scheme. The outcomes are not themselves mandatory rules. However, they are factors which BSB regulated persons or unregistered barristers should have in mind when considering how the core duties, conduct rules, etc, should be applied in particular circumstances.

3.118 The BSB will take into account whether or not an outcome has, or might have been, adversely affected when considering how to respond to alleged breaches of the core duties, conduct rules or bar qualification rules.

Code of conduct: Core duties

3.119 The ten core duties are reproduced below:

> 'CD1 You must observe your duty to the court in the administration of justice.
>
> CD2 You must act in the best interests of each client.
>
> CD3 You must act with honesty, and with integrity.
>
> CD4 You must maintain your independence.
>
> CD5 You must not behave in a way which is likely to diminish the trust and confidence which the public places in you or in the profession.
>
> CD6 You must keep the affairs of each client confidential.
>
> CD7 You must provide a competent standard of work and service to each client.
>
> CD8 You must not discriminate unlawfully against any person.
>
> CD9 You must be open and co-operative with your regulators.
>
> CD10 You must take reasonable steps to manage your practice, or carry out your role within your practice, competently and in such a way as to achieve compliance with your legal and regulatory obligations.'

Compliance with all ten core duties is required, as the rules are mandatory.

3.120 The core duties are generally not presented in order of precedence, subject to certain specified exceptions. For example, CD1 overrides any other core duty.

3.121 The duty to act in the client's best interests (CD2) is clearly a central and important requirement generally. It is also relevant when giving advice on tax planning arrangements.

3.122 For example, it must be highly questionable whether it would ever be in a client's best interests to participate in an artificial and/or potentially abusive tax avoidance scheme. On that basis, barristers who give advice on such schemes run the risk of breaching CD2.

3.123 Furthermore, the requirement that barristers do not behave in a way that is likely to diminish the trust and confidence which the public places in them or in the profession (CD5) will be particularly apposite in the context of advice on tax planning arrangements.

3.124 Public awareness of tax avoidance and 'unacceptable' (in HMRC's view) tax planning has increased in recent years following publicity by HMRC and the media of numerous 'high profile' cases concerning tax schemes and arrangements that were ultimately unsuccessful. The participants of some schemes have included well-known celebrities.

3.125 Barristers who are instructed to advise on proposed tax planning arrangements will therefore need to take various factors into account when considering whether to accept such instructions.

3.126 For example, if a barrister gives an opinion that a proposed scheme or arrangement will achieve its tax objectives, but that scheme or arrangement is later found to be abusive and/or is successfully challenged by HMRC in the courts, would this bring the profession into disrepute, and therefore constitute a breach of CD5? In addition, should the instructions have been accepted in the first place (ie how was the scheme or arrangement likely to be perceived by the public)?

3.127 Furthermore, tax barristers will need to carefully consider the public's possible perception of the professionals who are proposing and/or promoting tax planning schemes or arrangements, before accepting instructions from them.

3.128 For example, a number of tax planning 'boutiques' have had their schemes and arrangements defeated by HMRC in the courts. Tax barristers will need to consider whether acceptance of instructions by such boutiques etc, might breach CD5. The BSB Handbook states the following in its guidance (at gC126):

> 'Your obligations under CD5 require you not to act in *an association* with a person where, merely by being associated with such person, you may reasonably be considered as bringing the profession into disrepute or otherwise diminishing the trust that the public places in you and your profession.'

3.129 In addition to the core duties, the BSB Handbook lists the following conduct rules:

C1. You and the court;

C2. Behaving ethically;

C3. You and your client;

C4. You and your regulator;

C5. You and your practice.

3.130 Each conduct rule is underpinned by outcomes, rules and guidance. For example, the following are of relevance to barristers advising on tax planning:

- Outcome C11 – 'Clients' best interests are protected and promoted by those acting for them' (oC11).
- Guidance C36 – 'Your duty is to your client, not to your professional client or other intermediary (if any)' (gC36).

- Rule C20 – 'Where you are a BSB authorised individual, you are personally responsible for your own conduct and for your professional work. You must use your own professional judgment in relation to those matters on which you are instructed and be able to justify your decisions and actions. You must do this notwithstanding the views of your client, professional client, employer or any other person' (rC20).

3.131 Outcomes, rules and guidance should also be considered in the context of conduct rules, core duties, etc. For example, conduct rule 1 ('You and the court') includes as its outcomes (at oC5): 'The public has confidence in the administration of justice and in those who serve it'. This outcome is also of relevance in the context of CD5 (see **3.128**).

The 'cab-rank' rule

3.132 The 'cab-rank' rule (rC29) applies to instructions from professional clients. Where the instructions are appropriate (taking into account experience, seniority and/or field of practice), the barrister is required (subject to certain exceptions; see **3.103**) to accept those instructions, irrespective of:

- the identity of the client;
- the nature of the case to which the instructions relate;
- whether the client is paying privately or is publicly funded; and
- any belief or opinion which the barrister may have formed as to the character, reputation, cause, conduct, guilt or innocence of the client.

It follows that (for example) barristers should generally not join the tax planning 'cab rank' by making themselves available to advise on such matters that are outside their experience and/or expertise.

3.133 However, there are certain exceptions to the cab-rank rule (rC30). These include where the barrister is required to refuse to accept the instructions pursuant to Rule rC21 (see below), or where accepting the instructions would require the barrister to do any foreign work. There is also an exception if the barrister has not been offered a proper fee for the relevant services. In determining whether or not a fee is 'proper' for these purposes, it is necessary to consider the complexity, length and difficulty of the case; the barrister's ability, experience and seniority; and the expenses which the barrister will incur.

3.134 Rule rC21 concerns the acceptance of instructions. It provides that instructions to act must not be accepted broadly if (among other things) there is an actual or potential conflict of interest; or the instructions require the barrister to act other than in accordance with the law or the provisions of the BSB Handbook; or the barrister is not competent to handle the particular matter or otherwise does not have enough experience to handle the matter; or there is a real prospect that the barrister is not going to be able to maintain independence.

The BSB Handbook can be viewed and downloaded from the BSB's website[16].

APPENDIX: SRA HANDBOOK (REPLACED ON 25 NOVEMBER 2019)

3.135 From October 2011 to November 2019, the SRA Handbook set out the standards and requirements that the SRA expected its regulated community to achieve and observe, for the benefit of the clients they served and in the public interest.

3.136 As indicated at **3.34**, the SRA Handbook was replaced by the SRA Standards and Regulations, which came into effect on 25 November 2019.

SRA Handbook: Principles

3.137 There are the ten principles in the SRA Handbook, which apply to those who are regulated by the SRA and underpin all aspects of practice. The principles define the 'fundamental ethical and professional standards' expected by the SRA of all firms (and in some circumstances they apply outside practice).

However, compliance with the principles is subject to any overriding legal obligations.

3.138 The ten principles are reproduced below:

'(1) uphold the rule of law and the proper administration of justice;

(2) act with integrity;

(3) not allow your independence to be compromised;

(4) all act in the best interests of each client;

(5) provide a proper standard of service to your clients;

(6) behave in a way that maintains the trust the public places in you and in the provision of legal services;

(7) comply with your legal and regulatory obligations and deal with your regulators and ombudsmen in an open, timely and co-operative manner;

(8) run your business or carry out your role in the business effectively and in accordance with proper governance and sound financial and risk management principles;

16 See tinyurl.com/BSB-Handbook.

(9) run your business or carry out your role in the business in a way that encourages equality of opportunity and respect for diversity; and

(10) protect client money and assets.'

As the principles are mandatory, they must all be considered.

3.139 In the context of tax planning advice, the principles of potential relevance in most cases are principles (4) and (6) (see below), and also principles (1) and (2).

3.140 However, solicitors must (for example) meet the competencies set out in the SRA competent statement and should not go beyond their professional capabilities without obtaining expert assistance.

3.141 Acting in the best interests of each client (principle (4)) requires solicitors to act in good faith and do their best for clients.

3.142 In the context of tax planning for clients, solicitors will need to consider (for example) whether recommending tax planning arrangements which are 'high risk' (including seeking to achieve results that are contrary to the clear intention of Parliament in enacting relevant legislation, and/or are highly artificial or contrived and seek to exploit shortcomings in the relevant legislation) and which are likely to be challenged by HMRC would breach this principle.

3.143 Principle (4) also includes the requirement to observe a duty of confidentiality to the client, and obligations with regard to conflicts of interest.

3.144 Principle (6) may be problematic for solicitors who (for example) design and/or implement tax planning arrangements for clients which are likely to be considered abusive and/or which seek to exploit loopholes in the tax legislation. The recent negative publicity surrounding tax avoidance 'schemes' is such that undertaking those activities might be regarded as a breach of principle (6), as it risks bringing the solicitor or the legal profession into disrepute.

The SRA Handbook principles' document can be accessed via the SRA website[17].

SRA Handbook: Code of conduct

3.145 The SRA Handbook's code of conduct section contains 'outcomes' required of individuals, firms and in-house practices, which are mandatory and are aimed at ensuring compliance with the principles in the particular contexts covered by the various chapters in the code.

17 See www.sra.org.uk/solicitors/handbook/handbookprinciples/content.page.

3.146 The outcomes may be achieved in various ways, depending on the circumstances. The SRA have therefore supplemented the mandatory outcomes with non-mandatory 'indicative behaviours' to aid compliance.

3.147 The indicative behaviours set out in the code of conduct are non-exhaustive, and the SRA recognises that the outcomes can be achieved in other ways, depending on the nature of the firm, the particular circumstances and the needs of their particular clients.

3.148 The code of conduct is divided into five sections (ie 'You and your client'; 'You and your business'; 'You and your regulator'; 'You and others'; and 'Application, waivers and interpretation'), which in turn are divided into a total of 15 chapters, as follows:

1. **Client care**

   The outcomes required to demonstrate that the SRA principles have been applied to client care include some of particular relevance in the context of tax planning advice. For example:

   - O(1.2) 'you provide services to your clients in a manner which protects their interests in their matter, subject to the proper administration of justice';
   - O(1.4) 'you have the resources, skills and procedures to carry out your clients' instructions';
   - O(1.12) 'clients are in a position to make informed decisions about the services they need, how their matter will be handled and the options available to them'.

   The indicative behaviours (IBs) which may tend to show that the outcomes have been achieved and the principles therefore complied with in dealing with the client's matter include IB(1.7), which is 'considering whether you should decline to act or cease to act because you cannot act in the client's best interests'.

   Solicitors who receive instructions to advise on tax planning arrangements which may be susceptible to challenge by HMRC as avoidance or unacceptable planning should ensure they can demonstrate that IB(1.7) has been taken into account.

2. **Equality and diversity**

3. **Conflicts of interest**

   This chapter dealing with the proper handling of conflicts of interest includes the following outcome, which prohibits acting in conflict situations (O(3.4)): 'you do not act if there is an own interest conflict or a significant risk of an own interest conflict'.

An 'own interest conflict' means any situation where a firm's or individual's duty to act in the best interests of any client in relation to a matter conflicts, or there is a significant risk that it may conflict, with the firm's or individual's own interests in relation to that or a related matter.

In the context of tax planning, this would mean that (for example) a firm giving planning advice to a client that might be considered abusive or outside the spirit of the legislation could bring the firm (and profession) into disrepute, such that there might be a significant risk of an own interest conflict.

4. **Confidentiality and disclosure**

This includes the following outcome (O(4.1)): 'you keep the affairs of clients confidential unless disclosure is required or permitted by law or the client consents'. This may be relevant (for example) when considering the extent of disclosure required in relation to tax planning arrangements entered into by a client, such as under DOTAS (see **Chapter 4**).

5. **Your client and the court**

6. **Your client and introductions to third parties**

This chapter deals with circumstances where firms or individuals wish to refer their clients to third parties. This may be relevant where (for example) a firm does not have the relevant expertise to advise on particular tax planning arrangements and wishes to refer the client to specialist tax advice.

The outcomes of particular relevance in this context include:

- O(6.1) – 'whenever you recommend that a client uses a particular person or business, your recommendation is in the best interests of the client and does not compromise your independence';
- O(6.3) – 'clients are in a position to make informed decisions about how to pursue their matter'.

Referring the client to a specialist in the above circumstances does not necessarily absolve the firm or individual from further responsibility in the matter. For example, indicative behaviour IB(6.3) advocates: 'having effective systems in place for assessing whether any arrangement complies with the statutory and regulatory requirements'.

7. **Management of your business**

This section, which concerns the management and supervision of firms and in-house practices, states the following in relation to outsourcing client matters, which may be relevant to tax planning advice (O(7.10)): 'where you outsource legal activities or any operational functions that are critical to the delivery of any legal activities, you ensure such outsourcing:

(a) does not adversely affect your ability to comply with, or the SRA's ability to monitor your compliance with, your obligations in the Handbook;

(b) is subject to contractual arrangements that enable the SRA or its agent to obtain information from, inspect the records (including electronic records) of, or enter the premises of, the third party, in relation to the outsourced activities or functions;

(c) does not alter your obligations towards your clients; and

(d) does not cause you to breach the conditions with which you must comply in order to be authorised and to remain so'.

8. **Publicity**

The manner in which a firm, in-house practice etc, is publicised must not be misleading, and must be sufficiently informative to ensure that clients and others can make informed choices.

The following outcome may be relevant when promoting tax planning services involving arrangements which may be considered to be potentially abusive or high risk (O(8.1)):

> 'your publicity in relation to your firm or in-house practice or for any other business is accurate and not misleading and is not likely to diminish the trust the public places in you and in the provision of legal services'.

9. **Fee sharing and referrals**

10. **You and your regulator**

11. **Relations with third parties**

12. **Separate businesses**

13. **Application and waivers provisions**

13A. **Practice overseas**

Individuals or bodies practising overseas must comply with the SRA overseas rules[18]. However, in certain circumstances it will also be necessary to comply with some provisions in the code of conduct.

14. **Interpretation**

15. **Transitional provisions**

---

18 See www.sra.org.uk/solicitors/handbook/introoverseasrules.

3.149 Detailed commentary on the code of conduct is beyond the scope of this chapter. Reference should be made to the SRA website, which includes the full text of the SRA code of conduct[19].

The last version of the SRA Handbook prior to being replaced by the SRA Standards and Regulations was published on 6 December 2018. It can be viewed or downloaded from the SRA website[20].

19 At www.sra.org.uk/solicitors/handbook/code/resources.page.

20 See www.sra.org.uk/solicitors/handbook/welcome.page.

Chapter 4

Disclosure of tax avoidance schemes

Hartley Foster, Partner, Fieldfisher LLP

SIGNPOSTS

DOTAS and DOITAS:

- Purpose of the regimes: (originally) information gathering and (now) deterring the promotion or use of arrangements that fall within their ambit (see **4.32**).
- Key concepts: 'promoter' (see **4.37**), 'tax advantage' (see **4.44–4.56**), 'main benefit' (see **4.57–4.59**), 'hallmarks' (see **4.77–4.110**).
- Legislation: *Pt 7* of the *Finance Act 2004* (DOTAS) and *Sch 17* to the *Finance (No 2) Act 2017* (DOITAS) (see **4.320**).
- Enforcement of the rules (see **4.241–4.265**):
  - Orders that a scheme be deemed notifiable (*FA 2004, s 306A*) or is notifiable (*FA 2004, s 314A*)
  - Information gathering regime
  - Penalty regime.

POTAS:

- Purpose of the regime: to change the behaviours of 'high risk' promoters and users (see **4.279**).
- Key concepts: 'Conduct Notice' (see **4.280**), 'Monitoring Notice' (see **4.308**), 'Stop Notice' (see **4.283**), 'relevant defeats' (see **4.290–4.294**).
- Legislation: *Finance Act 2014, Pt 5* and *Schs 34* to *36* (see **4.276–4.283**).

INTRODUCTION

General

4.1 A common theme that arises in relation to the countering of 'tax avoidance' by governments is that of information gathering. Tax professionals need to be aware of this, not least because obligations are often imposed both on the professional and on the client. There exists a plethora of regimes, both national and international, by which fiscal authorities seek to ensure that they have sufficient information to counteract tax avoidance. Internationally, the measures include the US's Foreign Account Tax Compliance Act (FATCA), under which foreign financial institutions and certain other non-financial foreign entities must report on the foreign assets held by their United States account holders or be subject to withholding taxes, the EU's Council Directive 2011/16 (known as 'DAC6'), which imposes reporting obligations on 'reportable cross border arrangements', and the Common Reporting Standard (CRS), a coordinated international approach to facilitate exchange of financial information globally. DAC6 is addressed in **Chapter 11**.

4.2 The focus of this chapter is on the domestic regime that applies in the UK with regard to the disclosure of tax avoidance schemes.

The regimes

4.3 There are three separate disclosure regimes for:

- direct taxes;
- National Insurance Contributions (NICs); and
- VAT.

There are also disclosure regimes for SDLT[1], ATED, IHT and the apprenticeship levy. HMRC's guidance on the regimes is available at www.gov.uk/government/publications/disclosure-of-tax-avoidance-schemes-guidance.

4.4 The primary focus of this chapter is on the Disclosure of Tax Avoidance Schemes rules that apply to direct taxes (the 'DOTAS rules').

4.5 For NICs, section 132A of the *Social Security Administration Act 1992* was inserted by *section 7* of the *National Contributions Act 2006* with effect from 30 March 2006 and the *National Insurance Contributions*

1 From 1 November 2012, the descriptions of SDLT arrangements required to be disclosed were extended so that they cover schemes intended to be used for non-residential or residential property of any value, subject to the following exceptions: (a) arrangements that were first made available for implementation before 1 April 2010 unless those arrangements fall within certain descriptions (see HMRC guidance at para 9.7.2); (b) arrangements falling within a 'white list', which includes the single use of a number of statutory reliefs (see HMRC guidance at paras 9.7–9.10). Available at https://assets.publishing.service.gov.uk/government/uploads/system/uploads/attachment_data/file/701190/DOTAS-March.pdf.

(Application of Part 7 of the Finance Act 2004) Regulations 2007, SI 2007/785 were introduced with effect from 1 May 2007. In broad terms, these provisions mirror (with minor modifications) the disclosure regime as it applies to income tax; and, where there is both a NICs advantage and an income tax advantage, only one notification (which identifies both advantages) needs to be made. Accordingly, the NICs provisions are not addressed in detail in this chapter.

4.6 The Disclosure of VAT Avoidance Scheme rules (DVATS) were introduced in 2004. *Section 19* and *Schedule 2* to the *Finance Act 2004* inserted *Schedule 11A* (Disclosure of Avoidance Schemes) into the *Value Added Tax Act 1994*; and the *Value Added Tax (Disclosure of Avoidance Schemes) (Designations) Order 2004, SI 2004/1933*, designated eight schemes that were notifiable. The DVATS rules applied between 1 August 2004 and 31 December 2017. They operated in a fundamentally different way to the DOTAS rules that applied to direct taxes and that were introduced at the same time. Under DVATS, the duty to notify was imposed on the end users, rather than on the promoters of the schemes, and the date for notification was after the VAT return for the period in which the relevant transactions had taken place had been filed, rather than prior to the relevant transactions having taken place.

4.7 *Finance (No 2) Act 2017* introduced a new disclosure system, with an effective date of 1 January 2018, that applies to the majority of indirect taxes: Disclosure of Indirect Tax Avoidance Schemes (DOITAS). In very large part, the DOITAS rules mirror the DOTAS rules. Accordingly, DOITAS is not addressed in detail in this chapter. A key concept that applies in the DOTAS regime is 'hallmarks'. There are three hallmarks that apply specifically with regard to VAT and these are described at **4.77** et seq below.

Disclosure of Tax Avoidance Schemes

4.8 The direct tax DOTAS rules were introduced in 2004 by *Pt 7* of *FA 2004* and three statutory instruments[2].

4.9 Whilst the basic framework has remained constant, there have been many legislative changes made to the DOTAS rules since their introduction. The secondary legislation, in particular, has been substantially revised since 2004. In addition, the compliance obligations, the exigibility and quantum of penalties, and HMRC's powers have been expanded considerably.

4.10 HMRC guidance entitled 'Disclosure of Tax Avoidance Schemes: guidance' (the 'DOTAS Guidance') was published on 14 May 2014. It has been

2 The *Tax Avoidance Schemes (Prescribed Descriptions of Arrangements) Regulations 2004 SI 2004/1863*; the *Tax Avoidance Schemes (Information) Regulations 2004 SI 2004/1864*; and the *Tax Avoidance Schemes (Promoters and Prescribed Circumstances) Regulations 2004, SI 2004/1865*.

amended several times since publication[3]. Certain parts of the DOTAS Guidance have the force of law (and this is explained in more detail below)[4].

Structure of the chapter

4.11 Following this introductory section, this chapter comprises seven sections:

4.12 (1) From GAAR to DOTAS – in this section, a brief summary of the history leading to the introduction of the DOTAS regime is set out.

4.13 (2) The purpose of DOTAS – the potential purposes of having a disclosure regime in relation to tax avoidance are summarised. It is considered that the primary purpose of DOTAS has changed from being that of information gathering to that of deterrence.

4.14 (3) The DOTAS rules – the key concepts underlying the DOTAS rules, including 'tax advantage', 'promoter' and 'hallmarks' are addressed in this section.

4.15 (4) Enforcement of the DOTAS rules – in this section, HMRC's powers of investigation regarding, and enforcement of, the DOTAS rules are summarised.

4.16 (5) Penalties – the penalties that are exigible in relation to breaches of the DOTAS rules are set out.

4.17 (6) Promoters of Tax Avoidance Schemes – this section describes the Promoters of Tax Avoidance Schemes (POTAS) rules that were introduced with the aim of changing the behaviours of 'high risk' promoters of tax avoidance schemes.

4.18 (7) *Finance Act 2021* – in this section, the proposed changes to, inter alia, DOTAS and POTAS are described briefly.

All statutory references in this chapter are to the *Finance Act 2004* (*FA 2004*), unless stated otherwise.

(1) FROM GAAR TO DOTAS

4.19 Although there were certain statutory provisions (such as *Finance Act 1951, s 32* with regards to profits tax and *Finance Act 1960, ss 28, 29 and 43* (which became *ss 703* to *709* of the *Income and Corporation Taxes Act 1988*) that applied to certain transactions in securities) that enabled the Inland Revenue to levy tax on transactions that were not otherwise expressly subject

3 On 2 September 2015, 13 January 2016, 17 October 2016, 7 December 2017, 28 February 2018 and 20 April 2018.

4 See also https://assets.publishing.service.gov.uk/government/uploads/system/uploads/attachment_data/file/701190/DOTAS-March.pdf.

to tax (by counteracting the tax advantage), until the 1990s, the standard approach to countering tax avoidance in the UK involved either introducing bespoke legislation or litigating on a case-by-case basis after individual tax planning structures had come to light[5]. For the tax authorities, the latter approach – litigation – had the potential benefit of ensuring that there was no 'leakage' of tax. As the ultimate court's decision would apply retrospectively, the tax collected should not fall short of what the taxing authority intended to collect via the original legislative provisions. But, with litigation, came risks: uncertainty for a number of years; substantial expense; and potential defeat. Although the government would be able to overturn defeat in the courts by legislation, and did so on many occasions[6], considerable sums in tax could have been 'lost'[7] in the meantime.

4.20 As regards the approach of enacting remedial 'anti-avoidance' provisions, it was perceived by many in the Inland Revenue and in the government that it simply resulted in 'squeezing the balloon in one area only to see a new bulge emerge in another'[8]: as the new legislation was introduced, so were new structures designed with the aim of circumventing its effect[9].

4.21 Moreover, generally, there would be only a comparatively short period available for Parliamentary consideration of the relevant Finance Bill. This meant also that there was a risk that the legislation may not meet its aim entirely. Also, and in any event, this approach, inevitably, added complexity to the taxing legislation. The targeted 'anti-avoidance' legislative approach tended to be operated by superimposing a further layer of rules on to the existing ones,

---

5 See the comments of the Paymaster General, Dawn Primarolo, in answer to a Parliamentary Question on tax avoidance (HC Deb 30 November 1999 c174W).

6 For example, after the House of Lord's decision in *Ingram v Inland Revenue Commissioners* [2000] 1 AC 293, the government amended the gifts with reservation of benefit rules (*Finance Act 1986, s 102*) with the aim of ensuring that taxpayers could not, in future, benefit from the scheme that was used in that case.

7 Strictly, the tax was never due; this is 'lost' in the sense of not having been collected, but expected by the taxing authority to have been collected.

8 Dave Hartnett, then Director General at HM Revenue & Customs (Address to CIOT as part of 75th anniversary celebrations, 19 July 2005).

9 Fully retrospective anti-avoidance legislation (ie legislation that takes effect before the intention to legislate has been announced) is not unlawful, but it is only rarely introduced in the UK. It was, for example, introduced by the *Finance Act 1978, s 31*, in relation to which a challenge in the European Court of Human Rights failed (*A, B, C and D v the United Kingdom,* Application/Requête No 8531/79 (1981) 23 DR 203). More recently, in *R (on the application of Huitson) v Revenue and Customs Commissioners* [2011] QB 174, the Administrative Court held that the importance of ensuring that a Double Taxation Agreement should not be permitted to assist the avoidance of income tax was so fundamental that retrospective legislation to curtail it was justified.
'Partially retrospective' legislation (where it is announced, say in a Pre-Budget Report, that a statute that alters the results of a past event for the future, ie from the date that, say, the Finance Act comes into force) is standard with regard to tax avoidance and particularly with regard to targeted anti-avoidance rules. By accelerating the date from which revenues will start to flow from the legislation, this approach mitigates the adverse effects of defects in the legislation for fiscal authorities.

by which it was intended that, ultimately, there would be 'a mass of detailed rules which it is hoped will tie up the taxpayer in a net from which he cannot escape'[10].

4.22 Various legislative methods of addressing these issues were considered by governments over the years. In his first Budget following the 1997 General Election, the new Chancellor, Gordon Brown, announced that, alongside a number of individual measures to counter avoidance, the case for the introduction of a General Anti-Avoidance Rule (GAAR) would be considered:

> 'The tax burden avoided by the few falls on the many … A Government committed to the proper funding of public services will not tolerate the avoidance of taxation, and we will be relentless in our war against tax avoidance. I have instructed the Inland Revenue to carry out a wide-ranging review of areas of tax avoidance, with a view to further legislation in future Finance Bills.
>
> I have specifically asked the Revenue to consider a general anti-avoidance rule.'

4.23 In October 1998, the Inland Revenue published a consultative document in respect of the introduction of a GAAR[11]; and in January 1999, HM Customs & Excise published a consultation document on the introduction of a 'mini-GAAR' that would be aimed at tackling tax avoidance in the construction industry[12].

---

10 See Lord Hoffmann, writing extra-judicially ('Tax Avoidance', *British Tax Review* 2005, 2, pp 197–206), where he said:

'It is not only literalism on the part of the judges which leads to what the Revenue regard as tax avoidance. There is also the way in which taxing statutes are often drafted. Judges sometimes draw a distinction between acceptable tax avoidance, like giving up smoking, and unacceptable tax avoidance, like schemes with platinum sponge. The difference, said Lord Templeman in *IRC v Challenge Corp Ltd*, lies in the fact that in one case the taxpayer actually reorders his affairs: he stops buying the taxed commodity, or he receives less income or incurs more expense. In the other case, the taxpayer still buys the taxed commodity or receives the same income, but structures the transaction to fall outside the taxing statute. This distinction is, if I may say so, based upon sound instinct, but it depends upon the assumption that Parliament imposes taxation by reference to economic and other events in the real world. If only this were true. But Parliament, for various reasons, sometimes leaves the taxpayer a choice of achieving the same economic result by two different methods, one of which may attract tax and the other not. Worse still, Parliament may not be content to describe the economic event which should attract tax because it does not trust the courts to understand such a concept and apply it in a practical way. Instead, it enacts a mass of detailed rules which it is hoped will tie up the taxpayer in a net from which he cannot escape. But sometimes there are holes in the net and the courts find that they cannot plug them by appealing to the economic event which, at a higher level of generality, it appears that Parliament wished to tax. It is one thing to give the statute a purposive construction. It is another to rectify the terms of highly prescriptive legislation in order to include provisions which might have been included but are not actually there.'

11 Inland Revenue Press Notice 127/98, 5 October 1998.

12 It was entitled 'A VAT mini 'GAAR' in construction services'.

4.24 Ultimately, the government decided against implementing a GAAR[13]. However, concerns regarding tax avoidance remained; and, in its 2004 Budget, the government announced, as an alternative to a GAAR, a new 'disclosure regime', whereby tax avoidance schemes would be required to be disclosed to the revenue departments.

4.25 In his Budget speech on 17 March 2004, the Chancellor said:

> 'It has been put to me that we should now introduce a general anti-avoidance rule. I do not at this stage intend to introduce this but I will today close loopholes in partnerships, finance leasing and VAT and make it a requirement – as in the USA – that accountancy firms and those promoting schemes register them with the Inland Revenue.'

4.26 The press notice (PN 05) supplied more detail:

> **'Tackling Tax Avoidance**
>
> The Government is introducing a new disclosure measure to counter large-scale avoidance of direct taxes. This will require those who devise and market certain avoidance schemes to provide the Inland Revenue with details of these schemes. This will improve transparency and allow the Inland Revenue to make a swifter and more targeted response to deliberate abuses of the tax system.
>
> This will be complemented by measures to improve transparency in VAT transactions. A register of VAT abusive avoidance schemes will be published, and businesses with an annual turnover of £600,000 or more will be required to disclose use of these schemes to Customs & Excise. Businesses with an annual turnover of £10 million or more will also be required to disclose details of VAT schemes and arrangements that meet certain criteria.'

4.27 The *Finance Bill 2004* contained, in *clause 19* and *Schedule 2*, the government's proposed disclosure measures in relation to VAT, and, in *clauses 306 to 319*, its proposed measures in relation to income tax, corporation tax, capital gains tax and other direct taxes including Stamp Duty Land Tax and Stamp Duty Reserve Tax. There were two key differences between the direct tax and indirect tax measures. The first was as to timing; the second as regards on whom the duty to notify was imposed. The VAT provisions required the VAT registered trader to notify the tax authorities of the fact that he had entered into transactions of a broadly specified kind within 30 days of the due date for filing the relevant VAT return. The direct taxes measures imposed the obligations primarily on the 'promoter' of the schemes; and the obligation to notify arose from the date that the promoter made available the arrangements.

13 HM Customs & Excise/Inland Revenue Budget press notice CW3, 9 March 1999.

4.28 In broad terms, as regards the direct tax measures, the draft DOTAS rules comprised wide definitions in the primary legislation, the ambit of which was restricted by conditions imposed by secondary legislation. Draft secondary legislation was published on 17 May 2004. It was the subject of considerable criticism by tax practitioners. This was for various reasons, including that the detailed mathematical formula (T + B + C = 0) that it included had the consequences that, for example, building society accounts constituted potentially notifiable products whilst certain gilt strips did not. The May 2004 draft secondary legislation was withdrawn. Revised draft secondary legislation was published on 9 July 2004, namely the draft *Tax Avoidance Schemes (Promoters and Prescribed Circumstances) Regulations 2004*, the *Tax Avoidance Schemes (Prescribed Descriptions of Arrangements) Regulations 2004* and the *Tax Avoidance Schemes (Information) Regulations 2004*[14].

4.29 The primary consequences of the Parliamentary Debates in respect of the *Finance Bill 2004* were to restrict the scope of the arrangements to which the new provisions were to apply and to narrow the definition of 'promoter'.

4.30 The *Finance Act 2004* received Royal Assent on 22 July 2004. The *Tax Avoidance Schemes (Prescribed Descriptions of Arrangements) Regulations 2004, SI 2004/1863*, the *Tax Avoidance Schemes (Information) Regulations 2004, SI 2004/1864* and the *Tax Avoidance Schemes (Promoters and Prescribed Circumstances) Regulations 2004, SI 2004/1865* were laid before the House of Commons on 22 July 2004 and came into force on 1 August 2004.

4.31 The first date on which notifications under the DOTAS rules were required to be made was 30 September 2004[15].

(2) THE PURPOSE OF DOTAS

4.32 Viewed in isolation, DOTAS is simply a reporting system that requires information in respect of tax avoidance schemes to be provided to HMRC earlier than it would be, had that information been disclosed via the tax return[16]. It has no impact on whether the scheme has the intended fiscal consequences, or not. Nor, per se, does DOTAS have a deterrence function,

14 Under the 'negative resolution procedure', which has the consequence that the provisions are not necessarily debated in the House of Commons.

15 *Tax Avoidance Schemes (Information) Regulations 2004, SI 2004/1864, reg 4(7).*

16 The government has always made it clear that a main benefit of the DOTAS rules would be an ability to use the information to change the law to counteract arrangements that it considered to be undesirable. As a general rule, the introduction of retrospective legislation to counteract avoidance is rare; and so being able to act swiftly to counteract arrangements by prospective legislative change is of considerable value to the fiscal authorities. Following the introduction of DOTAS, the government introduced a number of targeted anti-avoidance measures that were informed by information disclosed under the regime. An early example is the provisions relating to financial instruments in the *Finance Act 2006, Sch 6*.

in the sense of deterring either the promotion or the use of arrangements that fall within its ambit. Before introducing the DOTAS regime, the government stated expressly that disclosure would not invite any adverse judgment about the nature of the arrangements: 'the fact that a disclosure has been made will not be taken to be an admission by a promoter or user that the arrangements constitute tax avoidance'[17].

4.33 Since its introduction, there have been two major developments of the DOTAS regime.

4.34 The first development was as regards its ambit and the second was as regards its purpose. As originally enacted, the DOTAS legislation had a narrow ambit. The DOTAS rules in relation to direct taxes were limited to arrangements 'connected with employment' and those 'in relation to financial products'; and the indirect tax provisions applied only to taxable persons with an annual turnover in excess of £600,000 who used one (or more) of eight designated schemes[18]. In 2006, the ambit of the DOTAS rules was increased significantly; and that ambit has been expanded further subsequently.

4.35 Secondly, it has become increasingly clear that the government and HMRC are no longer neutral about arrangements that fall within the DOTAS regime. When introducing the changes in 2006, the government stated that it believed the disclosure regime had contributed to a sharp decline in marketed tax avoidance. Particularly with the further changes that were introduced in 2014, DOTAS has become one of HMRC's key deterrence weapons against tax avoidance. Now, falling within the DOTAS regime brings with it the government's express disapproval.

4.36 Notification under DOTAS brings with it a number of concomitant consequences. For the taxpayer, these include the potential:

(i) to be issued with an accelerated payment notice (APN)[19]; and

(ii) to be penalised and named and shamed under the 'serial tax avoiders' legislation[20].

---

17 *Hansard* HC Standing Committee A Debates, col 712 (22 June 2004).

18 *Value Added Tax Act 1994, Sch 11A, para 7(4)(a)*. The eight schemes that had been designated were described in the *Value Added Tax (Disclosure of Avoidance Schemes) (Designations) Order 2004, SI 2004/1933, Sch 1*.

19 In Working Paper No 11, 'Evaluation of HMRC anti-avoidance and operational measures' (September 2017), The Office for Budget Responsibility noted at para 4.16 that: '*It appears that the threat of receiving an AP notice has acted as a stronger deterrent than originally assumed. The number of avoidance schemes disclosed under DOTAS and declared usages of DOTAS schemes on tax returns, though already on a downward trend prior to the introduction of APs, has fallen significantly faster since … HMRC estimates that the number of DOTAS scheme usages has fallen by over a half due to the deterrent effect of AP notices'. In R (on the application of Rowe and Others) v HMRC* [2018] STC 462, Arden LJ noted at 481: 'Parliament clearly intended that the new [APN] regime would change taxpayers' behaviour so as to deter or reduce the use of these [marketed tax avoidance] schemes. It is the premise of the new regime that the use of such schemes is in effect anti-social behaviour'.

20 The serial tax avoiders regime is set out in the *Finance Act 2016, s 159, Sch 18*.

Additionally, with regard to a company, there is the potential to lose the ability to tender for government contracts. Also, a director of a company can be made jointly and severally liable for a company's tax liabilities, if the company has entered into tax avoidance arrangements and there is a risk that the company may enter insolvency (by service of a 'joint liability notice'[21]).

4.37 For the promoter, there is the potential to fall within the draconian rules that apply to 'high risk promoters'[22].

4.38 HMRC's disclosure statistics demonstrate a significant downward trend in the number of schemes that have been notified under DOTAS and show that, particularly since 2014, the number of schemes notified under the DOTAS rules each year is very small. HMRC consider that that is because promoters are no longer complying with the DOTAS rules. In a paper entitled 'Use of marketed tax avoidance schemes in the UK'[23], HMRC asserted that:

> 'Promoters of avoidance schemes are legally required to disclose their schemes to HMRC. But they are increasingly unlikely to do so, so that they can continue to market them before HMRC can stop them. In the last two years [ie 2018 to 2020], the majority of avoidance schemes were only disclosed to HMRC after we used our legal powers to force them to be disclosed.'

Financial Year	*Financial*	*Employment*	*Main Regime*	*NICs*	*IHT*	*SDLT*	*ATED*	*Total*
2004/05	340	163	0	0	0	0	0	503
2005/06	94	28	0	0	0	485	0	607
2006/07	29	7	125	0	0	185	0	346
2007/08	2	0	205	23	0	70	0	300
2008/09	0	0	102	<5	0	28	0	130 to 134
2009/10	0	0	116	6	0	61	0	183
2010/11	0	0	97	11	0	21	0	129
2011/12	0	0	116	17	<5	13	0	146 to 150
2012/13	0	0	59	7	<5	18	0	84 to 89
2013/14	0	0	28	7	<5	10	<5	45 to 53
2014[24]	0	0	<5	0	0	<5	0	0 to 8

21 Under the *Finance Act 2020, Sch 13.*
22 *Finance Act 2014, Pt 5, Schs 34–36.*
23 Published on 26 November 2020.
24 This pertains to the six-month period between 1 April to 30 September 2014.

2015/16	Not published	Not published	Not published	Not published	Not published	Not published	Not published	Not published
2016/17	Not published	Not published	Not published	Not published	Not published	Not published	Not published	Not published
2017/18	Not published	Not published	Not published	Not published	Not published	Not published	Not published	15
2018/19[25]	Not published	Not published	Not published	Not published	Not published	Not published	Not published	16

(3) THE DOTAS RULES

Introductory

4.39 These rules cover income tax, corporation tax (including amounts assessable as if they were corporation tax, such as the bank levy), capital gains tax, apprenticeship levy[26], the annual tax on enveloped dwellings (ATED)[27], stamp duty land tax, stamp duty reserve tax and inheritance tax.

Notifiable arrangements

4.40 The primary legislation that introduced the DOTAS regime establishes the broad parameters of its scope. It does not incorporate a definition of a tax avoidance transaction. Instead, the concept of 'notifiable arrangements' is the basis of the DOTAS rules. It is only notifiable arrangements (or 'notifiable proposals', which are any proposals for arrangements which, if entered into, would be notifiable arrangements[28]) that give rise to the obligation (on three classes of person: (1) promoters; (2) persons dealing with non-UK promoters; and (3) parties to a transaction where there is no promoter) to make a notification to HMRC.

4.41 The term 'notifiable arrangements' is defined in *section 306(1)*. There are three key attributes to the concept, namely, that the arrangements:

25 HMRC regularly published disclosure statistics data during, and for, the period 1 August 2004 to 30 September 2014. That information is no longer published. Passing reference to the numbers of DOTAS disclosures made in 2017/18 and 2018/19 is to be found in the Annual Accounts and Reports 2018/19. It is not clear whether these numbers include disclosures that have been made under DOITAS.

26 With effect from 15 September 2016 (*para (da)* being inserted in the definition of 'tax' in *FA 2004, s 318* by the *Finance Act 2016, s 104(1)*).

27 With effect from 17 July 2013 (*Finance Act 2013, s 168, Sch 35, para 2* amending the definition of 'tax' in *FA 2004, s 318*).

28 *FA 2004, s 306(2)*. It is stated at para 3.5 of the DOTAS Guidance, that a person makes a scheme available for implementation if and when: 'the scheme is fully designed, it is capable of implementation in practice, and he/she communicates information about the scheme to potential clients suggesting that they consider entering into transactions forming part of the scheme'.

- must fall within any description prescribed by the Treasury by regulations[29];
- enable, or might be expected to enable, any person to obtain an advantage in relation to any tax that is so prescribed in relation to arrangements of that description[30];and
- are such that the main benefit, or one of the main benefits, that might be expected to arise from them is the obtaining of that advantage[31].

4.42 'Arrangements' and 'tax advantage' are widely defined, as discussed below.

4.43 The 'main benefit' requirement restricts the scope of the regime to an extent. However, the main restrictions on the ambit of the DOTAS rules are contained in the regulations. As stated above, the primary legislation does not define a tax avoidance transaction. The precise scope of the DOTAS regime is delineated by the regulations, which seek to encapsulate those features that the government considers are common to arrangements that it wishes to monitor (and potentially address by legislation and/or litigation). A consequence of this somewhat paradoxical approach[32] is a degree of fluidity; the relevant secondary legislation has been amended several times since 2004. In this section, the attributes prescribed by the primary legislation (tax advantage and main benefit) are addressed first; and the regulations are analysed subsequently.

'Tax advantage'

4.44 The terms 'advantage' and 'arrangements' are defined in *section 318.*

4.45 The term 'arrangements' is widely defined, as including 'any scheme, transaction or series of transactions'. In *HMRC v Hyrax Resourcing Ltd and Others* [2019] UKFTT 175 (TC), the Tribunal held that, in determining whether there were arrangements, any steps that 'must have … been part of the scheme user's expectations' were all part of the arrangements. It is considered that it is highly unlikely that a pre-planned transaction or set of transactions would not constitute an arrangement.

4.46 The definition of 'advantage' is based on the meaning of 'tax advantage', as it appeared in *section 709* of the *Income and Corporation Tax Act 1988*[33].

---

29 *FA 2004, s 306(1)(a).*

30 *FA 2004, s 306(1)(b).*

31 *FA 2004, s 306(1)(c).*

32 The original aim of the DOTAS regime was to enable HMRC to obtain information regarding schemes of which it was not previously aware. Yet, the way in which the DOTAS regime has been enacted means that government needs to be aware of the arrangements in order to be able to define those characteristics that are intrinsic to the arrangements in respect of which it wishes to obtain information.

33 See now, *Income Tax Act 2007, s 683* and *Corporation Tax Act 2010, s 732.*

4.47 It is defined as meaning 'in relation to any tax':

'(a) Relief or increased relief from, or repayment or increased repayment of, that tax, or the avoidance or the avoidance or reduction of a charge to tax or an assessment to that tax or the avoidance of a possible assessment to that tax,

(b) the deferral of any payment of tax or the advancement of any repayment of tax, or

(c) the avoidance of any obligation to deduct or account for any tax.'

4.48 As with *section 709*, no comparator is specified in the first limb. However, the definition of 'tax advantage' advanced by Lord Wilberforce in *IRC v Parker* [1966] AC 141, which described a contrast position between receiving something in a non-taxable way which could have been received in a taxable way, has been referred to in virtually all subsequent cases where the issue has been considered.

4.49 Lord Wilberforce said, at 178G:

> '… The paragraph, as I understand it, presupposes a situation in which an assessment to tax, or increased tax, either is made or may possibly be made, that the taxpayer is in a position to resist the assessment by saying that the way in which he received what it is sought to tax, prevents him from being taxed on it; and that the Revenue is in a position to reply that if he had received what it is sought to tax in another way he would have had to bear tax. In other words, there must be a contrast, as regards the "receipts", between the actual case where these accrue in a non-taxable way with a possible accruer in a taxable way, and, unless this contrast exists, the existence of the advantage is not established.'[34]

4.50 For example:

(a) In *Cleary v Inland Revenue Commissioners* [1968] AC 766, the House of Lords held that the sale of shares by the taxpayer to her company enabled her to obtain a tax advantage when compared to the tax consequences of the company, instead, paying her a dividend equal to the sale price of the shares. Viscount Dilhorne referred to Lord Wilberforce's analysis, and said:

> 'The definition does not require the contrast of like with like … and to give it such an interpretation would narrow the scope of the section considerably. … That the appellant received £60,500 in such a way

34 The case concerned *Finance Act 1960, s 43(4)(g)*, which defined 'tax advantage' as follows: '"tax advantage" means a relief or increased relief from, or repayment or increased repayment of, income tax, or the avoidance or reduction of an assessment to income tax or the avoidance of a possible assessment thereto, whether the avoidance or reduction is effected by receipts accruing in such a way that the recipient does not pay or bear tax on them, or by a deduction in computing profits or gains'.

that she did not pay or bear tax on it, is not disputed. It could have been distributed to her by way of dividend and, if it had been, she would have been liable to tax. There is thus in this case the contrast to which Lord Wilberforce referred. It is clear that in consequence of a transaction in securities she avoided a possible assessment to income tax, the possible assessment being that which would have been made if she had received the sum by way of dividend. She therefore obtained a tax advantage within the meaning of the section.'

(b) In *Emery v Inland Revenue Commissioners* [1981] STC 151, Nourse J said, with regard to the term 'tax advantage', as defined in *section 466(1)* of the *Income and Corporation Taxes Act 1970*, that:

> 'It is now well established that in all these cases where it is necessary to determine whether a tax advantage has been obtained a start must be made with the … passage in the speech of Lord Wilberforce in *Inland Revenue Commissioners v Parker* …'[35]

It was held that a tax advantage is obtained if the taxpayer receives something in a non-taxable form, even though he might equally have received it in some other non-taxable form, provided always that he could have received it in some third way which would have resulted in its being subject to tax. There is no requirement that the taxpayer must be in a legally identical position; his being placed in an economically similar (but for the tax) position is sufficient.

4.51 The DOTAS Guidance[36] at para 6.2.2, refers, with approval, to Lord Justice Parker's comment in *Inland Revenue Commissioners v Trustees of the Sema Group Pension Fund* [2003] STC 95, at 114*j*, that:

> '… what the draftsman was manifestly trying to do when defining "tax advantage" in s 709(1) was to cover every situation in which the taxpayer vis-à-vis the Revenue is improved in consequence of the particular transaction or transactions.'

4.52 Whilst it is considered that that is too broad (and too nebulous to provide any assistance), nonetheless, the few cases in which there has been consideration of the term 'tax advantage' in the context of *section 306* demonstrate that seeking to persuade a Tribunal that there is not a tax advantage in respect of a fiscally motivated structure that has not been notified under DOTAS will not be easy.

4.53 In *HMRC v Hyrax Resourcing Ltd and Others* [2019] UKFTT 175 (TC), the respondents sought to distinguish *Parker*, by asserting that the definition considered by Lord Wilberforce was crucially different to that in

35 At 171j to 172a.

36 At https://assets.publishing.service.gov.uk/government/uploads/system/uploads/attachment_data/file/701190/DOTAS-March.pdf.

section 309, because the former contained, but the latter omitted, the following words:

> '... whether the avoidance or reduction is effected by receipts accruing in such a way that the recipient does not pay or bear tax on them, or by a deduction in computing profits or gains.'

4.54 That argument was rejected by the Tribunal, at para 185:

> '... I do not accept that those additional words do make any significant difference to the meaning of "tax advantage" in the two Finance Acts. Both definitions make it clear that they are contrasting two situations: one which has lower tax bill than the other. Both definitions require the "contrast" situation to be identified. The additional words in the 1960 Act are there simply to make it clear that the contrast exists where the lower tax bill is not the result of receiving something free of tax, but by having increased expenses or deductions. I would say that those additional words are unnecessary as that meaning is implicit in the first part of the definition, but it is irrelevant to this application where there is no question of a deduction in computations.'

4.55 The Tribunal also rejected the respondents' argument that the contrast analysis can be applied only if a scheme user was in the identical legal position if he used the scheme compared to the position if he had not used it:

> '196. It is a matter of statutory construction. The statute itself does not refer to a contrast situation; it is merely implicit because the statute talks of relief/avoidance/reduction, all of which terms indicate that there would be a contrast situation without the relief/avoidance/reduction. The statute therefore does not define the contrast situation: it does not expressly state whether the contrast situation must be legally or only economically, identical or only similar, to the actual situation which arises.
>
> ...
>
> 198. The aim of the legislation was clearly to combat tax avoidance. It is well understood ... that there may be tax avoidance where a person adopts a scheme which puts them in a similar economic position to the non-scheme position, but with a lower tax liability. To interpret "tax advantage" as requiring the contrast situation only to be one where the scheme user was in an identical legal position to the one actually used would be to largely deprive the legislation of much of its effect. It is obvious the objective of tax avoidance is to put the avoider into an economically similar position (but with less tax) than he would otherwise be in, and so it seems obvious to me that Parliament intended the contrast situation to include those that were merely economically similar to the actual situation. Parliament intended the legislation to effectively combat tax avoidance.

> 199. … I think that it is clear that Parliament intended to refer to economically similar contrast situations (as well as legally identical ones). A layman, including promoters and users of the scheme, when considering a scheme would consider its economic reality and not its legal form and should understand "tax advantage" in the same way.'

4.56 *Section 306(1)(b)* refers to the arrangements enabling, or 'might be expected to enable', any person to obtain a tax advantage. In *HMRC v Curzon Capital Ltd* [2019] SFTD 506, the Tribunal held that it was not necessary to answer the question whether the arrangements 'enabled' tax avoidance in order to determine whether they were notifiable under the DOTAS rules. That would require a detailed analysis of the arrangements, including, potentially, a final determination of their effect by litigation. The Tribunal said:

> 'The more relevant question is whether they "might be expected to enable" it. Clearly that was the stated expectation … but is that sufficient? To put the point more broadly, whose expectation is to be considered in this context? It seems to me that this question must be considered in the light of the policy behind the provisions in general, and that policy would be stultified if a detailed examination had to be carried out into the robustness of any scheme in order to form a view as to whether, from the point of view of some notional observer with particular attributes, it "might be expected to enable" a tax advantage to be obtained; the better view in a case such as the present is, I think, that if the arrangements are presented in such a way as to claim that a tax advantage will (or may) flow from using them, then unless the claim is clearly ridiculous, it can fairly be said that the arrangements "might be expected to enable" the advantage to be obtained.'

'Main benefit'

4.57 *Section 306(1)(c)* introduces a 'main benefit' threshold; and, accordingly, the difficult question of when a benefit is a 'main benefit' arises. In contrast to *section 306(1)(b)*, which involves a comparison between the actual arrangements and a hypothetical set of arrangements, *section 306(1)(c)* involves an analysis of the actual arrangements. If a tax advantage, as defined, arises from the arrangements, then that will be a benefit. Whether it is 'the' or 'a' main benefit will be a question of fact.

4.58 Little further assistance is provided in the DOTAS Guidance, where it is stated at para 6.3:

> 'The advantage is one of the main benefits of the arrangements if it is a significant or important element of the benefits and not incidental or insubstantial.
>
> …
>
> In our experience those who plan tax arrangements fully understand the tax advantage such schemes are intended to achieve.

Therefore we expect it will be obvious (with or without detailed explanation) to any potential client what the relationship is between the tax advantage and any other financial benefits of the product they are buying.

The test is objective and considers the value of the expected tax advantage compared to the value of any other benefits likely to be enjoyed.'

4.59 The dictionary definition of 'main' includes the following: 'principal, chief, pre-eminent'. Based on that definition, there can only be more than one main benefit if there are benefits that are all equal in pre-eminence. If one benefit is clearly of greater importance than all the others, then, by definition, its pre-eminence must preclude any other benefit from being a main benefit. Arguably, if a transaction has a preponderant non-fiscal benefit, then the fact that it also confers a significant tax advantage is not sufficient to satisfy the test in *section 306(1)(c)*. The main benefit of the arrangement is the former, not the avoidance of tax. With a transaction such as acquiring a company or purchasing a property, it is unlikely that obtaining a tax advantage is normally a main benefit of the transaction as a whole. The main benefit of the transaction is likely to be a commercial one. It is considered that, in such a case, even if there are steps undertaken in that transaction that have a pure fiscal motivation, unless those steps form a discrete whole, the main benefit test should be applied to the overall transaction and would not be satisfied.

The Regulations

4.60 A significant amount of ordinary tax planning would be notifiable under DOTAS by reference to *section 306(1)(b)* and *(c)* solus. The limits on the definition of notifiable arrangements are primarily provided by the descriptions of notifiable arrangements in the Regulations prescribed by the Treasury under *section 306(1)(a)*.

The 2004 Regulations

4.61 The original Regulations to which *section 306(1)(a)* referred were the *Tax Avoidance Schemes (Prescribed Descriptions of Arrangements) Regulations 2004, SI 2004/1863*. They came into force on 1 August 2004; and were amended shortly thereafter by the *Tax Avoidance Schemes (Prescribed Descriptions of Arrangements) (Amendment) Regulations 2004, SI 2004/2429*, which came into force on 30 September 2004[37].

4.62 *SI 2004/1863* limited the scope of the regime to arrangements 'connected with employment' and those 'in relation to financial products'. The descriptions of the two forms of notifiable arrangements were broadly expressed.

---

37 *SI 2004/2429, reg 3* introduced a definition of 'premium fee' and *reg 5* introduced 'excluded arrangements'.

'Connected with employment'

4.63 With regard to arrangements 'connected with employment', arrangements that give rise to a tax advantage for an employee, for an employer or for any other person by reason of the employee's employment were to be disclosed, where they 'involved' one or more of three additional elements – securities or associated rights, payments to trustees or intermediaries or loans. These three additional elements were defined in detail.

'Financial products'

4.64 With the 'financial products' limb, it was necessary to establish whether the expected tax advantage arose to a significant degree from the inclusion in the arrangements of 'specified financial products', as defined in *Sch 1, Pt 2, para 7*.

4.65 The products specified in *para 7* included shares, loans, derivative contracts and stock lending arrangements; *para 7* also included a broad 'sweeping-up' provision under which contracts that, alone or in combination with one or more other contracts in substance, represented the making of a loan and fell to be accounted for on that basis, constituted specified financial products. *Paragraph 7(2)* specifically excluded assets held within Individual Savings Accounts or personal equity plans, with the consequence that, if the only financial products involved in the arrangements were one or both, then the arrangements would not fall within the financial products limb.

Exclusion

4.66 Arrangements were excluded from being notifiable if they met two (and in some cases three) tests. These were:

- the premium fee test;
- the confidentiality test; and
- if appropriate, the open market test.

The aim of the tests

4.67 The aim of the tests was to seek to distinguish between 'ordinary' bespoke tax planning (where the taxpayer pays for advice in respect of his affairs and for the implementation of such advice) and 'off the peg' advice, where the taxpayer typically pays (in addition) the equivalent of a 'finder's fee', that is, an additional fee for making the intellectual property of the elements of the scheme itself available (which is a hallmark of a pre-packaged scheme of a substantially uniform nature) and where the promoter is likely to want to keep the details of the scheme hidden from other potential promoters. It was only the latter type of advice that was intended to be notifiable.

'Premium fee'

4.68 The definition of 'premium fee' in the draft legislation published in July 2004 had three elements, the third of which related expressly to the quantum of the fee charged. That third requirement was removed from the legislation, leaving only as 'premium fees': (a) fees which are '*to a significant extent attributable*' to the tax advantage; and (b) fees which are '*contingent on the tax advantage*'. In the Inland Revenue Guidance, it was stated that the first of these required a comparison of the fee that is chargeable by virtue of the tax element in the arrangements with that which would be charged normally by the adviser for the sort of advice in question. It was confirmed that increased fees chargeable because of the adviser's location, the size of the transaction, the adviser's skills, the scarcity of appropriately skilled staff (in the case of complex areas of advice), a special negotiation resulting in an increased fee, or the urgency of the advice, may not be premium fees chargeable by virtue of the tax avoidance element. Nor would fees linked to tax saved or tax repayment obtained, if it was the normal practice of the adviser concerned to charge on this basis, necessarily be premium fees[38].

4.69 The premium fee test was a hypothetical one: whether the arrangements are likely to command the payment of a fee, the amount of which is contingent on or attributable to a tax saving by a client with experience of purchasing sophisticated tax services. If so, then the premium fee test is failed (even if no premium fee was actually charged by the particular promoter); and the scheme was reportable under the DOTAS rules. However, as a promoter was only likely to be able to charge a premium fee or keep a product secret from its competitors when that product was novel, arrangements that were within the DOTAS regime when first devised, arguably, would cease to be after their implementation by a number of taxpayers.

4.70 The premium fee exclusion originally applied only in respect of financial products. The *Tax Avoidance Schemes (Prescribed Descriptions of Arrangements) (Amendment) Regulations 2004, SI 2004/2429* inserted *paragraph 5A* into *SI 2004/1863*, so as to extend the premium fee exclusion to cover employment arrangements, with effect from 30 September 2004.

'Everyday tax advice'

4.71 The Inland Revenue authorised an official statement by it to be published in the Chartered Institute of Taxation Technical Note of 23 August 2004, with the aim of confirming that there is no requirement to disclose 'everyday tax advice':

> 'We can confirm again that we do not intend promoters or employers to have to disclose everyday advice and arrangements.

38 'Detailed meaning of specified financial product, "Premium Fee Definition"', Appendix 1, Inland Revenue Guidance.

> …
>
> We confirm the assurances we have given in the past, that where a person merely provides advice as to how the tax system operates in particular circumstances then that activity on its own does not trigger a disclosure requirement on the part of the adviser.'

Certain examples of what would constitute everyday arrangements were included in the note, albeit without any further clarification. In the context of employment products, these included: 'salary sacrifice arrangements for cars, computers, childcare vouchers or pension funds' and 'standard dual contract arrangements'[39].

The 2006 Regulations

4.72 In the December 2005 Pre-Budget Report it was announced that the 2004 Regulations would be repealed and that new regulations would be enacted. Drafts of the new regulations were published on 28 April 2006, with comments invited by 31 May 2006.

4.73 The *Tax Avoidance Schemes (Prescribed Descriptions of Arrangements) Regulations 2006, SI 2006/1543* (the '*2006 Regulations*') were laid before the House of Commons on 15 June 2006 and came into force on 1 August 2006.

4.74 *Regulation 18* of the *2006 Regulations* revoked the *Tax Avoidance Schemes (Prescribed Descriptions of Arrangements) Regulations 2004* and the *Tax Avoidance Schemes (Prescribed Descriptions of Arrangements) (Amendment) Regulations 2004*.

4.75 In the Explanatory Note to the *2006 Regulations*, it was stated:

> '7.5 Part 7 applies across all of the direct taxes. However, the Government has targeted the disclosure rules at the areas at high risk from avoidance.
>
> 7.6 The arrangements prescribed in secondary legislation in relation to income tax, corporation tax and capital gains tax were limited to two areas, employment and financial products. Disclosure was a new concept and there were inevitable uncertainties as to how it would operate in practice. Consequently, the Government decided to limit the scope to the highest risk areas.
>
> 7.7 Monitoring of the disclosure regime in relation to income tax, corporation tax and capital gains tax has identified three risks:
>
> - significant avoidance exists outside these areas. For example, measures were announced in the Pre-Budget report 2005 to

39 The statement has not been withdrawn, but, as it was issued by reference to secondary legislation that has been revoked, it is considered that an assertion that there is a legitimate expectation that reliance can be placed on it is unlikely to succeed.

combat significant avoidance of corporation tax involving the use of intangible assets. There has also been a series of measures combating avoidance within the leasing regime. Both of these areas are outside the current scope of the disclosure regime;

- there is evidence that the "filters" used within the descriptions of arrangements to target schemes that are potentially avoidance may not capture all of the schemes that the regime was intended to capture; and
- the time limit for disclosing schemes where no promoter is involved (by the filing date of the return to use the scheme, compared to the normal time limit for promoted schemes of within 5 days of the scheme being marketed or implemented) severely affects the objective of the disclosure regime to obtain information in close to real time.

7.8 In order to counter these risks regulations will:

- extend the disclosure regime to the whole of income tax, corporation tax and capital gains tax;
- employ a suite of seven descriptions of arrangements (commonly referred to as "hallmarks") to target new and innovative schemes, standardised tax products and two specific high risk areas: schemes designed to create tax losses for individuals and leasing arrangements; and
- reduce the time limit for notifying schemes where no promoter is involved to within 30 days of the first transaction implementing the scheme.'

4.76 *Regulation 5* of the *2006 Regulations* is entitled 'Prescribed descriptions of arrangements'. *Regulation 5(1)* provides:

'(1) The following arrangements are prescribed for the purposes of Part 7 of the FA 2004 (disclosure of tax avoidance schemes)—

(a) in relation to income tax, corporation tax and capital gains tax, any arrangements which fall within any description specified in a provision of these Regulations listed in paragraph (2); …'

4.77 *Regulation 5(2)* identifies the provisions and the relevant descriptions or hallmarks. The *2006 Regulations*, as enacted, introduced five generic hallmarks:

- confidentiality involving a promoter;
- confidentiality where no promoter involved;
- premium fee;
- off-market terms; and
- standardised tax products;

and three particular hallmarks, each of which targeted a specific perceived high-risk area, namely:

- leasing schemes;
- income tax loss schemes; and
- pensions contributions.

4.78 A number of these hallmarks was amended in 2013 (by the *Tax Avoidance Schemes (Prescribed Descriptions of Arrangements) (Amendment) Regulations 2013, SI 2013/2595*) and a number was amended in 2016 (by the *Tax Avoidance Schemes (Prescribed Descriptions of Arrangements) (Amendment) Regulations 2016, SI 2016/99*).

4.79 Each of the hallmarks that is in force as at the date of writing is analysed in turn.

Description 1: confidentiality in cases involving a promoter

4.80 *Regulation 6* of the *2006 Regulations* provides:

'(1) Arrangements are prescribed if—

(a) any element of the arrangements (including the way in which the arrangements are structured) gives rise to the tax advantage expected to be obtained under the arrangements; and

(b) it might reasonably be expected that a promoter would wish the way in which that element of those arrangements secures, or might secure, a tax advantage to be kept confidential from any other promoter at any time following the material date.

(2) Arrangements are prescribed if it might reasonably be expected that a promoter would, but for the requirements of these Regulations, wish to keep the way in which any element of those arrangements (including the way in which the arrangements are structured) that secures, or might secure, the tax advantage confidential from HMRC at any time following the material date, and a reason for doing so is to facilitate repeated or continued use of the same element, or substantially the same element, in the future'[40].

40 With effect from 4 November 2013, *reg 3* of the *Tax Avoidance Schemes (Prescribed Descriptions of Arrangements) (Amendment) Regulations 2013, SI 2013/2595* amended *reg 6(2)* as follows:

'(a) for "if the promoter would" substitute "if it might reasonably be expected that a promoter would"; and

(b) for "the way in which the element of these arrangements" substitute "the way in which any element of those arrangements (including the way in which the arrangements are structured)'

and inserted *para (2A)*.

(2A) Cases where arrangements will be prescribed under paragraph (2) include, but are not limited to, where—

(a) a promoter does not provide to the user of the arrangements ("the user"), or prevents or discourages the user from retaining, any promotional materials, data or written professional advice relating to those arrangements; and

(b) it might reasonably be expected that the reason for doing so is to keep the arrangements confidential from HMRC in order to facilitate repeated or continued use of any element of those arrangements.'[41]

4.81 The hallmark has two limbs: (a) confidential from other promoters; and (b) confidential from HMRC.

Confidential from other promoters

4.82 Paragraph 7.3.2 of the DOTAS Guidance provides HMRC's perspective on the test. According to HMRC, it requires the person with the duty to disclose to ask themselves the hypothetical question:

> 'Might it reasonably be expected that any promoter of the arrangements would wish the way in which any element of those arrangements (including the way in which they are structured) gives rise to and secures, or might secure, the expected tax advantage to be kept confidential from any other promoter at any time following the material date?'

4.83 HMRC considers that the test is whether a hypothetical promoter would want to keep the arrangements (or an element of them) confidential; the attitude to confidentiality of the particular promoter of the scheme is not the defining factor. According to the DOTAS Guidance, promoters should apply a two-step approach. First, the promoter should consider its own position; and, in that regard:

> 'The test would be answered in the affirmative if an element of the scheme were sufficiently new and innovative that a promoter would want the details to remain secret in order to maintain their competitive advantage and ability to earn fees.'

4.84 If the promoter concludes that it would not want to keep the arrangements confidential from another promoter, then it should consider, nonetheless, whether another (hypothetical) promoter would wish to keep the arrangements confidential. In applying the second step, the promoter should attribute to the hypothetical promoter the knowledge and information that the promoter itself holds, and only that information and knowledge, and it

41 This hallmark was extended to cover inheritance tax with effect from 23 February 2016.

should assume that the hypothetical promoter will take a 'reasonable view of its obligations to disclose proposals and arrangements under DOTAS'.

4.85 It is the confidential nature of the fiscal element of the arrangements that is determinative, not the parties to the transaction or the quantum of the consideration, for example. Accordingly, the fact that a promoter generally would ask clients to sign a confidentiality agreement is not determinative. HMRC state that the 'test is unrelated to any general rule or agreement by a client that they keep advice confidential', but that 'The use of an explicit confidentiality agreement before revealing full details of the scheme to a client by advisers who do not normally use such agreements may indicate that the test is met'. HMRC accept that the test is not met if the scheme is reasonably well known in the tax community. That would be so even if the particular promoter would ask clients to sign a confidentiality agreement in respect of the scheme. The knowledge of the scheme can be demonstrated by, for example, articles in the tax press, textbooks or case law.

Confidential from HMRC

Promoters

4.86 This second limb of the confidentiality test applies if a promoter might reasonably expect (qua a hypothetical promoter) to keep any element of the relevant arrangements confidential from HMRC in order to facilitate repeated or continued use of the same element, or substantially the same element, in the future.

4.87 HMRC state that the test requires the promoter to ask the hypothetical questions[42]:

> 'Might it reasonably be expected that any promoter of the arrangements would wish the way in which any element of those arrangements (including the way they are structured) gives rise to, or might secure, the expected tax advantage to be kept confidential from HMRC?
>
> Is a reason for doing so to facilitate the repeated or continued use of that element, or substantially the same element, in the future? (This may be, for example, in order to secure fee income in the future ...)',

and that a promoter will answer the relevant questions in one of the following ways:

> 'I wish to keep an element of the scheme confidential from HMRC in order to facilitate repeated or continued use of that element, or substantially the same element, in future, or
>
> I do not wish to keep any element of the scheme confidential in order to facilitate repeated or continued use of that element, or substantially

42 DOTAS Guidance, para 7.3.3.

the same element, in the future but, and disregarding any obligation of confidentiality, I nevertheless wish to keep it confidential from HMRC for other reasons, or

I do not wish to keep any element of the scheme confidential from HMRC.'

If the promoter's answer falls within the second or third options, then there is no obligation to notify by reference to this hallmark.

4.88 If a scheme is not notified, factors that HMRC state that it could consider as being indicative that the promoter wanted to keep it confidential from HMRC (and accordingly that this hallmark was met) include:

> 'How new, innovative and aggressive the scheme is. Schemes that promoters are aware to be known to HMRC are not caught by the hallmark. These can be evidenced from, for example, technical guidance notes, case law, or past correspondence with a case officer in HMRC where the detail of how the scheme works has been made clear.
>
> Whether a promoter imposes an obligation upon potential clients, whether in writing or verbally, to keep the details of the scheme confidential from third parties including HMRC. This factor would not be considered if the agreement is a general agreement.
>
> Whether a promoter does not provide to, or otherwise prevents or discourages the user from, retaining promotional materials, data or written professional advice so that such information cannot be provided by the user to HMRC.
>
> Whether confidentially agreements, general or specific, between a promoter and client allow the client to disclose information to HMRC without referral to the promoter.
>
> The use of explicit warnings in marketing material or other communications to a client to the effect that the scheme may have a limited "shelf life" because Parliament may act to close it once it became known the degree of co-operation to requests for information from HMRC concerning a specific scheme and the reasons for not providing information.'

Users

4.89 *Regulation 6(3)* of the *2006 Regulations* imposes the second limb of this hallmark (confidential from HMRC) on users in two circumstances:

(a) where there is a promoter, but the promoter is non-resident and fails to notify; and

(b) where the promoter is not treated as a promoter, because the exemption for lawyers by reason of legal professional privilege applies.

In contrast to hallmark 2 (confidentiality where no promoter involved), which applies only to a scheme user which is a business that is not a small- or medium-sized business (SME)[43], this hallmark applies to all users; it applies, accordingly, to individuals and SMEs.

If either of the *reg 6(3)* preconditions is met, then this hallmark applies if the scheme user would, but for the disclosure rules, wish to keep the way that the tax-saving element secures the tax advantage confidential from HMRC at any time following the material date.

4.90 HMRC recommends that scheme users ask themselves:

> '[D]o I wish to keep confidential from HMRC the way any element of the arrangements (including the way they are structured) gives rise to and secures, or might secure, the expected tax advantage at any time following the material date?'[44]

4.91 Where this limb of the hallmark is considered in relation to promoters, the reason for wanting to keep the tax-saving element confidential is relevant. For the hallmark to apply, the reason must be to facilitate repeated or continued use of the same element, or substantially the same element, in the future. The reason it might reasonably be expected that the scheme user would want to keep the tax-saving element confidential from HMRC is not relevant. It is considered that the test here is in respect of a reasonable user, rather than 'the' user. Accordingly, the test is not met simply because a particular scheme user has a general disinclination to disclose any aspect of his financial affairs, whether to HMRC or elsewhere.

Description 2: Confidentiality where no promoter involved

4.92 This hallmark is defined in *reg 7* of the *2006 Regulations*. It applies in respect of arrangements where:

(a) no person is a promoter in relation to them;

(b) the intended user of the arrangements is a business that is not an SME;

(c) any element of the arrangements (including the way in which the arrangements are structured) gives rise to the tax advantage expected to be obtained under the arrangements;

(d) it might reasonably be expected that the user of those arrangements wishes the way in which that element is expected to secure a tax advantage to be kept confidential from HMRC at any time following the material date;

43 SMEs are defined by reference to the European Commission Recommendations of 6 May 2003 (2003/361/EC), with some modifications. To be a medium-sized company, the entity must employ fewer than 250 employees and either have an annual turnover of €50m or less or have net assets of €43m or less.

44 DOTAS Guidance, para 7.3.3.

(e) a reason for the user's wishing to keep that element confidential from HMRC is to:

   (i) facilitate repeated or continued use of the same element, or substantially the same element, in the future;

   (ii) reduce the risk of HMRC using that information to open an enquiry into any return or account which a person is required by or under any enactment to deliver to HMRC; or

   (iii) reduce the risk of HMRC using that information to withhold payment of all or any part of an amount claimed separately from a return under either *s 261B* of the *Taxation of Chargeable Gains Act 1992* (treating trade loss etc, as a CGT loss) or *ss 59–155* of the *Income Tax Act 2007* (loss relief).

4.93 *Regulations 2, 6* and *8* of the *Tax Avoidance Schemes (Prescribed Descriptions of Arrangements) (Amendment) Regulations 2013, SI 2013/2595* introduced a second limb to this hallmark with effect from 4 November 2013.

4.94 Arrangements are also prescribed if:

(a) the first three preconditions specified above (at **4.92** (a) to (c)) are met; and

(b) if there had been a promoter in relation to the arrangements, it might reasonably have been expected that it would, but for the requirements of the regulations, wish to have kept the way in which any element of the arrangements (including the way in which the arrangements were structured) that secured the tax advantage confidential from HMRC at any time following the material date, and a reason for doing so would be to facilitate repeated or continued use of the same element, or substantially the same element, in the future.

4.95 The second limb of the hallmark was added due to a concern expressed by HMRC that banks in particular had been developing and using (unnotified) schemes in-house, which schemes they then subsequently recommended to their clients.

4.96 This hallmark applies only to schemes that are devised for use 'in-house' for businesses that are not SMEs.

4.97 In the DOTAS Guidance, it is stated at para 7.4.2 that:

> 'So the test for a person using an in-house scheme are, having entered into a transaction forming part of the arrangements:
>
> - "do I wish to keep confidential from HMRC
> - would any user wish to keep confidential from HMRC
> - the way any element of the arrangements (including the way they are structured) gives rise to and secures the expected tax advantage …

- … at any time following the material date?" …
- "Is a reason for doing so to:
  - facilitate the repeated or continued use of that element in the future?…
  - reduce the risk that HMRC might open an enquiry into any return or account that I am required to make?
  - reduce the risk that HMRC might withhold some or all of a repayment sought in a claim outside a return in respect of losses under s 216B Taxation of Chargeable Gains Act 1992 (trade loss treated as a capital loss) or Part 4 Income Tax Act 2007 (loss relief)?""

Description 3: Premium Fee

4.98 *Regulation 8* of the *2006 Regulations* provides:

'**8.— Description 3: Premium Fee**

(1) Arrangements are prescribed if they are such that it might reasonably be expected that a promoter or a person connected with a promoter of arrangements that are the same as, or substantially similar to, the arrangements in question, would, but for the requirements of these Regulations, be able to obtain a premium fee from a person experienced in receiving services of the type being provided.

But arrangements are not prescribed by this regulation if—

(a) no person is a promoter in relation to them; and

(b) the tax advantage which may be obtained under the arrangements is intended to be obtained by an individual or a business which is a small or medium-sized enterprise.

(2) For the purposes of paragraph (1), and in relation to any arrangements, a "premium fee" is a fee chargeable by virtue of any element of the arrangements (including the way in which they are structured) from which the tax advantage expected to be obtained arises, and which is—

(a) to a significant extent attributable to that tax advantage, or

(b) to any extent contingent upon the obtaining of that tax advantage as a matter of law.'[45]

45 The *Tax Avoidance Schemes (Prescribed Descriptions of Arrangements) (Amendment) Regulations 2010, SI 2010/2834, reg 7* amended *reg 8* with effect from 1 January 2011 as follows:

'…

(2) In paragraph (1) for "to disclose information under" substitute "of".

(3) In paragraph (2)(b) after "advantage" insert "as a matter of law".

4.99 A premium fee is a fee that is chargeable by virtue of any element of the arrangements (including the way in which they are structured) from which a tax advantage is expected to arise and which is either:

(a) to a significant extent attributable to the tax advantage; or

(b) to any extent contingent on obtaining the tax advantage, as a matter of law.

4.100 According to HMRC, this hallmark provides no more than 'a broad attempt to identify tax advice that is innovative and valuable'. The hallmark works on the assumption that if a promoter is able to devise and market an innovative tax arrangement that other promoters are not aware of, then potential scheme users will be prepared to pay more to the promoter for that scheme.

4.101 The premium fee description was amended with effect from 1 January 2011 to reduce the number of unnecessary notifications, by adding the phrase 'as a matter of law'. HMRC recognised that almost any fee obtained in relation to tax planning could be said, at least to some extent, to be contingent on obtaining a tax advantage. 'As a matter of law' is intended to narrow the ambit of the hallmark, by limiting its being met to only the situation where the fee is contingent upon the scheme delivering the expected tax advantage, ie where the tax analysis is correct. Accordingly, if the promoter's terms provide that a fee is payable even if the scheme is unsuccessful, it is not a premium fee under this limb. HMRC state that the hallmark will not apply to the situation where the fee is contingent wholly on factors other than the tax analysis being correct, such as 'salary sacrifice situations where the fee depends on the number of employees entering the scheme'[46].

4.102 Although the test is a hypothetical one, HMRC considers that it is met if the promoter charges a premium fee[47]. In contrast, the fact that the promoter does not charge a premium fee does not mean that the test is not met, according to HMRC.

4.103 HMRC consider that a fee is not a premium fee solely on account of factors such as:

- the adviser's location;
- the urgency of the advice;
- the size of the transaction;
- the skill or reputation of the adviser or the scarcity of appropriately skilled staff; or
- the number of users who sign up to the scheme[48].

4.104 In *The Commissioners for Her Majesty's Revenue and Customs v EDF Tax Limited (In Creditors' Voluntary Liquidation)* [2020] SFTD 161, the

46 DOTAS Guidance, para 7.5.3.
47 DOTAS Guidance, para 7.5.2.
48 DOTAS Guidance, para 7.5.3.

Tribunal noted that the absolute amount of the fee charged was calculated by reference to the amount of money paid into the scheme. Its analysis was as follows:

> '118. The amount paid into the scheme was not the amount of the expected tax advantage; the expected tax advantage could only have been about 50% of that sum (on the assumption that the directors were higher rate taxpayers). So is it right to say that the fee was chargeable by virtue of any element of the arrangements (including the way in which they were structured) from which the tax advantage expected to be obtained arose? I find it is. The fee was charged by reference to the sum paid into the scheme; the absolute sum paid into the scheme was itself directly related to the tax advantage expected to be obtained (in the sense that the more paid in, the greater that tax advantage). In other words, the amount of the fee related directly to the amount of the expected tax advantage.
>
> 119 I am aware that the fee charged to 2020 does not entirely fit with this analysis, but it was clear that even that fee was charged as a percentage of the reward and did not relate to the amount of work undertaken. It makes no difference to my overall conclusion that the fees were charged in relation to the expected tax advantage.
>
> *Fee attributable to tax advantage?*
>
> 120. Further, I find the fee paid was to a significant extent attributable to the expected tax advantage. I find this because I find that, on the basis of the evidence in front of me the only reasonable explanation for the payment of fees which normally amounted to 12–13% of the amount paid to the directors and about (very approximately) of about quarter of the expected tax advantage was that the users' directors perceived the payment of the fees as being significantly cheaper than payment of the tax on their earnings. In other words, the fee was paid because the directors and scheme users expected to obtain the tax advantage. It would make no sense whatsoever for the directors and scheme users to have paid such large fees unless there was such an expectation, as to pay the fees and remain liable for the tax on the award paid to the directors would leave them in a much worse economic position than if a cash award had been made to the directors.
>
> *Premium fee reasonably expected?*
>
> 121. In conclusion, the fees paid were within the definition of "premium fee". And I agree with HMRC that the evidence that premium fees were paid proves that it might reasonably be expected that a promoter of the arrangements the subject of this appeal (or substantially similar ones) would be able to obtain a premium fee from a person experienced in receiving services of the type being provided.'

Users

4.105 If there is no promoter and the expected tax advantage is intended to be obtained by an individual or an SME, the hallmark is not met[49].

Description 4: off-market terms

4.106 This hallmark was repealed with effect from 1 January 2011[50]. For completeness, a brief explanation is provided. This hallmark was described under *reg* 9. It prescribed arrangements where:

(a) the tax advantage arose, to more than an incidental degree, from the inclusion of a financial product;

(b) a promoter or someone connected with him became a party to the financial product; and

(c) the price of the financial product differed significantly from what might reasonably have been expected in the open market.

'Financial product' was widely defined. It included, for example, a share, a loan, a derivative contract and a stock lending arrangement within the meaning of *s 263B* of the *Taxation of Chargeable Gains Act 1992*.

Description 5: standardised tax products

4.107 *Regulation 10* of the *2006 Regulations* provides:

> **'10.— Description 5: standardised tax products**
>
> (1) Subject to regulation 11, arrangements are prescribed if a promoter makes the arrangements available for implementation by more than one person and the conditions in paragraph (2) are met.
>
> (2) The conditions are that an informed observer (having studied the arrangements and having regard to all relevant circumstances) could reasonably be expected to conclude that—
>
> (a) the arrangements have standardised, or substantially standardised, documentation—
>
> (i) the purpose of which is to enable a person to implement the arrangements;
>
> (ii) the form of which is determined by the promoter; and
>
> (iii) the substance of which does not need to be tailored, to any material extent, to enable a person to implement the arrangements;

49 *2006 Regulations, reg 8(1)(a)* and *(b)*.
50 By *reg 8* of *SI 2010/2834*.

(b) a person implementing the arrangements must enter into a specific transaction or series of specific transactions;

(c) the transaction or series of transactions is standardised, or substantially standardised, in form; and

(d) either the main purpose of the arrangements is to enable a person to obtain a tax advantage or the arrangements would be unlikely to be entered into but for the expectation of obtaining a tax advantage.'[51]

4.108 According to the DOTAS Guidance, the hallmark contained in *reg 10* is intended to capture 'mass-marketed schemes' and the fundamental characteristic of standardised tax products is stated to be their 'ease of replication'.

This hallmark only applies where there is a promoter.

Subject to certain specified exemptions, arrangements fall within the provisions if:

(a) they have standardised documents to enable the client to implement the scheme;

(b) the form of the documents is determined by the promoter, and not tailored, to any material extent, to reflect the circumstances of the client;

(c) a client must enter into a specific transaction or series of transactions that are standardised, or substantially standardised in form; and

(d) either the main purpose of the arrangements is to enable a person to obtain a tax advantage, or the arrangements would be unlikely to be entered into but for the expectation of obtaining a tax advantage.

4.109 With effect from 23 February 2016, the test as to whether arrangements are a tax product is whether an informed observer (having studied the arrangements) could reasonably conclude that this is the case, having considered all the above aspects.

HMRC considers that the hypothetical informed observer is not an expert or tax practitioner. The informed observer is 'a person', rather than a client of the promoter. He is independent, has all relevant knowledge of the scheme and sufficient knowledge and skill to understand both the scheme and the relevant legislation. The informed observer is deemed to have access to all information available to the scheme promoter.

4.110 According to para 7.6.5 of the DOTAS Guidance, the 'relevant circumstances' that the informed observer must take into account include:

51 *SI 2016/99* substituted the wording in *reg 10*, with effect from 23 February 2016.

(a) commercial factors, such as the commercial (as opposed to tax) benefits expected to arise from the scheme; and

(b) the terms of the documents and the substance of the product.

HMRC guidance[52]

4.111 Standardised products are those that have been pre-prepared and which require little, if any, modification to suit individual clients. HMRC describe such schemes as follows:

> 'Schemes with this replication characteristic have variously been described to us as "shrink-wrapped" or "plug and play" schemes.
>
> Essentially, all the client purchases is a prepared tax product that requires little, if any, modification to suit his circumstances. To adopt it would not require him or her to receive significant additional professional advice or services.'[53]

4.112 It is considered that the corollary of that guidance is that, if the relevant transactions or documents need significant consideration of the particular client's circumstances before they can be undertaken, then, even if there is a similarity as regards the product that may be provided to multiple clients, that is not sufficient for this hallmark to be met.

4.113 In *R (on the application of Root2 Tax Limited) v First-Tier Tribunal (Tax Chamber)* [2018] EWHC 1254 (Admin), the High Court held that the fact that the documents were not authored by the promoter was irrelevant. It held that *reg 10(2)(ii)* requires only that the form of the documentation is 'determined' by the promoter.

Excepted arrangements

4.114 *Regulation 11* of the *2006 Regulations* specifies arrangements that are excepted from being standardised products:

- arrangements that consist solely of one or more plant or machinery leases;
- an enterprise investment scheme;
- arrangements using a venture capital trust;
- arrangements qualifying under the corporate venturing scheme;
- arrangements qualifying for community investment tax relief;

52 This is not defined in the DOTAS Guidance; and it is unclear whether it is intended by HMRC to refer to the DOTAS Guidance itself. It is also unclear as to whether HMRC consider that an informed observer must take into account erroneous HMRC Guidance and, if so, whether he should treat it as erroneous or not.

53 DOTAS Guidance, para 7.6.2.

- an individual savings account (ISA);
- an approved share incentive plan;
- an approved share option scheme;
- an approved company share option plan (CSOP) scheme;
- the grant of one or more options qualifying as an Enterprise Management Incentive, together with such other steps as reasonably necessary to facilitate it;
- a registered pension scheme;
- an overseas pension scheme in respect of which tax relief is granted in the UK under *s 615* of the *Income and Corporation Taxes Act 1988*;
- a relevant non-UK pension scheme;
- a scheme for periodical payments of personal injury damages to which *s 731* of the *Income Tax (Trading and Other Income) Act 2005* applies; and
- financial products that fall outside the financial products hallmark because of the Code of Practice for Banks exception.

Description 6: loss schemes

4.115 This hallmark applies where all the following apply:

- The promoter expects more than one individual to implement the same or substantially the same arrangements.
- The arrangements are such that an informed observer (having studied the arrangements and having regard to all relevant circumstances) could reasonably conclude that each of the following apply:
  - the main benefit or one of the main benefits which could be expected to accrue to some or all of the individuals participating in the arrangements is the provision of losses; and
  - the arrangements (including the way that they are structured) contain an element which is, or elements which are, unlikely to have been entered into by the individuals concerned were it not for the provision of those losses; and
  - those individuals would be expected to use those losses to reduce their CGT or income tax liability[54].

54 *Regulation 12* was amended by the *Tax Avoidance Schemes (Prescribed Descriptions of Arrangements) (Amendment) Regulations 2016, SI 2016/99, reg 8*, with effect from 23 February 2016.

4.116 HMRC has stated that this hallmark is 'intended to capture various loss creation schemes that are typically used by wealthy individuals'[55].

4.117 It is confirmed in the DOTAS Guidance that the terms 'informed observer' and 'relevant circumstances' have the same meaning as in hallmark 5.

4.118 Whether the provision of losses is one of the main benefits[56] of the arrangements is an objective test that requires a comparison of the value of the tax advantage arising from the expected losses with the value of any other benefits arising from the scheme. To be a main benefit, the advantage arising from the losses must be, at the least, a significant element of the overall benefits.

4.119 Whether an informed observer could reasonably conclude that the arrangements would have been entered into without the provision of losses will require the observer to assess whether the arrangements include any uncommercial transactions, such as steps undertaken solely to generate losses. The informed observer should consider the difference between any economic losses and any tax losses, and whether any losses arise in the context of a commercial transaction or an avoidance scheme.

4.120 According to HMRC, the main expected benefit of the scheme will be to generate losses for individuals where it is reasonable to expect that the tax relief anticipated by the investors is greater than the amount of the investment that represents 'real personal risk'[57]. Accordingly, limited or non-recourse financing of investment arrangements may mean that the hallmark is met.

4.121 As with hallmark 5, this hallmark only applies where there is a promoter.

Description 7: leasing arrangements

4.122 *Regulations 13, 15, 16* and *17* of the *2006 Regulations* prescribe the seventh hallmark that concerns leasing arrangements.

4.123 Hallmark 7 applies with effect from 1 August 2006 to both promoters and in-house schemes.

4.124 Arrangements are not prescribed if:

- no person is a promoter in relation to them; and
- the tax advantage which may be obtained under the arrangements is intended to be obtained by an individual or an SME.

4.125 Under hallmark 7, arrangements are prescribed where all the following apply:

---

55 DOTAS Guidance, para 7.7.2.

56 Prior to 23 February 2016, the requirement was to consider whether the provision of losses was *the* main benefit, rather than *a* main benefit.

57 DOTAS Guidance, para 7.7.5.

(a) the arrangements include a plant or machinery lease;

(b) one of the specified additional conditions (in *reg 15*) is met;

(c) the relevant value condition (under *reg 16*) is met; and

(d) the lease is not a short-term lease (as defined in *reg 17*).

Meaning of plant or machinery lease

4.126 *Regulation 14* of the *2006 Regulations* provided a definition of 'plant or machinery lease'. It was revoked, with effect from 1 January 2011, by *SI 2010/2834*. The definition in *s 70K* of the *Capital Allowances Act 2001* is, effectively, the definition that is adopted in the DOTAS Guidance[58]. In *s 70K*, it is stated that a plant or machinery lease, for these purposes, is:

- any agreement or arrangement under which a person grants to another person the right to use plant or machinery for a period, and which, in accordance with generally accepted accounting practice, falls (or would fall) to be treated as a lease; or
- any other agreement or arrangement to the extent that, in accordance with generally accepted accounting practice, it falls (or would fall) to be treated as a lease, and the agreement or arrangement conveys (or falls, or would fall, to be regarded as conveying) the right to use an asset, and the asset is plant or machinery.

4.127 In the DOTAS Guidance, it is stated that a finance lease where the plant or machinery is the subject of a sale and finance leaseback (as defined in the *Capital Allowances Act 2001, s 221*) also falls within the definition.

Additional conditions

4.128 One of the three additional conditions set out in *reg 15* of the *2006 Regulations* must be satisfied in order for the arrangements to fall within hallmark 7.

Condition 1

4.129 One party to the lease has the right to claim plant and machinery allowances under the *Capital Allowances Act 2001* for the expenditure incurred on the plant or machinery, and another party to the lease is outside the charge to corporation tax (*reg 15(1)–(3)*). According to the DOTAS Guidance, a lease satisfies this additional condition if both of those requirements are met, regardless of whether there are other parties to the lease who satisfy neither of the conditions, but a party who acts merely as a guarantor under the lease is

58 DOTAS Guidance, para 7.8.3.

disregarded for the purposes of determining whether there is a party who is not within the charge to corporation tax[59].

Condition 2

4.130 The arrangements include a provision designed to remove the whole or greater part of the lessor's risk of sustaining a loss if payments due under the lease were not made in accordance with its terms, and that provision involves money or a money debt (*reg 15(4)*). 'Money' and 'money debt' have the same meanings as they are used in *s 702(6)* of the *Income Tax (Earnings and Pensions) Act 2003* (*ITEPA 2003*).

Condition 3

4.131 The arrangements involve either a sale and finance leaseback or a lease and finance leaseback unless either:

(a) the arrangement involves a sale and finance leaseback, and the assets are new and unused when acquired or created and that acquisition/creation was no more than four months before the sale; or

(b) the assets are:

  (i) fixtures in buildings or leased with land (unless they are used for storage and production); or

  (ii) do not exceed half of the value of the total leased assets and the rent payable under the lease is not directly or indirectly dependent on the availability of capital allowances.

For these purposes, 'used for storage and production' means:

(a) storing, moving or displaying goods intended to be sold in a trade;

(b) manufacturing goods or materials or subjecting them to a process;

(c) storing goods or materials which are:

  (i) to be used in the manufacture of other goods or materials;

  (ii) to be subjected to a process in the course of a trade;

  (iii) finished goods which have not yet been delivered to a purchaser; or

  (iv) imported goods, on their arrival in the UK.

4.132 HMRC provide two examples in the DOTAS Guidance (at para 7.8.8):

> 'If a factory is sold and leased back where the production line plant in the factory has a value of over £25m (or contains equipment with an individual value of over £10m) it will need to be disclosed.

59 DOTAS Guidance, para 7.8.6.

But the sale and leaseback of an office block costing £100m with £35m of plant or machinery that does not meet the definition of 'plant used for storage or production' will not need to be disclosed under this condition.'

The relevant value condition

4.133 *Regulation 16* of the *2006 Regulations* provides that the relevant value condition is met if either:

- the lower of the cost to the lessor or the market value of any one asset leased under the arrangements is at least £10m; or
- the aggregate of the lower of the cost to the lessor or the market value of all the plant or machinery leased under the arrangements is at least £25m.

4.134 In the DOTAS Guidance, it is stated that facilities to lease assets with an individual value of £10m or to the aggregate value of at least £25m are caught by this test, even if there is no guarantee that the £25m threshold will be reached; they should be disclosed when the facilities are made available[60].

Short-term leases

4.135 A short-term lease is a lease with a term of two years or less. Leases with a term of two years or less are not treated as short-term leases if either:

- the lessee has an option to extend the lease beyond two years; or
- other arrangements are entered into that either contemplate extension of the lease beyond two years or which provide for the assets to be leased to a person connected with the lessee, with the effect that the aggregate term of the letting to the lessee group is more than two years.

Description 8: employment income provided through third parties

4.136 *Regulation 18* of the *2006 Regulations* was introduced with effect from 4 November 2013[61]. Its aim is to ensure that schemes that attempt to circumvent the disguised remuneration rules in *Pt 7A* of *ITEPA 2003* are notified to HMRC.

4.137 *Regulation 18* provides as follows:

> **'18. — Description 8: Employment income provided through third parties**

60 DOTAS Guidance, para 7.8.4.

61 By the *Tax Avoidance Schemes (Prescribed Descriptions of Arrangements) (Amendment) Regulations 2013, SI 2013/2595, reg 10.*

(1) Arrangements are prescribed if—

(a) Conditions 1 and 2 are met and Condition 3 is not met; or

(b) Conditions 1, 2 and 3 are met and at least one of Conditions 4 and 5 is met.

(2) Condition 1 is met if the arrangements involve at least one of the following—

(a) a relevant third person taking a relevant step under section 554B;

(b) any person taking a relevant step under section 554C or 554D; or

(c) B taking a step under section 554Z18 or 554Z19.

(3) Condition 2 is met if the main benefit, or one of the main benefits, of the arrangements is that an amount that would otherwise count as employment income under section 554Z2(1) is reduced or eliminated.

(4) Condition 3 is met if, by reason of at least one of sections 554E to 554X or regulations made under section 554Y, Chapter 2 of Part 7A does not apply.

(5) Condition 4 is met if the arrangements involve one or more contrived or abnormal steps without which the main benefit in paragraph (3) would not be obtained.

(6) Condition 5 is met if the arrangements involve—

(a) a relevant step being treated as taking place; and

(b) Chapter 2 of Part 7A applying as a consequence of sub-paragraph (a).

(7) In this regulation—

(a) references to sections or Parts are to those in ITEPA unless otherwise stated;

(b) "B" has the meaning given for Part 7A by sections 554A(1)(a) and 554Z17(7) read together;

(c) "contrived or abnormal" has the same meaning as in section 207 of the Finance Act 2013; and

(d) "relevant third person" has the same meaning as in section 554A(7).'

4.138 Hallmark 8 applies to both promoted schemes and those designed in-house. There is no exclusion for SMEs in respect of in-house schemes; the hallmark applies to all sizes of business.

4.139 It applies if either:

- Conditions 1 and 2 are met and Condition 3 is not met; or
- Conditions 1, 2 and 3 are met and either Condition 4 or Condition 5 is met.

4.140 Condition 1 is met if the arrangements involve the taking of one of three relevant steps under *Pt 7A* of *ITEPA 2003*. Condition 1 is a wide provision.

4.141 The potential breadth of hallmark 8 is narrowed by Condition 2, which is a main benefit test. Condition 2 is met if one of the main benefits of the arrangements is that an amount that would otherwise count as employment income under *s 554Z2(1)* of *ITEPA 2003* is reduced or eliminated. If *Pt 7A* applies, then there will be an amount counting as employment income under *s 554Z2(1)*; and if the arrangements do not have the benefit of reducing or eliminating such income, then Condition 2 will not be satisfied.

4.142 HMRC provides a number of examples of the application of the two tests at paras 7.9.7 to 7.9.11 of the DOTAS Guidance. These include, for example:

> '*Example: relevant step by employer*
>
> If an employer makes a normal salary payment to an employee, this will be a relevant step under section 554C and will thus meet Condition 1.
>
> However, an employer is not (except in certain unusual circumstances) a relevant third person, and so the salary payment will not trigger Part 7A.
>
> This is a consequence of the arrangements. But reduction or elimination of Part 7A income is not the main benefit, or one of the main benefits, of the arrangements. Therefore Condition 2 is not met.'

4.143 Condition 3 is met if, by reason of at least one of the *Pt 7A* exclusions, *Pt 7A* does not apply.

4.144 Condition 4 is met if the arrangements involve one or more contrived or abnormal steps without which the main benefit of the arrangements would not be obtained. HMRC state in the DOTAS Guidance that the words 'contrived' and 'abnormal' have the same meaning as in *s 207* of the *Finance Act 2013*, which pertains to the General Anti Abuse Rule. The words are not defined in either statute. HMRC asserts that they 'will be applied in their normal sense'[62]. Transactions that differ significantly from the commercial norm may be considered by HMRC to involve contrived or abnormal steps. As a general rule, HMRC regards the following as examples of contrived or abnormal steps:

62 DOTAS Guidance, para 7.9.14.

- circular cash flows;
- the disposal of assets if the disposal has no purpose other than to secure a desired result; and/or
- the involvement of third parties for no purpose other than to secure a desired result.

4.145 The aim of Conditions 3 and 4 is to seek to ensure that tax planning that aims to take advantage of the *Pt 7A* exclusions is notifiable.

4.146 Condition 5 is defined in *re 18(6)* as the 'deliberate fall-back charge' condition. It seeks to catch arrangements that have the aim of deferring tax by excluding an up-front charge for the price of a later fall-back charge.

Description 9: financial products

4.147 *Regulation 19* of the *2006 Regulations* was introduced with effect from 23 February 2016[63]. Its focus is specifically on financial products. Arrangements are prescribed under hallmark 9 if the following conditions are met:

(a) the arrangements include at least one specified financial product; and

(b) the arrangements are such that an informed observer (having studied the arrangements and having regard to all relevant circumstances) could reasonably conclude that:

  (i) one of the main benefits of including such a product in the arrangements is to give rise to a tax advantage; and either:

    (x) such a product contains at least one term that is unlikely to have been entered into by the parties were it not for the tax advantage; or

    (y) the arrangements involve one or more contrived or abnormal steps, without which the tax advantage could not be obtained.

Specified financial products

4.148 *Regulation 20* of the *2006 Regulations* provides that the following are specified financial products:

(a) loans;

(b) shares;

(c) derivative contracts within the meaning of *s 576* of the *Corporation Tax Act 2009* (*CTA 2009*);

63 By the *Tax Avoidance Schemes (Prescribed Descriptions of Arrangements) (Amendment) Regulations 2016, SI 2016/99.*

(d) repos in respect of securities within the meaning of *s 263A(A1)* of the *Taxation of Chargeable Gains Act 1992* (*TCGA 1992*);

(e) creditor repos, creditor quasi-repos, debtor repos and debtor quasi-repos (within *ss 543, 544, 548* and *549* of *CTA 2009* respectively);

(f) stock-lending arrangements within *s 263B(1)* of *TCGA 1992*;

(g) alternative finance arrangements within *Chapter 6* of *CTA 2009* or *Pt 10A* of the *Income Tax Act 2007*; and

(h) contracts that, whether alone or in combination with one or more other contracts, in substance represent the making of a loan, or the advancing or depositing of money, and fall to be accounted for on that basis under UK GAAP or International Accounting Standards (or would if the relevant person were a company).

Exclusions

4.149 There are exclusions for financial products whose terms require the product to be held for a minimum period or provide that it can only be redeemed after a permitted period. Similarly, products whose terms provide for conversion into, or redemption in, a currency other than sterling, are excluded[64].

4.150 Arrangements are excluded from this hallmark under *reg 19* if the promoter is a participating entity (or part of a participating group) for the purposes of the rules relating to the Code of Practice on Taxation for Banks in *s 286* of the *Finance Act 2014* and HMRC has confirmed (or could reasonably be expected to confirm) to the promoter that the arrangements are acceptable under that Code.

4.151 In the DOTAS Guidance, HMRC illustrates the application of this hallmark by describing certain products and arrangements that do not fall within its ambit (assuming ordinary, commercial use)[65].

4.152 These include:

(a) Issuing debt rather than equity to raise financing, including via quoted Eurobonds:

> 'The issuing of securities is a commercial practice. The genuine raising of finance by way of debt, including through the use of quoted Eurobonds, rather than equity has a commercial purpose and benefit. HMRC considers that the benefit of paying interest on a security with commercial terms, without being required to withhold income tax from the interest, is not important or significant compared with

64 For example, bonds that include a term to ensure that they are not qualifying corporate bonds, are excluded.

65 At para 7.10.10.

the main benefit of the arrangements, which is to raise or maintain working capital. HMRC also does not consider that such finance is unlikely to have been raised without the tax advantage of being entitled to pay interest without withholding income tax. The tax advantage of not being required to account for withholding tax is not one of the main benefits of the arrangements therefore *s 306(1)(c)* of the *Finance Act 2004* is not satisfied and the financial products hallmark does not need to be considered.'

(b) Excluded indexed securities:

'HMRC accepts that there is commercial demand for investments which include terms providing investment returns based on a specified index and that some investors prefer not to take direct ownership of the underlying assets. Excluded indexed securities are taxed under the capital gains rules. There is HMRC guidance on the tax treatment of Excluded Indexed Securities in the Savings and Investment Income Manual at SAIM3050. While the tax advantage is arguably a main benefit of holding excluded indexed securities, HMRC's view is that these products, whose investment returns are determined by the value of certain assets, would be commercially viable without this favourable tax treatment.

Consequently, HMRC does not take the view that it would be reasonable for an informed observer to conclude that investors would be unlikely to choose to have their investment returns determined in this way, were it not for the tax advantages of investing in such securities nor that it involves any contrived or abnormal steps.

HMRC would expect an informed observer to conclude that neither condition 3 nor condition 4 is met.'

(c) Carrying out a partition demerger:

'Arrangements consisting of a reorganisation of share capital of a holding company into different classes of share to reflect different interests in a group before a demerger should not be caught by the hallmark.

The main benefit of the demerger is the commercial outcome. HMRC does not consider it would be reasonable for an informed observer to conclude that either condition 3 or condition 4 is met where there is a commercially-driven reorganisation.'

The VAT hallmarks

4.153 The *Indirect Taxes (Notifiable Arrangements) Regulations 2017, SI 2017/1216* specify four VAT Hallmarks.

(1) Retail supplies – splitting and value shifting

4.154 This hallmark is intended to capture arrangements that split up a supply to a retail customer with the aim of enabling him to benefit from a different VAT treatment for those supplies[66].

4.155 An arrangement is a notifiable arrangement if:

(a) a person ('A') makes a supply ('supply 1') of goods or services to a retail customer ('C');

(b) A, or another person ('B'), makes a supply ('supply 2') of other goods or services to the same customer, C; and

(c) either Condition 1 or Condition 2 is met in relation to those supplies, and Condition 3 is met.

4.156 Condition 1 is met if:

(a) were both supplies treated as a single supply, then that supply would be taxable[67]; and

(b) one or both of the supplies is 'non-taxable'[68].

4.157 Condition 2 is met if:

(a) were both supplies treated as a single supply, then that supply would be exempt; and

(b) one or both of the supplies is taxable[69].

4.158 Condition 3 is met if it would be reasonable to conclude that at least two of the following seven conditions apply:

(1) C would not agree to receive supply 1 without also agreeing to receive supply 2;

(2) where supply 2 is made to C by B, B makes the supply with the agreement of A;

(3) supply 1 and supply 2 would be made as a single supply or part of a single supply were it not for a VAT advantage which is obtained, or which may be obtained, by making those supplies separately;

(4) the business model of A or B (or both) assumes that:

- only A will make supply 1 to C;
- only A or B (as the case may be) will make supply 2 to C, and
- the agreements to make the supplies will be entered into with C at or about the same time;

66 *SI 2017/1216, reg 4.*

67 At either the standard or reduced rate.

68 Meaning either reduced-rated, zero-rated or exempt, but excluding exempt supplies that are taxable at the higher rate of Insurance Premium Tax.

69 At the standard, reduced or zero rate.

(5) at least one of the supplies is dependent on the other;

(6) were the supplies made as a single supply or part of a single supply to C, then they would be made at or about the same price as the total price of supply 1 and supply 2 that are made to C; or

(7) a higher profit is generated from whichever of supply 1 or supply 2 is the supply which obtains the greater VAT advantage.

4.159 The 'be reasonable to conclude' test in Condition 3 imposes the test of an independent informed observer, who has studied the arrangements. It applies in a similar way to the equivalent test in the DOTAS rules.

4.160 The following example is provided by HMRC:

> 'An operator of a holiday park provides residential facilities to holidaymakers for a standard weekly charge which is standard rated. It then decides to provide its services from two companies. Company A provides the holiday accommodation and Company B provides various services to the holidaymaker such as water and electricity. The overall weekly charge to the holidaymaker does not change and the holidaymaker has no practical choice but to accept and pay for B's services. The aim is that B's services will be charged at the zero and reduced rates, whilst A's services are standard rated.'[70]

(2) Offshore supplies – insurance and finance

4.161 Arrangements that seek to enable businesses that make exempt supplies of insurance or finance to recover the input tax by routing the supplies via businesses outside the EU fall within this hallmark. The hallmark is intended to cover 'offshore loops', where (1) a UK-based business supplies insurance or financial services to a non-EU business; and (2) insurance or financial services are then supplied to EU customers by the non-EU business, with the non-EU business relying on the supplies made by the UK-based business in order to make these supplies of services.

4.162 *Regulation 5* of *SI 2017/1216* provides that an arrangement is notifiable if:

(a) a person, D, who carries on business in the United Kingdom (UK) makes an exempt supply of services to a relevant business person[71], E, who belongs outside the European Union (EU);

70 Notice 799 (March 2019), para 7.6.8.

71 *Section 7A(4)* of the *Value Added Tax Act 1994* (*VATA 1994*) defines a 'relevant business person', in relation to a supply of services, as meaning: (i) a taxable person within the meaning of Art 9 of Directive 2006/112/EC; (ii) a person registered under *VATA 1994,* or the equivalent legislation in another Member State; or (iii) a person registered under an Act of Tynwald in the Isle of Man for the purposes of any tax imposed by or under an Act of Tynwald which corresponds to VAT, where those services are received by the person otherwise than wholly for private purposes.

(b) E makes a supply of services to F, who belongs in the EU, where the supply would be exempt if it was made in the UK;

(c) the supply which D makes to E is used to make the supply by E to F; and

(d) a supply of services is made by D to E or E to F notwithstanding that the supply:

 (i) is incorporated within a supply made by another person;

 (ii) is split into separate supplies; or

 (iii) is effected by means of a chain of supplies involving one or more intermediate suppliers.

4.163 HMRC provides a number of examples. These include:

> '*Example 1*
>
> Company A is an insurer in the UK and Company B is an insurance intermediary in the UK; they sell insurance policies to UK customers. Company A is advised to set up an associate insurance business, Company C, in a non-EU country that will act as the underwriter of policies sold to UK customers. Company B now gives its intermediary services to Company C and is able to recover its input tax on its costs as a result of it "exporting" its services.
>
> Company A still bears the main insurance risk through re-insurance of Company C and, together with Company B, gives most of the resources and expertise needed. This structure satisfies tests 1 to 3 and, from the circumstances, its main aim is to obtain the tax advantage of Company B recovering its input tax. So this is a notifiable arrangement subject to any "grandfathering").
>
> If Company A was further advised to insert an additional non-EU intermediary between Companies B and C, this would still trigger a disclosure because of the clarification set out in tests 1 to 3 regarding intermediate suppliers.'[72]

4.164 This hallmark will be amended by *reg 87* of the *Value Added Tax (Miscellaneous Amendments and Revocations) (EU Exit) Regulations 2019, SI 2019/59*, in due course, so that it provides relevantly as follows:

(a) a person, D, who carries on business in the UK makes an exempt supply of services to a relevant business person, E, who belongs outside the UK; and

(b) E makes a supply of services to F, who belongs in the UK, and the supply is exempt or would be exempt if it was made in the UK.

72 Notice 799 (March 2019), para 7.7.9.

(3) Offshore supplies—relevant business persons

4.165 This hallmark is intended to apply to arrangements where services are routed outside the UK in order to ensure that a UK or EU customer does not suffer irrecoverable VAT.

4.166 *Regulation 6* of *SI 2017/1216* provides that an arrangement is a notifiable arrangement if:

(a) a person, G, who carries on business in the UK makes a supply of services to a relevant business person, H, who belongs outside the EU;

(b) the supply by G to H would be taxable[73] were H a relevant business person who belongs in the UK;

(c) H makes a supply of services to a person, I who belongs in the EU and the supply:

  (i) would be an exempt supply if made in the UK, or

  (ii) is made in the place where H belongs;

(d) the supply that G makes to H is used to make the supply by H to I; and

(e) a supply of services is made by G to H or H to I notwithstanding that the supply:

  (i) is incorporated within a supply made by another person;

  (ii) is split into separate supplies; or

  (iii) is effected by means of a chain of supplies involving one or more intermediate suppliers.

4.167 HMRC provides two examples:

> '*Example 1:*
>
> Company D arranges loans for UK individuals from UK lenders I, receiving commission from the latter. The commission is consideration for D's supplies of exempt financial intermediary services to I.
>
> D incurs substantial input VAT on advertising costs from UK supplier G which it cannot recover.
>
> On the basis of tax advice received, D sets up an associated company H outside the EU, which contracts with the lenders in D's place. H sub-contracts the actual intermediation work to D. H also buys in the advertising from G, obtaining it free of VAT since H belongs outside the EU. The new structure does not deliver any significant non-tax benefits.
>
> The conditions are met and the hallmark applies. It is therefore notifiable subject to any grandfathering.

73 At the standard or reduced rate of VAT.

Example 2:

Company J in the UK gives tax advice services to wealthy UK individuals L. In order to avoid charging VAT on these services, J sets up associated company K outside the EU, and arranges for L to contract with K for the tax advice service, with K sub-contracting the service to company J. J does not charge VAT to K since its service to K is treated as supplied where K belongs, outside the EU. K does not charge VAT to customers L under the place of supply rules.

The conditions are met and the hallmark applies. It is therefore notifiable subject to any grandfathering.'[74]

(4) Options to tax – land

4.168 This hallmark covers arrangements that prematurely end an option to tax a property by seeking to ensure that the anti-avoidance rules that displace the option to tax apply.

4.169 *Regulation 7* of *SI 2017/1216* provides that an arrangement is a notifiable arrangement if:

(a) a person, J, has exercised the option to tax in respect of land,[75] which option has not been revoked;

(b) fewer than 20 years have expired since the date on which the option had effect;

(c) a supply is made in respect of the land by:

  (i) J, or

  (ii) a relevant associate[76] of J, such that

  (iii) the supply is not a taxable supply by virtue of the *Value Added Tax Act 1994* (*VATA 1994*), *Sch 10, Pt 1, para 12(1)*[77].

4.170 HMRC provides the following example:

'*Example*

A business opted to tax a property enabling it to recover VAT on construction costs. A consequence of opting is that it must charge VAT on any supplies of the building by way of rent, sale and so on.

---

74 Notice 799 (March 2019), para 7.8.2.

75 See *VATA 1994, Sch 10, Pt 1, para 2*,

76 *VATA 1994, Sch 10, para 3* defines a 'relevant associate' as a body corporate that:

  (a) was a member of the same VAT group as the opter at the time that the option first had effect;

  (b) was a member of the same VAT group as the opter at any later time when the opter had a relevant interest in the land; or

  (c) was in the same VAT group as another relevant associate of the opter at a time when that relevant associate held a relevant interest in the land.

77 *Paragraph 12(1)* is an anti-avoidance provision that disapplies the option to tax.

After ten years, the business wishes to let the property to a business that cannot recover VAT, for example a bank or insurance company. In order to attract these tenants the business wants to avoid having to charge VAT on the rent. It is unable to revoke the option until 20 years has passed since opting. An adviser suggests a scheme to "wash out" the option to tax on the property before the 20-year period has elapsed.

The new tenant provides the business with finance for refurbishment works on the building costing £300,000. This creates the conditions for the option to tax not to apply to the lease to the new tenant (under the anti-avoidance provision in *VATA 1994, Sch 10, para 12*).

The input VAT on the original building construction is not adjusted since the capital goods scheme adjustment period expired at the end of ten years. The tax advantage gained from not having to charge VAT on the rent greatly outweighs the irrecoverable input tax suffered on the refurbishment.

The hallmark conditions above are met, and since one of the main benefits expected from the arrangements is obtaining this advantage, these would be notifiable arrangements unless grandfathering applies …

There could be a similar example in which no overall tax advantage is expected or where a VAT advantage might not be expected to be a main benefit. In such a case the hallmark description might be met but the arrangements would not need to be disclosed because the overarching tax advantage and main benefit tests would not be met.'[78]

Promoter

4.171 The primary obligation to notify a scheme under the DOTAS rules falls on the 'promoter'.

4.172 A promoter is defined in *s 307* as:

'(1) For the purposes of this Part a person is a promoter—

(a) in relation to a notifiable proposal, if, in the course of a relevant business, the person ("P")—

(i) is to any extent responsible for the design of the proposed arrangements,

(ii) makes a firm approach to another person ("C") in relation to the notifiable proposal with a view to P making the notifiable proposal available for implementation by C or any other person, or

(iii) makes the notifiable proposal available for implementation by other persons, and

78 Notice 799 (March 2019), para 7.9.4.

(b) in relation to notifiable arrangements, if he is by virtue of paragraph (a)(ii) or (iii) a promoter in relation to a notifiable proposal which is implemented by those arrangements or if, in the course of a relevant business, he is to any extent responsible for—

(i) the design of the arrangements, or

(ii) the organisation or management of the arrangements.'

4.173 The basic definition in *s 307* is reduced in scope by the *Tax Avoidance Schemes (Promoters and Prescribed Circumstances) Regulations 2004* (the '*Promoters Regulations*'), which introduce exclusions. The exclusions are addressed at **4.197** below.

4.174 There are two broad categories of promoter: those who 'design' schemes and those who are involved in implementing them. The latter category, implementers, has three sub-categories. *Section 307* defines a promoter as any person who, in the course of a 'relevant business':

(a) is responsible, to any extent, for the design of the proposed or actual arrangements (a 'scheme designer');

(b) makes a firm approach to another person with a view to making a scheme available for implementation by that person or others (the maker of a 'firm approach');

(c) makes a notifiable proposal available for implementation by another person (a 'scheme implementer'); or

(d) is responsible, to any extent, for the organisation or management of a scheme (a 'scheme organiser').

Relevant business

4.175 *Section 307(2)* defines 'relevant business' as any trade, profession or business that:

(a) involves providing 'services relating to taxation' to others; or

(b) is carried on by a bank (as defined by the *Corporation Tax Act 2010, s 1120*) or a securities house (as defined by the *Corporation Tax Act 2010, s 1009(3)*).

The latter limb was included to ensure that banks who are involved in the marketing or implementation of schemes, but who do not provide tax advice, are, nonetheless, within the DOTAS rules.

4.176 The meaning of relevant business was considered by the Tribunal in *HMRC v Curzon Capital Ltd* [2019] SFTD 506. The Tribunal held, at para 91, that the phrase 'services relating to taxation' is a very broad one and does not require the business to provide taxation services:

> 'In the context of the overall scheme of Part 7 ..., I consider that they were. I accept that CCL had no expertise in the area of taxation and its services were, and were characterised ... as administration services, though it also carried out some marketing activities as summarised above. However, the phrase "services relating to taxation" is in my view sufficiently broad in meaning to cover the activity of administering a tax avoidance scheme, even when doing so without any clear knowledge of the detailed way in which it is intended to work.'

4.177 Accountants, lawyers and Independent financial advisers (IFAs), for example, can be promoters.

Design promoters

4.178 In the guidance that was published on the introduction of the DOTAS rules, HMRC indicated that it considered that any contribution to the design would suffice to make a person a promoter (assuming that the other tests were met). It said: 'An adviser who is consulted on the design and gives an opinion that it achieves its intended effect, without offering any suggestions for changes, is not a designer', but 'an adviser who is consulted and explains why the design does not work or offers suggestions for changes to it may be a designer ...'[79].

4.179 In *The Commissioners for Her Majesty's Revenue and Customs v EDF Tax Limited (In Creditors' Voluntary Liquidation)* [2019] UKFTT 598 (TC), the Tribunal held that EDF was a promoter under *section 307(1)(b)(i)* by reason of its having claimed that it was. The Tribunal said:

> '... by their own admission, they were to some extent responsible for the design of the arrangements: their letters state that they are giving the advice and in the solution letter, they state that they had devised the solution in partnership with leading counsel. Even without that statement, it seems more likely than not that EDF were largely responsible for the design of the arrangements which they were promoting. Not only did they write all the letters and provide all the material for execution, they were paid an extremely large fee.'

Exceptions

4.180 There are, however, three exceptions to the definition of a 'design promoter' set out in the *Promoters Regulations*. These reduce its ambit significantly. The aim of these exceptions is, according to HMRC, to ensure that only those 'at the heart of' a scheme are required to notify it under the DOTAS rules.

79 Inland Revenue Guidance, Appendix 3, section (a).

(1) The 'non-adviser'

4.181 This applies to a person who is responsible to any extent for the design of the arrangements, but who does not provide tax advice as part of his duties relating to the arrangements[80]. It applies only to those whose business involves the provision of services relating to taxation. HMRC state that the exception does not apply to banks or securities houses[81].

4.182 HMRC has provided two examples of when it considers that this exception is likely to apply:

> 'where a promoter consults:
>
> a law firm (which has a business that includes giving tax advice) in relation to company law – the law firm will not become a promoter as long as it provides no tax advice (other than benign advice) in the course of carrying out its responsibilities
>
> [an] accounting firm in relation to accounting aspects of a scheme – the firm is not a promoter so long as it provides no tax advice in the course of carrying out its responsibilities.'

(2) The 'benign test'

4.183 The aim of this test is to seek to ensure that those who provide tax advice on the effects or implications of a structure, without having any input into its design, are excluded from being promoters. *Regulation 4(2)* provides that a person who gives tax or NICs advice on the arrangements, but is not responsible to any extent for the design of any element of the arrangements that gives rise to the tax advantage, is excluded from being a promoter. The benign test is often met by, for example, tax lawyers or accountants who are asked to advise a client on what may be the tax consequences for that client in relation to an arrangement that has been designed by a promoter.

4.184 HMRC provides the following example of when the benign test applies:

> 'For example, a promoter may seek advice from an accounting or law firm on whether two companies are 'connected' for any purpose of the Taxes Acts. Provided the advice goes no further than explaining the interpretation of words used in tax legislation, it would be benign, as would advice on general compliance requirements, and so on.'[82]

4.185 It is considered that this is a limited, and not overly helpful, example in the context of understanding whether the provision of advice in relation to an arrangement gives rises to an obligation to notify under DOTAS. A more

80 *Promoters Regulations, reg 4(3).*
81 DOTAS Guidance, para 3.4.2.
82 DOTAS Guidance, para 3.4.1.

realistic, and common, example would be tax Counsel being asked to advise a client as to which, out of several proposed, options is optimal. It is considered that simply answering the question by stating that 'X is to be preferred' cannot be said to be providing input into its design[83].

(3) The 'ignorance test'

4.186 A person who is responsible for the design of some of the tax-saving elements of an arrangement and who could not reasonably be expected to have sufficient information to enable him to know whether a notification is required or to provide all the information required in a notification is excluded, under *reg 4(4)*. This exception is intended to exclude those who are insufficiently involved to be able to decide whether or not notification is required.

4.187 These three exceptions (the non-adviser, benign and ignorance tests) only apply to design promoters. They do not apply to persons who are promoters because they make a notifiable proposal available for implementation by another person or because they organise or manage the implementation of a scheme.

'A firm approach'

4.188 This limb of the definition of 'promoter' was introduced by the *Finance Act 2010*, with effect from 1 January 2011. It was introduced with the aim of ensuring that notifications are made to HMRC as early as possible; it gives rise to an obligation to notify as soon as steps are taken to market the scheme, irrespective of whether that scheme is made available for implementation or not[84]. The 'makes a firm approach' test was introduced to ensure that disclosure of a marketed scheme is triggered as soon as a promoter takes any steps to market the scheme to potential clients.

4.189 HMRC considered that, prior to its introduction, there were examples of promoters taking steps to ensure that notification was not made until virtually the point where it was implemented, so as to ensure that the obligation under 'making available' was not (technically) breached.

4.190 Under *s 307*, a person ('P') is a promoter where the following three cumulative tests are satisfied:

(1) P '*makes a marketing contact*' with another person, C, in relation to the scheme.

P makes a marketing contact with C if P:

83 In any event, if the advice is provided by a legal adviser, then he is likely to be excluded from being a promoter by reason of *reg 6*, which stops professional legal advisers from being promoters if their involvement is such that they cannot produce all the prescribed information because aspects of it are privileged. See further **4.200–4.204** below.

84 DOTAS Guidance, para 14.3.

(a) communicates information about the scheme to C;

(b) the communication is made with a view to C (or any other person) entering into transactions forming part of the arrangements; and

(c) the information communicated includes an explanation of any tax advantage that a person might be expected to obtain from using the arrangements[85].

It is stated in DOTAS Guidance that it is sufficient that the general nature of the tax advantage is communicated and that it is not necessary for the scheme to be explained in full[86].

'C' is not defined in *s 307*. It is stated in the DOTAS Guidance that, for these purposes, C can be the client, an introducer or co-promoter.

(2) At the time of the marketing contact, the scheme is '*substantially designed*'.

'Substantially designed' is defined at *s 307(4C)*. It provides that the scheme must have been sufficiently developed for it to be reasonable to believe that a person who wished to obtain the tax advantage communicated might enter into those or similar transactions.

DOTAS Guidance (at para 3.6.2) provides further detail of HMRC's perspective with regard to the test:

> 'This test must be read in conjunction with the first test. If the first test is met a person will have communicated information to third parties about a scheme, including information about an expected tax advantage, with a view to persons entering into the scheme. This second test asks whether the design is worked up to the point that it would be reasonable to conclude that the combination of transactions envisaged in the design would be used to deliver the advantage to anyone wishing to secure the advantage communicated, without the design requiring further, substantial, amendment. In practice, this point will normally coincide with the point where a promoter has sufficient confidence in the tax analysis of the scheme to market it.
>
> It does not matter whether:
>
> - the detailed design is communicated to potential clients …
> - the scheme is eventually implemented in that form …
> - potential clients choose not to enter the scheme for reasons unconnected with the design …

85 *FA 2004, s 307(4B)*. See also DOTAS Guidance, para 3.6.1.

86 DOTAS Guidance, para 3.6.1.

- the scheme is capable of being implemented in practice … at this time, for example, the design of the scheme may include a loan – it does not matter whether or not an actual loan provider is in place at this point.'

(3) P makes the marketing contact with a view to making the scheme available for implementation by C or by any other person.

HMRC consider that this limb of the test requires P to make a marketing contact with a view to making the scheme available himself (ie with a view to obtaining clients who will buy the scheme from him). A person who is simply an 'introducer' (ie a person who solicits clients for another person (the promoter) will not meet this test[87]).

HMRC v Curzon Capital Ltd [2019] SFTD 506 concerned Curzon Capital Ltd (CCL), a company that had been invited by the arranger of a tax planning scheme, NM, to provide financial administration services in relation to arrangements that were designed to reduce the taxable income of participating individuals. It liaised with new participants, dealt with invoices, operated bank accounts and distributed information to the participants to enable them to complete their tax returns; and it also, in order to generate further administration fees for itself, sent out marketing material to other IFAs. The Tribunal held that CCL was acting in the course of a relevant business in carrying out its activities in relation to the arrangements. However, it did not make the firm approach with a view to itself making the scheme available for implementation. Accordingly, as the activities were not within *s 307(1)(a)(ii)* or *(iii)*, the company was not a promoter of the arrangements within *s 307(1)(b)*. The Tribunal referred to para 3.6.3 of the DOTAS Guidance with approval:

> 'This highlights the significance which HMRC place upon it being "P" himself (in this case CCL) who would actually provide the scheme, if implemented following the firm approach. I consider their guidance to be correct in this regard. In the present case, if any firm approach made by CCL had matured into the implementation of the Arrangements by any client of the relevant IFAs, it is quite clear that the scheme would have been made available for implementation by NM (from whom the scheme would have been "bought"), and not by CCL. Accordingly, I consider that CCL was not a promoter of the Arrangements by reference to *section 307(1)(b)*, applying *section 307(1)(a)(ii)*.'

A 'scheme implementer'

4.191 The somewhat imprecise expression 'making available' is not defined in the legislation; it has remained in the legislation since the introduction of the

87 DOTAS Guidance, para 3.3.

DOTAS rules. In the original guidance, two examples of 'making available' that also would not be treated as 'designer' were provided: 'Designer of "solution" obtains introduction to client from adviser for fee'; and 'Adviser distributes 'solution' designed by another'[88]. It is considered that these would now be likely to fall within the firm approach test.

4.192 HMRC has stated that this limb is retained to cover the circumstances where a promoter makes a scheme available for implementation by clients without having previously marketed it (and thereby come within the firm approach test).

4.193 An example provided by HMRC is:

> 'For example, a promoter may offer a client a "packaged solution". By "packaged solution" we refer to the situation where a promoter does not actively market a scheme, but has a ready developed planning solution (ie a scheme) on a solutions database or similar system which is rolled out, with or without modification, to a specific client in response to an approach from that client. In our view a scheme is made available for implementation at the point when all the elements necessary for implementation of the scheme are in place and a communication is made to a client suggesting the client might consider entering into transactions forming part of the scheme, but it does not matter whether full details of the scheme are communicated at that time.'[89]

A scheme organiser

4.194 A person is a promoter qua scheme organiser if, in the course of a relevant business, he is to any extent responsible for the organisation and management of notifiable arrangements[90]. A person cannot be a promoter qua scheme organiser in relation to notifiable proposals.

4.195 In *HMRC v Hyrax Resourcing Ltd* [2019] SFTD 536, HMRC asserted that Hyrax managed and organised the arrangements and/or made the arrangements available for implementation by other persons. The Tribunal held that it made the arrangements available for implementation by other persons, because it was the counterparty to all the relevant contracts (the purpose of which was tax avoidance). It added, *obiter*, that the natural inference from Hyrax being the counterparty was that it was also the organiser and manager of the arrangements.

4.196 If there are separate designers and organisers and managers, then often they will be co-promoters. If the co-promoter rule applies (see **4.219** below), it is not necessary that both persons make a DOTAS notification.

88 '*Further guidance on definition of promoters*', section (a), Appendix 3, Inland Revenue Guidance.

89 DOTAS Guidance, para 14.3.2.

90 Under *FA 2004, s 307(1)(b)(ii)*.

General exclusions from the definition of 'promoter'

4.197 The *Promoters Regulations* prescribe certain exclusions:

(1) Companies that provide services in connection with notifiable proposals or arrangements only to other group members

4.198 *Regulation 2* of the *Promoters Regulations* provides that companies that provide services in relation to notifiable proposals or notifiable arrangements only to other members of the same group of companies are excluded from being promoters.

(2) Employees of promoters or of participants in notifiable arrangements

4.199 *Regulation 3* of the *Promoters Regulations* provides that a person is not to be treated as a promoter in relation to a notifiable proposal or notifiable arrangements where he is an employee of a promoter or a person that enters into any transaction that forms part of the proposed arrangements. This exception was amended with effect from 17 April 2015[91] to ensure that UK resident employees of offshore promoters who fail to make a disclosure are not excluded from the definition of promoter. Such employees will be treated as promoters if they carry out any of the activities of the promoter.

(3) Legal professional privilege

4.200 *Section 314(1)* provides: 'Nothing in this Part requires any person to disclose to the Board any privileged information'[92].

In its draft guidance note issued on 17 May 2004, the Inland Revenue indicated that professional legal advisers should disclose a summary of the tax planning proposal, having redacted the clients' details. It was pointed out by a number of commentators and the Law Society that that would breach legal advisers' duty to maintain legal professional privilege (LPP)[93]; and the Law Society issued guidance to its members stating that they did not have to disclose legally privileged material. There were also concerns expressed on behalf of the accountancy profession that the rules bestowed an unfair competitive advantage on lawyers, given that legal advice privilege protects communications between

91 *Regulation 3(4)*: 'This regulation does not apply where, but for this paragraph, it would result in a duty under *section 309* falling on any person', inserted by the *Tax Avoidance Schemes (Promoters and Prescribed Circumstances) (Amendment) Regulations 2015, SI 2015/945*.

92 See further, **Chapter 7**.

93 See Patrick Cannon, 'Legal Professional Privilege "Lite"', *Taxation*, 10 June 2004; and Sarah Falk and Sean Jeffrey, 'Privilege and the Disclosure Regime', *Tax Journal*, 8 November 2004, Issue 764, 5.

a professional legal adviser and his client made in connection with the giving of legal advice to the client. It does not protect communications between an accountant, for example, and his client made in connection with the giving of legal advice to the client.

4.201 On 6 October 2014, the Inland Revenue issued a press release in which it was explained that amending legislation would be introduced. *Regulation 6* of the *Promoters Regulations* came into force on 14 October 2004. It provides:

> 'A person is not to be treated as a promoter in relation to a notifiable proposal or notifiable arrangements where his involvement with the proposal or arrangements is such that he is not required to provide all of the information prescribed in regulation 4(1) of the Tax Avoidance Schemes (Information) Regulations 2012 by virtue of section 314 (legal professional privilege).'[94]

4.202 *Regulation 6* stops professional legal advisers from being promoters if their involvement is such that they cannot produce all the prescribed information because aspects of it are privileged. As most (if not all) 'bespoke' advice emanating from professional legal advisers will be privileged, and an anonymous précis of the advice also would be privileged, the effect of *reg 6* is to remove such advisers from the category of promoters in such circumstances. This exclusion means that professional legal advisers are unlikely to be promoters unless the client waives LPP. Thus, unless there is another promoter, or the client waives LPP[95], the obligation to notify will fall on the user of the scheme.

4.203 The relevant section of the Law Society guidance to solicitors provides as follows[96]:

> 'In light of the exception for privileged information that exists in the DOTAS regime, the Law Society has taken advice from leading Counsel as to the extent of solicitors' disclosure obligations under the regime.
>
> We are of the view that, in many cases, information that you would otherwise be required to disclose under the tax avoidance regulations would be subject to legal professional privilege (LPP). Such information would not have to be disclosed to HMRC.
>
> …
>
> Legal professional privilege has been recognised by the House of Lords as a fundamental human right. It is the privilege of the client and, unless unambiguously waived by the client, must be asserted by you. You must uphold privilege until such time as any unambiguous waiver has been expressly communicated to you by your client.

94 As amended by the *Tax Avoidance Schemes (Information) Regulations 2012, SI 2012/1836*, with effect from 1 September 2012.

95 LPP belongs to the client. It gives rise to a duty on the solicitor to protect it. The solicitor cannot waive LPP; that is a right possessed only by the client.

96 *Disclosure of tax avoidance schemes* (revised, 11 May 2011).

If you have advised clients about affairs which give rise to a notifiable proposal or notifiable arrangements under the DOTAS regime, it is likely that the services which you provide to your client in connection with the proposal or arrangements will involve legal advice about how the scheme should be constructed and/or the likelihood that a scheme which is constructed in a particular way will achieve its objective of obtaining a tax advantage.

In these circumstances, if you disclose the prescribed information sought by HMRC including the principal features of a proposed scheme, you are likely both to be disclosing the fact that your client has consulted you for legal advice on a particular subject, and to be revealing (directly or indirectly) the substance of privileged communications passing between you and your client for the purpose of obtaining and giving that legal advice.

You should also bear in mind that the form in which a disclosure takes place is immaterial. It is not the position that legal professional privilege will not be breached just because you do not provide copies of actual documents or planning advice to HMRC. Nor is it the case that legal advice privilege will not be breached merely because under the disclosure rules only facts or information about the features of a particular proposal are revealed rather than the actual advice given.

The Law Society considers that you should ask yourself whether any information that you would be required to disclose to HMRC under the DOTAS regime forms part of, or would otherwise reveal, the substance or subject matter of confidential communications that have passed between you and your clients for the purpose of obtaining and giving legal advice.

If the answer to that question is yes then the information will usually be subject to the privilege exception to disclosure of information set out in *section 314* of the *Finance Act 2004.*

In such cases, the privileged information should not be disclosed unless you are aware that your client has waived the privilege. The position is not altered by the fact that you may give similar advice to several clients.

The effect of [*The Tax Avoidance Schemes (Promoters, Prescribed Circumstances and Information) (Amendment) Regulations 2004*] is to stop lawyers from being treated as promoters where they would be unable to comply with the rules without breaching legal professional privilege.

In cases where these regulations apply, unless there is another promoter who can fulfil the obligation to disclose without breaching privilege, the scheme must be disclosed by your client when they enter into any transaction forming part of it.

It is our view that privilege will not prevent your client disclosing details of a scheme which they are implementing and setting out what they consider to be the tax effect of the scheme. This is because in a client's hands neither the facts as to what has been done nor the arguments on which a scheme is based are privileged. However, the advice your client received from you on the merits of the scheme and how it should be constructed would be privileged as is any information which identifies or is capable of identifying the fact that legal advice has been taken (this would include information on related issues such as the identity of the lawyer etc) …'

4.204 The LPP exclusion is disregarded for the purpose of determining whether an arrangement falls within hallmarks 1, 2, 3 or 7[97].

Professional advisers

4.205 When advising in relation to DOTAS, professional advisers need to be cognisant of the various measures (both legislative and regulatory) that have been introduced with the aim of deterring those who advise in relation to tax matters from advising in relation to the avoidance of tax. A detailed examination of these matters is outside the scope of this chapter, but there are two particular measures that professional advisers need to be aware of before advising in this field: (1) the 'enabler penalty' legislation; and (2) the Professional Conduct in Relation to Taxation (PCRT).

4.206 Solicitors also need to be aware of the Warning Notice that was issued by the Solicitors Regulation Authority on 21 September 2017 and updated on 25 November 2019 (the 'SRA Notice').

(1) The enabler penalty legislation

4.207 *Schedule 16* to the *Finance (No 2) Act 2017* provides for the imposition of a penalty on each person who 'enabled' the arrangements where:

(a) a person ('T') has entered into abusive tax arrangements; and

(b) T incurs a defeat in respect of the arrangements.

4.208 *Part 4* of *Schedule 16* defines five categories of persons who 'enabled' the arrangements. The categories include 'designers of arrangements', which is very widely designed and can encompass specialist tax advisers who provide advice with regard to arrangements. If the conditions are met, the penalty is 'the total amount or value of all the relevant consideration received or receivable by that person'[98].

97 *2006 Regulations, reg 5(3).*
98 *Finance (No 2) Act 2017, Sch 16, para 15(1).*

(2) The PCRT

4.209 In March 2015, the government asked:

> 'the regulatory bodies who police professional standards to take on a greater lead and responsibility in setting and enforcing clear professional standards around the facilitation and promotion of avoidance to protect the reputation of the tax and accountancy profession and to act for the greater public good.'

4.210 In response, various tax and accountancy bodies jointly issued a revised PCRT[99]. Solicitors are also required to abide by the PCRT. The SRA Notice requires solicitors to 'be familiar with the PCRT and adhere to its standards'[100]. The PCRT contains the following requirement, at para 2.29:

> '**Tax planning arrangements**
>
> Members must not create, encourage or promote tax planning arrangements or structures that (i) set out to achieve results that are contrary to the clear intention of Parliament in enacting relevant legislation and/or (ii) are highly artificial or highly contrived and seek to exploit shortcomings within the relevant legislation.'[101]

4.211 There are similarities between this prohibition and (a) arrangements that are counteracted by the GAAR and (b) the conduct that can give rise to the imposition of enabler penalties. However, there are important differences. In particular, in the GAAR, reference to the 'intention of Parliament' was excluded, due to 'the established principle of statutory interpretation in the UK which holds that the intention of Parliament can be discerned only from the language of the legislation itself'[102]. As Lord Hoffmann, writing extra-judicially, said:

> '… tax avoidance in the sense of transactions successfully structured to avoid a tax which parliament intended to impose should be a contradiction in terms. The only way in which parliament can express an intention to impose a tax is by a statute, which means that such a tax is to be imposed. If that is what parliament means, the courts should be trusted to give effect to its intention. Any other approach will lead us into dangerous and unpredictable territory.'[103]

4.212 An example of an occasion where the inclusion of reference to the intention of Parliament in the PCRT would be problematic for tax advisers is

99 The Association of Accounting Technicians, Association of Chartered Certified Accountants, Association of Taxation Technicians, Chartered Institute of Taxation, Institute of Chartered Accountants in England and Wales, Institute of Chartered Accountants of Scotland and the Society of Trust and Estate Practitioners.

100 Published on 21 September 2017 and updated on 25 November 2019.

101 1 November 2016.

102 See Graham Aaronson QC, *GAAR Study: A Study to Consider whether a General Anti-Avoidance Rule should be introduced into the UK Tax System* (2011) at para 5.17.

103 [2005] *British Tax Review* 195.

the tax avoidance structure known as SHIPS 2, which was considered in *Mayes v HM Revenue & Customs* [2011] STC 1269. The object of the scheme was to minimise the income tax liabilities of higher rate taxpayers and their liabilities for CGT; and, as the Court of Appeal noted, at para 9:

> 'An unusual feature of this case is that the series of pre-planned steps, which HMRC say include artificial, unreal and uncommercial tax-avoidance insertions, are built on or structured around a set of provisions in ICTA for the taxation of life assurance policies: and those provisions operate on a basis and in a manner that can fairly be described as artificial, unreal and uncommercial.'

4.213 The High Court and the Court of Appeal held, albeit with great reluctance, that the scheme had the tax consequences intended by its designer, and noted that such tax consequences were, concomitantly, contrary to the clear intention of Parliament. For example:

> 'Lord Justice Thomas:
>
> 100. I agree with the judgment of Lord Justice Mummery which sets out with great clarity why the appeal and cross appeal have to be dismissed. However, for the reasons given by Lord Justice Toulson, my concurrence is reluctant. The higher rate taxpayers with large earnings or significant investment income who have taken advantage of the scheme have received benefits that cannot possibly have been intended and which must be paid for by other taxpayers. It must be for Parliament to consider the wider implications of the decision as it relates to the way in which revenue legislation is structured and drafted.
>
> Lord Justice Toulson:
>
> 101. I also agree. On the corresponding deficiency issue I add a brief summary to explain the reason for my reluctant concurrence in a result which instinctively seems wrong, because it bears no relation to commercial reality and results in a windfall which Parliament cannot have foreseen or intended.'

4.214 SHIPS 2 was a highly artificial arrangement, but it was, nonetheless, a legally effective way of avoiding tax. Had the current version of the PCRT been in force at the relevant time, a specialist tax adviser asked to advise his client on whether the arrangement achieved the intended purpose could have found himself in the iniquitous position of being caught between the Scylla of the prohibition, as a matter of professional conduct, against advising that the arrangement was legally effective and the Charybdis of being under a contractual duty to provide that advice.

4.215 The position is particularly acute for solicitors, as the SRA Notice not only goes considerably further than the PCRT, it is also more complex and raises a number of questions that it does not answer[104]. It is stated in the SRA Notice that:

> 'When advising a client on avoidance of tax schemes you should make clear that any avoidance arrangements the client enters into might deliver tax outcomes that were never envisaged or intended by Parliament and may be challenged. You should be clear as to the legal implications, the costs and penalties of non-compliance should the arrangement fail.
>
> You should also consider your own position in advising or facilitating such an arrangement. It is likely that, should the arrangement fail, your conduct will be called into question. To be involved in such arrangements is likely to reflect badly on you and to damage public confidence in those delivering legal services. You will leave yourself open to the risk of disciplinary proceedings as well as committing a criminal offence.'

4.216 It is wholly unclear what is meant by 'to be involved in such arrangements'. The dictionary definition of 'involve' as a transitive verb is 'to engage as a participant'. That suggests that it only means 'participating in such arrangements'. But the context and the references to 'when advising a client' suggests that that literal interpretation cannot be correct, and that, instead, a purposive interpretation is needed. Perhaps it means advising on? Or facilitating? Or promoting? Or implementing? Or conducting litigation in respect of? Or perhaps it is intended to encompass all of these activities. That the SRA Notice is wholly unclear in relation to these matters is entirely unsatisfactory.

4.217 It is also wholly unclear as to which criminal offence the SRA considers arises, when it arises or how[105]. Yet, despite that it is said that a criminal offence, 'will' have been committed by a solicitor. It seems to be being stated that the SRA's position is that if a solicitor advises in relation to an avoidance structure that subsequently 'fails' (whatever that means) then he will have committed a criminal offence. Leaving aside that the SRA is unable to indicate which criminal offence it considers has been committed, that position is clearly wrong as a general proposition. Advancing an argument as to why

---

104 However, whether it is binding on solicitors is moot, particularly given that it is in conflict with the Code of Conduct. See Michael Blackwell, *Conduct Unbefitting: Solicitors, the SRA and Tax Avoidance*, BTR 2019, 1, 31–54 for a detailed analysis of the SRA Notice. Mr Blackwell considers that, as the SRA Notice would need to have been approved by the Legal Services Board as an alteration of 'regulatory arrangements of an approved regulator', but was not, it is not enforceable. He also expresses the view: 'The rule of law is most significantly violated by the SRA attempting to limit the issues on which legal advice is available to citizens. It is also arguably violated by providing a warning notice that is so muddled that it lacks a clear guidance value'.

105 The SRA was unable to provide any clarification or explanation in response to the author's requests and stated only that 'it would be outside the scope of the warning notice to specify the types of criminal offences that may be committed … as these are often complex matters that are adjudicated by the relevant courts and tribunals depending on the individual facts of each case'.

an avoidance scheme (or even an 'aggressive avoidance scheme' or an abusive arrangement) may work does not constitute *per se* the putting forward of a case that is improper or not properly arguable. Still less can it be said *per se* to be criminal[106].

4.218 Moreover, whilst it is correct that HMRC's 'win-rate' in avoidance cases is very high, it cannot be said that no avoidance case can succeed (with the consequence that no solicitor could advise properly that any structure 'may' achieve its aim). In the Budget 2014: policy costings, a win-rate of 80% was used to enable an estimate of the financial impact of APNs on the exchequer to be calculated; and that figure is used elsewhere in publications issued by HMRC[107]. But, whilst an 80% success rate is high, nonetheless, as Lady Justice Arden noted in *R (on the Application of Rowe and Others) v Her Majesty's Revenue and Customs* [2018] STC 462, it is indicative of the fact: 'that there are a significant percentage of cases where HMRC does not succeed in showing that the scheme is ineffective for tax purposes'[108].

Co-promoters

4.219 Given the width of the definition of promoter and the fact that the steps of devising a scheme, opining on it, amending it and marketing it are often undertaken by more than one person, it is not uncommon for a number of persons to fall within the definition of promoter in relation to the same scheme.

4.220 *Section 308(4)–(4C)* provides for exemptions where there are two or more promoters in respect of the same scheme. The rules apply in two circumstances:

(1) Where a co-promoter exists at the time of the disclosure:

106 Moreover, if it were to be the case that the test of criminality is whether there is a 'failing' in the sense that the ultimate court concludes that the arrangement does not achieve the purpose intended by the designer, then there would be an argument that Art 7 of the European Convention on Human Rights (ECHR) precludes its application.

107 See, for example, 'HMRC Fast Facts: record revenues for the UK', May 2014 Bulletin (amended July 2014).

108 At para 91. To understand properly what percentage of avoidance schemes do not achieve their purpose, it would be necessary also to: (a) exclude from 'HMRC wins' those cases that fail solely on the facts, because the scheme has not been properly implemented, and (b) take into account the cases that have not been taken to litigation (and the reasons why). A hermeneutical approach to '80% HMRC wins' would also consider whether HMRC has an inherent structural advantage, and, if so, its value. HMRC is a 'repeat player' whilst most taxpayers are 'one-shotters' (adopting the terminology used by Galanter, 'Why the haves come out ahead: Speculations on the limits of legal change' (1974) 9 *Law & Society Review* 95). The Tax Law Review Committee noted that being a repeat player gave the Inland Revenue the ability to litigate those cases that it was most likely to win, when there were multiple taxpayers in relation to the same issue, or similar issues (*The Tax Appeal System* (IFS, 1996), paras 2.24 to 2.33).

A promoter (P2) is exempt from making a notification under DOTAS where:

(a) another promoter (P1) discloses the scheme information to HMRC;

(b) P2 holds evidence that notification has been made[109]; and

(c) P1 has provided the identity and address of P2 to HMRC before P2's duty to notify has arisen.

(2) Where a person becomes a co-promoter after the time of disclosure:

P2 is exempt from making a disclosure where:

(a) P1 notifies the scheme and an SRN is allocated to it; and

(b) P2 holds evidence about the notification and the SRN[110].

4.221 Promoters who wish to rely on notification by a co-promoter will need to satisfy themselves that the notification was correct and made within the required time limit, so as to ensure that they are not at risk of penalties consequent on any such default by the co-promoter.

No promoter

4.222 As stated above, the primary obligation to notify rests on the promoter. However, there are three circumstances when the end-user of the scheme has a duty to notify:

(1) The promoter is a lawyer and the LPP exception precludes his notifying the scheme (see **4.199** above).

(2) There is a non-UK resident promoter who does not notify the scheme and there is no UK resident promoter.

(3) There is no promoter, because, for example, the arrangements have been developed in-house for use within that entity or corporate group to which it belongs.

4.223 HMRC consider that the legislation applies extra-territorially. Non-UK resident promoters remain, in theory, subject to the notification obligations. However, when the DOTAS rules were introduced, it was recognised that, in practice: (a) they may not comply; and (b) enforcing compliance may not be straightforward. Accordingly, if the non-UK resident promoter does not notify and there is no UK resident promoter or UK resident employee of the promoter who is treated as a promoter, it is the client who must make a notification. That

109 HMRC state that, normally, it would expect P2 to possess a copy of the disclosure made by P1. DOTAS Guidance, para 14.2.2.

110 HMRC state that, normally, it would expect P2 to possess a copy of the disclosure made by P1 and the SRN. DOTAS Guidance, para 14.2.2.

must be done within five business days of entering into the first transaction implementing a notifiable arrangement[111]. There is no exclusion for individuals or SMEs from this obligation.

Introducers

4.224 The *Finance Act 2010* introduced the concept of an 'introducer'. An introducer is defined in *s 307(1A)* as a person who 'makes a marketing contact' in relation to a scheme that is notifiable under DOTAS. In many cases, a person will fall within both the definition of introducer and the definition of promoter. A 'pure' introducer will not have been involved in the design of the scheme and, indeed, may not know how it is intended to work; this is often the case with IFAs, who liaise between promoters and users.

4.225 HMRC can require an introducer to:

(a) opine on whether the proposal or arrangements are notifiable, and, if not, explain why not[112]; and

(b) provide prescribed information in relation to:

   (i) each person who has provided it with any information relating to a proposal; and

   (ii) any persons to whom it has made a marketing contact in relation to the proposal[113].

4.226 The prescribed information to be provided in relation to the latter is their names and addresses[114]. This power applies only in respect of proposals; it does not apply in respect of arrangements. It enables HMRC to monitor potential users of avoidance schemes.

Obligations on a promoter

4.227 Promoters are required, under *s 308(3)*, to provide to HMRC prescribed information pertaining to notifiable arrangements. *Section 308(3)* provides:

> 'A person who is a promoter in relation to notifiable arrangements must, within the prescribed period after the date on which he first becomes aware of any transaction forming part of the notifiable arrangements, provide the

111 *FA 2004, s 309* and the *Tax Avoidance Schemes (Information) Regulations 2012, SI 2012/1836, reg 5(4)*.

112 Under *FA 2004, s 313A*, as amended by *Finance Act 2010, s 56, Sch 17*, with effect from 1 January 2011.

113 *FA 2004, s 313C*, as inserted by *Finance Act 2010, s 56, Sch 17*, with effect from 1 January 2011.

114 *Tax Avoidance Schemes (Information) Regulations 2012, SI 2012/1836, reg 15*, as amended by the *Tax Avoidance Schemes (Information) (Amendment) Regulations 2015, SI 2015/948, reg 12*.

Board with prescribed information relating to those arrangements, unless those arrangements implement a proposal in respect of which notice has been given under subsection (1).'

4.228 *Section 316* provides that HMRC may specify the form and manner in which the information is to be provided to it. The relevant regulations have been amended several times since 2004.

4.229 The *Tax Avoidance Schemes (Information) Regulations 2012, SI 2012/1836*, as amended by *SI 2013/2592*, apply with effect from 1 September 2012. *Regulation 4, SI 2012/1836* provides:

> **'Prescribed information in respect of notifiable proposals and arrangements**
>
> (1) The information which must be provided to HMRC by a promoter under section 308(1) or (3) (duties of promoter) in respect of a notifiable proposal or notifiable arrangements is sufficient information as might reasonably be expected to enable an officer of HMRC to comprehend the manner in which the proposal or arrangements are intended to operate, including—
>
> (a) the promoter's name and address;
>
> (b) details of the provision of the Arrangements Regulations, the ATED Arrangements Regulations, the IHT Arrangements Regulations or the SDLT Arrangements Regulations by virtue of which the arrangements or the proposed arrangements are notifiable;
>
> (c) a summary of the arrangements or proposed arrangements and the name (if any) by which they are known;
>
> (d) information explaining each element of the arrangements or proposed arrangements (including the way in which they are structured) from which the tax advantage expected to be obtained under those arrangements arises; and
>
> (e) the statutory provisions, relating to any of the prescribed taxes, on which that tax advantage is based.
>
> …
>
> (5) In this regulation—
>
> "the Arrangements Regulations" means the Tax Avoidance Schemes (Prescribed Descriptions of Arrangements) Regulations 2006;
>
> …'

4.230 *Section 308(1)* imposes the equivalent obligation on promoters in relation to notifiable proposals.

4.231 It is specified at para 1.4.3 of the DOTAS Guidance that the information required under *section 308(1)* must be provided to HMRC on Form AAG1. That part of the DOTAS Guidance that specifies the form and manner for providing specified information has the force of law[115].

4.232 Promoters must notify a notifiable proposal to HMRC within five business days of the 'relevant date', which is the earliest of the dates when the promoter:

(a) makes a firm approach to another person with a view to making the scheme available for implementation by that person or others;

(b) makes a notifiable proposal available for implementation by another person; or

(c) becomes aware of any transaction implementing the proposal[116].

4.233 HMRC has stated that it considers that the third of these dates is likely to apply only when a scheme is 'wholly bespoke', by which it means:

> 'an arrangement designed by an interactive process in response to a client's specific tax management issue, where it may be that at no point can the scheme be said to be made available for implementation.'[117]

In such circumstances, the implementation itself is the trigger for disclosure.

4.234 A promoter must also notify notifiable arrangements within five business days of first becoming aware of any transaction forming part of notifiable arrangements, unless they implement a proposal that has already been notified[118].

Scheme Reference Numbers

4.235 Where a person makes a disclosure of a notifiable proposal or arrangements, under *s 311*, HMRC may within 90 days[119] allocate a reference number (a 'Scheme Reference Number' (SRN)) to the proposal or arrangements and, if it does so, HMRC must notify that number to that person and to any other person who is a promoter in relation to the proposal or arrangements and whose identity has been notified to HMRC.

4.236 *Section 311(2)* provides:

> 'The allocation of a reference number to any notifiable arrangements (or proposed notifiable arrangements) is not to be regarded as constituting any indication by the Board that the arrangements could as a matter of law result in the obtaining by any person of a tax advantage.'

115 See DOTAS Guidance, para 1.2.
116 *Information Regulations, reg 5(4).*
117 DOTAS Guidance, para 14.3.3.
118 *FA 2004, s 308(3)* and *Information Regulations, reg 5(5).*
119 Prior to 26 March 2015 the period was 30 days.

Obligations on the promoter in relation to the SRN

4.237 *Section 312* imposes a duty on the promoter to notify its clients of the SRN. A promoter who provides (or has provided) services to any person ('the client') in connection with notifiable arrangements must provide the client with prescribed information (on Form AAG 6) within 30 days of the relevant date, being the later of:

(a) the date on which the promoter first becomes aware of any transaction forming part of the arrangements; or

(b) the date on which the SRN is notified to the promoter by HMRC.

4.238 The information that a promoter must supply to its clients is:

- his name and address;
- the name, or a brief description of the notifiable arrangements or proposal;
- the SRN; and
- the date that the SRN was sent by the promoter to the client.

Obligations on the users as regards the SRN

4.239 Any person who is party to notifiable arrangements to which an SRN has been allocated must include the SRN in his tax return and must notify HMRC of the tax year in which the tax advantage is expected to be obtained[120]. That obligation applies for each year in respect of which the person expects to obtain a tax advantage. If a person is not otherwise obliged to submit a tax return, notification is to be made on Form AAG4.

4.240 The *Finance Act 2008* inserted *s 312A* into the *Finance Act 2004* with effect from 1 November 2008[121]. Under *s 312A*, there is an obligation on clients to notify SRNs to other users in two circumstances:

(1) Reasonable expectation

Under *s 312A(2)*, a client is obliged to pass on the SRN to any other person whom the client might reasonably be expected to know is, or is likely to be, a party to the scheme and who might reasonably be expected to gain a tax advantage from the scheme.

This must be done within 30 business days of the client first becoming aware of any transaction implementing the scheme or, if later, receiving the SRN from the promoter. The obligation applies regardless of whether or not the client itself participates in the scheme.

120 *FA 2004, s 313* and *Information Regulations, reg 9.*

121 Save as regards SDLT. The obligation as regards SDLT was with effect from 1 April 2010 (by virtue of *SI 2010/409*).

It is stated in the DOTAS Guidance that HMRC consider that the obligation to notify the SRN to others under *s 312A(2)* applies only where the client has 'sufficient commercial connection with [the other person] to have a reasonable expectation that they will gain a tax advantage from the scheme'[122].

HMRC's examples of this include:

> '*Example 1: sale and leaseback with a finance house*
>
> A company which is not subject to UK corporation tax seeks to reduce costs on equipment. It buys a disclosable leasing scheme from a promoter (thereby becoming their "client"). Under the scheme it purchases equipment and then enters into a sale and leaseback arrangement with a UK finance house.
>
> The finance house not the company, obtains the tax advantage, as defined, but the company seeks to share in the capital allowances the finance house can claim.
>
> The promoter is required to provide the company with the scheme reference number.
>
> As the company can reasonably be expected to know that the finance house is a party to, and expects to gain a tax advantage from, the scheme, it must provide them with the scheme reference number.'

(2) *Employees*

Where the client is an employer and a promoter has provided it with an SRN, it is required to pass the information to each of its employees who might reasonably be expected to receive an advantage as a result of the scheme.

Under *s 312A(2A)*[123], the employer must also provide the SRN to employees in circumstances when it is the employer who might reasonably be expected to gain a tax advantage in relation to the employment of those employees by entering into the scheme. It is not necessary in these circumstances for those employees to themselves be expected to gain a tax advantage by reason of the arrangements.

The SRN must be provided to the employees within 30 days of receipt on Form AAG7.

If the client of a promoter is an employer and the scheme is intended to result in a tax or NICs advantage in relation to the employment of one or more directors or employees, either for the employer or the employees (or both), the employer is required, under *s 313ZC*, to make an annual report to HMRC, on Form AAG8, that provides information about

---

122 At para 17.3.2.

123 Inserted by *Finance Act 2015, s 117, Sch 17*, with effect from 26 March 2015.

'relevant employees'. Relevant employees are employees who might be reasonably expected to obtain a tax or NICs advantage from the scheme or employees in relation to whose employment the employer might reasonably expected to obtain a tax or NICs advantage from the scheme.

The information to be provided includes:

- the employer's name, address and tax reference number;
- the name, address and national insurance number of each relevant employee;
- the tax year in which the relevant employee obtained or expects to obtain the advantage;
- the SRN;
- the name and address of the promoter; and
- the name given to the notifiable arrangement.

(4) ENFORCEMENT OF THE DOTAS RULES

4.241 HMRC's powers to investigate and to enforce compliance with the DOTAS rules have been expanded considerably over the years. In particular, the *Finance Act 2007* provided HMRC with a range of investigatory powers in relation to non-disclosed schemes and powers to apply to the Tribunal for orders that a scheme be treated as notifiable.

4.242 In December 2006, a technical note[124] and draft legislation were circulated. HMRC stated that the new powers were necessary because there was evidence that a significant minority of promoters were failing to comply with their obligations under the disclosure regime.

4.243 Subsequently, *s 108* of the *Finance Act 2007* introduced *ss 306A, 308A, 313A, 313B, 314A* and *317A* to the *Finance Act 2004*. There have been a number of extensions made subsequently to the information powers and to the obligations imposed on promoters, introducers and clients:

(1) *Finance Act 2010* introduced amendments in respect of introducers. An additional information power in respect of introducers (*s 313C*) was introduced; and the powers under *ss 313A* and *313B* were extended to introducers. *Finance Act 2010* also introduced *s 313ZA* (duty on the promoter to provide details of clients).

(2) *Finance Act 2013* introduced *s 312B* (duty of client to provide information to promoter) and *s 313ZB*, which enables HMRC to seek further information from promoters where the client is suspected not to be the only party to a disclosed scheme.

124 'Ensuring Compliance with the Tax Avoidance Disclosure Regime' (18 December 2006).

(3) *Finance Act 2014* introduced *ss 310A* and *310B*, which provide HMRC with a power to require further information or documents to be provided.

(4) *Finance Act 2015* introduced an obligation on promoters to notify HMRC of changes in respect of schemes that had been notified (*s 310C*), increased HMRC's powers in relation to introducers (by amending *s 313C*), and provided HMRC with increased powers to publish information about avoidance schemes and promoters (*s 316C*).

4.244 HMRC's primary investigatory powers comprise:

- pre-disclosure enquiries (*ss 313A* and *313B*);
- request for introducer to provide information (*s 313C*); and
- request for supplemental information (*ss 308A, 310A* and *310B*).

These are addressed in turn below.

4.245 The powers under *ss 313A, 313B* and *313C* apply where a scheme has not been notified; and the powers under *sections 308A, 310A* and *310B* apply where a scheme has been notified. *Sections 308A, 310A* and *310B* enable HMRC to obtain information beyond that which is prescribed (in the *Information Regulations*). They expand the obligations of promoters and users under the DOTAS rules.

4.246 HMRC's enforcement powers enable applications to be made to the Tribunal for either:

- an order that a scheme be deemed notifiable, where there is doubt as to notifiability (*s 306A*); or
- an order that a scheme is notifiable (*s 314A*).

Pre-disclosure enquiries

Section 313A

4.247 *Section 313A* enables HMRC to require that a suspected promoter or introducer, P, states whether he considers that the scheme is notifiable and, if not, to provide the reasons for this conclusion. Prior to its introduction, HMRC described *s 313A* as simply codification of its existing practice. If HMRC obtained information that suggested that a notifiable scheme might not have been disclosed, an explanation would be requested. However, not all promoters responded by providing a full explanation. Hence, the statutory power was required.

4.248 The reasons provided as to why the scheme is not notifiable must refer to the relevant legislative provisions of DOTAS and explain why they do not apply, providing sufficient information to enable HMRC to confirm this view. *Section 313A(3)(b)* provides that, in giving reasons, it is not sufficient to refer to the fact that a lawyer or other professional has given an opinion. However, a person who summarised the reasons why a lawyer advised that the scheme would not be notifiable would, almost certainly, be waiving LPP in the underlying advice by so doing. It is considered that, for that reason, HMRC cannot use its power under *s 313A* to compel a person to provide a summary of the advice received from a lawyer.

4.249 HMRC has indicated that, with regard to an introducer, it anticipates that his reply to a *s 313A* notice will be that the scheme is not notifiable by him, because he is an introducer, and not a promoter. HMRC state that this power has been extended to introducers, because, where a person is advertising a scheme, HMRC may not know who is the promoter and 'it is important to find out who the promoter is'[125]. There is, however, as HMRC accept, no obligation on the introducer to identify the promoter under *s 313A*. If the introducer refuses to identify the promoter voluntarily post receipt of a notice under *s 313A*, then HMRC may serve a notice under *s 313C* compelling him to provide the promoter's name and address.

Section 313B

4.250 *Section 313B* allows HMRC to apply to the Tribunal for an order requiring P to provide specified information or documents in support of its statement of reasons. HMRC's powers under *s 313B* are derivative on their powers under *s 313A*. HMRC state that: 'the information or documents required at this preliminary stage are those which are required to test whether or not a scheme is disclosable by that person, not information that describes how the scheme works'[126]. In the circumstance in which *s 313B* applies, that distinction may be difficult to maintain.

Request for introducer to provide information

4.251 Where HMRC suspects a person of acting as an introducer for a notifiable scheme that has not been disclosed, *s 313C* enables it to serve a notice on that person, requiring him to provide the name and address of any person who has provided him with any information about the scheme and of any persons with whom he has made a marketing contact. The power, accordingly, enables HMRC to identify both promoters and users of undisclosed schemes.

---

125 DOTAS Guidance, para 21.4.1.
126 DOTAS Guidance, para 21.4.1.

Request for supplemental information

Section 308A

4.252 This provision applies where there has been a notification, but HMRC believes that insufficient prescribed information has been provided. *Section 308A* enables HMRC to apply to the Tribunal for an order requiring the promoter to provide specified additional information or documents. The Tribunal may only make the requested order if they are satisfied that HMRC either:

(a) has reasonable grounds for suspecting that the information or documents sought form part of the information prescribed under the *Tax Avoidance Schemes (Information) Regulations 2004*; or

(b) has reasonable grounds for suspecting that the information or documents will 'support or explain' the prescribed information.

Given that the Regulations impose an obligation on the promoter to provide: 'sufficient information as might reasonably be expected to enable an officer of the Board to comprehend the manner in which the proposal is intended to operate', it is unclear what would fall only within the latter category of documents.

Sections 310A and *310B*

4.253 Where the promoter has provided the prescribed information about a notifiable proposal or arrangement, HMRC may require him to provide additional documents or further information about the proposal or arrangement within 10 working days or such longer period as HMRC may allow. HMRC provides the following example:

> 'HMRC may require the promoter to supply a detailed analysis of the financial transactions undertaken by a typical client as part of a scheme along with the documentation for those financial transactions.'[127]

4.254 *Section 310A* also applies either where the relevant person who has provided the notification is a person dealing with a promoter outside the UK or where the arrangements do not involve a promoter and HMRC that the relevant person has not provided all the prescribed information. (If a promoter is involved and HMRC consider that he has not provided sufficient prescribed information, the relevant power available to HMRC will be under *s 308A*).

4.255 If the person fails to provide information or documents required on service of a notice under *s 310A*, HMRC may apply to the Tribunal for an order requiring that to be provided. The Tribunal only needs to be satisfied that HMRC has reasonable grounds for suspecting that the information or documents '*will*

127 DOTAS Guidance, para 21.7.

assist' it in considering the notifiable proposals or arrangements, in order to make the order.

Sections 306A and *314A*

4.256 These enforcement provisions were introduced, according to HMRC, to address its concern that a minority of promoters was not complying with the disclosure obligations. Prior to the enactment of *Finance Act 2007*, there was no mechanism to force notification, save that a penalty was exigible for failure to notify, if it was established that notification under DOTAS should have been made. In the only such case that was heard – *Mercury Tax Group* [2009] STC (SCD) 307, HMRC's application for a penalty was unsuccessful[128]. The Special Commissioner held that the scheme was not notifiable; and added, *obiter*, that Mercury had a reasonable excuse for not notifying, because it relied on Counsel's opinion and, accordingly, 'If therefore I am wrong in deciding that the scheme is not notifiable and a penalty is payable I would fix the amount at nil'[129].

4.257 HMRC may apply to the Tribunal for an order that arrangements or a proposal are to be treated as notifiable (under *s 306A*) or an order that arrangements or a proposal are notifiable (under *se 314A*)[130].

4.258 To date, there have been six applications for orders made by HMRC to the Tribunal:

(1) *HMRC v Root2 Tax Ltd* [2017] UKFTT 696 (TC)[131];

(2) *HMRC v Hyrax Resourcing Ltd* [2019] UKFTT 175 (TC);

(3) *HMRC v EDF Tax Limited (In Creditors' Voluntary Liquidation)* [2019] UKFTT 598 (TC);

(4) *HMRC v Curzon Capital Ltd* [2019] SFTD 506[132];

(5) *HMRC v White Collar Financial Ltd* [2020] UKFTT 459 (TC); and

(6) *HMRC v Opus Bestpay Ltd* [2020] UKFTT 408 (TC).

In each of these cases, the Tribunal held that the relevant scheme was notifiable under the DOTAS regime. In *Curzon Capital*, the order was not granted because the Tribunal held that Curzon Capital Ltd was not a promoter.

---

128 This case concerned the *2004 Regulations*. The scheme was not notified within the relevant time limit under these regulations. It was notified after the *2006 Regulations* expanded the ambit of the DOTAS rules.

129 At para 13.

130 With effect from 19 July 2007; these sections being inserted by the *Finance Act 2007, s 108*.

131 See Andrew Hubbard, 'Changing landscape', *Taxation*, 28 September 2017, p 20.

132 In HMRC's Annual Report and Accounts 2018/19, it is stated, at page 32, that: 'Since 2014, we have been investigating more than 100 people involved in promoting tax avoidance. We've taken litigation action against promoters for failing to disclose their avoidance schemes, with five cases heard in the last year, prompting around 20 others to disclose to avoid similar litigation'.

4.259 An order under *s 314A* has retrospective (and prospective) effect. It has the effect of confirming that a scheme not only is, but always was, notifiable within the time limits prescribed in *s 308(3)* and the Regulations made thereunder. An order under *s 306A* is prospective only. It has the effect of deeming that the scheme comprises notifiable arrangements with effect from the date of the order.

Section 306A

4.260 *Section 306A* provides, relevantly, that:

> '(3) On an application the tribunal may make the order only if satisfied that HMRC—
>
> (a) have taken all reasonable steps to establish whether the proposal or arrangements are notifiable, and
>
> (b) have reasonable grounds for suspecting that the proposal or arrangements may be notifiable.
>
> (4) Reasonable steps under subsection (3)(a) may (but need not) include taking action under section 313A or 313B.
>
> (5) Grounds for suspicion under subsection (3)(b) may include—
>
> (a) the fact that the relevant arrangements fall within a description prescribed under section 306(1)(a);
>
> (b) an attempt by the promoter to avoid or delay providing information or documents about the proposal or arrangements under or by virtue of section 313A or 313B;
>
> (c) the promoter's failure to comply with a requirement under or by virtue of section 313A or 313B in relation to another proposal or other arrangements.'

4.261 The consequence of *s 306A* is that arrangements are notifiable under DOTAS if either they satisfy the relevant conditions or HMRC have reasonable grounds to suspect that they satisfy these conditions. That means that an arrangement need not be notifiable in order for HMRC to require that it be disclosed. Provided that HMRC reasonably suspects that it is (and the promoter's failure to provide information in relation to a different scheme, for example, is prescribed as a ground for suspicion), the Tribunal may make the order, even if the arrangement is not notifiable[133].

Section 314A

4.262 *Section 314A(3)* provides:

133 In the Consultation Draft, it was proposed that the Special Commissioners could make an order only if they were satisfied that the scheme was notifiable.

'On an application the tribunal may make the order only if satisfied that *section 306(1)(a)* to *(c)* apply to the relevant arrangements.'

4.263 Accordingly, in contrast to *s 306A*, an order under *s 314A* can be granted only if the Tribunal is satisfied that the scheme is notifiable under the DOTAS rules. In *Hyrax*, the Tribunal accepted the respondents' submissions that, because the consequence of an order under *s 314A* is that the scheme always was notifiable, which means that the promoter potentially becomes subject to the imposition of a daily penalty that is backdated to a date a number of years prior: *s 314A* is: (a) penal; and (b) is to be categorised as giving rise to criminal proceedings for the purposes of Article 6 of the European Convention on Human Rights (ECHR). Accordingly, any ambiguity in the legislation must be interpreted in favour of those sought to be penalised[134]; and the respondent to HMRC's application has the right 'to be informed promptly, in a language which he understands and in detail, of the nature and cause of the accusation against him'[135].

4.264 There is a six-year time limit that applies in relation to the making of an application by HMRC for a *s 314A* order (under the *Taxes Management Act 1970, s 103(4)*).

Appeals in respect of sections 306A and 314A

4.265 *Section 11* of the *Tribunals, Courts and Enforcement Act 2007* (*TCEA 2007*) provides (so far as material):

'Right to appeal to Upper Tribunal

(1) For the purposes of subsection (2), the reference to a right of appeal is to a right to appeal to the Upper Tribunal on any point of law arising from a decision made by the First-tier Tribunal other than an excluded decision.

(2) Any party to a case has a right of appeal, subject to subsection (8)[136].

(3) That right may be exercised only with permission (or, in Northern Ireland, leave).'

For the purposes of *section 11(1)* of *TCEA 2007*, an 'excluded decision' includes 'any decision of the First-tier Tribunal that is of a description specified in an order made by the Lord Chancellor'.

134 See *ESS Production Ltd (in administration) v Sully* [2005] EWCA Civ 554.

135 Article 6(3)(a) of ECHR. Although not addressed in the decision, another right that arises under Art 6(3) is the right to legal assistance, which is to be provided free if the interests of justice require it. It seems that a potential consequence of the decision is that a respondent to an application for an order under *s 314A* may apply for legal aid in relation to its defence of the application.

136 The limitation in *TCEA 2007, s 11(8)* is not material for these purposes.

The *Appeal (Excluded Decisions) Order 2009, SI 2009/275* (the '*Excluded Decisions Order*') was made on 5 February 2009 and came into force on 1 April 2009. It provides that:

> 'For the purposes of sections 11(1) and 13(1) of the Tribunals, Courts and Enforcement Act 2007, the following decisions of the First-tier Tribunal or the Upper Tribunal are excluded decisions—
>
> [...]
>
> (i) any decision under section 306A (doubt as to notifiability), 308A (supplemental information), 313B (reasons for non-disclosure: supporting information) or 314A (order to disclose) of the Finance Act 2004.'

As a result of the *Excluded Decisions Order*, a Tribunal's decision in relation to an application under *s 306A* or an application under *s 314A* is an 'excluded decision', with the result that there is no right of appeal to the Upper Tribunal under *s 11(1)* of *TCEA 2007*. The only potential remedy available is the right to seek judicial review. To date, there have been no judicial review applications heard in respect of orders issued by the Tribunal under either *s 306A* or *s 314A*[137].

(5) PENALTIES

Introduction

4.266 A detailed analysis of the penalty provisions is outside the scope of this chapter. In broad terms, there are three categories of penalties that are relevant to the DOTAS rules. These are:

(1) penalties for failing to notify a scheme;

(2) penalties for failing to provide information; and

(3) user penalties.

Penalties for failing to notify a scheme

4.267 A consequence of an order under *s 314A* is that the arrangements are, and were, notifiable. Consequently, a result of an order under *s 314A* having been made is that the promoter potentially becomes subject to the imposition of a daily penalty for failure to notify under *section 308* that is backdated to the date on which, it has been determined by the issuance of the order, the promoter had a duty to notify. That date can be a number of years

137 The Administrative Court refused the application by Root2 Tax Ltd for permission to apply for judicial review: *R (on the application of Root2 Tax Ltd) v First-tier Tribunal (Tax Chamber)* [2018] EWHC 1254 (Admin).

prior to the issuance of the order. The backdated penalty cannot be mitigated by notification of the arrangements by the promoter subsequent to issuance of the Tribunal's order under *s 314A*. An order under *s 306A* has prospective effect only.

4.268 In order for a penalty to be imposed in relation to a failure to notify, an application must be made by HMRC to the Tribunal, under *s 100C* of the *Taxes Management Act 1970* (*TMA 1970*). Any penalty determined by the Tribunal in proceedings under that section is to be treated as if it were tax charged in an assessment and due and payable[138]. The quantum of the penalty is to be determined by the Tribunal, 'after taking into account of all relevant considerations'[139]. These include: 'the desirability of its being set at a level which appears appropriate for deterring the person, or other persons, from similar failures to comply' in future and the amount of any fees received in connection with the arrangements. As at the date of writing, there has been no judicial consideration of these provisions.

Penalties for failing to provide information

4.269 Penalties are exigible (on promoters, intermediaries and clients) in relation to a failure to provide prescribed information by the due date and in the form and manner specified. These apply, for example, to:

(a) a promoter who does not respond to a notice issued under *s 313A*;

(b) a promoter who does not provide his client with a SRN;

(c) an introducer who does not provide, when required to do so, the identity of the person who supplied them with information about the scheme or persons with whom the introducer has made marketing contacts; and

(d) a client who fails to provide the SRN to any other person whom he might reasonably expect to be a party to the scheme and expected to obtain a tax advantage from using it (this includes an employer who fails to provide the SRN to an employee for a scheme implemented by the employer in relation to that employee's employment).

4.270 For all these information penalties, a Tribunal may determine an initial penalty for each failure of an amount not exceeding £5,000. HMRC may determine a daily penalty, not exceeding £600, for each day that each failure to provide information continues after an initial penalty has been determined by the Tribunal[140].

138 Under *TMA 1970, s 100C(3)*.

139 *TMA 1970, s 98C(2ZB)*.

140 In certain circumstances, the daily penalty can be increased to £5,000.

User penalties

4.271 A scheme user who fails to comply with a *s 313* obligation to report an SRN and related information (on a return or separately, as prescribed in the *Information Regulations*) is liable to a penalty of:

(a) £5,000 per scheme for a first occasion;

(b) £7,500 per scheme on the second occasion within three years (whether or not it relates to the same scheme involved in the previous occasion); and

(c) £10,000 per scheme on the third and subsequent occasions (whether or not the failure relates to schemes involved in a previous occasion.

(6) FROM DOTAS TO POTAS

4.272 In 2012, a consultation: 'Lifting the Lid on Tax Avoidance Schemes' was undertaken. As part of that consultation, introducing a DOTAS hallmark for 'high-risk' promoters was discussed. The government concluded from the consultation that there were some promoters who 'would commonly encourage tax advisers' clients to enter into avoidance schemes, attempt to impose conditions of confidentiality on clients and disrupt the relationship between the tax adviser and their client'. A further consultation: 'Raising the stakes on tax avoidance' commenced on 12 August 2013. The Exchequer Secretary to the Treasury emphasised that the purpose of the new rules would be deterrence:

> 'This government is committed to tackling tax avoidance and the proposals in this consultation will allow HMRC to further close in on the cowboy advisers promoting these high-risk schemes.
>
> HMRC is successful in over 80 per cent of the avoidance cases they take to court so we want to deter taxpayers from using these often unsuccessful schemes and ensure that they pay the tax that is due.
>
> The vast majority of tax advisers are not high risk and have moved away from selling aggressive avoidance schemes, but there is still a minority that persists in promoting these schemes. We want to make life as difficult as we can for them …'

4.273 It was stated in the consultation paper that:

> 'There are some advisers who promote tax avoidance schemes and are not or do not want to be transparent with HMRC – these advisers are potentially high-risk promoters. Instead they commonly display other behaviours that are detrimental to the fairness of the tax system such as:
>
> - designing, marketing or implementing products that on analysis have negligible probability of working;
> - relying on non-co-operation with HMRC to achieve a tax advantage for their clients selling products that rely on concealment and mis-description of elements to succeed.'

4.274 Proposals to address the behaviour of high-risk promoters of tax avoidance schemes were set out. These included:

- specific information powers for high-risk promoters;
- penalties for failure to comply with information powers; and
- 'naming and shaming' high-risk promoters.

4.275 In January 2014, draft legislation, Explanatory Notes, and a Tax Information and Impact Note (TIIN) were published. It was indicated in the TIIN that it was estimated that there were approximately 20 businesses that may become subject to the high-risk regime.

4.276 The Promoters of Tax Avoidance Schemes (POTAS) legislation was introduced by *Pt 5* and *Schs 34–36* to the *Finance Act 2014* (*FA 2014*)[141]. It was amended by *Sch 19* to the *Finance Act 2015*[142] and amended again by *s 160* of the *Finance Act 2016*. Further changes are anticipated to be introduced by the *Finance Act 2021*.

4.277 The POTAS regime is complex. Its aim is clearly, as the Exchequer Secretary to the Treasury indicated, 'to make life as difficult as we can for' high-risk promoters; and, reflecting that aim, considerable discretion is bestowed on HMRC, with few protections, such as rights of appeal, being provided to its subjects.

4.278 Guidance on the POTAS rules was published on 28 May 2014 (the 'POTAS Guidance')[143]. According to HMRC, the objectives of the POTAS regime:

> 'are to change the behaviour of a small and persistent minority of promoters of avoidance schemes who exhibit certain behaviours, and to aim to deter the development and use of avoidance schemes by influencing the behaviour of promoters, their intermediaries and clients.'

The POTAS regime

Introduction

4.279 The POTAS rules are provided by *Pt 5* and *Schs 34–36* to *FA 2014*. They adopt, with some amendments, many of the definitions that are used in the DOTAS rules. The POTAS rules enable HMRC to issue to a high-risk promoter a 'conduct notice' that specifies steps that the promoter must take to change its behaviour and that which the promoter should, or should not, be doing.

141 The *National Insurance Contributions Act 2015* applies *Part 5* of *FA 2014* to NICs with effect from 12 April 2015.

142 With effect from 26 March 2015.

143 Revised guidance was published on 12 February 2015; and re-revised guidance was published on 2 September 2015. The guidance has not been amended to take account of *FA 2014, s 237A*, which was inserted by *Finance Act 2016, s 160*.

Failure to comply with a conduct notice may result in the promoter being issued with a 'monitoring notice'. A promoter that is subject to a monitoring notice is referred to as a 'monitored promoter'. Names of monitored promoters may be published by HMRC, together with details of how the conduct notice was breached. A monitored promoter is also required to publish his monitored status to clients.

Conduct notices

4.280 A promoter who has met one or more of the specified threshold conditions in the previous three years may be considered for a conduct notice.

Promoter

4.281 'Promoter' is defined at *s 235* of *FA 2014*. It is similar to the definition under the DOTAS rules. A person is a promoter in relation to proposed arrangements if he:

- is responsible for the design of the proposal;
- makes a firm approach to another person in relation to the proposal; or
- makes the proposal available for implementation by another person.

4.282 There is no equivalent provision to *reg 6* of the *Tax Avoidance Schemes (Promoters and Prescribed Circumstances) Regulations 2004*, which provides that a person is not to be treated as a promoter in relation to a notifiable proposal or notifiable arrangements where his involvement with the proposal or arrangements is such that he is not required to provide all of the prescribed information by virtue of LPP. Accordingly, a lawyer may be a promoter under POTAS and not a promoter under DOTAS in relation to the same arrangements. There is a limited exclusion for lawyers (and others) provided by the *Promoters of Tax Avoidance Schemes (Prescribed Circumstances under Section 235) Regulations 2015, SI 2015/130*. The Regulations provide that a person will not be treated as a promoter in relation to an avoidance scheme if his only involvement in the scheme is to have been responsible to some extent for either the design of proposed arrangements or the design, organisation or management of arrangements. Such a person will be excluded from being a promoter within the POTAS regime if he does not also provide tax advice in connection with the scheme or could not reasonably be expected to know that the arrangements are an avoidance scheme. HMRC provides the following example in the POTAS Guidance[144]:

> 'As an example of how these regulations apply, they will prevent a lawyer, whose only involvement in designing and developing an avoidance scheme

144 At para 1.4.

is to give independent legal advice on a discrete element of the scheme not relating to tax, from being treated as a promoter in relation to that scheme.'

The threshold conditions in Schedule 34

4.283 There are 11 threshold conditions specified in *Sch 34* to *FA 2014*; these are as follows:

(1) publication of information about the promoter as a deliberate tax defaulter;

(2) the promoter being named in a report for a breach of the Code of Practice on Taxation for Banks;

(3) the promoter receiving a conduct notice as a dishonest tax agent[145];

(4) the promoter failing to comply with certain obligations under DOTAS;

(5) the promoter having been charged with a relevant offence, unless he has been acquitted, the charge has been dismissed or the proceedings have been discontinued. The offences to be taken into account primarily pertain to fraudulent conduct and include the common law offence of cheating in relation to the public revenue;

(6) the majority of the GAAR Advisory Panel has provided an opinion that entering into one of the promoter's tax avoidance schemes is not a reasonable course of action;

(7) the promoter has been found guilty of misconduct of a prescribed kind by a specified professional body (which includes, for example the ICAEW, the Law Society, and the Bar Council) that has taken action against him and imposed a penalty;

(8) a sanction has been imposed on the promoter by virtue of misconduct by the Financial Conduct Authority or the Financial Services Authority;

(9) the promoter has failed to comply with an information notice issued by HMRC under any of *paras 1, 2, 5* or *5A* of *Sch 36* to the *Finance Act 2008*;

(10) the promoter has imposed restrictive contractual terms on another person, such as requiring a client to keep details of a tax avoidance scheme confidential from HMRC; and

(11) the promoter has continued to market a tax avoidance scheme after being given a notice to stop by HMRC (a 'stop notice'). A stop notice may be given where the promoter promotes arrangements that are in substance the same as arrangements in respect of which a person has been given a follower notice[146], which has not been withdrawn. A stop notice must

145 Under *Finance Act 2012, Sch 38, para 4.*
146 Under *FA 2004, s 204.*

specify the arrangements which are the subject of the follower notice, specify the relevant judicial ruling and explain the effect of the stop notice.

Section 237A

4.284 *Section 237A* of *FA 2014* provides an additional route to the issuance of a conduct notice[147]. A conduct notice will be issued to a person, P, if five conditions are met:

(1) P is carrying on a business as a promoter[148].

(2) There have been a number of 'relevant defeats' in relation to P, either:

   (a) three in the last three years;

   (b) two at a time when a 'single defeat notice' had effect; or

   (c) one at a time when a 'double defeat notice' had effect.

(3) The authorised officer is not already required to make a determination as to whether the breach of a threshold condition under the original POTAS regime is 'significant'.

(4) The meeting of the second condition (relevant defeats) is determined to be significant by the authorised officer.

(5) It cannot be concluded that it would be inappropriate, having regard to the extent of the impact that P's activities as a promoter are likely to have on the collection of tax, to give P a conduct notice[149].

4.285 The 'relevant defeat' conditions are specific to *section 237A*. The 'significance' test and the 'tax impact' test are common to the original POTAS regime as well (and are addressed at **4.296** and **4.299** respectively below).

Relevant defeat

Defeat

4.286 The following constitute 'defeat' of arrangements[150]:

(1) Condition A (GAAR counteractions) is met where there is a final counteraction of a tax advantage under the GAAR.

(2) Condition B (follower notices) is met where a follower notice has been issued; and either the denied tax advantage has been corrected by the taxpayer or the denied tax advantage has been counteracted by HMRC and the counteraction is final.

147 *Finance Act 2016* inserted *ss 237A–237D* into *FA 2014*.
148 *FA 2014, s 237A(1)*.
149 *FA 2014, s 237A(10)*.
150 *FA 2014, Sch 34A, para 10*.

(3) Condition C (DOTAS arrangements) is met where the arrangements are notifiable under the DOTAS rules, and the relevant tax advantage has been counteracted by adjustments having been made to the taxpayer's position on the basis that the whole or part of the tax advantage does not arise, which adjustments are final.

(4) Condition D (DOTAS arrangements) is met where the arrangements are notifiable under the DOITAS rules, and the relevant tax advantage has been counteracted by adjustments having been made to the taxable person's position on the basis that the whole or part of the tax advantage does not arise, which adjustments are final.

(5) Condition E (DOTAS arrangements where another party is expected to obtain a tax advantage) is met where:

- (a) the arrangements are notifiable under DOITAS;
- (b) 'S', makes supplies of goods or services to 'T', a taxable person;
- (c) T is a party to the notifiable arrangements;
- (d) the arrangements relate to S's VAT position;
- (e) T is expected to obtain a tax advantage as a result of the arrangements;
- (f) the tax advantage has been counteracted; and
- (g) that counteraction is final.

(6) Condition F (relevant judicial rulings) is met where:

- (a) a person has claimed a tax advantage;
- (b) that tax advantage would not arise if a particular 'avoidance-related rule' was applicable; and
- (c) there is a final judicial ruling that that avoidance-related rule applies.

An 'avoidance-related rule'[151] is, broadly, a provision that either requires consideration of whether the transaction had a tax avoidance purpose or whether the benefits of the transaction were obtaining a tax advantage or varies a person's tax treatment depending on whether or not their action had a commercial purpose.

'Relevant'

4.287 A defeat is 'relevant' if:

(a) the defeated arrangements are 'promoted arrangements' in relation to P (arrangements will be promoted arrangements in relation to P if P is

151 Defined in *FA 2014, Sch 34A, para 25*.

carrying on the business of a promoter, has promoted the arrangements and the arrangements enable a person to obtain a tax[152] advantage and have as a (or the) main benefit the obtaining of that tax advantage); and

(b) either:

(i) the defeated arrangement is not related to any other arrangements; or

(ii) the rules in relation to related arrangements in *Sch 34A, para 5* apply.

4.288 Arrangements are related to each other if they are 'substantially the same'. Arrangements that have, for example, been allocated the same DOTAS scheme reference number will be substantially the same.

4.289 If the arrangements are related arrangements and one of the three Cases set out in *Sch 34A, para 5* applies, there will be one relevant defeat that is treated as applying to all users of related arrangements. The Cases are:

(1) Case 1 is that any of the Conditions A to E defeats (as described at **4.286** above) applies to any of the arrangements and the tax advantage is counteracted by a final judicial ruling.

(2) Case 2 is that Condition F applies to any of the arrangements.

(3) Case 3 is that at least 75%, but less than 100%, of the related arrangements has been defeated and there is no final judicial ruling upholding the asserted tax advantage in respect of any of the related arrangements.

Defeat notices

4.290 When HMRC become aware of one or more relevant defeats that occurred in the past three years, it may issue the promoter with a defeat notice[153].

4.291 A 'single defeat notice' can be issued by HMRC where a relevant defeat occurred in the past three years; and a 'double defeat notice' can be issued by HMRC where two relevant defeats occurred in the past three years. The defeat notice must be issued within 90 days of HMRC becoming aware of the relevant defeat.

4.292 It will be set out in the defeat notice:

(a) when the 'look-forward' period begins and ends; and

(b) the statutory consequences of two further relevant defeats (or in the case of a double defeat notice, one further relevant defeat) occurring in the

152 *FA 2014, Sch 34A, para 3(2)* defines 'tax' as including all the taxes listed at *FA 2014, s 283* (income tax, CGT, corporation tax, petroleum revenue tax, apprenticeship levy, inheritance tax, SDLT, SDRT and ATED) and VAT.

153 Under *FA 2014, s 241A*.

look-forward period, which will be, subject to the other conditions being met, the issuance of a conduct notice[154].

4.293 The look-forward period is akin to a period of probation. It is a five-year period that commences on the day after the day on which the defeat notice is given and ends five years later. This is except in circumstance where the original defeat notice has been overturned and a second defeat notice has been issued subsequently; in this particular circumstance, the look-forward period ends five years after the date of the further relevant defeat[155].

4.294 A defeat notice can be overturned only if the relevant defeat is a Case 3 relevant defeat and a final judicial ruling that upholds the asserted tax advantage in relation to any of the arrangements is issued[156]. For that reason, a conduct notice, that has as its basis a Case 3 relevant defeat, is described as a 'provisional' conduct notice[157]. HMRC cannot take steps to issue a monitoring notice if the terms of a provisional conduct notice are breached, but can take those breaches into account if and when that conduct notice is no longer provisional (because, subsequently, there have been sufficient 34)[158].

The 'safeguards'

4.295 There are two tests (the significance test and the tax impact test) that the HMRC officer must consider, in order, when exercising his duty to issue a conduct notice because one or more threshold conditions are met[159].

(1) The significance test

4.296 If the threshold condition that has been breached is one of the following: (i) deliberate tax defaulters; (ii) breach of the Banking Code of Practice; (iii) dishonest tax agents; (iv) persons charged with certain offences; or (v) issuance of a GAAR opinion notice, then that breach must be regarded as significant[160].

4.297 With regard to the other threshold conditions, the officer must determine whether the breach is 'significant in view of the purposes of' the POTAS regime[161]. HMRC consider that a condition is significant unless it is trivial and a one-off or occasional. It is stated in the POTAS Guidance:

154 *FA 2014, s 241A(8).*

155 *FA 2014, s 241A(10)(b).*

156 *FA 2014, s 241B.*

157 *FA 2014, s 237C.*

158 *FA 2014, s 242(6), (7).*

159 The significance test and the tax impact test are described in the POTAS Guidance as 'safeguards'. Given that they constitute limited restrictions on the HMRC officer's discretion in limited circumstances, and there is no right of appeal in relation to the application of the tests by the officer, it is considered that describing them as safeguards is inapposite.

160 *FA 2014, s 237(9).*

161 *FA 2014, s 237(5).*

> 'In considering whether meeting the condition is significant, an authorised officer will be realistic and will take into account that all organisations will make mistakes from time to time that will result in isolated or trivial failures to meet obligations. However this would not prevent an authorised officer from concluding that the meeting of one or more threshold conditions repeatedly or as part of a consistent pattern is to be regarded as significant, although each individual failure might not have been determined to be significant if viewed in isolation.
>
> So, for example, an officer may decide that isolated or trivial failures to meet DOTAS obligations, such as being a few days late with a disclosure, are not significant.'

4.298 The examples in relation to the DOTAS condition emphasise that HMRC consider that, for a failure not to be significant it must be: (a) trivial; (b) excusable; and (c) isolated:

> 'Promoter A only makes one or two disclosures a year under DOTAS. The promoter makes a firm approach to a potential customer about a notifiable arrangement on 1 August 2015 and should have disclosed it by 6 August to HMRC. The person who usually makes the DOTAS disclosures is on leave and no-one else can make the disclosure, consequently Promoter A agrees in writing that the disclosure is made a week late on the 13 August. Although a threshold condition has been met this would not be regarded as significant.
>
> Promoter E has made its first disclosure and has to provide its first quarterly client list to HMRC. It misjudges the final date for submitting the client list and as a consequence accepts in writing that it submitted the list two days late. Although a threshold condition has been met this would not be regarded as significant.'

(2) The tax impact test

4.299 In the event that the HMRC officer concludes that the meeting of one or more of the threshold conditions is significant[162], he must issue a conduct notice unless he concludes that, 'having regard to the extent of the impact that [the promoter's] activities as a promoter are likely to have on the collection of tax, it is inappropriate' to do so.

4.300 In the POTAS Guidance, it is stated that 'A conduct notice will not be issued if the authorised officer considers that the promoter's activities are unlikely to notably affect the collection of tax'. According to the TIIN, the predicted financial impact of the POTAS regime would be at least £5m in 2014/15 and at least £35m in each of the following three years. It was indicated also that it was anticipated that about 20 persons would be made subject to the POTAS regime. It is not known the extent to which these estimates are accurate, but, on

162 *FA 2014, s 237(8)*.

the assumption that they are entirely accurate, it would mean that, in 2014/15, the average financial impact of the POTAS regime per POTAS promoter was (at least) £250,000. In 2014/15, £517.7bn tax revenues were collected in the UK[163]. Accordingly, *ex hypothesi* 'collection of tax' meaning *total* collection of tax, it would be all but impossible for any POTAS promoter's activities to ever 'notably affect the collection of tax'. It is reasonable to assume, however, that HMRC is unlikely to adopt a similar analysis when considering the tax impact test, as it would mean that the test could rarely, if ever, be satisfied.

4.301 No details regarding HMRC's approach are provided in the POTAS Guidance, save that it is emphasised by HMRC that the significance test is a gateway to the second test, the tax impact test; and so the financial consequences are not limited to those that may arise from the breach of the threshold condition. It is stated that:

> 'The extent of the impact of the promoter's activities on the collection of tax will depend on the impact all of the promoter's activities would be likely to have. The authorised officer is not limited to considering the likely tax impact of the promoter's business activities, in the course of which it met one or more threshold conditions. On this basis it is not possible to provide comprehensive examples.'[164]

4.302 Examples of when HMRC considers that the significance test is met demonstrate that that test can be met where the financial impact of the breach of a threshold condition is unlikely to be significant in the context of tax collection. For example:

> 'Promoter C also makes around 15 disclosures under DOTAS each calendar year and has regular contact with the HMRC DOTAS team as well as several people able to make disclosures. It suffers a disastrous computer failure on 8 March 2015 for two weeks and as a result misses the deadlines for three separate disclosures. The promoter agrees in writing that it submitted the information late when disclosures are eventually made in April. Promoter C does not contact the HMRC DOTAS team to inform them of the computer failure and to make alternative arrangements for making disclosures. … In the absence of remedial action the promoter has met the threshold condition and it is significant.'[165]

4.303 Once the significant test has been met, all of Promoter C's activities will be considered by HMRC when applying the tax impact test. It is stated in the POTAS Guidance:

> 'When applying this test, the authorised officer is also obliged to take into account the likely impact of all of the promoter's activities on the collection of relevant contributions …'[166]

163 HMRC Annual Reports and Accounts 2014/15.
164 POTAS Guidance, para 2.2.3.
165 POTAS Guidance, para 2.2.2.
166 POTAS Guidance, para 2.2.3.

Contents of a conduct notice

4.304 *Section 238* of *FA 2014* prescribes the purposes for which conditions may be imposed by a conduct notice. These are to ensure that the promoter:

(a) provides adequate information to his clients about relevant proposals, and relevant arrangements, in relation to which he is a promoter;

(b) provides adequate information about relevant proposals, in relation to which he is a promoter, to intermediaries;

(c) meets his obligations under specified disclosure provisions, namely *ss 308, 312, 313ZA, 313ZB* and *Sch 36, Pt 1* to the *Finance Act 2004*;

(d) does not discourage others from complying with any obligation to disclose to HMRC information of a description specified in the notice;

(e) does not enter into agreements with other persons that impose restrictive contractual terms which require clients to enter into confidentiality agreements or contribute to a fighting fund whilst restricting them from settling matters with HMRC;

(f) does not promote schemes which rely on one or more contrived or abnormal steps to produce a tax advantage; and

(g) does not fail to comply with any stop notice.

4.305 There is no requirement in the legislation that the conditions imposed by the conduct notice reflect or have any connection with the particular threshold condition that has occasioned the notice being issued. The content of the conduct notice is at the discretion of the authorised officer. However, the conduct notice will be bespoke to the specific promoter; and the recipient must be given an opportunity to comment on the proposed terms of the notice before it is issued. According to the POTAS Guidance:

> 'HMRC expects that in most circumstances there will be discussions with a promoter that has met a threshold condition, with the aim of understanding why that happened and agreeing on appropriate standards for the future. HMRC will aim to develop a working relationship with promoters … The authorised officer must give the promoter an opportunity to comment on the proposed terms of the conduct notice before finalising its terms …'

4.306 A conduct notice has a maximum length of two years. It can be amended or withdrawn by HMRC, having taken into account the promoter's compliance with it. In order for a conduct notice to be withdrawn, the promoter needs to demonstrate, to HMRC's satisfaction, that his behaviours and conduct have improved in relation to the areas specified in the notice. The promoter's compliance with the obligations imposed on him under the notice will be monitored by HMRC. *Section 262* of *FA 2014* provides HMRC with an information power that can be used to this end. It enables an HMRC officer to issue a notice to the promoter requiring him to provide information or documents that are reasonably required to check that he is complying with the conduct notice. It is stated in the POTAS Guidance:

> 'There is no limit on the number of times or the frequency with which this power can be used, subject to the requirement that the power must be used reasonably. The authorised officer will balance the need for proper oversight of the conditions imposed in the conduct notice in order to ensure the promoter operates within the terms of the notice with the cost and inconvenience to the promoter of complying with requests for information and documents.'[167]

4.307 There is no right of appeal against the issue of a conduct notice. The only remedy available to a recipient would be an application for judicial review (a non-statutory remedy), on the basis that the conditions imposed are unreasonable; *s 238(3)* imposes a reasonableness safeguard: 'A notice may include only conditions that it is reasonable to impose' for one of the prescribed purposes.

Monitoring notices

4.308 A promoter who fails to comply with the terms of a conduct notice may be issued with a 'monitoring notice'. A promoter who is subject to a monitoring notice is referred to as a 'monitored promoter'[168]. Monitored promoters are subject to a strict compliance regime.

4.309 Monitoring notices impose stringent obligations, not only on the monitored promoter, but on its clients. The obligations on the promoter include an obligation to inform clients of its monitored promoter status and provide them with a Promoter Reference Number (PRN). In turn, there is an obligation on clients to put the PRN on their tax returns or otherwise report the PRN to HMRC. There are specific information powers and a specific penalty regime that apply to monitored promoters, their clients and intermediaries. The 'standard' defences of reasonable care and reasonable excuse to the imposition of penalties are strictly limited in relation to the monitored promoter regime. HMRC is permitted to publish the names of monitored promoters and details of how the relevant conduct notice was breached by each monitored promoter[169]. The clear aim of these provisions is to deter clients from using the services of monitored promoters.

4.310 Issuance of a monitoring notice requires the approval of the Tribunal. If a promoter fails to comply with one or more conditions in a conduct notice, HMRC may apply to the Tribunal for it to approve the issuance of a monitoring notice. Notice must be given to the potential recipient, who is to be given a reasonable opportunity to make representations to the Tribunal, including

167 POTAS Guidance, para 2.5.

168 *FA 2014, s 244(5)*.

169 Under *FA 2014, s 248(1)* and *(4)* respectively.

representations about the reasonableness of the conditions in the conduct notice that HMRC considers has been breached. It is for the Tribunal to decide whether there should be a hearing or only written representations made. There is a right of appeal (to the Upper Tribunal) against a Tribunal's decision to approve a monitoring notice being issued.

4.311 A monitored promoter also has the right to make a request to HMRC that the monitoring notice should be withdrawn[170]. A request for withdrawal cannot be made before 12 months after the end of the appeal period. The appeal period ends at the end of the period during which an appeal against the Tribunal's decision to approve the issuance of the notice can be made or, if there is an appeal, when that appeal has been finally determined.

4.312 In deciding whether or not to agree to withdraw the monitoring notice, the HMRC officer must take the following into account:

(a) whether, during the period in which the monitoring notice has had effect, the promoter has engaged in behaviour of a sort that could be regulated by imposing conditions in a conduct notice;

(b) whether it is likely that the promoter will engage in such behaviour in future; and

(c) whether the promoter has complied, or failed to comply, with all the obligations imposed on it as a monitored promoter since the monitoring notice took effect[171].

4.313 The officer must also consider, when deciding to withdraw the notice, whether to issue a follow-on conduct notice that would be take effect immediately after the cessation of the monitoring notice. If the officer refuses to withdraw the monitoring notice, he must explain to the monitored promoter his reasons for this. The monitored promoter has a right to appeal the decision to the Tribunal.

Publicity

4.314 It is stated in the POTAS Guidance that:

> 'A key principle of the regime that applies to monitored promoters is that clients, potential clients and intermediaries should be aware of the promoter's status.'[172]

Reflecting that principle, the regime both enables HMRC to publish information regarding monitored promoters and requires monitored promoters to publicise their monitored status (and the reasons for it).

---

170 Under *FA 2014, s 245.*
171 *FA 2014, s 245(5).*
172 At para 3.8.

4.315 The information that HMRC may publish[173] is:

- the promoter's name and business address;
- the nature of his business;
- any other information that makes clear the monitored promoter's identity, such as any name used in the promoter's business, as well as any previous names or pseudonyms; and
- a statement of the conditions in the conduct notice that were breached.

4.316 It is stated in the POTAS Guidance that: 'as a general rule HMRC will publish the information on its website with due prominence'[174].

4.317 A monitored promoter is required to inform both existing and potential new clients: (a) that it is a monitored promoter; and (b) which conditions in a conduct notice it has failed to meet[175]. It must also publish the same information, and its PRN, on:

(a) its website;

(b) any other websites that promote or provide information about its activities;

(c) any publication or correspondence containing information about schemes offered or promoted by the promoter (save correspondence with HMRC);

(d) any publication or correspondence which is shown, given or sent to existing, new or prospective clients or existing, new or prospective intermediaries in relation to any schemes;

(e) any correspondence concerning any schemes with a professional body to which the monitored promoter belongs or used to belong or of which the promoter is a prospective member; and

(f) any correspondence with a regulatory authority concerning the promoter's conduct in respect of any schemes.

4.318 The information published by the monitored promoter on its website must[176]:

- appear in a prominent position;
- if in writing, be legible;
- if in an audiovisual format, be clearly audible or visible;

173 After the monitored promoter's rights of appeal against the Tribunal's approval of the monitoring notice have been exhausted.

174 At para 3.8.

175 Under *FA 2014, s 249(1)*.

176 Under *reg 3* of the *Finance Act 2014 (High Risk Promoters Prescribed Information) Regulations 2015, SI 2015/549*.

- not in any way be concealed; and
- not be presented in a way that promotes the activity of tax avoidance.

(7) FINANCE ACT 2021

4.319 On 21 July 2020, HMRC published a consultation document entitled 'Tackling Promoters of Tax Avoidance'. It contains proposed changes to, inter alia, DOTAS and POTAS. The changes were first announced in December 2019 and at Budget 2020, the government announced that the revisions would be made in the *Finance Act 2021*. Draft legislation was also published on 21 July 2020.

DOTAS

4.320 It is intended that the relevant section and schedule of *Finance Act 2021* will amend the notification obligations in respect of DOTAS and DOITAS (*Ch 8* of *Pt 7* of the *Finance Act 2004* and *Sch 17* to the *Finance (No 2) Act 2017* respectively) by providing that when HMRC reasonably suspect that a person has failed to disclose proposals or arrangements which should have been notified to them, and the main purpose, or one of the main purposes of arrangements, is the obtaining of a tax advantage, HMRC may issue a notice to anyone they suspect of being involved in the supply of the arrangements requiring the person to satisfy HMRC within 30 days, or any longer period HMRC agree, that the proposal or arrangements are not disclosable. If HMRC is not satisfied, it may issue an SRN in respect of the proposal or arrangements.

POTAS

4.321 The proposed amendments will provide HMRC with the power to issue stop notices to promoters at an earlier stage and in a wider range of circumstances.

4.322 If the *Finance Act 2021* is introduced in accordance with the draft legislation, then the following will apply.

- If HMRC issues a 'stop notice' to a named promoter under the proposed legislation, then that person must immediately stop promoting the arrangements or proposed arrangements specified in the notice.
- HMRC can issue a stop notice if the officer suspects that the person is promoting arrangements or proposals for arrangements that meet conditions A and B. Condition A is met if one (or more) of the following circumstances apply to the arrangements (or proposed arrangements):
  - (a) had they been implemented before 5 April 2019 then they would have been likely to cause a person to be treated as taking a 'relevant step' under the disguised remuneration rules in *Pt 7A* of

ITEPA 2003, for the purposes of the loan charge rules in *Finance (No 2) Act 2017, Sch 11, Pt 1, para 1(1)*;

(b) had they been implemented before 5 April 2019, they would have been likely to cause a 'relevant benefit' to be treated as arising under the disguised trading income rules in the *Income Tax (Trading and Other Income) Act 2005, ss 23A–23H* for the purposes of the loan charge rules; or

(c) they are similar in form or effect to arrangements that have been notified under DOTAS or DOITAS or to arrangements in respect of which a follower notice has been issued.

- Condition B is met if:

  (a) the arrangements (or proposed arrangements) have been or are likely to be marketed as capable of enabling a person to obtain a tax advantage, and

  (b) it is more likely than not that they will fail to produce the tax advantage.

- A promoter who is made subject to a stop notice will be able to request that the stop notice be lifted. If HMRC declines to withdraw the stop notice following representations by the promoter, the promoter can appeal to the Tribunal.

4.323 HMRC will also be able to publish the names of the promoters and details of the scheme where a stop notice has been issued.

4.324 It is intended also that the ambit of POTAS will be extended to encompass individuals who control, or significantly influence, entities that carry on promotion activities.

Chapter 5

Contract: terms of engagement

SIGNPOSTS

- Contract law determines rights and obligations between the tax professional and client in the letter of engagement (LOE) (see **5.16–5.26**).
- Terms to be covered in a contract: checklist (see **5.27–5.29**).
- Breach of contract will entitle the client to be put in the position the client would have been in had the contract been properly performed (eg no tax liability, interest and penalties) (the compensatory principle) (see **5.128–5.136**).
- Importance of certainty of express contract terms (eg as to fees, scope of work, time of performance, limitation of liability), certainty as to consequences arising from breach and/or termination of a contract, liability and exclusion clauses (see **5.61–5.66**).
- Terms implied as a matter of law in consumer contracts (eg services to be provided with reasonable skill and care, within a reasonable time, for reasonable payment) (see **5.67–5.71**).
- Exclusion and limitation of liability: reasonableness/consumer and non-consumer contracts (see **5.81–5.98**).
- Interpretation of contract terms (purposive and commercial approach, intention of the parties) (see **5.125–5.127**).
- Breach of contract (express and implied terms, rights arising on breach), quantification of loss, causation of loss and mitigation of loss, contributory negligence by claimant limiting recovery of loss (see **5.128–5.136**).
- *Consumer Rights Act 2015* (*CRA 2015*) 'consumer' who is an individual acting for purposes that are wholly or mainly outside that individual's trade, business, craft or profession entitled to rights under *CRA 2015*. Services must be performed with 'reasonable care and skill' and also 'within a reasonable time'. Unfair term not effective in contract. A term is unfair if, 'contrary

to the requirement of good faith, it causes a significant imbalance in the parties' rights and obligations under the contract to the detriment of the consumer' (see **5.74–5.80**).

- *Limitation Act 1980*: claims time barred after six years from accrual of cause of action (see **5.164–5.166**).

INTRODUCTION

Why does Contract law have relevance to the tax professional?

5.1 Contract law is important in the context of the regulation of tax professionals as it can impose financial liabilities due to failure to perform the contract, eg failure to provide services to the required standard of competence, failure to pay for services.

5.2 It is one of the indirect ways in which tax professionals are regulated (see **Chapter 2** at **2.16** et seq).

5.3 Contract law imposes civil liability on a tax professional who is in breach of it.

5.4 Contract law seeks to put the claimant (either party to the contract) in the position the claimant would have been had the contract been properly performed. This can be expensive.

General comments

5.5 Contract law is an inescapable reality of business life for any professional adviser, whether an accountant, tax adviser, lawyer or client (professional or otherwise).

5.6 Typically, a contract will govern the rights and obligations of each party, such as the nature and scope of professional services to be provided to a client; whilst the client's primary obligation will be to pay fees for such services.

5.7 Essentially, a contract is about binding reciprocal promises between two or more persons to a contract.

5.8 Contracts are highly relevant to the advice given by a professional adviser in terms of the services provided to our clients (whether accounting, audit, tax or legal advice).

5.9 The contract should determine the scope and basis of the terms of engagement and define the ambit of the advice relating to accounting, audit, tax or legal work; and how much the client is required to pay.

5.10 Contracts will also be relevant to the implementation of professional advice such as structuring a transaction for clients, eg for the purchase and sale of residential or commercial property, assets, shares, commercial supply chain transactions (the supply of goods or services). These contracts if properly negotiated will contain express terms relating to promises concerning the subject matter of the contract (eg valid title to the asset, no defects, full records relating to the business, no liabilities).

Focus of this chapter

5.11 This chapter is concerned with the contractual liability of a professional adviser for the performance of their services. A contract is often about allocating the risk of loss between the parties.

5.12 The focus of this chapter is on the general framework of a typical contract which a professional adviser might enter into with a client (whether a business or non-business recipient).

5.13 Of course, much of what is said in this chapter will also be relevant to the contracts which a person may enter into on an everyday basis for the supply and receipt of goods and/or services.

5.14 Obviously, contracts deal with a variety of different relationships, such as that between employer and employee, the transfer of goods, loan agreements, etc, and the reader should make reference to specialist books on these topics and/or a specialist professional adviser since such a relationship is regulated by specific legislation and case law.

5.15 This chapter explains the relevant laws of England. The laws of Scotland and Wales are outside the scope of this book. **Chapter 6** explains the law of negligence which will be relevant if a claim is made for services that do not meet the requisite professional standard, and no claim is available for breach of contract for that loss.

WHY ARE CONTRACTS IMPORTANT TO TAX PROFESSIONALS?

Professional requirement

5.16 Any person who provides professional services will invariably be expected to enter into a contract, an engagement letter (LOE), with their client.

5.17 The function of a contract will assist professional advisers to demonstrate that they have complied with their professional obligations (ie by clearly establishing the nature and basis of the service, their obligations to the client and the obligations of the client in order to ensure that the parties are dealing on a straightforward and transparent basis).

5.18 In this regard, the professional bodies have set out a range of expectations on their members, which include the following (and see generally **Chapter 3** on the PCRT for tax advisers):

- **Accountants:** Institute of Chartered Accountants of England and Wales (ICAEW)

  The ICAEW's Code of Ethics[1] (the 'Code') states that a professional accountant must comply with the fundamental principles set out in the Code, which includes 'Integrity – to be straightforward and honest in all professional and business relationships'[2].

- **Tax Advisers:** Chartered Institute of Taxation (CIOT) / Association of Taxation Technicians (ATT)

  The *Professional Rules and Practice Guidelines* (effective from 9 November 2018)[3] require each member: 'To be straightforward and honest in all professional and business relationships' (at para 2.1). The guidance emphasises the importance of an engagement letter (at para 4.5.1) stating:

  > 'On accepting instructions, a member is strongly recommended to issue an engagement letter to the client at the outset of the engagement and review it regularly. The engagement letter can be used to manage client expectations and it, or related correspondence, should also clearly set out the basis upon which fees are charged, the scope and nature of the assignment. The client should be asked for their formal agreement. This provides significant protection to a member and is likely to be an important document in any dispute. When the scope of the engagement changes significantly a new letter of engagement may be required. For more information, see the guidance Engagement Letters for Tax Practitioners which can be found on the CIOT and ATT websites.'

  The Professional Rules state in respect of Charging for Services (para 8.1.1.1):

  > 'Before undertaking any work on behalf of any new or existing client, a member should ensure that the client clearly understands the basis on which fees will be charged and how expenses incurred on behalf of the client will be treated. It will usually be appropriate to set these matters out in the letter of engagement.'

1 Available at www.icaew.com/technical/ethics/icaew-code-of-ethics/icaew-code-of-ethics#:~:text=%20ICAEW%20Code%20of%20Ethics%20from%201%20January,on%20aspects%20of%20the%20Code%20of...%20More%20.

2 See Part A – General Application of this Code, at para 100.5.

3 See www.tax.org.uk/sites/default/files/181109%20PRPG.pdf.

Specific guidance has been issued by CIOT and ATT on Engagement Letters, including in respect of proposed content[4].

- **Solicitors:** Solicitors Regulation Authority (SRA)

  The SRA Code of Conduct for Solicitors (the SRA Standards and Regulations came into effect on 25 November 2019)[5] sets out the principles and code by which Solicitors must conduct themselves[6]. In terms of maintaining trust and integrity the SRA Code states (at para 1.3) that: 'You perform all undertakings given by you, and do so within an agreed timescale or if no timescale has been agreed then within a reasonable amount of time'. The SRA Code requires at the time of engagement that the solicitor advises the client about, inter alia, pricing of services (at para 8.7), complaints (at para 8.3).

- **Barristers:** Bar Standards Board (BSB)

  The BSB Code of Conduct for barristers[7] sets out the principles and code by which barristers must conduct themselves. In this regard, it states (Part 2 – B at CD3*)* You must act with honesty, and with integrity'. Under Part 2 – C3 'Outcomes' at oC13: 'Clients know what to expect and understand the advice they are given' and at oC18 'Clients are adequately informed as to the terms on which work is to be done'.

  Under rC22:

  > 'Where you first accept *instructions* to act in a matter:
  >
  > .1 you must, subject to Rule rC23, confirm in writing acceptance of the *instructions* and the terms and/or basis on which you will be acting, including the basis of charging[8];...'

---

4 See www.tax.org.uk/professional-standards/professional-standards-%E2%80%93-full-listing/engagement-letters.

5 Updated 20 March 2020: www.sra.org.uk/globalassets/documents/sra/standards-regulations.pdf?version=4a1aba.

6 A solicitor must act: '1. in a way that upholds the constitutional principle of the rule of law, and the proper administration of justice. 2. in a way that upholds public trust and confidence in the solicitors' profession and in legal services provided by authorised persons. 3. with independence. 4. with honesty. 5. with integrity. 6. in a way that encourages equality, diversity and inclusion. 7. in the best interests of each client'. SRA Principles at p 5, 'SRA Standards and Regulations'.

7 See BSB Handbook at www.barstandardsboard.org.uk/for-barristers/bsb-handbook-and-code-guidance/the-bsb-handbook.html.

8 The Guidance to the BSB Code states 'gC75 Compliance with the requirement in Rule rC22 to set out the terms and/or basis upon which you will be acting may be achieved by including a reference or link to the relevant terms in your written communication of acceptance. You may, for example, refer the client or professional client (as the case may be) to the terms of service set out on your website or to standard terms of service set out on the Bar Council's website (in which regard, please also refer to the guidance on the use of the standard terms of service). Where you agree to do your work on terms and conditions that have been proposed to you by the client or by the professional client, you should confirm in writing that that is the basis on which your work is done. Where there are competing sets of terms and conditions, which terms have been agreed and are the basis of your retainer will be a matter to be determined in accordance with the law of contract'.

Commercial requirement

5.19 The nature of any commercial relationship, whereby services are provided for reward will result in the creation of a contractual relationship.

5.20 A contract will determine what each person is required to provide under the terms of that relationship. It will often allocate risk between the parties.

5.21 The existence of a written contract between the supplier and recipient promotes certainty and transparency in the relationship with the objective of ensuring that no disputes arise during the contract and that the mutual expectations of the parties are met.

5.22 If disputes do arise it can help to determine the dispute sometimes in a shorter time (and thereby keeping down costs).

5.23 It can also set out mechanisms for dispute resolution such as mediation and alternative dispute resolution (ADR).

Legal requirements

5.24 A contract can be created orally between parties.

5.25 However, a written contract will assist in resolving disputes as it provides the starting evidence as to what was agreed.

5.26 It also enables compliance with relevant regulations that impose specific requirements in connection with the content of information to be provided to a client. For example, where 'services'[9] are subject to the *Provision of Services Regulations 2009, SI 2009/2999* (see www.legislation.gov.uk).

TYPICAL TERMS OF BUSINESS FOR SUPPLY OF PROFESSIONAL SERVICES

5.27 The terms of business for a professional service provider will vary between each provider and client due to the nature of the services being supplied. A client will often accept an adviser's standard LOE without amendment (subject to agreeing the nature of the work to be done, fees and limitation of liability) but sometimes the terms of the standard LOE will negotiated by the client (or their representatives). When the standard LOE is altered it is important to give careful consideration to the effect of the amendments before reaching any final and binding agreement.

9 Regulation 2(1) states: '"service" means any self-employed economic activity normally provided for remuneration'.

5.28 A detailed review for each profession and any terms in a LOE is beyond the scope of this book; however, reference should be made to the professional standards which should be met.

5.29 By way of overview, contracts should typically cover the following material matters between the contracting parties:

(1) *Definitions*

The purpose of this section will be to define key terms used in the contract, such as identifying the commencement date of the contract.

(2) *Scope of Services*

This section of the contract should identify the scope and nature of the services to be provided to the recipient (either in the terms of the contract or by reference to an engagement letter with the client). This part of the contract should explain to whom the services are being provided (eg solely to the contracting party and/or to a third party).

(3) *Delivery*

This section should identify when the services are to be provided to the recipient.

(4) *Reliance*

This section should explain on what basis the recipient is entitled to rely on the services provided under the contract. Typically, this will be by reference to final written advice and not oral or draft advice.

(5) *Client obligations*

This section should explain to the client their specific obligations under the contract. For example, that the client will supply information and documents on transactions, corporate structure, etc, to enable the adviser to discharge their obligations under the contract. That the client should discharge their obligations on a timely basis, and that the client should ensure all information given to the adviser is accurate and complete.

(6) *Fees*

This section should explain the financial payments that must be made to the provider of the services, and the time when such fees are to be paid. The clause should explain, among other things, that any estimate is not binding, how the fees have been calculated, whether time spent travelling which is referable to the services is recoverable.

(7) *Expenses*

This section should explain the type of expenses and the basis on which expenses are recoverable from the client.

(8) *Taxes*

This section should explain that any fees invoiced to the client will be subject to applicable taxes, such as Value Added Tax, and that these are payable in addition. The section should also require the recipient to provide evidence of their VAT status, ie whether a business or non-business recipient.

(9) *Invoices and payment*

This section should explain when the supplier is entitled to invoice the client (eg monthly) and when the client is required to pay the fees (eg within 14 or 30 days etc). If the client fails to pay the fees the clause should explain the consequences, eg interest payable at the rate set by law.

(10) *Confidentiality*

This section should explain the basis on which the parties will share confidential information for the purpose of enabling the services to be provided to the client. Such a clause will typically state that confidential information will not be disclosed to any third party except as permitted by the clause and as required by law (eg by court order, information notice issued under the *Finance Act 2008, Sch.36*). For example, if the professional adviser will need to work with third parties in order to deliver the services, then this must be expressly dealt with in the contract (eg by the client agreeing to the sharing of such information to the adviser's network of advisers, subcontractor or IT service providers).

(11) *Intellectual Property Rights*

This section should explain who owns any intellectual property rights (ie copyright) in the work product which is provided to the client. For example, the client will usually be granted a licence to use the material for internal purposes.

(12) *Data Protection/General Data Protection Regulation (GDPR)*

This section should state that each party will comply with all applicable data protection legislation in relation to personal data shared under the contract. If personal data is to be provided, then the person sharing it must have authority to do so. The contract should also explain how any data is processed under the agreement (typically by reference to a privacy statement), when data transfers and processing are permitted.

(13) *Liability: scope*

This section should explain that any liability for errors in the services is limited solely to the recipient of the services (as defined by the contract). The contract should also identify the limitation on liability (eg financial limits) and that no liability for any loss will arise if that loss is attributable to the client failing to discharge their obligations under the contract (eg by failing to provide accurate and timely information on transactions, financial data, etc). This type of clause should seek to identify precisely the nature of the losses covered and excluded. Typical losses which are sought to be excluded relate to loss of data, loss of profit, goodwill, business opportunity, savings or benefits, indirect and consequential loss. It should be noted that some losses cannot be limited by law (eg liability attributable to a person's liability for death or personal injury caused by that person's negligence).

(14) *Liability: cap*

This section should explain the provider's total liability (including interest) for all claims connected with the services or the agreement (including in respect of any claim for negligence). For example, some contracts may seek to limit the liability for losses to a multiple of the fees paid for the services or a specific amount (whichever is the greater).

(15) *Liability: claims*

A clause should state that any claims for loss are brought against the provider of the services, but cannot be brought against any individual employee or member of the firm (eg if an LLP is providing the services).

(16) *Liability: third parties*

The contract should explain the circumstances in which any liability for losses under the contract will be reduced by reference to the liabilities of another person. For example, if the client is also entitled to claim against a third party then the liability of the provider under the contract will be reduced by reference to, inter alia, the extent of the responsibility of the third party for the loss.

(17) *Third party service providers*

This clause of the contract should explain whether the supplier will use third parties to provide the services to the client under the contract, and if so, on what basis.

(18) *Documents and deliverables*

This clause should explain whether the provider is entitled to retain copies of information and documents provided by the client for the purposes of the contract (including for how long the material can be retained).

(19) *Termination*

This clause should explain the circumstances in which the contract between the parties can be terminated. The type of circumstances might include:

- Immediate termination where: (i) there is a material breach of contract which is not remedied within a specified number of days; (ii) a party is unable to pays its debts or becomes insolvent; (iii) performance of the agreement may breach a legal or regulatory requirement.
- Written notice, eg on giving 28 days' notice.

A termination clause should explain the amount of fees payable on termination and the basis for such payment (eg time spent). The clause should also explain which clauses in the agreement will continue to apply (eg liability, payment of fees, confidentiality, ownership of intellectual property rights, data protection, liability, dispute resolution, general clauses (eg entire agreement), interpretation clause).

(20) *Dispute resolution*

This clause should explain how the parties will resolve any disputes arising in connection with the contract. For example, it should require the parties to seek to resolve the dispute by discussion, negotiation and mediation prior to the issue of any legal proceedings.

(21) *Governing Law*

This clause should state that the contract is governed by the laws of England, and that it is subject to the exclusive jurisdiction of the English courts.

(22) *Limitation Period*

This clause should stipulate the time limit for bringing any claims under the contract.

(23) *General*

This clause should generally cover the following matters:

- *Entire agreement:* the contract is the entire agreement between the parties in respect of the services to be provided (specifically that any prior agreement, representations, statements or discussions do not form part of the contract) (ie any statements, representations which are binding on the parties must only be identified in the contract);
- *Amendment:* a term of the agreement can only be altered if specifically agreed in writing between the parties;
- *Assignment:* no assignment of the rights or benefits arising under the contract are permitted without prior written agreement;
- *Novation:* if a party to the contract is to be replaced this is called a novation. A novation occurs where one party transfers all of the party's obligations and benefits under a contract to a third

party. A novation should not be permitted without prior written agreement.

- *Rights of third parties:* unless otherwise specifically agreed in the contract, a person who is not a party to the agreement has no rights under the *Contracts (Rights of Third Parties) Act 1999* to enforce any term of the agreement.
- *Regulated services:* whether any of the services provided under the contract are regulated and if so the basis on which the services are regulated (eg legal services provided by a solicitor are regulated in accordance with the Solicitors Regulation Authority (SRA) Standards and Regulations).

(24) *Complaints*

The contract should explain how a client makes a complaint about the provision of services under the contract (eg a designated individual within the firm responsible for quality assurance). It should be noted that where services are provided by a person/firm that are regulated then the contract should direct the client to the relevant professional regulator. In this regard, complaints about the following professional service providers can be made to their Regulator:

- Institute of Chartered Accountants in England & Wales
- SRA regulated services
- Chartered Institute of Taxation (CTA)
- Association of Tax Technicians (ATT)
- Society of Trust and Estate Practitioners (STEP)
- Bar Standards Board (BSB).

For regulated legal service providers, complaints can also be made to the legal ombudsman[10]. However, this is outside the scope of this book.

CONTRACT FORMATION

Offer and acceptance

5.30 A contract creates binding obligations (legally enforceable promises) between two or more persons for the supply of services.

5.31 A contract comes into existence when an unconditional offer is made by a person and that offer is unequivocally accepted by the recipient of the offer.

10 See www.legalombudsman.org.uk/helping-the-public.

5.32 Each contracting party must give 'consideration'[11] for the other parties' undertakings otherwise there will be no contract, unless it is by way of a deed[12].

5.33 The contracting parties must also have capacity (ie not be a minor and not be under any mental incapacity) to enter into the contract otherwise the agreement will potentially be unenforceable[13].

5.34 The following commentary identifies the nature of the main constituent elements of a contract, and how a contract is formed in the context of professional transactions.

5.35 A detailed discussion of these matters is beyond the scope of this chapter and professional advice should be taken where appropriate.

Offer distinguished from invitation to treat

5.36 An offer by a person to enter into a contract must be distinguished from what is called an 'invitation to treat', since such an invitation by itself is not capable of forming a binding offer to contract which when accepted unequivocally can give rise to a legally enforceable agreement.

5.37 An invitation to treat is often a preliminary stage in the process towards the conclusion of a contract, since it is merely an invitation to another person to make an offer which is capable of being accepted. Giving a potential client a price range is likely to be an invitation to treat whereas after an inquiry from a potential client who wants you to act saying 'I will carry out the work we agreed for £x' is likely to be an offer which is capable of forming a binding contact. As lawyers often say 'it all depends on the facts!', and clearly these type of disputes can be easily avoided by only having written terms of engagement which excludes any prior statements and representations.

5.38 Generally, an offer must be communicated to the recipient in such terms that the offer must be clear with the intention that it should be binding

11 'A quid pro quo' for the deal in the Bargain Theory of Contract.

12 HM Land Registry's Practice guide 8: execution of deeds (Sept 2020), at para 1.2 states:
'To be a deed the document must:
- be in writing
- make clear on its face that it is intended to be a deed by the person making it or the parties to it. This can be done by the document describing itself as a deed or expressing itself to be executed as a deed 'or otherwise'
- be validly executed as a deed by the person making it or one or more of the parties to it (*section 1* of the *Law of Property (Miscellaneous Provisions) Act 1989*).'

See www.gov.uk/government/publications/execution-of-deeds/practice-guide-8-execution-of-deeds.

13 The age of a party may be relevant. A contract with an 'infant' (someone under the age of 18 in England) may be void. Specialist advice is needed where this is an issue.

on unequivocal acceptance, ie there should be an intention to create legal relations. Written terms of engagement are necessary because such a document will provide proof of the basis of engagement.

Acceptance

5.39 For an offer to be accepted, so as to form a binding contract, there must usually be an acceptance that is unqualified and communicated (eg the client accepts the terms by signing and returning a copy of the contract to the adviser).

5.40 If any new terms are offered then the recipient has effectively made a counter offer which supersedes the original offer, and itself becomes an offer capable of acceptance.

5.41 It is generally necessary for the acceptance to be communicated to the person making the offer, and the general rule is that acceptance has no effect until it is communicated to the offeror[14].

5.42 Silence is usually not indicative of acceptance[15]. This is in contrast to the theoretical position in some continental countries[16].

5.43 However, there is a general principle that postal acceptance of an offer is effective[17].

5.44 A postal acceptance is only effective if it is reasonable to use the post and/or the terms of the acceptance use the postal system in accordance with its terms.

5.45 If instantaneous forms of communication are used, acceptance is only effective when the acceptance is actually communicated to the offeror[18].

5.46 Instantaneous methods of communication would include email, telephone and, by extension, video conferencing[19].

---

14 *Entores Ltd v Miles Far East Corp* [1955] 2 QB 327; *Brinkibon Ltd v Stahag Stahl and Stahlwaren handel sgesellschaft* [1983] 2 AC 34.

15 *Felthouse v Bindley* (1862) 142 ER 1037.

16 *Cf* Germany and Norway and see, eg Daniel A Nye, 'Formation of Contracts: The Law in Norway', Vol 12, No 2, North Carolina Journal of International Law and Commercial Regulation (https://core.ac.uk/download/pdf/151515821.pdf).

17 *Adams v Lindsell* (1818) 1 B & Ald 681; *Henthorn v Fraser* [1892] 2 Ch 27.

18 *Brinkibon* [1983] 1 AC 34.

19 In *Brinkibon*, Lord Wilberforce commented: 'No universal rule can cover all such cases; they must be resolved by reference to the intention of the parties, by sound business practice and in some cases by a judgment where the risk should lie'.

FEES: CONSIDERATION

5.47 The undertakings given by each contracting party must be supported by consideration (eg cash) (unless made by execution of a Deed)[20].

5.48 In other words, a benefit must be given by one party to the person promising to supply services[21]. Each party must at least have a benefit or detriment under the contract. This is the nature of the bargain which is struck in order for an enforceable contract to come into existence. 'Consideration' is traditionally defined in terms of benefit to the promisor or detriment to the promisee. Lord Lindley expressed it in the following way in the Privy Council decision in *Fleming v Bank of New Zealand* [1900] AC 577 at 586, quoting from the judgment of Lush J in *Currie v Misa* (1875) LR 10 Exch 153 at 162: 'A valuable consideration in the sense of the law, may consist either in some right, interest, profit, or benefit accruing to the one party, or some forbearance, detriment, loss, or responsibility, given, suffered, or undertaken by the other …'. The classic statement is that a promise to pay a peppercorn rent is good consideration. In *Chappell & Co Ltd v Nestle & Co Ltd* [1960] AC 87, where Lord Somervell, at p 114, said: 'a peppercorn does not cease to be good consideration if it is established that the promisee does not like pepper and will throw away the corn'.

5.49 The consideration must come from the person seeking to enforce the promise[22]. Further, the consideration must have value which can be nominal[23]. For example, a payment of £1 for a valuable promise would be sufficient consideration for a binding contract. However, as a general rule, performing an act which is already a pre-existing obligation is not sufficient consideration[24].

CONTRACT FORMALITIES AND FREEDOM TO CONTRACT

5.50 Generally, in English Law, there are no formalities for the creation of a valid contract, such as a requirement that the contract is made in writing, although there are a number of statutory exceptions which are beyond the scope of this book[25].

---

20 An instrument is a deed if it is clear on its face it is a deed and is to take effect as a deed and is executed as a deed. An instrument is executed as a deed if it is signed by the individual making it, witnessed and delivered (essentially 'delivery' means an act indicating that the deed is binding on the person making it): see the *Law of Property (Miscellaneous Provisions) Act 1989, s 1*.

21 *O'Sullivan v Management Agency & Music Ltd* [1985] QB 428.

22 *Cf England v Davidson* (1840) 11 Ad & E 856; *Collins v Godefroy* (1831) 1 B & Ad 950; *Williams v Roffey Bros & Nicholls (Contractors) Ltd* [1991] 1 QB 1.

23 *Wild v Tucker* [1914] 3 KB 36.

24 *Stilk v Myrick* (1809) 2 Camp 317.

25 Under the *Law of Property (Miscellaneous Provisions) Act 1989, s 2*, a contract for the sale or other disposition of an interest in land can only be made in writing.

5.51 The law of England generally imposes no written formalities.

5.52 The parties to a contract are generally entitled to contract on whatever terms they wish to be bound in respect of the provision of services and supply of goods[26]. The courts will not intervene to improve the bargain made under a contract[27].

5.53 However, there are some restrictions on the terms of a contract which may be imposed by public policy considerations (eg the non-enforcement of penalty clauses in a contract, or terms which are unfair in a consumer contract) which statute imposes. The terms of a consumer contract are subject to the *CRA 2015* (see **5.74** et seq).

5.54 Once the parties have signed a contract, generally they cannot then resile from the contract[28], unless, for example, it is a 'consumer contract' governed by the *Consumer Contracts (Information Cancellation and Additional Charges) Regulations 2013, SI 2013/3134*[29].

---

26 See *Printing and Numerical Registering Co v Sampson* (1874-1875) LR 19 Eq 462 where Sir George Jessel MR (at 465) stated: 'if there is one thing which more than another policy requires is that men of full age and competent understanding shall have the utmost liberty of contracting, and that their contracts when entered into freely and voluntarily shall be held sacred and shall be enforced by Courts of justice. Therefore, you have this paramount public policy to consider – that you are not lightly to interfere with this freedom of contract'.

27 *Prime Sight Ltd v Lavarello* [2013] UKPC 22.

28 See *Saunders v Anglia Building Society* [1971] AC 1004 at 1015–1016, [1970] 3 All ER 961 at 963, HL, per Lord Reid, at 1020 and 966–967 per Viscount Dilhorne, at 1025–1027 and 971–973 per Lord Wilberforce and at 1034 and 978–979 per Lord Pearson.

29 The *2013 Regulations* apply to contracts between traders and consumers (see *reg 4*). Some provisions of the Regulations apply only to on-premises contracts, some only to off-premises contracts, and some only to distance contracts; these terms are defined in *reg 5*. *Part 2* of the Regulations requires traders to provide information to consumers in relation to contracts concluded between them. *Regulation 9* and *Sch 1* specify the information (including the main characteristics of the goods or service, the identity of the trader and the total price) which a trader must provider to a consumer before entering into an on-premises contract. *Regulations 10, 13* and *Sch 2* specify the information required for an off-premises contract or a distance contract (including delivery arrangements, the trader's complaint handling policy, if there is one, and cancellation rights). *Regulations 12* and *16* require the trader to provide the consumer with a copy of the signed contract or confirmation of the contract, within a reasonable time after the conclusion of the contract. *Regulation 18* provides that a term is implied into the contract between the trader and the consumer that the trader has complied with the information requirements in *regs 9–14* and *16*. *Part 3* of the Regulations contains provisions concerning a consumer's right to cancel a distance or off-premises contract without giving any reason or incurring any costs other than those specified. *Regulation 29* establishes the right to cancel. *Regulation 30* provides for a cancellation period of 14 days calculated from the date of conclusion of the contract or the date of delivery, according to the type of contract. *Regulation 31* provides that the cancellation period may be extended by up to 12 months if the trader does not provide the consumer with the information on cancellation rights specified in *Sch 2*. *Regulation 34* requires the trader to pay a refund to the consumer within 14 days of being informed of the cancellation. *Regulations 36* and *37* provide that the consumer loses the right to cancel where a service or digital content is supplied during the cancellation period, if the consumer acknowledged that the right would be lost in those circumstances. The Regulations are available at www.legislation.gov.uk.

REPRESENTATIONS PRIOR TO CONTRACT

5.55 Prior to the parties entering into a contract they will usually have discussions and a negotiation about the nature of what will be supplied under the contract.

5.56 It is possible for representations made during the course of such pre-formal contract discussions to become a term of the contract.

5.57 Whether a statement is a term of the contract will turn on whether the parties intended it to be an actual term of the contract; but this is assessed on an objective basis by reference to the conduct of the parties, their words and behaviour.

5.58 The test is whether an intelligent bystander would reasonably infer that a 'warranty' was intended[30].

5.59 In *Inntrepreneur Pub Co Ltd v East Crown Ltd* [2000] 2 Lloyd's Rep 611, Lightman J, at para [10] stated:

> '(1) a pre-contractual statement will only be treated as having contractual effect if the evidence shows that parties intended this to be the case. Intention is a question of fact to be decided by looking at the totality of the evidence;
>
> (2) the test is the ordinary objective test for the formation of a contract: what is relevant is not the subjective thought of one party but what a reasonable outside observer would infer from all the circumstances;
>
> (3) in deciding the question of intention, one important consideration will be whether the statement is followed by further negotiations and a written contract not containing any term corresponding to the statement. In such a case, it will be harder to infer that the statement was intended to have contractual effect because the prima facie assumption will be that the written contract includes all the terms the parties wanted to be binding between them;
>
> (4) a further important factor will be the lapse of time between the statement and the making of the formal contract. The longer the interval, the greater the presumption must be that the parties did not intend the statement to have contractual effect in relation to a subsequent deal;
>
> (5) a representation of fact is much more likely intended to have contractual effect than a statement of future fact or a future forecast.'

5.60 If pre-contract discussions do not form a term of the contract, it is nonetheless possible that a remedy may exist for any incorrect representation on the basis of misrepresentation (eg under the *Misrepresentation Act 1967*)[31].

30 In *Oscar Chess Ltd v Williams* [1957] 1 WLR 370, at 375 per Denning LJ, as he then was.
31 See the *Misrepresentation Act 1967* at www.legislation.gov.uk.

A contract will often include what is called an 'entire agreement' clause which states that it operates to exclude representations, statements, collateral warranties or proof of extraneous terms that, even if agreed in the course of negotiations, were not included in the parties' final written agreement. In *Inntrepreneur Pub Co v East Crown Ltd* [2000] 2 Lloyd's Rep 611, Lightman J explained at [7]:

> 'The purpose of an entire agreement clause is to preclude a party to a written agreement from threshing through the undergrowth and finding in the course of negotiations some (chance) remark or statement (often long forgotten or difficult to recall or explain) on which to found a claim such as the present to the existence of a collateral warranty. The entire agreement clause obviates the occasion for any such search and the peril to the contracting parties posed by the need which may arise in its absence to conduct such a search. For such a clause constitutes a binding agreement between the parties that the full contractual terms are to be found in the document containing the clause and not elsewhere, and that accordingly any promises or assurances made in the course of negotiations (which in the absence of such a clause might have effect as a collateral warranty) shall have no contractual force, save insofar as they are reflected and given effect in that document. The operation of the clause is not to render evidence of the collateral warranty inadmissible in evidence … It is to denude what would otherwise constitute a collateral warranty of legal effect.'

However, an entire agreement clause has been held not to prevent the implication of terms upon the ordinary principles relating to terms that can be implied into a contract as a matter of law. In *JN Hipwell & Son v Szurek* [2018] EWCA Civ 674 the Court of Appeal stated at [26], that it was well established that a term may be implied where it is necessary to give business efficacy to the contract even if the contract contains an entire agreement clause[32].

EXPRESS TERMS OF A CONTRACT

5.61 Generally, the terms of the contract will not be effective unless and until agreed as part of the acceptance process.

5.62 The agreement of clear and express terms to a contract ensures that there is certainty for both parties, and in consequence this should avoid any dispute on interpretation of the scope of the clauses to the contract. For example, it is particularly important for a tax professional to be precisely aware of the facts in respect of which advice or tax services are sought, and to identify clearly the client who is relying on the advice. An express term should usually be incorporated into the engagement letter to the effect that:

32 See also *Seadrill Management Services Ltd v OAO Gazprom* [2010] EWCA Civ 691, at [27]–[28] (per Moore-Bick LJ) and *Harrison v Shepherd Homes Ltd* [2011] EWHC 1811 (TCC), at [65] (per Ramsey J).

> 'The Tax Professional shall act only for the Client and the Tax Professional's duty is: (i) limited to the Client and no responsibility is assumed by the Tax Professional to any third party; (ii) limited to the matters stated in the advice on the basis of the facts disclosed in instructions from the client to the Tax Professional and reliance may not be placed on advice in relation to other circumstances; (iii) limited to the laws in force in England as applied by the English courts; and (iv) as at the date the advice is given.'

5.63 Sometimes terms will be incorporated by reference to a document, which are referred to in the offer letter (LOE), for example, a contract which is made subject to the standard terms of the supplier or settled by a representative body such as a trade association. A tax professional may wish to include assumptions concerning the relevant facts which are being advised on for the purpose of providing tax advice to a client. Such factual assumptions perform an important role because:

- they ensure that the client reviews the assumptions and identifies to the tax professional whether they are correct and if not, then this will identify what impact the facts have on the nature of the tax advice to be provided;
- if any of the assumptions are wrong and the client has not notified the tax professional then this should assist in limiting the liability of the tax professional.

An illustrative list of assumptions is provided in **Appendix 5**. Such assumptions could be incorporated into the engagement letter as follows:

> 'The assumptions in Appendix X (subject to any explicit agreement to the contrary or matter set out in the advice explicitly or implicitly) have been made (inter alia) for the purposes of any advice provided under the terms of engagement, in addition to those made explicitly or implicitly made in any advice (whether in writing or otherwise).'

5.64 Where reliance is placed on the incorporation of terms into a contract by reference to a standard term document, it is important that professional advice should be taken to ensure the contract is valid.

5.65 To the extent any terms in a standard terms document are incompatible with any rule of law they will generally be excluded[33].

The approach which the parties, lawyers and a court should adopt to interpret the terms of a contract are discussed below. It is important to ensure that there is absolute clarity between the parties as to the terms and conditions incorporated into the contract. This is to ensure that there is no 'battle of forms' between the parties. For example, Party A (the advisory firm) may state that its terms and conditions referred to in a clause to the contract contained the type of limitation and exclusion of liability clauses which might be expected.

33 For example, under the *Unfair Contract Terms Act 1977* and the *Unfair Terms in Consumer Contracts Regulations 1999, SI 1999/2083*: see www.legislation.gov.uk.

However, Party B (the client) may argue that Party A's acceptance of the offer incorporated Party B's terms and conditions which did not contain any limitation or exclusion clauses in Party A's favour. Such disputes often occur in cases where each of the parties send their offer and acceptance with the specifications for that transaction or services (such as fee and delivery date) on the front of the forms, and the standard terms and conditions on the back.

5.66 The best practice is to require the client to return a signed acknowledgement of the LOE, which states that the client has read the engagement letter, terms and conditions of engagement and that the contents are accepted. If advice is provided to a client prior to the return of the signed engagement letter, it is necessary to ensure that the terms of engagement sent to the client include an express term which states that the client's instruction of the tax professional is deemed to be accepted on the terms of engagement even if not returned prior to the provision of any advice. However, such engagements should be the exception rather than the norm.

IMPLIED TERMS OF A CONTRACT

General

5.67 The term of a contract may also be incorporated into a contract for the purposes of giving 'business efficacy' to a transaction[34], where the term is necessary to make the agreement work[35], or where statute requires a term to be implied. These aspects are discussed below.

Term implied 'in fact' by the court: 'business efficacy'

5.68 Whether a term is to be implied into a contract is a matter of law for a court.

5.69 However, any term that would otherwise be implied must give way to an inconsistent express term of the contract[36].

5.70 Whether or not a term is implied will usually depend upon the intention of the parties as collected from the words of the agreement, the surrounding circumstances and commercial common sense.

5.71 The relevant legal principles on the implication of a term into a contract are provided in the Supreme Court decision in *Marks & Spencer plc*

34 In *Shirlaw v Southern Foundries Ltd* [1939] 2KB 206, at [227] MacKinnon LJ stated: 'Prima facie that which in any contract is left to be implied and need not be expressed is something so obvious that it goes without saying: so that, if while the parties were making their bargain, an officious bystander were to suggest some express provision for it in their agreement, they would testily supress him with a common "Oh, of course!"' (affirmed [1940] AC 701).

35 See *Luxor (Eastbourne) Ltd v Cooper* [1941] AC 108.

36 See *Marks & Spencer plc v BNP Paribas Securities Services Trust Co (Jersey) Ltd* [2015] UKSC 72 at [28] per Lord Neuberger.

v BNP Paribas Securities Services Trust Co (Jersey) Ltd [2015] UKSC 72 at [16]–[31] (Lord Neuberger (with whom Lords Sumption and Hodge agreed)):

> '16. There have, of course, been many judicial observations as to the nature of the requirements which have to be satisfied before a term can be implied into a detailed commercial contract. They include three classic statements, which have been frequently quoted in law books and judgments. In *The Moorcock* (1889) 14 PD 64, 68, Bowen LJ observed that in all the cases where a term had been implied, "it will be found that … the law is raising an implication from the presumed intention of the parties with the object of giving the transaction such efficacy as both parties must have intended that at all events it should have". In *Reigate v Union Manufacturing Co (Ramsbottom) Ltd* [1918] 1 KB 592, 605, Scrutton LJ said that "[a] term can only be implied if it is necessary in the business sense to give efficacy to the contract". He added that a term would only be implied if "it is such a term that it can confidently be said that if at the time the contract was being negotiated" the parties had been asked what would happen in a certain event, they would both have replied "Of course, so and so will happen; we did not trouble to say that; it is too clear". And in *Shirlaw v Southern Foundries* (1926) Ltd [1939] 2 KB 206, 227, MacKinnon LJ observed that, "[p]rima facie that which in any contract is left to be implied and need not be expressed is something so obvious that it goes without saying". Reflecting what Scrutton LJ had said 20 years earlier, MacKinnon LJ also famously added that a term would only be implied "if, while the parties were making their bargain, an officious bystander were to suggest some express provision for it in their agreement, they would testily suppress him with a common 'Oh, of course!'".
>
> 17. Support for the notion that a term will only be implied if it satisfies the test of business necessity is to be found in a number of observations made in the House of Lords. Notable examples included Lord Pearson (with whom Lord Guest and Lord Diplock agreed) in *Trollope & Colls Ltd v North West Metropolitan Regional Hospital Board* [1973] 1 WLR 601, 609, and Lord Wilberforce, Lord Cross, Lord Salmon and Lord Edmund-Davies in Liverpool City Council v Irwin [1977] AC 230, 254, 258, 262 and 266 respectively. More recently, the test of "necessary to give business efficacy" to the contract in issue was mentioned by Lady Hale in Geys at para 55 and by Lord Carnwath in *Arnold v Britton* [2015] 2 WLR 1593, para 112.
>
> 18. In the Privy Council case of *BP Refinery (Westernport) Pty Ltd v President, Councillors and Ratepayers of the Shire of Hastings* (1977) 52 ALJR 20, [1977] UKPC 13, 26, Lord Simon (speaking for the majority, which included Viscount Dilhorne and Lord Keith) said that:
>
>> "[F]or a term to be implied, the following conditions (which may overlap) must be satisfied: (1) it must be reasonable and equitable; (2) it must be necessary to give business efficacy to the contract, so that no term will be implied if the contract is effective without it; (3) it must be so obvious

that 'it goes without saying'; (4) it must be capable of clear expression; (5) it must not contradict any express term of the contract."

19. In *Philips Electronique Grand Public SA v British Sky Broadcasting Ltd* [1995] EMLR 472, 481, Sir Thomas Bingham MR set out Lord Simon's formulation, and described it as a summary which "distil[led] the essence of much learning on implied terms" but whose "simplicity could be almost misleading". Sir Thomas then explained that it was "difficult to infer with confidence what the parties must have intended when they have entered into a lengthy and carefully-drafted contract but have omitted to make provision for the matter in issue", because "it may well be doubtful whether the omission was the result of the parties' oversight or of their deliberate decision", or indeed the parties might suspect that "they are unlikely to agree on what is to happen in a certain … eventuality" and "may well choose to leave the matter uncovered in their contract in the hope that the eventuality will not occur". Sir Thomas went on to say this at p 482:

> "The question of whether a term should be implied, and if so what, almost inevitably arises after a crisis has been reached in the performance of the contract. So the court comes to the task of implication with the benefit of hindsight, and it is tempting for the court then to fashion a term which will reflect the merits of the situation as they then appear. Tempting, but wrong. [He then quoted the observations of Scrutton LJ in Reigate, and continued] [I]t is not enough to show that had the parties foreseen the eventuality which in fact occurred they would have wished to make provision for it, unless it can also be shown either that there was only one contractual solution or that one of several possible solutions would without doubt have been preferred …"

20. Sir Thomas's approach in *Philips* was consistent with his reasoning, as Bingham LJ in the earlier case *The APJ Priti* [1987] 2 Lloyd's Rep 37, 42, where he rejected the argument that a warranty, to the effect that the port declared was prospectively safe, could be implied into a voyage charter-party. His reasons for rejecting the implication were "because the omission of an express warranty may well have been deliberate, because such an implied term is not necessary for the business efficacy of the charter and because such an implied term would at best lie uneasily beside the express terms of the charter".

21. In my judgment, the judicial observations so far considered represent a clear, consistent and principled approach. It could be dangerous to reformulate the principles, but I would add six comments on the summary given by Lord Simon in *BP Refinery* as extended by Sir Thomas Bingham in *Philips* and exemplified in *The APJ Priti*. First, in *Equitable Life Assurance Society v Hyman* [2002] 1 AC 408, 459, Lord Steyn rightly observed that the implication of a term was "not critically dependent on proof of an actual intention of the parties" when negotiating the contract. If one approaches the question by reference to what the parties would have agreed, one is

not strictly concerned with the hypothetical answer of the actual parties, but with that of notional reasonable people in the position of the parties at the time at which they were contracting. Secondly, a term should not be implied into a detailed commercial contract merely because it appears fair or merely because one considers that the parties would have agreed it if it had been suggested to them. Those are necessary but not sufficient grounds for including a term. However, and thirdly, it is questionable whether Lord Simon's first requirement, reasonableness and equitableness, will usually, if ever, add anything: if a term satisfies the other requirements, it is hard to think that it would not be reasonable and equitable. Fourthly, as Lord Hoffmann I think suggested in *Attorney General of Belize v Belize Telecom Ltd* [2009] 1 WLR 1988, para 27, although Lord Simon's requirements are otherwise cumulative, I would accept that business necessity and obviousness, his second and third requirements, can be alternatives in the sense that only one of them needs to be satisfied, although I suspect that in practice it would be a rare case where only one of those two requirements would be satisfied. Fifthly, if one approaches the issue by reference to the officious bystander, it is "vital to formulate the question to be posed by [him] with the utmost care", to quote from *Lewison, The Interpretation of Contracts* 5th ed (2011), para 6.09. Sixthly, necessity for business efficacy involves a value judgment. It is rightly common ground on this appeal that the test is not one of "absolute necessity", not least because the necessity is judged by reference to business efficacy. It may well be that a more helpful way of putting Lord Simon's second requirement is, as suggested by Lord Sumption in argument, that a term can only be implied if, without the term, the contract would lack commercial or practical coherence.

22. Before leaving this issue of general principle, it is appropriate to refer a little further to *Belize Telecom*, where Lord Hoffmann suggested that the process of implying terms into a contract was part of the exercise of the construction, or interpretation, of the contract. In summary, he said at para 21 that "[t]here is only one question: is that what the instrument, read as a whole against the relevant background, would reasonably be understood to mean?". There are two points to be made about that observation.

23. First, the notion that a term will be implied if a reasonable reader of the contract, knowing all its provisions and the surrounding circumstances, would understand it to be implied is quite acceptable, provided that (i) the reasonable reader is treated as reading the contract at the time it was made and (ii) he would consider the term to be so obvious as to go without saying or to be necessary for business efficacy. (The difference between what the reasonable reader would understand and what the parties, acting reasonably, would agree, appears to me to be a notional distinction without a practical difference.) The first proviso emphasises that the question whether a term is implied is to be judged at the date the contract is made. The second proviso is important because otherwise Lord Hoffmann's formulation may be interpreted as suggesting that reasonableness is a sufficient ground for

implying a term. (For the same reason, it would be wrong to treat Lord Steyn's statement in *Equitable Life Assurance Society v Hyman* [2002] 1 AC 408, 459 that a term will be implied if it is "essential to give effect to the reasonable expectations of the parties" as diluting the test of necessity. That is clear from what Lord Steyn said earlier on the same page, namely that "[t]he legal test for the implication of … a term is … strict necessity", which he described as a "stringent test".)

24. It is necessary to emphasise that there has been no dilution of the requirements which have to be satisfied before a term will be implied, because it is apparent that *Belize Telecom* has been interpreted by both academic lawyers and judges as having changed the law. Examples of academic articles include C Peters, The implication of terms in fact [2009] CLJ 513, P Davies, Recent developments in the Law of Implied Terms [2010] LMCLQ 140, J McCaughran, Implied terms: the journey of the man on the Clapham Omnibus [2011] CLJ 607, and JW Carter and W Courtney, Belize Telecom: a reply to Professor McLauchlan [2015] LMCLQ 245). And in *Foo Jong Peng v Phua Kiah Mai* [2012] 4 SLR 1267, paras 34-36, the Singapore Court of Appeal refused to follow the reasoning in *Belize* at least in so far as "it suggest[ed] that the traditional 'business efficacy' and 'officious bystander' tests are not central to the implication of terms" (reasoning which was followed in *Sembcorp Marine Ltd v PPL Holdings Pte Ltd* [2013] SGCA 43). The Singapore Court of Appeal were in my view right to hold that the law governing the circumstances in which a term will be implied into a contract remains unchanged following *Belize Telecom.*

25. The second point to be made about what was said in *Belize Telecom* concerns the suggestion that the process of implying a term is part of the exercise of interpretation. Although some support may arguably be found for such a view in *Trollope* at p 609, the first clear expression of that view to which we were referred was in *Banque Bruxelles Lambert SA v Eagle Star Insurance Co Ltd* [1997] AC 191, 212, where Lord Hoffmann suggested that the issue of whether to imply a term into a contract was "one of construction of the agreement as a whole in its commercial setting". Lord Steyn quoted this passage with approval in *Equitable Life* at p 459, and, as just mentioned, Lord Hoffmann took this proposition further in *Belize Telecom*, paras 17-27. Thus, at para 18, he said that "the implication of the term is not an addition to the instrument. It only spells out what the instrument means"; and at para 23, he referred to "The danger … in detaching the phrase 'necessary to give business efficacy' from the basic process of construction". Whether or not one agrees with that approach as a matter of principle must depend on what precisely one understands by the word "construction".

26. I accept that both (i) construing the words which the parties have used in their contract and (ii) implying terms into the contract, involve determining the scope and meaning of the contract. However, Lord Hoffmann's analysis in *Belize Telecom* could obscure the fact that construing the words used

and implying additional words are different processes governed by different rules.

27. Of course, it is fair to say that the factors to be taken into account on an issue of construction, namely the words used in the contract, the surrounding circumstances known to both parties at the time of the contract, commercial common sense, and the reasonable reader or reasonable parties, are also taken into account on an issue of implication. However, that does not mean that the exercise of implication should be properly classified as part of the exercise of interpretation, let alone that it should be carried out at the same time as interpretation. When one is implying a term or a phrase, one is not construing words, as the words to be implied are ex hypothesi not there to be construed; and to speak of construing the contract as a whole, including the implied terms, is not helpful, not least because it begs the question as to what construction actually means in this context.

28. In most, possibly all, disputes about whether a term should be implied into a contract, it is only after the process of construing the express words is complete that the issue of an implied term falls to be considered. Until one has decided what the parties have expressly agreed, it is difficult to see how one can set about deciding whether a term should be implied and if so what term. This appeal is just such a case. Further, given that it is a cardinal rule that no term can be implied into a contract if it contradicts an express term, it would seem logically to follow that, until the express terms of a contract have been construed, it is, at least normally, not sensibly possible to decide whether a further term should be implied. Having said that, I accept Lord Carnwath's point in para 71 to the extent that in some cases it could conceivably be appropriate to reconsider the interpretation of the express terms of a contract once one has decided whether to imply a term, but, even if that is right, it does not alter the fact that the express terms of a contract must be interpreted before one can consider any question of implication.

29. In any event, the process of implication involves a rather different exercise from that of construction. As Sir Thomas Bingham trenchantly explained in *Philips* at p 481:

> "The courts' usual role in contractual interpretation is, by resolving ambiguities or reconciling apparent inconsistencies, to attribute the true meaning to the language in which the parties themselves have expressed their contract. The implication of contract terms involves a different and altogether more ambitious undertaking: the interpolation of terms to deal with matters for which, ex hypothesi, the parties themselves have made no provision. It is because the implication of terms is so potentially intrusive that the law imposes strict constraints on the exercise of this extraordinary power."

30. It is of some interest to see how implication was dealt with in the recent case in this court of *Aberdeen City Council v Stewart Milne Group Ltd*

2012 SLT 205. At para 20, Lord Hope described the implication of a term into the contract in that case as "the product of the way I would interpret this contract". And at para 33, Lord Clarke said that the point at issue should be resolved "by holding that such a term should be implied rather than by a process of interpretation". He added that "[t]he result is of course the same".

31. It is true that *Belize Telecom* was a unanimous decision of the Judicial Committee of the Privy Council and that the judgment was given by Lord Hoffmann, whose contributions in so many areas of law have been outstanding. However, it is apparent that Lord Hoffmann's observations in *Belize Telecom*, paras 17–27 are open to more than one interpretation on the two points identified in paras 23–24 and 25–30 above, and that some of those interpretations are wrong in law. In those circumstances, the right course for us to take is to say that those observations should henceforth be treated as a characteristically inspired discussion rather than authoritative guidance on the law of implied terms.'

TERM IMPLIED BY STATUTE

Introductory

5.72 In certain circumstances terms are implied by operation of law into both non-consumer and consumer contracts.

Non-consumer contracts

5.73 In relation to non-consumer contracts[37] under *the Supply of Goods & Services Act 1982* the following terms are implied:

- *Section 13* states: 'In a [relevant contract for the supply of a service] where the supplier is acting in the course of a business, there is an implied term that the supplier will carry out the service with reasonable care and skill'.
- *Section 14* provides that for such a contract if the time for the service to be carried out is not fixed by the contract, left to be fixed in a manner agreed by the contract or determined by the course of dealing between the parties, there is an implied term that the supplier will carry out the service within a reasonable time.
- *Section 15* provides that where the consideration for the service is not determined by the contract, left to be determined in a manner agreed by the contract or determined by the course of dealing between the parties,

37 The *Supply of Goods & Services Act 1982, s 12(1)* provides that: '... a "[relevant contract for the supply of a service]" means ... a contract under which a person ("the supplier") agrees to carry out a service, other than a contract to which *Chapter 4* of Part 1 of the *Consumer Rights Act 2015* applies'. See the 1982 Act at www.legislation.gov.uk.

there is an implied term that the party contracting with the supplier will pay a reasonable charge.

- *Section 16* provides that where a right, duty or liability would arise under a [relevant contract for the supply of a service], it may be negatived or varied by express agreement, or by the course of dealing between the parties, or by such usage as binds both parties to the contract.

Consumer Rights Act 2015: consumers

5.74 The *CRA 2015* controls unfair terms in a 'consumer contract', which is a contract between a 'trader' and 'consumer'; and the effect of the legislation is to deem that specific minimum terms are incorporated into the contract[38].

5.75 A trader is a person acting for purposes relating to that person's trade, business or profession[39]. Accordingly, a tax professional is subject to the terms of *CRA 2015* when dealing with a consumer.

5.76 A 'consumer' is 'an individual acting for purposes that are wholly or mainly outside that individual's trade, business, craft or profession'[40].

5.77 The protection conferred by the legislation is not extended to an individual who enters into a contract as part of their business (eg advice on structuring the disposal of business assets).

5.78 A trader claiming that an individual was not acting for purposes wholly or mainly outside the individual's trade, business, craft or profession must prove it[41].

5.79 The *CRA 2015* ensures that a trader's liability under the contract cannot be excluded or restricted in respect of supply of services (or sale of goods)[42].

5.80 *Part 1, Ch 4* of *CRA 2015* deals with a 'contract to supply a service', and it provides the following protection for a consumer:

(1) The contract is treated as including a term that the trader must perform the service with reasonable care and skill[43].

---

38 See *CRA 2015* at www.legislation.gov.uk.

39 *CRA 2015, s 2(2).*

40 *CRA 2015, s 2(3).*

41 *CRA 2015, s 2(4).*

42 *Part 1. Ch 4* of *CRA 2015* (*s 54*) does not affect any enactment or rule of law that imposes a stricter duty on the trader. The provisions on services are subject to any other enactment which defines or restricts the rights, duties or liabilities arising in connection with a service of any description.

43 *CRA 2015, s 49.*

(2) Information about the trader or service is binding on the trader[44]. Anything that is said or written to the consumer, by or on behalf of the trader, about the trader or the service, if:

   (a) it is taken into account by the consumer when deciding to enter into the contract[45]; or

   (b) it is taken into account by the consumer when making any decision about the service after entering into the contract.

(3) A reasonable price to be paid for the service (which is a question of fact)[46]. This requirement applies to a contract to supply a service if:

   (a) the consumer has not paid a price or other consideration for the service;

   (b) the contract does not expressly fix a price or other consideration, and does not say how it is to be fixed; and

   (c) anything that is to be treated under *section 50* of *CRA 2015* (see 2 above) as included in the contract does not fix a price or other consideration either.

(4) Service to be performed within a reasonable time (which is a question of fact)[47]. This requirement is imposed if:

   (a) the contract does not expressly fix the time for the service to be performed, and does not say how it is to be fixed; and

   (b) information that is to be treated under *section 50* of *CRA 2015* (see point 2 above) as included in the contract does not fix the time either.

EXCLUSION OF LIABILITY AND LIMITATION OF LIABILITY: UCTA 1977

5.81 The express terms of a contract will usually be enforced by a court unless there is a specific rule of the common law or statute which allows a court to intervene and mitigate what otherwise be regarded as an unfair result for a contracting party.

---

44 *CRA 2015, s 50.*

45 *CRA 2015, s 50(2)* states: 'Anything taken into account by the consumer as mentioned in subsection (1)(a) or (b) is subject to—

(a) anything that qualified it and was said or written to the consumer by the trader on the same occasion, and

(b) any change to it that has been expressly agreed between the consumer and the trader (before entering into the contract or later).'

46 *CRA 2015, s 51.*

47 *CRA 2015, s 52.*

5.82 The terms of a contract may seek to specifically exclude liability and/or limit liability arising under the contract. However, such clauses are likely to be interpreted on a restrictive basis against the party seeking to rely on the clause in cases of ambiguity. Under the '*contra proferentem*' principle, where there is ambiguity in a provision then its interpretation will be resolved against the party who put the clause forward and who relies upon it. In *Nobahar-Cookson v Hut Group Ltd* [2016] EWCA Civ 128 Briggs LJ (as he then was) stated as follows at [14]:

> '... and the contra proferentem rule in its classic form was by no means limited to, or even mainly about, exclusion clauses. It was a rule designed to resolve ambiguities against the party who prepared the document in which the clause appeared, or prepared the particular clause, or against the person for whose benefit the clause operates: see *Lewison*, (op. cit.) [then *The Interpretation of Contracts* (5th ed., 2011)] at paragraph 7.08(b) at page 391 and the admirable historical introduction which precedes it.'

5.83 If the exclusion clause is incorporated into the contract, the next issue will be whether the term applies to actually exclude liability for the events which have occurred.

5.84 Under the *Unfair Contract Terms Act 1977* (*UCTA 1977*) (which now applies only to non-consumer contracts) various categories of exclusion clauses are rendered ineffective[48].

5.85 In relation to consumer contracts, protection is provided on a more extensive basis by the *CRA 2015* (see **5.99**). *UCTA 1977* is relevant to the obligations of accountants, tax advisers, lawyers and generally anyone carrying on a business activity. Where *UCTA 1977* applies to render ineffective the exclusion of liability for negligence or liability arising under a contract then *UCTA 1977* will also apply as follows (*s 13(1)*):

> '(1) To the extent that this Part of this Act prevents the exclusion or restriction of any liability it also prevents—
>
> (a) making the liability or its enforcement subject to restrictive or onerous conditions;
>
> (b) excluding or restricting any right or remedy in respect of the liability, or subjecting a person to any prejudice in consequence of his pursuing any such right or remedy;
>
> (c) excluding or restricting rules of evidence or procedure;
>
> and (to that extent) sections 2, 6 and 7 also prevent excluding or restricting liability by reference to terms and notices which exclude or restrict the relevant obligation or duty.

48 See *UCTA 1977* at www.legislation.gov.uk.

(2) But an agreement in writing to submit present or future differences to arbitration is not to be treated under this Part of this Act as excluding or restricting any liability.'

5.86 The net effect of *section 13(2)* of *UCTA 1977* is that if the parties agree to submit a dispute to arbitration it is not treated as excluding or restricting liability.

5.87 However, if the contract stipulates that a complaint must be made within a specified time then it will operate as a restriction (*s 13(1)(a)*).

5.88 Further, if the contract prevents the client from withholding part of the fees in respect of services supplied then that will be a restriction (*s 13(1)(b)*).

Business liabilities

5.89 *Section 1(3)* of *UTCA 1977* states that it applies to a 'business liability':

> 'In the case of both contract and tort, sections 2 to 7 apply (except where the contrary is stated in section 6(4)) only to business liability, that is liability for breach of obligations or duties arising—
>
> (a) from things done or to be done by a person in the course of a business (whether his own business or another's); or
>
> (b) from the occupation of premises used for business purposes of the occupier;
>
> and references to liability are to be read accordingly …'

Liability for negligence

5.90 Under *UCTA 1977*, a contract cannot exclude or restrict liability for death or personal injury resulting from negligence[49].

5.91 Further, an exclusion clause in the case of other loss or damage cannot exclude or restrict liability for negligence except in so far as the term or notice satisfies the requirement of reasonableness[50]. See **5.95** for a discussion on 'reasonableness'.

5.92 The legislation specifically provides that where a contract term or notice purports to exclude or restrict liability for negligence a person's agreement to or awareness of it is not of itself to be taken as indicating that person's voluntary acceptance of any risk[51].

49 *UCTA 1977, s 2(1).*
50 *UCTA 1977, s 2(2).*
51 *UCTA 1977, s 2(3).*

Liability arising under contract

5.93 If a person is dealing on another person's written standard terms of business, then *UCTA 1977* applies to ensure that the standard terms cannot exclude or restrict liability unless the term satisfies the requirement of reasonableness.

5.94 *Section 3* of *UCTA 1977* states:

'(1) This section applies as between contracting parties where one of them deals … on the other's written standard terms of business.

(2) As against that party, the other cannot by reference to any contract term—

(a) when himself in breach of contract, exclude or restrict any liability of his in respect of the breach; or

(b) claim to be entitled—

(i) to render a contractual performance substantially different from that which was reasonably expected of him, or

(ii) in respect of the whole or any part of his contractual obligation, to render no performance at all,

except in so far as (in any of the cases mentioned above in this subsection) the contract term satisfies the requirement of reasonableness.'

Reasonableness

5.95 As discussed above an exclusion or limitation clause will be rendered ineffective under *UCTA 1977* to the extent the clause fails the test of 'reasonableness'. In this regard, *section 11* states:

'(1) In relation to a contract term, the requirement of reasonableness for the purposes of this Part of this Act … is that the term shall have been a fair and reasonable one to be included having regard to the circumstances which were, or ought reasonably to have been, known to or in the contemplation of the parties when the contract was made.

…

(3) In relation to a notice (not being a notice having contractual effect), the requirement of reasonableness under this Act is that it should be fair and reasonable to allow reliance on it, having regard to all the circumstances obtaining when the liability arose or (but for the notice) would have arisen.

(4) Where by reference to a contract term or notice a person seeks to restrict liability to a specified sum of money, and the question arises

(under this or any other Act) whether the term or notice satisfies the requirement of reasonableness, regard shall be had in particular … to—

(a) the resources which he could expect to be available to him for the purpose of meeting the liability should it arise; and

(b) how far it was open to him to cover himself by insurance.

(5) It is for those claiming that a contract term or notice satisfies the requirement of reasonableness to show that it does.'

5.96 Particular points to note in respect of the 'reasonableness' test is that reasonableness should be assessed at the time the contract is entered into by the parties. A court is entitled to take into account all matters which will be relevant to determining the issue.

5.97 *UCTA 1977* contains guidelines in *Schedule 2* which are relevant where there is a sale/hire-purchase of goods and where contracts are entered into under which title to goods pass.

5.98 These guidelines, adapted below to the provision of professional services, provide some helpful guidance to the matters to be taken into account:

- the strength of the bargaining positions of the parties relative to each other, taking into account (among other things) alternative means by which the customer's requirements could have been met;
- whether the customer received an inducement to agree to the term, or in accepting it had an opportunity of entering into a similar contract with other persons, but without having to accept a similar term;
- whether the customer knew or ought reasonably to have known of the existence and extent of the term (having regard, among other things, to any custom of the trade and any previous course of dealing between the parties);
- where the term excludes or restricts any relevant liability if some condition is not complied with, whether it was reasonable at the time of the contract to expect that compliance with that condition would be practicable;
- whether the services were designed or adapted to the special order of the customer.

EXCLUSION OF LIABILITY, LIMITATION OF LIABILITY, UNFAIR TERMS: CRA 2015

5.99 The *CRA 2015* controls unfair terms in a 'consumer contract', which is a contract between a 'trader' and 'consumer'.

5.100 A trader is a person acting for purposes relating to that person's trade, business or profession[52].

5.101 Whereas a 'consumer' is 'an individual acting for purposes that are wholly or mainly outside that individual's trade, business, craft or profession'[53].

5.102 The protection conferred by the legislation is not extended to an individual who enters into a contract as part of their business.

5.103 A trader claiming that an individual was not acting for purposes wholly or mainly outside the individual's trade, business, craft or profession must prove it[54].

5.104 A trader must ensure that a written term of a consumer contract, or a consumer notice in writing, is transparent[55].

5.105 The *CRA 2015* ensures that a trader's liability cannot be excluded or restricted in respect of the sale of goods and services[56].

5.106 *Part 1, Ch 4* of *CRA 2015* deals with a 'contract to supply a service'.

5.107 *Section 57* of *CRA 2015* provides that a term of a contract to supply services is not binding on the consumer to the extent that it would exclude:

(a) the trader's liability arising under *section 49* (service to be performed with reasonable care and skill);

(b) the trader's liability arising under *section 50* (information about trader or service to be binding).

5.108 Further, a term of a contract to supply services is not binding on the consumer to the extent that it would restrict the trader's liability arising under any of *sections 49* and *50* and, where they apply, *sections 51* and *52* (reasonable price and reasonable time), if it would prevent the consumer in an appropriate case from recovering the price paid or the value of any other consideration.

5.109 A term of a contract to supply services is not binding on the consumer to the extent that it would:

- exclude or restrict a right or remedy in respect of a liability under any of *sections 49–52*;
- make such a right or remedy or its enforcement subject to a restrictive or onerous condition;

52 *CRA 2015, s 2(2).*

53 *CRA 2015, s 2(3).*

54 *CRA 2015, s 2(4).*

55 *CRA 2015, s 68.*

56 *Part 4* of *CRA 2015* (*s 54*) does not affect any enactment or rule of law that imposes a stricter duty on the trader. The provisions on services are subject to any other enactment which defines or restricts the rights, duties or liabilities arising in connection with a service of any description.

- allow a trader to put a person at a disadvantage as a result of pursuing such a right or remedy; or
- exclude or restrict rules of evidence or procedure.

Negligence

5.110 A trader cannot by a term of a consumer contract or by a consumer notice exclude or restrict liability for death or personal injury resulting from negligence[57]. In this regard, 'negligence' means the breach of, inter alia[58]:

> '(a) any obligation to take reasonable care or exercise reasonable skill in the performance of a contract where the obligation arises from an express or implied term of the contract,
>
> (b) a common law duty to take reasonable care or exercise reasonable skill …'

Unfair terms

5.111 The *CRA 2015* also renders invalid a term of a consumer contract which is an 'unfair term' and an 'unfair consumer notice'[59].

5.112 The legislation (*s 62*) states what is 'unfair' as follows:

> '(4) A term is unfair if, contrary to the requirement of good faith, it causes a significant imbalance in the parties' rights and obligations under the contract to the detriment of the consumer.
>
> (5) Whether a term is fair is to be determined—
>
> (a) taking into account the nature of the subject matter of the contract, and
>
> (b) by reference to all the circumstances existing when the term was agreed and to all of the other terms of the contract or of any other contract on which it depends.
>
> (6) A notice is unfair if, contrary to the requirement of good faith, it causes a significant imbalance in the parties' rights and obligations to the detriment of the consumer.
>
> (7) Whether a notice is fair is to be determined—
>
> (a) taking into account the nature of the subject matter of the notice, and

57 *CRA 2015, s 65(1)*.

58 *CRA 2015, s 65(4)*.

59 *CRA 2015, s 62(1), (2)*. *Section 62(3)* states the consumer may rely on the term or notice if the consumer chooses to do so.

(b) by reference to all the circumstances existing when the rights or obligations to which it relates arose and to the terms of any contract on which it depends.'

5.113 It is important to appreciate that the test of 'fairness' applies not only to standard term contracts but also applies to contracts where the terms have been directly negotiated with the consumer.

Fairness

5.114 The test of fairness in *CRA 2015* has been adopted from the predecessor Regulations[60] and EU Directive[61] which provided the foundation stone for these consumer rights.

5.115 The *CRA 2015* uses very similar language to the EU Directive.

5.116 The test for fairness is the same as it was under the Regulations and the leading decisions on 'fairness'[62].

5.117 In *Cavendish Square Holding BV v Talal El Makdessi*, a decision of the Supreme Court, Lord Neuberger stated:

> '105. … The Regulations give effect to Council Directive 93/13/EEC on unfair terms in consumer contracts, and these rather opaque provisions are lifted word for word from articles 3 and 4 of the Directive. The effect of the Regulations was considered by the House of Lords in *Director General of Fair Trading v First National Bank plc* [2001] UKHL 52] [2002] 1 AC 481. But it is sufficient now to refer to *Aziz v Caixa d'Estalvis de Catalunya, Tarragona i Manresa* (Case C-415/11) [2013] 3 CMLR 89, which is the leading case on the topic in the Court of Justice of the European Union. *Aziz* was a reference from a Spanish court seeking guidance on the criteria for determining the fairness of three provisions in a loan agreement. They provided for (i) the acceleration of the repayment schedule in the event of the borrower's default, (ii) the charging of default interest, and (iii) the unilateral certification by the lender of the amount due for the purpose of legal proceedings. The judgment of the Court of Justice is authority for the following propositions:
>
> (1) The test of "significant imbalance" and "good faith" in article 3 of the Directive (regulation 5(1) of the 1999 Regulations) "merely defines in a general way the factors that render unfair a contractual term that has not been individually negotiated" (para 67). A significant element of judgment is left to the national court, to exercise in the light of the circumstances of each case.

60 *Unfair Terms in Consumer Contracts Regulations 1999.*

61 EC Directive 93/13 on 'Unfair Terms in Consumer Contracts'.

62 These are *Director General of Fair Trading v First National Bank plc* [2001] UKHL 52, *Aziz v Caixa d'Estalvis de Catalunya* [2013] EUECJ C-415/11 and *Cavendish Square Holding BV v Talal El Makdessi* [2015] UKSC 67.

(2) The question whether there is a "significant imbalance in the parties' rights" depends mainly on whether the consumer is being deprived of an advantage which he would enjoy under national law in the absence of the contractual provision (paras 68, 75). In other words, this element of the test is concerned with provisions derogating from the legal position of the consumer under national law.

(3) However, a provision derogating from the legal position of the consumer under national law will not necessarily be treated as unfair. The imbalance must arise "contrary to the requirements of good faith". That will depend on "whether the seller or supplier, dealing fairly and equitably with the consumer, could reasonably assume that the consumer would have agreed to such a term in individual contract negotiations" (para 69).

(4) …'

In the *First National Bank* case, Lord Bingham (at para 17) stated:

> 'The requirement of good faith in this context is one of fair and open dealing. Openness requires that the terms should be expressed fully, clearly and legibly, containing no concealed pitfalls or traps. Appropriate prominence should be given to terms which might operate disadvantageously to the customer. Fair dealing requires that a supplier should not, whether deliberately or unconsciously, take advantage of the consumer's necessity, indigence, lack of experience, unfamiliarity with the subject matter of the contract, weak bargaining position or any other factor listed in or analogous to those listed in Schedule 2 to the Regulations. Good faith in this context is not an artificial or technical concept; nor, since Lord Mansfield was its champion, is it a concept wholly unfamiliar to British lawyers. It looks to good standards of commercial morality and practice. Regulation 4(1) lays down a composite test, covering both the making and the substance of the contract, and must be applied bearing clearly in mind the objective which the Regulations are designed to promote.'

5.118 It should be noted that the *CRA 2015* does not permit a consumer to invoke its protection just because the consumer has made a bad bargain.

Terms of a contract subject to requirement of fairness

5.119 The effect of *CRA 2015* is that almost any term in a consumer contract can be assessed for fairness (eg disputes clause, liquidated damages clause).

5.120 *Section 64* excludes from the test for 'fairness' the following terms of a contract:

'(1) A term of a consumer contract may not be assessed for fairness under section 62 to the extent that—

(a) it specifies the main subject matter of the contract, or

(b) the assessment is of the appropriateness of the price payable under the contract by comparison with the goods, digital content or services supplied under it.

(2) Subsection (1) excludes a term from an assessment under section 62 only if it is transparent and prominent.

(3) A term is transparent for the purposes of this Part if it is expressed in plain and intelligible language and (in the case of a written term) is legible.

(4) A term is prominent for the purposes of this section if it is brought to the consumer's attention in such a way that an average consumer would be aware of the term.

(5) In subsection (4) "average consumer" means a consumer who is reasonably well-informed, observant and circumspect.'

5.121 Where a term of a consumer contract is not binding on the consumer the contract continues, so far as practicable, to have effect in every other respect[63].

Illustrative list of unfair terms

5.122 *CRA 2015* provides an indicative and non-exhaustive list of terms of consumer contracts that may be regarded as unfair[64]:

(1) A term which has the object or effect of excluding or limiting the trader's liability in the event of the death of or personal injury to the consumer resulting from an act or omission of the trader.

(2) A term which has the object or effect of inappropriately excluding or limiting the legal rights of the consumer in relation to the trader or another party in the event of total or partial non-performance or inadequate performance by the trader of any of the contractual obligations, including the option of offsetting a debt owed to the trader against any claim which the consumer may have against the trader.

(3) A term which has the object or effect of making an agreement binding on the consumer in a case where the provision of services by the trader is subject to a condition whose realisation depends on the trader's will alone.

(4) A term which has the object or effect of permitting the trader to retain sums paid by the consumer where the consumer decides not to conclude or perform the contract, without providing for the consumer to receive compensation of an equivalent amount from the trader where the trader is the party cancelling the contract.

---

63 *CRA 2015, s 67.*

64 *CRA 2015, s 63* and *Sch 2, Pt 1.*

(5) A term which has the object or effect of requiring that, where the consumer decides not to conclude or perform the contract, the consumer must pay the trader a disproportionately high sum in compensation or for services which have not been supplied.

(6) A term which has the object or effect of requiring a consumer who fails to fulfil his obligations under the contract to pay a disproportionately high sum in compensation.

(7) A term which has the object or effect of authorising the trader to dissolve the contract on a discretionary basis where the same facility is not granted to the consumer, or permitting the trader to retain the sums paid for services not yet supplied by the trader where it is the trader who dissolves the contract.

(8) A term which has the object or effect of enabling the trader to terminate a contract of indeterminate duration without reasonable notice except where there are serious grounds for doing so.

(9) A term which has the object or effect of automatically extending a contract of fixed duration where the consumer does not indicate otherwise, when the deadline fixed for the consumer to express a desire not to extend the contract is unreasonably early.

(10) A term which has the object or effect of irrevocably binding the consumer to terms with which the consumer has had no real opportunity of becoming acquainted before the conclusion of the contract.

(11) A term which has the object or effect of enabling the trader to alter the terms of the contract unilaterally without a valid reason which is specified in the contract.

(12) A term which has the object or effect of permitting the trader to determine the characteristics of the subject matter of the contract after the consumer has become bound by it.

(13) A term which has the object or effect of enabling the trader to alter unilaterally without a valid reason any characteristics of the goods, digital content or services to be provided.

(14) A term which has the object or effect of giving the trader the discretion to decide the price payable under the contract after the consumer has become bound by it, where no price or method of determining the price is agreed when the consumer becomes bound.

(15) A term which has the object or effect of permitting a trader to increase the price of goods, digital content or services without giving the consumer the right to cancel the contract if the final price is too high in relation to the price agreed when the contract was concluded.

(16) A term which has the object or effect of giving the trader the right to determine whether the goods, digital content or services supplied are in

conformity with the contract, or giving the trader the exclusive right to interpret any term of the contract.

(17) A term which has the object or effect of limiting the trader's obligation to respect commitments undertaken by the trader's agents or making the trader's commitments subject to compliance with a particular formality.

(18) A term which has the object or effect of obliging the consumer to fulfil all of the consumer's obligations where the trader does not perform the trader's obligations.

(19) A term which has the object or effect of allowing the trader to transfer the trader's rights and obligations under the contract, where this may reduce the guarantees for the consumer, without the consumer's agreement.

(20) A term which has the object or effect of excluding or hindering the consumer's right to take legal action or exercise any other legal remedy, in particular by:

- (a) requiring the consumer to take disputes exclusively to arbitration not covered by legal provisions;
- (b) unduly restricting the evidence available to the consumer; or
- (c) imposing on the consumer a burden of proof which, according to the applicable law, should lie with another party to the contract.

THIRD PARTY RIGHTS

5.123 A person who is not party to a contract (ie a third party) is not usually entitled to enforce the terms of the contract, and neither can obligations be imposed on a third party.

5.124 Under *section 1(1)* of the *Contracts (Rights of Third Parties) Act 1999*[65] (which applies to contracts made on or after 11 May 2000), a person who is not a party to the contract may enforce a term of the contract if:

- (a) the contract expressly provides that he may; or
- (b) the term purports to confer a benefit on him.

It should usually be the case that a contract for the provision of professional services will exclude third party rights. The rights of a third party will only ever be relevant if the contract explicitly states that 'X' is entitled to enforce the contract. Under *section1(3)* the third party must be expressly identified in the contract by name, as a member of a class or as answering a particular description but need not be in existence when the contract is entered into. In particular, *section 1(4)* emphasises that *section 1* does not confer a right on

65 See www.legislation.gov.uk.

a third party to enforce a term of a contract otherwise than subject to, and in accordance with, any other relevant terms of the contract.

INTERPRETATION OF CONTRACTS

5.125 A written contract should always be used to govern the relationship between the parties; and in respect of such a contract the court will not allow a party to seek to rely on evidence which operates to amend, vary or contradict the written agreement[66]. In determining the objective meaning of the language used in a contract, it is necessary not only to analyse the words used but also to consider the contract as a whole and, depending on the nature, formality and quality of drafting of the contract, give more or less weight to elements of the wider context in reaching a view as to that objective meaning. Sophisticated or complex agreements drafted by skilled professionals are likely to be interpreted principally by textual analysis unless a provision lacks clarity or is apparently illogical or incoherent[67].

5.126 The correct approach to the interpretation of a contract and the specific clauses was identified by the Upper Tribunal in *Ingenious Games LLP and Others v Revenue and Customs Commissioners* [2019] UKUT 226 (TCC) (26 July 2019).

5.127 In the *Ingenious* case, Falk J stated as to the non-tax legal interpretation of contracts:

> '[79] The basic principles to be applied to the construction of written contracts have been set out in a number of relatively recent Supreme Court judgments, namely *Rainy Sky SA v Kookmin Bank* [2011] UKSC 50, [2012] 1 All ER 1137, [2011] 1 WLR 2900, *Arnold v Britton* [2015] UKSC 36, [2016] 1 All ER 1, [2015] AC 1619, and *Wood v Capita Insurance Services Ltd* [2017] UKSC 24, [2017] 4 All ER 615, [2017] AC 1173 where Lord Neuberger PSC summarised the approach to be taken at [10] to [15]:

66 This is the 'parole evidence rule'. In *Shogun Finance Ltd v Hudson* [2003] UKHL 62 Lord Hobhouse at [49] stated: 'The rule that other evidence may not be adduced to contradict the provisions of a contract contained in a written document is fundamental to the mercantile law of this country; the bargain is the document; the certainty of the contract depends on it. The relevant principle is well summarised in Phipson on Evidence, paragraphs 42-11 and 42-12: "When the parties have deliberately put their agreement into writing, it is conclusively presumed between themselves and their privies that they intend the writing to form a full and final statement of their intentions, and one which should be placed beyond the reach of future controversy, bad faith or treacherous memory." (See also *Bank of Australasia v Palmer* [1897] AC 540, per Lord Morris at p.545.) This rule is one of the great strengths of English commercial law and is one of the main reasons for the international success of English law in preference to laxer systems which do not provide the same certainty.'

67 See *Wood v Capita Insurance Services Ltd* [2017] UKSC 24, per Lord Hodge JSC at [9]–[13] and *National Bank of Kazakhstan v Bank of New York Mellon* [2018] EWCA Civ 1390, per Hamblen LJ at [39]–40].

"[10] The court's task is to ascertain the objective meaning of the language which the parties have chosen to express their agreement. It has long been accepted that this is not a literalist exercise focused solely on a parsing of the wording of the particular clause but that the court must consider the contract as a whole and, depending on the nature, formality and quality of drafting of the contract, give more or less weight to elements of the wider context in reaching its view as to that objective meaning. In *Prenn v Simmonds* [1971] 3 All ER 237 at 239–241, [1971] 1 WLR 1381 at 1383–1385 and in *Reardon Smith Line Ltd v Yngvar Hansen-Tangen* [1976] 3 All ER 570 at 575, [1976] 1 WLR 989 at 997 Lord Wilberforce affirmed the potential relevance to the task of interpreting the parties' contract of the factual background known to the parties at or before the date of the contract, excluding evidence of the prior negotiations. When in his celebrated judgment in *Investors Compensation Scheme Ltd v West Bromwich Building Society* [1998] 1 All ER 98 at 114–115, [1998] 1 WLR 896 at 912–913 Lord Hoffmann reformulated the principles of contractual interpretation, some saw his second principle, which allowed consideration of the whole relevant factual background available to the parties at the time of the contract, as signalling a break with the past. But Lord Bingham in an extra-judicial writing, 'A new thing under the sun? The interpretation of contracts and the ICS decision' (2008) 12 Edin LR 374–390, persuasively demonstrated that the idea of the court putting itself in the shoes of the contracting parties had a long pedigree.

[11] Lord Clarke elegantly summarised the approach to construction in *Rainy Sky* [2012] 1 All ER 1137, [2011] 1 WLR 2900 (at [21]f). In *Arnold* [2016] 1 All ER 1, [2015] AC 1619 all of the judgments confirmed the approach in *Rainy Sky* (Lord Neuberger paras [13]–[14]; Lord Hodge para [76]; and Lord Carnwath para [108]). Interpretation is, as Lord Clarke stated in *Rainy Sky* (para [21]), a unitary exercise; where there are rival meanings, the court can give weight to the implications of rival constructions by reaching a view as to which construction is more consistent with business common sense. But, in striking a balance between the indications given by the language and the implications of the competing constructions the court must consider the quality of drafting of the clause (*Rainy Sky* para [26], citing Mance LJ in *Gan Insurance Co Ltd v Tai Ping Insurance Co Ltd (No 2)* [2001] EWCA Civ 1047, [2001] 2 All ER (Comm) 299, [2002] Lloyd's Rep IR 667 (at [13], [16]); and it must also be alive to the possibility that one side may have agreed to something which with hindsight did not serve his interest: *Arnold* (paras [20], [77]). Similarly, the court must not lose sight of the possibility that a provision may be a negotiated compromise or that the negotiators were not able to agree more precise terms.

[12] This unitary exercise involves an iterative process by which each suggested interpretation is checked against the provisions of the contract and its commercial consequences are investigated: *Arnold* para [77]

> citing *Re Sigma Finance Corp* [2009] UKSC 2, [2010] 1 All ER 571, [2010] BCC 40 (at [12]) per Lord Mance. To my mind once one has read the language in dispute and the relevant parts of the contract that provide its context, it does not matter whether the more detailed analysis commences with the factual background and the implications of rival constructions or a close examination of the relevant language in the contract, so long as the court balances the indications given by each.
>
> [13] Textualism and contextualism are not conflicting paradigms in a battle for exclusive occupation of the field of contractual interpretation. Rather, the lawyer and the judge, when interpreting any contract, can use them as tools to ascertain the objective meaning of the language which the parties have chosen to express their agreement. The extent to which each tool will assist the court in its task will vary according to the circumstances of the particular agreement or agreements. Some agreements may be successfully interpreted principally by textual analysis, for example because of their sophistication and complexity and because they have been negotiated and prepared with the assistance of skilled professionals. The correct interpretation of other contracts may be achieved by a greater emphasis on the factual matrix, for example because of their informality, brevity or the absence of skilled professional assistance. But negotiators of complex formal contracts may often not achieve a logical and coherent text because of, for example, the conflicting aims of the parties, failures of communication, differing drafting practices, or deadlines which require the parties to compromise in order to reach agreement. There may often therefore be provisions in a detailed professionally drawn contract which lack clarity and the lawyer or judge in interpreting such provisions may be particularly helped by considering the factual matrix and the purpose of similar provisions in contracts of the same type. The iterative process, of which Lord Mance spoke in *Re Sigma Finance Corp* (above), assists the lawyer or judge to ascertain the objective meaning of disputed provisions.
>
> [14] On the approach to contractual interpretation, *Rainy Sky* and *Arnold* were saying the same thing.
>
> [15] The recent history of the common law of contractual interpretation is one of continuity rather than change. One of the attractions of English law as a legal system of choice in commercial matters is its stability and continuity, particularly in contractual interpretation."

[80] In *Arnold v Britton* at [15] Lord Neuberger said that when interpreting a written contract, the court is concerned to "identify the intention of the parties by reference to what a reasonable person having all the background knowledge which would have been available to the parties would have understood them to be using the language in the contract to mean" (citing Lord Hoffmann in *Chartbrook Ltd v Persimmon Homes Ltd (Chartbrook Ltd and anor, Pt 20 defendants)* [2009] UKHL 38, [2009] 4 All ER 677,

[2009] AC 1101 (at [14])), by focusing on the meaning of the relevant words, in the documentary, factual and commercial context.

...

[107] We are therefore not persuaded that, as a matter of contractual construction, the FTT was correct in adopting a 'composite agreement' approach without reference to *Ramsay*. In our view, the starting position for the FTT in construing the contracts should have been to consider them separately in accordance with the basic principles set out at [79] and [80] above.

[108] However, where a number of contracts are entered into together, at the very least the existence of the other contracts is part of the factual background known to the parties at or before the date of the contract, as referred to by Lord Neuberger at [10] of *Wood v Capita* (quoted at [79] above) and commonly referred to as the "factual matrix". The existence of the other contracts is therefore a relevant part of the factual matrix when construing any one of them. Furthermore, where the contracts specifically cross-refer or there are other indications that they are intended to operate only as a package, then that fact will be relevant.'

BREACH OF CONTRACT

5.128 All terms of a contract must be performed by the parties to the contract.

5.129 However, the consequences of a failure to perform a particular term of the contract will depend on its classification. This is not always obvious and the terminology is not always used in a consistent way.

5.130 If a party fails to perform a promise under the contract, then it will usually entitle a party to claim financial compensation by way of damages.

5.131 However, the right to terminate a contract is only allowed if there is a breach of a 'condition' or in the case of a 'intermediate' or 'innominate' term where the breach is sufficiently serious.

5.132 The injured party will not be allowed to terminate the contract if he does something unequivocal to affirm the contract (ie intends to keep it on foot)[68].

5.133 If a party is in breach of a 'warranty' then the right is solely for the injured party to claim damages. It is open to the contracting parties to identify

68 See *The Kanchenjunga* [1990] 1 Lloyd's Rep 391, 398, per Lord Goff. Where one party, having two alternative and inconsistent courses of action open to him, acts in a way consistent only with him having chosen one of those courses, he will be held to have elected to abandon the other.

in their written agreement whether a particular term of the contract should be treated as a 'condition'[69].

5.134 The law as to the circumstances in which breach of an innominate, or intermediate, term of a contract will be 'repudiatory', in the sense of entitling the innocent party to elect to terminate the contract, is set out in *Valilas v Januzaj* [2014] EWCA Civ 436 at [59] by Arden LJ, who stated[70]:

> 'The common law adopts open-textured expressions for the principle used to identify the cases in which one contracting party ("the victim") can claim that the actions of the other contracting party justify the termination of the contract. I will use the formulation that asks whether the victim has been deprived of substantially the whole of the benefit of the contract. The expression "going to the root of the contract" conveys the same point: the failure must be compared with the whole of the consideration of the contract and not just a part of it. There are other similar expressions. I do not myself criticise the vagueness of these expressions of the principle since I do not consider that any satisfactory fixed rule could be formulated in this field.'

5.135 In the same case, Floyd LJ, with whose judgment Arden LJ expressed agreement, said at [54]:

> 'Whether a breach or threatened breach does give rise to a right to terminate involves a multi-factorial assessment involving the nature of the contract and the relationship it creates, the nature of the term, the kind and degree of the breach and the consequences of the breach for the injured party: see the passage from the majority decision of the High Court of Australia in *Koompahtoo Local Aboriginal Land Council v Sanpine Pty Ltd* [2007] HCA 61 (2007) 82 AJLR 345 at [54] cited by Lewison LJ in *Telford Homes (Creekside) Ltd v Ampurius Nu Holdings* [2013] EWCA Civ 577 at [50].'

5.136 Whether or not a person can terminate the contract for breach of an intermediate term is a multi-factorial question, which will turn on consideration of these issues:

69 Note that merely calling a clause a 'condition' does not necessarily make it an actual condition giving an injured party the right to terminate the contract: see *Schuler (L) AG v Wickman Machine Tool Sales Ltd* [1974] AC 235, HL. In this case the contract contained clauses which were inconsistent with the use of the term 'condition' for the particular clause. Further, a contractual interpretation which produces an absurd or even unreasonable result is likely to be wrong. If commercial parties intend such an absurd or unreasonable result, it will ordinarily take clear and unambiguous language to achieve that result. In *Wickman Machine* Tools, Lord Reid said at p 251: 'The fact that a particular construction leads to a very unreasonable result must be a relevant consideration. The more unreasonable the result the more unlikely it is that the parties can have intended it, and if they do intend it the more necessary it is that they shall make that intention abundantly clear'.

70 See also *Hongkong Fir Shipping Co Ltd v Kawasaki Kisen Kaisha Ltd* [1962] 2 QB 26 (CA), *Telford Homes (Creekside) Ltd v Ampurius Nu Homes Holdings Ltd* [2013] EWCA Civ 577.

- What benefit was the injured party intended to obtain from performance of the contract?
- What is the effect of the breach on the injured party?
- What financial loss has the breach caused?
- How much of the intended benefit under the contract has the injured party already received?
- Can the injured party be adequately compensated by an award of damages?
- Is the breach likely to be repeated?
- Will the guilty party resume compliance with his obligations?
- Has the breach fundamentally changed the value of future performance of the guilty party's outstanding obligations?

DAMAGES

Compensatory principle

5.137 Where there is a breach of contract the injured party is entitled to damages, which is based on a compensatory principle, so that the innocent party is put in the position it would have been in if the contract had been performed.

5.138 There have been a number of cases in recent times where the compensatory principle has been discussed and the test re-formulated[71].

5.139 In *The Golden Victory* [2007] UKHL12, the issue was whether, in assessing damages for anticipatory breach of a long-term charter party, it was necessary to take account of the fact that, by the time the damages came to be assessed, it was known that if performance of the contract had been continued, the contract would not have run its full term, but would have been lawfully cancelled as a result of the outbreak of the Second Gulf War.

5.140 Lord Scott (in the majority) said (at paras 29–36):

> '29. … The fundamental principle governing the quantum of damages for breach of contract is long established and not in dispute. The damages should compensate the victim of the breach for the loss of his contractual bargain. The principle was succinctly stated by Parke B in *Robinson v Harman* (1848) 1 Exch 850, 855 and remains as valid now as it was then …
>
> If the contract is a contract for performance over a period, whether for the performance of personal services, or for supply of goods, or, as here, a time charter, the assessment of damages for breach must proceed on the

71 See also *Bunge SA v Nidera BV* [2015] UKSC 43.

same principle, namely, the victim of the breach should be placed, so far as damages can do it, in the position he would have been in had the contract been performed.

…

32 … The underlying principle is that the victim of a breach of contract is entitled to damages representing the value of the contractual benefit to which he was entitled but of which he has been deprived. He is entitled to be put in the same position, so far as money can do it, as if the contract had been performed. …

…

The lodestar is that the damages should represent the value of the contractual benefits of which the claimant had been deprived by the breach of contract, no less but also no more.'

5.141 The court held applying the compensatory principle it was necessary to take account of the outbreak of war even though, at the time of the shipowner's acceptance of the charterer's renunciation, the outbreak of war could not have been foreseen as more than a possibility.

5.142 That was because, if the contract had been performed, it would have been terminated prematurely once the war began. Accordingly, the value of the contractual rights of which the shipowner had been deprived by the charterer's repudiation was the hire which would have been earned at the charter rate up until the date of the outbreak of war, but no further. Hire beyond that date would never have been earned.

5.143 As can be seen, the compensatory principle can operate to reduce or extinguish the innocent party's claim for damages.

5.144 Damages are assessed at the date of breach of the contract[72].

5.145 It is possible for the parties to a contract to agree that a specified sum will be paid by a party in the event of a breach of contract.

5.146 Such a sum is regarded as a liquidated damages clause, and enforceable by the injured party.

5.147 However, if the clause is actually a penalty clause then it will not be enforceable[73].

Mitigation

5.148 The compensatory principle is subject to the requirement that the innocent party must act reasonably in order to mitigate or reduce his loss.

72 *SC Confectia SA v Miss Mania Wholesale Ltd* [2014] EWCA Civ 1484, at [17] per Beatson LJ.
73 See *Makdessi v Cavendish Square Holdings BV* [2015] UKSC 67, at [32].

5.149 An injured party cannot recover damages against a repudiator '... which he could reasonably have avoided by taking reasonable commercial steps to mitigate his loss'[74].

5.150 The rationale of the rule is one of simple commercial fairness. The injured party owes no duty to the repudiator, but fairness requires that he should not ordinarily be permitted to rely on his own unreasonable and uncommercial conduct to increase the loss falling on the repudiator[75].

Causation/remoteness of damage

5.151 A person who breaches a contract is liable for such damage resulting from his breach if, at the time of making the contract, a reasonable person in his shoes would have had damage of that kind in mind as not unlikely to result from a breach.

5.152 The classic statement of the rules regarding remoteness of damage in contract is given in *Hadley v Baxendale* [1854] 9 Ex 341 by Alderson B:

> 'Where two parties have made a contract which one of them has broken, the damages which the other party ought to receive in respect of such breach of contract should be such as may fairly and reasonably be considered either as arising naturally, i.e. according to the usual course of things, from such breach of contract itself, such as may reasonably be supposed to have been in the contemplation of both parties, at the time they made the contract as the probable result of the breach of it. Now, if the special circumstances under which the contract was actually made were communicated by the plaintiffs to the defendants, and thus known to both parties, the damages resulting from the breach of such a contract, which they would reasonably contemplate, would be the amount of injury which would ordinarily follow from a breach of contract under these special circumstances so known and communicated ...'

5.153 The first limb of the rule relating to losses identified above are those that arise 'in the usual course of things' and the second limb of the rule in relation to losses recoverable only because they were contemplated by the parties.

5.154 Where a contract is discharged by reason of one party's breach, and that party's unperformed obligation is of a kind for which there exists an available market in which the innocent party could obtain a substitute contract, the innocent party's loss will ordinarily be measured by the extent to which his financial position would be worse off under the substitute contract than under the original contract. Where damages are assessed on this basis it is not necessary for the innocent party actually to enter into a replacement contract at all[76].

---

74 See *The Golden Victory* [2007] UKHL 12 at [10].
75 See *The Golden Victory* [2007] UKHL 12 at [10].
76 See *The Golden Victory* [2007] UKHL 12 at [10].

5.155 In *Wellesly Partners LLP v Withers LLP*[77] the Court of Appeal summarised the law on recoverability of losses in these terms (at 69–71):

> '69. The rule which controls what damage is recoverable in contract has been reviewed and analysed in many decisions since *Hadley v Baxendale* (1854) 9 E. 341. The rule was restated by the Court of Appeal in *Victoria Laundry*, re-examined by the House of Lords in *The Heron II* [1969] 1 AC 350 and most recently considered by the House in *The Achilleas* [[2008] UKHL 48]. It remains the basic rule that a contract breaker is liable for damage resulting from his breach if, at the time of making the contract, a reasonable person in his shoes would have had damage of that kind in mind as not unlikely to result from a breach. The principle is founded on the notion that the parties, in the absence of special provision in the contract, would normally expect a contract breaker to be assuming responsibility for damage which would reasonably be contemplated to result from a breach. *The Achilleas* shows that there may be cases where, based on the individual circumstances surrounding the making of the contract, this assumed expectation is not well founded. Thus, in that case, charterers of a ship were not liable for all the consequences of a late redelivery of the vessel, which had forced the owners to renegotiate a more favourable rate for a follow-on charter. The commercial pressure to renegotiate had arisen because of unusually and highly volatile market rates. According to Lord Hoffmann (see paragraph 23), with whom Lord Hope agreed, departure from the ordinary test was justified because the loss claimed would have been completely unquantifiable at the date of the contract and because the general understanding of the market was that the claimed loss was not recoverable. The charterer could not reasonably be taken to have assumed responsibility for the particular loss claimed. Lord Hoffman recognised that the mere fact that losses were unforeseeably large did not exclude recovery if loss of that type would fall within one or other of the rules in *Hadley v Baxendale* (see paragraph 21). Nevertheless there was also what he called an "exclusive principle" which meant that there could be some foreseeable losses for which the contract breaker would not be liable because they were not the kind or type of loss for which he can be treated as having assumed responsibility (*ibid*). Whether a type of loss was different is determined by asking whether it reflects what would reasonably have been regarded as significant for the purpose of the risk being undertaken (paragraph 22). Lord Hoffmann did, however, point out that:
>
> > "... cases of departure from the ordinary foreseeability rule based on individual circumstances will be unusual, but limitations on the extent of liability in particular types of contract arising out of general expectations in certain markets, such as banking and shipping are likely to be more common."
>
> 70. Lord Rodger, with whom Lady Hale agreed, felt able to bring the case within the traditional remoteness rule, holding that the loss in

77 [2015] EWCA Civ 1146, [2016] Ch 529.

question stemmed from an unusual occurrence of which the charterers were unaware and could not have been foreseen as being likely to arise out of the delay in question. He felt it unnecessary to deal with questions of assumption of responsibility in those circumstances (see paragraphs 60 and 63).

71. The speech of Lord Walker contains passages which appear to approve the "assumption of responsibility" approach of Lord Hoffman and Lord Hope: see for example his approval of the proposition that foreseeability itself is not a satisfactory test at paragraph 79. At paragraph 87, however, he allies himself in addition with the reasoning of Lord Rodger. I have not found it necessary to delve further into the question of whether this means that the true ratio of the decision is that given by Lord Hoffmann or Lord Rodger, or whether there are two inconsistent ratios.'

Contributory negligence

5.156 If a person is in breach of a contractual duty of care, which would also be liable under the laws of negligence, then the amount of the damages will be reduced to reflect any contributory negligence by the claimant[78].

5.157 In *Forsikringsaktieselskapet Vesta v Butcher* [1989] AC 852, 860-867, 875, 879, the Court of Appeal adopted the three categories of breach described by Hobhouse J, as he then was, in the first instance judgment ([1986] 2 All ER 488, 508):

'(1) Where the defendant's liability arises from some contractual provision which does not depend on negligence on the part of the defendant.

(2) Where the defendant's liability arises from a contractual obligation which is expressed in terms of taking care (or its equivalent) but does not correspond to a common law duty to take care which would exist in the given case independently of contract.

(3) Where the defendant's liability in contract is the same as his liability in the tort of negligence independently of the existence of any contract.'

5.158 For the first category, the defendant cannot utilise the defence of contributory negligence.

5.159 In respect of the second, it may only avail itself of the defence if there is a *Hedley Byrne*-type relationship between the parties.

5.160 If the third category exists, the defence of contributory negligence is conceptually available to a defendant as long as it is made out on the facts.

The nature of this defence is discussed further in **Chapter 6**.

78 *Forsikringsaktieselskapet Vesta v Butcher* [1989] AC 852.

ENFORCEMENT OF A CONSUMER CONTRACT: CRA 2015

5.161 If the contract is governed by *CRA 2015* then the consumer not only has the rights provided for under general contract law (eg damages) but by virtue of statute the following further rights are conferred[79]:

- If the service does not conform to the contract, the consumer's rights are: (a) the right to require repeat performance; (b) the right to a price reduction[80].
- If the trader is in breach of a term that requires to be treated as included in the contract but that does not relate to the service, the consumer has the right to a price reduction[81].
- If the trader is in breach of what the contract requires in respect of performance within a reasonable time, the consumer has the right to a price reduction[82].

Right to repeat performance

5.162 The right to require repeat performance is a right to require the trader to perform the service again, to the extent necessary to complete its performance in conformity with the contract[83]. If the consumer requires such repeat performance, the trader must provide it within a reasonable time and without significant inconvenience to the consumer (and the trader must bear any necessary costs incurred in doing so)[84]. But the consumer cannot demand repeat performance if completing performance of the service in conformity with the contract is impossible[85].

Right to price reduction

5.163 The right to a price reduction is the right to require the trader to reduce the price (including up to the full amount) to the consumer by an appropriate amount (including the right to receive a refund for anything already paid above the reduced amount)[86]. A consumer who has the right to require repeat performance is only entitled to a price reduction in one of these situations[87]:

(a) because the consumer cannot require repeat performance; or

---

79 *CRA 2015, s 54(6).*
80 *CRA 2015, s 54(3).*
81 *CRA 2015, s 54(4).*
82 *CRA 2015, s 54(5).*
83 *CRA 2015, s 55(1).*
84 *CRA 2015, s 55(2).*
85 *CRA 2015, s 55(3).*
86 *CRA 2015, s 56(1), (2).*
87 *CRA 2015, s 56(3).*

(b) the consumer has required repeat performance, but the trader is in breach of the requirement to do it within a reasonable time and without significant inconvenience to the consumer.

A refund must be given without undue delay, and in any event within 14 days from when the trader agrees that the consumer is entitled to a refund[88].

LIMITATION PERIOD

5.164 A claim for breach of contract must be issued within six years[89]. This is because the cause of action accrues on the date of the breach of contract, and the limitation period runs from this date.

5.165 In *Coburn v Colledge* [1897] 1 QB 702, the Court of Appeal found that a solicitor's cause of action accrues as soon as the work for which payment is sought has been completed. However, for solicitors it is not possible to effectively continue proceedings for payment on a bill until after the bill has been assessed. *Section 70* of the *Solicitors Act 1974* provides that:

> '(1) Where before the expiration of one month from the delivery of a solicitor's bill an application is made by the party chargeable with the bill, the High Court shall, without requiring any sum to be paid into court, order that the bill be assessed and that no action be commenced on the bill until the assessment is completed.
>
> (2) Where no such application is made before the expiration of the period mentioned in subsection (1), then, on an application being made by the solicitor or, subject to subsections (3) and (4), by the party chargeable with the bill, the court may on such terms, if any, as it thinks fit (not being terms as to the costs of the assessment), order—
>
> (a) that the bill be assessed; and
>
> (b) that no action be commenced on the bill, and that any action already commenced be stayed, until the assessment is completed.'

5.166 In contrast, while a claim for negligence (in tort) must be brought within six years from the date on which the damage/loss is suffered; however, such a claim may be made in respect of latent damage in circumstances where the claimant does not have knowledge of all material facts within the six-year period[90]. This is discussed in **Chapter 6**.

88 *CRA 2015, s* 56(4).
89 *Limitation Act 1980, s 5.*
90 *Limitation Act 1980, s 14A.*

Chapter 6

Negligence and the tax professional

SIGNPOSTS

- The tax professional owes a duty of care in tort law to clients and to some third parties (not to provide negligent advice) (see **6.30–6.51**).
- The tax professional must provide services to the standard of competence expected of a tax practitioner (which includes giving accurate and correct advice, having up-to-date knowledge, appraising a client of relevant risks, adhering to professional standards in the giving of advice –see **Chapter 3** (PCRT) (see **6.15–6.29**).
- Damages for negligence seek to put the injured party (the client or possibly a third party) back in the position that party would have been in if the negligent advice had not been given; however, damages may be awarded for loss of chance which can be costly (see **6.75–6.90**).
- Liability can be limited under the terms of a contract of engagement (see **6.70–6.74**).
- Claims are time limited to six years unless time is extended under the *Latent Damage Act 1986* to a further three years from discovering a loss, or from the date when the claimant should reasonably have known of his or her loss (see **6.106–6.111**).

INTRODUCTORY – TORT IN THE CONTEXT OF THE REGULATION OF TAX PROFESSIONALS

6.1 Tort law is important in the context of the regulation of tax professionals. It is one of the indirect ways in which tax professionals are regulated (see **2.28** to **2.32**).

6.2 Tort law imposes civil liability on a tax professional who is in breach of it. Tort law seeks to put the injured party, known as the claimant, in the position the claimant would have been in had there been no breach. This can be expensive.

6.3 Such claims tend to come from third parties[1] rather than from the client. Clients will usually claim under the contract with the tax professional which seeks to put the claimant in the position the claimant would have been in had the contract been performed properly. However, a claim in tort can be beneficial where a claim in contract would otherwise be time barred under the *Limitation Act 1980* (see **6.106** et seq).

6.4 Such liability or, more accurately, the possibility of it, has an impact on the behaviour of tax professionals as they do not want to incur the liability and its cost or reputational risk (any claim will inevitably increase the cost of professional indemnity insurance).

6.5 The professional bodies require the tax professional to carry professional indemnity insurance to cover such liability. It is important to always check that an adviser has insurance cover.

6.6 Because claims mainly come from third parties it can be difficult to protect against claims through contractual terms as almost by definition there will be no contract.

The *Consumer Rights Act 2015* and the *Provision of Services Regulations 2009, SI 2009/2999* must be borne in mind. These are discussed in **Chapter 5** at **5.26** and **5.74** et seq.

6.7 The main tortious liability that arises for tax professionals is for negligent advice, which is the main focus of this chapter. The Law Society has issued specific guidance for solicitors advising on tax (24 August 2020) (see www.lawsociety.org.uk/topics/tax/guidance-for-solicitors-advising-on-tax).

INTRODUCTION TO NEGLIGENCE

6.8 The law of negligence is an area of law which needs to be considered on an active basis by any professional adviser.

6.9 An understanding of the law of negligence will hopefully assist the adviser in never being the subject of a claim for loss arising from their advice (or if a claim is made, then the adviser is in a position to defend against the allegations).

6.10 Unfortunately, for some practitioners there will be errors in the advice (whether through innocent or negligent error) provided to a client, and on the basis of that advice the client incurs an economic loss (eg a tax liability, interest and penalties). In these circumstances there will be an allegation that the advice was negligent and that the adviser is liable for the loss.

1 See, eg *White v Jones* [1995] 2 AC 207 where the House of Lords allowed recovery by a disappointed beneficiary under a will of compensation for a lost legacy which the solicitor had been instructed by the testator to prepare. There was no direct contractual nexus between the claimant and the solicitor.

6.11 In any negligence claim the relevant question is whether a reasonably competent specialist tax adviser (whether lawyer, ICAEW, CTA, TEP, etc) at the time in question, with particular expertise in the relevant area of tax, applying proper skill and care, could have competently advised as the adviser did regarding the particular planning or other tax issue, eg the availability of entrepreneurs' relief or substantial shareholding relief. If the answer to that question is 'yes', there is no negligence just because other reasonably competent tax professionals of equivalent expertise would have taken a different view or advised in different terms. In other words, was the advice within the spectrum of advice that a reasonably competent tax professional could have properly given?

6.12 The rest of this chapter explains the requirements for a negligence claim in respect of professional advisers. It does so by reference to:

- duty of care;
- standard of the duty of care;
- causation;
- defences;
- damages;
- limitation of liability.

6.13 This chapter explains the relevant laws of England. The laws of Wales, Scotland and Northern Ireland are outside the scope of this book.

6.14 **Chapter 2** explains the law of negligence which will be relevant if a claim is made for services that do not meet the requisite professional standard (see **2.29**). The requisite rules as to professional standards will be considered next followed by the law of negligence.

PROFESSIONAL STANDARDS

6.15 Any person who provides professional services is expected to provide their services to the level of competence required by a professional adviser. **Chapter 3** provides a detailed review of the standards imposed by professional bodies in the context of the PCRT.

In this regard, the following expectations are established by the professional bodies:

Accountants

6.16 The Institute of Chartered Accountants of England and Wales (ICAEW): The ICAEW's Code of Ethics[2] (the 'Code') at Part 1 states:

2 1 January 2020: available at www.icaew.com/technical/ethics/icaew-code-of-ethics/icaew-code-of-ethics.

'SUBSECTION 113 – PROFESSIONAL COMPETENCE AND DUE CARE

R113.1 A professional accountant shall comply with the principle of professional competence and due care, which requires an accountant to:

(a) Attain and maintain professional knowledge and skill at the level required to ensure that a client or employing organisation receives competent professional service, based on current technical and professional standards and relevant legislation; and

(b) Act diligently and in accordance with applicable technical and professional standards.

113.1 A1 Serving clients and employing organisations with professional competence requires the exercise of sound judgment in applying professional knowledge and skill when undertaking professional activities.

113.1 A2 Maintaining professional competence requires a continuing awareness and an understanding of relevant technical, professional and business developments. Continuing professional development enables a professional accountant to develop and maintain the capabilities to perform competently within the professional environment

113.1 A3 Diligence encompasses the responsibility to act in accordance with the requirements of an assignment, carefully, thoroughly and on a timely basis.

R113.2 In complying with the principle of professional competence and due care, a professional accountant shall take reasonable steps to ensure that those working in a professional capacity under the accountant's authority have appropriate training and supervision.

R113.3 Where appropriate, a professional accountant shall make clients, the employing organisation, or other users of the accountant's professional services or activities, aware of the limitations inherent in the services or activities.'

Tax advisers

6.17 The Chartered Institute of Taxation (CIOT) / Association of Taxation Technicians (ATT): The *Professional Rules and Practice Guidelines* (effective from 9 November 2018) states:

'1.6 A member owes a duty to their clients (including those clients for whom they act on a reduced fee or no fee basis) to act with reasonable care and skill, honesty, integrity, impartiality and professionalism. These obligations are also owed to a member's employers, employees, partners, co-directors and generally.

...

5.1 Duty of care

5.1.1 A member has a duty of care to their client which is recognised in law. A member must exercise reasonable skill and care when acting for a client. An engagement letter or other correspondence with the client may limit or define a member's duty of care.

...

5.6 Consultation and second opinions

5.6.1 A member is encouraged to consult with fellow professionals when advising clients, where appropriate, such as where they are giving significant opinion/advice, to ensure that relevant skill and judgement is applied. This may be obtained by requesting an independent view from a colleague, or by instructing another member or tax counsel. In addition, in any case where the risks for a member (assessed in terms of professional reputation or financial exposure of their practice) of giving wrong advice are high, a member should consider taking a second opinion. It is a matter of judgement for a member whether a second opinion is necessary in any particular situation. If a member relies on a second opinion, evidence of it should be retained on the client file. Client confidentiality rules, especially those concerning consent, must be taken into account. A significant opinion/advice is one in respect of which either:

- The amount of tax at stake, or potentially at stake, in relation to the matters advised on is significant for a client and there is a real risk that a contrary view to that taken by a member on those matters could be reached; or
- The matters advised on are, for some other reason, of sufficient importance to a client to merit obtaining a second opinion.

5.7 Form and content of advice

5.7.1 On deciding on the form of advice provided to a client, a member should exercise professional judgement and should consider such factors as the following:

- The importance of the transaction and amounts involved;
- The specific or general nature of the client's enquiry;
- The time available for development and submission of the advice;
- The technical complications presented;
- The existence of authorities and precedents;
- The tax sophistication of the client;
- The need to seek other professional advice.

5.7.2 Advice should normally be given in writing. If a member gives advice in meetings or by telephone, a member should consider carefully whether to confirm in writing. This will allow a client the chance to correct any mistaken assumptions set out in the note and to have a written record of the advice given.

5.7.3 Unless set out in a separate document (such as terms and conditions or an engagement letter) an advice communication should normally set out:

- The purpose for which the advice is required and the client's objectives;
- The background facts and assumptions on which the advice is based and whether or not the facts have been verified by the adviser;
- The alternatives open to the client;
- The risks associated with the advice;
- Relevant caveats and exclusions.

5.7.4 The advice and associated working papers should be consistent with PCRT and in particular, the standards for tax planning.

5.7.5 When formulating advice, a member should refer to the relevant taxation legislation and the practice of HMRC. Due regard should also be given to case law.

5.7.6 A member should make it clear that the advice given is current and may be affected by subsequent changes in the law. To reduce the risk of misunderstanding, a member may wish to make it clear in the engagement letter that no responsibility is accepted to inform a client automatically that advice previously given, by either a member or a predecessor, has been affected by a change in the law but that they are willing to receive instructions to reconsider such advice[3].'

Solicitors: Solicitors Regulation Authority (SRA)

6.18 The SRA Code of Conduct for Solicitors[4] sets out the principles and code by which solicitors must conduct themselves[5]. The SRA Code deals with service and competence as follows (www.sra.org.uk/solicitors/standards-regulations/code-conduct-solicitors):

---

3 *McMahon v Grant Thornton UK LLP* [2020] CSOH 50.

4 At www.sra.org.uk/solicitors/standards-regulations/code-conduct-solicitors.

5 A solicitor must act: '1. in a way that upholds the constitutional principle of the rule of law, and the proper administration of justice. 2. in a way that upholds public trust and confidence in the solicitors' profession and in legal services provided by authorised persons. 3. with independence. 4. with honesty. 5. with integrity. 6. in a way that encourages equality, diversity and inclusion. 7. in the best interests of each client'. SRA Principles at p 5, 'SRA Standards and Regulations' (updated 20 March 2019).

'3 Service and Competence

3.1 You only act for clients on instructions from the client, or from someone properly authorised to provide instructions on their behalf. If you have reason to suspect that the instructions do not represent your client's wishes, you do not act unless you have satisfied yourself that they do. However, in circumstances where you have legal authority to act notwithstanding that it is not possible to obtain or ascertain the instructions of your client, then you are subject to the overriding obligation to protect your client's best interests.

3.2 You ensure that the service you provide to clients is competent and delivered in a timely manner.

3.3 You maintain your competence to carry out your role and keep your professional knowledge and skills up to date.

3.4 You consider and take account of your client's attributes, needs and circumstances.

3.5 Where you supervise or manage others providing legal services:

(a) you remain accountable for the work carried out through them; and

(b) you effectively supervise work being done for clients.

3.6 You ensure that the individuals you manage are competent to carry out their role, and keep their professional knowledge and skills, as well as understanding of their legal, ethical and regulatory obligations, up to date.'

6.19 The SRA has issued a Warning Notice, 'Tax avoidance – your duties' (21 September 2017, updated 25 November 2019)[6], which applies to:

> 'All those we regulate involved either directly or indirectly advising clients about tax, handling client matters or transactions involving them in the design, implementation, organisation or management of tax affairs, schemes or arrangements.'

6.20 The effect of the notice is to require those regulated by the SRA to adhere to the Professional Conduct in Relation to Taxation (PCRT) (which establishes tax planning standards to be adhered to by professional advisers (see, generally, **Chapter 3** and **6.22** below). The Warning Notice states, among other things:

> **'Professional conduct in relation to taxation**
>
> Accountancy bodies have worked with HMRC to produce a statement of Professional Conduct in Relation to Taxation (PCRT). This is published on the websites of the accountancy bodies (and is liable to change). We

6 Available at www.sra.org.uk/solicitors/guidance/tax-avoidance-duties.

welcome this statement and say that: "These standards reflect our own principles, particularly that solicitors must be honest and act with integrity and uphold the rule of law."

We therefore expect you to be familiar with the PCRT and adhere to its standards.

Where you consider that a scheme is likely to be found to be abusive, you can advise a client to this effect. Where a scheme can reasonably be argued not to be abusive, you can advise a client to this effect, facilitate the scheme where so instructed by a client properly advised as to the risks, and litigate on behalf of a client as to the legality of the scheme where you can do so in a manner consistent with your duty to the Court.

It is for the relevant courts and tribunals to adjudicate on the legality of tax avoidance schemes. However, where schemes are found to be abusive, or where there is no finding but schemes contain indicators of abuse (such as, but not limited to, misleading conduct or the indicators set out in the GAAR or PCRT), and solicitors have facilitated such schemes, whether by providing supportive advice which advocates the use of such schemes, or does not sufficiently highlight the associated risks or otherwise, we will see this, on the face of things, as evidence of breach of the SRA Principles and are likely to investigate. If a solicitor gives advice to the effect that a scheme is likely to be found to be abusive and takes no steps to give effect to such a scheme, it is unlikely that enforcement action would be taken.'

Barristers: Bar Standards Board (BSB)

6.21 The BSB Code of Conduct for Barristers[7] sets out the principles and code by which Barristers must conduct themselves. In this regard, as to service delivery the Code states:

'CD7 You must provide a competent standard of work and service to each client [CD7]'

...

'gC38 'CD7 requires not only that you provide a competent standard of work but also a competent standard of service to your client. Rule rC15 is not exhaustive of what you must do to ensure your compliance with CD2 and CD7. By way of example, a competent standard of work and of service also includes:

.1 treating each client with courtesy and consideration; and

.2 seeking to advise your client, in terms they can understand; and

7 'Part 2: Code of Conduct' of the BSB Handbook (version 4.3), at www.barstandardsboard.org.uk/uploads/assets/f0d114af-9c5a-4be4-9dbffa9f80b1e47f/8c50a665-79ee-4bfa-b36eb5c138798d72/Part-2-Code-of-Conduct18092019092228.pdf.

.3 taking all reasonable steps to avoid incurring unnecessary expense; and

.4 reading your instructions promptly. This may be important if there is a time limit or limitation period. If you fail to read your instructions promptly, it is possible that you will not be aware of the time limit until it is too late.'

Professional Conduct in Relation to Taxation (PCRT)

6.22 The PCRT sets out the principles and standards of behaviour that all members and students must follow in their tax work, where regulated by professional bodies. The PCRT was introduced and is applied by (and adopted by the SRA – see **6.20** above):

- Association of Accounting Technicians (AAT);
- Association of Chartered Certified Accountants (ACCA);
- Association of Taxation Technicians (ATT);
- Chartered Institute of Taxation (CIOT);
- Institute of Chartered Accountants in England and Wales (ICAEW);
- Institute of Chartered Accountants of Scotland (ICAS);
- Society of Trust and Estate Practitioners (STEP).

6.23 The 'Professional Rules and Practice Guidelines' published by CIOT (effective from 9 November 2018) state:

'**2.9 Compliance with Professional Conduct in Relation to Taxation (PCRT)**

2.9.1 A member must conduct their tax work in accordance with PCRT (see the CIOT and ATT websites).'

The same position will be applied across all professional bodies. As to the quality of service the PCRT imposes these requirements[8]:

'2.2 A member must comply with the following Fundamental Principles.

...

- Professional competence and due care

  To maintain professional knowledge and skill at the level required to ensure that a client or employer receives competent professional service based on current developments in practice, legislation and techniques and act diligently and in accordance with applicable technical and professional standards.'

...

8 PCRT, ICAEW at www.icaew.com/-/media/corporate/files/technical/tax/pcrt/pcrt.ashx.

Professional competence and due care

2.8 A member has a professional duty to carry out their work within the scope of their engagement and with the requisite skill and care. A member should take care not to stray beyond the agreed terms of the engagement; if they do exceed the scope, they should agree revised terms with their client and check that their professional indemnity insurance covers the enhanced work.

2.9 A member is free to choose whether or not to act for a client both generally and as regards specific activities. However, where a member chooses to limit or amend the scope of services, they provide to a client they should make this clear in writing.

2.10 When advising a client, a member has a duty to serve that client's interests within the relevant legal and regulatory framework.

2.11 A member must carry out their work with a proper regard for the technical and professional standards expected. In particular, a member must not undertake professional work which they are not competent to perform unless they obtain appropriate assistance from a suitably qualified specialist.

2.12 A member who is giving what they believe to be a significant opinion to a client should consider obtaining a second opinion to support the advice. Where the second opinion is to be obtained externally, due regard must be had to client confidentiality.

2.13 Advice should be given in the context of the commercial and other non-tax objectives and the facts and circumstances of the client.

2.14 On occasions there may be more than one tenable interpretation of the law. Each case should be considered on its own individual facts and circumstances.

…

3 THE STANDARDS FOR TAX PLANNING

3.1 In order to protect the reputation of members, the wider profession, and ensure that public interest concerns are met, the PCRT bodies have developed further Standards that members must observe when advising on UK tax planning. These seek to build on the Fundamental Principles set out above, focussing in particular on integrity, professional competence and behaviour. The Standards are a supplement to, and not a substitute for, the five Fundamental Principles. These standards have been developed in the specific context of the UK including the role of Parliament of making tax law, of HMRC in administering it, and the courts in enforcing it, and the roles of their devolved equivalents.

3.2 The Standards are set out below:

- Client Specific

  Tax planning must be specific to the particular client's facts and circumstances. Clients must be alerted to the wider risks and the implications of any courses of action.

- Lawful

  At all times members must act lawfully and with integrity and expect the same from their clients. Tax planning should be based on a realistic assessment of the facts and on a credible view of the law. Members should draw their clients' attention to where the law is materially uncertain, for example because HMRC is known to take a different view of the law. Members should consider taking further advice appropriate to the risks and circumstances of the particular case, for example where litigation is likely.

- Disclosure and transparency

  Tax advice must not rely for its effectiveness on HMRC having less than the relevant facts. Any disclosure must fairly represent all relevant facts.

- Advising on tax planning arrangements

  Members must not create, encourage or promote tax planning arrangements or structures that: i) set out to achieve results that are contrary to the clear intention of Parliament in enacting relevant legislation; and/or ii) are highly artificial or highly contrived and seek to exploit shortcomings within the relevant legislation.

- Professional judgement and appropriate documentation

  Applying these requirements to particular client advisory situations requires members to exercise professional judgement on a number of matters. Members should keep notes on a timely basis of the rationale for the judgments exercised in seeking to adhere to these requirements.

...

Tax planning arrangements

3.9 Where a member has a genuine and reasonable uncertainty as to whether particular planning is in breach of this Standard, the member should:

- document the detailed reasoning and evidence sufficiently to be able to demonstrate why they took the view that any planning was not in breach of this Standard;
- include in their client advice an assessment of uncertainties and risks involved in the planning see Standard Lawful above; and
- include in their client advice an assessment of the relevant disclosures that should be made to HMRC in order to enable it, should it wish to do so, to make any reasonable enquiries – see Standard Disclosure and transparency above.'

Taxation Disciplinary Board

6.24 Failure to comply with the PCRT may result in the professional being referred to the Taxation Disciplinary Board (TDB) (see https://tax-board.org.uk). The aims of the TDB are to investigate complaints and take action against CIOT, ATT and IIT members who have breached professional standards; provided inadequate professional service; or behaved in an unbecoming manner.

6.25 Upon receipt of a complaint under Part 3 of the Taxation Disciplinary Board Scheme Regulations 2014[9] at Regulation 3.1, the TDB 'will consider such Complaint, inquiry or information in accordance with these Regulations'. Under Regulation 3.2 the initial consideration of the Complaint shall be undertaken by a Reviewer, who may decide to take no action in accordance with Regulations 3.3,[6] 3.4[7] or 3.5[8]:

'3.3 No Complaint, inquiry or information shall be considered where it is lodged in excess of 24 months after the last incident relied on or in excess of 24 months from when that last incident became known to the Complainant, unless in the opinion of the Reviewer:

(a) there are issues of such public interest that pursuing the Complaint is appropriate;

(b) the Complaint raised is of sufficient importance or gravity that pursuing the Complaint is appropriate; or

(c) there is a valid reason for the delay in the Complaint being brought to the attention of the TDB.

3.4 If the Reviewer considers that a Complaint, inquiry or information does not fall within the jurisdiction of the Scheme or Regulations, he shall take no further action.

3.5 If the Reviewer considers that the Complaint, inquiry or information is vexatious or of such a minor nature that, in his view,

9 As amended 29 November 2016, available at https://tax-board.org.uk/taxation-disciplinary-board-scheme-regulations.

it would not if proved merit a sufficiently serious sanction to justify prosecution, the Reviewer may determine that no further action shall be taken.'

6.26 If the Reviewer determines to take no further action under Regulations 3.3, 3.4 or 3.5, he shall immediately inform the Complainant. If a Complainant is dissatisfied with the Reviewer's decision, the Complainant may by written notice to the Reviewer request that the Complaint be referred to an Investigatory Assessor (who may uphold the decision of the Reviewer or order the Reviewer to refer the matter to an Investigation Committee). Under Regulation 3.8 'if, however, the Reviewer refers a report of the Complaint to an Investigation Committee to consider, he shall first provide the Defendant with an opportunity to comment on the Complaint'. The Defendant will have 21 days to respond to the Reviewer's request. If the Defendant fails to respond the Reviewer may refer the case to an Investigation Committee. Following determination of any referral the Investigatory Assessor shall give written reasons for his determination to the Reviewer and the Complainant or Defendant within 28 days. An Investigation Committee must consider whether the Complaint discloses a prima facie case under Regulations 5.1[9] and 5.2[10]. For this purpose, the rules state:

'5.1 The Investigation Committee shall consider whether the Complaint discloses a Prima Facie Case.

5.2 A Prima Facie Case can include, but is not limited to a case involving:

(a) a breach of professional standards and guidelines; or

(b) inadequate professional service; or

(c) Conduct Unbefitting.'

6.27 The Investigation Committee may reach any of the following decisions under Part 4, Regulation 5(4):

'(a) in circumstances where it finds that no Prima Facie Case has been made out, rule that the Complaint be rejected;

(b) in circumstances where it finds that a Prima Facie Case has been made out, but the Complaint is of such a minor nature that, in the Investigation Committee's view, it would not if proved merit a sufficiently serious sanction to justify prosecution, rule that the Complaint shall lie on file for the period of three years starting from the date of its decision;

(c) before deciding whether to make the direction provided for in Regulation 5.4(b) above, the Committee may take into account any facts or matters which have been considered by an Investigation Committee on previous occasions in relation to the Defendant, in respect of which, although a Prima Facie Case has been made out, either no further action was taken or the Complaint was ordered to lie on file. If it is decided to refer the Complaint to the Disciplinary Tribunal,

(i) the Investigation Committee shall state in its written reasons for its decision that a material factor in its decision to refer the Complaint to the Disciplinary Tribunal was that there had been a previous Complaint made against the Defendant in respect of which it had been ordered that no further action be taken or that the Complaint had been ordered to lie on file;

(ii) in respect of any previous Complaint which was ordered to lie on file pursuant to Regulation 5.2(b) above, the Investigation Committee may order that the said earlier Complaint should now go forward to the Disciplinary Tribunal together with the current Complaint;

(iii) in respect of any other previous Complaint, the Investigation Committee shall make no order;

(d) in circumstances where it finds that a Prima Facie Case has been made out, rule that no further action be taken if, in its opinion, the evidence is not of sufficient strength to establish the facts in question before a Disciplinary Tribunal;

(e) where it considers that a Prima Facie Case has been made out, refer the whole or appropriate part of the Complaint to the Disciplinary Tribunal.'

6.28 The Investigation Committee may refer the Complaint to the Disciplinary Tribunal under Regulation 5.4(e) having provided written reasons under Regulation 5.7 (which reasons must address the specific issues identified in Regulation 5.4(d)). A Disciplinary Tribunal must conduct any hearing in accordance with Regulation 18 (governing conduct of the hearing) and make its determinations (as required by Regulation 20) including imposing the burden of proof on the presenter under Regulation 20.3 to prove his case against the tax professional on the Civil Standard (ie balance of probabilities), as required by Regulation 20.4.

6.29 The Disciplinary Tribunal is required to take the following matters into account, and it has the power to impose the following sanctions under Regulation 20.6 if the charges are proved:

'(a) the Clerk [to the Tribunal] shall inform the Disciplinary Tribunal of any previous cases in which the Investigation Committee found a Prima Facie Case against the Member but ruled that no action should be taken;

(b) the Clerk shall inform the Disciplinary Tribunal of any previous disciplinary findings against the Defendant and of any orders made

(c) the Clerk shall inform the Disciplinary Tribunal of any interim order made by the Interim Orders Panel in connection with the same Complaint

(d) the Defendant or his representative shall be allowed to address the Disciplinary Tribunal in mitigation

(e) the Disciplinary Tribunal must take into consideration any previous cases where a Prima Facie Case was found but no action was taken against the Defendant, the past disciplinary record (if any) of the Defendant, the Disciplinary Tribunal's view as to the nature and gravity of the charges (so far as they are proved) and any other circumstances the Disciplinary Tribunal considers to be relevant. The Tribunal shall also take into account the Indicative Sanctions Guidance issued by the Board.

(f) The Disciplinary Tribunal may:

(i) order the Complaint to rest on file for 3 years

(ii) require the Defendant to apologise to the Complainant or another party

(iii) warn the Defendant as to his future conduct

(iv) censure the Defendant

(v) fine the Defendant a sum not exceeding £20,000 for each proven Charge

(vi) suspend the Defendant from membership of any Participant. Such suspension may be for a fixed period of no less than one month to a maximum period of two years. Any period of suspension imposed by an Interim Orders Panel in relation to the same Complaint shall be taken into account when determining any further period of suspension

(vii) expel the Defendant from membership of any Participant

(viii) order the Defendant to pay a sum or sums as compensation to a limit of £5,000

(ix) impose conditions on the Defendant

(x) recommend the suspension or removal of the Defendant from any register maintained by the Participants

(xi) impose such other sanctions as are appropriate to students, associates or any other persons or bodies subject to the jurisdiction of the Participants

(xii) order the Defendant to pay a sum by way of costs, including any costs referable to any decision made by the Interim Orders Panel.

(g) In awarding costs as above under Regulation 20.6(f)(xii), the Disciplinary Tribunal must have regard to any relevant guidance issued by the Board.'

DUTY OF CARE: OVERVIEW

General

6.30 An adviser is subject to the law of negligence if a duty of care is owed to a person. That person will usually be the client who is the recipient of the advice. However, it is also likely that a duty of care is owed to a third party in circumstances where the adviser can foresee that damage will be caused to a third party by negligent advice.

6.31 In cases involving pure economic loss, a duty of care will be imposed if three criteria are met. There must be:

- reasonable foreseeability of damage;
- a relationship of sufficient 'proximity' between the party owing the duty and the party to whom it is owed; and
- the imposition of the duty of care contended for should be just and reasonable in all the circumstances.

6.32 In *Caparo Plc v Dickman* [1990] 2 AC 605 (at pp 620 to 621), a decision of the House of Lords, Lord Bridge stated the position as follows:

> 'The salient feature of all these cases is that the defendant giving advice or information was fully aware of the nature of the transaction which the plaintiff had in contemplation, knew that the advice or information would be communicated to him directly or indirectly and knew that it was very likely that the plaintiff would rely on that advice or information in deciding whether or not to engage in the transaction in contemplation. In these circumstances the defendant could clearly be expected, subject always to the effect of any disclaimer of responsibility, specifically to anticipate that the plaintiff would rely on the advice or information given by the defendant for the very purpose for which he did in the event rely on it. So also the plaintiff, subject again to the effect of any disclaimer, would in that situation reasonably suppose that he was entitled to rely on the advice or information given by the defendant for the very purpose for which he did in the event rely on it.'

6.33 Lord Oliver, in *Caparo*, referred to the conditions, whose presence would indicate the existence of 'The necessary relationship between the maker of a statement or giver of advice (the adviser) and the recipient who acts in reliance upon it (the advisee)':

> '(1) the advice is required for a purpose, whether particularly specified or generally described, which is made known, either actually or inferentially, to the adviser at the time the advice is given; (2) the adviser knows, either actually or inferentially, that his advice will be communicated to the advisee, either specifically or as a member of an ascertainable class, in order that it should be used by the advisee for that purpose; (3) it is known, either

actually or inferentially, that the advice so communicated is likely to be acted upon by the advisee for that purpose without independent inquiry, and (4) it is so acted upon by the advisee to his detriment.'

Duty of care: scope of the retainer

6.34 The starting point in considering breach of duty by a professional is the terms of the professional's terms of engagement (ie the retainer)[11]. A retainer is a contract and as such the terms of the contract will be relevant in determining the liability of the adviser. If the contract is silent on the nature of the standard of service to be provided, it will be an implied term of such retainer that the adviser will exercise reasonable skill and care in giving their advice (see **Chapter 5** at **5.67** et seq). As such, the professional adviser's duty of care in negligence can be co-extensive with the duty in contract to the client and third parties.

6.35 In *Mehjoo v Harben Barker* [2014] EWCA Civ 358, Lewison LJ at [69] comments on the requirement to accurately identity the extent of an adviser's duties by examining the terms of the retainer[12]:

> 'there is no such thing as a general retainer in that sense. The expression "my solicitor" is as meaningless as the expression "my tailor" or "my bookmaker" in establishing any general duty ... The extent of his duties depends upon the terms and limits of that retainer and any duty of care to be implied must be related to what he is instructed to do.'

6.36 The effect of the retainer in the context of a solicitor has been explained in these terms, in *Credit Lyonnais v Russell Jones & Walker* [2002] EWHC 1310 (Ch), Laddie J said at [28]:

> 'A solicitor is not a general insurer against his client's legal problems. His duties are defined by the terms of the agreed retainer. This is the normal case although *White v Jones* [1995] 2 AC 207 suggests that obligations may occasionally arise outside the terms of the retainer or where there is no retainer at all. Ignoring such exceptions, the solicitor only has to expend time and effort in what he has been engaged to do and for which the client has agreed to pay. He is under no general obligation to expend time and effort on issues outside the retainer. However, if, in the course of doing that for which he is retained, he becomes aware of a risk or a potential risk to the client, it is his duty to inform the client. In doing that he is neither going beyond the scope of his instructions nor is he doing "extra" work for which he is not to be paid. He is simply reporting back to the client on issues of concern which he learns of as a result of, and in the course of, carrying out his express instructions. In relation to this I was struck by the analogy drawn by Mr Seitler. If a dentist is asked to treat a patient's tooth and, on looking into the latter's mouth, he notices that an adjacent tooth is in need of treatment, it is his duty to warn the patient accordingly. So too, if in the course of carrying out instructions within his area of competence a

> lawyer notices or ought to notice a problem or risk for the client of which it is reasonable to assume the client may not be aware, the lawyer must warn him.'

6.37 In *Altus Group Ltd v Baker Tilly Tax & Advisory Services and Another* [2015] EWHC 12 (Ch) [at 69] the High Court held that the same approach should apply to tax advisers.

6.38 In *Mehjoo v Harben Barker and Another*[10] the Court of Appeal held that [23] '… there is no such thing as a general retainer and the terms and limits of the retainer and any consequent duty of care therefore depend on what the professional is instructed to do …'. As stated, in *Mehjoo* an accountant is not therefore under a general roving duty to have regard to and to advise on all aspects of the claimant's affairs absent a request to do so by the client. In that case the Court of Appeal held that an accountancy firm did not have a general duty to recommend sophisticated tax planning to a client. The retainer never required the accountant to give the client tax planning advice on possible ways of minimising or eliminating the rate of CGT applicable to the disposal of shares. There was some evidence that the accountant had nonetheless given some tax advice in respect of various matters, but this was relatively routine, even if pro-active, and the accountant never held himself out as a specialist in tax planning or that he would have been competent to do so.

6.39 In *Mehjoo*, the Court of Appeal drew a distinction (at para 40) between routine tax advice and sophisticated tax planning advice (which was not part of the retainer):

> '… routine tax advice of this kind, though an important part of an accountant's ordinary duties, is not what this case is about. … much of the difficulty with the judge's analysis of the scope of [the accountant's] HB's retainer and duty of care stems from a failure to differentiate between the tax advice of the kind which [the accountant] gave to [the client] on the occasions referred to by the judge and the much more sophisticated form of tax planning exemplified by the [Bearer Warrant Shares] BWS which often involves a re-formulation of the transaction in order to bring about particular tax consequences rather than a mitigation of the tax liability which the transaction will otherwise produce.'

6.40 The Court of Appeal concluded:

> 'As I have already explained, the giving of general tax advice (such as the availability of reliefs) was undoubtedly part of the existing retainer but it is difficult to see why a positive duty to advise on such matters should be extended in this case (by October 2004) to include a duty to give specialist tax planning advice as understood by the judge. HB were not and had never held themselves out to be specialist tax planners; and had never given Mr Mehjoo advice of that sort. It is therefore surprising to say the least that

10 [2014] EWCA Civ 358.

from a course of conduct which did not involve tax planning, they should be taken to have assumed a positive duty to give advice of that kind.'

6.41 In *Hurlingham Estates Ltd v Wilde & Partners* [1997] STC 627 the issue was whether a solicitor engaged to carry out a conveyancing transaction was under a duty to advise his client of the existence of a potential tax charge which would be avoided by re-structuring the transaction. The solicitor was held liable because the solicitor should have known about the tax charge (albeit the solicitor was a conveyancing specialist and not a tax specialist). Lightman J said:

> 'The test to be derived from the authorities is whether, having regard to the terms of the retainer in all the circumstances which were known or should reasonably have been known by [the solicitor], [the solicitor] should reasonably have appreciated that [the client] needed his advice and guidance in respect of the tax liabilities to which entry into the transaction would expose it. The circumstances include the relevant business experience of [the client], and the ready availability to [the client] and likely recourse by [the client] to other advice.'

6.42 In *Hurlingham*, the existence of the tax charge was something which the judge held should have been known to the solicitor and which he should have warned his client about. In *Mehjoo* (discussed above), the claimant knew about the tax charge and was told that schemes might exist to reduce it. However, the accountants did not know what those schemes were, nor could they be expected to do so. As discussed in **Chapter 5**, the terms of engagement must clearly identify the nature and scope of the services to be provided to the client. There is much to be said for a contract also stating what is excluded from the retainer, even if it is to say that the advice is solely on X tax and excludes all other taxes relevant to the proposed advice (if this is the limitation of the advice). Further, the contract should also state that there is no obligation to provide any update to a client once the services are performed.

STANDARD OF CARE: OVERVIEW

6.43 It is well established that a solicitor in providing tax services owes his client a duty to exercise the skill and care reasonably to be expected of an experienced specialist tax solicitor[11]. If the retainer does not exclude tax, a solicitor may be considered negligent if their advice does not address relevant tax matters that arise in relation to the transaction[12].

6.44 The same standard will be applied to any tax adviser (whether regulated via CIOT, STEP, ATT, ICAEW). The relevant question is to ask, 'whether reasonable practitioners professing the expertise of the adviser could properly have given advice in the terms they did'.

11 Per Oliver J in *Midland Bank Trust Co Ltd v Hett Stubbs and Kemp* [1979] Ch 384 at 403.

12 See *Mason v Mills and Reeve* [2012] EWCA Civ 498.

6.45 In *Saif Ali v Sidney Mitchell & Co* [1980] AC 199, concerning a barrister's liability in negligence, Lord Diplock observed, at 220:

> 'No matter what profession it may be, the common law does not impose on those who practise it any liability for damage resulting from what in the result turns out to have been errors of judgment unless the error was such as no reasonably well informed and competent member of that profession could have made.'

6.46 The standard of the advice is to be determined by reference to the nature of the skills which the adviser professes to have in the particular area of expertise.

6.47 In this regard, for tax specialist Queen's Counsel, the question is whether a reasonably competent tax QC, applying proper care and skill to the task (eg providing an opinion, or settling and advising on a draft letter), could have done as he did. Where a person provides advice without seeking to rely on a third-party adviser, then that person will be held to the same high standard to be expected of a QC if that person holds themselves out as providing *that* quality and standard of service (ie the services of a QC).

6.48 In *Matrix Securities Ltd v Theodore Goddard (a firm) and David Goldberg QC* [1998] PNLR 280, the High Court analysed the position of a QC and lawyers who were engaged to provide a client with a clearance letter to be submitted to HMRC. The client sued for professional negligence in relation to the clearance letter. The High Court stated (in respect of the objective of the letter being to seek to persuade the Revenue to grant a clearance in circumstances where they could not go back on it) at 321:

> 'In relation to that objective I hold that the duty of TG [the solicitors] and Mr Goldberg [the QC] was to exercise such skill and care as a reasonably competent practitioner in the relevant sector of the profession would have done with a view to securing such a clearance [ie clearance from HMRC for a tax arrangement]. I do not accept that their duties were to secure a clearance which was 100 per cent reliable, or to do so if the exercise of reasonable skill and care could achieve such a thing. That formulation turns the common law position set out in *Saif Ali* by Lord Diplock on its head. Instead of imposing legal liability on the professional only if he does that which no reasonably competent member of the relevant profession or part of the profession would have done in the same situation, he would be rendered liable for breach of duty if he omitted anything which any one of the reasonably competent members of the relevant group or class would have done, even if, as might be the case in an area involving judgment as between different choices, the steps that a number of different reasonably competent members of the profession would reasonably have taken would be incompatible with each other. That is not the law. Mr Slater pays lip service to Lord Diplock's observation, and to one of its sources *Bolam v Friern Hospital Management Committee* [1957] 1 W.L.R. 582, but he submits that

the scope for acceptable error in a case such as this, with professionals of such high skill and experience, is very small indeed … I approach the case on the footing that the standard of competence by which Mr Goldberg is to be judged is that of the rather small and select group of silks specialising in tax matters, and for TG it is that of firms of solicitors with specialist tax departments. I agree that the standard for both Mr Goldberg and TG is a high standard. But I cannot accept [counsel for the plaintiffs]'s reversal of the basic common law formulation of the duty, which led him at one point to accept my formulation of his proposition as being that they could possibly have been right and still negligent but they could not have been wrong and not negligent.'

6.49 The standard of care to be expected of the professional adviser will turn on whether the adviser put themselves forward as providing a top-level specialist service.

6.50 In *Herrmann v Withers LLP* [2012] EWHC 1492 (Ch) Newey J (as he then was) said (at para 67):

> 'It is common ground that, in considering whether Withers were negligent, I should have regard to the fact that they are a City of London firm and pride themselves on offering an excellent service to their clients. In *Hicks v Russell Jones & Walker* [2007] EWHC 940 (Ch), Henderson J said (at paragraph 138(3)) that it would be "absurd" to judge the firm with which he was concerned, which had "experience in the fields of commercial litigation and insolvency, including the conduct of complex appeals", by the same standard as a small country firm. Withers accepted that it would be similarly inappropriate to judge them by the same standard as a small country firm.'

6.51 In this regard, any professional tax adviser who holds themselves out as being a top-end specialist adviser will be judged by that standard. This approach was specifically adopted by the High Court in *Altus Group Ltd v Baker Tilly Tax & Advisory Services and Another* [2015] EWHC 12 (Ch), where the Judge commented (at 82):

> 'It is that standing that brings clients to them and those with whom they are in competition. They are reasonably to be judged by the standards appropriate to that standing. The defendants are reasonably to be expected to have much greater technical resources than an "ordinary" firm of accountants and as a result to be aware of relevant impending changes to tax legislation.'

WOULD A SIGNIFICANT BODY OF REASONABLE PRACTITIONERS HAVE ACTED AS THE DEFENDANT DID?

6.52 If a significant body of reasonable practitioners would have acted as the professional adviser did, then there is no breach of duty even if some other advisers might have acted differently, for example by giving more detailed advice.

6.53 In *Bolitho v City and Hackney HA* [1998] AC 232 at 241H Lord Browne-Wilkinson said:

> '… the use of these adjectives – responsible, reasonable and respectable – all show that the court has to be satisfied that the exponents of the body of opinion relied upon can demonstrate that such opinion has a logical basis. In particular in cases involving, as they so often do, the weighing of risks against benefits, the judge before accepting a body of opinion as being responsible, reasonable or respectable, will need to be satisfied that, in forming their views the experts have directed their minds to the question of comparative risks and benefits and have reached a defensible conclusion on the matter.'

6.54 He continued at 243B:

> '… *In the vast majority of cases the fact that distinguished experts in the field are of a particular opinion will demonstrate the reasonableness of that opinion.* In particular where there are questions of assessment of the relative risks and benefits of adopting a particular medical practice, a reasonable view necessarily presupposes that the relative risks and benefits have been weighed by the experts in forming their opinions. *But if, in a rare case, it can be demonstrated that the professional opinion is not capable of withstanding logical analysis, the judge is entitled to hold that the body of opinion is not reasonable or responsible.*
>
> *I emphasise that in my view it will very seldom be right for a judge to reach the conclusion that views genuinely held by a competent medical expert are unreasonable.* The assessment of medical risks and benefits is a matter of clinical judgement which a judge would not normally be able to make without expert evidence. As the quotation from Lord Scarman makes clear, *it would be wrong to allow such assessment to deteriorate into seeking to persuade the judge to prefer one of two views both of which are capable of being logically supported …*' [Emphasis added]

Provision of information

6.55 Any adviser who provides information to a client must take reasonable care in ensuring that information is correct.

6.56 In *SAAMCO v York Montague Ltd*[13], Lord Hoffmann (at 214D) of the judgment said:

> '[The principle] is that a person under a duty to take reasonable care to provide information on which someone else will decide upon a course

13 *South Australia Asset Management Corp v York Montague Ltd (sub nom Banque Bruxelles Lambert SA v Eagle Star Insurance Co Ltd)* [1997] AC 191 (HL) ('*SAAMCO*').

of action is, if negligent, not generally regarded as responsible for all the consequences of that course of action. He is responsible only for the consequences of the information being wrong …

The principle thus stated distinguishes *between a duty to provide information for the purpose of enabling someone else to decide upon a course of action and a duty to advise someone as to what course of action he should take.* If the duty is to advise whether or not a course of action should be taken, the adviser must take reasonable care to consider all the potential consequences of that course of action. If he is negligent, he will therefore be responsible for all the foreseeable loss which is a consequence of that course of action having been taken. If his duty is only to supply information, he must take reasonable care to ensure that the information is correct and, if he is negligent, will be responsible for all the foreseeable consequences of the information being wrong.' [Emphasis added]

6.57 In *BPE Solicitors v Hughes – Holland* [2017] UKSC 21, a decision of the Supreme Court, Lord Sumption, at [40], emphasised the nature of the consequences which flow from advice and the provision of information by an adviser, as follows:

'[40] In cases falling within Lord Hoffmann's "advice" category, it is left to the adviser to consider what matters should be taken into account in deciding whether to enter into the transaction. His duty is to consider all relevant matters and not only specific factors in the decision. If one of those matters is negligently ignored or misjudged, and this proves to be critical to the decision, the client will in principle be entitled to recover all loss flowing from the transaction which he should have protected his client against. The House of Lords might have said of the "advice" cases that the client was entitled to the losses flowing from the transaction if they were not just attributable to risks within the scope of the adviser's duty but to risks which had been negligently assessed by the adviser. In the great majority of cases, this would have assimilated the two categories. An "adviser" would simply have been legally responsible for a wider range of informational errors. But in a case where the adviser is responsible for guiding the whole decision-making process, there is a certain pragmatic justice in the test that the Appellate Committee preferred. If the adviser has a duty to protect his client (so far as due care can do it) against the full range of risks associated with a potential transaction, the client will not have retained responsibility for any of them. The adviser's responsibility extends to the decision. If the adviser has negligently assessed risk A, the result is that the overall riskiness of the transaction has been understated. If the client would not have entered into the transaction on a careful assessment of its overall merits, the fact that the loss may have resulted from risks B, C or D should not matter.'

6.58 The position of the adviser is to be contrasted with the 'information' category. Lord Sumption continued:

'[41] By comparison, in the "information" category, a professional adviser *contributes a limited part of the material* on which his client will rely in deciding whether to enter into a prospective transaction, *but the process of identifying the other relevant considerations and the overall assessment of the commercial merits of the transaction are exclusively matters for the client* (or possibly his other advisers) …' [Emphasis added]

STANDARD OF CARE: ERROR IN PROVIDING ASSURANCE

6.59 In *Halsall v Champion Consulting Ltd* [2017] EWHC 1079, a decision of the High Court, the adviser was held to be in breach of the duty of care in respect of a 'tax scheme' because the adviser provided an assurance that the scheme would work effectively. Each expert witness agreed that if a professional adviser gave a guarantee on the efficacy of a tax scheme it would not be reasonable.

6.60 In summary, the following points can be derived from the expert witness evidence:

- An adviser who provides tax advice would at a minimum be expected to advise on how the scheme was intended to operate, how HMRC would view it, the importance of valuation (if relevant), the risks of HMRC challenge and the worst-case scenario in the event of a successful challenge.
- If a professional adviser gives a guarantee he would not regard it as reasonable.
- If the guarantee was in the context of 'come on, it's so good, if it doesn't work I'll pay the tax', that would not be reasonably competent advice.
- If an adviser says, 'this is a tax scheme, I've reviewed it and you going into it is a no-brainer', then that would not be advice that a reasonable adviser would give.

6.61 In *Halsall*, the judge stated at [123]:

'The fact that some of the companies succeeded and that some of the schemes went unchallenged by the Revenue is in my view irrelevant to the question of whether the reasonably competent tax adviser would have given an unconditional assurance that the charity shell scheme would work effectively.'

STANDARD OF CARE: BREACH OF DUTY TO GIVE RISK WARNINGS

6.62 A professional adviser must not only provide non-negligent advice, but must also where relevant ensure that the client is aware of the risks associated with relying on the adviser's advice (eg it cannot be guaranteed that HMRC will accept the adviser's interpretation of the legislation, and the consequences of HMRC failing to accept the adviser's interpretation (ie additional tax, possible penalties)).

6.63 Clearly, any tax adviser is providing a client with advice on the interpretation and application of tax laws in return for payment. This means that the client is entitled to expect that the tax advice includes an assessment of the risks associated with such advice.

6.64 In *Barker v Baxendale Walker Solicitors (a firm)* [2017] EWCA Civ 2056, at [64], the Court of Appeal expressed the position as follows in respect of a solicitor, which applies with equal force to a tax adviser:

> 'In this case, legal advice was the very service which was being provided and which was being relied upon. There can be no separation between the advice and any appropriate caveats as to risk. They are one and the same. The lawyer as part of the legal advice he is providing, must evaluate the legal position and determine whether in all of the circumstances, he should advise his client that there is a significant risk that the view he has taken about the substantive matter in question may be wrong …'

6.65 As to risk warnings, the question is whether a reasonably careful practitioner with the degree of expertise claimed by that practitioner should warn the client of the risk that the advice will fail to deliver the intended tax advantages. The issue of risk warnings arise even in circumstances where a professional gives advice which a reasonably competent person with the persons' expertise could have done so.

6.66 Nonetheless, an adviser can be negligent where in the light of all the circumstances no reasonably competent adviser in the position of the adviser would have failed to give the specific warning that there was a significant risk that the advice/planning would fail to be tax effective.

6.67 In *Barker v Baxendale Walker Solicitors (a firm) and Others* [EWCA] Civ 2056, the Court of Appeal (at paras 60–61) put the matter in these terms in respect of a solicitor but there is no reason to suppose a different test applies to another professional adviser:

> 'It is important to appreciate that the court is considering what advice ought to have been given by the reasonably competent practitioner in the particular factual circumstances at the time. Of course, the advice which a reasonably competent solicitor would give in the circumstances turns substantially upon the view that he could take of the provision on which it turns. It is also dependent upon whether contrary arguments as to construction are of sufficient significance to require specific mention when taken with the degree of risk inherent in the circumstances and the importance in those circumstances of a balanced view of the provision. As Salmon LJ noted in *Dixie v Parsons* the question turns in part upon the likelihood or otherwise of a dispute.

It seems to me that the following principles are likely to apply:

(i) The question of whether a solicitor is in breach of a duty to explain the risk that a court may come to a different interpretation from that which he advises is correct is highly fact sensitive: (*Queen Elizabeth, Hermann, Balogun* and *Levicom* cases);

(ii) If the construction of the provision is clear, it is very likely that whatever the circumstances, the threshold of "significant risk" will not be met and it will not be necessary to caveat the advice given and explain the risks involved;

(iii) However, depending on the circumstances, it is perfectly possible to be correct about the construction of a provision or, at least, not negligent in that regard, but nevertheless to be under a duty to point out the risks involved and to have been negligent in not having done so (*Levicom* and *Balogun* cases);

(iv) It is more likely that there will be a duty to point out the risks, or to put the matter another way, that a reasonably competent solicitor would not fail to point them out when advising, if litigation is already on foot or the point has already been taken, although this need not necessarily be the case (the *Queen Elizabeth* case to be compared with *Balogun*); and

(v) The issue is not one of percentages or whether opposing possible constructions are "finely balanced" but is more nuanced.'

6.68 The question of whether there is a 'significant risk' turns on, amongst other things:

- the likely competing construction of the applicable statutory provision or arising from the interaction of statutory provisions;
- the factual circumstances including:
  - the nature of the arrangements and its purpose (ie commercial or artificial);
  - the amount at stake;
  - the risk of challenge by HMRC;
  - the risk of a court taking a different view.

6.69 Very often these issues involve issues of mixed fact and law to be determined by the court applying the standard of the reasonably competent adviser. The evidence of an expert witness in professional negligence proceedings is likely to be crucial to demonstrate that the advice either met or fell short of the standard of a reasonably competent adviser. In *Kennedy v Cordia (Services) LLP* [2016] UKSC 6 the Supreme Court has given helpful guidance on the admissibility of expert evidence where it said (at para 44):

'There are in our view four considerations which govern the admissibility of skilled evidence:

(i) whether the proposed skilled evidence will assist the court in its task:

(ii) whether the witness has the necessary knowledge and experience;

(iii) whether the witness is impartial in his presentation and assessment of the evidence; and

(iv) whether there is a reliable body of knowledge or experience to underpin the expert's evidence.'

EXCLUSION OF LIABILITY AND LIMITATION OF LIABILITY: (UCTA 1977) AND CRA 2015

Overview

6.70 As to the general position of the *Unfair Contract Terms Act 1977* (*UCTA 1977*), see **Chapter 5** at **5.81** et seq.

6.71 A limitation clause is usually to be identified in the retainer letter, and generally takes this form:

> 'any claim for breach of contract, breach of duty or fault of negligence or otherwise whatsoever arising out of or in connection with this engagement shall be brought against the adviser within six years of the act or omission alleged to have caused the loss in question.'

6.72 Such a clause is subject to the requirement of reasonableness in *section 11* of *UCTA 1977* and *section 61* of the *Consumer Rights Act 2015* (*CRA 2015*)[14] since it purports to exclude liability for negligence. The requirement of reasonableness as set out in *section 11* of *UCTA 1977* is that the term 'shall have been a fair and reasonable one to be included having regard to the circumstances which were, ought reasonably to have been, known to or in the contemplation of the parties when the contract was made'. By virtue of *section 11(5)* of *UCTA 1977*, it is for the defendant to show that a contract term satisfies the requirement of reasonableness. *Section 64* of *CRA 2015* states:

> **'64 Exclusion from assessment of fairness**
>
> (1) A term of a consumer contract may not be assessed for fairness under section 62 to the extent that—
>
> (a) it specifies the main subject matter of the contract, or
>
> (b) the assessment is of the appropriateness of the price payable under the contract by comparison with the goods, digital content or services supplied under it.

14 For *UCTA 1977* and *CRA 2015*, see www.legislation.gov.uk.

(2) Subsection (1) excludes a term from an assessment under section 62 only if it is transparent and prominent.'

6.73 *Section 62* of *CRA 2015* states:

'62 Requirement for contract terms and notices to be fair

(1) An unfair term of a consumer contract is not binding on the consumer.

(2) An unfair consumer notice is not binding on the consumer.

(3) This does not prevent the consumer from relying on the term or notice if the consumer chooses to do so.

(4) A term is unfair if, contrary to the requirement of good faith, it causes a significant imbalance in the parties' rights and obligations under the contract to the detriment of the consumer.

(5) Whether a term is fair is to be determined—

- (a) taking into account the nature of the subject matter of the contract, and
- (b) by reference to all the circumstances existing when the term was agreed and to all of the other terms of the contract or of any other contract on which it depends.

(6) A notice is unfair if, contrary to the requirement of good faith, it causes a significant imbalance in the parties' rights and obligations to the detriment of the consumer.

(7) Whether a notice is fair is to be determined—

- (a) taking into account the nature of the subject matter of the notice, and
- (b) by reference to all the circumstances existing when the rights or obligations to which it relates arose and to the terms of any contract on which it depends.

(8) This section does not affect the operation of—

- (a) section 31 (exclusion of liability: goods contracts),
- (b) section 47 (exclusion of liability: digital content contracts),
- (c) section 57 (exclusion of liability: services contracts), or
- (d) section 65 (exclusion of negligence liability).'

Liability for negligence

6.74 Under *UCTA 1977* and *section 65* of *CRA 2015*, a contract cannot exclude or restrict liability for death or personal injury resulting from negligence. Further, an exclusion clause in the case of other loss or damage cannot exclude or restrict liability for negligence except in so far as the term or notice satisfies the requirement of reasonableness. The legislation specifically provides that where a contract term or notice purports to exclude or restrict liability for negligence a person's agreement to or awareness of it is not of itself to be taken as indicating that person's voluntary acceptance of any risk.

DAMAGES

6.75 We are concerned here with recovery of economic loss rather than loss resulting from physical damage. English law has traditionally been reluctant to allow recovery for 'pure economic loss' but this is subject to exceptions (see below).

6.76 Pure economic loss is financial damage resulting from the negligent act of another person without any associated or consequential physical damage to a person or property. The classic authority for the recovery of economic loss in tort for negligent misstatement is *Hedley Byrne v Heller* (1964) AC 465 (HL).

6.77 Common examples of pure economic loss are:

- incurring a liability (such as tax, interest and penalties);
- expenditure;
- loss of profit, profitability; or
- loss of some other form of financial gain such as a legacy.

6.78 Fashions in recovery for pure economic loss come and go. The relationship to the duty of care must also be borne in mind.

Compensatory principle

6.79 The general principle, in tort, is that the court should award that sum of money which will put the party who has been injured, or who has suffered, in the same position as he would have been in if he had not sustained the wrong for which he is now getting his compensation or reparation.

6.80 Consideration must also be given to whether a claimant would also allege 'loss of chance' in claiming compensation (ie that the claimant would have entered into a different transaction or other form of tax planning) (see **6.96** below).

6.81 Where a defendant is under concurrent liability for negligence in contract and tort for pecuniary loss, the contractual test for remoteness applies to both causes of action[15].

15 *Wellesley Partners LLP v Withers LLP* [2015] EWCA Civ 1146.

6.82 Where a claim is brought only for negligence, because a contractual claim would be out of time, a claimant cannot benefit from a broader test for remoteness after the contractual limitation period has expired than if he had started his proceedings earlier when a contractual claim was still open to him. In these circumstances a claimant can recover only for such loss as was in the reasonable contemplation of both the client and the adviser at the time when the client retained the adviser.

6.83 The distinction between a contractual claim and for a negligence claim is succinctly explained by the Court of Appeal in *Wemyss v Karim* [2016] EWCA Civ 27, at [23]–[28] where Lewison LJ commented:

> '23. Before delving into the details of the way in which the damages claim was put I think that it is necessary to set out a few principles. The claim was put both as a claim for breach of warranty (i.e. a claim in contract) and also as a claim for misrepresentation (i.e. a claim in tort). The measure of damages differs according to which cause of action is in play. In the case of a claim that there has been a breach of warranty about the quality of an asset that is sold, the measure of damages is the difference between the true value of the asset and its value with the quality as warranted. But in the case of a claim in tort, the measure of damages is the difference between the true value of the asset and the price paid. The point was put clearly by Lord Denning MR in *Doyle v Olby (Ironmongers) Ltd* [1969] 2 QB 158:
>
>> "On principle the distinction seems to be this: in contract, the defendant has made a promise and broken it. The object of damages is to put the plaintiff in as good a position, as far as money can do it, as if the promise had been performed. In fraud, the defendant has been guilty of a deliberate wrong by inducing the plaintiff to act to his detriment. The object of damages is to compensate the plaintiff for all the loss he has suffered, so far, again, as money can do it."
>
> 24. As Professor Treitel explained in 'Damages for Deceit' (1969) 32 M.L.R. 556, 558-559 in a passage approved by Lord Steyn in *Smith New Court Ltd v Citibank NA* [1997] AC 254, 282:
>
>> "If the plaintiff's bargain would have been a bad one, even on the assumption that the representation was true, he will do best under the tortious measure. If, on the assumption that the representation was true, his bargain would have been a good one, he will do best under the first contractual measure (under which he may recover something even if the actual value of what he has recovered is greater than the price)."
>
> 25. Suppose that A owns a painting that he tells B was painted by a famous artist. If it had been, it would be worth £10,000. B pays £8,000 for it. It was not in fact painted by the famous artist and was only worth £100. If B can establish that what A said was a contractual warranty, then he is entitled to £10,000 – £100 = £9,900. But if he can only establish that the statement was an actionable misrepresentation, then he is entitled to £8,000 – £100 =

£7,900, although if the misrepresentation was (or is treated as) fraudulent he may be entitled to consequential losses as well. Changing the facts, perhaps unrealistically, if the painting as warranted would have been worth £10,000 but is in fact worth £8,000, then on the contractual measure the buyer who paid £8,000 will recover £2,000; but on the tortious measure will recover nothing.

26. There is one further important difference between a claim in contract for breach of warranty and a claim in tort for misrepresentation. In the case of a claim for misrepresentation the claimant must show that he relied on the representation in deciding to enter into the contract (although the representation need not be the sole cause of the decision). However, in the case of a claim for breach of warranty all that the claimant needs to prove is that the warranty has been broken. As Slade LJ said in *Harlingdon and Leinster Enterprises Ltd v Christopher Hull Fine Art Ltd* [1991] 1 QB 564:

> "If a party to a contract wishes to claim relief in respect of a misrepresentation as to a matter which did not constitute a term of the contract, his claim will fail unless he is able to show that he relied on this representation in entering into the contract; in general, however, if a party wishes to claim relief in respect of a breach of *a term* of the contract (whether it be a condition or warranty) he need prove no actual reliance.' [Emphasis in original]

27. There is one other point that I should make at this stage. At [54] the judge observed that in a "no transaction" case the loss "is generally assessed as the difference between what was paid and the true value of the asset acquired". In the case of a claim in tort this is undoubtedly correct. But if the claim is put in contract, whether this proposition is correct depends on the term of the contract that has been broken. The "no transaction" point usually arises in the context of claims for professional negligence (normally in relation either to valuation or conveyancing). Such a claim may be framed in tort or in contract. But the essential point is that the contractual term in question is almost invariably an implied term to the effect that the professional will act with reasonable skill and care. So, in the case of a valuation, the implied term does not amount to a warranty that the valuation is correct. It is no more than a warranty that the valuer has used reasonable skill and care in reaching his valuation figure. It is for that reason that the measure of damages in a typical "no transaction" case is the same whether the claim is framed in contract or in tort. But this case is different. In this case Mr Karim was entitled to claim on the basis that the information given to him was warranted to be true; not merely that care had been taken in providing it.

28. In principle, therefore, Mr Karim is entitled to be put into the position in which he would have been if the business had had the turnover and profit warranted.

29. Two particular heads of loss were argued before the judge. The first related to a loan that Mr Karim said that he had taken from a company associated with Mr Wemyss in order to set up or expand a personal injury department. The argument was that if the business had had the turnover and profitability warranted the loan would not have been necessary. The judge rejected that argument for a number of reasons. He said at [55]:

> "Firstly, a warranty as to turnover and/or profit in a period before completion is not the same as a warranty that the LLP as a corporate entity would have any particular level of assets or capital at the date of completion such as might provide capital for future expansion. Nor is it a warranty that the firm will continue to have a particular turnover or earn a particular level of profits at any time after completion, such as might have generated capital for the new business".'

Losses in a professional negligence claim

6.84 The question of what damages are recoverable in a case where, 'but for', the negligence of a professional adviser a client would not have embarked on some course of action is not straightforward. To answer this question it is necessary to understand the House of Lords' decision in *SAAMCO*[16], which makes a distinction between 'information' cases (sometimes referred to as 'category 1' cases) and 'advice' cases (sometimes referred to as 'category 2' cases) and what is generally referred to as the '*SAAMCO* cap', namely the principle that in an 'information' case the recoverable damages exclude losses which would still have been suffered even if the erroneous information had been correct.

6.85 In summary, the Court of Appeal has expressed the *SAAMCO* principles as follows in *Manchester Building Society v Grant Thornton UK LLP* [2019] EWCA Civ 40 (at 54):

> 'The application of the *SAAMCO* principle may generally be addressed by considering the following:
>
> (1) It is first necessary to consider whether it is an "advice" case or an "information" case. This is a necessary first step because the scope of the duty, and therefore the measure of liability, is different in the two cases.
>
> (2) It will be an "advice" case if it can be shown that it has been "left to the adviser to consider what matters should be taken into account in deciding whether to enter into the transaction", that "his duty is to consider all relevant matters and not only specific matters in the decision" and that he is "responsible for guiding the whole decision making process".

16 *South Australia Asset Management Corpn v York Montague Ltd* [1997] AC 191, see **6.56** above.

(3) If it is an "advice" case, then the negligent adviser will have assumed responsibility for the decision to enter the transaction and will be responsible for all the foreseeable financial consequences of entering into the transaction.

(4) If it is not an "advice" case, then it is an "information" case and responsibility will not have been assumed for the decision to enter the transaction.

(5) If it is an "information" case, the negligent adviser/information provider will only be responsible for the foreseeable financial consequences of the advice and/or information being wrong.

(6) This involves a consideration of what losses would have been suffered if the advice and/or information had been correct. It is only losses which would not have been suffered in such circumstances that are recoverable.'

6.86 In *SAAMCO* the court drew a distinction between a person who provides information and a person who gives advice. In this regard, Lord Hoffmann stated (at p 214):

> 'It is that a person under a duty to take reasonable care to provide information on which someone else will decide upon a course of action is, if negligent, not generally regarded as responsible for all the consequences of that course of action. He is responsible only for the consequences of the information being wrong. A duty of care which imposes upon the informant responsibility for losses which would have occurred even if the information which he gave had been correct is not in my view fair and reasonable as between the parties. It is therefore inappropriate either as an implied term of a contract or as a tortious duty arising from the relationship between them.
>
> The principle thus stated distinguishes between a duty to *provide information* for the purpose of enabling someone else to decide upon a course of action and a duty to *advise* someone as to what course of action he should take. If the duty is to advise whether or not a course of action should be taken, the adviser must take reasonable care to consider all the potential consequences of that course of action. If he is negligent, he will therefore be responsible for all the foreseeable loss which is a consequence of that course of action having been taken. If his duty is only to supply information, he must take reasonable care to ensure that the information is correct and, if he is negligent, will be responsible for all the foreseeable consequences of the information being wrong.' [Emphasis in original]

6.87 In *BPE Solicitors v Hughes-Holland* [2017] UKSC 21 the Supreme Court provided further guidance on the distinction between the two SAAMCO categories. This case concerned whether a firm of solicitors that drafted transactional documentation was liable to its client for the losses they suffered after having lent money in respect of a proposed property development.

6.88 Lord Sumption commented as follows:

> '39. Turning to the distinction between advice and information, this has given rise to confusion largely because of the descriptive inadequacy of these labels. On the face of it they are neither distinct nor mutually exclusive categories. Information given by a professional man to his client is usually a specific form of advice, and most advice will involve conveying information. Neither label really corresponds to the contents of the bottle. The nature of the distinction is, however, clear from its place in Lord Hoffmann's analysis as well as from his language.
>
> 40. In cases falling within Lord Hoffmann's "advice" category, it is left to the adviser to consider what matters should be taken into account in deciding whether to enter into the transaction. His duty is to consider all relevant matters and not only specific factors in the decision. If one of those matters is negligently ignored or misjudged, and this proves to be critical to the decision, the client will in principle be entitled to recover all loss flowing from the transaction which he should have protected his client against. The House of Lords might have said of the "advice" cases that the client was entitled to the losses flowing from the transaction if they were not just attributable to risks within the scope of the adviser's duty but to risks which had been negligently assessed by the adviser. In the great majority of cases, this would have assimilated the two categories. An "adviser" would simply have been legally responsible for a wider range of informational errors. But in a case where the adviser is responsible for guiding the whole decision-making process, there is a certain pragmatic justice in the test that the Appellate Committee preferred. If the adviser has a duty to protect his client (so far as due care can do it) against the full range of risks associated with a potential transaction, the client will not have retained responsibility for any of them. The adviser's responsibility extends to the decision. If the adviser has negligently assessed risk A, the result is that the overall riskiness of the transaction has been understated. If the client would not have entered into the transaction on a careful assessment of its overall merits, the fact that the loss may have resulted from risks B, C or D should not matter.
>
> 41. By comparison, in the "information" category, a professional adviser contributes a limited part of the material on which his client will rely in deciding whether to enter into a prospective transaction, but the process of identifying the other relevant considerations and the overall assessment of the commercial merits of the transaction are exclusively matters for the client (or possibly his other advisers). In such a case, as Lord Hoffmann explained in *Nykredit*, the defendant's legal responsibility does not extend to the decision itself. It follows that even if the material which the defendant supplied is known to be critical to the decision to enter into the transaction, he is liable only for the financial consequences of its being wrong and not for the financial consequences of the claimant entering into the transaction so far as these are greater. Otherwise the defendant would become the

underwriter of the financial fortunes of the whole transaction by virtue of having assumed a duty of care in relation to just one element of someone else's decision.

42. What is clear is that the fact that the material contributed by the defendant is known to be critical to the claimant's decision whether to enter into the transaction does not itself turn it into an "advice" case. Otherwise all "no transaction" cases would give rise to liability for the entire foreseeable loss flowing from the transaction, which is the very proposition rejected in *SAAMCO*. I respectfully agree with the careful analysis of this point by Rix LJ, giving the leading judgment in the Court of Appeal in *Haugesund Kommune v Depfa ACS Bank (Wikborg Rein & Co, Part 20 defendant) (No 2)* [2011] 3 All ER 655. The facts of that case were that a firm of lawyers had negligently advised that a Norwegian local authority had legal capacity to enter into a loan agreement, when it did not. A local authority's legal capacity to borrow might fairly be thought fundamental to any decision to lend it money, and the evidence was that but for the lawyer's advice the bank would not have lent. But under Norwegian law the debt would not have been enforceable against the assets of the authority even if legal capacity had existed, making the debt in effect one of honour only. Rix LJ held that it was an "information" case because legal capacity was only one factor in a wider assessment of whether to lend the money, with which the lawyers were not concerned. At para 75, he said:

> "It is of course true that Depfa would not have entered into the transactions at all unless it could be advised that the contracts were valid and within the kommunes' capacity. In effect, that causal connection between advice and loss goes without saying in all such cases. It is not in itself the reason for finding that the scope of duty concerned embraces all the loss consequential upon entering into the transaction concerned. For these reasons it does not seem to me that it is a sufficient explanation for characterising a case as a category 2 [sc 'advice'] case to say that, without the forthcoming albeit negligent advice, the transaction concerned would not have been 'viable'. That is simply another way of saying that, if the claimant had not received the advice it did, it would not have entered into the transaction.'"

6.89 In *Manchester Building Society v Grant Thornton UK LLP* [2019] EWCA Civ 40[17], the Court of Appeal considered the liability of an auditor for losses incurred on long term interest rate swap agreements which were entered into in reliance upon negligent accounting advice and which were closed out at a loss when the negligent advice came to light.

6.90 The Court (at 51–53) commented:

'51 In order to recover the foreseeable loss suffered as a result of entering into the transaction it is necessary to show that it is an "advice" case. An

17 See also *Assetco Plc v Grant Thornton UK LLP* [2020] EWCA Civ 1151.

"advice" case is where "it is left to the adviser to consider what matters should be taken into account in deciding whether to enter into the transaction. His duty is to consider all relevant matters and not only specific matters in the decision". He is "responsible for guiding the whole decision-making process" (para 40). In such circumstances "the adviser's responsibility extends to the decision" to enter the transaction and he is liable for the foreseeable losses flowing from having entered into it.

52 Unless the adviser is "responsible for guiding the whole decision-making process" in the way described, it is an "information" case. In an "information" case the adviser or information provider is not responsible for the decision to enter into the transaction and is accordingly not responsible for all the foreseeable financial consequences of so doing. He is only responsible for the foreseeable financial consequences of the information or advice being wrong (para 41).

53 In order to determine what are the foreseeable financial consequences of the information or advice being wrong it is necessary to exclude all losses which would have been suffered if the information or advice had been correct – the "*SAAMCO* cap". As Lord Sumption explains at para 45, this is "a tool for giving effect to the distinction between (i) loss flowing from the fact that as a result of the defendant's negligence the information was wrong and (ii) loss flowing from the decision to enter into the transaction at all". It reflects "the award of loss which is within the scope of the defendant's duty" rather than "the exclusion of loss which is outside it" (para 46).'

CONTRIBUTORY NEGLIGENCE

6.91 If a person is in breach of a contractual duty of care, which would also be liable under the laws of negligence then the amount of the damages will be reduced to reflect any contributory negligence by the claimant. In *Forsikringsaktieselskapet Vesta v Butcher* [1989] AC 852, 860-867, 875, 879, the Court of Appeal adopted the three categories of breach described by Hobhouse J as he then was in the first instance judgment ([1986] 2 All ER 488, 508):

'(1) Where the defendant's liability arises from some contractual provision which does not depend on negligence on the part of the defendant.

(2) Where the defendant's liability arises from a contractual obligation which is expressed in terms of taking care (or its equivalent) but does not correspond to a common law duty to take care which would exist in the given case independently of contract.

(3) Where the defendant's liability in contract is the same as his liability in the tort of negligence independently of the existence of any contract.'

6.92 For the first category, the defendant cannot utilise the defence of contributory negligence.

6.93 In respect of the second, the defendant may only avail itself of the defence if there is a *Hedley Byrne* type relationship between the parties.

6.94 If the third category exists, the defence of contributory negligence is conceptually available to a defendant if it is made out on the facts.

6.95 The *Law Reform (Contributory Negligence) Act 1945, s1(1)* deals with the apportionment of liability in the case of contributory negligence which enables a court to restrict the amount of damages recoverable by reference to the claimant's share in responsibility for the damage. The subsection states:

> '(1) Where any person suffers damage as the result partly of his own fault and partly of the fault of any other person or persons, a claim in respect of that damage shall not be defeated by reason of the fault of the person suffering the damage, but the damages recoverable in respect thereof shall be reduced to such extent as the court thinks just and equitable having regard to the claimant's share in the responsibility for the damage:
>
> Provided that—
>
> (a) this subsection shall not operate to defeat any defence arising under a contract;
>
> (b) where any contract or enactment providing for the limitation of liability is applicable to the claim, the amount of damages recoverable by the claimant by virtue of this subsection shall not exceed the maximum limit so applicable.'

The provisions of the 1945 Act apply to contractual liability where it is based on a failure to take reasonable care and that failure also comprised negligence under the law of tort.

LOSS OF CHANCE

6.96 A breach of duty by a professional adviser may involve an allegation that there has been an omission by the adviser (eg the failure to advise on an alternative planning arrangement). In these circumstances, had the breach not occurred, the extent of any loss may depend on the actions of a third party.

6.97 In determining the level of losses, the court will consider two issues:

- The claimant must prove on the balance of probabilities what he would have done if the breach of duty had not occurred. (This may be called the primary causation issue.)
- If the claimant discharges the burden on the primary causation issue, the damages will be assessed on the basis of the value of the chance that the third party would have acted in such a way as to confer the benefit.

6.98 In a tax context where there is an alternative basis for saving tax, then: (i) the court must decide on the balance of probabilities whether the claimant would have implemented the alternative planning; and (ii), if the court finds that the claimant would have implemented it, it must assess the chance that the alternative planning would have been successful in mitigating the amount of tax paid by the claimant (ie the chance that HMRC would not have made a successful challenge to the planning).

6.99 The position has been explained by the High Court in *Altus Group Ltd v Baker Tilly Tax & Advisory Services and Another* [2015] EWHC 12 (Ch) in these terms (at para 60):

> 'If the claimant can prove that, but for the defendants' breach of duty, it would have implemented the New LLP Proposal [the alternative tax planning], the benefit it would have gained from that scheme will depend on the prospects of it being successfully challenged. If the scheme had not been successfully challenged, the claimant would as a matter of fact have paid less tax. The resulting financial loss is no less real than, for example, the loss resulting from the loss of the opportunity to negotiate a more advantageous settlement of a dispute. In the latter case, the loss is not illusory merely because it might be said that the settlement actually achieved accurately reflected the strict legal merits of the dispute. I shall consider below whether there is something special about tax cases.'

6.100 The relevant approach on a loss of chance claim is set out in the judgment of Stuart-Smith LJ in *Allied Maples Group Ltd v Simmons & Simmons* [1995] 1 WLR 1602, at 1609–11:

> '[W]here the plaintiffs' loss depends upon the actions of an independent third party, it is necessary to consider as a matter of law what it is necessary to establish as a matter of causation, and where causation ends and quantification of damage begins.
>
> (1) What has to be proved to establish a causal link between the negligence of the defendants and the loss sustained by the plaintiffs depends in the first instance on whether the negligence consists of some positive act or misfeasance, or an omission or non-feasance. In the former case, the question of causation is one of historical fact. The court has to determine on the balance of probability whether the defendant's act, for example the careless driving, caused the plaintiff's loss consisting of his broken leg. Once established on balance of probability, that fact is taken as true and the plaintiff recovers his damage in full. …
>
> (2) If the defendant's negligence consists of an omission … causation depends, not upon a question of historical fact, but on the answer to the hypothetical question, what would the plaintiff have done if the equipment had been provided or the instruction or advice given? This can only be a matter of inference to be determined from all the circumstances. …

Although the question is a hypothetical one, it is well established that the plaintiff must prove on balance of probability that he would have taken action to obtain the benefit or avoid the risk. But again, if he does establish that, there is no discount because the balance is only just tipped in his favour. …

(3) In many cases the plaintiff's loss depends on the hypothetical action of a third party, either in addition to action by the plaintiff, as in this case, or independently of it. In such a case, does the plaintiff have to prove on balance of probability, as Mr. Jackson submits, that the third party would have acted so as to confer the benefit or avoid the risk to the plaintiff, or can the plaintiff succeed provided he shows that he had a substantial chance rather than a speculative one, the evaluation of the substantial chance being a question of quantification of damages?

Although there is not a great deal of authority, and none in the Court of Appeal, relating to solicitors failing to give advice which is directly in point, I have no doubt that Mr. Jackson's submission is wrong and the second alternative is correct.'

6.101 This suggests that the correct approach will generally be to assess the chance of the scheme succeeding or failing upon a challenge, although there may be cases where it is appropriate to determine the legal point[18].

6.102 In *Altus Group Ltd* (at **6.99** above), the Court stated that: 'The fact that one of the contingencies on which the outcome was dependent was a judicial decision by the First-tier Tribunal or Upper Tribunal would not by itself preclude the "loss of a chance" approach'.

6.103 The usual principle is that, where the chance in question relates to the outcome of other judicial proceedings if they had been fought, it is inappropriate to try those proceedings as a trial within a trial[19].

6.104 Of course, if the law on a point is clear, it will be inappropriate to proceed on the assumption that the court or tribunal would have got it wrong.

6.105 The fact that the efficacy of the claimant's hypothetical conduct in achieving a benefit or avoiding a risk would have turned on a point of law does not by itself make the 'loss of a chance' approach inappropriate, although in a suitable case the appropriate course might be to resolve the point of tax law.

LIMITATION PERIOD

6.106 A claim for negligence must be issued within six years from the date on which the cause of action accrued (*Limitation Act 1980, s 2* (*LA 1980*))[20].

18 *Altus Group Ltd* at [62].

19 *Dixon v Clement Jones Solicitors* [2004] EWCA Civ 1005, per Rix LJ at [27].

20 See www.legislation.gov.uk.

This effectively means that the claim must be brought within six years from the date on which the damage/loss is suffered. However, such a claim may be made in respect of latent damage in circumstances where the claimant does not have knowledge of all material facts within the six-year period.

6.107 For example, if a person enters into a transaction which it is advised to have specific tax advantages (but unknown to the person it does not qualify), then the person will incur damage from the date of the transaction because there will be a liability to tax. Accordingly, this is the primary limitation period.

6.108 If the client is not aware of the damage it is nonetheless possible for the limitation period to be extended under *section 14A* of *LA 1980*. See also **6.118** below.

6.109 *Section 14A* may save a negligence action if the claimants can show that they did not have 'the knowledge required for bringing an action in damages' in the period, being three years before the claim was issued.

6.110 The effect of *section 14A* is to result in a further limitation period running against a person, but only in circumstances where that person would have had to have knowledge, or reasonably be expected to have had knowledge that:

- he or she suffered damage; and
- this loss was attributable to an act or omission of the adviser.

6.111 In these circumstances, in the context of professional advice, the damage will be that the person is liable for tax (eg because the arrangements entered into did not satisfy the relevant statutory requirements). Once a person knew or should have known that he suffered that damage, he would have realised that the advice he had been given by the adviser was defective (which was due to reliance on their advice). However, to start the period of limitation, the person does not need to know that their advice was negligent, ie that it was such as no reasonably competent tax adviser of appropriate expertise could have given (*LA 1980, s 14A(9)*).

WHEN IS DAMAGE SUFFERED?

6.112 *Section 2* of *LA 1980* provides that 'an action founded on tort shall not be brought after the expiration of six years from the date on which the cause of action accrued'.

6.113 The time when a person suffers damage is fact sensitive. The potential points in time, include when a person relies on the advice and enters into a tax planning arrangement, disposes of an asset, acquires an asset and when HMRC issue an assessment.

6.114 Is damage only suffered when a court or tribunal issues an adverse finding in respect of tax planning arrangements? The answer is no, because interest will start to run from when HMRC issues an adverse decision or tax assessment. In *Integral Memory Plc v Haines Watts* [2012] STI 1385 it was stated at para 32:

> 'The claimant's liability to pay interest on the unpaid NIC to HMRC was in no relevant sense contingent. A contingent liability is a liability which, by reason of something done by the person bound, may or may not arise depending on the happening of a future event … That was not the position in the present case. There was either an actual liability to pay NIC and interest on arrears or there was not. The existence of such liability is not contingent on HMRC succeeding or failing in a tax tribunal … All the tribunal or court is deciding is whether or not there is an actual liability … The fallacy … is demonstrated by [counsel's] submission that where a debt is incurred, but disputed, and court proceedings follow, the liability is contingent until the court gives judgment in favour of the creditor … That submission is clearly wrong.'

Further guidance is provided by the cases of *Pegasus Management Holdings SCA v Ernst & Young* [2010] EWCA Civ 181 and *Shore v Sedgwick Financial Services Ltd* [2008] EWCA Civ 863.

6.115 In *Pegasus* there was a claim for damages for professional negligence in respect of the alleged failure of Ernst & Young to give the claimants proper tax planning advice. Ernst & Young advised Mr Bradbury to set up the claimant company in order to qualify for tax relief, which Mr Bradbury did in March 1998. The claimant company then acquired a business and the alleged negligence was failing to advise the company that it should acquire the business through another route.

6.116 Rimer LJ said:

> '[81] It is correct that even without such a structure, there was no certainty that Mr Bradbury would suffer the Adverse Consequence. He could have sought to ensure that all Pegasus's purchases of qualifying trades were by way of asset purchases rather than share purchases. There must, however, be an uncertainty that he could achieve that in the case of every acquisition; and to the extent that it could not, the risk of the Adverse Consequence remained. The alleged flaw in the E & Y 's advice was therefore a material one, which immediately reduced Mr Bradbury's flexibility. It left him in a materially worse commercial position that he ought to have been in by inhibiting the way in which he might go about acquiring qualifying trades. He was so disadvantaged immediately upon the completion of the transaction. He was so disadvantaged not because his shares in Pegasus were then worth less than he paid for them; but because the shares did not give him the control of a company with characteristics that would be proof against the Adverse Consequence … Moreover, once April 6, 1998 … was passed, the defect was incapable of cure. Mr Bradbury *was not thereby inevitably doomed to suffer the Adverse Consequence; but he was thereby tied into a commercially disadvantageous straitjacket.* [Emphasis added]

[82] Did E & Y's alleged failure cause Mr Bradbury actual damage for the purposes of completing the tort of negligence that forms the basis of his claim? … There is a clear line of Court of Appeal authority that damage sufficient to complete the tort of negligence will or may be caused in a "wrong transaction" case by the fact that, as a result of the defendant's negligence, the claimant has not received what he ought to have received. It is, in particular, not necessary to show that the claimant is immediately put into a position in which he is financially worse off than he would have been had the defendant not been negligent …

[83] … I agree … that the "wrong transaction" cases do not represent any exception from the general *tort principle that actual damage must be suffered before the tort is complete.*' [Emphasis added]

6.117 In *Shore*, Dyson LJ said at para 42:

'… I do not accept that the transaction cases can be distinguished as [counsel] contends. It is true that none of them concerned a transaction in which it was possible that the claimant would be better off financially as a result of the negligence than he would have been but for the negligence. But the essence of the reasoning in those cases is that *the fact that the risk to which the claimant was exposed by the defendant's negligence might not eventuate did not mean that the claimant did not suffer loss as a result of being exposed to that risk.…* The fact that the financial benefits accruing to Mr Shaw from the PFW scheme might not be less than those accruing to him from the Avesta scheme did not mean that he did not suffer loss when he invested in the scheme and was then and there exposed to the risk that they might be less. It is the possibility of actual financial harm that constitutes the loss. That possibility is present even if there is also the possibility that the claimant will be financially better off as a result of being exposed to the risk.' [Emphasis added]

LATENT DAMAGE

6.118 Where the claim is outside the six-year period, any claimant will need to show that the claim in tort is brought within three years from the starting date pursuant to *section 14A* of *LA 1980*. The 'starting date' is defined in *subsection (5)* as:

'the earliest date on which the plaintiff or any person in whom the cause of action was vested before him first had both the knowledge required for bringing an action for damages in respect of the relevant damage and a right to bring such an action.'

6.119 In *Jacobs v Sesame* [2014] EWCA Civ 1410 (CA), the defendant, a financial adviser, advised the claimant to invest £65,000 in a bond. Its representative led her to believe that there was no chance of her receiving less than £65,000 when the investment period elapsed. The claimant surrendered the bond in February 2012 when its value was approximately £53,000. On the issue of limitation, it was asserted that the claimant had sufficient knowledge to bring a claim in July 2009. The claimant contended that it was not until 2012 that she had known either that she had suffered a loss or that she might have received inappropriate advice. The Court of Appeal held (at para 29) that the starting point of any enquiry whether a claimant could rely upon the special time limit made available by *section 14A*, was to identify the damage in respect of which indemnity was claimed.

6.120 *Section 14A* of *LA 1980* applies to an action for damages for negligence other than a personal injury claim and provides, insofar as material:

> '(3) An action to which this section applies shall not be brought after the expiration of the period applicable in accordance with subsection (4) below.
>
> (4) That period is either—
>
> (a) six years from the date on which the cause of action accrued; or
>
> (b) three years from the starting date as defined by subsection (5) below, if that period expires later than the period mentioned in paragraph (a) above.
>
> (5) For the purposes of this section, the starting date for reckoning the period of limitation under subsection (4)(b) above is the earliest date on which the plaintiff or any person in whom the cause of action was vested before him first had both the knowledge required for bringing an action for damages in respect of the relevant damage and a right to bring such an action.
>
> (6) In subsection (5) above "the knowledge required for bringing an action for damages in respect of the relevant damage" means knowledge both—
>
> (a) of the material facts about the damage in respect of which damages are claimed; and
>
> (b) of the other facts relevant to the current action mentioned in subsection (8) below.
>
> (7) For the purpose of subsection (6)(a) above, the material facts about the damage are such facts about the damage as would lead a reasonable person who had suffered such damage to consider it sufficiently serious to justify his instituting proceedings for damages against a defendant who did not dispute liability and was able to satisfy a judgment.
>
> (8) The other facts referred to in subsection (6)(b) above are—
>
> (a) that the damage was attributable in whole or in part to the act or omission which is alleged to constitute negligence; and

(b) the identity of the defendant; and

(c) if it is alleged that the act or omission was that of a person other than the defendant, the identity of that person and the additional facts supporting the bringing of an action against the defendant.

(9) Knowledge that any acts or omissions did or did not, as a matter of law, involve negligence is irrelevant for the purposes of subsection (5) above.

(10) For the purposes of this section a person's knowledge included knowledge which he might reasonably have been expected to acquire—

(a) from facts observable or ascertainable by him; or

(b) from facts ascertainable by him with the help of appropriate expert advice which it is reasonable for him to seek;

but a person shall not be taken by virtue of this subsection to have knowledge of a fact ascertainable only with the help of expert advice so long as he has taken all reasonable steps to obtain (and, where appropriate, to act on) that advice.'

6.121 The threshold for knowledge under *section 14A* must not be placed too high, and a court should approach the question of whether a claimant had the requisite knowledge in a common-sense way.

6.122 Hence, in *Halford v Brookes* [1991] 1 WLR 428, Lord Donaldson MR stated as follows (at 443):

> 'In this context "knowledge" clearly does not mean "know for certain and beyond possibility of contradiction." It does, however, mean "know with sufficient confidence to justify embarking on the preliminaries to the issue of a writ, such as submitting a claim to the proposed defendant, taking legal and other advice and collecting evidence." Suspicion, particularly if it is vague and unsupported, will indeed not be enough, but reasonable belief will normally suffice.'

6.123 And in *Spencer-Ward v Humberts* [1995] 06 EG 148, Bingham LJ said (at 151):

> 'It is, I think, necessary that issues on this section [14A] should be approached in a broad common-sense way, bearing in mind the object of the section and the injustice that it was intended to mitigate. There is a danger of being too clever and it would usually be possible to find some fact of which a plaintiff did not become sure until later. It would be a pity if a desire to be indulgent to plaintiffs led the court to be unfair to defendants.'

6.124 In *Hallam-Eames v Merrett Syndicates Ltd* [2001] Lloyd's Rep PN 178 at 181, considering the extent of the knowledge required, Hoffmann LJ emphasised the statutory wording 'attributable … to the act or omission which is alleged to constitute negligence' and continued:

> 'In other words, the act or omission of which the plaintiff must have knowledge must be that which is causally relevant for the purposes of an allegation of negligence … It is this idea of causal relevance which various judges of this court have tried to express by saying the plaintiff must know the "essence of the act or omission to which the injury is attributable" (Purchas LJ in *Nash v Eli Lilly & Co* [1993] 1 WLR 782, 799) or "the essential thrust of the case" (Sir Thomas Bingham MR in *Dobbie v Medway Health Authority* [1991] 1 WLR 428, 1238[21]) or that "one should look at the way the plaintiff puts his case, distil what he is complaining about and ask whether he had in broad terms knowledge of the facts on which that complaint is based" (Hoffmann LJ in *Broadley v Guy Clapham & Co* [1993] 4 Med LR 328, 332).'

6.125 There are two aspects to knowledge for this purpose: the degree of certainty and the degree of detail. As to the degree of certainty the applicable test set out in *Halford* v *Brookes* was approved by Lord Nicholls in *Haward v Fawcetts* [2006] UKHL 9 at para 9 of the judgment:

> '… thus, as to the degree of certainty required, Lord Donaldson … gave valuable guidance in *Halford v Brookes* … He noted that knowledge does not mean knowing for certain and beyond possibility of contradiction. It means *knowing with sufficient confidence to justify embarking on the preliminaries* to the issue of the claim form, such as submitting a claim to the proposed defendant, *taking advice and collecting evidence*. "Suspicion, particularly if it is vague and unsupported, will indeed not be enough but reasonable belief will normally suffice." In other words, *the claimant must know enough for it to be reasonable to begin to investigate further.*' [Emphasis added]

6.126 As to the degree of detail, in *Haward,* Lord Nicholls said that the claimant must know there was a real possibility the damage was caused by ('attributable to') the acts or omissions alleged to constitute negligence; in that case the giving of flawed advice. He said (at para 21) that:

> 'For time to start running there needs to have *been something which would reasonably cause Mr Haward to start asking questions about the advice he was given.*' [Emphasis added]

LONG-STOP

6.127 *Section 14B* of *LA 1980* imposes a long-stop date for the issue of proceedings.

---

21 *Dobbie v Medway Health Authority* [1994] 1 WLR 1234, [1994] 4 All ER 450, [1994] 5 WLUK 116, [1994] PIQR P353, [1994] 5 Med LR 160, (1994) 144 NLJ 828.

6.128 An action in respect of a breach of duty more than 15 years old at the date proceedings were issued, even if at that date no damage had arisen from that breach of duty is time barred.

6.129 *Section 14B* provides that for claims in negligence:

> '(1) An action for damages for negligence, other than one to which section 11 of this Act applies, shall not be brought after the expiration of fifteen years from the date (or, if more than one, from the last of the dates) on which there occurred any act or omission—
>
> (a) which is alleged to constitute negligence; and
>
> (b) to which the damage in respect of which damages are claimed is alleged to be attributable (in whole or in part).
>
> (2) This section bars the right of action in a case to which subsection (1) above applies notwithstanding that—
>
> (a) the cause of action has not yet accrued; or
>
> (b) where section 14A of this Act applies to the action, the date which is for the purposes of that section the starting date for reckoning the period mentioned in subsection (4)(b) of that section has not yet occurred;
>
> before the end of the period of limitation prescribed by this section.'

CONCLUSION

6.130 To minimise the risk of any allegation of tax negligence, it is essential that the tax professional:

- enters into clear written terms of engagement with the client which identifies the scope and nature of the service being provided and what is excluded from the retainer; and caveats any advice by reference to assumptions which are brought to the attention of the client as part of the terms and conditions of engagement;
- understands the facts relevant to the client and the objectives of the client;
- only advises on an area of law where the tax professional is a specialist;
- keeps up to date in the adviser's specialist area of practice; and
- complies with relevant professional standards imposed by a professional body (eg the PCRT).

Chapter 7

Privilege in tax disputes

George Gillham, Partner, and Christopher Kientzler, Barrister, Fieldfisher LLP

SIGNPOSTS

Introduction

- Legal professional privilege can protect some communications between client and lawyer, and in certain situations third parties such as tax advisers, from being seen or used by HMRC in litigation. This is to allow taxpayers to receive candid advice (see **7.1–7.2**).
- Privilege will be relevant to HMRC and taxpayers in particular contexts but mainly when HMRC exercise their information powers under *Schedule 36* to the *Finance Act 2008* (*FA 2008*), or in Tribunal proceedings (see **7.3** and **7.16–7.40**).
- Mistakes in disclosing privileged material can jeopardise a client's position. Privilege only applies in specific limited situations to communications with tax advisors and accountants (see **7.7–7.8** and **7.72–7.95** and **7.123–7.129**).
- This chapter deals with common law privilege as applied in England & Wales although parallel rights exist in Scottish law (see **7.10**).
- Privilege is a complicated and fact-sensitive area and will often require specialist advice (see **7.11–7.13** and **7.195–7.202**).
- No adverse inference should be drawn from someone relying on privilege (see **7.14** and **7.15**).

HMRC's information powers in FA 2008, Sch 36 privilege and its analogs

- *Schedule 36* to *FA 2008* sets out HMRC's statutory information gathering powers, which involve the use of an information notice (see **7.16–7.40**).

- Taxpayers can resist disclosing documents and information sought in an information notice on the basis that the material sought is privileged, and there are prescriptive processes that have to be followed in those circumstances (see **7.16–7.33**).
- Disclosure under an information notice can also be resisted where information relates to the conduct of an appeal (see **7.34–7.35**). It can also be resisted where a document is an auditor's or a tax adviser's document (see **7.36–7.40**). These are statutory analogs of privilege. They can be relied upon when HMRC are exercising their information powers but not when disclosure is sought in litigation (see **7.18** and **7.19**).

Communications must be confidential to be privileged

- For privilege to apply, a communication must be confidential which will often be the case unless confidentiality is lost (see **7.41–7.47**).

Two heads of privilege

- There are two different types of legal professional privilege which are related but have different rules. Broadly, legal advice privilege has the benefit of covering communications at any point, but the disadvantage that it only covers client-lawyer communications or communications evidencing qualifying advice. Litigation privilege can cover third party communications when made for a litigation purpose and when litigation is 'in the air' (see **7.48**).

Legal advice privilege (LAP)

- LAP applies to communications passing between a client and lawyers, acting in their professional capacity, in connection with the provision of legal advice (see **7.49–7.59**).
- Its scope is limited due to the restricted meaning of 'lawyer' and 'client' (see **7.72–7.80**).
- LAP is less important in tax disputes but can sometimes have a bearing such as when a 'main purpose' test applies, or as a fall-back when litigation privilege does not apply (see **7.57**).
- LAP covers two categories of communications: communications between lawyers and clients for the dominant purpose of seeking or giving legal advice (Category A) and communications that evidence the substance of such communications (Category B) (see **7.62–7.69**).

- Where there is a series of communications it may be that the whole series is covered rather than individual pieces, but it is important to keep in mind that giving or receiving legal advice must be the dominant purpose of the communication (see **7.62–7.64**).
- Category B comes with its own nuances (see **7.65–7.69**).
- The meaning of 'lawyer' and 'legal adviser' excludes tax advisers for various reasons so that communications with those professionals are not covered by LAP (see **7.72–7.80**).
- Communications with third parties are not covered by LAP unless the third parties are a mere conduit (see **7.81–7.87**).
- Complications arise where there are composite communications involving more than just client and lawyer, leading to particular treatments of a lawyer's response, an email from a client to a lawyer and others, meetings with lawyers and others (see **7.88–7.95**).
- The meaning of 'client' is restricted in a corporate context; the decision in *Three Rivers (No 5)* discussed (see **7.99–7.114**).
- Attachments to emails should generally be treated as separate communications (see **7.115**).

Litigation privilege (LP)

- LP protects communications between a party to a dispute and their lawyers and third parties where the communications are made for the sole or dominant purpose of obtaining information or advice in connection with existing or contemplated litigation (see **7.116–7.145**).
- LP is only available in litigation, which does not include investigatory or inquisitorial processes (see **7.146–7.147**).

Exceptions to privilege

- There are exceptions to privilege, which mean that privilege that would have applied, does not apply in certain circumstances (see **7.148**).
- Privilege can be lost or waived intentionally or unintentionally in a number of ways, which include sharing a privileged document, and advisers should be aware of the possible pitfalls (see **7.149–7.183**).

- As a result, advisers should be careful to take into account various considerations before sharing privileged material with HMRC (see **7.184–7.188**).
- Acts of Parliament sometimes provide that legal privilege does not apply, and privilege may not be applicable to communications made for an illegal or nefarious purpose (see **7.189–7.193**).

INTRODUCTION

General

7.1 Legal professional privilege is a fundamental right of the client whose privilege it is. Generally, privileged documents cannot be ordered to be provided by the party whose privilege it is, in respect of an HMRC enquiry or litigation, unless this is as a result of a waiver. The fact that such documents might be highly relevant does not entail their production. Accordingly, a tax professional who is a legal adviser is under an absolute obligation not to disclose any privileged communications without waiver of privilege (see in *DAC Beachcroft LLP v HMRC*[1] where HMRC were refused access to certain documents in respect of a third-party information notice issued under *FA 2008, Sch 36*). Legal professional privilege can protect some communications between client and solicitors, barristers, or foreign lawyers ('Lawyers'), and in certain situations third parties such as tax advisers, from being seen or used by HMRC, other taxpayers, the tax tribunals, or the courts. Protected communications can encompass emails, letters, notes, what was said at meetings and also a witness's recollections of phone calls; they need not be in written form, but usually are. Privilege is a valuable right but discerning what is and is not privileged is difficult in the context of any dispute with HMRC.

7.2 The purpose of privilege is, 'that a person can seek and obtain legal advice with candour and full disclosure, secure in the knowledge that the communications involved can never be used against that person'[2].

7.3 When HMRC exercises its information powers and makes a request for information and documents under *Schedule 36* to *FA 2008*, a taxpayer or third party can object to disclosure of a communication if it is covered

1 *DAC Beachcroft LLP v The Commissioners for Her Majesty's Revenue and Customs* [2018] UKFTT 0502 (TC).

2 *R (on the application of Prudential plc and Another) v Special Commissioner of Income Tax and Another* [2013] UKSC 1, at [39], [2013] 2 AC 185, at 219. See also Gosforth CJ in *R v Derby Magistrates' Court, ex p B* [1996] AC 487, at 507, 508; Lord Hoffmann in *R (on the application of Morgan Grenfell & Co Ltd) v Special Commissioners of Income Tax* [2002] UKHL 21, at [7], [2003] 1 AC 563, at 607(HL); Lord Scott in *Three Rivers DC v Bank of England (No 6)* [2004] UKHL 48, at [29]–[33], [2005] 1 AC 610, at 647–649.

by privilege[3] (see more at **7.20–7.33** below). In addition, in setting out and defining HMRC's powers to obtain information during an enquiry or otherwise from taxpayers and third parties, Parliament has provided statutory analogs under *Schedule 36* to *FA 2008* (see **7.34–7.40** below). One of these analogs protects certain communications with tax advisers, which are otherwise only covered by privilege in limited circumstances, but does so on a narrow footing (see **7.36–7.40**).

7.4 In proceedings in the First-tier Tribunal (Tax Chamber) (FTT), a party cannot be compelled to allow inspection of documents that are privileged[4]. An informal request for information and documents by HMRC can (and in many instances probably ought to) be politely declined by the taxpayer or their adviser insofar as documents are privileged; see **7.149–7.188** below. In the context of a criminal investigation, where special procedure material may be obtained by a police officer from a Lawyer, privileged material is still protected from compulsory disclosure[5].

7.5 While the FTT was originally intended to provide a speedier, lower-cost, and less formal forum for resolution of tax matters than the courts, HMRC is typically much less resource-constrained than individual taxpayers. That allows HMRC to put pressure on taxpayers and their agents in contentious proceedings. So, in a litigation context, privilege can be particularly precious.

7.6 HMRC also can assert privilege; privileged material can be withheld when a taxpayer applies for an order for inspection or disclosure of such material. Similarly, where a taxpayer makes a data access request in respect of information held by HMRC, privileged material (such as legal advice received by HMRC) is excluded from the requirement to provide information[6]. Although not strictly a matter of privilege, HMRC may also refuse to disclose information where this would potentially jeopardise an ongoing investigation (this is a common reason for non-disclosure in criminal investigations).

7.7 Mistakes made by disclosing privileged materials can jeopardise a client's position, because privilege in those documents can then be lost (see **7.149–7.183**).

---

3 *FA 2008, s 113, Sch 36, para 23*. See also: *R (on the application of Morgan Grenfell & Co Ltd) v Special Commissioners of Income Tax* [2002] UKHL 21, in relation to a call for documents of taxpayer and others under *TMA 1970, s 20* (now repealed and replaced by *FA 2008, s 113, Sch 36*).

4 *Rule 27(3)* of the *Tribunal Procedure (First-tier Tribunal) (Tax Chamber) Rules 2009, SI 2009/273 (L1)*. See *Janet Addo v The Commissioners for Her Majesty's Revenue & Customs* [2018] UKFTT 530.

5 The *Police and Criminal Evidence Act 1984, s 9* provides a constable the power to obtain special procedure material defined in *s 14(2)* as not including privileged material as defined in *s 10*.

6 *General Data Protection Regulation (EU) 2016/679, Art 15* sets out the right to access and Member States can make exemptions under *Art 23*. The *Data Protection Act 2018, Sch 2, para 19* provides a privilege exemption which applies to the listed GDPR provisions, including GDPR, Art 15 (see *Sch 2, para 6*). See *Gaines-Cooper v Revenue and Customs Commissioners* [2017] EWHC 868 (Ch) is an interesting example but note that it is based on previous law.

7.8 Privilege only applies in very specific circumstances to communications with tax advisers, or accountants (see **7.72–7.95** and **7.123–7.129** in particular). Nevertheless, it is a relevant topic for any tax adviser involved in tax disputes, because it limits and decides what documents HMRC and taxpayers may inspect. Tax advisers who are not involved in disputes, but give advice on matters that may later end in dispute, are also aided in understanding the rules of privilege because proper attention to questions of privilege can prevent time-consuming and costly disputes down the line (see Case studies 2 (at **7.196**) and 3 (at **7.197**) by way of example). As a result, tax advisers should attempt to obtain a clear understanding of when privilege does apply, when it can be asserted, and when it might be in clients' best interests to involve a Lawyer; so that any advice, or document that is created, is covered by privilege.

7.9 It is important, however, to remember that privilege belongs to the client and not the Lawyer[7] or other adviser. This means that an adviser cannot refuse to disclose privileged material where the client insists that the material is disclosed; although giving clear warnings as to the downsides of doing so are advisable for professional liability reasons if nothing else.

7.10 While rights similar to privilege exist in Scottish law[8], this chapter only covers common law legal professional privilege as interpreted in England and Wales; and the specific provisions under *Schedule 36* to *FA 2008*, which latter are applicable throughout the United Kingdom.

Privilege is a difficult area which may require specialist advice

7.11 Privilege is a creature of common law[9] and is therefore mainly contained in case law but, in some cases, legislation has fully or partially codified[10], and occasionally extended, its application[11]. It is thus a complicated subject with no comprehensive statutory code to which tax advisers may refer.

---

7 *Ventouris v Mountain* [1991] 1 WLR 607, at 611 and Lord Neuberger in *R (on the application of Prudential plc and Another) v Special Commissioner of Income Tax and Another* [2013] UKSC 1, at [22], [2013] 2 AC 185, at 216 (Bingham LJ).

8 More often referred to as 'confidentiality in communications'. See Lord Reed's exposition in the Inner House of the Court of Sessions in *Narden Services Ltd v Inverness Retail and Business Park Ltd* [2008] CSIH 14, 2008 SC 335, at [11].

9 See Taylor CJ's summary in *R v Derby Magistrates' Court, ex p B* [1996] AC 487, at 504–507.

10 *Police and Criminal Evidence Act 1984, s 10*, interpreted as demonstrating Parliament's intention to reflect common law principles: *R v Central Criminal Court, ex p Francis & Francis* [1989] AC 346, at 392, 295.

11 *Copyright, Designs and Patents Act 1988, s 280, Trade Marks Act 1994, s 87* and *Administration of Justice Act 1985, s 33*, and see *R (on the application of Prudential plc and Another) v Special Commissioner of Income Tax and Another* [2013] UKSC 1, at 218 at [35], and 225 at [68].

7.12 In addition, as will be seen below and as is demonstrated by the case studies at the end of this this chapter (see **7.195–7.202**), the incidence of privilege is exceptionally fact sensitive.

7.13 For these reasons, privilege can trip up the unwary. The aim of this chapter is to introduce the reader to the subject in the tax context and provide examples, and a flavour, of the difficulties and risks that can arise. To avoid any issues, it may be advisable to seek advice from a specialist litigation lawyer save in the simplest cases.

No adverse inference

7.14 It is worth mentioning at the outset, that, doctrinally, insistence on the rights associated with privilege '... does not enable the court to draw an adverse inference against the person who maintains his privilege'[12]. HMRC explicitly recognises privilege in its current Litigation and Settlement Strategy (LSS) and states that '[i]t is unlikely that HMRC will need to see a copy of any legal advice obtained by a customer'[13]. This is an assertion that is not always borne out in practice but, in the view of the authors, HMRC's frequent demands for details of privileged communications is probably because their officers do not understand how easily privilege is lost (rather than because they do). The LSS also states that 'HMRC should not interpret a decision by a customer not to waive [privilege] over legal advice as a sign of non-collaboration ...'[14]. The authors have not seen evidence to support that this is not the case.

7.15 Meanwhile, in relation to this latter point, the FTT, rightly or wrongly, appears in a recent case to have been willing to draw an 'adverse inference' because of non-disclosure of document which turned out not to be privileged but over which privilege had been asserted[15]. The issue had arisen shortly before the main hearing and rather than seeking an adjournment to allow inspection of the documents, HMRC requested that an 'an adverse inference' be drawn in coming to conclusions of fact on the nature of advice received; the FTT agreed[16]. The decision has not been appealed from the FTT and is therefore not binding. The authors respectfully suggest that this decision is not good law and should not be followed.

---

12 *Wentworth v Lloyd* (1864) 10 HLC 589. Mentioned in *Oxford Gene Technology Ltd v Affymetrix Inc (No 2)* [2001] RPC 18, at [21] (CA).

13 HMRC's 'Resolving tax disputes – Commentary on the litigation and settlement strategy' (October 2017) under the heading 'Legal Professional Privilege' (p 30). See also headings 'Paragraph 13' (p 28) and 'Handling Disputes' (p 5). Available at: https://assets.publishing.service.gov.uk/government/uploads/system/uploads/attachment_data/file/655344/HMRC_Resolving_tax_disputes.pdf (last accessed on 19 November 2020).

14 'Resolving tax disputes – Commentary on the litigation and settlement strategy' (above), under the heading 'Legal Professional Privilege' (p 30).

15 *Conegate Ltd v The Commissioners for Her Majesty's Revenue & Customs* [2018] UKFTT 82 (TC), see paras [8], [33]–[35] in particular.

16 *Conegate* (above).

HMRC'S INFORMATION POWERS IN FA 2008, SCH 36, PRIVILEGE AND ITS ANALOGS

General

7.16 *Schedule 36* of *FA 2008* sets out HMRC's statutory information-gathering powers. This section explains how privilege and certain statutory analogs of it interact with HMRC's powers to obtain information, most commonly during an enquiry and usually before any dispute in the FTT. All references to 'paragraphs' under this heading are to paragraphs under *Schedule 36* unless indicated otherwise.

7.17 An information notice[17] under the Schedule can be used to compel a taxpayer or third party to disclose information to HMRC. HMRC will sometimes first ask for information in general correspondence and if it is not supplied (or if they seek information from a third party) serve an information notice. An information notice compels a taxpayer, third party, or financial institution to provide the information and documents requested in the notice by a particular date. However, an information notice (as defined in *para 6*) can only properly be sent if certain conditions are met. The conditions are specific according to whether a notice is given to taxpayer, a third party, or a financial institution. For example, an information notice to taxpayer can only request information or a document if it is 'reasonably required'. A third-party notice must state the name of the taxpayer in respect of whom information is requested unless HMRC has obtained permission from the FTT that it need not do so. Taxpayers can resist disclosing information where the request falls outside various conditions set out in *Schedule 36* by appealing to the FTT; though in the experience of the authors issues can usually be resolved in dialogue with HMRC.

7.18 As mentioned above, this chapter is only focused on those conditions (or bases for resisting disclosure) which relate to privilege, or are similar to it. An information notice does not require the disclosure of privileged information or documents (see **7.20–7.33**), information of documents relevant to the conduct of an appeal (see **7.34–7.35**), or certain auditor's or tax adviser's documents (see **7.36–7.40**).

7.19 It is important to remember that the effect of these statutory grounds is confined to information notices. HMRC can still apply for a direction from the FTT for inspection of any document during an appeal[18], or hearing, if the information or document is not subject to privilege; even if they could not seek it under their information powers. The taxpayer can, of course, also make such an application for disclosure of a document during an appeal or hearing. Such applications are subject to their own limitations such as a

17 As defined in *FA 2008, Sch 36, para 6.*

18 Which the Tribunal can grant under the case management powers set out in *rule 5(3)(d)* of the *Tribunal Procedure (First-tier Tribunal) (Tax Chamber) Rules 2009, SI 2009/273 (L1)*).

requirement that they be relevant to an issue in the case. HMRC's disclosure practices have occasionally been subject to considerable criticism in the past[19] but it is fair to say that, in the authors' experience, they have improved in recent years.

Resisting disclosure because the information is privileged (under common law)

7.20 HMRC may request, whether knowingly or unknowingly, privileged material in an information notice. However, *paragraph 23(1)* states that '[a]n information notice does not require a person: (a) to provide privileged information, or (b) to produce any part of a document that is privileged'. *Subparagraph (2)* makes clear that information or a document is privileged insofar as privilege attaches to it.

7.21 Where a dispute arises over whether something is, in fact, privileged, regulations provide for an appeal mechanism to the FTT[20]. This is a different process to appealing an information notice under *Part 5* of *Schedule 36* (such as on the basis that the information sought is not reasonably required).

7.22 The Regulations are very prescriptive and should be carefully reviewed in each instance.

7.23 Generally, in relation to information notices[21], the formal process is that on receipt of the information notice the taxpayer, third party, or person acting on their behalf (the 'recipient') must specify each document which is in dispute, in a list, with a description of the nature and contents of that document[22].

7.24 The list must be produced by the date given on HMRC's information notice[23].

7.25 The list must be served on HMRC[24].

7.26 Proof of service of the application must also be given to HMRC[25]. Service must take place within a reasonable time, to be agreed between the recipient and HMRC, but it cannot be more than 20 working days after the date given in the notice for providing information or producing documents[26].

---

19 *Test Claimants in the Thin Cap Group Litigation v Revenue and Customs Commissioners* [2009] EWHC 2908 (Ch) at [246]–[247], [2010] STC 301, 376.

20 *Information Notice: Resolution of Disputes as to Privileged Communications Regulations 2009, SI 2009/1916.*

21 *2009/1916, reg 5(2)(a).*

22 *2009/1916, reg 5(2).*

23 *2009/1916, reg 5(2)(b).*

24 *2009/1916, reg 5(6)).*

25 *2009/1916, reg 5(7).*

26 *2009/1916, reg 5(3).*

7.27 In drawing up the list, the recipient is not required to give a description of a document or type of document where the description 'would itself give rise to a dispute over privilege'[27].

7.28 This slightly cryptic statement is likely to mean that where the description itself contains information, which is arguably privileged, the recipient is not required to give that description. Doing so might waive privilege (see **7.149–7.187** below).

7.29 Then, within 20 working days of receiving the list, HMRC must notify the person who served the list of any documents on the list that it requires to be produced and which it considers are not privileged[28].

7.30 On receipt of HMRC's response, the recipient must make an application to the FTT to consider and resolve the dispute and must include copies of the documents which remain in dispute with the application[29].

7.31 An application must be made within a reasonable time to be agreed between HMRC and the recipient but must not be later than 20 working days of the date of the date of HMRC's notification that it disputes the claim to privilege[30].

7.32 It is vital that the recipient does not send the disputed documents to HMRC, even if the FTT has been provided with them, because this will result in the loss of privilege.

7.33 The FTT is under an obligation to withhold the documents from HMRC until it has made a decision as to whether they are privileged.

Resisting disclosure of information that relates to the conduct of an appeal

7.34 If HMRC could request and rely on every bit of advice a taxpayer receives during litigation (without the contrary being true), it would have an unfair advantage in the conduct of litigation. Accordingly, *paragraph 19(1)(a)* protects information and documents 'relating to the conduct of any pending appeal relating to tax' from disclosure under service of an information notice. This only covers documents that are brought into existence for the purposes of the preparation and presentation of the appeal[31].

7.35 This provision is therefore limited, and in practice the limitation is very significant. *Paragraph 19(1)(a)* only applies once an appeal has been

27 *2009/1916, reg 5(4).*
28 *2009/1916, reg 5(5).*
29 *2009/1916, reg 5(7).*
30 *Monarch Assurance Co Ltd v Special Comrs* [1986] STC 311.
31 *Three Rivers DC v Bank of England (No 6)* [2004] UKHL 48, at [24], [2005] 1 AC 610, at 646.

made and does not cover the, potentially much more significant, information and documents created when litigation is in contemplation. Therefore, it is not the same as litigation privilege, which is discussed at **7.116–7.147** below.

Resisting disclosure because the document is an auditor's or tax adviser's document

7.36 As has been mentioned, and as discussed in greater detail later in this chapter, privilege usually does not cover communications with non-lawyers such as accountants, tax advisers or auditors, notwithstanding that such communications could contain material which would be protected by privilege had it been provided by a Lawyer.

7.37 Therefore, as a policy matter, *paragraph 24* provides that an auditor cannot be required to provide information held in connection with the performance of carrying out a statutory audit or to produce documents that are his property and that were created in the course of carrying out a statutory audit.

7.38 *Paragraph 25* provides that a tax adviser cannot be required to produce documents that are his or her property, and which consist of 'relevant communications'.

7.39 Relevant communications are those with the taxpayer client made for the purpose of giving (by the tax adviser) or obtaining (by the client) advice on that client's tax affairs.

7.40 There are, in practice, quite extensive limitations under *paragraph 26* on the protection offered by *paragraphs 24* and *25*. Thus, working papers, and documents showing how a particular entry on a return or in particular accounts were arrived at, are not covered. Information which could tell HMRC the address or identity of a client or the identity of a previous adviser also falls outside the protection of *paragraphs 24* and *25*.

COMMUNICATIONS MUST BE CONFIDENTIAL TO BE PRIVILEGED

7.41 It is a fundamental prerequisite that communications must be confidential in order to qualify for privilege, but confidential material is not necessarily privileged[32].

32 *Anderson v Bank of British Columbia* (1876) 2 Ch D 644, at 648 per Jessel MR and *BBGP Managing General Partner Ltd v Babcock & Brown Global Partners* [2011] Ch 296, at [48].

7.42 Confidentiality is readily established in Lawyer-client relationships[33] and it is generally going to be the case that legal advice is confidential[34].

7.43 In the tax context, confidentiality is likely to exist in many instances[35]. It has been observed in the highest courts that a '… client's financial or tax position or the financial or tax position of members of his family, may well be relevant to the way in which he asks his solicitor to structure a property transaction … People have a legitimate interest in keeping such matters private'[36].

7.44 In the context of litigation privilege (see **7.116** et seq below), it has been suggested that the threshold for meeting confidentiality is low: that is, that material remains confidential 'in the sense that it is not properly available for use'[37].

7.45 The objective for advisers and representatives should always be to ensure the confidential nature of communications, documents and information is not lost.

7.46 In practice, confidentiality (and loss of it) is only likely to be an issue where legal advice has been given to a wider audience (such as legal advice to various participants in an avoidance scheme), or where privileged material has become publicly available (for example, by being leaked by a third party as were the 'Panama Papers').

7.47 In the privilege context, certain information is deemed not to be confidential (although it might otherwise be confidential) and therefore not privileged: examples are the identity of the client and the existence of a retainer[38].

THE TWO HEADS OF PRIVILEGE

General

7.48 There are two sub-heads[39] of privilege: legal advice privilege (LAP) and litigation privilege (LP). The effect is similar but, as will become clear, the

33 *BBGP Managing General Partner Ltd v Babcock & Brown Global Partners* [2011] Ch 296, at [48].

34 *Section 18(1)* of the *Commissioners for Revenue and Customs Act 2005* in respect of HMRC. However, also note underlying common law duties: *R (Ingenious Media Holdings plc and Another) v Revenue and Customs Commissioners* [2016] UKSC 54, at [26]–[29].

35 *Three Rivers DC v Bank of England (No 6)* [2004] UKHL 48, at [55], [2005] 1 AC 610, at 651 (Lord Rodger).

36 *Bourns Inc v Raychem Corp* [1999] 3 All ER 154, 167-8. See R Pattenden, *The law of Professional-Client Confidentiality* (2nd edn, 2016), OUP, Oxford, para 15.42, *cf* 15.68.

37 *Bursill v Tanner* (1885) 16 QBD 1, 4, *Pascal v Galinski* [1970] 1 QB 38, *cf Thorson v Jones* (1973) 38 DLR (3d) 312. See B Thanki and ors, *The Law of Privilege* (3rd edn, 2018), OUP, Oxford, at 2.86.

38 *R (on the application of Prudential plc and Another) v Special Commissioner of Income Tax and Another* [2013] UKSC 1, at [17], [2013] 2 AC 185, at 215.

39 Lord Carswell in *Three Rivers DC v Bank of England (No 6)* [2004] UKHL 48, at [105], [2015] 1 AC 610, at 677.

way these two sub-heads operate is somewhat different. Each sub-head comes with its own limitations and rules which determine whether a communication is privileged. These rules and limitations are dealt with at **7.49–7.147** below. In very simple terms, LAP has the benefit of covering communications at any point but the disadvantage that it only covers client-Lawyer communications or communications evidencing qualifying advice; whereas LP can cover third-party communications (including potentially those with tax advisers) but is only engaged when made for a litigation purpose and when litigation is in the air.

LEGAL ADVICE PRIVILEGE

General

7.49 In general terms LAP applies to communications passing between a client and Lawyers, acting in their professional capacity, in connection with the provision of legal advice[40]. Certain conditions apply which limit its application further. These conditions are discussed at **7.63** et seq.

7.50 The principal limitation on this head of privilege, in the tax context, is that LAP only covers communications between clients, (who are narrowly defined – see **7.96** below), and Lawyers. It does not cover communications with third parties and/or tax advisers or accountants (see **7.72–7.80** below).

7.51 LAP can often play a relatively small role in the tax context.

7.52 In disputes with HMRC the advice a person has received will sometimes have little bearing on the ultimate settlement. This is because the cost of litigation is high, costs recovery is limited, and there is always some uncertainty about outcome, so many taxpayers ultimately conclude that there is an acceptable price for certainty.

7.53 In addition, taxpayers may, after due consideration, be prepared to share positive tax advice with HMRC, where the advice has been properly and carefully followed, unless sharing it runs the risk of exposing other privileged material.

7.54 Often the circumstance in which the taxpayer will wish to protect such advice against disclosure is where it relates to a tax-efficient structure and the advice is nuanced in its discussion of tax risk and the prospects of the structure surviving HMRC challenge – because disclosing such advice would give HMRC the advantage of knowing where to apply pressure. But such advice is often covered by the statutory exemption in any event (see **7.36–7.40** above).

40 *R (on the application of Prudential plc and Another) v Special Commissioner of Income Tax and Another* [2013] UKSC 1, at [19], [2013] 2 AC 185, at 215, making reference to *Three Rivers DC v Bank of England (No 6)* [2004] UKHL 48, at [38], [2005] 1 AC 610, at 615 (Lord Scott).

7.55 To the extent that the ultimate conclusion in a dispute with HMRC is that some additional tax is payable the fact that legal advice was sought, and followed, may allow for the reduction or elimination of penalties. In these circumstances, taxpayers can consider the approach of indicating that the taxpayer had sought privileged advice without disclosing the advice itself. Note that, in the experience of the authors, HMRC are now more aggressively testing the substance of such indications ('When was the advice given? By whom? To whom? In what form? What precisely did the advice address?') than they were five or ten years ago.

7.56 Making reference to advice is different to relying on it, although one has to be extremely careful not to be taken to have waived privilege by such an admission[41] (see **7.149–7.183** below).

7.57 However, in certain circumstances, the content of advice a taxpayer has requested and received really does matter. This is where tax legislation contains a 'main purpose' test[42] since advice rendered may have bearing on the answers to that test. It may also matter in the context of other anti-avoidance legislation, such as the general anti-avoidance rule in *section 207* of the *Finance Act 2013*, or, in certain instances where the motive defence in the transfer of assets code is at issue.

7.58 LAP can also feature as a fall-back option on advice received by HMRC or taxpayers at a stage when LP has not yet been engaged, or where there is some doubt over whether it existed at the relevant date. In certain circumstances, LAP can also be very wide, and cover something that would otherwise not be covered, which is when that document would reveal the nature of qualifying advice received.

7.59 This section explains what categories of communications are covered by LAP (at **7.60**) and how these categories have been interpreted and applied in case law to particular facts and circumstances (at **7.62–7.69**). It goes to explain that LAP does not cover legal advice provided by accountants and tax advisers and the case law and policy reasons behind this (at **7.72–7.80**). It then discusses typical LAP issues, such as problems that involve communications with third parties (at **7.81–7.87**), and the analysis that should be applied to composite communications involving more than just Lawyers and their clients (at **7.88**), responses to Lawyers (at **7.89**), emails from clients and Lawyers to others (at **7.90–7.92**) and meetings (at **7.93–7.95**). It then discusses the identity

41 *Bourns Inc v Raychem Corp and Another* [1999] 3 All ER 154, at 166–167. The distinction between reference to advice and reliance upon it has been described as being 'so slippery that it is almost impossible to apply': *ARX v Controller of Income Tax* [2016] SGGA 56, at [56] (Singapore Court of Appeal).

42 For example: *Taxation of Chargeable Gains Act 1992, ss 16A, 103K, 137, 139, 140B*; *Corporation Tax Act 2009, s 831* (The genuine commercial transaction requirement and clearance); *Finance Act 2003, s 65* (Incorporation of limited liability partnership); *Limited Liability Partnerships Act 2000, s 12* (stamp duty); *Finance Act 1986, s 77* (Acquisition of target company's share capital).

of the 'client' in a corporate context and the difficulties that can thereby arise (at **7.96–7.98**). Finally, the section discusses the controversies surrounding LAP arising from a case called *Three Rivers (No 5)* (at **7.99–7.114**) and the treatment of attachments to communications (at **7.115**).

What is covered by LAP?

7.60 LAP attaches to two categories of communications. Category A is communications passing between the client and legal advisers (whether or not through any intermediary) for the dominant purpose of seeking or obtaining legal advice; and Category B is documents which evidence the substance of such a communication[43].

7.61 Where a document is intended to be a communication, which is covered by LAP but is not actually communicated, it might still qualify for LAP[44].

Category A: the approach to determining whether a communication is seeking legal advice

7.62 Category A covers 'communication … for the purposes of seeking legal advice'. In determining what documents fall within this wording, courts have rejected:

> '… a narrow or nit-picking approach to documents and [have] ruled out an approach which takes a record of a communication sentence by sentence and extends the cloak of privilege to one and withholds it from another.'[45]

Therefore:

> '[w]here information is passed by the solicitor or client to the other as part of the continuum aimed at keeping both informed so that advice may be sought and given as required, privilege will attach … [but] [i]t may be that applying this test to any series of communications might isolate occasional letters or notes which could not be said to enjoy privilege.'[46]

43 *Three Rivers District Council and Others v Governor and Company of the Bank of England (No 5)* [2003] EWCA Civ 474, at [19]. The complete wording stems from the declaration of the CA which is set out in *Three Rivers DC and Others v Governor and Company of the Bank of England (No 6)* [2004] UKHL 48, at [14], [2005] 1 AC 610, at 643. At the time of writing, *Three Rivers (No 5)* (CA) remains good law (at least in certain respects) despite some criticism.

44 Lord Carswell in *Three Rivers DC v Bank of England (No 6)* [2004] UKHL 48, at [72], [2005] 1 AC 610, at 633, repeating *Three Rivers District Council and Others v Governor and Company of the Bank of England (No 5)* [2003] EWCA Civ 474, at [21], [2003] QB 1556, at 1575.

45 Lord Bingham CJ in *R v Manchester Crown Court, ex p Rogers* [1999] 1 WLR 832, at 839.

46 Taylor LJ in *Balabel v Air India* [1988] Ch 317, at 330F and330H.

Paragraph 8 of *Schedule 36* to *FA 2008* provides that, upon application, the Tribunal shall direct which part or parts of a document (if any) shall be disclosed so that the legislation is drafted on the basis that privilege does not necessarily apply to the whole of a document[47].

Category A: the purpose of seeking legal advice must be the dominant purpose of the communication

7.63 On the current state of the law, the purpose of seeking or giving legal advice must be the 'dominant' purpose of the communication[48]. This requirement causes difficulty both to commentators and the courts; the Court of Appeal reached different points of view in 2018[49] and 2020[50]. However, at the time of writing[51], the communication must made with the dominant purpose of giving or obtaining legal advice for LAP to apply. While the fact that the communication was sent to a Lawyer may be a 'starting point', to evidence such a dominant purpose, this is not decisive.

7.64 For example, if the dominant purpose of a communication is to obtain the commercial views of non-Lawyer addressees, then it will not be privileged even if a subsidiary purpose is simultaneously to obtain legal advice from the lawyer addressee(s)[52].

Category B: documents evidencing the substance of communications

7.65 Category B documents 'which evidence the substance of a communication', might sensibly be understood to mean, 'any document prepared by a Lawyer or a client from which there might be inferred the nature of the advice sought or given'[53].

7.66 By way of example of LAP, in *DAC Beachcroft LLP v HMRC*[54] engagement letters including the names of clients (information which was

47 *DAC Beachcroft LLP v The Commissioners for Her Majesty's Revenue and Customs* [2018] UKFTT 0502 (TC), at [22].

48 *R (on the application of Jet2.com Ltd) v Civil Aviation Authority* [2020] EWCA Civ 35, at [96].

49 The necessity of the test was doubted in *Director of the Serious Fraud Office v Eurasian Natural Resources Corp Ltd* [2018] EWCA Civ 2006, at [132], [2019] 1 WLR 791, at 842, however, these were obiter comments and not binding and have since been discounted in *R (on the application of Jet2.com Ltd) v CAA* [2020] EWCA Civ 35 (see [88]–[90]).

50 *R (on the application of Jet2.com Ltd) v CAA* [2020] EWCA Civ 35, at [96].

51 It has been held by binding Court of Appeal authority, which only the Supreme Court can overrule.

52 *R (on the application of Jet2.com Ltd) v CAA* [2020] EWCA Civ 35, at [100 ii].

53 *Pratt Holdings v Commissioners of Taxation* (2004) 207 ALR 217, at [20] (Federal Court of Australia). As a common law authority, the case has some persuasive effect.

54 *DAC Beachcroft LLP v The Commissioners for Her Majesty's Revenue and Customs* [2018] UKFTT 0502 (TC).

valuable to HMRC), did not qualify for privilege, although the sections that set out the scope of instructions were privileged[55] as these would evidence the nature of the advice sought. Where the client (note the limited interpretation of 'client' addressed at **7.96–7.114** below) prepares a factual summary for the purpose of giving advice, this summary can be privileged if it is part of the necessary information exchange[56].

7.67 It should be noted that the Court of Appeal, in recently reviewing LAP, did not expressly repeat the formulation which the authors have used for this category. However, the Court did recognise that any communication passing on, considering, or applying advice covered by LAP internally is also covered by LAP[57]. The Court observed that LAP attaches to communications from a Lawyer to a third party, containing information provided by the client to the lawyer which is covered by LAP, and which the client has given the lawyer authority to disclose[58]. In addition, the Court did not disapprove of *Three Rivers (No 5)*, from which the formulation stems. Consequently, the authors still consider it to be an accurate statement of principle.

7.68 While there is doubtful judicial authority to the effect that where a document was created before the need to seek legal advice arose, but disclosing it would reveal the advice sought or given, the pre-existing document might be privileged[59]. The authors consider that pre-existing documents that fall within Category B would not be covered. This is because the Court of Appeal has decided that the communication must be made for the dominant purpose of seeking or obtaining legal advice. In addition, if such a document accompanied advice, in light of the court's approach to treating attachments to emails (see **7.115** below), it is doubtful that LAP applies. That said, if the document itself is a communication which was made for the dominant purpose of seeking or obtaining legal advice, it may be covered.

7.69 As part of Category B, a Lawyer's working papers are also regarded as being covered by LAP[60], though there is as yet unresolved conflicting opinion on whether this is an application of Category B and therefore limited to that scope, or a special class covering everything no matter whether it evidences the substance of the communications with the client.

55 *DAC Beachcroft LLP* , at [55] and [56] and see specific documents listed in [57] as examples.

56 *The Southwark and Vauxhall Water Company v Quick* (1878) 3 QBD 315.

57 *R (on the application of Jet2.com Ltd) v CAA* [2020] EWCA Civ 35, at [45].

58 *R (on the application of Jet2.com Ltd) v CAA* (above).

59 *Behague v The Commissioners for Her Majesty's Revenue & Customs* [2013] UKFTT 596 (TC), at [34].

60 *Balabel v Air India* [1988] CH 317, at 323.

The meaning of 'legal advice and assistance'

7.70 'Legal advice' means, 'telling the client the law'[61] but it also includes 'advice as to what should prudently and sensibly be done in a relevant legal context'[62]; that is, 'advice on the application of law'[63].

7.71 There will be marginal cases that move between legal and business advice.

> 'In cases of doubt … [one] should ask whether the advice relates to the rights, liabilities, obligations or remedies of the client either under private law or under public law. If it does not, then … legal advice privilege would not apply. If it does so relate then … [one] should ask [oneself] whether the communication falls within the policy underlying the justification for legal advice privilege in our law. Is the occasion on which the communication takes place and is the purpose for which it takes place such as to make it reasonable to expect the privilege to apply? The criterion must … be an objective one.'[64]

It has been suggested that 'giving of advice in a commercial context through a lawyer's eyes' would satisfy this test[65].

The meaning of 'lawyer' or 'legal adviser'

7.72 Importantly, LAP only covers communications passing between client and solicitor (including in-house lawyer[66]), barrister, or foreign lawyer[67], and individuals, such as trainees or paralegals, working under their supervision. LAP extends to communications with foreign lawyers whether or not they are 'in-house' and thus employees of a particular company or organisation, and the court will not enquire into how or why the foreign lawyer is regulated or what standards apply to the foreign lawyer under the local law, but it must be clear that they are acting in a professional capacity[68].

7.73 For LAP to apply, being a 'Lawyer' is not enough, and the adviser must be acting in the course of his or her professional relationship and within the scope of his or her professional duties. Thus, legal advice provided by an accountant, tax adviser, or other professional does not attract LAP[69].

---

61 Taylor LJ in *Balabel v Air India* [1988] Ch 317, at 329.

62 *Balabel v Air India*, endorsed by Lord Scott in *Three Rivers DC v Governor and Company of the Bank of England (No 6)* [2004] UKHL 48, at [38], [2005] 1 AC 610, at 651.

63 *R (on the application of Jet2.com Ltd) v CAA* [2020] EWCA Civ 35, at [68].

64 Lord Scott in *Three Rivers DC v Governor and Company of the Bank of England (No 6)* [2004] UKHL 48, at [38], [2005] 1 AC 610, at 651.

65 *R (on the application of Jet2.com Ltd) v CAA* [2020] EWCA Civ 35, at [100 ii].

66 *R (on the application of Jet2.com Ltd) v CAA* [2020] EWCA Civ 35, at [44].

67 See Lord Neuberger in *R (on the application of Prudential plc) v Special Commissioner of Income Tax* [2013] UKSC 1, at [45], [2013] 2 AC 185, at 220.

68 See *PJSC Tatneft v Bogolyubov* and Others [2020] EWHC 2437 (Comm), at [57].

69 *R (on the application of Prudential plc) v Special Commissioner of Income Tax* [2013] UKSC 1, [2013] 2 AC 185.

7.74 In 2013, the UK Supreme Court grappled with this question in *Prudential v HMRC*[70]. The majority of the judges acknowledged that this distinction is not necessarily a rational approach, but policy considerations mean this should be a matter for Parliament and not the courts.

7.75 The issue involves some inherent policy debates. Lawyers' daily practice is generally closer to legal advisory work than that of accountants and tax advisers.

7.76 Solicitors and barristers are specifically trained in the administration and giving of legal advice services. Alongside that training come higher duties to the court and tough statutory and regulatory control that goes beyond ethics codes and encompasses a series of specific criminal offences.

7.77 Since Lawyers are rarely in charge of general tax compliance, their advice would, in theory, be more independent and robust since it is not reliant on continued compliance business. Of course, formally trained tax advisers and accountants adhere to high standards; but there are issues defining dividing lines between who does, in theory, meet the same standard and who does not.

7.78 The background to the decision is that extending LAP to tax advisers would represent a widening of the common law. It is only relatively recently (in common law terms) that advice about tax law has been regularly sought from accountants[71]. It is also only recently that privilege has really developed outside the litigation context since non-judicial bodies, such as HMRC, only obtained information-seeking powers in the 20th century[72]. Though this change took place relatively long ago, nevertheless, in common law terms the Supreme Court was not assisted by ancient precedent.

7.79 The conclusion of the majority of the Supreme Court in *Prudential v HMRC* was thus that the matter is much more appropriately dealt with by legislation (which might involve further statutory regulation of the accounting and tax adviser professions) on the back of proper consultation. The authors consider that since the financial crisis of 2008 and the resultant change in attitudes towards taxation, there is little political appetite for widening the cloak of confidentiality when it comes to tax advice.

7.80 As discussed at **7.36–7.40** above, *Schedule 36* to *FA 2008* does provide a limited carve-out in respect of tax advisers.

70 *R (on the application of Prudential plc) v Special Commissioner of Income Tax* [2013] UKSC 1, [2013] 2 AC 185.

71 *R (on the application of Prudential plc) v Special Commissioner of Income Tax* [2013] UKSC 1, at [121], [2013] 2 AC 185, at 239 (per Lord Sumption).

72 *Three Rivers DC v Governor and Company of the Bank of England (No 6)* [2005] 1 AC 610, at 614 (argument by the parties).

Issues that arise in case of communications with third parties

7.81 The treatment of communications with third parties will frequently cause complications in practice.

Communications between clients and third parties and lawyers and third parties

7.82 First, the Court of Appeal has been very clear that communications must be between client and Lawyer, and cannot be between Lawyer and third parties[73], or client and third parties, for LAP to apply[74].

7.83 In *Director of the Serious Fraud Office v Eurasian Natural Resources Corpn Ltd*, the Court of Appeal stated the view that previous case law had decided that communications from 'agents of the client' would not attract privilege but that communications from 'mere intermediaries' would do so. Previous case law took the view that:

> '[i]f the representative is a person employed as an agent on the part of the client to obtain the legal advice of the solicitor, of course he stands in exactly the same position as the client as regards protection, and his communications with the solicitor stand in the same position as the communications of his principal with the solicitor.'[75]

However, the situation is different if those persons were active agents of the client. Communications from them would not be privileged. If 'they were employed on behalf of the clients … to do certain work, but that work was not the communicating with the solicitor to obtain legal advice … their communications cannot be protected …'[76].

7.84 There is, accordingly, a slight nuance, since when a client or Lawyer communicates through an 'intermediary', LAP still attaches to that communication[77]. If a client asks a third person to write a letter to a solicitor (presumably providing its content), and sends a letter through a third person, or gives a verbal message to a person, or asks third persons to deliver information[78], the communication continues to be covered.

---

73 *Wheeler v Le Marchant* (1881) 17 Ch D 675, at 680–681, 682–683 and, importantly, 684–685. See also discussion in *Three Rivers DC v Governor and Company of the Bank of England (No 5)* [2003] EWCA Civ 474, at [18] and [19]. See also *Director of the Serious Fraud Office v Eurasian Natural Resources Corpn Ltd (Law Society intervening)* [2018] EWCA Civ 2006, at [[67]–[81] and comments at [123]–[130].

74 *Three Rivers DC v Governor and Company of the Bank of England (No 5)* [2003] EWCA Civ 474, at [18] and [21].

75 *Wheeler v Le Marchant* (1881) 17 Ch D 675, at 684.

76 *Wheeler v Le Marchant* (1881) 17 Ch D 675.

77 *Three Rivers DC v Governor and Company of the Bank of England (No 5)* [2003] EWCA Civ 474, at [19], [2003] 3 WLR 667, at 1575.

78 *Anderson v British Bank of Columbia* (1876) 2 Ch D 644, at 649.

7.85 Such an 'intermediary', confusingly called an 'agent' in some cases, must be a mere channel or conduit of information. As soon as he has to consider whether he needs to act himself on the communication[79], or brings material into existence[80], he is no longer an 'intermediary'.

7.86 However, under Category B, if a communication evidences the contents of a document covered under Category A, it may still be covered by LAP. Thus, it has been explicitly recognised that communication passing on, considering, or applying that advice internally is covered by LAP[81].

7.87 Equally, LAP attaches to communications from a Lawyer to a third party containing information provided by the client to the lawyer which is covered by LAP and which the client has given the lawyer authority to disclose[82].

Composite communications (copying in Lawyers and third parties)

7.88 Second, there is a common issue that arises in terms of composite communications. Thus, emails may often include Lawyers, but also other individuals involved in a matter.

Lawyer's response

7.89 A response from a Lawyer, if it contains legal advice, will almost certainly be privileged, even if it is copied to more than one addressee. Again, whilst the dominant purpose test applies, given the wide scope of 'legal advice' and 'continuum of communications', the court will be extremely reluctant to engage in the exercise of determining whether, in respect of a specific document or communication, the dominant purpose was the provision of legal (rather than non-legal) advice[83].

Email from client to Lawyer and others

7.90 Meanwhile, communication from the client to the Lawyer and others would be treated differently. In case of multi-addressee communications, each communication to each recipient should be considered as separate bilateral communication between the sender and each recipient, and not as a whole.

7.91 Lord Justice Hickinbottom has stated that:

> '[w]here the purpose of the sender is simultaneously to obtain from various individuals both legal advice and non-legal advice/input, it is difficult to

79 *Jones v Great Central Railway* [1910] AC 4, 6 (HL).

80 *Price Waterhouse v BCII* [1992] BCLC 583, 589.

81 *R (on the application of Jet2.com Ltd) v CAA* [2020] EWCA Civ 35, at [45].

82 *R (on the application of Jet2.com Ltd) v CAA* [2020] EWCA Civ 35, at [45].

83 *R (on the application of Jet2.com Ltd) v CAA* [2020] EWCA Civ 35, at [100 iii].

see why the form of the request (in a single, multi-addressee email on the one hand, or in separate emails on the other) in itself should be relevant as to whether the communications to the non-lawyers should be privileged. That is not to say, of course, that the form may not in some cases reveal the true purpose of the communication, eg it may appear from the form of the email that the dominant purpose of the email is to settle the instructions to the lawyer who has merely been copied in by way of information, or to the contrary that the dominant purpose of sending the email to the non-lawyers is to obtain their substantive (non-lawyer) input in any event.'[84]

7.92 In his Lordship's view:

> '[T]here is some benefit in [considering] whether, if the email were sent to the lawyer alone, it would have been privileged. If no, then the question of whether any of the other emails are privileged hardly arises. If yes, then the question arises as to whether any of the emails to the non-lawyers are privileged, because (eg) its dominant purpose is to obtain instructions or disseminate legal advice.'[85]

Meetings with Lawyers and others

7.93 The mere presence of a Lawyer at a meeting, perhaps only on the off-chance that his or her legal input might be required, is insufficient to render the whole meeting the subject of LAP such that none of its contents (including any notes, minutes or record of the meeting) are disclosable.

7.94 If the dominant purpose of the meeting is to obtain legal advice, unless anything is said outside that legal context, the contents of the meeting will be privileged.

7.95 If the dominant purpose of the discussions is commercial, or otherwise non-legal, then the meeting and its contents will not generally be privileged; although any legal advice sought or given within the meeting may be. It is likely that, where not inextricably intermingled, the non-privileged part will be severable (and, on disclosure, redactable)[86].

The meaning of 'client'

7.96 A well-established but controversial principle in English law is that employees of a client are primarily considered to be in the same position as any other third party. Therefore, any communication between a Lawyer and an employee of a corporate client is not privileged unless the employee

84 *R (on the application of Jet2.com Ltd) v CAA* [2020] EWCA Civ 35, at [100 iv].
85 *R (on the application of Jet2.com Ltd) v CAA* [2020] EWCA Civ 35, at [100 v].
86 *R (on the application of Jet2.com Ltd) v CAA* [2020] EWCA Civ 35, at [100 viii].

was tasked with 'seeking and receiving advice on behalf of the client'[87] or 'instructing' the Lawyer[88]. The controversy over this point is addressed at **7.99** and, in particular, **7.105–7.114** below.

7.97 In *Taylor Made Consulting Ltd v HMRC* [2014] UKFTT 903 (TC) it was decided that communications between the employer of an in-house solicitor and the employer's clients were not legally privileged, even if they had been produced by the employed solicitor. Only communications between an in-house solicitor and his employer were potentially subject to legal LAP.

7.98 The state of the law is particularly problematic in the tax context since working relationships will frequently involve tripartite or multi-angular relationships between clients, tax advisers and Lawyers. In addition, accounting or compliance departments of larger corporates will often not have the requisite authorisation but will often be communicating with Lawyers about various tax matters. We note that LP more amply covers such situations.

The case of Three Rivers (No 5) and its controversies

7.99 A key case in this area, which has been cited above, is *Three Rivers (No 5)*[89]. The background to the case is that, in the context of an inquiry, the Bank of England asked a team within the bank (the 'BIU') to carry out internal investigations in order to submit a response to the inquiry. The BIU were assisted by (external) Lawyers.

7.100 Claimants in a later lawsuit against the Bank seeking damages sought disclosure of the documents that were created as part of the internal investigation. It was accepted that LAP did not cover reports prepared by third parties and sent to Lawyers[90]; they were disclosed.

7.101 The Court in *Three Rivers (No 5)* was deciding whether documents that had been prepared by employees and ex-employees of the Bank, who were not tasked with carrying on the investigation as part of the BIU, were privileged.

87 The CA in *Director of the Serious Fraud Office v Eurasian Natural Resources Corpn Ltd (Law Society intervening)* [2018] EWCA Civ 2006, at [123], [2019] 1 WLR 791, at 838, states that this is its conclusion as to *Three Rivers (No 5)*, and no mention is made of the requirement that the employee must be authorised to 'provide instructions' which had been the approach taken by Andrews J in the first instance decision [2017] EWHC 1017 (QB) at [41], [2017] 1 WLR 4205, at 4215.

88 See paras [64], [89] at *In re RBS Rights Issue Litigation* [2016] EWHC 3161 (Ch), [2017] 1 WLR 1991.

89 *Three Rivers DC v Governor and Company of the Bank of England (No 5)* [2003] EWCA Civ 474; [2003] QB 1556.

90 *Three Rivers DC v Governor and Company of the Bank of England (No 5)* [2003] EWCA Civ 474, at [1], [2003] QB 1556, at 1561.

7.102 Some documents were 'preparatory' documents, and were never communicated to the Lawyers, but their contents were used in communications with the Lawyers.

7.103 The Court of Appeal set out the two categories mentioned at **7.60** et seq above, which are:

- Category A being communications passing between the client and legal advisers (whether or not through any intermediary) for the dominant purposes of seeking or obtaining legal advice; and
- Category B being documents which evidence the substance of such a communication.

7.104 The Court added that documents intended to be Category A and B communications, but which were not, in fact, communicated to the Lawyers, were also covered.

7.105 Secondly, the Court of Appeal decided that communications with employees and ex-employees who were not tasked with seeking legal advice (or giving instructions) were not covered. This latter ruling provoked controversy both amongst academics and Lawyers. An application for leave to appeal was made but permission was refused[91].

7.106 However, approximately one year later, another case within the *Three Rivers* litigation ('*No 6*') reached the House of Lords. This appeal was over a narrow issue, namely, whether in that case, communications between the people tasked with carrying out the internal investigation and the Lawyers were protected by LAP[92].

7.107 However, the House of Lords framed its decision on much wider 'policy' terms[93].

7.108 Submissions were made by interested parties seeking 'guidance' on the narrow approach of the Court of Appeal in *Three Rivers (No 5)* to the identity of the 'client'; ie whether and to what extent this excluded employees and ex-employees who were not part of the BIU.

7.109 The House of Lords allowed submissions to be made on this point despite it not being an issue in the appeal. However, the court decided not to give an opinion on this point. Lord Carswell said that 'I do not propose to express any opinion [on this issue]. Having said that, I am not to be taken to have approved the decision in *Three Rivers (No 5),* and I would reserve

91 *Three Rivers DC v Bank of England (No 6)* [2004] UKHL 48, at [15], [2005] 1 AC 610, at 644 (Lord Scott).

92 *Three Rivers DC v Bank of England (No 6)* [2004] UKHL 48, at [20], [2005] 1 AC 610, at 645 (Lord Scott).

93 *Three Rivers DC v Bank of England (No 6)* [2004] UKHL 48, at [2], [2005] 1 AC 610, at 640 (Lord Scott).

my position on its correctness'[94]. Lord Scott said nothing should be read as 'approval or disapproval'[95] of *Three Rivers (No 5)*.

7.110 *Three Rivers (No 5)* is thus a continuing source of legal awkwardness. The authors suggest that the first part of the decision, concerning Category A and Category B, continues to be good law. The authors respectfully suggest, however, that insofar as the decision does address 'presentational material' in the context of LAP the decision is to be approached with some care.

7.111 The authors also note that the narrow meaning of 'client' espoused in *Three Rivers (No 5)*, namely that it includes only those specifically tasked with seeking legal advice and not others who may receive it within an organisation, remains the law. But it is highly controversial because it can significantly and capriciously limit the effect of privilege in a corporate client scenario. While the Court of Appeal has recently questioned it[96], only the Supreme Court can overrule the decision.

7.112 The refusal of the House of Lords to allow an appeal gives the judgment additional formal respectability. *Three Rivers (No 5)*, as a decision of the Court of Appeal, is binding both on lower courts and the Court of Appeal. However, it is fair to say that the House of Lords in *Three Rivers (No 6)* did not enthusiastically endorse it.

7.113 In 2016, an attempt was made to distinguish it on the basis the case dealt with the unusual situation where employees who were not tasked with communicating with Lawyers supplied information to those who were. It was, so the argument went, therefore not applicable to cases where the employees who were not specifically authorised to seek legal advice nevertheless communicated directly with Lawyers; that attempt failed and the High Court decided the case was of 'general application'[97].

7.114 While sensitive to the criticisms of the decision[98], the court felt bound by *Three Rivers (No 5)*. Where the recipient Lawyer is in-house, and the 'client' is an employee within a company (or within HMRC for that matter), this may be less of an issue since it is less likely to be the case on the facts that employees were not tasked with seeking legal advice from their in-house Lawyer[99].

---

94 *Three Rivers DC v Bank of England (No 6)* [2004] UKHL 48, at [118], [2005] 1 AC 610, at 682 (Lord Carswell).

95 *Three Rivers DC v Bank of England (No 6)* [2004] UKHL 48, at [48], [2005] 1 AC 610, at 654 (Lord Scott).

96 *R (on the application of Jet2.com Ltd) v CAA* [2020] EWCA Civ 35, at [47–59], see in particular [57]. Also see *SFO v Eurasia Natural Resources* [2018] EWCA Civ 2006, at [127], [2019] 1 WLR 791, at 840.

97 *The RBS Rights Issue Litigation* [2016] EWHC 3161 (Ch), at [54], [2017] 1 WLR 1991, at 2002.

98 *The RBS Rights Issue Litigation* [2016] EWHC 3161 (Ch), at [63], [2017] 1 WLR 1991, at 2004.

99 *R (on the application of Jet2.com Ltd) v CAA* [2020] EWCA Civ 35, at [59].

Communications – the treatment of attachments

7.115 As far as attachments are concerned, while an email and attachment can be regarded as a single communication, separate consideration will need to be given to the attachment, given that it will have been received or created by the sender, and therefore may require discrete consideration[100].

LITIGATION PRIVILEGE

General

7.116 LP has a greater importance in tax than LAP, at least when a dispute has arisen with HMRC.

7.117 This section outlines the category of communications covered by LP (at **7.118**), and the general rules as to when such communications are covered (at **7.119**). Certain situations are discussed in particular including communications between Lawyer and client and accountant or tax adviser and client (at **7.120–7.128**), and the client and third parties (at **7.129**). The section then goes on to discuss particular conditions that must also be met, including that the communication must contain information and advice (at **7.130–7.133**), and must be made for the sole or dominant purpose (at **7.134–7.139**) of ongoing or contemplated (at **7.140–7.145**) litigation (at **7.146–7.147**).

Category of communications covered by LP

7.118 LP protects communications between a party to a dispute and their Lawyers and third parties where the communications are for the purpose of obtaining information or advice in connection with existing or contemplated litigation.

When are these communications protected by LP?

7.119 Such communications are, however, covered only where and when the following restrictions are satisfied:

(a) litigation must be in progress or in contemplation;

(b) the communications must have been made for the sole or dominant purpose of conducting that litigation;

(c) the litigation must be adversarial, not investigative or inquisitorial[101].

---

100 *R (on the application of Jet2.com Ltd) v CAA* [2020] EWCA Civ 35, at [107].

101 *Three Rivers DC v Governor and Company of the Bank of England (No 6)* [2004] UKHL 48, at [102], [2005] 1 AC 610, at 675. See discussion in *WH Holding Ltd, West Ham United Football Club Ltd v E20 Stadium LLP* [2018] EWCA Civ 2652, at [11].

The types of relationships that are covered

Communications between parties or their solicitors and third parties

7.120 LP covers communications between parties to a dispute (HMRC or the taxpayer) and their Lawyers and third parties, and also covers other documents created for, or on behalf of, the client or their lawyer. There is no separate head of privilege that covers communications within a company[102].

7.121 Repackaging these terms into more practical parcels, the following picture emerges.

7.122 First, LP covers communications between parties to a dispute and their Lawyer. This is often concurrent with LAP.

7.123 Second, as regards communications between a Lawyer (or an accountant providing litigation support services in relation to a dispute) and a third party: these are instances where LP can arise – communications between accountants and Lawyers, Lawyers representing an individual partner of a Limited Liability Partnership and communicating with the designated member of the partnership, Lawyers communicating with trustees in relation to a beneficiary's tax affairs, and so on.

7.124 It was noted in *Prince Jefri Bolkiah v KPMG* that it was 'conceded by KPMG that an accountant who provides litigation support services of the kind which they provided to Prince Jefri must be treated for present purposes in the same way as a solicitor'[103], but that is not, in the authors' view, authority for any novel proposition as to the nature of the privilege that covers communications between a client and their accountant in relation to a dispute.

7.125 *Prudential*, when first heard before the Special Commissioners, dealt with LAP and appears to have been argued on the basis that LP could be available to accountants[104].

7.126 The issue was touched on, but not definitively resolved in the Tax Chamber of the Upper Tribunal (UT) in *HMRC v Muhammed Katib*. In this case, the parties made submissions on the basis that LP existed in a case where there was no LAP since the advice was not given by a Lawyer. The UT acknowledged that there 'might' be LP[105].

---

102 See *WH Holding Ltd, West Ham United Football Club Ltd v E20 Stadium LLP* [2018] EWCA Civ 2652, at [26]–[27].

103 *Prince Jefri Bolkiah v KPMG (A Firm)* [1999] 2 AC 222, at 234.

104 *R (Prudential plc and Another) v Special Commissioner of Income Tax and Another (Institute of Chartered Accountants in England and Wales and others intervening)* [2010] EWCA Civ 1094, at [54], [2011] QB 669, at 689.

105 *The Commissioners for Her Majesty's Revenue & Customs v Muhammed Katib* [2019] UKUT 189 (TCC).

7.127 The authors accordingly consider that in FTT appeals, where accountants may effectively act in the same way as a solicitor with conduct of the litigation, or a barrister performing the advocacy, and legislation or delegated legislation provides for this[106], as a matter of policy it makes sense to accord communications between a client and an accountant the same treatment as communications between Lawyers and accountants with their clients.

7.128 Third, communications between client (or party) and third persons for the dominant purpose of obtaining legal advice or information in connection with or conducing or adding the conduct of commenced or reasonably contemplated litigation, are also covered by LP.

7.129 Therefore, where a taxpayer contacts his accountant, a trustee, a designated member or partner, or an employer, under these circumstances, even if the Lawyer did not request it[107], or the client to third-party communications never reached the Lawyer[108], LP is still capable of applying.

When are documents covered: communications for the purpose of obtaining information or advice in connection with existing or contemplated litigation?

Information or advice

7.130 This element needs little explanation. However, it is important to keep in mind that facts, and the opinions of expert witnesses, cannot be shielded by privilege. This would frustrate any attempt to establish the salient facts in litigation.

7.131 In practical terms, where a Lawyer interviews an accountant or an expert witness to establish how and why a transaction was carried out, this would be covered if the dominant purpose test (dealt with below) was met. However, the accountant could still be compelled to give evidence on how the transaction was carried out, since there is no property in a witness; and an expert witness could be compelled to give evidence about facts and his opinions[109].

7.132 That said, a Lawyer cannot be compelled to disclose his opinion on the likelihood of success of a case[110].

106 *Legal Services Act 2007, Sch 2, paras 3(2)* and *4(2)*. See then the provisions of *Tribunals, Courts and Enforcement Act 2007, s 3, Sch 5, para 9*, then see *Tribunal Rules, rule 11*. See *Porter and Co v Revenue and Customs Commissioners* [2018] UKFTT 264 (TC).

107 *Southwark and Vauxhall Water Company v Quick* (1878) 3 QBD 315, at 320 and 322.

108 *Southwark and Vauxhall Water Company v Quick*, at 315, 320 and 323.

109 *In Re L (A Minor) (Police Investigation: Privilege)* [1997] AC 16, at 25 and 34.

110 *In Re L*, at 25.

7.133 One effect of privilege may be that the other party cannot conveniently find out the facts and arguments at the other party's disposal by requesting communications about them. But that does not mean the underlying and pre-existing factual basis cannot be sought through disclosure, investigation, or compelling witnesses.

The sole or dominant purpose

7.134 Reading principle and restriction together, the purpose for which the communication must be made is required to be for the sole or dominant purpose of conducting litigation.

7.135 The Court of Appeal in *Three Rivers (No 5)* suggests the question of dominant purpose is to be assessed objectively on the evidence[111]. That decision concerns LAP and must be treated carefully (see **7.99–7.114**), but it is suggested that it could find application in courts and tribunals.

7.136 The conduct of litigation is not a well-defined phrase, even in a regulatory context. It includes, the authors suggest, work around commencing (drafting, lodging, serving) conducting or defending proceedings.

7.137 Conducting litigation will include deciding whether to litigate and includes whether to settle the dispute giving rise to litigation: 'deciding whether to litigate … also includes [deciding] whether to settle the dispute giving rise to the litigation'[112].

7.138 Where two persons are simply conducting private discussions on a commercial settlement, LP does not apply. This has only recently been clarified in case law[113] and it remains to be seen how it will apply in the tax context.

7.139 It is important to remember that the dominant purpose must be linked to the proceedings in respect of which privilege is asserted. Thus, where an employee settles a potential employment claim with his employer, and HMRC issues an information notice in an enquiry into the tax affairs of the employee, the employee cannot resist disclosure of relevant documents to HMRC in the context of the tax enquiry on the basis that the older employee-employer communications were covered by LP. For the purposes of the tax enquiry, they are not.

111 [2003] EWCA Civ 474, [2003] QB 1556.

112 *WH Holding Ltd, West Ham United Football Club Ltd v E20 Stadium LLP* [2018] EWCA Civ 2652, at [12], [27] and see [12]–[27] for discussion.

113 *WH Holding Ltd v E20 Stadium LLP* [2018] EWCA Civ 2652, at [18]–[22].

The point at which litigation is in progress or contemplation

7.140 For LP to apply, at the time of the communication, litigation must already be live or be in reasonable contemplation[114] (or be 'anticipated'[115], 'pending'[116], 'apprehended'[117] or 'threatened'[118]).

7.141 The 'contemplation' is that of the taxpayer[119] but the court will apply the test objectively[120] to the circumstances of the case. The exact meaning of the phrase is 'difficult to express in words' but a 'mere possibility' of litigation or 'a distinct possibility that sooner or later someone might make a claim' or 'a general apprehension of future litigation' is not enough[121]. However, a 'real likelihood'[122] of litigation is enough in counterpoint to a 'a mere possibility' and there does not, for example, need to be a greater than 50% chance of litigation[123].

7.142 The question of whether litigation is in contemplation will thus be dependent on the facts of each case.

7.143 Generally, it will be more difficult to establish that litigation is in contemplation when HMRC merely amends a return, or opens an enquiry into a return, or issues a discovery assessment, or a closure notice, or a partial closure notice. It will be more straightforward to establish that litigation is in contemplation when an appeal of an HMRC decision is made, or a review of a decision is requested from HMRC, or an application to the Tribunal for an order that a closure notice be made is threatened.

7.144 That said, it is theoretically possible that litigation can be in reasonable contemplation when a tax return is submitted, for example, when a taxpayer has participated in a particularly aggressive DOTAS reportable tax scheme.

---

114 *Wheeler v Le Merchant* (1881) 17 Ch 675, at 681. *Three Rivers DC and Others v Governor and Company of the Bank of England (No 6)* [2004] UKHL 48, at [29], [52], [65], [102], [2005] 1 AC 610, at 647, 654, 660, 675. See also *WH Holding v E20 Stadium LLP* [2018] EWCA Civ 2652, at [26].

115 *Birmingham and Midland Motor Omnibus Company Ltd v London and North Western Railway Co* [1913] 3 KB 850, at 856.

116 *Wheeler v Le Marchant* (1881) 17 Ch 675, 683. *Three Rivers DC v Governor and Company of the Bank of England (No 6)* [2004] UKHL 48, at [52], [2005] 1 AC 610, at 654.

117 *Waugh v British Railways Board* [1980] AC 521, at 542.

118 *Anderson v Bank of British Columbia* (1876) 2 Ch D 644, at 655.

119 That is, the 'party'. See *Plummers Ltd v Debenhams plc* [1986] BCLC 447, at 454 (per Millet J).

120 *Dadourian Group International Inc v Simms* [2008] EWHC 1784 (Ch), at [87].

121 *United States v Philip Morris Inc (No 1)* [2004] EWCA Civ 330, at [68], [2004] 1 CLC 811, at 856. Cited in *AXA Seguros SA De CV v Allianz Insurance plc (t/a Allianz Global Risks)* [2011] EWHC 268 (Comm), at [13].

122 *SFO v Eurasia Natural Resources* [2018] EWCA Civ 2006, at [92], [2019] 1 WLR 791, at 828.

123 *United States v Philip Morris Inc (No 1)* [2004] EWCA Civ 330, at [68], [2004] 1 CLC 811, at 856. Cited in *Westminster International BV and Others v Dornoch Ltd and Others* [2009] EWCA Civ 1323, at [15] and *Rawlinson and Hunter Trustees SA and Others v Akers and Another* [2014] EWCA Civ 136, at [13].

7.145 This is distinct from the provisions under *paragraph 19* of *Schedule 36* to *FA 2008* (discussed above), which only provide cover once an appeal has been made.

The limits of 'litigation': not investigative or inquisitorial

7.146 Litigation must be adversarial and not investigative or inquisitorial. Proceedings before the FTT, High Court or and the criminal courts are adversarial, so that, so long as litigation before any of them is in reasonable contemplation, no real issues would arise.

7.147 However, the dividing line is not always clear. In the tax context, it is suggested that the only decisive factor is whether an appeal against a decision has been made, or a judicial review application has been made, or is in reasonable contemplation. For this reason, mediating a dispute with HMRC before a decision is made by HMRC and appealed by the taxpayer (albeit that appeal need not be notified to the Tribunal) is something that requires caution.

EXCEPTIONS TO PRIVILEGE AND LOSS OF PRIVILEGE

General

7.148 Generally, a client has the right to object to any outsider seeing a communication for any purpose, unless one of the exceptions below applies[124]. However, even if all the conditions which we have discussed above are met, and a document is privileged on the face of it, there are exceptions to the rules and privilege can be lost, or can no longer be claimed, in certain circumstances (see **7.149–7.187**). There are also circumstances where privilege does not apply because of legislation (see **7.189**), because the communication was made for an illegal or nefarious purpose (see **7.190–7.193**), or some other reason (see **7.194**).

Waiver or loss of privilege

7.149 Privilege can no longer be asserted where it has been waived or lost.

7.150 The safest approach is to assume before disclosing communications that once privileged material is divulged to an opponent (or even seen by the opponent), whether accidentally, unintentionally or intentionally, privilege will be lost[125].

---

124 *Guinness-Peat Ltd v Fitzroy Robinson Partnership* [1987] 1 WLR 1027 (CA), at 1044–1045.

125 *R (on the application of Prudential plc and Another) v Special Commissioner of Income Tax and Another* [2013] UKSC 1, at [17], [2013] 2 AC 185, at 215.

7.151 In practice, matters are slightly more complicated. If HMRC claims that privilege has been waived, or lost, such a claim should be closely examined before accepting it as true.

7.152 The rules surrounding loss of privilege have no common thread, and are both highly complex and fact sensitive, but Mr Justice Leggat[126] sought to define circumstances in which privilege can be lost. The authors gratefully borrow these definitions, and respectfully add some additional comments in some places.

7.153 First, a party who by suing his legal adviser puts their confidential relationship in issue cannot claim privilege as against that legal adviser in relation to information relevant to the determination of that issue[127]. Note, however, that privilege over legal advice remains intact in a dispute with the legal adviser over their fees[128].

7.154 Second, because privilege only protects information which is confidential (see **7.41–7.47** above), if the information concerned ceases to be confidential, privilege cannot be claimed. Where a party does an act that has the effect of making information public, this has sometimes been described as a waiver of privilege[129] but it is more accurate to say that privilege cannot be claimed because confidentiality has been lost.

7.155 Third, where a party comes into possession of privileged material by any means, even if without the knowledge or consent of the other party, the receiving party is free to use such material subject to the equitable jurisdiction of the court to restrain a breach of confidence. The FTT is unlikely to have an equitable jurisdiction to give relief for breach of confidence, but such relief can be sought from the High Court most commonly by applying for an injunction, though this is costly. The authors tentatively suggest that if the FTT were faced with the question, and no High Court relief were place, it ought to consider its general obligations to act in accordance with the law of confidence and the overriding objective to deal with cases fairly and justly.

7.156 Fourth, if one party either expressly consents to the use of privileged material by another party or chooses to disclose the information to the other party in circumstances which imply consent to its use, privilege is lost. Such a waiver may be either general or limited in scope.

7.157 In concluding this discussion of privilege, there are two connected extensions to privilege that are worth mentioning in passing here as they can serve a practical purpose. These extensions preserve privilege in circumstances where there is a joint or common interest in the privileged material: they are called 'joint interest privilege' and 'common interest

126 As he then was. See *Serdar Mohammed v Ministry of Defence* [2013] EWHC 4478 (QB).
127 The governing principle is one of fairness: *Paragon Finance v Freshfields* [1999] 1 WLR 1183.
128 Eg the *Solicitor Act 1974, s 70.*
129 *Goldstone v Williams* (1899) 1 Ch 47.

privilege'. In essence, they allow one person to share privileged material with another person without waiving privilege as against a third. The authors note that these two extensions come with further intricacies and ambiguities, which are not dealt with here.

7.158 Joint interest privilege only arises when a joint interest exists at the time the privileged communication comes into existence. It means that privilege does not exist as between the parties, but it does mean that one party cannot assert privilege against the other party in respect of anything within the joint interest.

7.159 Common interest privilege is residual, that is, it applies if joint interest privilege does not. It arises at the point of disclosure and not at the point of creation (provided there is a contemporaneous common interest) which can be important.

Case study 1

7.160 Taxpayer Lucy is receiving litigation advice, and decides to share that advice with taxpayer Dave, who is a litigant in a case which has been joined with her case as part of a group appeal. Dave can insist as against HMRC that the advice shared by Lucy is privileged under joint interest privilege.

Where Lucy received tax advice several years ago, and within the litigation, Lucy and Dave have the same interest in seeing this advice, and Lucy shares it with Dave, common interest privilege might apply against others such as HMRC.

In both cases, it might be advisable for Lucy to impose contractual restrictions on Dave as regards safeguarding confidentiality of the advice, and its use.

7.161 Fifth, where a party waives privilege in the first sense above, by deliberately deploying material in proceedings, the party also loses the right to assert privilege in relation to other material relating to the same subject matter[130].

7.162 In *PCP Capital Partners LLP and Another v Barclays Bank plc* [2020] EWHC 1393 (Comm), the High Court was asked to determine whether there had been a waiver of privilege in circumstances where a witness statement made references to legal advice. Waksman J commented as to the situations in which there is not a waiver of privilege (at paras 48 to 50):

130 *Great Atlantic Insurance Co v Home Insurance Co* [1981] 1 WLR 529. The underlying principle is one of fairness to prevent 'cherry picking': *Brennan v Sunderland City Council* [2009] ICR 479, at [16], 483–484.

'As to the question of waiver itself, it is not easy to find a succinct and clear definition of when it arises, going beyond general statements to the effect, for example, that the party alleged to have waived them has deployed them in some way as part of its case. But on any view in my judgment, first, the reference to the legal advice must be sufficient (a point I return to below) and second, the party waiving must be relying on that reference in some way to support or advance his case on an issue that the court has to decide.

I give two examples of what is clearly not waiver. First, a purely narrative reference to the giving of legal advice does not constitute waiver. This is because, on any view, there is no reliance upon it in relation to an issue in the case. Nor does a mere reference to the fact of legal advice along these lines, "My solicitor gave me detailed advice. The following day I entered into the contract". That is not waiver, however tempting it may be to say that what is really being said is "I entered into the contract as a result of that legal advice". The corresponding point is that if that latter expression is used, then there will be waiver.

I next turn to the vexed question which still confounds the law of privilege, namely the idea that, quite apart from reliance, waiver cannot arise if the reference is to the "effect" of the legal advice as opposed to its "contents". The judicial disquiet to which this distinction has given rise is well-summarised in *Passmore on Privilege* 4th Edition, at paragraphs 7-224 to 7-242.'

At para 60, after a careful review of the case law, the judge concluded that the correct approach to determining whether there has been a waiver is:

'… to deal with matters of principle, in my judgment the correct approach to applying the content/effect distinction is this: the application of the content/effect distinction, as a means of determining whether there has been a waiver or not, cannot be applied mechanistically. Its application has to be viewed and made through the prism of (a) whether there is any reliance on the privileged material adverted to; (b) what the purpose of that reliance is; and (c) the particular context of the case in question. This is an acutely fact-sensitive exercise. To be clear, this means that in a particular case, the fact that only the conclusion of the legal advice referred to is stated as opposed to the detail of the contents may not prevent there being a waiver.'

7.163 In practice, it is this circumstance that causes the greatest number of problems. Parties must tread very carefully since 'deploying', and relying on, privileged material can open up the whole of that material, and other privileged material, for examination by the FTT or courts and by HMRC.

7.164 This is because 'where a party is deploying … material which would otherwise be privileged, the opposite party and the court must have an opportunity to satisfy themselves that what the party has chosen to release from privilege represents the whole material relevant to the issue in question'[131]. But this is not to, say that there is '... a rule that a party who waves privilege in relation to one communication is taken to wave privilege in relation to all, [it does, however, mean that] a party may not waive privilege in such a partial and selective manner that unfairness or misunderstanding may result'[132].

7.165 The most dangerous aspect of this fifth type of waiver is that if such waiver takes place, it can go beyond one document to encompass separate privileged documents[133] that are relevant to the same transaction, issue or purpose[134].

7.166 The process for establishing what has, or has not, been waived has been set out in the High Court as follows[135].

7.167 Identify the 'transaction' in respect of which the disclosure has been made.

7.168 That transaction may be identifiable simply from the nature of the disclosure made — for example, advice given by counsel on a single occasion. In some cases, the purpose of the disclosure of privileged material may 'provide a realistic, objectively determinable definition of the "transaction"'[136].

7.169 Equally, it may be apparent from that material, or from other available material, that the transaction is wider than that which is immediately apparent. If it does, then the whole of the wider transaction must be disclosed.

7.170 When that has been done, further disclosure will be necessary if that is necessary in order to avoid unfairness or misunderstanding of what has been disclosed.

7.171 The authors note that the purpose of the voluntary disclosure, which has prompted the contention that privilege in other material has been collaterally waived, is an important consideration in the assessment of what constitutes the relevant 'transaction'[137].

---

131 Mustill J in *Nea Karteria Maritime Co Ltd v Atlantic and Great Lakes Steamship Corporation* [1981] Comm LR 138, at 139. Approved in *Great Atlantic Insurance Co v Home Insurance Co* [1981] 1 WLR 529, at 538.

132 Bingham CJ in *Paragon Finance v Freshfields* [1999] 1 WLR 1183, at 1188.

133 Auld LJ, *R v Secretary of State for Transport, ex p Factortame Ltd (Discovery)* (1997) 9 Admin LR 591, at 599 (HC).

134 As a helpful example see, generally, *Fulham Leisure Holdings v Nicholson Graham & Jones* [2006] EWHC 158 (Ch), [2006] 2 All ER 599. It is suggested there that this is essentially a very fact-sensitive question reliant on considerations of 'fairness'. See application in *Fisher v The Commissioners for Her Majesty's Revenue & Customs* [2012] UKFTT 335 (TC), at [71] and discussion in B Thanki and ors, *The Law of Privilege* (3rd edn, 2018), OUP, Oxford, paras 5.129–5.133 for a helpful review of authorities.

135 *Fulham Leisure Holdings Ltd v Nicholson Graham & Jones* [2006] EWHC 158 (Ch), [2006] 2 All ER 599, at [11].

136 *Fulham Leisure Holdings Ltd v Nicholson Graham & Jones* [2006] EWHC 158 (Ch), [2006] 2 All ER 599, at [18].

137 *R (on the application of Jet2.com Ltd) v CAA* [2020] EWCA Civ 35, at [114].

7.172 It may also be helpful to keep in mind that '… waiver of privilege in one communication waives privilege in that transaction but not in the underlying topics …'[138].

7.173 In practice, the case law in this area is highly fact sensitive, and the legal principles are not straightforward to navigate.

7.174 The FTT and courts will consider the matter in light of 'fairness'[139]. As part of that assessment, it seems, if the purpose of the waiver were 'modest', fairness would dictate that privilege covering material of the same transaction has not been waived[140].

7.175 It is not entirely clear what is meant by 'modest'. The authors suggest that it might mean where disclosure may have been made to make a party look good in a communication; but without the disclosure itself having a significant impact on issues of fact or law involved in the dispute.

7.176 To illustrate the effect of the waiver rules, it may be helpful to consider *Conegate v HMRC*[141] a persuasive (but not binding) FTT decision.

7.177 In *Conegate*, a taxpayer had disclosed some email correspondence with its lawyers. Some of the legal advice received in relation to a transaction was also summarised in a witness statement. This set out the fact that advice was received on inadvertent and unnecessary Capital Gains Tax (CGT) consequences, that advice had been that an alternative that was blocked by the *Companies Act 2006*, and mentioned that there had been a conclusion that the 'only feasible' alternative that remained was the transaction that the taxpayer undertook. It did not say what the advice on the 'only feasible alternative' actually was.

7.178 HMRC argued that the taxpayer had waived privilege. The FTT approached the question of waiver based on whether sufficient reliance was placed on the privileged material to constitute waiver as a composite question of achieving fairness between the parties[142].

7.179 The FTT decided that the witness statement referred to advice, in order to make the case that it was because of that advice that the taxpayer had taken the steps the taxpayer had taken in the circumstances[143]. In this regard, although the way the reasoning was expressed may not have been identical to that of Waksman J in *PCP Capital Partners* (see **7.162**) but the conclusion appears to be consistent with that authority. The FTT found that it would be

138 *Holyoake v Candy* [2017] EWHC 387 (Ch), at [54].

139 *Paragon Finance v Freshfields* [1999] 1 WLR 1183.

140 *R (on the application of Jet2.com Ltd) v CAA* [2020] EWCA Civ 35, at [119].

141 *Conegate Ltd v The Commissioners for Her Majesty's Revenue & Customs* [2018] UKFTT 82 (TC).

142 *Conegate Ltd*, at [29]. Applying Elias J's approach in *Brennan and Others v Sunderland City Council and Others* [2009] ICR 479, at [67].

143 *Conegate Ltd*, at [30].

unfair to allege advice led directly to particular steps without HMRC having an opportunity to examine the documents: privilege had been lost[144].

7.180 In *Fisher v HMRC*, the FTT held that deployment of legal advice and the consequential waiver of privilege did not extend to advice that had been given after a transaction. It observed that the waiver of privilege in respect of one document would only encompass other documents that are relevant to the same issue in the appeal. Thus, privilege is not waived merely because the other documents are relevant to the appeal as a whole or some other issue in it[145].

7.181 In *HMRC v Muhammed Katib*, HMRC invited the UT to issue general guidance to the FTT to the effect that a formal waiver of privilege should be required in cases where a taxpayer is relying on the averred failings of professional advisers in support of an application for permission to make a late appeal[146].

7.182 The UT refused to give guidance and rejected HMRC's submission that an application for a late appeal will necessarily fail 'in the absence of a signed, formal waiver of privilege'[147]. However, the UT did state that 'in most cases, a litigant seeking permission to make a late appeal on the grounds that previous advisers were deficient will face an uphill task and should expect to provide a full account of exchanges and communications with those advisers. It will often be impossible to give the requisite full account without waiving privilege'[148].

7.183 While it is always a client's privilege in most cases waiver of privilege by a Lawyer acting for him cannot, generally, be reversed despite privilege being the right of the client.

Sharing privileged material

7.184 As referred to at **7.53** above, however, just because a party has the right not to disclose documents does not always mean they have to be withheld.

7.185 There can be many reasons one might choose to share privileged material, either because the advice is helpful, or a taxpayer was wrongly advised and is seeking to reduce or eliminate penalties (though this is not an easy argument to make), or because the process with HMRC is collaborative. However, one must be extremely careful because of the categories of waiver.

---

144 *Conegate Ltd*, at [30].

145 *Fisher v The Commissioners for Her Majesty's Revenue & Customs* [2012] UKFTT 335 (TC), at [71].

146 *The Commissioners for HM Revenue and Customs v Muhammed Hafeez Katib* [2019] UKUT 0189 (TCC), at [45].

147 *The Commissioners for HM Revenue and Customs v Muhammed Hafeez Katib*, at [50].

148 *The Commissioners for HM Revenue and Customs v Muhammed Hafeez Katib*, at [49].

7.186 Before disclosing privileged material (whether formally or informally), it is advisable to consider and/or seek advice on whether the documents are actually privileged; and, if a privileged document is to be disclosed, to what extent privilege is waived in respect of other documents or communication and how the other party (HMRC) might view any of the material for which privilege has been waived or could be waived.

7.187 Finally, one must consider whether the privileged documents disclose further matters, currently not under enquiry, which could be brought into the enquiry. Waiver, the scope of the word 'transaction' and what is 'fair', is notoriously fact sensitive.

7.188 Some of the authorities are not easy to navigate, and it still appears to be in development, so that this is an area where if there are risks, it is highly advisable to seek legal advice especially as an accountant.

Situations where privilege is overridden by statute

7.189 It should be noted in passing that statute can override privilege[149] although a statutory power requiring the production of a document would generally be deemed to exclude the right to demand privileged material unless this is explicitly provided for in primary legislation[150].

Privilege cannot be relied on if the communication took place for or in connection with a nefarious purpose

7.190 Where a person consults a Lawyer in furtherance of a criminal purpose (or, it has been suggested, where there is an 'iniquity' that puts advice or conduct of the Lawyer outside the normal scope of the Lawyer's engagement or renders it an abuse of the relationship[151]), then, whether or not the Lawyer knowingly assists in the furtherance of such purpose, the communications between the client and the solicitor do not attract privilege[152].

7.191 This may become an issue in the context of actual fraudulent tax schemes, although the authors note that, in practice, it is unlikely that truly fraudulent individuals have sought advice from a Lawyer.

---

149 *R (on the application of Prudential plc and Another) v Special Commissioner of Income Tax and Another* [2013] UKSC 1, at [17], [2013] 2 AC 185, at 215.

150 *R (on the application of Morgan Grenfell & Co Ltd) v Special Commissioners of Income Tax* [2002] UKHL 21, at [8].

151 *JSC BTA Bank v Ablayzov* [2014] EWHC 2788 (Comm), at [93], [2014] 2 CLC 263, at 291: this case concerned allegations of concealment and deceit that is dishonest or fraudulent conduct.

152 *Kuwait Airways Corpn v Iraqi Airways Co (No 6)* [2005] EWCA Civ 286, at [14] (CA), [2005] 1 WLR 2734, at 2738. It may be assumed that the same applies in relation to advice of counsel.

7.192 However, courts will not lightly deprive parties of privilege[153] and have made it clear that consulting a 'solicitor about an intended course of action in order to be advised on whether it is legitimate or not … or [laying before him] the facts relating to a charge of fraud, actual made or anticipated … is a very different thing from consulting him in order to learn how to plan, execute, or stifle and actual fraud'[154].

7.193 Anecdotally, clients do sometimes unwittingly suggest a course of conduct that could constitute the criminal offence of Cheating the Public Revenue. However, they invariably refrain from adopting that course of conduct on it being explained to them that what they are suggesting is legally improper; and that were they to proceed with it a substantial prison sentence could result.

Other miscellaneous exceptions

7.194 For the sake of completeness, it should be noted that there are a number of other exceptions to privilege (eg in a probate case where the validity of a will is contested) which do not commonly apply in the context of tax advice and litigation.

CASE STUDIES 2–7

Background facts

7.195 An individual client is subject to an HMRC enquiry into the sale of a chattel which sale generated substantial liabilities to CGT. The asset having been acquired before 31 March 1982, the correct value of the asset at that date is in point. If the correct value is high, the CGT is reduced. If the correct value is low, the CGT is increased.

Case study 2

7.196 The client is advised in relation to the enquiry over a period of time by a solicitor and an accountant. The client discusses the matter by email (copying in both solicitor and accountant), telephone (conference calls), and also in person with the solicitor and accountant together. Both also respond to the client with advice.

Each email with the solicitor and the accountant must be viewed as a separate communication notwithstanding that each is copied into the email. Communications with, and the responses the individual receives in relation to the enquiry from the solicitor, are protected by LAP so long

153 *R v Cox and Railton* (1884) 14 QBD 153, 176 and, slightly more recently, in *R v Snaresbrook Crown Court, ex p DPP* [1988] 1 QB 532, at 538.

154 Lord Sumner in *O'Rourke v Darbishire* [1920] AC 581, at 613 (HL).

as they seek or contain advice on the law or what should reasonably or sensibly be done in a legal context, or evidence it and are made for the dominant purpose of seeking such advice.

Where an email is sent by the individual to the accountant copying in the solicitor, or the accountant is copied into the email to the solicitor, it would be covered by LAP insofar as it would be covered by LAP if it had been sent to the solicitor alone. If it would not be covered under such circumstances, it would only be covered if its dominant purpose is to obtain instructions or disseminate legal advice.

The responses from the accountant are less likely to be protected by LAP unless made for the dominant purpose of obtaining instructions. They may also be covered by *FA 2008, Sch 36, paragraph 25* if they are 'relevant communications' (ie the giving or obtaining of advice about the tax affairs of the individual). Since, however, they are more likely to be about enquiry strategy than tax advice at this stage, careful analysis will be required to discern whether they are protected from disclosure under this head.

Conference calls would be covered by LAP insofar as they were made to give or obtain legal advice.

Case study 3

7.197 The solicitor then retires and comes off the roll but continues to make contributions to the enquiry process. The accountant continues to advise. The client discusses the matter by email (all copied), telephone (conference calls), and also in person with the former solicitor and accountant together. Both also respond to the client with advice.

The responses the individual receives in relation to the enquiry from the former solicitor are not protected by LAP. Given that the status of the former solicitor is at this point unclear, it is equally unclear whether these are relevant communications such that the protections of *FA 2008, Sch 36, paragraph 25* are available. (Is the former solicitor, in this context, a tax adviser? Only possibly so. And bear in mind he is not a member of a professional institute.) The same analysis as the previous scenario applies to communications to and from the accountant.

Case study 4

7.198 The enquiry carries on for some time but eventually the client, accountant and former solicitor decide that enough is enough and instruct a second solicitor, a specialist in tax disputes, to deal with the ongoing enquiry. That specialist solicitor discusses the matter by email (all copied), telephone (conference calls), and also in person with the client, former solicitor, and accountant together. Both of the latter also respond to the client with advice. That specialist solicitor also contacts by email, telephone and in person with the former solicitor and accountant separately.

Communications with, and the responses the individual receives in relation to the enquiry from the specialist solicitor are protected by LAP insofar as they contain or evidence legal advice and the dominant purpose of giving or receiving legal advice. The same analysis as the previous scenario applies to responses from the former solicitor and accountant to the client.

It is more complicated when one comes to the communications between the specialist solicitor and the accountant, and the specialist solicitor and the former solicitor, when the client is not part of the circle, because the status of the communications depends on the capacity in which those communications are made (in particular in response) by the accountant and former solicitor. In the case of the former solicitor, if he is acting as mere intermediary ('I'll get those documents from the client for you as you request') his responses would arguably be covered by LAP, but note that pre-existing documents are unlikely to be covered. If the former solicitor is acting as an adviser ('I'll think about that and advise the client and get back to you with what we decide') his responses would arguably not be covered by LAP. The responses from the accountant are not protected by LAP nor would they appear to be covered by *FA 2008, Sch 36, paragraph 25* because they are not between the accountant and his client. Meanwhile, where the communication from the specialist solicitor, to the former solicitor and accountant, contains information provided by the client to the specialist solicitor, which is covered by LAP and which the client has given the lawyer authority to disclose it, would be covered by LAP.

Case study 5

7.199 The decision is taken by the client, on advice from the specialist solicitor, that further correspondence is pointless and that the case is heading to the Tribunal. The specialist solicitor thereafter discusses the matter by email (all copied), telephone (conference calls), and also in person with the client, former solicitor, and accountant together and separately. Both of the latter also respond to the client with advice.

The responses the individual receives in relation to the enquiry from the specialist solicitor at this stage are protected by LP. The taxpayer is likely to be able to claim that litigation is in contemplation. If in issue and HMRC presses the point, the taxpayer may be able to claim that the engagement of a specialist tax disputes solicitor evidences such contemplation; but the taxpayer would, ideally, be able to point to non-privileged correspondence with HMRC, rather than the content of advice he received since this could lead to issues of waiver. HMRC could argue the advice was deployed and that it was right to see the advice. Even if the advice only contains advice on the ways to force the issue to a tribunal dispute, depending on the exact content there may be a risk of wider advice being opened up.

The responses from the former solicitor and accountant are now also quite possibly protected by LP insofar they are made for the dominant purpose of information and advice in connection with the conducting the litigation. The communications between the specialist solicitor and the accountant, and between the specialist solicitor and the former solicitor, are also protected by LP.

Case study 6

7.200 One email exchange passes between different parties. Initially, the specialist solicitor gives legal advice to the client copying in the former solicitor and accountant. The former solicitor has then taken out all other recipients and emailed the accountant within that chain. At a later stage, this email is forwarded again to the specialist solicitor who forwards it, with his own comments, to the individual.

The initial email by the specialist solicitor is likely to be covered by both LP and LAP. The private exchange between former solicitor and accountant is not covered by LP. However, the email from the specialist solicitor to the individual is covered by LP. However, if the private exchange between former solicitor and accountant discusses the specialist solicitor's advice so as to evidence what that advice was, a claim of LAP may attach to it or part of it.

Case study 7

7.201 A decision is elicited from HMRC and an appeal is lodged. The specialist solicitor thereafter discusses the matter by email (all copied), telephone (conference calls) and also in person with the client, counsel, former solicitor, and accountant together and separately. Both of the latter also respond to the client with advice.

The responses the individual receives in relation to the enquiry from the specialist solicitor are protected by litigation privilege. The responses from the former solicitor and accountant are also protected by LP. The communications between the specialist solicitor and the accountant, and between the specialist solicitor and the former solicitor, and between the specialist solicitor and counsel, are also protected by LP.

Comment on case studies

7.202 Thus, even if the same personnel are involved, the capacity in which the communication is made by an individual, and the nature of the communication, and the circumstances in which the communication is made, may cause one to reach a different conclusion about whether a communication is protected from disclosure.

Chapter 8

Criminal investigations and prosecution

David Bloom, Sonn Macmillan Walker solicitors

SIGNPOSTS

- **Introduction** – overview followed by analysis of the criminal standard and burden of proof; explanation of criminal liability and the accused's state of mind; consideration of direct, indirect and strict liability tax offences and new civil recovery orders (see **8.1–8.90**).
- **Criminal investigations** – explanation of HMRC's civil investigation procedures and what makes criminal investigations more likely; consideration of prevalence and diversity of HMRC criminal investigations (see **8.91–8.123**).
- **The criminal investigatory powers of HMRC** – detailed analysis of powers authorising the lawful search and seizure of material, or its compulsory production and disclosure, and the power of arrest. Includes the *Police and Criminal Evidence Act 1984 (PACE 1984), the Serious Organised Crime and Police Act 2005 (SOCPA 2005)*, the *Taxes Management Act 1970 (TMA 1970)*, and the *Proceeds of Crime Act 2002 (POCA 2002)* (see **8.124–8.186**).
- **Dealing with a 'dawn raid' and challenging court orders** – detailed checklist of the practical steps to be taken by the tax professional at every stage of a search and routes of challenge in the courts explained (see **8.187–8.209**).
- **Interviews under caution and the role of the legal professional** – the tax professional and the interview process, including the implication of the *PACE 1984* caution, and the role of the legal adviser (see **8.210–8.239**).
- **The charging decision** – the limited options available to the suspect explained; the tests the prosecution must apply before any criminal charge made are explained; out-of-court disposals and how charges can be challenged are considered (see **8.240–8.259**).

- **Criminal prosecutions** – different venues for criminal proceedings explained and the court process is analysed (see **8.260–8.295**).
- **Criminal trials** – a brief review of the sequence of the criminal trial (see **8.296–8.297**).
- **Sentence and confiscation** – approach of the sentencing judge considered, and confiscation regime reviewed (see **8.298–8.316**).
- **Key points** – a list of key points (see **8.317**).

INTRODUCTION

Overview

8.1 This chapter considers the criminal justice system, its processes and procedures, from initial investigations through to prosecution in the criminal courts. It does not pretend to be comprehensive but aims to provide practical guidance and topics of interest to the tax professional. The practitioner facing a specific criminal allegation ought to seek immediate professional advice.

8.2 Accountants, both certified and chartered CTAs, are the most readily identifiable tax professionals but 'tax agent' has a wide statutory definition and refers to an individual who, in the course of business, assists other persons (ie clients) with their tax affairs.

8.3 Auditors, bankers, bookkeepers, and lawyers may provide tax assistance that could include:

- advising a client in relation to tax;
- acting or purporting to act as agent on behalf of a client in relation to tax;
- assisting with any document that a client is likely to rely on to determine a person's tax position; and
- assistance that is given for non-tax purposes, if it is given with the knowledge that it will be, or is likely to be, used by a client in connection with the client's tax affairs.

(*Finance Act 2012 (FA 2012), Sch 38, s 2*)

8.4 Aside from being a victim of a crime, the tax professional may be concerned in criminal cases:

- *Directly* as the subject of a criminal investigation and/or court proceedings.

- *Indirectly* where his client is the focus of criminal allegations and/or the tax professional is required to provide a witness statement for/against.
- *Independently* as an expert who assists the court.

8.5 This chapter focuses on direct and indirect involvement and is aimed at the tax professional unfamiliar with the criminal law and its processes.

8.6 The tax professional who appears as an expert witness in a criminal court will be aware of his duties as an expert witness, codified in the amended *Criminal Procedure Rules* (*CrimPR*), *Pt 19*[1].

8.7 The *CrimPR* and the *Criminal Practice Directions* (*CPD*) provide the procedural rules and codes of practice binding on every court, prosecution and defence and together promote the consistent administration of justice.

8.8 A criminal prosecution is the strongest action open to the tax authorities and can result in:

- a fine, community punishment or sentence of imprisonment;
- a criminal record, with implications on future employment prospects, including eligibility to be appointed as a company director and professional disqualification;
- the loss of anonymity, with the potential for reputational damage; and
- proceedings to recover underlying lost tax.

8.9 If these consequences represent the 'grave' in terms of the criminal justice system, the 'cradle' is the preceding investigation in which relevant incriminating material will have been gathered by an investigating law enforcement authority.

8.10 The tax professional is most likely to be concerned with criminal investigations conducted by Her Majesty's Revenue & Customs (HMRC), but the City of London police, Serious Fraud Office (SFO), Financial Conduct Authority (FCA), or National Crime Agency (NCA) could all initiate and lead the investigation or work in conjunction with each other.

8.11 In the case of HMRC's criminal investigations in England and Wales, the decision of whether to bring a criminal prosecution is made by the Crown Prosecution Service (CPS), an independent prosecuting authority.

8.12 As we shall see in this chapter, the first a criminal suspect might know of an investigation is when officers attend their home address or place of work in the early hours with a court order. The legal provisions that allow for 'dawn raids' and practical steps that ought to be considered by the tax professional or his client in this situation will be outlined.

1 See www.justice.gov.uk/courts/procedure-rules/criminal/docs/2015/crim-proc-rules-2015-part-19.pdf.

8.13 The formal interview 'under caution' allows a suspect to comment on the allegation(s) and raise his defence if he so wishes. The investigator may have had days or weeks to plan for this interrogation and the role of the solicitor in safeguarding the interests of the suspect will be considered.

8.14 After the officers have completed their investigations and concluded all reasonable lines of enquiry, they will send the results of their efforts to the CPS. The tests and factors that Crown Prosecutors must apply in deciding whether to charge an individual or company will be explained.

8.15 Once charged, a 'suspect' becomes a 'defendant' who will be asked to enter a plea at court. If the defendant is contesting the allegation(s), the case will be adjourned for a trial and the most relevant aspects of court proceedings, including the disclosure regime and sentencing principles, will be outlined.

8.16 Before delving into criminal investigations and prosecutions, it is first necessary to explain what is meant by criminal liability and the 'standard' and 'burden' with regard to proving an offence in a criminal court.

Criminal liability

8.17 Criminal liability is composed of three basic elements:

- a guilty act or omission, known in Latin as '*actus reus*';
- a guilty mind or '*mens rea*'; and
- a valid defence that negates criminal liability even if the elements of the offence (ie the *actus reus* and *mens rea*) are present.

8.18 This reflects the legal maxim (in Latin) '*actus non facit reum nisi mens sit rea';* which means, 'the act will not make a person guilty unless the mind is also guilty': eg a person cannot be guilty of murder if he accidentally runs over and kills someone. The *mens rea* for murder requires an intention to kill or cause very serious bodily injury. An accident will render the requisite legal intent for the offence of murder absent.

8.19 Most criminal offences are unambiguous in terms of what specific act and state of mind must be present. However, some offences that are likely to concern the tax professional do not require specific intent on the part of the accused: eg money laundering offences, contrary to *POCA 2002, ss 327–329*, can be committed when the accused conceals, arranges or acquires 'criminal property', ie property which he knows or suspects constitutes or represents a benefit to him from his criminal conduct.

States of mind

8.20 *Intention* describes a state of mind as to the consequences, eg the accused intends to make a gain. A person 'intends' to cause a specific result if he acts to bring it about. In such circumstances, it is immaterial that his chances of success are small.

8.21 *Knowledge* is usually used in relation to circumstances, eg the possession of criminal property, and includes 'shutting one's eyes to an obvious means of knowledge' or 'deliberately refraining from making inquiries the results of which the person does not care to have'[2].

8.22 *Belief* is a state of mind by which a person thinks that X is the case. It is 'a more positive frame of mind than suspicion'[3].

8.23 *Suspicion* is a state of mind by which the person in question thinks that X may be the case[4]. It requires the prosecution to prove that an accused thought that there was a real possibility that a specific circumstance was the case, even though the accused could not prove or be sure about it.

8.24 Many criminal offences, which may concern the tax professional, will centre around his probity or that of his taxpaying client. Since 2017, the issue of dishonesty in criminal law has undergone a major revision.

8.25 *Dishonesty*: the starting point remains that the trial judge is discouraged from defining this nebulous concept to a jury even where it is an ingredient of the criminal offence to be decided. Where a jury asks for assistance, the judge ought now to follow the decision in *R v Barton and Booth* [2020] EWCA Crim 575.

8.26 The Court of Appeal in that case confirmed that the criminal law test of dishonesty is that (unanimously said in passing) by the Supreme Court in *Ivey v Genting Casinos* [2017] UKSC 67, namely:

(a) what was the accused's actual state of knowledge or belief as to the facts; and

(b) was his conduct dishonest by the standards of ordinary decent people?

8.27 *Barton and Booth* was a landmark decision for recalibrating the relationship between the subjective and objective elements of dishonesty. An accused can still introduce evidence of his perceptions of the honesty of his conduct. But the jury will now be directed that what an accused believed is not determinative of whether his conduct was dishonest by objective standards. In other words, there is no requirement for the prosecution to show that the accused recognised that his conduct was dishonest.

Proving the elements of the offence

The criminal standard and burden of proof

8.28 Viscount Sankey, in *Woolmington v DPP* [1935] UKHL 1, called the presumption of innocence the 'one golden thread' that exists with only minor qualification throughout the 'web' of criminal proceedings.

2 *Westminster City Council v Croyalgrange Ltd* (1986) 83 Cr App R 155.

3 *R (Errington) v Metropolitan Police Authority* [2006] EWHC 1155 Admin.

4 *A and Others v Secretary of State for the Home Department* [2004] EWCA Civ 1123.

8.29 There is no burden on the accused to prove his innocence. The burden is on the prosecution to prove the guilt of the accused. To do this, the prosecution must prove to the very high criminal standard every element of every offence that it alleges the accused has committed. This ensures that every effort is made to remove the risk of mistakes of facts that could result in the conviction of the innocent.

What is the criminal standard of proof?

8.30 The expression 'beyond reasonable doubt' may come to mind but the Judicial Studies Board's Crown Court Compendium (July 2020) makes clear that the trial judge should not refer to this particular phrase unless an advocate has used it. In those circumstances, the judge should tell the jury that it means the same as being 'sure'.

8.31 Members of a jury may scratch their heads at these familiar but imprecise expressions which lend themselves to subjective interpretations. The criminal justice system is predicated on an impartial determination of the facts to this exacting standard.

8.32 But it is fair to ask, just how sure must a jury be of the accused's guilt to safely convict? If the jury wrote a note asking that question, the judge would explain that the law does not require absolute certainty for an accused to be convicted. Common sense makes plain that it is virtually impossible to prove anything to this degree. But it is not enough to convict on the basis that the accused is probably guilty or even very probably guilty.

8.33 As Denning J (as he then was) explained in *Miller v Minister of Pensions*[5]: 'the … degree of cogency … required in a criminal case before an accused person is found guilty is well settled'. It need not reach certainty, but it must carry a high degree of probability. Proof beyond reasonable doubt does not mean proof beyond the shadow of a doubt. The law would fail to protect the community if it admitted fanciful possibilities to deflect the course of justice. If the evidence is so strong against a man as to leave only a remote possibility in his favour which can be dismissed with the sentence 'of course it is possible, but not in the least probable', the case is proved, but nothing short of that will suffice.

8.34 These remarks have been repeatedly approved by the Court of Appeal (see *R v Scott Smith*[6]).

8.35 An accused ought not, therefore, be convicted if there remains any doubt about any part of the prosecution case where such a doubt is more than merely fanciful or far-fetched or based only on an extremely remote possibility. Put another way: if any residual doubt is not realistic, an accused ought to be found guilty.

---

5 [1947] 2 All ER 372, at [373]

6 [2012] EWCA Crim 702, at [15] to [17].

8.36 By contrast in civil proceedings, a lower standard of proof applies. Lord Nicholls confirmed the civil standard of proof in the context of a family case[7]: 'The balance of probability standard means that a court is satisfied an event occurred if the court considers that, on the evidence, the occurrence of the event was more likely than not'.

8.37 This means that a higher bar must be surmounted by law enforcement authorities, such as HMRC, that wish to secure a criminal conviction than if they wish to establish facts before a civil court.

Vicarious liability for a company

8.38 The House of Lords in *Salomon v Salomon & Co Ltd* [1897] AC 22 confirmed the company law principle that every company has its own legal identity, which is not the same as the identities of its shareholders, directors, parent or subsidiary companies.

8.39 The liabilities of the company are distinct from the liabilities of the shareholders or directors; and, conversely, the assets of the company do not belong to the shareholders or directors individually, regardless of whether or not the shareholder holds 100% of the shares.

8.40 This corporate veil may be pierced to prevent the abuse of corporate legal personality, eg where the company is used to evade the law, as identified by Lord Sumption in *Prest v Petrodel Resources Ltd* [2013] UKSC 34.

8.41 A company is though capable of being prosecuted and corporate liability may be established, depending on the offence, with respect to:

- vicarious liability for the acts of a company's employees or agents; or
- non-vicarious liability arising from the 'identification principle' where the offender was a 'directing mind' and will of the company, ie 'controlling officers' of the company.

The 'directing mind' principle

8.42 *Tesco Supermarkets v Nattrass*[8] remains the leading authority confirming the 'directing mind' principle of corporate liability.

8.43 Tesco was offering a discount on washing powder which was advertised on posters displayed in stores. Once they ran out of the lower priced product the stores began to replace it with the regularly priced stock. The manager failed to take the signs down and a customer was charged at the higher price. Tesco was charged under the *Trade Descriptions Act 1968, s 24(1)* for falsely advertising the price of washing powder.

---

7 *In re H (Minors)* [1966] AC 563, at [586].
8 [1972] AC 153.

8.44 In its defence, Tesco argued that it had taken all reasonable precautions and undertaken all due diligence, and that the conduct of the manager could not attach liability to the corporation.

8.45 The House of Lords accepted the defence and found that the manager was not a 'directing mind' of the corporation and his conduct was not attributable to the corporation. The corporation had done all it could to enforce the rules regarding advertising and Tesco was acquitted. Lord Reid held that, 'Then the person who acts is not speaking or acting for the company. He is acting as the company and his mind which directs his acts is the mind of the company. If it is a guilty mind, then that guilt is the guilt of the company.'

Direct and indirect and strict liability tax offences

8.46 The tax professional will be aware that his clients – individual or companies – could commit direct or indirect taxes offences, or that he himself could face accusations of wrongdoing by law enforcement authorities due to his proximity and position of trust.

8.47 Direct tax is charged directly on the income or wealth of the person (eg income tax). Indirect tax is imposed on the price of goods and services (eg Value Added Tax).

8.48 The fraudulent evasion of either of these types of tax is contrary to specific Acts of Parliament: ie for income tax, the offence is contrary to the *TMA 1970, s 106A;* while for VAT, the offence is contrary to the *Value Added Tax Act 1994* (*VATA 1994*), *s 72*.

8.49 While most criminal offences require a guilty act and mind, some do not. These are called 'strict liability offences' and are committed irrespective of the state mind of the accused.

8.50 Some examples that might be relevant to the tax professional include failure to:

- provide information when requested, contrary to the *Customs and Excise Management Act 1979* (*CEMA 1979*), *s 167*;
- pay a VAT security, contrary to *VATA 1994, s 72(11)*;
- declare offshore income tax and capital gains in accordance with *TMA 1970, ss 7* and *8* (following the insertion of *ss 106B–106H* by *Finance Act 2016* (*FA 2016*), *s 166)*;
- prevent facilitation of tax evasion, contrary to the *Criminal Finances Act 2017* (*CFA 2017*), *Pt 3* (see **Chapter 9**).

8.51 The common feature of these offences is that whilst HMRC must demonstrate the specific failure or instances of non-compliance on the part of the taxpayer to the high criminal standard, it does not have to prove the taxpayer's guilty mind to secure a criminal conviction.

8.52 Some strict liability offences have statutory defences provided within the Act of Parliament: eg reasonable excuse or where the accused has carried out due diligence. But, generally, there are few defences available, because as with other strict liability offences in general, eg speeding, the law was framed specifically to discourage the evasion of responsibility once the act was established.

Failure to prevent the facilitation of tax evasion

8.53 This offence, also known as the Corporate Criminal Offence (CCO), was introduced on 30 September 2017 to increase tax transparency. Whilst it was previously a criminal offence to evade tax and/or assist in the evasion of UK tax, the new provisions contained in *Part 3* of the *CFA 2017* introduced the offence of failing to prevent the facilitation of tax evasion. This means that if a person 'associated' to a company in the course of their duties is found to have assisted a third party to evade tax, then the company could be guilty of this corporate offence.

8.54 The successful prosecution of a company can lead to an unlimited fine and/or criminal record for its directors in addition to considerable reputational damage. The company does have a full statutory defence if it can prove that, when the UK tax facilitation offence was being committed, it had in place 'reasonable prevention procedures in place'. This defence is analogous to the 'adequate procedures' defence that can protect companies charged with failing to prevent bribery under the *Bribery Act 2010, s 7*.

8.55 HMRC has announced that, as of 13 October 2020, they had 13 CCO investigations open and a further 18 'live opportunities are currently under review', meaning that they were considering whether to open an investigation[9].

8.56 HMRC have disclosed that these 31 investigations and 'opportunities' span 10 different business sectors, including the financial sector. These businesses are inherently at risk of an HMRC CCO investigation if one of their clients is implicated in a financial crime.

8.57 They will have to consider having an appropriate CCO policy to mitigate this risk and which is properly implemented. A reasonable CCO preventative policy will likely include a statement confirming the company's values and commitment to prevent the facilitation of tax evasion. It will explain how risks are assessed, recorded and reviewed and staff receive relevant training. They will also have to notify the FCA of any investigation.

---

9 See www.gov.uk/government/publications/number-of-live-corporate-criminal-offences-investigations/number-of-live-corporate-criminal-offences-investigations.

Value Added Tax offences

8.58 As VAT is likely to be the indirect tax of most interest to the tax professional, it is worth setting out some specific offences in more detail:

- **Fraudulent evasion of VAT** (*VATA 1994, s 72(1)*)

  A person who is knowingly concerned in, or is taking steps with a view to, the fraudulent evasion of VAT by him or any other person is liable under this offence. A person's conduct may amount to fraudulent evasion under this provision if he understates payments due for a prescribed accounting period. In certain circumstances the overclaiming of VAT (eg a refund in respect of bad debts) may also result in fraudulent evasion.

- **Production, furnishing or sending of false documents and statements** (*VATA 1994, s 72(3)*)

  The offender commits this offence if his intention is to deceive, though he is also liable if he knowingly or recklessly makes a false statement.

- **Conduct which must have involved an offence** (*VATA 1994, s 72(8)*)

  Where a person's conduct during any specified period must have involved the commission by him of one or more of the offences listed in *section 72*, then, regardless of whether the specifics of the offence(s) are known, he is guilty of an offence. The purpose of this provision is to cover cases where it can be proved that an offence has been committed during a period spanning a number of prescribed accounting periods, but it is not clear to what extent it was committed in any particular prescribed accounting period within the total period concerned.

- **The possession and dealing in goods on which VAT has been evaded** (*VATA 1994, s 72(10)*)

  A person commits this offence if, having reason to believe that tax has been or will be evaded on them, he either acquires possession of any goods; deals with any goods; or accepts the supply of any services.

Example 8.1: Non-payment of VAT security (VATA 1994, s 72(11))

8.59 Mr A is the director and sole shareholder of company X Ltd. Mr Z provides Mr A and X Ltd with professional tax advice. On 1 May, X Ltd received a Notice of Requirement (NoR) to pay a security in the sum of £10,000.

The VAT security regime

8.60 Where HMRC has cause to believe that current and/or future payments of VAT will not be made by a person or body corporate as they become due, HMRC may decide to serve on the person or body corporate a NoR. Once paid, the security is held by HMRC.

8.61 If there is a current VAT debt on file, the security may be used to offset that debt. If future payments of VAT are not paid when they become due, HMRC is able to take the payment from the security held. In this way, the security regime operates to secure payments due to the public purse.

8.62 A criminal offence is committed when a person or a body corporate makes taxable supplies after having been served with a NoR if he/she/it does not pay the security amount.

8.63 The security is required immediately but the person or body corporate has a period of 30 days in which to:

(a) provide further information to the original HMRC decision-maker; or

(b) ask for an internal HMRC review; or

(c) lodge an appeal to the First-tier Tribunal (Tax).

The practical (although not necessarily strictly legal) effect of (a), (b) or (c) is that the requirement for the bond security is suspended as trading may still be prohibited unless a bond paid.

The criminal offence

8.64 The offence is committed contrary to *VATA 1994, s 72(11)*: 'If any person supplies or is supplied with goods or services in contravention of *paragraph 4(2)* of *Schedule 11*, he shall be liable on summary conviction to a maximum penalty of £20,000'.

8.65 *VATA 1994, Sch 11, para 4(2)* states:

> 'If they think it necessary for the protection of the revenue, the Commissioners may require a taxable person, as a condition of his supplying or being supplied with goods or services under a taxable supply, to give security, or further security, for the payment of any VAT that is or may become due from (a) the taxable person; or (b) any person by or to whom relevant goods or services are supplied.'

8.66 *CEMA 1979, s 171(4)* states:

> 'Where an offence under any enactment relating to an assigned matter which has been committed by a body corporate is proved to have been committed with the consent or connivance of, or to be attributable to any neglect on the part of, any director, manager, secretary or other similar officer of the body corporate or any person purporting to act in any such capacity, he as well as the body

corporate shall be guilty of that offence and shall be liable to be proceeded against and punished accordingly.'

8.67 'Assigned matter' is defined in *CEMA 1979, s 1(1)* as: '… any matter in relation to which the Commissioners, or officers of Revenue and Customs, have a power or duty …'.

8.68 The provisions combine to mean that this is a strict liability offence and X Ltd can be guilty if Mr A (its directing mind) was at least negligent in not taking sufficient steps to ensure compliance with HMRC's requirement to pay the sum of £10,000 (in the example above).

Civil recovery

8.69 Before considering criminal investigations and prosecutions, the tax professional ought to be aware of non-criminal conviction-based asset forfeiture, ie civil recovery.

8.70 Civil recovery is the name given to the powers conferred by *POCA 2002, Pt 5* whereby a law enforcement authority can:

(a) recover in civil proceedings before the High Court property which is, or represents, property obtained through unlawful conduct; or

(b) enable the forfeiting in the magistrates' court of property which is, or represents, property obtained through unlawful conduct, or which is intended to be used in unlawful conduct (*POCA 2002, s 240(1)*).

8.71 'Unlawful conduct' is defined as conduct which is unlawful under the criminal law of the relevant part of the UK or, if it occurs abroad, both is unlawful under the criminal law of the foreign country and, if it had occurred in a part of the UK, would be unlawful under the criminal law of that part (*POCA 2002, s 241*).

8.72 As we have seen, to secure a criminal conviction, the prosecution must meet a high standard; by contrast, the court must decide on a balance of probabilities whether it is proved that any matters alleged to constitute unlawful conduct have occurred (*POCA 2002, s 241(3)*).

8.73 As we will see, criminal investigations can be protracted, and the court process drawn out with the result in the hands of a jury for more serious offences. The civil route offers law enforcement authorities a relatively cheap and quick alternative before a judge.

8.74 Finally, new powers, eg unexplained wealth orders (UWOs), in their 'investigative toolkit' (*POCA 2002, Pt 8*) and new provisions, eg account freezing orders (AFOs), introduced by the *Criminal Finance Act 2017*, have made civil recovery increasingly popular with HMRC and other agencies : ie in the 2019 to 2020 period, law enforcement agencies in England and Wales froze £208m covering over 812 bank and building society accounts through the use of AFOs (see HM Treasury's 'National risk assessment of money laundering and terrorist financing 2020').

Principles derived from case authorities

8.75 Prior to reviewing UWOs and AFOs, it is worth mentioning some key principles from important civil recovery cases:

- In *R (on the application of the Director of the Assets Recovery Agency) v Jia Jin He (No 2)* [2004] EWHC 3021 (Admin) it was noted that criminal conduct may be regarded as inherently less probable than non-criminal conduct, and courts should look for 'cogent evidence' before deciding this test had been met.
- While a claim for civil recovery cannot be maintained *solely* upon the basis that a defendant has no identifiable lawful income to warrant his lifestyle (*Director of the Assets Recovery Agency v Green* [2005] EWHC 3168 (Admin) at [47]), a lack of lawful income to support the defendant's lifestyle may be a very relevant factor in painting the overall picture (*Olupitan and Others v Assets Recovery Agency* [2008] EWCA Civ 104, per Carnwath LJ at [16] and [30]).
- Similarly, while the burden of proof is on the law enforcement authority to show that the property in question was obtained by, or in return for, unlawful conduct, and not for the defendant to show that the property was obtained lawfully, the ability or not of a person to show that the source was not unlawful conduct is likely to be relevant (*Serious Organised Crime Agency v Bosworth* [2010] EWHC 645 (QB) at [56]).
- In *R v Anwoir* [2008] EWCA Crim 1354 [2009] per Latham LJ at [21], the Court of Appeal held that where the Crown seeks to prove that property derives from crime by evidence of the circumstances in which the property is handled, it must be 'such as to give rise to the irresistible inference that it can only be derived from crime'.
- Some balance to this can be found in *NCA v Baker* [2020] EWHC 822 (Admin) per Mrs Justice Lang at [97] that the use of complex offshore corporate structures or trusts is not per se a ground for believing that they have been set up, or are being used, for wrongful purposes. The Court of Appeal refused to grant the NCA permission to appeal this first significant UWO decision.

Unexplained Wealth Orders

8.76 Unexplained Wealth Orders (UWOs) are a new investigative tool aimed at tackling money laundering and economic crime (*POCA 2002, ss 363A–363T*).

8.77 A lacuna in the *POCA 2002* provisions meant that law enforcement authorities were sometimes unable to freeze or recover assets even when they had reasonable grounds to suspect the identified assets represented the proceeds of crime due to their inability to obtain evidence from overseas jurisdictions.

8.78 UWOs were intended to correct this but do not confer a new power to recover assets; rather they compel an individual or company to provide information or documentation explaining the origins of assets (valued in excess of £50,000) that appear to be disproportionate to their known income.

8.79 Failure to provide a full response can give rise to a presumption that the property is recoverable in any subsequent civil recovery proceedings.

8.80 A UWO creates therefore a reverse burden on the respondent to prove the legitimacy of the income used to acquire the property and reduces the investigative burden on the enforcement agencies.

8.81 To prevent the property in question being dissipated, a UWO application may be made to a High Court judge sitting in private in the absence of the respondent and will be made if the court is satisfied, on the balance of probabilities, that the legislative preconditions are met.

8.82 The court can, when issuing an UWO, make an interim freezing order (IFO) if it considers it necessary to safeguard against the frustration of any future recovery order.

Account Freezing and Forfeiture Orders

8.83 Prior to the recent *POCA 2002* amendments, the contents of bank and building society accounts could be confiscated following a conviction or recovered under civil recovery powers where the value was more than £10,000 and on an application to High Court. Where neither of these conditions applied, there was no formal mechanism for recovering the funds.

8.84 The account freezing and forfeiture provisions provide a formal regime (*POCA 2002, ss 303Z1–303Z19*). These are broadly based on the cash forfeiture procedures (*POCA 2002, Ch 3*) and proceedings similarly take place in the first instance in the magistrate's court. Any appeal is heard in the Crown Court.

8.85 The starting point where funds are held in a bank account is for the law enforcement officer to apply to freeze the credit balance (above £1,000) of a bank or build society account that has a head office or branch in the UK in accordance with the *Magistrates' Court (Freezing and Forfeiture of Money in Bank and Building Society Accounts) Rules 2017, SI 2017/1297.*

8.86 The court may make this freezing order if it is satisfied that there are 'reasonable grounds to suspect' money in the account is recoverable property (ie property obtained through unlawful conduct) or intended for use in unlawful conduct. This is an objective test and there must be a nexus between the suspicions and the funds in question.

8.87 The account can be frozen for a maximum of two years. The account holder can seek to vary or discharge the freezing order or apply to draw down reasonable living expenses, legal fees (unlike cash forfeiture cases), or access funds to enable the continuation of a trade.

8.88 Before the expiry of the two-year period, if the enforcement officer wishes to recover the frozen funds, he must apply to the court for an account forfeiture order. He will have to satisfy the court on the balance of probabilities that the money is recoverable property or intended for use in crime before ordering its forfeiture.

8.89 In a contested forfeiture hearing, the court will be presented with competing explanations of the source of the disputed frozen funds and expert evidence, such as a forensic account, may be called.

8.90 In response to a freedom of information request, HMRC has confirmed that it froze 166 bank and building society accounts in the 2019/20 tax year to March 25, preventing individuals' access to or withdrawals from £19.5m suspected to have been derived from tax fraud and other crimes. This was a dramatic increase on the 60 orders covering £8m it froze in 2018/19.

CRIMINAL INVESTIGATIONS

Civil investigation of suspected tax fraud: COP9 procedure

8.91 HMRC reserves the right to conduct criminal investigations in all the areas for which it has responsibility.

8.92 However, its policy is to deal with instances of suspected fraud where possible using the civil investigation procedures under Code of Practice 9 (COP9)[10].

8.93 This procedure relies on the taxpayer cooperating with HMRC and disclosing fraudulent activities.

8.94 It is cost effective for HMRC to be in receipt of the taxpayer's incriminating information from the outset and enter a contractual arrangement with the taxpayer for the recovery of evaded tax.

8.95 Once a COP9 letter has been sent by HMRC to the taxpayer, the taxpayer will have 60 days from the day of receipt to:

- fully cooperate with the process and accept the offer of a contract, called the 'Contractual Disclosure Facility' (CDF); or

10 'Guidance – HMRC's criminal investigation policy' (May 2019), available at www.gov.uk/government/publications/criminal-investigation/hmrc-criminal-investigation-policy.

- formally reject the offer.

8.96 The taxpayer might reject the offer if he does not reasonably believe his deliberate conduct led to a loss of tax.

8.97 If the taxpayer rejects the CDF offer, makes no response or only partially cooperates in the civil investigation, HMRC can initiate a criminal investigation if it considers it appropriate.

8.98 In accepting the offer, the taxpayer is admitting to HMRC that a specified amount of tax has been lost and is recoverable, including interest and associated penalties that may have been evaded.

8.99 The taxpayer must provide an 'Outline Disclosure' declaration within the same 60-day period containing:

- a brief description of the frauds they have committed;
- a formal admission of deliberately bringing about a loss of tax;
- any non-fraudulent irregularities;
- any proposals for a payment on account.

8.100 If HMRC accepts the Outline Disclosure, the taxpayer is required to make progress towards a formal disclosure, which will include:

- Certificate of Full Disclosure.
- Statement of assets and liabilities.
- Certificate of bank accounts operated.
- Certificate of debit and credit cards operated.

8.101 Under the terms of the contract, the taxpayer will not be criminally investigated or prosecuted by HMRC for matters covered by the Outline Disclosure. Full cooperation will likely ensure a greater reduction in any penalty found to be due and avoid other civil sanctions such as insolvency. This route can also lessen the potential for adverse publicity to the taxpayer.

8.102 Whilst HMRC cannot accept a monetary settlement and then institute criminal proceedings, the CPS are not precluded from initiating proceedings, eg for false accounting based on the same facts[11].

8.103 The CPS retains prosecutorial discretion and is not bound by a civil route preferred by HMRC. However, the taxpayer may be able to argue that there was an 'abuse of process' if he were induced to settle with HMRC and acted to his own detriment with a legitimate expectation that he would not be prosecuted.

11 See *R v Werner (Laurence Ian)* [1998] STC 550 (CA (Crim Div)).

Cases where a criminal investigation is more likely

8.104 According to HMRC's published policy, criminal investigations are reserved for cases where it needs to send a strong deterrent message or where the conduct involved is such that only a criminal sanction is appropriate. For these purposes, a 'criminal investigation' means any process:

- for considering whether an offence has been committed;
- for discovering by whom an offence has been committed; and
- as a result of which an offence is alleged to have been committed.

(*Commissioners for Revenue and Customs Act 2005, s 21(2A)*).

8.105 HMRC's policy confirms that cases or conduct likely to result in a criminal investigation include:

- where deliberate concealment, deception, conspiracy or corruption is suspected;
- cases involving the use of false or forged documents;
- cases involving importation or exportation breaching prohibitions or restrictions;
- where the accused has committed previous criminal offences or unlawful conduct that resulted in civil penalties;
- cases involving theft or the misuse or unlawful destruction of HMRC documents;
- where there is evidence of assault on, threats to, or the impersonation of HMRC officials;
- where there is a link to suspected wider criminality, whether domestic or international, involving offences not under the administration of HMRC;
- cases of organised criminal gangs attacking the tax system or systematic frauds where losses represent a serious threat to the tax base, including conspiracy;
- where an individual holds a position of trust or responsibility;
- where money laundering is suspected, particularly where professional advisers provide the means to put tainted money out of reach of law enforcement. In this situation, HMRC takes a particularly severe attitude as a dishonest accountant is considered a source of 'infection' likely to have assisted multiple clients in the commission of serious fraud. Where a tax professional is criminally investigated and subsequently prosecuted, HMRC has the right to be selective in pursuing his clients[12];

12 *R v IRC, ex p Mead* [1992] STC 482.

- where materially false statements are made, or materially false documents are provided, during a civil investigation: for example in 1987, the former British champion jockey Lester Piggott receiving a three-year prison sentence after pleading guilty to failing to declare income tax on almost £3m of earnings. An aggravating feature had been that after two previous tax investigations, Piggott had signed false statements of assets;
- finally, in relation to a tax avoidance scheme, where reliance is placed on a false or altered document – or such reliance or material facts are misrepresented – to enhance the credibility of such a scheme. Although an avoidance scheme would normally be investigated by HMRC under a civil procedure, HMRC will initiate a prosecution in appropriate circumstances.

8.106 HMRC has made clear that certain offences will almost always be criminally investigated and prosecuted rather than be dealt with by means of the COP9 route.

8.107 These include:

- VAT missing trader intra-community (MTIC) fraud involving the importation and onward sale of small high-value components such as mobile phones and computer chips;
- VAT bogus registration repayment fraud; and
- organised tax credit fraud.

8.108 When HMRC is determining whether a case should be investigated using the civil fraud investigation procedures under COP9 or via the criminal investigation route, significant weight will be attached to the extent to which the taxpayer has made complete and unprompted disclosure of the offence committed.

8.109 The tax professional will note that HMRC can conduct simultaneous criminal and civil investigations (HMRC internal manual, Specialist Investigations Operational Guidance, SIOG6105).

8.110 The *Commissioners for Revenue and Customs Act 2005, s 17* allows for information obtained by HMRC in connection with one function (ie as part of a civil investigation) to be used in connection with any other function (ie a parallel criminal investigation).

8.111 An abuse of civil powers by HMRC can lead to the exclusion of potentially significant evidence in criminal proceedings.

Covid-19-related frauds

8.112 On 7 September 2020, Jim Harra gave evidence to the Public Accounts Committee about Coronavirus Job Retention Scheme payments. Harra, HMRC's Chief Executive, told Members of Parliament, 'We have made an assumption for the purposes of our planning that the error and fraud rate in this scheme could be between 5% and 10%'.

8.113 At that time, 9.6 million workers were covered by the UK furlough scheme and the programme had cost the UK Government £35.4bn.

8.114 Harra made the distinction between employers who have made legitimate mistakes in compiling their claims during a challenging time and confirmed that HMRC's focus would be in tackling abuse and fraud.

8.115 Harra confirmed that HMRC was looking into 27,000 'high-risk' cases where they believe a serious error has been made in the amount employers have claimed.

8.116 Since the *Finance Act 2020* received Royal Assent in July 2020, HMRC has had powers to claw back grants that employers are not entitled to. It remains to be seen how effective this will be and whether the estimated 'missing' £1.75bn to £3.5bn is, in fact, the tip of the iceberg. On 23 October 2020, the National Audit in its report 'Implementing employment support schemes in response to the COVID-19 pandemic' on the extension of the furlough scheme, noted that HMRC will not know the actual levels of fraud and error until the end of 2021 at the earliest.

8.117 HMRC will also be actively investigating potentially fraudulently claims under the Bounce Back Loan Scheme, which could represent an even bigger sum, and, probably, to a significantly lesser extent, the Coronavirus Business Interruption Loan Scheme.

8.118 The tax professional has an obligation to notify any suspicion of fraud first to his internal Money Laundering Reporting Officer, who in turn must consider a report to the National Crime Agency.

Prevalence of HMRC criminal investigations

8.119 HMRC's criminal investigations represent a fraction of the cases that pass through the criminal justice system each year.

8.120 Between October 2019 and September 2020, 1.19 million individuals (defined by the Ministry of Justice as being both people and companies) were prosecuted at magistrates' courts in England and Wales. Covid-19 effected the third and fourth quarters of this period in particular. Between April 2019 and March 2020, 1.49 million individuals were prosecuted or dealt with by means of 'out of court' disposals, according to the government's quarterly statistics[13].

8.121 In 2019, HMRC's fraud investigations led to some 600 individuals being convicted for their part in tax crimes and HMRC commenced new

13 Available at https://assets.publishing.service.gov.uk/government/uploads/system/uploads/attachment_data/file/962357/criminal-justice-statistics-quarterly-sept-2020.pdf.

criminal investigations into more than 610 individuals during the calendar year, according to HMRC's Annual Report published January 2020[14].

8.122 HMRC's 2019 Annual Report does illustrate the range of criminal offences it investigates:

- Two wealthy professionals who attempted to steal more than £60m through a fraudulent tax avoidance scheme which claimed to invest in HIV research and conservation and were jailed for a total of 14 and a half years.
- A Berkshire-based gang that stole £34m in VAT and laundered £87m, the proceeds from selling illicit alcohol through bank accounts in Britain, Cyprus, Hong Kong, Dubai and other countries and were jailed for more than 46 years.
- A fugitive £17m tax fraudster who was tracked down to Prague and brought back to the UK to serve his eight-year sentence.
- Five people, including the former owners of a Sussex petrol station, who were sentenced for distributing and selling an estimated 4.8 million litres of illicit fuel to unsuspecting motorists, including haulage companies across the South East.
- The jailing of a former Top Gear mechanic who helped father and son tax cheats escape from the UK via ferry and Eurotunnel prior to sentencing for a £1m VAT fraud.
- A charity treasurer who tried to steal more than £330,000 in a Gift Aid repayment fraud and spent the money on lavish cruise holidays.
- Joint work with Interpol to take apart a pan-European crime gang involved in cigarette trafficking, drug smuggling and money laundering.

Stated aim of HMRC 'Compliance Handbook'

8.123

> 'The aim of the Compliance Handbook is to give you clear and comprehensive guidance to help you and external customers understand and apply the penalties and compliance powers introduced by FA 2007 to FA 2013. The guidance is in two sections: The technical guidance (CH1 – CH199999) explains the legislation and the overall policy about the way it should be applied. The operational guidance (CH200000 onwards) explains how to use the penalties and powers in your job. We are still developing this manual and we will add further guidance as it is produced for all compliance matters, both technical and operational.' (Compliance Handbook, updated

14 See www.gov.uk/government/news/busted-hmrc-reveals-biggest-criminal-cases-of-year-2019.

12 November 2020, available at www.gov.uk/hmrc-internal-manuals/compliance-handbook)

THE CRIMINAL INVESTIGATORY POWERS OF HMRC

Answering law enforcement authority initial enquiries

8.124 Any law enforcement authority may initially informally contact the tax professional and enquire as to whether he possesses material relevant to a criminal investigation concerning a specific taxpayer.

8.125 The tax professional may instinctively wish to provide information but ought to treat casual requests with utmost caution.

8.126 Where the taxpayer is aware that he is the subject of an investigation and specifically instructs the tax professional to interact with an investigating officer on his behalf, the tax professional will want to make clear the remit of his instructions.

8.127 It may be prudent for the tax professional to obtain his own independent legal advice before providing any information.

8.128 The tax professional, who is put on notice of a criminal investigation concerning a client's business or personal affairs by a law enforcement officer, may wish to consider making a suspicious activity report (SAR) to the NCA.

8.129 The suspicions of an investigating officer will not automatically result in the tax professional forming the same suspicions. But at a minimum, the practitioner may wish to audit the relevant 'know your client' (KYC) information and undertake additional anti-money laundering (AML) checks.

8.130 The tax professional will need to consider carefully whether knowledge of a criminal investigation into a client's tax affairs by a law enforcement authority is a notifiable incident in terms of his own professional indemnity insurance. Appropriate client confidentiality must be maintained for the purpose of any disclosures of information to an insurer.

8.131 A tax practitioner must at all times take proper care to ensure that he does not become concerned in an arrangement which he knows or suspects facilitates (by whatever means) the acquisition, retention, use or control of criminal property by or on behalf of another person when assisting clients (*POCA 2002, s 328*).

8.132 The money laundering risk areas that a tax practitioner may encounter in practice include:

- a client's refusal to correct errors (both for the past and on an ongoing basis);

- a client's deliberate under-declaration of profits/income/gain or deliberate overstatement of expenses/losses.

8.133 There will be no question of criminality where the taxpayer has adopted in good faith, honestly and, without misstatement, a technical position with which HMRC disagrees.

Complying with notices and court orders

8.134 Law enforcement officers can apply under a myriad of different laws to the criminal courts for orders that have the effect of compelling the provision of information: eg production orders issued pursuant to *TMA 1970, s 20BA.*

8.135 In addition, under certain investigative powers they can issue notices: eg disclosure notices issued pursuant to *SOCPA 2005, s 61.*

8.136 In most cases, an officer will apply to court without the other party ('*ex parte*') being present. In all cases, a court order will clearly state the time frame for compliance and the recipient must establish answers to key questions without delay.

Four key questions to ask on receipt of any court order

8.137

(1) What statutory provision underlies the court order?

(2) What does the court order require the recipient to do?

(3) What would be the consequence of not complying with the court order?

(4) Are there any defects in the court order?

8.138 A 'defect' could include an order which is drafted too widely, which could be grounds for quashing it: eg *Gittins v Central Criminal Court* [2011] EWHC 131 (Admin); *Power-Hynes v Norwich Magistrates Court and the Chief Constable of Norfolk* [2009] EWHC 1512 (Admin).

Disclosure notices and search warrants – SOCPA 2005, s 61

8.139 Disclosure notice: this may be issued where the law enforcement authority:

- has reasonable grounds for suspecting that a 'relevant offence' is being committed;
- knows the person to whom it is directed has information; and
- has reasonable grounds for suspecting that information is likely to be of substantial value to the investigation.

8.140 'Relevant offences' include bribery, failure to prevent the facilitation of tax evasion as well as other tax offences.

8.141 The recipient of a disclosure notice has to produce documents relevant to the investigation; 'answer questions with respect to any matter relevant to the investigation', and 'provide information with respect to any such matter as is specified in the notice'.

8.142 The disclosure notice will contain information on how the respondent is to provide the information requested and by what date. The process for challenging the lawfulness of the notice is by way of judicial review to the High Court.

8.143 Two criminal offences were created in relation to these notices:

- Failing to comply with the requirements set out in a disclosure notice is punishable by a maximum sentence of 51 weeks' imprisonment.
- Making a false or misleading statement in response to the requirements imposed by a disclosure notice is punishable by a maximum of two years' imprisonment.

8.144 Search warrants: if the recipient of a disclosure notice fails to comply with its terms, HMRC or any other law enforcement authority can apply to the magistrates' court for a warrant of entry. This will allow the seizure of any documents that appear to be of a description specified in the disclosure notice.

8.145 The tax professional will note that a warrant can also be issued by the court, pursuant to *SOCPA 2005, s 66(2)*, if the law enforcement authority can show on the balance of probabilities that it is not practicable to issue a disclosure notice or where the service of a disclosure notice might seriously prejudice the investigation.

Production orders – TMA 1970, s 20BA

8.146 Under these provisions, inserted by the *Finance Act 2000* to expedite HMRC obtaining tax information, HMRC officers may apply to a circuit judge of the Crown Court to compel an individual or company to produce material if:

- there are reasonable grounds for suspecting that an offence involving serious fraud in connection with, or in relation to, tax is being, has been or is about to be committed; and
- documents which may be required as evidence for the purposes of any proceedings in respect of such an offence are, or may be, in the power or possession of any person.

8.147 The recipient of a production order will generally be afforded ten working days to comply or face contempt of court proceedings.

8.148 It is a criminal offence to falsify, conceal, destroy, or otherwise dispose of (or permit the same to happen to) any document required by a *section 20BA* order punishable by up to two years' imprisonment and/or a fine.

8.149 The specific procedural rules governing applications for production order and for resolving disputes concerning legally privileged material are contained within the *Orders for the Delivery of Documents (Procedure) Regulations 2000, SI 2000/2875* ('the *2000 Regulations').*

8.150 HMRC must give notice of its intention to apply for an order no less than five working days before the hearing of the application and the notice must specify:

- the date, time, and place for hearing the application;
- the documents which are the subject of the application;
- a description of the suspected offence to which the application relates; and
- the name of the person suspected of the offence.

8.151 The recipient is entitled to appear and be heard at this hearing unless the judge is satisfied that this would seriously prejudice the investigation, in which case the application will be made *ex parte.*

8.152 A recipient of the notice of intention to apply for an order must not:

- conceal, destroy, alter or dispose any document to which the application relates:
  - until after the application is dismissed or abandoned; or
  - until after any order is complied with;
- disclose to any other person, information, or any other matter likely to prejudice the investigation of the offence to which the application relates. This does not prevent the recipient of this notice from seeking legal advice.

8.153 Where the recipient of this notice is a professional legal adviser, he may discuss the fact of the application with his client for the purpose of providing legal advice.

8.154 There is no equivalent statutory protection safeguarding the tax professional who receives this notice and wishes to consult his client[15].

8.155 *Regulation 7* of the *2000 Regulations* sets out the procedure for the resolution of disputes as to legal privilege:

15 See *R (on an application of Prudential plc) v Special Commissioner of Income Tax* [2013] UKSC 1.

- If there is a dispute as to whether any document or parts of documents are protected by legal privilege, the person concerned may apply to the court to resolve the dispute.
- HMRC is entitled to five days' notice of this hearing and all the contested documents must be lodged with the court.
- If the court upholds the claim for legal privilege, in whole or in part, the costs of the application are to be met by HMRC.

8.156 HMRC does not have a statutory duty to provide copies or inventories of documents produced in obeyance of a *section 20BA* order. But where an original document is delivered to HMRC and it is of a nature that a copy is sufficient (either for use as evidence at a trial for an offence, for forensic examination or for investigation of an offence), the original must not be retained longer than necessary to establish that fact and to obtain the copy.

PACE 1984 powers

8.157 Authorised HMRC officers can use the criminal investigation powers available under *PACE 1984* which fall into three broad categories:

- search premises and seize material;
- compel the production of material; and
- arrest suspects.

8.158 The first and second powers – search premises and seize material, and compel the production of material – can only be exercised pursuant to court orders.

Search warrants

8.159 A magistrates' court can issue a warrant pursuant to *PACE 1984, s 8* to allow the lawful search of premises by a law enforcement authority if it has reasonable grounds for believing that:

- an indictable tax offence has been committed; and
- there is material on the specified premises that is likely to be of substantial value (whether by itself or together with other material) to the investigation of the offence; and
- that the material is likely to be relevant (meaning admissible) evidence; and
- that it does not consist of (or include) items subject to legal privilege, excluded material or special procedure material; and
- that it is not practicable to communicate with any person entitled to grant entry to the premises;

- that it is practicable to communicate with a person entitled to grant entry to the premises, but it is not practicable to communicate with any person entitled to grant access to the evidence;
- that entry to the premises will not be granted unless a warrant is produced;
- that the purpose of a search may be frustrated or seriously prejudiced unless a constable arriving at the premises can secure immediate entry to them.

Timing of the search

8.160 Criticism of the early morning raid was considered by the Keith Committee in the early 1980s. One expert, in evidence to the Committee, maintained that the hours between 4.00 am and 7.00 am were the only hours when the hardened criminal could be guaranteed to be found at home. HMRC and other law enforcement agencies continue with raids in the early hours of the morning, usually around 7.00 am.

8.161 *PACE 1984, s 16* stipulates the requirements in relation to the execution of search warrants:

- A warrant is valid for three months from the date of issue.
- A warrant may be executed by any officer of HMRC.
- Entry and search must be at a reasonable hour unless the purpose of the search might be frustrated on entry at a reasonable hour.
- The warrant may authorise persons to accompany the investigator. Such persons have the same power as the officer they are accompanying but they may exercise these powers only in the company, and under the supervision, of an officer. The presence during a raid of unauthorised persons has been successfully challenged in judicial review proceedings.
- If the warrant is an all-premises warrant, premises which are not specified may not be entered or searched unless a senior officer has given written authority; nor may premises be entered or searched for a second or subsequent time under a warrant which authorises multiple entries unless a senior officer has given written authority.
- The officer must identify himself to the occupier of the premises if he is present at the time the warrant is executed, and if not, to any other who is present, and provide him with a copy of the warrant.
- If no person is present a copy of the warrant must be left in a prominent place.
- A search may only be carried out to the extent required for the purpose for which the warrant was issued.

- HMRC may download information from computers or it may remove them if necessary. This highlights the need for regular backing up of data.
- The officer must endorse the warrant, stating whether the articles sought were found and whether any articles were seized other than articles which were sought. HMRC must not remove documents which are subject to legal professional privilege. Disputed documents should be separately bagged and sealed for adjudication later.
- On completion of the search, a (*PACE 1984, s 8*) warrant has to be returned to the designated officer for the local justice area and a (*PACE 1984, Sch 1, para 12*) warrant to the appropriate officer of the court.
- A returned warrant must be kept for 12 months from its return, during which time it must be available for inspection by the occupier of the premises entered and searched.
- Computerised information must be provided in a form in which it can be taken away and in which it is visible and legible, or from which it can readily be produced in a visible and legible form.

Compelling the production of material

8.162 A court can order a tax professional to produce client material ('special procedure material') if it is satisfied that the documents are likely to be relevant evidence or of substantial value to an investigation into an offence (*PACE 1984, s 9, Sch 1*).

8.163 Special procedure material includes material acquired or created in the course of any trade, business, profession or other occupation for the purpose of any paid or unpaid office which is held (*PACE 1984, s 14(2)*): eg business records held by an accountant on a client's behalf or the accountant's working papers.

8.164 Special procedure material excludes material classified as 'excluded material' or items that are subject to 'legal professional privilege' (LPP) (see **Chapter 7**).

8.165 Excluded material includes personal records which a person has acquired or created in the course of any trade, business, profession or other occupation or for the purposes of any paid or unpaid office and which he holds in confidence (*PACE 1984, s 11(1)(a)*).

8.166 Items are subject to LPP if they are:

- Communications between a professional legal adviser and his client made in connection with the giving of legal advice to the client (LPP). This privilege does not extend to commercial or strategic advice given by a legal adviser.

- Communications between a professional legal adviser and his client made in connection with, or in contemplation of, legal proceedings and for the purposes of such proceedings ('Litigation Privilege'). This privilege extends to communication taken for the purpose of avoiding litigation[16]. It does not apply to items held with the intention of furthering a criminal purpose: eg a solicitor conspiring with a client to defraud HMRC.

8.167 Both types of protection are lost if confidential communications are sent to third parties, eg a client to his tax adviser.

8.168 A taxpayer who merely copies a legal adviser into email correspondence will not be able to sustain a claim that the communication in question is privileged.

Court procedure

8.169 Where a search is likely to uncover special procedure material of evidential value in criminal proceedings, the law enforcement officer must obtain a warrant signed by a circuit judge of the Crown Court for either the material's production or authority to search for it (*PACE 1984, Sch 1, para 12*).

8.170 Production Order applications are made by the law enforcement officer serving a copy of the application notice on the person or company with access to, or custody of, the material. The prescribed *CrimPR* form must be used by the officer.

8.171 The recipient of the notice must not destroy, conceal, alter or dispose of the material that the application relates to without leave from a judge or written permission from the law enforcement agency that has applied for the production order.

8.172 The conditions for granting the application (which must all be satisfied) are that:

- there are reasonable grounds for believing that an indictable offence has been committed;
- special procedure material exists on the specified premises or on premises occupied or controlled by a person specified in the application;
- the material is likely to be of substantial value to the investigation;
- other methods of obtaining the material have been tried without success or would be bound to fail;
- it is in the public interest to obtain the material.

16 *SFO v Eurasian Natural Resources Corporation Limited* [2018] EWCA Civ 2006.

8.173 If the judge is satisfied that these conditions have been met, he may make an order requiring the person who appears to be in possession of the material to produce it for removal, or to give access to it within a specified period, not to exceed seven days from the date of the order.

8.174 **Search warrant application:** if the judge is satisfied that that the preconditions have been met (and one of the following further pre-conditions applies), he can issue a search warrant for the special procedure material the applicant seeks if:

- it has not been practicable to communicate with any person to grant entry to the premises or material; or
- the material contains information which is subject to a restriction on disclosure and is likely to be disclosed in breach of that restriction if a warrant was not issued; or
- service of a notice may seriously prejudice the investigation.

8.175 Failure to comply with a production order can result in the respondent committing the offence of contempt of court in addition to the court issuing a search warrant authorising entry and the seizure of the requested material.

8.176 The process for challenging the lawfulness of this order is by way of judicial review to the High Court and the underlying information can be sought.

Power of arrest

8.177 Arrests can only be made only by HMRC officers, who have been trained and authorised to use this power. At any time HMRC has approximately 1,500 officers with the power of arrest.

8.178 The same legal test applies to HMRC officers as to police constables when executing an arrest of a person.

8.179 Under *PACE 1984, s 24* an officer may arrest an individual without a warrant if he reasonably suspects the person of being guilty of an offence, or if he reasonably believes he is committing an offence or about to commit one.

8.180 The officer must reasonably believe that it is necessary to arrest the individual for any of the following reasons:

- to ascertain the person's name and address;
- to prevent the person causing or suffering physical injury, loss or damage to property or committing an offence against public decency;
- to allow prompt and effective investigation of an offence;
- to prevent the person disappearing and thus avoid prosecution.

8.181 In *Parker v The Chief Constable of Essex Police* [2018] EWCA Civ 2788, an appeal which involved the entertainer Michael Barrymore, Sir Brian Leveson PQBD summarised the relevant legal principles (at [115]):

> 'The bar for reasonable cause to suspect set out in s 24(2) of [*PACE 1984*] is a low one. It is lower than a prima facie case and far less than the evidence required to convict … Further, prima facie proof consists of admissible evidence, while suspicion may take account of matters that could not be put in evidence … Suspicion may be based on assertions that turn out to be wrong … The factors in the mind of the arresting officer fall to be considered cumulatively …'

8.182 This appeal reaffirmed the Court of Appeal's decision in *Hayes v The Chief Constable of Merseyside Police* [2011] EWCA Civ 911, in that what is required for 'necessity' is actual belief that an arrest is necessary and objectively that such belief is reasonable.

8.183 Where a person is arrested, an officer may enter and search any premises occupied and/or controlled by him if the officer suspects that there is evidence on the premises relating to the offence for which the individual has been arrested.

8.184 There is no right to have a lawyer present at the time of arrest, but if a suspect is held in police custody or any other premises, he has the right to independent legal advice and to consult a solicitor privately.

8.185 It is rare for law enforcement authorities to confirm to the press the name of a suspect in a criminal investigation. If a suspect is charged, the principle of open justice usually allows for the press reporting of the court proceedings.

8.186 In *ZXC v Bloomberg* [2020] EWCA Civ 611, Simon LJ, having reviewed the case authorities (at [119]), concluded that '… it is possible now to say that, in general, a person does have a reasonable expectation of privacy in a police investigation up to the point of charge'.

DEALING WITH A 'DAWN RAID': A CHECKLIST

Pre-planning for a raid

8.187

- Frontline staff, ie reception staff, and those who normally arrive at work early should be familiar with the raid response plan (which should also be included in an Office Manual) and be clear as to which senior staff must be contacted first.

Initial entry

8.188

- When a law enforcement officer seeks entry, staff should be polite; officers are likely to be equipped with body-worn video recording and any comment could be used in subsequent court proceedings.
- Ask for officers to wait until you can seek legal advice before proceeding. Officers are not legally obliged to wait but may do so if you can provide a time frame and waiting will not unreasonably delay the search.
- Ask for a copy of the order to check:
  - the statutory power that is asserted;
  - the date of issuance;
  - the details are correct in terms of the premises specified to be searched;
  - the details of who the court has authorised to enter the premises;
  - what precise material may be searched for and seized;
  - what is said in relation to material which might be subject to LPP.
- If you are satisfied that the court order gives the investigating officer the power to enter and search the premises and/or you have received legal advice to this effect, you should not obstruct the officers in their search or prevent access to material.
- If you are not satisfied and believe the search is unlawful, you should make representations to that effect and make sure that these are recorded.
- Irrespective of any concerns about the lawfulness of the search, nothing should be done physically to impede the search and no documentation or electronic files should be destroyed or concealed. Such actions can be grounds for arrest.
- If the officers will not wait for your lawyer, allocate senior staff members to shadow the investigating officers and video record their actions and make a written record of documents or material seized, in addition to:
  - all the officers' requests and questions;
  - any answers provided;
  - any original material seized or copied by officers.
- Email all employees to inform them:
  - to be professional and courteous in their dealings with the officers;
  - not to volunteer information or documents, without obtaining prior legal advice;

   - not to delete, destroy or conceal any documentation or data;
   - to suspend immediately any routine document destruction until further notice;
   - not to advise any third party of the search;
   - a breach of these requirements could be a criminal offence and/or a serious disciplinary offence.

During the search

8.189

- Ask the investigating officers what they are looking for and, where possible, decide together the processes by which the search will take place.
- A senior member of staff ought to:
   - direct officers to where material listed in the warrant is kept;
   - direct them away from irrelevant rooms or privileged material; and
   - ensure that the search is being carried out with minimal disturbance to the premises and that only reasonable force is used if necessary, for example, to open locked filing cabinets.
- Do not volunteer documents not expressly requested by officers.
- A lawful investigation requires that the premises be searched only to the extent required for the purpose for which the warrant was issued. A search cannot:
   - be made in places where the items specified in the warrant could not possibly be found; or
   - conducted for longer than necessary to find them.
- Ensure that officers do not seize or copy:
   - documents falling outside the scope of the investigation; and
   - documents subject to LPP.
- Notify an official if you think any item requested is covered by legal privilege. Provide officers with substantiating information about the specific items (eg the author and its addressee as well as its purpose and the circumstances of its preparation) without revealing the contents. Any item subject to LPP should not be seized by law enforcement officers. If privilege cannot be claimed, the material will form part of the continuing investigation. In case of disagreement, insist on your objections being noted by the officer and request that the 'blue bag' process (see **8.191** below) be used until its status is determined.

- If the investigating officers want to ask questions of staff, establish the basis on which they propose to ask questions. During the search this should be restricted to questions to assist in complying with the terms of the warrant or order, such as identifying where relevant material is kept, eg 'Where would I find document X? or 'What is the password for Y?'. Any other questioning should be done in the presence of a lawyer.
- A search warrant may allow officers to search staff without arresting them. Body searches must be carried out by an officer of the same gender.
- Investigating officers must only retain an original material when a photograph or copy is not sufficient. This includes documents stored electronically as well as in paper form. Officers will usually take an image of the server on-site but could take it away. Mobile electronic devices, including personal devices (eg smartphones, tablets and laptops) which receive work communications, will routinely be seized and imaged later. All data on all electronic devices should be backed up off-site or within Cloud storage facilities.

After the search

8.190

- When documents are seized following a search, the investigating officers must make a detailed record of the search. A copy of this inventory must be provided upon request within a reasonable time frame.
- You can request access to seized documents/items and copies.
- If access is denied, reproduce as best you can a copy of all material seized during the search so your legal team can advise you of the potential criminal implications and your specific exposure.
- Seized material may be returned at the end of the investigation, but application can also be made to the court, eg to the magistrates' court under the *Police (Property) Act 1897, s 1*.
- Any tax professionals subject to a dawn raid should consider a press release to mitigate against potential adverse publicity and reputational damage. This will typically stress cooperation.

Dawn raids – five key points

8.191

(1) Examine the wording of any court order.

(2) Instruct your lawyer to attend in person or provide telephone advice.

(3) Emphasise your cooperation and do not impede a lawful search.

(4) Identify any legally privileged material.

(5) Make a detailed contemporaneous note of what is seized, what is asked and what is answered.

'Blue bag' process

8.192 To preserve the integrity of material where legal professional privilege arises, an established protocol exists to resolve disputes that are not resolved during the search.

8.193 The material will be placed in a blue plastic bag and sealed, and the investigating officers will instruct independent lawyers to provide their opinion on whether the material is properly subject to LPP and therefore ought not be disclosed. The law enforcement authority bears the cost of instructing counsel for this purpose.

8.194 The material will be taken by the agency and will remain sealed until the dispute is resolved, or in the case of inextricably linked material, until it can be separated by independent counsel.

8.195 The tax professional whose documents have been quarantined in this way has the right to be present at the review of the material. He can apply to court for the material to be returned.

8.196 This process was approved by the court in *R v Customs and Excise Comrs, ex p Popely & Harris* [1999] STC 1016.

Applying for the return of seized property

8.197 An individual or company can make a free-standing application to the magistrates' court for the return of seized property under the *Police (Property) Act 1897, s 1*. These proceedings are regulated by *CrimPR, r 47*.

8.198 Notice is filed with the court detailing the applicant's legal 'interest', ie setting out ownership of the property he wants returned.

8.199 *PACE 1984, s 22(1)* allows the retention by law enforcement officers of any property which has been seized 'so long as it is necessary in all the circumstances.'

8.200 While anything seized for the purposes of a criminal investigation may be retained for use as evidence at a trial or for forensic examination or for investigation in connection with an offence, 'nothing may be retained for either of those purposes … if a photograph or copy would be sufficient for that purpose' (*PACE 1984, s 22(2)* and *(4)*).

8.201 The court can exercise its discretion and order the return of original documents where copies can be taken, and a criminal investigation will not otherwise be hindered.

Challenging search warrant and court orders

8.202 The recipient of a search warrant or production order made without notice may wish to challenge its validity by way of judicial review to the High Court, eg due to a perceived procedural impropriety. This will most likely be a lengthy and costly process.

8.203 The quicker remedy can be to seek redress in the court that made the order and apply for its discharge.

8.204 Orders secured in private mean the applicant must make 'full and frank' disclosure to the court during the hearing when the application is made. Anything less than full candour can lead to the court subsequently quashing the order.

8.205 If an order is obtained without notice, the recipient of the order can request all the information used in support of the applications, as well as the reasons giving for granting the applications[17].

8.206 The courts have emphasised that for a search warrant to be issued it is necessary for the law enforcement agency to meet the legislative requirements.

8.207 In the lead case of *R (S, F and L) v Chief Constable of British Transport Police* [2013] EWHC 2189 (Admin), a practising solicitor (S) and partner in the claimant solicitors' firm (F), together with another firm of solicitors (L) sought to quash search warrants and the seizure of excluded material and special procedure material. The High Court quashed the warrants and commented that the legislative safeguards meant that 'there has to be a very rigorous procedure both in preparing an information for the application for a search warrant and also when a judge is considering it'.

8.208 If material has been obtained under an order that has been quashed because the order itself was unlawfully obtained, then, on usual principles, the material collected should be returned with no copies kept; eg the search warrant case of *R (Cook) v Serious Organised Crime Agency* [2011] 1 WLR 144.

8.209 However, in certain prescribed circumstances, despite a warrant having been discharged, the material seized may still be retained whilst another properly formulated application is made.

INTERVIEWS UNDER CAUTION AND THE ROLE OF THE LEGAL PROFESSIONAL

8.210 Not every prosecution is preceded by a dawn raid or arrest. Investigating law enforcement officers might consider a search unnecessary where, for example, they already possess incriminating material as a result

17 *R (Rawlinson and Hunter Trustees) v Central Criminal Court; R (Tchenguiz) v SFO* [2013] 1 WLR 1634.

of another investigation or from an informer or by a third party, such as a bank under *FA 2008, Sch 36(2)*. An arrest may be unnecessary if a suspect is cooperating. In such circumstances the evidential jigsaw may be all but complete.

8.211 The final stage of the investigation is to give the suspect the opportunity at least to comment on the criminal allegation in a formal interview 'under caution'.

8.212 As has been seen, *PACE 1984* underpins legal provisions in relation to criminal investigations: eg the production of material, search and seizures of material, and arrests.

8.213 The *1984 Act* is supported by codes of practice that detail the standards to be applied when officers exercise and carry out the relevant powers and duties. *PACE 1984, Code C* covers the requirements for the detention, treatment and questioning of suspects. Persons other than police officers, ie HMRC officers, 'who are charged with the duty of investigating offences or charging offenders' are under a duty to have regard to any relevant provisions of the codes of practice (*PACE 1984, s 67(9)*).

8.214 To conduct an interview under caution[18]:

> '[t]here must be some reasonable, objective grounds for the suspicion, based on known facts or information which are relevant to the likelihood the offence has been committed and the person to be questioned committed it.'

8.215 An interview under caution will take place with a suspect who has either been arrested or who is not under arrest but rather has attended voluntarily.

8.216 Voluntary interviews are commonly conducted by HMRC officer who will have invited a taxpayer or tax professional to attend by appointment with a solicitor if they wish.

8.217 For the interviewing officer, the interview gives the opportunity to obtain evidence (eg a confession) and information relevant to the criminal investigation.

8.218 For the suspect, it is the opportunity to answer the allegation and potentially eliminate himself or at least produce lines of enquiry leading the officer away from him.

The caution

8.219 The legal warning, the 'caution', must be administered where a person is suspected of committing a criminal offence and is to be questioned about that offence. This is to ensure that any answers (or silence) will be admissible in proceedings.

18 *PACE 1984, Code C, Note for Guidance 10A.*

8.220 A defence solicitor will give clear advice what the caution means and remind his client that the burden of proof rests with the investigating officers.

8.221 The caution is as follows[19]:

> 'You do not have to say anything. But it may harm your defence if you do not mention when questioned something which you later rely on in court. Anything you do say may be given in evidence.'

8.222 The caution has three parts:

- ***You do not have to say anything*** – A suspect can lawfully sit in silence and cannot be compelled to answer a question. The interviewing officer will ask the suspect to say at least 'no comment' after each question so he knows the question has been heard and the next question can be asked. The common law privilege against self-incrimination is also impliedly conferred under the *European Convention of Human Rights, art 6* which affords a person a fair trial.
- ***But it may harm your defence if you do not mention when questioned something which you later rely on in court*** – If the suspect has a defence and does not raise it at his first reasonable opportunity and relies on it at trial, an 'adverse inference' might be drawn (*Criminal Justice and Public Order Act 1994, s 34*); meaning a judge or jury may disbelieve the defence because it was not mentioned in response to the initial questioning.
- ***Anything you do say may be given in evidence*** – The suspect's responses during a properly conducted interview may be used as evidence against him in any subsequent criminal proceedings. Evidence obtained during the interview can only be used against the person being questioned, ie it cannot be used in evidence against another person such as a co-defendant or the company where the suspect is an employee. The interview will be audio recorded and may be filmed as well. Usually, a summary or transcript will be agreed that will have removed irrelevant questions and answers. A suspect who is charged will be entitled, free of charge, to a copy of their full interview recording which must be provided within a reasonable time frame.

Self-incrimination in criminal proceedings and pre-existing material

8.223 A suspect being investigated or defendant on trial cannot be forced to bear witness against himself. The position is different with regard to forcing disclosure of inculpatory material already in his possession: eg a computer or password.

19 *PACE 1984, Code C, para 16.5.*

8.224 In *R v S* [2008] EWCA Crim 2177, the Court of Appeal confirmed that it was an established principle that independently existing evidence did not normally engage the privilege against self-incrimination. That case concerned the disclosure of passwords to encrypted electronic devices.

8.225 In *Volaw Trust and Corporate Services Ltd v The Office of the Comptroller of Taxes*[20], the Privy Council confirmed this in relation to tax related matters. The case concerned compliance with tax notices where tax avoidance and evasion offences were suspected by the Norwegian tax authorities. It was determined that the notices did not engage the privilege against self-incrimination as they required the production of pre-existing documents.

The role of the legal professional

8.226 Where HMRC are the investigating agency, the letter inviting the taxpayer to an interview will make clear that the taxpayer is to be 'cautioned' and will suggest that he considers seeking legal representation.

8.227 Before the start of an interview, the officer may have had days, if not months, to examine documents and speak to witnesses and formulate an interview plan. He will have a strategy and likely checklist of points to cover.

8.228 The interviewing officer may want to disarm the suspect with 'new' information that he will hope results in admissions and/or self-incrimination. Exhibits will likely be presented and different techniques attempted to elicit comment if the suspect is exercising his right to silence: eg the interviewer might mix open and closed questions, introduce forced-choice questions, probe different topics using checkable facts to increase the suspect's discomfort or postulate as to likely sentencing outcomes.

8.229 The legal professional may have to repeatedly remind his client of his right to silence. Despite the monotony of the questioning, the investigating officer will continue asking questions as long as the process does not become oppressive and the questions remain relevant.

8.230 The right to information in advance of an interview ('pre-interview disclosure') remains relatively limited but can permit the defence solicitor to anticipate and advise on the likely line of questioning as well as the overall strength of the case.

8.231 Sufficient information must be provided to enable an understanding of the nature of the suspected offence and why the individual or company is suspected of committing it, 'in order to allow for the effective exercise of the rights of the defence' (*PACE 1984, Code C, para 11.1A*); and documents

20 *Volaw Trust and Corporate Services Ltd and its Directors and Others v The Office of the Comptroller of Taxes and Another* [2019] UKPC 29.

and materials that are essential to challenging the lawfulness of the arrest or detention must be made available (*PACE 1984, Code C, para 3.4(b)*).

8.232 *Note for Guidance 3ZA(b)* says the way in which documents and materials are 'made available' is a matter for the investigating officer to determine on a case-by-case basis having regard to the nature and volume of the documents and materials involved: eg they may be made available by supplying a copy or allowing the legal professional supervised access to view.

8.233 The suspect will typically exercise one of three options during interview:

- exercising his right to silence by answering 'no comment' to all questions asked;
- instructing his representative to prepare and read a statement on his behalf; or
- commenting fully by answering himself all questions asked of him.

8.234 A prepared statement or 'no comment' interview will invariably be the safest default option advised by the defence solicitor.

8.235 A person being interviewed, has an ongoing right to have the interview suspended to consult with his solicitor in private (*PACE, s 58(1)*). Where there has been limited pre-interview disclosure and new information is being drip fed during the course of the interview, the suspect may well wish to exercise this right and take a more informed view on whether to answer questions and/or set out a specific defence.

8.236 The solicitor can intervene in the interview only[21]:

- to seek clarification.
- to challenge an improper question to their client;
- to challenge the manner in which a question is put;
- to advise their client not to reply to particular questions;
- if they wish to give their client further legal advice.

8.237 Where a company is invited to attend an interview under caution, the company will be asked to nominate a person to answer questions on its behalf.

8.238 The legal representative of the company will have to ensure that he is not conflicted in representing the company as distinct from the nominated person. Investigators ought to confirm this prior to the start of any interview.

21 *PACE 1984, Code C, NfG 6D.*

8.239 Where the company has only one director and investigators suspect both the company and the director of committing criminal offences, two separate interviews ought to be conducted in order that the company director can comment on behalf of either the company or himself.

THE CHARGING DECISION

8.240 For an individual or company suspected of criminal wrongdoing, the wait for a decision can be interminable and intolerable. The investigating officer and CPS will not provide a 'running commentary' which will add to the frustration.

8.241 An aggrieved taxpayer could, after complaining first to HMRC, complain to the Adjudicator's Office regarding an unreasonable delay[22].

8.242 A criminal suspect could initiate judicial review proceedings in according with the pre-action protocol, citing the CPS's own guidance which confirms that investigations ought to be progressed expeditiously: eg the *Charging (The Director's Guidance) 2013* (May 2013) states (at para [3]): 'The police will undertake effective early investigations to ensure that the key evidence required to make informed decisions in cases is obtained as soon as possible …'.

8.243 The courts, however, have made clear the very high bar that must be overcome by claimants seeking to challenge the lawfulness of decisions taken by investigators or prosecutors[23].

8.244 The speed of an investigation was part of the claimants' challenges in *Soma Oil*[24]. The courts are very slow to close an investigation based on self-serving arguments advanced on behalf of a suspect that there is no prospect of an eventual prosecution.

8.245 The CPS charging guidance is complemented by the *Code for Crown Prosecutors* (October 2018), which asks prosecutors:

- Is there enough evidence against the defendant? (The 'evidential' stage.)
- Is it in the public interest for the CPS to bring the case to court? (The 'public interest' stage.)

8.246 The Crown Prosecutor must be satisfied that there is enough evidence to provide a realistic prospect of conviction against each suspect on each charge. This means considering the totality of the evidence, its reliability and credibility, including the impact of any likely defence or information put forward by the suspect.

---

22 See www.gov.uk/guidance/how-to-complain-to-the-adjudicators-office.

23 See *R (Soma Oil) v SFO* [2016] EWHC 2471 (Admin), at [54].

24 See para [39] and *R (on the application of C) v 'A' Magistrates' Court* [2006] EWHC 2352 (Admin), at [32].

8.247 If the decision maker's assessment is that the court would be more likely than not to convict the person, the evidential stage is passed and he can consider the public interest stage. If the evidential stage is not passed, the charge cannot proceed no matter how serious or sensitive it may be.

8.248 The Crown Prosecutor must weigh factors for and against prosecution fairly before arriving at an overall assessment of whether the proceedings against the suspect is in the public interest. Each case is unique and must be considered on its own facts.

8.249 Public interest factors that can affect the decision to prosecute include:

- the seriousness of the offence;
- the suspect's level of culpability;
- the circumstances of, and harm caused to, the victim;
- the age and maturity of the suspect;
- the impact on the community;
- whether prosecution is a proportionate response, eg is a nominal penalty likely?

8.250 If a tax professional is charged with a criminal offence, his lawyer may think it appropriate to make written representations to the CPS inviting a reconsideration of the charging decision.

8.251 The effectiveness of such representations will be fact specific. It may be contended that insufficient weight has been applied to public interest factors tending against prosecution or 'new' material exists that changes the evidential evaluation.

8.252 Wherever possible, the tax professional will hope to avoid a criminal prosecution and the immediate reputational damage, and thereafter the uncertainties of court proceedings and vagaries of jury decisions.

8.253 A conviction or caution for a financial offence will have career implications for the tax adviser, in addition to any criminal penalty that could be imposed on conviction.

8.254 The Institute of Chartered Accountants in England and Wales (ICAEW) insist that convictions for relevant offences listed in the *Money Laundering, Terrorist Financing and Transfer of Funds (Information on the Payer) Regulations 2017, SI 2017/692, Sch 3* must be disclosed. These include economic crimes such as fraud, bribery, dishonesty, tax offences and breaches of the money laundering regulations. Even non-scheduled offences may result in the ICAEW's Professional Conduct Department investigating.

Example 8.2: 'Out-of-court' disposal

8.255 A 19-year-old officer worker is caught on CCTV stealing £20 from a colleague's purse and the police are called. The young person detained and searched and found to be in possession of £20. He is arrested and taken to the police station.

8.256 In his interview under caution, he admits his actions and expresses his remorse which the interview officer considers to be genuine.

8.257 The officer updates his employer about the young man's admission and sorrow. Despite this, the employer confirms that he will be dismissed for gross misconduct.

8.258 The officer considers that there are strong mitigating factors: the cooperation and remorse expressed; the young man's age and immaturity; the opportunistic nature of the offence, ie lack of planning or premeditation; and the absence of any previous convictions, cautions, or reprimands as an adult or juvenile.

8.259 The officer is satisfied that despite the offence having been committed, the public interest could be satisfied by an out-of-court disposal, specifically the administration by a senior police officer of a caution, which would avoid the young man facing criminal proceedings that would result in a criminal conviction.

CRIMINAL PROSECUTIONS

8.260 According to Ministry of Justice statistics, between March 2018 and March 2019 some 1.19 million individuals were convicted of criminal offences and 82% of prosecutions were for 'summary' offences, ie decided in the magistrates' court.

8.261 Only a minority of criminal cases reach the Crown Court but those are evidently the most serious in nature and attract the most severe penalties.

8.262 Prior to the first appearance by a defendant in the magistrates' court, the CPS will provide the initial details of the prosecution case (IDPC) to the defence. This will contain details of the charge(s) and a summary of the allegation(s). It can contain witness statements but usually provides cursory information.

Magistrates' court

8.263 Magistrates normally sit in benches of three and make their decisions collectively. Each magistrate, irrespective of their experience, has the same voice in the decision-making process. The magistrate in the middle acts as the spokesperson for the whole bench and all dialogue goes through him or her and is addressed as 'Sir' or 'Madam'.

8.264 A single district judge, who is legally qualified, can sit instead of lay magistrates and has the same powers.

8.265 The magistrates' court has limited sentencing powers: it can send an accused to prison for up to six months (or up to twelve months in total for more than one offence).

8.266 Magistrates and district judges, and the lawyers who appear before them, do not wear wigs or gowns.

8.267 The following points should also be noted.

- For a 'summary offence', eg low-value criminal damage or a low-level assault, the magistrates will retain jurisdiction.
- For an offence which can be tried either in the magistrates' court or the Crown Court (an 'either-way offence'), eg fraud by false representation, the magistrates will determine the suitable venue by reference to the likely sentence on conviction. If the magistrates retain jurisdiction, and the defendant contests the allegation, the defendant may 'elect' to have his case heard by a jury in the Crown Court.
- If the defendant has been charged with an 'indictable offence', such as conspiracy to defraud or cheating the public revenue, the magistrates must send the case to be tried in the Crown Court.

8.268 Most criminal allegations likely to concern the tax professional, eg conspiracies to defraud or where significant sums are alleged to have been misappropriated, can only be tried in the Crown Court on an indictment.

Crown Court

8.269 A judge, usually addressed as 'Your Honour', presides over the proceedings.

8.270 During a trial, the judge will decide matters of law, in the absence of the jury, to ensure the fairness of the proceedings, eg whether certain evidence can be introduced. The jury decides factually on the significance of each piece of evidence which is presented, and ultimately determines if the defendant is guilty or not guilty to the criminal standard.

8.271 If the defendant is found guilty, the judge will proceed to pass sentence in accordance with any relevant sentencing guideline.

Court process

8.272 Regardless of the venue, the Crown is obliged to comply with the statutory disclosure regime.

8.273 After initially providing details of its case, the prosecution has four weeks in the magistrates' court to serve its case against the defendant, including all witness statements and exhibits it intends to rely on to prove each and every allegation.

8.274 If the defendant's case has been sent by the magistrates' court to the Crown Court or he has elected to have a trial in the Crown Court, the first hearing in the Crown Court is a 'Plea and Trial Preparatory Hearing'. At this hearing, the defendant will be 'arraigned', ie enter his plea to any offence listed and particularised on the indictment prepared by the Crown Prosecutor.

8.275 If the defendant pleads 'guilty', the judge may pass sentence immediately after listening to the facts of the offending and any mitigation advanced on his behalf. The judge may be persuaded by the defence to adjourn passing sentence and order Probation Services to prepare a (non-binding) pre-sentence report.

8.276 If the defendant pleads 'not guilty' in the Crown Court, the judge will adjourn the case for a trial, having pronounced a detailed timetable to ensure the effective preparation and readiness of the case by the prosecution and defence.

Disclosure

8.277 Disclosure is the process by which material collected by investigators is made available during the case first to the Crown Prosecutor and subsequently, subject to certain rules, to the defence team.

8.278 The prosecution and defence may make use of this material in preparation for and during a trial where it is potentially relevant to an issue, or issues, in a case.

8.279 When it works properly, the disclosure process enables the court to have all the relevant evidence before it as it decides on the guilt or innocence of an accused person. When the disclosure process does not work as it should, crucial evidence might not be heard, and miscarriages of justice can follow.

8.280 The disclosure regime is governed by the *Criminal Procedure and Investigations Act 1996 (CPIA 1996)*, accompanied by a code of practice. The statutory scheme must be adhered to by the prosecution and the defence.

8.281 The *CPIA 1996* provisions include:

- *Initial duty of prosecutor to disclosure* (*CPIA 1996, s 3*): the Crown must notify the defence that it has served its case and produce a schedule itemising material which it possesses but which it does not intend to rely on.

- *Defence statement* (*CPIA 1996, s 6A*): in the Crown Court, the defendant must set out plainly his defence in a statement served on the Crown and court in which he makes clear any issues of facts or law he disputes and identifies any alibi witness he intends to rely on at his trial. In the magistrates' court, service of a defence statement is optional. The statement can request specific material be disclosed.
- *Secondary disclosure by prosecutor* (*CPIA 1996, s 7*): the Crown must either provide the requested disclosure or explain on what basis the items do not satisfy the disclosure test.
- *Application by accused for disclosure* (*CPIA 1996, s 8*): if dissatisfied by the Crown's response, the defendant can apply to court for specific items of disclosure.
- *Faults in disclosure by the accused* (*CPIA 1996, s 11*): the judge, Crown Prosecutor or another defendant may comment on a failure by the accused with respect to his defence statement and the jury may draw such conclusions as it thinks proper in deciding whether the defendant is guilty.

8.282 The Crown is required to give the defence access to material obtained during the investigation which may be unused by the Crown as part of its case where such material is relevant to an issue in the case.

8.283 The House of Lords stated in *R v H and C*[25]:

> 'Fairness ordinarily requires that any material held by the prosecution which weakens its case or strengthens that of the defendant, if not relied on as part of its formal case against the defendant, should be disclosed to the defence. Bitter experience has shown that miscarriages of justice may occur where such material is withheld from disclosure. The golden rule is that full disclosure of such material should be made.'

The disclosure test

8.284 This principle of fairness is reflected in the single test for disclosure which requires Crown Prosecutors to 'disclose to the accused any prosecution material which has not previously been disclosed to the accused and which might reasonably be considered capable of undermining the case for the prosecution against the accused or of assisting the case for the accused' (*CPIA 1996, s 3(1)(a)*).

8.285 Prosecution material' is defined[26] as material which:

25 [2004] UKHL 3, [2004] 2 AC 134, [2004] 2 Cr App R 10.

26 *CPIA 1996, s 3(2)*.

- is in the prosecutor's possession, and came into his possession in connection with the case for the prosecution against the accused; or
- has been inspected in connection with the case for the prosecution against the accused.

8.286 The *CPIA 1996* Code of Practice (March 2015) identifies the general responsibilities relevant to this disclosure duty at (para 3.5):

> 'In conducting an investigation, the investigator should pursue all reasonable lines of inquiry, whether these point towards or away from the suspect. What is reasonable in each case will depend on the particular circumstances.'

8.287 Relevant material is defined (at para 2.1) as material that 'has some bearing on any offence under investigation or any person being investigated, or on the surrounding circumstances of the case, unless it is incapable of having any impact on the case'.

8.288 The tension will invariably be that the defence and prosecution interpret 'relevance' differently.

8.289 In *R v R*[27], Sir Brian Leveson PQBD summarised the relevant principles (at para 34):

> 'To fulfil its duty under s 3 [*CPIA 1996*], the prosecution must adopt a considered and appropriately resourced approach to giving initial disclosure. Such an approach must extend to and include the overall disclosure strategy, selection of software tools, identifying and isolating material that is subject to legal professional privilege (LPP) and proposing search terms to be applied.'

8.290 The tax professional may find himself involved in a criminal case involving a mass of data from electronic devices or accounting records. This material must be in the first instance sifted and analysed by investigating officers and a prosecution lawyer before being disclosed to the defence. This can be a laborious time-consuming process. The defence must play their part in defining the real issues in the case in the defence statement and only making appropriate requests for disclosable material.

8.291 In July 2018, the CPS published 'Disclosure – A guide to "reasonable lines of enquiry" and communications evidence' which confirms that the ultimate arbiter of lines of enquiry is the investigating officer. 'What represents a reasonable line of enquiry', the legal guidance concludes (at para [19]), 'is an investigative matter for the police and whilst the prosecution will do what they can to assist in identifying potential further enquiries, that ought not to be taken by the police as definitive or exhaustive'.

---

27 *R v R and Others* [2015] EWCA Crim 1941, [2016] 1 Cr App R 20.

8.292 In *R v S* [2008] EWCA Crim 21877, the Court of Appeal confirmed that 'reasonable lines of enquiry' do not require that mobile phones, for instance, should be examined as a matter of course in every case; confirming that 'the decision is fact specific in each and every case'.

8.293 Defence lawyers will review each item of material – served witness statements or exhibits, identified but not disclosed items, or missing items – and apply to the court for specific items of material that meet the disclosure test and have not been provided by the prosecution despite being requested in the defence statement (*CPIA 1996, s 8*).

8.294 Defence lawyers will manage bundles of used and unused prosecution material and obtain the defendant's instructions so that the defence case can be comprehensively presented at trial.

8.295 The defence may need to gather any exculpatory material and information, including from potential expert witnesses (eg forensic accountants) and non-expert witnesses, to present in the criminal trial.

CRIMINAL TRIALS

8.296 HMRC claims to be successful in around 90% of criminal cases it brings to trial. By contrast, the SFO conviction rate for the same period was 53% by defendant and 86% by case according to its annual report [28].

8.297 The order of events is as follows:

- Swearing in of the 12 members of the jury to decide the case on only the evidence that is presented in court during the trial (or 14 if the case is due to last more than four weeks with the last two members being discharged before the start of the evidence).
- Opening speech from the prosecution barrister outlining the nature of the case against the defendant.
- Prosecution witnesses called to give evidence 'in chief' and questioned first by the prosecutor and then cross-examined by the defence barrister. These witnesses may be re-examined by the prosecutor and the judge may ask questions or seek clarifications.
- The final prosecution witness is usually the investigating officer, who will confirm details of the investigation, eg the results of any searches and response provided by the defendant in his interview under caution.
- At the conclusion of the prosecution case, the defence may make a legal submission to the judge (in the absence of the jury) that there is no case for the defendant to answer due to there being either no evidence

28 'Annual Report and Accounts 2018–19', HC2400, available at www.sfo.gov.uk/wp-content/uploads/2019/07/SFO-Annual-Report-and-Accounts-2018-2019.pdf.

or insufficient evidence called by the prosecution to substantiate the offence(s). If successful, the judge will direct verdicts of not guilty and the defendant will be freed (pending any prosecution appeal); if unsuccessful, the trial will continue.

- Defence witnesses called to give evidence, starting with the defendant should he choose to testify. The defence witnesses will be questioned first by the defence barrister and then cross-examined by the prosecutor, before being re-examined by the defence and possible questions from the judge.
- The prosecution closing speech is followed by the defence closing speech.
- Summing up by the judge to jury of the factual issues and provision of legal directions.
- Jury retires to consider its verdict in private.
- Verdict: this must be unanimous, but a majority verdict of 11:1 or 10:2 will be accepted if it appears to the judge that the jury has had such period of time for deliberation as is reasonable having regard to the nature and complexity of the case and the jury has had at least two hours for deliberation (*Juries Act 1974, s 17*).
- No verdict: if the jury cannot reach a verdict, then the judge has the power to discharge the jury. The Crown may seek a re-trial with a new jury.
- Not guilty verdict: if the defendant has privately funded his defence, he may be able to recover some of his legal costs through a Defence Costs Order at the Legal Aid rate, if Legal Aid has been applied for and refused.
- Guilty verdict: the judge will proceed to sentence the defendant either with or without a pre-sentence report.
- At the conclusion of the trial, HMRC will seek to recover any tax lost as a result of the fraud even if the taxpayer has been acquitted of any criminal offence.

SENTENCING

The approach of the sentencing judge

8.298 Sanctions for criminal offences are decided by the courts in accordance with the sentences allowed for by the law and after taking account of any relevant Sentencing Council guideline (SGC).

8.299 In every case where the offender is aged 18 or over at the time of conviction, the court must have regard to the five purposes of sentencing contained in the *Criminal Justice Act 2003* (*CJA 2003*), *s 142(1)*:

- the punishment of offenders;
- the reduction of crime (including its reduction by deterrence);
- the reform and rehabilitation of offenders;
- the protection of the public; and
- the making of reparation by offenders to persons affected by their offence.

8.300 The *CJA 2003* does not indicate that any one purpose should be more important than any other and in practice they may all be relevant to a greater or lesser degree in any individual case. The judge has the task of determining the manner in which they apply but must start by considering the seriousness of the offence, the assessment of which will[29]:

- determine which of the sentencing thresholds has been crossed;
- indicate whether a custodial, community or other sentence is the most appropriate;
- be the key factor in deciding the length of a custodial sentence, the onerousness of requirements to be incorporated in a community sentence and the amount of any fine imposed.

8.301 A court is required to pass a sentence that is commensurate with the seriousness of the offence.

8.302 The seriousness of an offence is determined by two main parameters:

- the culpability of the offender;
- the harm caused or risked being caused by the offence.

8.303 The *Criminal Justice Act 2003, s 143(1)* provides:

> 'In considering the seriousness of any offence, the court must consider the offender's culpability in committing the offence and any harm which the offence caused, was intended to cause or might foreseeably have caused.'

8.304 Before passing sentence, the judge will hear submissions on mitigation by the prosecution and defence barristers and consider any relevant guidelines published by the Sentencing Council or else guidance from case authority. For most offenders likely to concern the tax professional, such as fraud or false accounting, the court will follow the SGC's 'Fraud, Bribery and Money Laundering Offences' guideline (effective from 1 October 2014):

- Applying the guideline requires the judge to determine the category of the offence by reference to a determination of the defendant's culpability before considering the harm caused by reference to the actual or intended pecuniary loss.

29 SGC, 'Overarching Principles: Seriousness', para 1.3.

- The level of culpability is determined by weighing up all the factors of the case to determine the offender's role and the extent to which the offending was planned and the sophistication with which it was carried out.
- Having qualified the defendant's role and quantified the loss, the judge will then consider any relevant aggravating (eg previous convictions) or mitigating factors (eg absence of previous conviction, remorse, sole or primary carer for dependent relatives).
- The judge will then apply any reduction for a guilty plea. If the accused has admitted his wrongdoing in his initial police interview and pleaded guilty at the earliest possible opportunity, he may receive the maximum one-third discount on the sentence he would otherwise have received.
- The judge finally will need to ensure the 'totality principle' is observed to ensure that the sentence cannot be appealed as being either wrong in law or manifestly excessive. All courts, when sentencing for more than a single offence, should pass a total sentence which reflects all the offending behaviour before it and is just and proportionate. It is usually impossible to arrive at a just and proportionate sentence for multiple offending simply by adding together notional single sentences. It is necessary to address the offending behaviour, together with the factors personal to the offender as a whole.

Confiscation proceedings

8.305 As part of the sentencing process, the judge could make a compensation order requiring the accused to recompense identifiable victims. In addition, he may be required to pay, or contribute towards, the prosecution's costs including those incurred at the investigation stage.

8.306 In the Crown Court, after the judge has made all other orders (including imposing an immediate period of imprisonment), the prosecution or the court can initiate confiscation proceedings if it believes it appropriate to do so. This has the effect of postponing the final part of the sentencing process to allow the prosecution's financial investigator (FI) to examine the defendant's financial circumstances. The FI will look to assess and then assert the extent to which the defendant benefitted from his offending and what assets he has available.

8.307 The confiscation process is widely maligned as costly and inefficient and lengthy as the FI carries out his investigation and the defendant replies.

8.308 Between 2014 and 2015, confiscation orders generated £155m according to the National Audit Office[30].

30 'Confiscation orders: progress review', HC 886, 11 March 2016.

8.309 The NAO estimates, however, that the annual cost of administering the end-to-end confiscation order process is around £100m.

8.310 The provisions governing this process are contained with *POCA 2002* and have been subject to extensive judicial clarification.

8.311 The Court of Appeal has approved a stepped approach to be taken in confiscation cases[31]:

(1) Ask whether the defendant has benefitted from his crime. (It may be benefit from the particular crime of which he has been convicted or, in some cases, benefit from his general criminal conduct.)

(2) If he has, the amount of the defendant's benefit or criminal proceeds must be determined.

(3) The assets available for realisation must be ascertained.

(4) The order must be for the amount of the benefit, or for the amount available, if that is smaller.

8.312 The court must also now ensure that any confiscation order is proportionate (*POCA 2002, s 6(5)* inserted in response to the case of *R v Waya* [2013] 2 Cr App R (S) 20).

8.313 Within the first step, the court must proceed as follows (*POCA 2002, s 4*):

- It must decide whether the defendant has a criminal lifestyle.
- If it decides that he has a criminal lifestyle it must decide whether he has benefited from his general criminal conduct.
- If it decides that he does not have a criminal lifestyle, it must decide whether he has benefited from his particular criminal conduct.

8.314 A defendant can have a criminal lifestyle either due to the nature of the offence or the nature of his previous offending.

8.315 Under *POCA 2002, Sch 2*, criminal lifestyle offences include fraudulent tax evasion, money laundering, blackmail or any offence of attempting, conspiring or inciting the commission of these offences.

8.316 The statutory provisions are routinely called 'draconian' because their effect is that the burden shifts to the accused to rebut assumptions and prove the legitimacy of income, expenditure and assets going back years. The implications for the family members of the accused or their business partners can be far reaching. It is essential that the tax professional facing confiscation proceedings, or interested parties, receive specialist legal advice at this stage as with all previous stages in the criminal justice process.

31 *R v Gangar* [2013] 1 Cr App R (S) 67A; modifying Lord Bingham's approach in *R v May* [2008] UKHL 28.

KEY POINTS

8.317

- HMRC reserves the right to conduct criminal investigations in all the areas for which it has responsibility but also to use its civil investigatory procedures. Certain conduct, particularly that which is an affront to the taxation system, makes a criminal investigation more likely.
- The criminal standard of proof means that an accused ought not to be convicted if there remains any doubt about any part of the prosecution case; specifically, where such a doubt is more than merely fanciful or far-fetched or based only on an extremely remote possibility. If any residual doubt is not realistic, an accused ought to be found guilty.
- The criminal standard is considerably higher than the civil standard, which requires satisfaction that an event was more likely to have occurred than not.
- A guilty mind is usually required for an individual or company to be criminally responsible for its actions but for strict liability tax offences this is not the case.
- *PACE 1984* production orders specifically exclude the production of items subject to legal professional privilege. Accordingly, this must be immediately flagged to officers conducting a search.
- Any court order must be forensically analysed to ensure that it has been lawfully obtained and its requirements are clearly understood. The recipient should undertake a thorough, document-by-document review to ensure that materials that fall outside the scope of an order are not disclosed.
- Preparation can be made to pre-empt and mitigate for the effects of a dawn raid. During a raid, a detailed contemporaneous record must be made documenting the actions of law enforcement officers and any objections voiced, especially in relation to excluded or privileged material.
- A solicitor should always be consulted, and ideally be present, prior to an interview under caution.
- Prosecution claims not to possess material that could assist the defence case or undermine the prosecution case should be robustly examined.
- A forensic accountant could be utilised by the defence from the initial stage through to the confiscation proceedings when challenges are made to the benefit figure and amount it is alleged that the defendant has available.

Chapter 9

Tax evasion and tax facilitation offences

SIGNPOSTS

- Corporate offence for facilitation of tax evasion by representatives of a business: statutory strict liability offence (subject to a single statutory defence) under the *Criminal Finances Act 2017* (*CFA 2017*) (see **9.21–9.23**).
- Purpose of *CFA 2017* is to prevent tax evasion occurring, and for businesses to implement procedures to prevent tax evasion (see **9.34**).
- Applies to UK and foreign tax evasion (see **9.23** and **9.24**).
- Statutory Defence: prevention procedures (see **9.34**).
- HMRC guidance and guiding principles relating to prevention procedures (see **9.29–9.33**):
  - risk assessment
  - proportionality of procedures
  - top level commitment
  - due diligence
  - communication and training
  - monitoring and review.

9.1 Tax evasion (also known as tax fraud) is a criminal offence under UK law. In July 2010 Treasury Minister David Gauke drew the following distinction between tax evasion and tax avoidance (HC Deb 12 July 2010 c706):

> 'Tax evasion occurs when someone acts against the law. Tax avoidance involves compliance with the letter but not the spirit of the law, and it is right that the Government seek to minimise that. Tax planning is a case of acting in both the spirit and the letter of the law. There is a distinction, although there will be occasions when the line is a little blurred.'

9.2 The distinction between tax avoidance, which is lawful, and tax evasion, which is not, is therefore of critical importance both to taxpayers and their advisers.

9.3 The key ingredient in any criminal offence, unless it is a strict liability offence relating to tax, is 'dishonesty'.

9.4 The issue of what constitutes dishonesty has been considered by the Court of Appeal in the leading case of *R v Ghosh* [1982] 3 WLR 110. In that case the court held that, in considering whether a person has been dishonest, the jury must ask itself two questions:

- Would the defendant be regarded as dishonest by the standards of reasonable and honest people? If not, the defendant should be acquitted.
- If the above is answered in the affirmative, the jury must then ask itself whether the defendant realised that his conduct would be regarded as dishonest by the ordinary standards of reasonable and honest people? The defendant should be convicted if he had this realisation. If not, he should be acquitted.

9.5 The test for dishonesty has been clarified by the Supreme Court in *Ivey v Genting Casinos (UK) Ltd t/a Crockfords v Genting* [2017] UKSC 67 unifying the principles for civil and criminal cases. Lord Hughes (with whom Lord Neuberger, Lady Hale, Lord Kerr and Lord Thomas agreed) stated as follows at [74]:

> '[74] These several considerations provide convincing grounds for holding that the second leg of the test propounded in *Ghosh* does not correctly represent the law and that directions based upon it ought no longer to be given. The test of dishonesty is as set out by Lord Nicholls in *Royal Brunei Airlines Sdn Bhd v Tan* and by Lord Hoffmann in *Barlow Clowes*: see para 62 above. *When dishonesty is in question the fact-finding tribunal must first ascertain (subjectively) the actual state of the individual's knowledge or belief as to the facts. The reasonableness or otherwise of his belief is a matter of evidence (often in practice determinative) going to whether he held the belief, but it is not an additional requirement that his belief must be reasonable; the question is whether it is genuinely held. When once his actual state of mind as to knowledge or belief as to facts is established, the question whether his conduct was honest or dishonest is to be determined by the fact-finder by applying the (objective) standards of ordinary decent people.* There is no requirement that the defendant must appreciate that what he has done is, by those standards, dishonest.' [Emphasis added]

9.6 Unlike a civil appeal, the Crown bears the legal burden of proof, which means that the Crown must prove that the accused person has committed the offence, and the standard of proof is beyond reasonable doubt. The governing principle of English criminal law is that the onus lies upon the prosecution in a criminal trial to prove all the elements of the offence with which the accused is charged.

9.7 Tax offences apply to the range of taxes, such as income tax, corporation tax and VAT, and also failing to make proper returns for the purpose of evading National Insurance contributions, while making false claims for state benefits or for the payment of government subsidies can constitute the offence of obtaining property by deception. **Chapter 8** examines criminal offences in detail.

9.8 All offences relating to tax matters can be prosecuted and punished under common or statute law such as the *Theft Acts 1968* and *1978*, and the *Fraud Act 2006*.

9.9 Tax offences carry potentially lengthy custodial terms and/or unlimited fines. In addition, the courts can order the confiscation of the benefit obtained from the crime. The measure used to calculate the quantum of benefit is usually punitive.

9.10 The Chief Secretary to the Treasury has stated: 'Tax evasion is a crime like any other. If people help a burglar, they are accomplices and criminals too. Now it will be the same for those that help tax evaders' (19 March 2015).

9.11 In the context of tax evasion, the number of prosecutions for tax evasion/tax fraud against individuals has increased markedly, and the figures do not reflect situations where a criminal investigation has been started and then subsequently a prosecution has not been brought by the Crown Prosecution Service (CPS):

Year	*Total number of persons prosecuted for tax evasion as result of HMRC criminal investigations*
2010/11	372
2011/12	501
2012/13	739
2013/14	880

(HM Treasury response to a written Parliamentary question to Chancellor of the Exchequer, February 2015.)

The year 2016 provides an illustrative flavour of HMRC prosecutions relating to tax fraud. This saw 679 individuals being convicted for their part in tax crimes, with sentences for 2016 totalling more than 730 years. HMRC published their ten most significant cases for that year, which included the following prosecutions:

- a group of film producers, accountants, financial advisers and investment bankers jailed for a total of 36 years for their part in a £2.2m film tax scheme fraud;
- three men jailed for a total of 27 years for a film fraud disguised as a tax avoidance scheme, which was intended to defraud taxpayers of £100m;

- three men – including an accountant and a construction firm boss jailed for a total of 19 years, after stealing £6.9m in a payroll fraud to fund lavish lifestyles;
- a criminal gang from the South East jailed for a total of 19 years, after getting caught red-handed with bundles of 'dirty' cash, as part of £15m made from selling alcohol illegally;
- two charity con men, who faked charitable donations to fraudulently claim more than £5m in Gift Aid repayments, were jailed for a combined total of 19 years;
- a gang of five men from the north of England, who used free public Wi-Fi to try to hide their £10m cigarette smuggling ring, were jailed for a total of 16 and a half years;
- a criminal gang, including a father and son, caught running a fuel fraud, evading more than £900,000 in duty and taxes by running an illegal filling station in the West Midlands, jailed for a combined total of more than nine and half years;
- a London couple who masterminded a nationwide counterfeit tobacco production racket capable of robbing the taxpayer of £1m a week, were jailed for a total of eight years;
- a cheating accountant who advised the media industry, was jailed for five years for a £6m tax fraud;
- four fraudsters from Forfar, Stoke-on-Trent and Spain, ordered to repay more than £111m in criminal profits. The men, who were part of an 18-strong criminal gang involved in a mobile phone VAT fraud, were sentenced between 2012 and 2014 to a total of 135 years in prison.

9.12 The majority of criminal investigations are initiated following the commencement of HMRC enquiries into the tax affairs of an individual and/or company, which have identified factual circumstances indicating that a criminal investigation should be undertaken. For these purposes a 'criminal investigation' means any process[1]:

- for considering whether an offence has been committed;
- for discovering by whom an offence has been committed; or
- as a result of which an offence is alleged to have been committed.

TAX FRAUD: OFFENCES IN OVERVIEW

9.13 There is no single criminal offence of committing tax evasion, ie tax fraud (set out overall in one place).

1 See the *Commissioners for Revenue and Customs Act 2005, s 21(2A)*.

9.14 A prosecution may be brought in either the magistrates' court or Crown Court but this depends on the nature of the offence.

9.15 The most serious offences will be heard in the Crown Court.

9.16 A prosecution for tax fraud in respect of direct taxes may be made under a variety of different offences, which are summarised below:

- Conspiracy to defraud (common law offence).

  Triable on indictment only.
- *Fraud Act 2006 (s 1).*

  Triable either way.

  Maximum: ten years' custody.
- False accounting: *Theft Act 1968 (s 17).*
- Fraudulent evasion of income tax: *Taxes Management Act 1970 (s 106A).*

  Triable either way.

  Maximum: seven years' custody.
- Cheating the public revenue (common law).

  Triable on indictment only.

  Maximum: life imprisonment.

  (Fraud, Bribery and Money Laundering Offences, Sentencing Council (effective 1 October 2014))
- Offences relating to offshore income, assets and activities.

  Maximum: on summary conviction up to 51 weeks imprisonment.

Cheating the public revenue

9.17 The principal offence for evading tax is cheating the public revenue, which is making a false statement tending to prejudice the Queen and the public revenue with the intent to defraud the Queen[2].

9.18 The offence includes the offence of causing to be delivered to an inspector of taxes accounts relating to the profits of a business that falsely and fraudulently state the profits to be less than they actually are.

9.19 Any individual who aids, abets, counsels or procures the cheating of the public revenue offence is also guilty of the actual offence (*Accessories and Abettors Act 1861, s 8*).

2 See *R v Hudson* [1956] 2 QB 252, cited with approval in *R v Mavji* [1987] 1 WLR 1388, 1391.

9.20 It is also an offence to attempt the above offences, conspire to commit them, or to perform an act capable of encouraging or assisting the commission of one of these offences, intending to encourage or assist in the offence, or believing that the offence will be committed and that the act will encourage or assist its commission (*Serious Crime Act 2007, s 45*).

OFFENCES FOR FAILURE TO PREVENT FACILITATION OF TAX EVASION

9.21 On 16 July 2015, the government published a consultation on holding corporations criminally responsible *for failing to prevent* their agents from facilitating tax evasion. Prosecutions are normally brought against an individual and not a corporate entity, but this new offence changes the position so that a corporation can be the subject of a criminal sanction, by way of imposition of a fine. The legislation was introduced by the *Criminal Finances Act 2017* (*CFA 2017*), which came into force with effect from 30 September 2017. The legislation (at www.legislation.gov.uk) makes the following activities an offence.

Failure to prevent facilitation of UK tax evasion offences

9.22 *CFA 2017, s 45* provides that a criminal offence is committed where:

> '(1) A relevant body (B) is guilty of an offence if a person associated with B commits a UK tax evasion facilitation offence when acting in the capacity of a person associated with B.'

In this regard, a UK tax evasion facilitation offence means (*CFA 2017, s 45(5)*):

> '(5) In this Part "UK tax evasion facilitation offence" means an offence under the law of any part of the United Kingdom consisting of:
>
> (a) being knowingly concerned in, or in taking steps with a view to, the fraudulent evasion of a tax by another person,
>
> (b) aiding, abetting, counselling or procuring the commission of a UK tax evasion offence, or
>
> (c) being involved art and part in the commission of an offence consisting of being knowingly concerned in, or in taking steps with a view to, the fraudulent evasion of a tax.'

UK tax evasion offence

9.23 The definition of 'UK tax evasion offence' in the context of UK tax evasion facilitation offence means (*CFA 2017, s 45(4)*):

> '(4) In this Part "UK tax evasion offence" means:

(a) an offence of cheating the public revenue, or

(b) an offence under the law of any part of the United Kingdom consisting of being knowingly concerned in, or in taking steps with a view to, the fraudulent evasion of a tax.'

FAILURE TO PREVENT FACILITATION OF FOREIGN TAX EVASION OFFENCES

9.24 *CFA 2017, s 46* provides that a criminal offence is committed where:

'(1) A relevant body (B) is guilty of an offence if at any time:

  (a) a person commits a foreign tax evasion facilitation offence when acting in the capacity of a person associated with B; and

  (b) any of the conditions in subsection (2) is satisfied.

(2) The conditions are:

  (a) that B is a body incorporated, or a partnership formed, under the law of any part of the United Kingdom;

  (b) that B carries on business or part of a business in the United Kingdom;

  (c) that any conduct constituting part of the foreign tax evasion facilitation offence takes place in the United Kingdom.'

Foreign tax evasion facilitation offence

9.25 For this purpose, the term 'foreign tax evasion facilitation offence' is defined as meaning (*CFA 2017, s 46(6)*):

'… conduct which:

(a) amounts to an offence under the law of a foreign country,

(b) relates to the commission by another person of a foreign tax evasion offence under that law, and

(c) would, if the foreign tax evasion offence were a UK tax evasion offence, amount to a UK tax evasion facilitation offence (see *s 45(5)* and *(6)*).'

9.26 The following points are particularly noteworthy in respect of the foreign tax evasion facilitation offence (drawn from HMRC's published guidance 'Corporate offences for failing to prevent criminal facilitation of tax evasion'[3]):

3 Published 6 September 2017 (updated 18 May 2018): see www.gov.uk/government/publications/corporate-offences-for-failing-to-prevent-criminal-facilitation-of-tax-evasion.

- **UK Nexus**: The offence can only be committed by a relevant body: incorporated under UK law, for example a limited company incorporated under UK law; carrying on a business or part of a business in the UK, for example a company incorporated under the law of France but operating from an office in Manchester; or whose associated person is located within the UK at the time of the criminal act that facilitates the evasion of the overseas tax, for example a company incorporated under German law whose employee helps another person to commit a foreign tax evasion offence whilst in London.
- **'Dual criminality'**: There are two stages of dual criminality. Firstly, the overseas jurisdiction must have an equivalent tax evasion offence at the taxpayer level and it must be the case that the actions carried out by the taxpayer would constitute a crime if they took place in the UK (an offence of being knowingly concerned in or taking steps with a view to the fraudulent evasion of the tax). Therefore, the corporate offence cannot be committed where the acts of the associated person would not be criminal if committed in the UK, regardless of what the foreign criminal law may be. Secondly, the overseas jurisdiction must have an equivalent offence covering the associated person's criminal act of facilitation, and it must be the case that the actions of the associated person would constitute a crime had they took place in the UK.

9.27 HMRC's guidance, 'Corporate offences for failing to prevent criminal facilitation of tax evasion' (above) states the following limitations in respect of a foreign offence:

> 'The legislation also requires that before proceedings for the foreign offence are commenced in England, Wales or Northern Ireland the personal consent of the Director of Public Prosecutions or the Director of the Serious Fraud Office must be gained[4]. Such consent would only be forthcoming where, having weighed up all factors, the prosecution was in the public interest.
>
> It is highly unlikely that a prosecution would be taken forward where a foreign tax was in some way incompatible with the UK's legal values, such as respect for human rights. It would also be very unlikely to be in the public interest to bring a prosecution where a foreign tax was discriminatory and applied on the basis of race, religion or gender.'

NO REQUIREMENT FOR ACTUAL LOSS OF TAX

9.28 It is particularly noteworthy that an offence can be committed under these provisions where a person dishonestly 'take steps with a view to' or

4 In relation to Scotland, the decision to prosecute is always taken by the Crown Office and Procurator Fiscal Service and so personal consent is not required in the legislation on the corporate offence. As a public body the Crown Office and Procurator Fiscal Service are bound by the *Human Rights Act 1998*.

'be knowingly concerned in' the evasion of the tax. For these offences to be committed it is not necessary that any tax actually be successfully evaded. Furthermore, a conviction at the taxpayer level is not a pre-requisite for bringing a prosecution against a relevant body. For example, a taxpayer may voluntarily come forward and make a full and honest disclosure to HMRC of their actions and it may not be in the interests of justice to criminally prosecute that individual. Where there is no criminal conviction of the taxpayer (stage 1) the prosecution would still have to prove during the prosecution of the relevant body, to the criminal standard of beyond all reasonable doubt, that the taxpayer level offence had been committed.

HMRC GUIDANCE

9.29 HMRC has published statutory guidance 'Tackling tax evasion: Government guidance for the corporate offences of failure to prevent the criminal facilitation of tax evasion' on the facilitation of tax evasion offences (the 'Guidance')[5].

9.30 It is a defence to the offences if a relevant body is able to establish that when the tax evasion was facilitated it either had in place such procedures as it was reasonable in all the circumstances to expect it to have, or it was not reasonable in all the circumstances to expect the relevant body to have any procedures in place. *Section 47* of *CFA 2017* imposes an obligation on the Chancellor of the Exchequer to prepare and publish guidance about the procedures that commercial organisations can put in place to prevent their employees from committing a tax evasion facilitation offence. The government has published guidance in accordance with this provision which assists in consideration of whether the reasonable procedures defence is available to an organisation. The guidance explains the policy behind the creation of the new offences and offers assistance on how corporations can institute proportionate procedures to prevent the commission of a criminal offence. Additionally, *section 47(7)* allows the Chancellor to approve and endorse guidance produced by a trade association that addresses sector-specific risks. The Guidance issued by HMRC has statutory force by virtue of the *Facilitation of Tax Evasion Offences (Guidance About Prevention) Regulations 2017, SI 2017/876.*

9.31 The Guidance provides the following overview of the offences (at para 1.3), stating that there are three stages that apply to both the domestic and foreign tax evasion facilitation offences (although it should be noted that there are additional requirements for the foreign offence set out above (including the 'dual criminality' requirement)):

5 Published 1 September 2017 with updates: available at https://assets.publishing.service.gov.uk/government/uploads/system/uploads/attachment_data/file/672231/Tackling-tax-evasion-corporate-offences.pdf.

> '**Stage one:** criminal tax evasion by a taxpayer (either a legal or natural person) under the existing law' (for example an offence of cheating the public revenue, or fraudulently evading the liability to pay VAT).'
>
> '**Stage two:** the criminal facilitation of the tax evasion by an "associated person" of the relevant body acting in that capacity' (this is criminal facilitation of the offence by a person acting on behalf of the corporation, whether by taking steps with a view to: being knowingly concerned in; or aiding, abetting, counselling, or procuring the tax evasion by the taxpayer).'
>
> '**Stage three:** the relevant body failed to prevent its representative from committing the criminal facilitation act' (this is the corporation's failure to take reasonable steps to prevent those who acted on its behalf from committing the criminal act outlined at stage two.'

9.32 Accordingly, as is apparent from the above, for a corporation to be liable it is necessary for there to be criminal tax evasion by a person, and for that evasion to have been facilitated by a person acting on behalf of the company.

9.33 The material defence for the corporation will be that it took reasonable steps to prevent the criminal facilitation.

STATUTORY DEFENCES

9.34 The legislation provides for the following defence for the corporate in respect of the UK tax evasion facilitation offence (*CFA 2017, s 45*):

> '(2) It is a defence for B to prove that, when the UK tax evasion facilitation offence was committed:
>
> (a) B had in place such prevention procedures as it was reasonable in all the circumstances to expect B to have in place, or
>
> (b) it was not reasonable in all the circumstances to expect B to have any prevention procedures in place.
>
> (3) In subsection (2) "prevention procedures" means procedures designed to prevent persons acting in the capacity of a person associated with B from committing UK tax evasion facilitation offences.'

9.35 A similar defence applies for the purposes of the foreign tax facilitation offence (see *CFA 2017, s 46*).

HMRC'S GUIDANCE: RELEVANT BODY TAKING REASONABLE STEPS TO PREVENT CRIMINAL FACILITATION

9.36 The Guidance (referred to at **9.29** above) contains guidance on the offence, and the following aspects are particularly noteworthy in the context of the defence relating to taking reasonable steps to prevent criminal facilitation.

9.37 In this regard, the document provides guidance on the type of approach that a corporation should consider adopting in order to ensure it has appropriate procedures in place.

9.38 The specific nature of any procedures adopted must be reasonable in all the circumstances, and this will be specific to each organisation. On this point the Guidance states (at Chapter 2 of the Guidance) that the prevention procedures which should be adopted by a person must be informed by reference to six specific principles:

> 'The Government considers that prevention procedures put in place by relevant bodies to prevent tax evasion from being committed on their behalf should be informed by the following six principles.
>
> - Risk assessment.
> - Proportionality of risk-based prevention procedures.
> - Top level commitment.
> - Due diligence.
> - Communication (including training).
> - Monitoring and review.'

9.39 The Guidance sets out the following principles for each organisation to consider in order to determine whether it has reasonable procedures in place to prevent criminal facilitation:

> **'Principle 1 – Risk assessment**
>
> The relevant body assesses the nature and extent of its exposure to the risk of those who act in the capacity of a person associated with it criminally facilitating tax evasion offences. The risk assessment is documented and kept under review.'
>
> **'Principle 2 – Proportionality of risk-based prevention procedures**
>
> Reasonable procedures for a relevant body to adopt to prevent persons acting in the capacity of a person associated with it from criminally facilitating tax evasion will be proportionate to the risk the relevant body faces of persons associated with it committing tax evasion facilitation offences. This will depend on the nature, scale and complexity of the relevant body's activities. We recognise that the reasonableness of prevention procedures should take account of the level of control and supervision the organisation is able to exercise over a particular person acting on its behalf, and the proximity of the person to the relevant body. The new offences do not require relevant bodies to undertake excessively burdensome procedures in

order to eradicate all risk, but they do demand more than mere lip-service to preventing the criminal facilitation of tax evasion.'

'Principles 3 – Top level commitment

The top-level management of a relevant body should be committed to preventing persons acting in the capacity of a person associated with it from engaging in criminal facilitation of tax evasion. They should foster a culture within the relevant body in which activity intended to facilitate tax evasion is never acceptable.'

'Principle 4 – Due diligence

The organisation applies due diligence procedures, taking an appropriate and risk-based approach, in respect of persons who perform or will perform services on behalf of the organisation, in order to mitigate identified risks.'

'Principle 5 – Communication (including training)

The organisation seeks to ensure that its prevention policies and procedures are communicated, embedded and understood throughout the organisation, through internal and external communication, including training. This is proportionate to the risk to which the organisation assesses that it is exposed.'

'Principle 6 – Monitoring and review

The organisation monitors and reviews its preventative procedures and makes improvements where necessary.'

HMRC GUIDANCE: SOME EXAMPLES

9.40 The Guidance (at pp 9 and 10) give the following illustrative examples of the different types of procedures which would be relevant for companies of varying sizes, complexity, industry focus and risk profile. HMRC state:

'For all the examples below it should be noted that the precise scale and nature of the tax evasion taking place would influence any decision to prosecute.

(1) Low/Medium risk

- A mid-size car parts maker ("UKCO") operating in the UK and Europe, entered into a sub-contracting arrangement with an UK distributor. The senior managers of the UK distributor created a false invoicing scheme with the assistance of a purchaser, allowing the purchaser to evade UK taxes due on its purchase of the car parts in the UK
- UKCO itself undertook a tax evasion focused risk assessment, identifying only low and medium level risks to the organisation,

subsequently implementing a number of prevention policies and procedures to mitigate the identified risks. UKCO had a clear policy against tax evasion, including terms and conditions within contracts with all third parties

- UKCO also carried out a due diligence assessment of its sub-contracting partner, but not for the entire supply chain. Nothing abnormal was detected during the due diligence test and consequently, UKCO had no reason to believe that the staff of the distributor were involved in a fraudulent tax scheme
- The UK distributor had no procedures to prevent tax evasion, in part because it is not required to do so in its jurisdiction.

In these circumstances, UKCO had undertaken a tax evasion facilitation risk assessment, had procedures and processes in place, as well as conducting a due diligence assessment of its sub-contracting partner. It is therefore unlikely that this company would have committed the offence as it could advance the defence of having reasonable procedures in place and articulating and evidencing what it had done, even if it did not conduct due diligence for the entire onward supply chain.

Whilst UKCO could have done more, it would not have been reasonable or proportionate to do so, the steps that it did take were proportionate to the risks it identified and faced.

(2) Higher risk

- As part of a large transaction an employee of a UK-based multinational bank knowingly referred a corporate client to an offshore accounting firm with the express intention of assisting the corporate client to set up a structure allowing the client to evade foreign income tax
- The bank, which had rigorous prevention procedures for money laundering and bribery procedures, undertook only a light-touch tax evasion risk assessment, nominally including the word "tax" into existing procedures and processes, but not effectively implementing them or reviewing tax fraud risks
- The bank undertook no tax evasion focussed due diligence assessment of the accounting firm to which the client was referred.

In these circumstances, although the bank could attempt to mount a defence of having reasonable procedures in place on paper for tackling the facilitation of tax evasion, in reality it had relied on unaltered money laundering and bribery procedures. Despite being in a high risk sector, it had also failed to undertake a thorough risk assessment, or follow Government or sector-focused guidance on the types of processes and procedures needed to mitigate risks. It is therefore likely that the bank would be found to have committed the new offence and would be unable to put forward a successful reasonable procedures defence.'

9.41 It is beyond the scope of this book to refer to all the illustrative examples given in the Guidance, and the recommendations which HMRC considers a relevant body should acknowledge for the purposes of formulating a policy to tackle tax evasion. Tax professionals will need to acquaint themselves and their clients with all relevant parts of the Guidance.

Chapter 10

Anti-money laundering

Arun Srivastava, Partner, Paul Hastings (Europe) LLP

SIGNPOSTS

- Tax advisors are the subject of increased focus for anti-money-laundering compliance issues (see **10.6**).
- A key aspect of anti-money laundering compliance is the 'risk-based approach' which requires that compliance procedures are calibrated according to the risks presented by particular clients, projects, transactions and products (see **10.19**).
- The *Money Laundering Regulations 2017* impose a number of obligations on firms (see **10.98**).
- The appropriate staffing and resourcing of a money laundering function is an important part of a firm's policies, controls and procedure (see **10.123**).
- The CCAB Guidance includes a Tax Appendix which contains supplementary guidance and should be consulted by tax practitioners as it offers an indication of the money laundering risk areas that a tax practitioner may encounter in practice (see **10.138**).
- STOP PRESS: The *Money Laundering and Terrorist Financing (Amendment) (EU Exit) Regulations 2020, SI 2020/991* update the existing *Money Laundering Regulations*. The principal amendments introduced by the provisions relate to trusts, in particular requiring additional trusts to be included on the trust register and extending the duty to report discrepancies in beneficial ownership to trusts (see *regs 5* and *7*).

INTRODUCTION

10.1 This chapter considers money laundering law and practice in the UK and its application to the tax adviser.

10.2 Tax advisers and accountants, in common with certain other professionals, are regarded as gatekeepers whose services can facilitate others to launder money. For this reason, firms practising in these sectors are not only subject to the general law prohibitions on money laundering contained in the *Proceeds of Crime Act 2002* (*POCA 2002*) but also fall within the regulated sector under the *Money Laundering, Terrorist Financing and Transfer of Funds (Information on the Payer) Regulations 2017, SI 2017/692* (*MLR 2017*). Firms that carry on business that falls within the definition of a 'tax adviser' under those Regulations must therefore have compliant anti-money laundering procedures in place to mitigate the risk that they will be used to facilitate money laundering.

10.3 Recent events such as the Panama Papers have highlighted the role that professional services firms, including accountants and professionals involved in the provision of tax advice, can play in facilitating wrong-doing and, in particular, the criminal evasion of taxes. The Panama Papers involved the leak of some 11.5 million documents from a Panamanian law firm (and corporate services provider), Mossack Fonseca, in April 2016. These documents provided client information on around 214,000 offshore entities, some of which are alleged to have been used for the purposes of facilitating unlawful tax evasion and other criminality. The Panama Papers leak is one of a number of scandals that have shone a light on the inner workings of some parts of the professional services industry. The issues that have come to light have influenced government policy and legislation. The result of this has been increased scrutiny of tax professionals and new laws and regulations that impact on and create obligations for the sector.

10.4 New requirements include important developments such as the *Criminal Finances Act 2017* (*CFA 2017*), which introduced a number of measures targeting tax evasion, money laundering, corruption and terrorist financing. These include the corporate offence of failing to prevent the facilitation of tax evasion, which requires firms to implement reasonable prevention procedures to mitigate the risk of facilitating tax evasion.

10.5 The use of the professional services sector to facilitate money laundering has also attracted attention at the European Union level. It prompted the European Parliament to carry out an inquiry into money laundering, tax avoidance and tax evasion in the course of 2017. The European Parliament's Report on its inquiry raised concerns that accountancy firms had played a role in recent tax scandals. The Report further concluded that in the context of anti-money laundering compliance, auditors and tax advisors remained insufficiently defined and regulated under the laws of the EU and in the laws of Member States.

10.6 The tax sector is accordingly under increased focus for anti-money laundering compliance issues. Under *reg 8* of the *Money Laundering, Terrorist Financing and Transfer of Funds (Information on the Payer) Regulations 2017*, 'auditors, insolvency practitioners, external accountants and tax advisers' are 'relevant persons' under the Regulations and are subject to specific requirements to have in place policies, controls and procedures to combat the risk that they will be used to facilitate money laundering or terrorist financing. A 'tax adviser' is defined as meaning a firm or sole practitioner who by way of business provides material aid or assistance or advice in connection with the tax affairs of other persons. Tax advisers form part of the Accountancy Service Providers (ASPs) sector. The ASP sector is regarded as having a high risk of money laundering.

10.7 In developing anti-money laundering compliance procedures, it is important for the sector to understand its susceptibility to money laundering and, accordingly, the reasons why tax advisers have been brought within the regulated sector under the Regulations. The UK is an attractive destination for money launderers, notwithstanding its long-established anti-money laundering legal and supervisory framework. The UK Government's National Risk Assessment on Money Laundering and Terrorist Financing of December 2020 (Risk Assessment) found that the size and complexity of the UK's financial sector mean that it is more exposed to criminality than financial sectors in other jurisdictions. The Risk Assessment found that laundering the proceeds of tax evasion together with the proceeds of fraud remain the largest known sources of criminal proceeds from offending in the UK, as well as the most common crime types. HMRC estimate that criminal tax evasion created a tax gap in 2018–19 of £4.6bn. This demonstrates the scale of the problem, given the need to integrate the proceeds of such offences into the legitimate financial system. The Risk Assessment identifies that the provision of tax advice provides clients with several means to launder money and poses a high risk. Particular risks, mentioned in the Risk Assessment in relation to the provision of tax advice, include risks of tax advisers advising clients on how to under-represent turnover or income to reduce tax liabilities and reclaiming funds from HMRC on a client's behalf when not entitled to do so.

10.8 In relation to the use of the professional services sector, the Risk Assessment notes that:

> 'Large amounts of criminal funds (often the proceeds of serious fraud or overseas corruption) continue to be laundered through the UK financial, professional services sectors and UK-registered corporate structures. The global nature of the financial system is exploited, often transferring funds through complex corporate vehicles and multiple offshore jurisdictions in order to hide the true beneficiary of the funds. This is regularly (wittingly or unwittingly) facilitated by professional services providers such as accountants, lawyers and transit and company service providers.'

10.9 Overall, the appeal of the ASP sector generally is the legitimacy and respectability that the use of a professional can confer. On the other hand, the risk of terrorist financing through the ASP is assessed as being low.

10.10 Criticisms have been made of the UK's supervisory structure, with Transparency International advocating in its 'Don't Look, Won't Find' Report that there should be a 'radical overhaul' of the UK's anti-money laundering system. The ASP sector in the UK is, in particular, subject to supervision by a patchwork of different supervisory bodies. Inconsistent supervision and enforcement of anti-money laundering obligation has, however, been largely addressed through the establishing of the Office for Professional Body Anti-Money Laundering Supervision, whose role is to supervise professional body supervisors and ensure the application of consistently high supervisory standards.

10.11 The Financial Action Task Force[1], in its Guidance to Accountants on the 'risk-based approach' to money laundering, identified the following services provided by ASPs as most useful to potential money launderers and therefore presenting the greatest vulnerabilities:

- financial and tax advice – criminals with a large amount of money to invest may pose as individuals hoping to minimise their tax liabilities or to place assets out of reach in order to avoid future liabilities;
- the creation of corporate vehicles or other complex legal arrangements (trusts, for example) – such structures may serve to confuse or disguise the links between the proceeds of crime and the perpetrator;
- buying or selling of property – property transfers can serve as either the cover for transfers of criminal property or may represent the final investment of these proceeds after their having passed through the laundering process;
- performing financial transactions – ASPs may be involved in effecting financial transactions for clients (for example, involving the purchase and sale of securities which involve criminal proceeds); and
- providing introductions to financial institutions – accountants may lend credibility to clients by introducing them to financial institutions.

10.12 It is in relation to these areas of risk, therefore, that tax advisers and other ASPs should focus their policies and procedures to mitigate the risk of facilitating money laundering and ensuring that they comply with their obligations under the *Money Laundering, Terrorist Financing and Transfer of Funds (Information on the Payer) Regulations 2017*.

1 The Financial Action Task Force (FATF) is an inter-governmental body which sets standards for anti-money laundering and terrorist financing laws internationally. National anti-money laundering legislation is influenced by FATF's Recommendations on Combatting Money Laundering and the Finance of Terrorism and Proliferation. Recommendation 12 of the 'old' Recommendations (now Recommendation 22) required that designated non-financial businesses and professionals (including accountants) be subject to additional anti-money laundering requirements.

10.13 The current UK anti-money laundering (AML) and counter-terrorism financing (CTF) framework has, of course, been shaped to a large extent by the five European Money Laundering Directives[2], which have in turn sought to implement the recommendations made by the Financial Action Task Force.

10.14 The law in the UK is based on the EU's Fourth Money Laundering Directive (4MLD)[3] as amended by the Fifth Money Laundering Directive (5MLD)[4]. The 4MLD was transposed in the UK through the *MLR 2017*, which came into force on 26 June 2017. These Regulations built on the framework established by the earlier *Money Laundering Regulations 2007* which they replaced. They have in particular focused more on the risk-based approach whilst preserving the architecture of the 2007 Regulations. The UK has, of course, now left the EU and will no longer be legally bound by EU Directives or other EU legislation. Anti-Money Laundering and Counter Terrorist Financing measures were addressed in the Trade and Co-operation Agreement entered into between the UK and the EU. The provisions in the Agreement principally cover the commitments by both parties to ensure transparency of beneficial ownership of corporate bodies and other legal entities and for the parties' respective authorities to co-operate in investigations and proceedings relating to the freezing and confiscation of property in criminal matters.

10.15 The EU is in the process of rapid consolidation of anti-money laundering supervision and laws. The EU's Sixth Money Laundering Directive (Directive (EU) 2018/1673 on combating money laundering by criminal law) (6MLD) will harmonise criminal law offences and sanctions across the EU. It will not, however, be implemented in the UK. The UK Government expressed the view that the UK was largely compliant with the provisions of the 6MLD, which as a criminal law provision would not have applied in the UK prior to Brexit in any event, unless the UK had expressly opted into it. Interestingly, Article 7 of 6MLD contains a novel provision for the 'Liability of Legal Persons' which imposes corporate criminal liability where a company has failed to properly supervise or control senior staff who have committed a money laundering offence. Since this applies to all business sectors and not just the regulated sector, it is likely to go beyond existing UK criminal law. The UK is, however, investigating a new corporate criminal liability offence of failure to prevent economic crime.

---

2 Directives 91/308/EEC, 2001/97/EC, 2005/60/EC, Directive 2015/849/EU and Directive (EU) 2018/843.

3 Directive (EU) 2015/849 of the European Parliament and of the Council of 20 May 2015 on the prevention of the use of the financial system for the purposes of money laundering or terrorist financing, amending Regulation (EU) No 648/2012 of the European Parliament and of the Council, and repealing Directive 2005/60/EC of the European Parliament and of the Council and Commission Directive 2006/70/EC.

4 Directive (EU) 2018/843 of the European Parliament and of the Council of 30 May 2018 amending Directive (EU) 2015/849 on the prevention of the use of the financial system for the purposes of money laundering or terrorist financing, and amending Directives 2009/138/EC and 2013/36/EU (Text with EEA relevance).

10.16 Although the UK has now left the EU, the background to the development of the EU Directives remains an important consideration in understanding the development of the UK's regulations. The terrorist attacks in Europe at the end of 2015 and the Panama Papers revelations in early 2016 prompted the European Union to amend the 4MLD to address specific concerns arising from these events. The 5MLD set out amendments to the 4MLD and was transposed in the UK through the *Money Laundering and Terrorist Financing (Amendment) Regulations 2019, SI 2019/1511*, which came into force on 10 January 2020, shortly before the UK left the EU.

10.17 This chapter provides an overview of the obligations that apply to accountants under the UK's anti-money laundering framework. It also provides an overview of requirements related to terrorist financing contained in the *Terrorism Act 2000*, which mirror the requirements of *POCA 2002* in many respects.

10.18 A key part of the anti-money laundering framework is the supervisory structure created by the *MLR 2017* whereby firms which fall within the scope of the regulations must be supervised for compliance by HMRC, the Financial Conduct Authority (FCA) or a professional body such as the Institute for Chartered Accountants for England and Wales. This chapter also considers the supervisory structure and guidance that has been issued for the sector as to how it should go about complying with its legal and regulatory obligations.

RISK ASSESSMENT

10.19 As already noted, a key aspect of anti-money laundering compliance is the 'risk-based approach' which requires that compliance procedures are calibrated according to the risks presented by particular clients, projects, transactions and products. The 4MLD has resulted in increased focus on firms implementing a risk-based approach. In order to assist firms in doing this, national governments have been required to publish risk assessments of money laundering and terrorist financing risks so that firms can combine this macro-level assessment of risk with their own microlevel assessment.

10.20 The UK's Home Office published the latest UK National Risk Assessment of Money Laundering and Terrorist Financing Risks in December 2020. Chapter 9 of the Risk Assessment covers ASPs, including tax advisers. The Risk Assessment categorises this sector as having a 'high' overall risk. Although the sector overall is rated 'high' risk, the risks posed to firms should also be considered on an individual basis.

10.21 The key threats and vulnerabilities that the Risk Assessment identified for accountants are as follows:

(1) *Company formation and termination* – the Risk Assessment identifies company formation and termination as the ASP sector's highest risk. The Home Office state in the Risk assessment that company formation

continues to be exploited by criminals to mask the ownership of assets or the transfer of assets between persons. These services are assessed to be higher risk where they are offered by ASPs as opposed to specialist company formation agents. This is because criminals may also access and exploit an ASP's wider services. Importantly in the context of the current economic downturn, the Risk Assessment also identifies the provision of company liquidation and associated services as an area of risk.

(2) *Mainstream accounting* – the Risk Assessment notes that accountancy services have also been exploited to provide a veneer of legitimacy to falsified accounts or documents used to conceal the source of funds. In some cases, this has been facilitated intentionally by accounting professionals, whereas in other cases it has been inadvertent. The Risk Assessment states that the risk of false accounting can arise in relation to both high-end and cash-based money laundering, with accountants involved in the account preparation or review processes for both small and large businesses.

(3) *Payroll services* – the Risk Assessment states that payroll services can provide criminals with a legitimate looking record of money movement. The risk of payroll services being used to laundering funds is considered to be high.

(4) *Misuse of client accounts* – the Risk Assessment identifies that there is a risk posed by accountants performing high-value financial transactions for clients with no clear business rationale involved, allowing criminals to transfer funds through bank accounts with little scrutiny as a means to complicate the audit trail.

(5) *Tax services* – as already noted, there is an increased focus on the provision of tax-related services. The Risk Assessment states that while tax services are unlikely to be used to launder the proceeds of other crimes, they are used to facilitate tax evasion and VAT fraud, the proceeds of which constitute criminal property under *POCA 2002*. The risks in the provision of tax advice are considered to be high because large amounts of funds can be claimed or undeclared and there is a high likelihood of tax advisers' services being used in this way.

(6) *Supervision, compliance and law enforcement respons*e – the Risk Assessment notes that the risk of inconsistent supervision of ASPs remain, albeit that the government has taken action to promote more effective supervision through the introduction of the Office for Professional Body Anti-Money Laundering Supervision, a role performed by the FCA.

10.22 The areas of risk identified by the Home Office in the UK's Risk Assessment are similar in scope to the areas identified by the Financial Action Task Force in its Guidance to Accountants which is referred to above. Under *reg 18* of the *Money Laundering, Terrorist Financing and Transfer of Funds*

(Information on the Payer) Regulations 2017, tax advisers must take appropriate steps to identify and assess the risks of money laundering and terrorist financing to which their business is subject. They must also prepare a written risk assessment taking account of risk factors relating to their customers, the countries or geographic areas in which they operate, their products or services, their transactions and delivery channels.

PROCEEDS OF CRIME ACT 2002

10.23 The principal UK criminal offences of money laundering are contained in *POCA 2002*. This is a lengthy statute and the money laundering offences are to be found in *Pt VII* (*ss 327–340*). The intention of *POCA 2002* was to consolidate the fragmented legislative structure that previously existed and to reform the offences relating to money laundering on a UK-wide basis. *POCA 2002* sets out the legal definition of the term 'money laundering' and sets out the specific money laundering offences. In summary, *POCA 2002* establishes that a person will commit a money laundering offence if he deals in any of the ways specified in *ss 327–329* (see below) with property that he knows or suspects is the product of criminal conduct as committed either in the UK or elsewhere. A person also commits an offence if he attempts, conspires or incites a person to commit one of the offences or aids, abets counsel or procures the commission of any of them.

10.24 The offences under *POCA 2002, ss 327–329* have been described as 'parasitic' offences. This is because they are predicated on the commission of another offence which has yielded proceeds, which then become the subject of a money laundering offence. The offences under *ss 327–329* apply generally to all individuals and entities. The Act also contains specific offences which apply only to businesses in the 'regulated sector'. The 'regulated sector' is a subset of businesses (corresponding to the business sectors subject to the *MLR 2017*) that have specific anti-money laundering responsibilities. Offences that apply in particular to the 'regulated sector' are the offences of 'Failure to disclose: regulated sector' (*s 330*), 'Failure to disclose: nominated officers in the regulated sector' (*s 331*) and 'Tipping off: regulated sector' (*s 333A*).

The POCA regulated sector

10.25 The definition of 'business in the regulated sector' is set out in Sch 9 to *POCA 2002*. Businesses which fall within this definition, so far as relevant to the ASP sector, include:

(1) the carrying on of statutory audit work by a statutory auditor under the *Companies Act 2006, Pt 42*;

(2) the activities of a person appointed to act as an insolvency practitioner under the *Insolvency Act 1986, s 388*;

(3) the provision of accountancy services by way of business;

(4) the provision of material aid or assistance or advice in connection with the tax affairs of other persons by a firm or sole practitioner, whether provided directly or through a third party, if the firm or sole practitioner by way of business provides (as the case may be) aid, assistance or advice in connection with the tax affairs of other persons;

(5) the creation, operation or management of trusts, companies or other similar structures;

(6) the carrying on of local audit work within the meaning of *Sch 5* to the *Local Audit and Accountability Act 2014* by any firm or individual who is a local auditor within the meaning of that Act; and

(7) acting or arranging for another person to act as a director or secretary of a company, as a partner of a partnership or in a similar position in relation to other legal persons, providing a registered office, business address, correspondence or administrative address or other related services for a company, partnership or other legal person or arrangement and acting or arranging for another person to act as a trustee of an express trust or similar legal arrangement or nominee shareholder for a person other than a company whose securities are listed on a regulated market.

In this chapter, reference to accountants can be taken to read accountants and auditors working in the regulated sector.

Principal money laundering offences

10.26 *POCA 2002* sets out three principal money laundering offences, which are:

(1) concealing, disguising, converting, transferring or removing from the jurisdiction property, which is or represents criminal property (*s 327*);

(2) entering into or becoming concerned in arrangements that a person knows or suspects will facilitate another person's acquisition, retention, use or control of criminal property (s 328); and

(3) acquiring, possessing or using criminal property (*s 329*).

10.27 A key ingredient of the above offences is that the conduct in question must be carried out in connection with 'criminal property'. The term 'criminal property' is defined in *s 340* of *POCA 2002* and, broadly, covers property that constitutes a person's benefit from 'criminal conduct'. The concepts of 'criminal property' and 'criminal conduct' are addressed further at **10.38–10.42** below.

10.28 The offences under *ss 327–329* can only be committed where a person knows or suspects that the property involved is criminal property or in the case of the offence under s 328 of *POCA 2002*, that the person knows or suspects that the arrangements concerned facilitate the acquisition, retention, use or control of criminal property. Knowledge or suspicion for these purposes is 'subjective' so that a person must actually know or suspect the relevant matters in order to commit an offence.

10.29 The UK operates a consent regime whereby a person can avoid the commission of one of the principal money laundering offences by making an authorised disclosure under *POCA 2002, s 338* and obtaining an appropriate consent to proceed. This applies in the case of each of the offences under *ss 327–329* of the Act. The consent regime is covered at **10.63–10.71** below.

Section 327: concealing, disguising or converting

10.30 Under *s 327(1)* of *POCA 2002* a person commits an offence if he conceals, disguises, converts, transfers or removes criminal property from the jurisdiction (the jurisdictions being respectively England and Wales, Scotland and Northern Ireland. Concealing or disguising criminal property includes concealing or disguising its nature, source, location, deposition, movement or ownership or any rights with respect to it (s 327(3)).

10.31 Prosecutions brought under *s 327* of *POCA 2002* cover a wide variety of factual circumstances. These range from cases involving employees of an investment management firm who set up bogus accounts into which they received proceeds from the redemption of customers' investments (*R v Price* [2008] EWCA Crim 590) to cases involving the conversion of cash from the sale of drugs (*R v Rouke* [2008] EWCA Crim 233).

10.32 Section 327 of *POCA 2002* has also been used to prosecute cases involving the proceeds of tax evasion, theft, bribery and fraud.

Section 328: concerned in arrangements

10.33 *Section 328* of *POCA 2002* makes it an offence for a person to enter into or become concerned in an arrangement that he knows, or suspects, facilitates the acquisition, retention, use or control of criminal property by or on behalf of another person.

10.34 This offence may typically be committed by a third party which becomes involved in another person's wrongdoing (for example *K Ltd v National Westminster Bank* [2007] 1 WLR 311). For professionals such as accountants, the offence under *s 328* is one which is most likely to be relevant to their activities as it criminalises the provision of services to clients where the services being provided facilitate the client's or another party's acquisition, retention, use or control of criminal property.

10.35 In order for an offence to be committed under *s 328*, a person must enter into or be concerned in an arrangement that in fact facilitates the acquisition, retention, use or control of criminal property (it is not sufficient that the offender merely suspects that it does). In *R v GH* [2015] 1 WLR 2126, the Supreme Court found that it does not matter whether criminal property exists when the relevant arrangement is entered into. What matters is that the property should be criminal property when the arrangement operates on it. Accordingly, an accountant's involvement in arrangements which are subsequently used to launder money will result in the commission of an offence at the time when the criminal property is used in the arrangements.

Section 329: acquisition, use and possession

10.36 Under *POCA 2002, s 329* it is an offence to acquire, use or have possession of criminal property. An offence can be committed by a person where he acquires, uses or has possession of the proceeds of his own criminal conduct. A defence is provided in *s 329(2)(c)* so that an offence is not committed where a person acquires, uses or has possession of property for adequate consideration. This defence is necessary in order to protect third parties who receive payment from funds that constitute criminal property. As indicated, the defence is only available where a person gives 'adequate consideration'. This is an important limitation. Consideration will not be regarded as 'adequate' where the value of the consideration is significantly less than the value of the property. Moreover, the defence is not available where a person provides goods or services which he knows or suspects may help another to carry out criminal conduct.

Criminal conduct and criminal property

10.37 The legal understanding of the term 'money laundering' revolves around the central concept of 'criminal property'. In order for one of the principal money laundering offences to be committed, some act must be carried out in relation to 'criminal property'. Under *POCA 2002, s 340(3)*, there are two main elements to criminal property:

- the property[5] must constitute a person's benefit from criminal conduct or it must represent such a benefit in whole or in part, directly or indirectly; and
- the alleged offender must know or suspect that the property constitutes criminal property. For these purposes, knowledge is actual knowledge and a person will be regarded as having a suspicion where it is more than merely fanciful that the relevant facts exist[6]. In both cases, the test is a

5 'Property' is defined in *POCA 2002, s 340(9)* as all property wherever situated, including cash, things in action and other intangible or incorporeal property.

6 See the case of *R v Da Silva* [2006] EWCA Crim 1654, where the court said that: 'It seems to us that the essential element in the word "suspect" and its affiliates, in this context, is that the defendant must think that there is a possibility, which is more than fanciful, that the relevant facts exist. A vague feeling of unease would not suffice'.

subjective one (ie whether the person in fact knows or suspects) and not an objective test.

10.38 Property that is alleged to be criminal property must have that quality at the time of the commission of the money laundering offence. It must therefore be obtained as a result of, or in connection with, criminal conduct that is separate from the conduct alleged to constitute the money laundering offence. In other words, there must be some separate underlying criminal conduct that produces criminal property before a money laundering offence can be committed.

10.39 Under *s 340(4)* it is immaterial who carried out the conduct, who benefited from it and when the conduct was engaged in. Property must be criminal property at the time of commission of the principal money laundering offence.

10.40 Criminal conduct is defined under *POCA 2002, s 340(2)* as conduct that constitutes an offence in any part of the UK or conduct which would constitute an offence in any part of the UK if it occurred there. The definition of 'criminal conduct' therefore includes conduct committed abroad, provided that this would have resulted in the commission of an offence if carried on in the UK and includes every crime on the statute book regardless of the seriousness of the crime. As a result, accountants in the UK have to be alert to a wide range of potential criminal activity. Some limits are imposed on the jurisdictional scope of the offences under *POCA 2002, ss 327–329*. For minor offences (ie those punishable with a term of imprisonment of 12 months or less), *POCA 2002* effectively requires dual criminality (ie that the underlying criminal conduct that gives rise to the criminal property being laundered, must be illegal both in the UK and the country in which the conduct occurred). Accordingly, with some exceptions, for such minor offences, no offence is committed where the alleged offender knew or believed that that underlying conduct that occurred outside the UK was not unlawful under the criminal law of the country in which the conduct occurred.

10.41 The jurisdictional scope of the principal money laundering offences under *POCA 2002* has been the subject of some debate. Broadly, criminal law has been applied on a territorial basis meaning that some element of the offence must occur in the UK for the conduct to be susceptible to prosecution in the UK. With money laundering offences, this has meant that while the underlying conduct giving rise to criminal proceeds may occur outside the UK, some element of the money laundering offence (eg arrangements relating to the laundering of the criminal funds or the transfer of those funds) must take place in the UK for the commission of an offence in the UK. The courts have, however, started to adopt a more flexible approach. In the case of *R v Rogers* [2014] EWCA Crim 1680, the Court of Appeal found that Parliament had intended *POCA 2002* to have extra-territorial effect and that a person who permitted use of his bank account in Spain for the receipt and withdrawal of criminally derived monies could be guilty of an offence under *POCA 2002*, *s 327* of converting criminal property, even though the conduct in question had taken place outside the UK.

10.42 Some uncertainty formerly existed as to whether tax evasion constitutes a predicate offence for money laundering purposes. This is on the basis that the funds in question are derived from a legitimate source and do not have a criminal origin. However, the case law in the UK has made clear that where a person engages in tax evasion, the tax not paid will constitute the proceeds of crime. This is on the basis that the person would have made a false declaration to HMRC and/or otherwise committed the offence of cheating the Revenue. Where a person cheats the Revenue by not paying tax on undeclared takings and obtains a pecuniary advantage as a result of criminal conduct this can amount to 'criminal property' within the meaning of *POCA 2002*[7]. In particular, *POCA 2002, s 340(6)* provides that if a person obtains a pecuniary advantage as a result of, or in connection with, conduct, he is taken to obtain as a result of, or in connection with, the conduct of a sum of money equal to the value of the pecuniary advantage. A person who unlawfully cheats the Revenue therefore obtains a benefit within *POCA 2002, s 340(3)*.

Disclosure and the consent regime

10.43 Where a person considers that he has committed a breach of any of the principal money laundering offences, or may get into a situation where a breach could occur, a reporting obligation is likely to arise.

10.45 Under *POCA 2002, s 330*, for a business in the regulated sector, an offence is committed unless suspicions of money laundering (knowledge, suspicion or reasonable grounds to suspect that another person is engaged in money laundering) are disclosed to the National Crime Agency (NCA) or to a Nominated Officer (being a person nominated internally to receive reports of such knowledge or suspicion) with a view to the Nominated Officer assessing whether to onward report to the NCA.

10.46 A disclosure might also be made as an 'authorised disclosure' under *POCA 2002, s 338*. A disclosure is an authorised disclosure if it is a disclosure to a constable (including NCA), a customs officer or a Nominated Officer that property is criminal property. An authorised disclosure is made where a reporter is seeking an appropriate consent to proceed with an act that would otherwise constitute a money laundering offence under *POCA 2002, ss 327–329* (a prohibited act).

10.47 An authorised disclosure may be made while doing the prohibited act provided that the person concerned had started to do the act at a time when he did not know or suspect that the act was prohibited. In such circumstances, the disclosure must be made on the person's own initiative as soon as practicable

7 See *R v IK* [2007] EWCA Crim 491.

after knowing or suspecting that property constitutes or represents a person's benefit from criminal conduct: *POCA 2002, s 338(2A)*.

10.48 The disclosure may also be made after the person carries out the prohibited act. In order for this to apply, the person concerned must have a reasonable excuse for failing to make the disclosure before doing the act and the disclosure must be made as soon as practicable. Where, for example, a person does not realise when he starts to conduct a transaction that criminal property was involved, the onus is on the person concerned to make an authorised disclosure as soon as possible when he does suspect.

10.49 According to the Suspicious Activity Reports (SARs) Annual Report for 2019, in the period April 2018 to March 2019 a total of 478,437 suspicious activity reports were made and an appropriate consent was sought in 34,543 cases.

Reporting suspicions – the regulated sector and POCA 2002, s 330

10.50 For tax advisers and other ASPs in the regulated sector, the key requirement in *POCA 2002, s 330* is that a report must be made as soon as possible if:

- the tax adviser or ASPs know or suspect or have reasonable grounds for knowing or suspecting that someone is engaged in money laundering; and
- the information on which they base their knowledge or suspicion has come to them in the course of their business in the regulated sector (ie in the course of providing accountancy services).

10.51 The offence under *s 330* can be committed both where a person has actual knowledge or suspicion and where a person has reasonable grounds to suspect money laundering.

10.52 The standard of 'reasonable grounds' is an objective standard. Liability can arise under *s 330* even where an accountant does not in fact know or suspect the relevant matters. It is sufficient for the prosecution to show that the accountant should have known or suspected.

10.53 The UK Government[8] justified this standard of liability on the basis that persons who are employed in the regulated sector, should be expected to exercise a higher level of diligence in handling transactions than those employed in other businesses. The introduction of such a wide failure to disclose offence was resisted by several ASP sector industry bodies.

10.54 Where a firm carries on activities, some of which are in the regulated sector and some of which are not, only the employees carrying on the regulated

8 Proceeds of Crime Consultation on Draft Legislation (Home Office, 2001).

sector activities are intended to be caught by the failure to disclose offence. The knowledge or suspicion may relate to a client, counterparty or any other person provided that the information or other matter giving rise to the knowledge or suspicion comes to a person in the course of the firm's regulated sector business.

10.55 In order to avoid the commission of an offence, the accountant must make the required disclosure (defined in *s 330(5)*) to a Nominated Officer (an internal disclosure) or the NCA as soon as is practicable. A Nominated Officer is a person nominated internally to receive disclosures under *POCA 2002, s 330(9)*.

10.56 From the perspective of the accountant, the act of disclosure to the Nominated Officer will be sufficient to discharge the accountant's employee duties under *s 330*. Once a disclosure has been made, the Nominated Officer must consider whether it is necessary to make an onward disclosure to the NCA. *Section 331* of the Act sets out a specific offence for Nominated Officers who will themselves be guilty of an offence if after having received notification pursuant to *s 330*, they fail to make a suspicious activity report to the NCA.

10.57 *Section 330* contains certain exceptions to liability for the failure to disclose offence. Under *s 330(7A)*, the offence of failure to disclose is not committed where a person in the regulated sector believes on reasonable grounds that the money laundering of which he has knowledge or suspicion is occurring outside the UK and is not unlawful under the criminal law in the jurisdiction in which it is taking place. This exception is subject to the condition that the conduct in question must not be of a description prescribed in an order made by the Secretary of State.

10.58 Under *s 330(6)(a)*, an offence is also not committed where a person has a reasonable excuse for not making the required disclosure. There is considerable uncertainty as to what would constitute a reasonable excuse. It has been suggested that a defence might be successful where the accountant has been subjected to threats and there would be violent consequences if he did report, but it should be said that care would need to be exercised before relying on this provision.

10.59 Where a person working for a tax adviser in the regulated sector has not received training on identifying suspicious transactions, this may found the basis of a defence for that employee. Under *POCA 2002, s 330(7)*, where the person concerned has not been provided with suitable training by his employer and did not have actual knowledge or suspicion of money laundering, no offence will be committed. However, a failure by an accounting firm in the regulated sector to provide training to employees may mean that the firm is in breach of its obligations under the *MLR 2017*.

10.60 Finally, legal advisers or a 'relevant professional adviser' are exempt from reporting if the information on which they would otherwise base their knowledge or suspicion came their way in privileged circumstances. A 'relevant professional adviser' includes an accountant, auditor or tax adviser who is a member of a relevant professional body. The scope of the exemption for information communicated in privileged circumstances was expanded to cover such relevant professional advisers following requests from the accountancy profession.

10.61 Care should be taken to establish whether privilege has attached as it only applies where information is communicated in connection with the giving by the adviser of legal advice to the client or by a person seeking legal advice or by a person in connection with legal proceedings or contemplated proceedings. Examples of situations could be advising directors on legal duties and liabilities, for example, wrongful trading under the *Insolvency Act 1986* or perhaps giving advice to a client on employment law. An accountant might meet the litigation advice condition if he represents a client at a tax tribunal.

Nominated Officers

10.62 A SAR may be made externally to the NCA or internally to the accountancy firm's Nominated Officer. A Nominated Officer is the individual who has been nominated to receive reports of money laundering suspicions by his firm. In most cases disclosures will, in the first instance, be made internally to the Nominated Officer and in most cases from the perspective of the employee that will be sufficient to discharge the employees' duties under *POCA 2002, s 330*. The role of the Nominated Officer in this connection is governed under *POCA 2002, s 331*, which sets out a specific offence for Nominated Officers who will themselves be guilty of an offence if after having received a SAR they fail to make a report to the NCA where the SAR gives rise to reasonable grounds for knowing or suspecting money laundering.

Consent

10.63 Upon the making of a disclosure to the NCA, the NCA has an initial notice period of seven working days, starting with the first working day after the disclosure is made, in which to consider the request for consent. Consent must either be given or refused within this seven-day notice period. If consent is not refused within this period, there will be a deemed consent to the carrying out of the prohibited act. If consent is refused, a further 31-day moratorium period will apply. Unless consent is refused again within this period, there will be a deemed consent to the carrying out of the act. As explained further below, where consent has been refused, NCA must keep its decision under review during the moratorium period and must give a consent where there is no longer any good reason for withholding it. This period of time may now be extended on application to the court under *POCA 2002, s 336A*.

10.64 Where a disclosure is made to the Nominated Officer, the Nominated Officer may grant consent to doing the prohibited act where the Nominated Officer has made a disclosure to the NCA and consent has been provided or the notice period or moratorium period referred to above has expired. The Nominated Officer will commit an offence if he provides consent without having obtained the consent from NCA.

Effect of consent

10.65 A consent to perform a prohibited act will only protect the person who has obtained the consent from otherwise committing a principal money laundering offence. A consent does not protect against the commission of some other criminal offence.

10.66 It will also not provide protection from civil claims against a firm that transfers property that is suspected to be criminal property (for example, because it suspects the property to be the proceeds of a fraud or other misappropriation of assets) by the owner of the assets.

10.67 Accordingly, the consent from the NCA will not necessarily protect an accountant or an accountancy firm from the risk of constructive trust liability. In such situations it would be prudent to approach the court for directions and/or a declaration from the court under CPR 40.20 (of the Court's Civil Procedure Rules). Directions and/or declaration may be sought in order to avoid constructive trust liability under the civil law. Moreover, the fact that the firm has made a SAR and received a consent to act may in itself be sufficient to rebut an assertion that it had somehow acted dishonestly in transferring assets or funds.

10.68 The operation of the consent regime has given rise to considerable practical problems, particularly for banks, although also relevant to accounting firms. Once a SAR is made the requirement not to continue involvement in a particular matter until consent for that involvement is forthcoming can present a significant challenge. For example, the firm is unable to operate the client's account as this could constitute a principal money laundering offence and potentially expose the firm to civil liability as a constructive trustee. On the other hand, a failure to implement a client's instructions could constitute a breach of the client's mandate and result in legal action against the firm for an injunction requiring the firm to comply with the mandate or for damages. From the perspective of an accountancy firm, the continued provision of services could result in the firm committing an offence under *POCA 2002, s 328*, of being concerned in arrangements.

10.69 The issues were more acute prior to the introduction of the notice and moratorium periods contained in *POCA 2002*. The leading case on issues pre *POCA 2002* is the *Bank of Scotland v A Ltd* [2001] 1 WLR 751. In this case, the Bank suspected that an account in the name of A Ltd was being used to launder criminal property. The Bank was concerned that paying funds in accordance with A Ltd's instructions could result in a money laundering offence and possible constructive trust liability but refusing to pay could result in a tipping-off offence as well as a civil claim against it for breach of mandate.

The Court of Appeal held that the appropriate course for the bank was to seek directions from the court with the Serious Fraud Office, rather than the customer, as respondent. The court could then use its powers to grant interim declarations in proceedings setting out the extent of the information which could be revealed to the customer.

10.70 Post *POCA 2002*, there have been several breach of contract claims brought by customers who have suffered an alleged loss as a result of a bank restricting access to their funds due to a suspicion of money laundering. The courts have given a degree of protection by establishing that the 'relevant suspicion' need not be based on reasonable grounds but is a subjective suspicion[9]. Further, in *Iraj Parvizi v Barclays Bank plc* [2014] EWHC B2 (QB), Master Bragge confirmed that suspicion need not be reasoned or thought out provided it was 'a clear belief' held by the disclosing person.

10.71 However, the *Serious Crime Act 2015* should render the debate about proof of suspicion obsolete by *s 37*, which came into force on 1 June 2015. There is now a statutory exclusion of civil liability for an authorised disclosure of suspicions of money laundering. This is achieved through amending *s 338* of *POCA 2002* to include the following additional words:

> 'where an authorised disclosure is made in good faith, no civil liability arises in respect of the disclosure on the part of the person by or on whose behalf it is made.'

This should remove the emphasis of any prospective claim away from proof of suspicion; instead, the question becomes was the disclosure made in good faith?

FAILURE TO PREVENT THE FACILITATION OF TAX EVASION UNDER CFA 2017

10.72 The *CFA 2017* was introduced as part of the government's reform of the UK's anti-money laundering framework. It made a number of amendments to *Part 5* of *POCA 2002*. In addition to this, *Part 3* of *CFA 2017* established two new corporate criminal offences of failing to prevent facilitation of UK and foreign tax evasion.[10] While the first offence applies to all businesses, wherever located, in respect of the facilitation of UK tax evasion, the second offence applies to businesses with a UK connection in respect of the facilitation of non-UK tax evasion. The offences are strict liability and require the existence of three elements, as described in more detail below, there is a statutory defence where at the time of the offence the relevant body had reasonable prevention procedures in place to prevent tax evasion facilitation offences or where it is unreasonable to expect such procedures.

9 See *Shah v HSBC Private Bank (UK) Ltd* [2012] EWHC 1283.

10 *CFA 2017, Pt 3, ss 44–52.*

10.73 The UK Government's National Risk Assessment of Money Laundering and Terrorist Financing Risks identifies tax services as one of the main areas of risk for the ASP sector. The government, in particular, refers to the risk that tax advisers can be utilised to facilitate tax evasion and VAT fraud. *Part 3* of *CFA 2017* is aimed at ensuring that firms have reasonable preventative measures in place to mitigate this risk. The requirements of *Part 3* of *CFA 2017* overlap with anti-money laundering requirements given that the procedures of tax evasion constitute criminal property under *POCA 2002*.

10.74 Under *CFA 2017*, a body corporate or partnership will be guilty of an offence if:

(1) a tax evasion offence is committed by a taxpayer (the tax evader);

(2) the offence is criminally facilitated by a third party (the facilitator) who is associated with the body corporate or partnership; and

(3) the body corporate or partnership has failed to prevent that facilitation.

10.75 'Associated persons' for these purposes are employees, agents and other persons who perform services for or on behalf of the business, such as contractors, suppliers, agents and intermediaries. The associated person must have criminally facilitated the tax evasion, in its capacity as an associated person, providing services to the business. Effectively, body corporate or partnerships will be vicariously liable for the criminal acts of their employees and others who act for or represent them.

10.76 However, to be guilty of the corporate offence, the last limb requires that the corporation has failed to prevent the facilitation. This means that if a corporation had put in place reasonable measures to prevent the facilitation, or where it is unreasonable to expect such procedures, it can escape liability.

10.77 HMRC has published guidance on the types of processes and procedures that a business can put in place to limit the risk of its 'associated persons' criminally facilitating tax evasion.[11] Under this guidance, HMRC explains that there are six guiding principles when establishing reasonable measures to prevent the facilitation of tax evasion. These are:

- risk assessment;
- proportionality of risk-based prevention procedures;
- top level commitment;
- due diligence;
- communication, including training; and
- monitoring and review.

11 HMRC Guidance – Failing to prevent criminal facilitation of tax evasion – government guidance on the criminal offences, dated 16 September 2017, last updated on 18 May 2018.

10.78 As noted above, undertaking a thorough risk assessment is key to AML policies. Businesses are required to undertake a rigorous risk assessment to identify the risks of facilitation of tax evasion within the organisation and the potential gaps in the existing control environment and policies. Robust measures and procedures should be based on this risk assessment. In addition, support from the organisation's board and training its staff appropriately will be essential.

10.79 In addition, to the three stages (at **10.74**) above, the foreign offence will be made out if there is a UK nexus and dual criminality.

10.80 A UK nexus will be established if the relevant body is: (i) incorporated in the UK; (ii) carries on business in the UK; or (iii) where any of the conduct constituting the facilitation of the foreign tax evasion takes place in the UK.

10.81 Dual criminality means that there is an equivalent offence to the tax evasion and facilitation in the local law, so that the conduct is illegal under both local law and UK law.

TERRORISM

10.82 Relevant anti-terrorism legislation broadly falls into two categories: legislation which provides for the imposition of penalties on those engaged in terrorist financing and legislation which aims to combat terrorism by freezing terrorist assets. One key difference between terrorist financing and money laundering is that money laundering relates to the proceeds of crime, whereas a terrorist money laundering offence may be committed in relation to the funds that have a legitimate source.

10.83 The *Terrorism Act 2000* (*TACT 2000*) includes a number of provisions relating to money laundering and in particular, makes it an offence to enter into or become concerned in an arrangement which facilitates the retention or control of terrorist property by concealment, removal from the jurisdiction, transfer to nominees or in any other way.

10.84 In the same way as accountants and others within the 'regulated sector' are obliged to report knowledge and suspicions of money laundering under *POCA 2002* there are corresponding requirements imposed on those persons to report information about offences committed under *TACT 2000*.

10.85 *TACT 2000* makes it an offence to provide or receive, or invite another person to provide, money or other property, intending or having reasonable cause to suspect that it may be used for the purposes of terrorism (*s 15*). Other offences created by *TACT 2000* relate to the use and possession of terrorist property (*s 16*) or the entering into of arrangements as a result of which money or other property is made available to another person for the purposes of terrorism (*s 17*). These three offences include a mental element in contrast to the strict liability money laundering offence created by *TACT 2000,* *s 18* entering into an arrangement which facilitates the retention or control of terrorist property.

10.86 For the purposes of these provisions, 'property' is defined on the same wide basis as it is in *POCA 2002*. 'Terrorist property' is defined to mean:

- money or other property which is likely to be used for the purposes of terrorism (including any resources of a proscribed organisation);
- proceeds of the commission of acts of terrorism; and
- proceeds of acts carried out for the purpose of terrorism.

It includes property which is wholly or partly directly or indirectly terrorist property.

10.87 The circumstances in which accountants will be required to report information about offences committed under *TACT 2000* are set out in *s 21A* as follows:

- when they know or suspect or have reasonable grounds for knowing or suspecting, that one of a number of specified offences have been committed (or have been attempted to be committed) by another person; and
- the information on which the knowledge or suspicion is based comes to him or her in the course of 'a business in the regulated sector'.

10.88 The reporting obligation operates in the same way as that under *POCA 2002*, meaning that, for an employee of a regulated firm, the obligation to report a suspicion is discharged by informing the firm's Money Laundering Reporting Office (MLRO) by means of the firm's internal reporting procedures. If the MLRO believes that the internal report contains grounds for suspicion, the MLRO has an obligation to report to the NCA. The offence of failing to disclose by a person in the regulated sector is punishable by a fine, or imprisonment of up to five years.

10.89 *TACT 2000* is broadly similar to *POCA 2002* in applying a single criminality test for its offences, that is, that an offence will be committed if a person has reasonable grounds to suspect that another person has engaged in money laundering or terrorist financing conduct either in the UK or overseas. Equivalent defences to those under *POCA* 2002 exist, including the privilege exceptions for professional advisers.

TIPPING OFF, PREJUDICING AN INVESTIGATION AND SUPER-SARS

10.90 Both *POCA 2002* and *TACT 2000* contain strict rules regarding the disclosure of information to third parties once a suspicion of money laundering is held. This is to ensure those suspected of involvement in such activity are not given opportunity to escape or destroy evidence before an investigation is conducted. *Section 333A* of *POCA 2002* (and an equivalent offence relating to terrorist financing contained in *TACT 2000, s 21D*) sets out an offence of tipping off once a SAR has been made. An accountant, or any other person in the regulated sector, must not:

- disclose that a disclosure has been made of information obtained in the course of the practice either to a constable, the NCA, an officer of HMRC or a Nominated Officer where the disclosure is likely to prejudice any investigation which might be conducted following the initial disclosure; or
- disclose that an investigation into allegations that a money laundering offence (which came to light in the course of the accountancy practice) has been committed, is being contemplated or is being carried out and the disclosure is likely to prejudice that investigation.

10.91 The risk of committing a tipping-off offence has created a practical impediment to financial institutions sharing information in order to resolve concerns around transactions or clients. This position has been addressed through the introduction of so-called 'super-SARs', which provide a framework within which institutions can exchange information in circumstances that might otherwise result in a disclosure that could amount to a tipping-off offence.

10.92 *Sections 333B–333D* of *POCA 2002* (and the equivalent *ss 21E–21G* of *TACT 2000*) contain exemptions that permit disclosures to be made in certain circumstances – for example, between employees, officers and partners of the same undertaking, between credit institutions, between financial institutions and between professional legal advisers.

10.93 There are separate offences under *POCA, s 342* and *TACT 2000, s 39*, which relate to prejudicing an investigation and which apply to the non-regulated sector. An offence is committed if a person knows that an investigation is being conducted and makes a disclosure which is likely to prejudice that investigation. The investigation may be for the purposes of confiscation, civil recovery or money laundering. In addition, under *s 342* of *POCA 2002* it is an offence where a person falsifies, conceals, destroys or otherwise disposes of documents relevant to an investigation knowing or suspecting that an investigation is being, or about to be, conducted.

10.94 As pointed out above, a recent innovation has been the super-SAR. This was introduced by *CFA 2017* which introduced new *ss 339ZB–339ZG* into *POCA 2002*, and new *ss 21CA–21CF* into the *Terrorist Act 2000* (*TA 2000*). The purpose of such super-SARs is to allow businesses in the regulated sector to share information with each other on a voluntary basis in relation to: (i) a suspicion that a person is engaged in money laundering; (ii) a suspicion that a person is involved in the commission of a terrorist financing offence; or (iii) in relation to the identification of terrorist property or its movement or use. The accountancy profession cannot currently make a super-SAR as the new provisions are limited to regulated firms that provide investment services and banks. The new provisions in *POCA 2002* and *TA 2000* allow information sharing to be instigated either by a regulated sector entity or the NCA. This can be done where the disclosure of the information will or may assist in determining any matter in connection with a suspicion that a person is engaged in money laundering.

10.95 In practical terms, where a regulated sector firm suspects money laundering, the super-SAR process allows it to send a request for disclosure to another regulated sector firm. The firm seeking disclosure will also need to notify the NCA of the intention to share information and indicate which regulated sector entities will be involved in the information sharing process. Once there is agreement between the parties to share information, information is disclosed to the party making the request. The party making the disclosure must be satisfied that the requested information will assist in determining any matter relating to a suspicion that a person is engaged in money laundering.

CLIENT CONFIDENTIALITY

10.96 Provisions in both *POCA 2002* and *TACT 2000* override the fundamental professional principle that accountants owe a duty of confidentiality to their clients. *Sections 337(1)* and *338(4)* of *POCA 2002* make it clear that any disclosure made by a person in the regulated sector which satisfies the three reporting conditions discussed earlier will not breach any restriction on the disclosure of information and will be a 'protected disclosure'. Where a person makes a report where any one of the conditions are not met, for example, an accountant makes a report on the basis of information that has not come his way during the course of his business, the accountant could leave himself open to an action by the client. An equivalent protection is provided by *TACT 2000, s 21B*, provided the information on which the reporter's knowledge or suspicion was obtained in the course of a business in the regulated sector the report will be a 'protected disclosure'.

THE MONEY LAUNDERING REGULATIONS

Introduction to the Money Laundering Regulations

10.97 The *Money Laundering, Terrorist financing and Transfer of Funds (Information on the Payer) Regulations 2017* (*MLR 2017*), which came into force on 26 June 2017, give effect in the UK to the EU's Fourth Money Laundering Directive (as amended).

10.98 The *MLR 2017* impose five main duties or obligations on firms and importantly legally enshrine the concept of a 'risk-based approach'. *Regulation 18* requires firms subject to the *MLR 2017* to prepare a written risk assessment which identifies and assesses the risk of money laundering and terrorist financing to which the firm is subject. In carrying out this assessment, firms must have regard to risk factors relating to their customers, the countries and geographical areas that they operate in, their products and services, their transactions and delivery channels. They also need to have regard to information issued by supervisory activities and must take the UK risk assessment into consideration.

10.99 In the context of preparing a risk assessment and identifying risks arising from geographic exposures, tax advisers should, in particular, have regard to the international standing of jurisdictions with which their clients or transactions have a nexus. The role of UK Crown Dependencies and Overseas Territories has been under scrutiny for some time and efforts have been made to improve transparency standards in these jurisdictions. The UK National Risk Assessment acknowledges the 'significant economic benefits' generated by the close economic ties between the UK and its Crown Dependencies and Overseas Territories while also stating that they continue to feature prominently in UK money laundering investigations and reporting. The Panama Papers episode highlighted the use of certain of these jurisdictions where corporate vehicles and offshore structures were used to further the criminal evasion of taxes. Concerns around transparency have been addressed through commitments by the jurisdictions to introduce publicly accessible registers of beneficial ownership of companies. The EU operates a list of non-cooperative tax jurisdictions, currently comprising 12 jurisdictions including Panama, in relation to which the EU states that it has major transparency concerns. In addition to this the EU maintains a list of third countries with weak anti-money laundering and terrorist financing regimes, which overlaps in part with the list of non-cooperative tax jurisdictions.

10.100 The other main requirements under the *MLR 2017* are as follows:

- *Customer due diligence measures* – Firms are required to carry out customer due diligence measures on a risk-sensitive basis. These measures must involve the identification and verification of customers and beneficial owners. Firms must also obtain information regarding the purpose and intended nature of the business relationship with the customer.

- *Internal polices, controls and procedures* – Firms must develop and maintain adequate and appropriate policies, controls and procedures to mitigate money laundering risks. These should cover risk management practices, internal controls and monitoring.

- *Record keeping* – Firms must make and retain records of their customer due diligence measures and transactions carried out by the firm, as evidence that they have complied with their legal and regulatory obligations.

- *Suspicious transactions and reporting procedures* – Firms must ensure that suspicious transactions are identified and reported to the firm's Money Laundering Reporting Officer, who may report the incident to the

National Crime Agency, which performs the role of the UK's financial intelligence unit.

- *Education and training to employees* – Firms must ensure that employees are adequately trained to identify suspicious transactions and are aware of the firm's money laundering risks.

10.101 The *MLR 2017* require that the approval of senior management be obtained for the adoption of policies, controls and procedures. The role of senior management is therefore important both formally under the *MLR 2017* and in setting the 'tone from the top'. Each of these duties is considered further below.

Scope of the Regulations

10.102 The offences under *POCA 2002* apply to all persons. The *MLR 2017*, on the other hand, are limited in scope, applying to persons engaged in certain types of activities. The rationale for this is that the specified sectors carry a greater risk of facilitating money laundering. The *MLR 2017* apply to 'relevant persons' acting in the course of business carried on by them in the UK. The full list of 'relevant persons' is set out below. Only certain of these activities will be relevant for the ASP sector as is explained below:

(a) credit institutions (as defined in *reg 10(1)*);

(b) financial institutions, which includes money service businesses (as defined in *reg 10(2)*);

(c) auditors, insolvency practitioners, external accountants and tax advisers;

(d) independent legal professionals, when participating in financial or real property transactions concerning:

    (i) the buying and selling of real property or business entities;

    (ii) the managing of client money, securities or other assets;

    (iii) the opening or management of bank, savings or securities accounts;

    (iv) the organisation of contributions necessary for the creation, operation or management of companies; or

    (v) the creation, operation or management of trusts, companies and similar structures;

(e) trust or company service providers, being persons who provide the following services to others:

    (i) forming companies or other legal persons;

    (ii) acting or arranging for another person to act as a director/secretary of a company, a partner of a partnership, or a similar position for other legal persons;

(iii) providing a registered office, business address, correspondence or administrative address or other related services for a company, partnership or any other legal person or arrangement; or

(iv) acting, or arranging for another person to act, as:

(A) a trustee of an express trust or similar legal arrangement; or

(B) a nominee shareholder for a person other than a company whose securities are admitted to trading on a regulated market.

(f) estate agents and letting agents (as defined in *reg 13*);

(g) high value dealers being a firm or sole trader who by way of business trades in goods (including auctioneers), who accept cash payments, in respect of any transaction, of €10,000 or more (whether the transaction is executed in a single operation or in a series of operations that appear to be linked);

(h) casinos, being the holder of a casino operating licence;

(i) art market participants;

(j) cryptoasset exchange providers; and

(k) custodian wallet providers.

10.103 Firms in the ASP sector are most likely to fall within the definition of a 'relevant person' and therefore become subject to the requirements of the *MLR 2017* under (c) or (e) above. In relation to (c), that is 'auditors, insolvency practitioners, external accountants and tax advisers', *reg 11* of the *MLR 2017* provides as follows:

'(a) "auditor" means any firm or individual who is:

(i) a statutory auditor within the meaning of Part 42 of the Companies Act 2006 (statutory auditors), when carrying out statutory audit work within the meaning of section 1210 of that Act (meaning of statutory auditor); or

(ii) a local auditor within the meaning of section 4(1) of the Local Audit and Accountability Act 2014 (general requirements for audit), when carrying out an audit required by that Act.

(b) "insolvency practitioner" means any firm or individual who acts as an insolvency practitioner within the meaning of section 388 of the Insolvency Act 1986 or article 3 of the Insolvency (Northern Ireland) Order 1989 (meaning of "act as insolvency practitioner").

(c) "external accountant" means a firm or sole practitioner who by way of business provides accountancy services to other persons, when providing such services.

(d) "tax adviser" means a firm or sole practitioner who by way of business provides material aid, or assistance or advice, in connection with the tax affairs of other persons, whether provided directly or through a third party, when providing such services.'

10.104 The definition of 'tax adviser' has been expanded by the changes introduced pursuant to the Fifth Money Laundering Directive. The provision of material aid or assistance in connection with another person's tax affairs is now within scope. The definition has also been expanded to cover the provision of services directly or through a third party to address the concern that advisors were not applying anti-money laundering checks where customers were introduced by another firm and not directly.

10.105 *Regulation 11(c)* of the *MLR 2017* defines an 'external accountant' as someone who provides accountancy services to other persons by way of business. As the CCAB Guidance (discussed in more detail below) points out, there is no definition given for the term accountancy services. For the purposes of the CCAB Guidance, it includes any service which involves the recording, review, analysis, calculation or reporting of financial information, and which is provided under arrangements other than a contract of employment.

Customer due diligence

10.106 The *MLR 2017* require firms to carry out customer due diligence measures when they:

- establish a business relationship;
- carry out an occasional transaction that amounts to the transfer of funds within the meaning of Article 3(9) of the EU Funds Transfer Regulations exceeding €1,000 or more or (other than for high value dealers and casinos) for occasional transactions that amount to €15,000 or more where they appear to be linked;
- suspect money laundering or terrorist financing; or
- doubt the veracity or adequacy of documents, data or information previously obtained for the purposes of identification or verification (*reg 27*).

Additionally, firms must apply customer due diligence measures on a risk-sensitive basis at 'other appropriate times' (*reg 27(8)*).

10.107 The precise nature of the customer due diligence measures that firms must apply are outlined below. However, broadly, a firm must:

- identify the customer and verify the customer's identity on the basis of documents, data or information obtained from a reliable and independent source;

- identify, where there is a beneficial owner who is not the customer, the beneficial owner and take reasonable measures to verify the identity of the beneficial owner so that the firm is satisfied that it knows who the beneficial owner is, including, in the case of a legal person, trust or similar legal arrangement, taking measures to understand the ownership and control structure of the person, trust or arrangement; and
- obtain information on the purpose and intended nature of the business relationship (*MLR 2017, reg 28*).

Beneficial owner

10.108 Broadly, a 'beneficial owner' is a person that has a 25% or higher interest in the customer, or any other person on whose behalf a transaction or activity is carried out. *Regulations 5* and *6* set out the definition of a 'beneficial owner'. The definition appears capable of capturing significant clients of customers as well as owners or controllers of customers. However, as set out above, it is not necessarily clear whether indirect clients should properly be treated as customers or as beneficial owners by a firm. In any event, it is submitted that due diligence measures should be carried out on direct customers of the firm, the owners or controllers of the firm and known indirect customers of the firm.

Customer

10.109 While the *MLR 2017* provide a list of circumstances in which CDD must be carried out, the absence of certain definitions can cause potential problems. For instance, the term 'customer' is not defined in the *MLR 2017*. Guidance issued by the Consultative Committee of Accountancy Bodies on Compliance with the *MLR 2017* states that customer due diligence should normally be carried out before entering into a business relationship or undertaking an occasional transaction. A business relationship is defined by the *MLR 2017* as a business, commercial or professional relationship between a firm and a customer, which arises out of the firm's business and is expected by the firm when contact is established to have an element of duration (*reg 4*). An 'occasional transaction' is defined as any transaction that is not carried out as part of a business relationship (*reg 3(1)*).

10.110 However, these definitions, whilst helpful, do not appear to answer all the possible questions as to whom a firm must classify as its 'customers'. For instance, it is not explicitly clear (although, following a cautious approach, arguably it should be assumed) that the client of a customer should also be treated by a firm as its customer, and due diligence measures applied, or whether such a person would more accurately be characterised as a 'beneficial owner'.

10.111 As well as the requirement that customer due diligence measures be carried out at the outset of a business relationship or prior to carrying out an occasional transaction, the *MLR 2017* also require measures to be applied when there is doubt as to previous information supplied, or where there is reason to suspect money laundering or terrorist financing. Additionally, measures are to be applied on a 'risk-based basis' at 'other appropriate times' (*reg 27(8)*). The *MLR 2017* also require a firm to keep the information it holds on customers up to date. It is clear, therefore, that the obligation on firms to ensure that they know who their clients are is an on-going one. The frequency of applying due diligence measures over the course of the relationship can be determined in line with the firm's risk-based approach, the concept of which is a central approach taken under the *MLR 2017* and the Fourth Money Laundering Directive.

Simplified due diligence

10.112 *Regulation 37* of the *MLR 2017* provides that a simplified due diligence (SDD) procedure may be carried out in relation to a particular business relationship or transaction if the firm determines that the business relationship or transaction presents a low degree of risk of money laundering and terrorist financing.

10.113 SDD is not a derogation from the need to perform customer due diligence measures. The *MLR 2017* are clear that where applying SDD firms must continue to comply with customer due diligence requirements under *reg 28* but that firms can adjust the extent, timing or type of measures that the firm undertakes. Firms applying SDD are also required to carry out sufficient monitoring of any business relationship or transactions which are subject to those measures, to enable firms to detect unusual or suspicious transactions.

10.114 The criteria to which firms must have regard in determining whether to apply SDD are:

(a) the firm's risk assessment carried out under *reg 18(1)*;

(b) relevant information made available to the firm by regulators or other bodies under *regs 17(9)* and/or *reg 47*; and

(c) the following risk factors:

  (i) customer risk factors including whether the customer:

  - is a public administration, or a publicly owned enterprise;
  - is an individual resident in a geographical area of lower risk;
  - is a credit institution or a financial institution which is:

    (A) subject to the requirements in national legislation implementing the Fourth AML Directive as an obliged entity (within the meaning of that Directive), and

    (B) supervised for compliance with those requirements in accordance with section 2 of Chapter VI of the Fourth AML Directive;

- is a company whose securities are listed on a regulated market, and the location of the regulated market;

(ii) product, service, transaction or delivery channel risk factors including whether the product or service is:

- a life insurance policy for which the premium is low;
- an insurance policy for a pension scheme which does not provide for an early surrender option, and cannot be used as collateral;
- a pension, superannuation or similar scheme which satisfies the following conditions:

  (A) the scheme provides retirement benefits to employees;

  (B) contributions to the scheme are made by way of deductions from wages; and

  (C) the scheme rules do not permit the assignment of a member's interest under the scheme;

- a financial product or service that provides appropriately defined and limited services to certain types of customers to increase access for financial inclusion purposes in an EEA state;
- a product where the risks of money laundering and terrorist financing are managed by other factors such as purse limits or transparency of ownership;
- a child trust fund within the meaning given by the *Child Trust Funds Act 2004, s 1(2)*;
- a junior ISA within the meaning given by the *Individual Savings Account Regulations 1998, SI 1998/1870, reg 2B*;

(iii) geographical risk factors including where the customer is resident, established or registered or in which it operates is:

- an EEA state;
- a third country which has effective systems to counter money laundering and terrorist financing;
- a third country identified by credible sources as having a low level of corruption or other criminal activity, such as terrorism (within the meaning of of *TACT 2000, s 1*), money laundering, and the production and supply of illicit drugs;
- a third country which, on the basis of credible sources, such as evaluations, detailed assessment reports or published follow-up reports published by the FATF, the IMF, the

World Bank, the OECD or other international bodies or non-+governmental organisations:

(A) has requirements to counter money laundering and terrorist financing that are consistent with the revised Recommendations published by the FATF in February 2012 and updated in October 2016; and

(B) effectively implements those Recommendations.

Enhanced due diligence

10.115 In addition to carrying out customer due diligence measures, the *MLR 2017* also require firms to apply enhanced due diligence measures (EDD) to a number of situations:

- where there is a high risk of money laundering or terrorist financing;
- in any business relationship or transaction with a person established in a high-risk country;
- in relation to correspondent relationships with credit institutions or financial institutions;
- where it is determined that a customer is a politically exposed person (PEP), or a family member or known close associate of a PEP;
- in any case where a customer provides false or stolen identification documents or information, and the relevant person proposes to continue to deal with that customer;
- where a transaction is complex and unusually large or there is an unusual pattern of transactions, and the transaction or transactions have no apparent economic or legal purpose; or
- in any other case which by its nature can present a higher risk of money laundering or terrorist financing;
- where EDD is to be applied, the firm must perform the following additional measures:

  (i) examine the background and purpose of the transaction;

  (ii) increase the degree and nature of monitoring of the business relationship in which the transaction is made;

  (iii) seek additional independent, reliable sources to verify information provided or made available;

  (iv) take additional measures to understand better the background, ownership and financial situation of the customer, and other parties to the transaction;

(v) take further steps to be satisfied that the transaction is consistent with the purpose and intended nature of the business relationship; and

(vi) increase the monitoring of the business relationship, including greater scrutiny of transactions.

Policies, controls and procedures

10.116 Under *reg 19* of the *MLR 2017*, firms must establish and maintain policies, controls and procedures to mitigate and effectively manage the risks of money laundering and terrorist financing identified in the risk assessment. The policies, controls and procedure must specifically include:

- risk management practices;
- internal controls;
- customer due diligence;
- reliance and record keeping; and
- monitoring and management of compliance.

10.117 The policies, controls and procedures adopted by a firm must be regularly reviewed and be proportionate to the size and risk of the firm. They should also provide for specific scrutiny where a transaction is complex or unusually large, or there is an unusual pattern of transaction and no apparent economic or legal purpose.

10.118 In addition, the senior management must approve such policies, controls and procedures and one person of senior management should be appointed as the officer responsible for compliance with the *MLR 2017*.The relevant supervisory authority needs to be informed of the appointment within 14 days.

10.119 Firms must also establish an independent audit function which is to examine and evaluate the adequacy and effectiveness of policies, controls and procedures, make appropriate recommendations and monitor compliance with those recommendations and carry out screenings of relevant employees, testing their integrity, skills and knowledge.

Record keeping

10.120 The *MLR 2017* require firms to make and keep records relating to their customer due diligence measures, that is, customer identification and verification procedures, and transactions carried out by the firm, as evidence that they have complied with their legal and regulatory obligations. Such evidence may also be used in any investigations conducted by the law enforcement bodies. The general rule is that all records must be retained for the 'prescribed period' of five years from the date the file is closed.

Internal reporting procedures

10.121 The *MLR 2017* require firms to ensure that any suspicious transactions identified are reported internally by staff to the firm's MLRO who must then determine whether it gives rise to knowledge or suspicion of money laundering or reasonable grounds for such knowledge or suspicion. Where such knowledge or grounds of suspicion are considered to exist, the MLRO must report such suspicious activity to NCA.

Training

10.122 The *MLR 2017* require firms to take appropriate measures to ensure that:

(1) all employees are aware of the risks of money laundering and terrorist financing, the relevant legislation, and their obligations under that legislation;

(2) all employees are given regular training in how to recognise and deal with suspicious transactions, and other activities or situations, that may be related to money laundering or terrorist financing; and

(3) the firm maintains written records of the measures taken under (1) and (2) above.

Resourcing and the MLRO

10.123 The appropriate staffing and resourcing of a money-laundering function is an important part of a firm's policies, controls and procedures. All firms are required to appoint a Money Laundering Reporting Officer (MLRO). As the CCAB Anti-Money Laundering Guidance for the Accountancy Sector (CCAB Guidance) states, the role of the MLRO is not defined in legislation but has traditionally included responsibility for internal controls and risk management. The CCAB Guidance further states that the MLRO should have the seniority, authority, governance responsibility, time, capacity and resources to fulfil the MLRO's brief.

10.124 The CCAB Guidance goes on to state that MLRO should:

- have oversight of, and be involved in AML and CTF risk assessments;
- take reasonable steps to access any relevant information about the business;
- obtain and use national and international findings to inform their performance of their role;
- create and maintain the business's risk-based approach to preventing money laundering and terrorist financing;

- support and coordinate management's focus on money laundering and terrorist financing risks in each individual business area. This involves developing and implementing systems, controls, policies and procedures that are appropriate to each business area;
- take reasonable steps to ensure the creation and maintenance of AML and CTF documentation;
- develop Customer Due Diligence policies and procedures;
- ensure the creation of the systems and controls needed to enable staff to make internal SARs in compliance with *POCA 2002*;
- receive internal SARs and make external SARs to the NCA;
- take remedial action where controls are ineffective;
- draw attention to the areas in which systems and controls are effective and where improvements could be made;
- take reasonable steps to establish and maintain adequate arrangements for awareness and training;
- receive the findings of relevant audits and compliance reviews (both internal and external) and communicate these to the board (or equivalent managing body); and
- report to the board (or equivalent managing body) at least annually, providing an assessment of the operations and effectiveness of the business' AML systems and controls. This should take the form of a written report. These written reports should be supplemented with regular ad hoc meetings or comprehensive management information to keep senior management engaged with AML compliance and up to date with relevant national and international developments in AML, including new areas of risk and regulatory practice. The board (or equivalent managing body) should be able to demonstrate that it has given proper consideration to the reports and ad hoc briefings provided by the MLRO and then take appropriate action to remedy any AML deficiencies highlighted.

The role of the MLRO and the MLRO's interaction with senior management within an organisation's governance structure are important features of an AML compliance framework.

Failure to comply with MLR 2017

10.125 Failure to comply with the requirements of the *MLR 2017* is a criminal offence which is punishable with up to two years' imprisonment, a fine or both. This offence is committed irrespective of whether any money laundering has taken place. It is also important to understand that in practice, where an offence is committed by a body corporate or partnership, for example, an offence may also have been committed by a director of the company or partner of the partnership. This will be the case where an offence is committed by a body corporate with the consent or connivance of an officer of the body corporate or can be attributed to neglect on the part of the director.

10.126 Failure to comply with the requirements of the MLR 2017 may also give rise to civil penalties imposed by the relevant supervisory authorities. The supervisory authorities are discussed further below.

10.127 The MLR 2017 provide that, in determining whether a person has complied with its requirements, the court may take account of any relevant supervisory or regulatory guidance. For the accountancy sector, the Guidance issued by the CCAB has been approved by HM Treasury for the purposes of the *MLR 2017*.

Supervisory authorities

10.128 Supervision and monitoring of compliance with *MLR 2017* is undertaken by a number of bodies. In particular, the Regulations designate certain bodies, such as the FCA, HMRC and certain professional bodies as 'supervisory authorities' and impose requirements on these bodies to monitor the firms they supervise and, where necessary, to adopt measures to ensure compliance by those firms with the requirements of the *MLR 2017*.

10.129 For accountants, bookkeepers, tax advisers and other financial advisers, the main supervisory bodies are:

- Association of Accounting Technicians;
- Association of Chartered Certified Accountants;
- Association of International Accountants;
- Association of Taxation Technicians;
- Chartered Institute of Management Accountants;
- Chartered Institute of Taxation;
- HMRC;
- Insolvency Practitioners Association;
- Institute of Certified Bookkeepers;
- Institute of Chartered Accountants in Ireland;
- Institute of Chartered Accountants in Scotland;
- Institute of Chartered Accountants of England and Wales;
- Institute of Financial Accountants; and
- International Association of Bookkeepers.

10.130 These supervisory bodies are in turn supervised by the Office for Professional Body Anti-Money laundering Supervision (OPBAS), a regulator set up in 2018 pursuant to the Oversight of Professional Body Anti-Money Laundering and Counter Terrorist Financing Supervision Regulations 2017, SI 2017/1301. OPBAS is intended to strengthen the UK's anti-money laundering supervisory regime and to ensure that professional body supervisors provide consistently high standards of AML supervision. The OPBAS sits within the FCA and oversees the above-listed bodies which are listed in *Sch 1* to *MLR 2017*. If a professional body wishes to become an AML supervisor, it needs to apply to OPBAS which will consider whether it meets the standards set out in *MLR 2017*. If it does, OPBAS will make a recommendation to HMRC to amend *Sch 1* to *MLR 2017* to give the body the formal role. OPBAS does not supervise members of professional bodies such as individual firms.

GUIDANCE ISSUED BY SUPERVISORY BODIES

10.131 In addition to the legislative provisions set out above, *ss 330* and *331* of *POCA 2002* and the *MLR 2017* enable HM Treasury to approve guidance issued by supervisory or other relevant bodies in relation to compliance with AML and CTF legal requirements. Under *s 330(8)* of the Act, in determining whether an offence of failure to disclose suspicions of money laundering has been committed, the court must have regard to guidance issued by a supervisory or other relevant body that has been approved by HM Treasury. Under *regs 76(6)* and *86(2)* of the *MLR 2017*, a court will have regard to guidance approved by HM Treasury in determining whether to impose a civil or criminal penalty for breaches of the *MLR 2017*.

10.132 The section below considers, in particular, the guidance issued by the CCAB[12] and the Financial Reporting Council (FRC)[13]. Guidance issued by both the CCAB and FRC have been approved by HM Treasury for these purposes which means that UK courts must take account of its contents when deciding whether a business committed an offence under *MLR 2017* or under *POCA 2002, ss 330* and *331*.

Anti-money laundering guidance for the accountancy sector

10.133 The CCAB Guidance provides that businesses (principally, auditors, insolvency practitioners, external accountants and tax advisers) need to establish systems that create an internal environment or culture where employees are aware of their responsibilities under the UK anti-money laundering regime and

12 The CCAB is made up of the ICAEW, ACCA, CIPFA, ICAS, Chartered Accountants Ireland and The Chartered Institute of Public Finance and Accountancy. Its guidance, 'Anti-Money Laundering Guidance for the Accountancy Sector', was published in March 2018 (the 'CCAB Guidance').

13 International Standard on Auditing (UK) 250 (Revised November 2019), Appendix: Money Laundering, Terrorist Financing and Proceeds of Crime Legislation in the United Kingdom.

where they understand that they are expected to fulfil those responsibilities with appropriate diligence. It is important that businesses have controls in place before establishing a client relationship or accepting an engagement. In deciding what systems to install, a business will need to consider a range of factors, including but not limited to:

- the type, scale and complexity of its operations;
- the geographical spread of client operations (including local AML regimes);
- the extent to which operations are linked to other organisations;
- the number of different business types it is involved in;
- the types of services it offers;
- its client profiles;
- the manner in which it sells its services;
- the types of business transactions it becomes involved in or advises on; and
- the risks associated with each area of its business in terms of the risks of the business or its services being used for money laundering or terrorist operations, or the risks of its clients and their counterparties being involved in such operations[14].

10.134 The CCAB Guidance notes that businesses should consider the nature of their practice when deciding how to carry out their risk assessment in line with the MLR and whether it should be simple or sophisticated. Where the practice is simple and the firm has few service lines and most clients fall into similar categories, a simple approach may be most appropriate for most clients, with the focus being on those clients that are atypical[15].

10.135 Under normal circumstances, if a prospective or existing client refuses to provide CDD information, the work must not proceed and any existing relationship with the client must be terminated. The CCAB Guidance notes that verification procedures may be completed during the establishment of a business relationship if it is necessary not to interrupt the normal course of business and that in some circumstances it may be necessary to carry out CDD while commencing work because the situation is so urgent. Such exceptional circumstances include:

- some insolvency appointments;
- appointments that involve ascertaining the client's legal position or defending them in legal proceedings;

14 CABB Guidance, section 4.5.
15 CABB Guidance, section 4.5.

- response to an urgent cyber incident; or
- when it is critically important to preserve or extract data or other assets without delay.

The CCAB Guidance also recommends that the above categories (and any others which may be appropriate depending on the business) must be carefully considered by the MLRO to ensure that the reasons for any extension are appropriate.

10.136 When deciding who is an appropriate person to be appointed to the role of MLRO within an accountancy firm, the CCAB Guidance suggests that an appropriately experienced individual might include an accounting firm principal (or similar in other businesses) or another senior and skilled person with sufficient authority to enable decisions to be taken independently[16].

10.137 The CCAB Guidance also provides a list of some of the more common instances where a firm acting in the accountancy industry may itself require a consent:

- acting as an insolvency office holder where there is knowledge or suspicion either that the assets may in whole or in part represent criminal property, or where the insolvent entity may enter into or become concerned in an arrangement under *s 328* of *POCA 2002*;
- designing and implementing trust and company structures for clients, including acting as trustees or company officers, where there is knowledge or suspicion that these structures are being, or may be about to be, used to launder money;
- acting on behalf of the client in the negotiation and implementation of transactions where these involve an element of criminal property being either bought or sold by a client, for example, corporate acquisitions;
- handling money in client accounts which is suspected to be of criminal origin; and
- providing outsourced business processing for clients where money is suspected to be of criminal origin[17].

Anti-money laundering guidance for the tax practitioner

10.138 The CABB Guidance includes a Tax Appendix which contains supplementary guidance and should be consulted by tax practitioners as it offers an indication of the money laundering risk areas that a tax practitioner may encounter in practice.

16 CABB Guidance, section 7.1.
17 CABB Guidance, section 8.5.

10.139 The Tax Appendix states that tax compliance services (that is assisting in the completion and submission of tax returns) should not be treated as being covered by the *MLR 2017* together with their tax advisory services. The Tax Appendix provides that tax practitioners need to be alert to the risk of assisting or facilitating the laundering of proceeds of crime whether through the evasion of taxes or otherwise.

10.140 A client's actions in respect of his tax affairs will create the proceeds of crime where he refuses to correct errors for the past or on an ongoing basis or where he deliberately makes an under declaration in respect of profits, income or gain, or makes a deliberate overstatement in respect of expenses or losses. Similarly, a money-laundering risk emerges where, during the course of dealing with a client's tax affairs, a tax practitioner realises that the client is holding the proceeds of crime[18].

10.141 A tax practitioner should be alert to the risk of assisting or facilitating the laundering of proceeds of crime whether through the evasion of taxes or otherwise. This risk should be appreciated particularly where a client puts significant importance on maintaining the anonymity of beneficiaries or owners or in keeping confidential the structure of a complex plan, ostensibly intended to minimise legally a tax liability, as there is the possibility that the funds involved are derived from the proceeds of crime[19].

10.142 A tax practitioner is not expected to be an expert in criminal law but there is an expectation that he will appreciate the boundary between deliberate understatement or other tax evasion and cases of error or differences in the interpretation of tax law. There will be no question of criminality where the client has adopted in good faith, honestly and without misstatement a technical position with which HMRC disagrees. The Tax Appendix states that the main areas where offences might arise are:

- tax evasion, including making false returns (involving supporting documents), accounts or financial statements or deliberate failure to submit returns; and
- deliberate refusal to correct known errors.

Anti-money laundering guidance for auditors

10.143 The Appendix to the International Standard on Auditing (UK) 250 summarises the requirements for auditors under the UK's anti-money laundering (AML) regime and contains guidance on an auditor's responsibilities in respect of AML and terrorist financing. This guidance was previously contained in a stand-alone document issued by the Auditing Practices Board but was added as an appendix to the FRC's International Standard on Auditing (UK)

18 Supplementary Anti-Money Laundering Guidance for Tax Practitioners (July 2019), section 4.1.

19 Supplementary Anti-Money Laundering Guidance for Tax Practitioners, section 4.2.

250 following the *MLR 2017*. An auditor will be considered to be within the regulated sector when conducting the audit of UK private or public companies, building societies, friendly societies, Lloyd's syndicate aggregate accounts, insurance undertakings, limited liability partnerships, qualifying partnerships[20] and any other such bodies prescribed by Order of the Secretary of State[21].

10.144 Examples of situations that may give rise to money laundering offences which auditors may encounter during the course of an audit include:

- offences that indicate dishonest behaviour, such as overpayments not returned;
- *Companies Act* offences that are criminal offences, such as illegal dividend payments;
- offences that involve saved costs, such as environmental offences; and
- offences where the client is the victim, such as where the client has been the victim of shoplifting.

10.145 Where an audit client has obtained legal advice indicating that certain actions or circumstances do not give rise to criminal conduct and as such cannot give rise to criminal property, an auditor may rely on this advice provided that it has been obtained from a suitably qualified and independent lawyer who was made aware of all material circumstances known to the auditor and the auditor followed industry standards on evidence and using an expert[22].

10.146 Due to the nature of an auditor's role, where a report has been made to the audit firm's MLRO and they have initiated further review, the auditor will need to be made aware of the results of any enquiries as these may have an impact on the audit report or the auditor's decision to accept reappointment as an auditor[23].

10.147 An auditor may sometime be required to make an application to obtain consent to perform an act which could otherwise constitute a principal money laundering offence. This would be required, for instance, where an auditor suspects that an audit report is necessary to allow financial statements to be issued in connection with a transaction involving the proceeds of crime, or if the auditor was to sign off on an auditor's report on financial statements for a company that was a front for illegal activity. In such circumstances the auditor might be involved in an arrangement which facilitated the acquisition, retention, use or control of criminal property under *POCA 2002, s 328*. In these circumstances the auditor would generally also need to obtain appropriate

20 Defined in the *Partnerships (Accounts) Regulations 2008, SI 2008/569*.

21 The definition of carrying out audit work in the regulated sector is provided in the *Companies Act 2006, s 1210*.

22 Appendix to the International Standard on Auditing (UK) 250, section 33.

23 Appendix (above), section 35.

consent from the NCA via its MLRO, as soon as is practicable[24]. Reporting to the NCA does not relieve the auditor from other statutory duties to report[25].

10.148 Where an auditor suspects that money laundering has occurred, the auditor will need to apply the concept of materiality when considering whether any report they have provided on the financial statements of a company needs to be qualified or modified. In doing this they should consider whether the crime itself has a material effect on the financial statements, whether the consequences of the crime have a material effect on the financial statements or whether the outcome of any subsequent investigation by the police or other investigatory body may have a material effect on the financial statements[26]. In deciding which action to take where the auditor believes money laundering has had a material impact, the auditor should be cautious of how and when any qualifications or modifications are introduced so as not to alert the money launderer and risk tipping off[27].

10.149 An auditor may wish to resign where they believe money laundering or indeed any illegality has taken place, particularly where they believe that a normal relationship of trust cannot be maintained. In such circumstances they should be conscious of conflicts between the requirement under *s 519* of the *Companies Act* for the auditor to deposit a statement at a company's registered office of any circumstances which they believe need to be brought to the attention of members or creditors and tipping off[28].

10.150 In respect of other businesses that are regulated under the AML regime (eg credit institutions and estate agents), auditors should, when auditing their financial statements, review the steps and processes taken by the entity to comply with the MLR, assess their effectiveness and obtain management representations concerning compliance.

10.151 If an auditor considers that a regulated client's systems may be ineffective, they should consider whether there is a responsibility to report a 'matter of material significance' to the regulator in compliance with ISA (UK) 250, Section B 'The Auditor's Right and Duty to Report to Regulators in the Financial Sector'. They should also consider the possible impact of fines if non-compliance is proven[29].

10.152 In contrast, where an entity's business lies outside the scope of the regulated sector, its management is not required to implement the MLR. The auditor is unlikely to consider anti-money laundering laws to have a material effect on the financial statement of the entity for the purposes of ISA (UK) 250, Section A.

24 Above, section 45.
25 Above, section 48.
26 Above, section 50.
27 Above, section 52.
28 Above, section 53.
29 Above, section 29.

APPLICATION OF PRIVILEGE TO THE ACCOUNTANCY PROFESSION

10.153 In the UK, different levels of privilege apply to communications involving professional legal advisers and relevant professional advisers such as accountants, auditors and tax advisers, who are members of a relevant professional body. Where privilege applies, a professional body will not be obliged to disclose information which they would otherwise be obliged to report under *POCA*, the *MLR* or other AML or CTF legislation, unless this information has been communicated or given with a view to furthering a criminal purpose.

10.154 Communications between a lawyer, a client and either of them and a third party, such as an accountant, auditor or tax adviser, are covered by litigation privilege, so long as the communications are for the dominant purpose of litigation which is existing or reasonably in prospect.

10.155 Legal advice given by professionally qualified lawyers, which is not related to any ongoing or foreseeable litigation, is covered by legal advice privilege. There was for some time a degree of uncertainty as to whether this privilege applied to other professional advisers who provide advice, particularly legal advice. This point was tested in the Supreme Court in *R (Prudential plc and Another) v Special Commissioner of Income Tax and Another*[30]. Prudential argued that it was not required to disclose documents to HM Revenue and Customs, which included tax advice from its accountants in relation to a tax avoidance scheme, as legal advice privilege attached to that advice. The Supreme Court rejected this argument and ruled that legal advice privilege should only apply in connection with advice provided by professional legal advisers, on the grounds that a change to the rules would make uncertain a principle that is clearly understood from previous authorities and it was for Parliament to legislate to alter the status quo.

10.156 Some solace was provided for the accountancy profession in the form of two dissenting judgments, which emphasised that privilege should be connected with a client's right to consult a professional legal adviser rather than members of a professional body. The dissenting judges also noted that accountants offering tax advice execute essentially the same function as tax lawyers.

10.157 Professional bodies, most notably the Institute for Chartered Accountants of England and Wales (ICAEW) responded negatively to the decision and committed to lobbying Parliament for a change that would level the playing field for the accountancy profession. The ICAEW has confirmed this as a priority in view of the *Legal Services Act 2007*. This Act provides for the creation of multi-disciplinary practices, the existence of which may serve to exacerbate the imbalance in privilege.

---

30 [2013] UKSC 1. The High Court and Court of Appeal both rejected Prudential's argument and the Supreme Court rejected Prudential's appeal.

Chapter 11

DAC 6

STOP PRESS

The Law in this area has changed but full details on its practical implementation are not available at the time of writing. Accordingly, the authors have decided to leave the chapter in place in its original form but preface it with this Stop Press. What next?

1. As the UK has now left the Transition Period and ceased to be (or to be treated as) a Member State, changes have been made to the UK legislation introducing DAC 6 requirements into UK Law which need to comply with the UK/EU and other international agreements.

2. HMRC have said in a letter to professional bodies and other stakeholders ('the Letter'):

   > 'Reporting under DAC 6 will still be required for a limited time, but only for arrangements which meet hallmarks under category D, in line with the UK's obligations under the FTA [Free Trade Agreement].
   >
   > In the coming year, the UK will consult on and implement the OECD's MDR as soon as practicable, to replace DAC 6 and transition from European to international rules.'

   The Hallmarks under Category D are set out at **11.216** below.

3. The changes were made by the *International Tax Enforcement (Disclosable Arrangements) (Amendment) (No 2) (EU Exit) Regulations 2020, SI 2020/1649*. These were made on 29 December 2020 and laid before the House of Commons on 30 December 2020.

4. According to the Letter, 'The changes will come into effect from 31 December 2020'.

5. The Explanatory Memorandum to SI 2020/1649 says (inter alia):

> **'2. Purpose of the instrument**
>
> 2.1 This instrument amends the International Tax Enforcement (Disclosable Arrangements) Regulations 2020 (SI 2020/25) (Existing Regulations). The Existing Regulations transposed Council Directive (EU) 2018/822 (Directive), which applied to the United Kingdom while it was a member of the European Union (a member state) and during the transition period. The Existing Regulations imposed obligations on taxpayers and their advisers, referred to in the Existing Regulations as "intermediaries", to report details of certain cross-border arrangements to HMRC. The amendments made by this instrument ensure that the relevant parts of the rules remain operative after the end of the transition period, whether or not the Free Trade Agreement (FTA) between the United Kingdom and the European Union is ratified. The amendments also ensure that the legislation is aligned with that agreement by limiting reporting to arrangements which would be reportable under the model rules developed by the Organisation for Economic Cooperation and Development.'

6. The Regulation came into force on 31 December 2020. This is less than the usual 21 days but the government considered that this is not an issue as the Negative Procedure for Statutory Instruments applies.

7. The Trade and Cooperation Agreement ('the TCA') contains provisions on Anti-Terrorism and Beneficial Ownership (see, eg Part Three Title X Anti-Money Laundering and Counter Terrorist Financing).

8. The Letter states:

> 'The text of the [TCA], which is available here[1] states that "A Party shall not weaken or reduce the level of protection provided for in its legislation at the end of the transition period below the level provided for by the standards and rules which have been agreed in the OECD at the end of the transition period, in relation to (a) the exchange of information … concerning … potential cross-border tax planning arrangements". The reference to OECD rules on exchange of information on cross-border arrangements is a reference to the OECD's model Mandatory Disclosure Rules (MDR). Therefore, under the terms of the FTA, the UK must not

1 See https://assets.publishing.service.gov.uk/government/uploads/system/uploads/attachment_data/file/948119/EU-UK_Trade_and_Cooperation_Agreement_24.12.2020.pdf.

> reduce the level of protection in its legislation below the level of protection afforded by the OECD's MDR.'

9. The Letter also tells us:

> '[T]he Government has decided to legislate for changes to SI 2020/25, to restrict reporting only to those arrangements, which would be reportable under the OECD's MDR. This means that only those arrangements which meet hallmarks under Category D of DAC 6 will need to be reported in the UK after the end of the transition period.'

10. The legislation implementing DAC 6 in the UK will be repealed in 2021. It is understood that it is intended to implement the OECD's MDR as soon as practicable. It is intended to consult on draft legislation to introduce MDR in the usual way. *Section 84* of *Finance Act 2019* gave HM Treasury power to make regulations for disclosure of information about certain arrangements. This includes DAC 6 but will also permit the implementation of the Organisation for Economic Co-operation and Development's (OECD) new model mandatory disclosure rules if it is decided to implement these.
11. HMRC will be updating the reporting guidance at IEIM600000 et seq to reflect the changes to the legislation.
12. This chapter will remain relevant to the application of DAC 6 from an EU perspective. Many UK advisers need to be aware of DAC 6 because UK clients will often have cross-border corporate and partnership structures where DAC 6 will remain a reporting obligation in those other Member States (and the UK adviser needs to be aware of these issues).

SIGNPOSTS

- An intermediary for a cross-border transaction involving an EU Member State may have an obligation to report (see **11.52–11.57**).
- Exemptions may be available for intermediaries with evidence that the relevant information has already been reported by another intermediary or relevant taxpayer (see **11.102–11.108**).
- When a cross-border transaction is first reported a unique reference, number called an Arrangement Reference Number (ARN) will be assigned (see **11.170–11.174**).
- Process.

- The information reported to HMRC under DAC 6 will be shared by HMRC with the other EU Member States (see **11.175**).
- Current rules remain for the present for hallmark D. Specific hallmarks concerning automatic exchange of information and beneficial ownership (see **11.156** and **11.216**).

INTRODUCTION

General

11.1 This chapter is concerned with the reporting requirements in EU Directive 2018/822 (known as DAC 6)[2] which have been enacted into UK law and impose reporting obligations on Tax Professionals. It is a form of direct regulation since it effectively forces the disclosure of tax planning which bears hallmarks that are regarded by the fisc as unacceptable; but, as explained below, DAC 6 goes beyond the disclosure of what is regarded as aggressive forms of planning. It has similarities to Disclosure of Tax Avoidance Schemes (DOTAS) (see **Chapter 4**) and Anti Money Laundering (AML) reporting (see **Chapter 10**). It is of European origin. The position post the transition period is mentioned at **11.24**. Note that this must be read in the light of the Stop Press above.

11.2 DAC 6 required legislation to be enacted by EU Member States[3] obliging 'intermediaries'[4] and sometimes taxpayers, to report information concerning cross-border arrangements falling within certain hallmarks to the relevant fisc. It should be noted that DAC 6 only applies to cross-border arrangements[5].

11.3 DAC 6 is a wide-ranging reporting requirement similar, as noted above, to DOTAS with penalties for non-compliance. It is not limited to just UK tax and related matters and so has a wider coverage than DOTAS.

What is DAC 6?

11.4 DAC 6 is an amendment to Directive 2011/16/EU[6], the Directive for Administrative Cooperation (DAC).

2 Council Directive (EU) 2018/822 of 25 May 2018 amending Directive 2011/16/EU as regards mandatory automatic exchange of information in the field of taxation in relation to reportable cross-border arrangements: available at https://eur-lex.europa.eu/legal-content/EN/TXT/PDF/?uri=CELEX:32018L0822&from=EN.

3 The UK was a Member State at the time.

4 The meaning of 'intermediary' is discussed at **11.52** et seq.

5 On reporting, see www.gov.uk/guidance/report-a-cross-border-arrangement-to-hmrc.

6 Council Directive 2011/16/EU of 15 February 2011 on administrative cooperation in the field of taxation and repealing Directive 77/799/EEC.

11.5 DAC 6 is the fifth Directive amending the DAC and is, therefore, if one includes the original DAC with the five amending Directives, the sixth DAC Directive matter. Hence, it is often referred to as DAC 6. This 'label' is used in this chapter for the convenience of the reader.

11.6 DAC 6 is, in one sense, an extension of the OECD's BEPS[7] Project, Action 12[8], on the disclosure of aggressive tax planning. However, DAC 6 is not limited to aggressive tax planning. It also applies to arrangements that would not generally be thought of as aggressive tax planning. The reporting requirements may be wider than just tax and can cover non-tax reporting other than for tax avoidance (see **11.156** et seq and the group of Hallmarks under Heading D. Specific hallmarks concerning automatic exchange of information and beneficial ownership).

11.7 DAC 6 came into force on 25 June 2018 as a matter of EU Law. The changes from 31 December 2020 affect the position in the UK as indicated in the Stop Press above.

Timing

11.8 Member States[9] had to enact implementing legislation for DAC 6 by 31 December 2019[10], for the provisions to apply from 1 July 2020. However, because of the coronavirus pandemic the reporting timing has been extended[11].

11.9 DAC 6 covers arrangements the first step of which was implemented after 25 June 2018[12], even though the obligation to report was originally not to apply until 1 July 2020.

11.10 Under the new EU deadlines, taxpayers need to report arrangements, the first step of which is implemented between 25 June 2018 and 30 June 2020, between 1 July 2020 and 30 November 2020 (extended from 31 August 2020). For arrangements, the first step of which is implemented between 1 July 2020 and 30 September 2020, the 30-day reporting period does not begin until 1 October 2020. (There is power to extend these deadlines for a further three months if the pandemic persists.) The position has been changed as indicated in the Stop Press above.

7 Base Erosion and Profit Shifting (see www.oecd.org/tax/beps).

8 Action 12 Mandatory Disclosure Rules (see www.oecd.org/tax/beps/beps-actions/action12).

9 Including the UK during the Transition Period.

10 The UK was late, the final regulations were laid on 13 January 2020.

11 See https://ec.europa.eu/taxation_customs/news/taxation-commission-proposes-postponement-taxation-rules-due-coronavirus-crisis_en.

12 This is the correct date.

11.11 HMRC have published guidance[13] broadly to the effect that taxpayers or intermediaries who make a DAC 6 report late, because of coronavirus difficulties arising, can have a reasonable excuse (and so will not be liable to penalties) provided the report is made without unreasonable delay after those difficulties are resolved[14].

UK IMPLEMENTATION OF DAC 6

11.12 Under the terms of the Withdrawal Agreement[15], the UK is obliged to abide by EU law until the end of the transition or implementation period[16]. This includes implementing DAC 6. The position has changed since the end of the transitional period and the Cooperation and Trade Agreement (CTA) as indicated in the Stop Press above.

11.13 Although the UK has reporting rules under DOTAS etc, DAC 6 is wider ranging. DOTAS is limited to arrangements that have an impact on UK tax, but DAC 6 is not. The rules are similar but not the same. Reports may well be due under both DAC 6 and DOTAS. Other reports may be due under the Common Reporting Standard (CRS) and Foreign Account Tax Compliance Act (FATCA).

11.14 No tax avoidance is required in some circumstances for DAC 6 to apply – see **11.156** et seq below.

11.15 For the UK policy on DAC 6 and related matters, see the Policy Paper of January 2020 entitled 'A report on "International Tax Enforcement: Disclosable Arrangements"'[17].

11.16 *Section 84* of *Finance Act 2019* (*FA 2019*) gave HM Treasury power to make regulations for disclosure of information about certain arrangements. This includes DAC 6 but will also permit the implementation of the Organisation for Economic Co-operation and Development's (OECD) new model mandatory disclosure rules if it is decided to implement these.

11.17 *Section 84* is headed 'International tax enforcement: disclosable arrangements'. *Subsection (1)* provides:

> 'The Treasury may, for the purpose of securing compliance with an obligation of the government of the United Kingdom under an international

---

13 See www.icaew.com/insights/tax-news/2020/may-2020/covid19-updated-guidance-on-DAC 6-and-reasonable-excuse.

14 On reporting, see www.gov.uk/guidance/report-a-cross-border-arrangement-to-hmrc.

15 See https://ec.europa.eu/info/european-union-and-united-kingdom-forging-new-partnership/eu-uk-withdrawal-agreement_en.

16 31 December 2020.

17 A report on how the power in *Finance Act 2019*, which enables regulations to implement Council Directive (EU) 2018/822, will be used in different EU Exit scenarios: at www.gov.uk/government/publications/international-tax-enforcement-disclosable-arrangements--2.

tax provision[18], make regulations requiring persons who participate[19] in arrangements[20] of a description specified in the regulations to disclose information about those arrangements.'

11.18 The regulations[21] (to be made by Statutory Instrument[22]) may specify the form and manner in which, and times at which, information is to be disclosed and require the information to be disclosed whether or not it relates to arrangements participated in before or after coming into the force of *section 84*. The regulations can also make provision as to penalties.

11.19 The regulations are subject to the negative resolution procedure unless they amend an Act etc, when they are subject to the affirmative resolution procedure[23].

11.20 No regulations may be made unless the Chancellor has laid a report before the Commons as to how the powers are to be exercised in the scenarios in *subsection (9)* concerning BREXIT.

'(8) No regulations may be made under this section unless the Chancellor of the Exchequer has laid before the House of Commons a report on how the powers in this section are to be exercised in each of the scenarios in subsection (9).

(9) The scenarios to be considered in the report under subsection (8) are—

(a) if either—

---

18 By *subsection (3)*: 'For the purposes of subsections (1) and (2)—
"international tax provision" means any provision of—
(a) any arrangements specified in an Order in Council made under section 173 of FA 2006 (international tax enforcement arrangements), or
(b) Council Directive 2011/16/EU of 15 February 2011 on administrative cooperation in the field of taxation and repealing Directive 77/799/EEC, as amended from time to time.'

19 By *subsection (3)*: '"participate", in relation to arrangements, includes being involved in, or facilitating, the arrangements in any way (for example, by receiving any benefit from them or by designing, marketing or providing services in connection with them, or arranging for others to do so)'.

20 By *subsection (3)*: '"arrangements" includes any scheme, transaction or series of transactions'.

21 '(2) Regulations under this section may—
(a) require information to be disclosed in such form and manner, and at such intervals, as may be specified in the regulations;
(b) require persons to disclose information about arrangements that they participated in before (as well as after) the coming into force of this section;
(c) provide for the imposition of penalties in respect of a contravention of, or non-compliance with, a requirement of the regulations, including provision about appeals in relation to the imposition of a penalty;
(d) make different provision for different purposes.'

22 *FA 2019, s 84(5)*: 'Regulations under this section are to be made by statutory instrument'.

23 *FA 2019, s 84(6)*: 'A statutory instrument containing regulations under this section which amend or repeal an enactment contained in an Act may not be made unless a draft of the instrument has been laid before, and approved by resolution of, the House of Commons'. *Subsection (7)*: 'A statutory instrument containing any other regulations under this section is subject to annulment in pursuance of a resolution of the House of Commons'.

(i) a negotiated withdrawal agreement, or

(ii) a framework for the future relationship with the European Union,

has not been ratified under section 13 of the European Union (Withdrawal) Act 2018 at the time of the United Kingdom ceasing to be a member of the European Union, and

(b) if both—

(i) a negotiated withdrawal agreement, and

(ii) a framework for the future relationship with the European Union,

have been ratified under section 13 of the European Union (Withdrawal) Act 2018 at the time of the United Kingdom ceasing to be a member of the European Union.'

11.21 The UK therefore needed regulations to be made to give practical effect to DAC 6.

11.22 *The International Tax Enforcement (Disclosable Arrangements) Regulations 2020, SI 2020/25* ('the Regulations'), were laid before Parliament on 13 January 2020, to take effect from 1 July 2020. These Regulations were published in draft on 22 July 2019, together with a consultation document. Some of the concerns raised by stakeholders in the consultation were addressed in the final *Regulations*. These have been changed as indicated in the Stop Press above.

11.23 Some guidance on reporting can be found at www.gov.uk/guidance/report-a-cross-border-arrangement-to-hmrc.

11.24 The government's report on International Tax Enforcement: Disclosable Arrangements (see **11.14**) included the statement that following the end of the transition period the government may amend, revoke or repeal the regulations. What change this would lead to can only be speculated upon. However, as the UK was prominent in the development of DAC 6, and will likely need higher government revenues, it is difficult to envisage the UK abandoning an approach which allows the identification of, and challenge to, offshore arrangements and the deterrence of aggressive tax avoidance. However, for the current UK government approach, see the Stop Press above.

WHO HAS TO MAKE A REPORT?

11.25 DAC 6 provides that the obligation to make a report falls on intermediaries, and in some cases on relevant taxpayers.

11.26 The meaning of 'intermediary' is discussed at **11.56** et seq.

11.27 The meaning of 'relevant taxpayer' is discussed at **11.57.**

Example 11.1

Dave, who operates in the UK and Ireland sells tax schemes involving BVI trusts and companies intended to confer a tax advantage to people in the UK and EU. Dave takes confidentiality undertakings and a tax related success fee when selling the schemes.

Dave has an obligation to report.

WHAT AND WHO IS COVERED? – GENERAL

Legislation

11.28 The Regulations have effect in relation to:

'(a) a *reportable cross-border arrangement* which is, or continues to be, made *available for implementation* or ready for implementation *on or after 1st July 2020*,

(b) a *reportable cross-border arrangement* in respect of which, *on or after 1st July 2020*, an *intermediary* within the second paragraph of Article 3(21) of the DAC *provided*, directly or by means of other persons, aid, assistance or advice with respect to designing, marketing, organising, making available for implementation or managing the implementation of the reportable cross-border arrangement, and

(c) a *reportable cross-border arrangement the first step in the implementation* of which was *made on or after 25th June 2018*[24].' [Emphasis added]

Regulation 3 concerns the reporting obligations of a UK intermediary.

Regulation 4 concerns the reporting obligations of a UK relevant taxpayer.

Regulation 5 imposes an annual reporting requirement on UK relevant taxpayers.

Some of the questions raised

11.29 The provision set out above raises several questions including the following:

- What is a reportable cross-border arrangement?
- When is the arrangement available?
- Who is an intermediary?

24 *Regulation 1(2).*

- Who is a relevant taxpayer? 'Relevant taxpayer' has the meaning given by Article 3(22) of the DAC.

These questions will be considered next, but this must be read with the discussion of the Regulations at **11.66** et seq below.

WHAT IS A REPORTABLE CROSS-BORDER ARRANGEMENT?

General

11.30 This term is defined in DAC 6 and that meaning is imported into the UK Regulations. This form of drafting tends to ensure compliance with EU requirements but does not always make for easy reading.

11.31 *Regulation 2(1)* tells us '"reportable cross-border arrangement" has the meaning given by Article 3(19) of the DAC'. This reads[25]:

> '19. "reportable cross-border arrangement" means any cross-border arrangement that contains at least one of the hallmarks set out in Annex IV.'

'Cross-border arrangement'

11.32 This raises the question as to what is meant by a 'cross-border arrangement'.

11.33 Paragraph 18 of Article 3 of the DAC makes provision about this. By *reg 2(1)* of the Regulations, 'cross-border arrangement' has the meaning given by Article 3(18) of the DAC.

11.34 This reads:

> '"cross-border arrangement" means *an arrangement* concerning *either more than one Member State or a Member State and a third country* where *at least one of the following conditions is met:*
>
> (a) not *all of the participants* in the arrangement are *resident* for tax purposes *in the same jurisdiction*;
>
> (b) one or more of the participants in the arrangement is *simultaneously resident* for tax purposes *in more than one jurisdiction*;
>
> (c) one or more of the participants in the arrangement carries on a *business in another jurisdiction through a permanent establishment* situated in that jurisdiction and the arrangement forms part or the whole *of the business* of that permanent establishment;

25 Council Directive 2018/822/EU and see https://ec.europa.eu/taxation_customs/sites/taxation/files/dac-6-council-directive-2018_en.pdf.

(d) one or more of the *participants in the arrangement carries on an activity in another jurisdiction* without being resident for tax purposes or creating a permanent establishment situated in that jurisdiction;

(e) such arrangement has a *possible impact on the automatic exchange of information or the identification of beneficial ownership.*

For the purposes of points 18 to 25 of this Article, Article 8ab and Annex IV, an arrangement shall also include a series of arrangements. An arrangement may comprise more than one step or part.' [Emphasis added]

What is an arrangement?

11.35 'Arrangement' is a word used in many contexts. It is often used in UK tax legislation[26] and often appears in Competition law in both the EU and UK.

11.36 The word 'arrangement' has been described as one of wide import[27]. In UK law it is not a 'word of art'[28].

11.37 The *Shorter Oxford Dictionary* defines 'arrangements' inter alia as 'a structural combination of things for a purpose et cetera … 6. disposition of measures for a particular purpose'.

11.38 An old case on a repealed statute can sometimes be helpful on this. The case is *British Basic Slag Ltd v Registrar of Restrictive Trading Agreements*[29]. This case considered the meaning of *section 6* of the *Restrictive Trade Practices Act 1956 which* referred to arrangements, but the Act *did not define what an 'arrangement' was*. The relevant issue was whether the judge was wrong to hold an arrangement existed when 'each [of the parties] has intentionally aroused in the other an expectation that he will act in a certain way'. It was argued that there must be mutuality in the acceptance of rights and obligations'.

11.39 The CA upheld the judge.

11.40 Willmer LJ said (at 739):

'I think it is highly significant that Parliament did not see fit to include any definition of "arrangement". I infer from this that it was intended that the word should be construed in its ordinary or popular sense. Though it may not be easy to put into words, everybody knows what is meant by an arrangement between two or more parties. If the arrangement is intended to be enforceable by legal proceedings, as in the case where it is made for good consideration, it may no doubt properly be described as an agreement. But the Act of 1956 clearly contemplates that there may be arrangements

26 For example, the settlement provisions.

27 See *Vinelott Butler v Wildin* [1989] STC 22.

28 See Lord Green MR (with whom Clawson and Goddard LJJ) agree in *IRC V Payne* (1940) 23 TC 610, at 626.

29 [1963] 1 WLR 727, [1963] 2 All ER 807, CA.

> which are not enforceable by legal proceedings, but which create only moral obligations or obligations binding in honour. This seems to me to be entirely consistent with the dictum of Upjohn J. to which I have already referred. Nor do I consider that there is any inconsistency between that, and the view expressed by the judge in the present case. For when each of two or more parties intentionally arouses in the others an expectation that he will act in a certain way, it seems to me that he incurs at least a moral obligation to do so. An arrangement as so defined is therefore something "whereby the parties to it accept mutual rights and obligations".'

11.41 Diplock LJ said (at 747) that there were many ways in which arrangements might be made. He continued:

> '... it is sufficient to constitute an arrangement between A and B, if (1) A makes a representation as to his future conduct with the expectation and intention that such conduct on his part will operate as an inducement to B to act in a particular way, (2) such representation is communicated to B, who has knowledge that A so expected and intended, and (3) such representation or A's conduct in fulfilment of it operates as an inducement, whether among other inducements or not, to B to act in that particular way.'

11.42 He also said (at 746):

> '"Arrangement" is not a term of art; under section 6(3) of the Act. I agree with my Lords that it bears the meaning that an ordinary educated man would ascribe to it. It involves a meeting of minds because under section 6(1) it has to be an arrangement "between two or more persons" and, since it must be an arrangement "under which restrictions are accepted by two or more parties", it involves mutuality and that each party, assuming he is a reasonable and conscientious man, would regard himself as being in some degree under a duty whether moral or legal to conduct himself in a particular way or not to conduct himself in a particular way as the case may be, at any rate so long as the other party or parties conducted themselves in the way contemplated by the arrangement.'

11.43 Accordingly, in the jargon, 'conscious parallelism' can be caught. Whether it can be proved in a tax context is a different matter, but it must always be remembered the onus of proof is on the taxpayer. Proving a negative is difficult but suitable documentation may help.

Series of Arrangements

11.44 The EU provision tells us that:

> 'For the purposes of points 18 to 25 of this Article, Article 8ab and Annex IV, an arrangement shall also include a series of arrangements. An arrangement may comprise more than one step or part.'

More than one Member State or a Member State and a third country

11.45 If everything is done in the UK, then there cannot be a cross-border arrangement as there cannot be 'an arrangement concerning either more than one Member State or a Member State and a third country'.

11.46 If there is an arrangement concerning the UK in the transitional period and the Channel Islands or the Isle of Man, there could be a cross-border arrangement as the Channel Island and the Isle of Man are not member states, but the UK is to be treated as one. After the end of the transition period, an arrangement between the UK and, say, Luxembourg[30] could be caught.

11.47 Some help can be found in the DOTAS Guidance at 6.2.1 Meaning of 'arrangements' (*FA 2004, s 318*) The meaning of 'arrangements' is not exhaustively defined in the primary legislation but includes any scheme, transaction or series of transactions.

Example 11.2

A number of transactions involving EU and other entities is proposed. intended to achieve a tax advantage. This would seem to constitute an arrangement as defined. If the arrangement were between the Channel Island, the BVI and the UK, after the transition period there would be no involvement of a Member State and, even if there were an arrangement, no obligation to report.

WHAT IS A CROSS-BORDER ARRANGEMENT?

11.48 An arrangement is a cross-border arrangement if it meets any of the following criteria:

- not all participants in the arrangement are tax resident in the same jurisdiction;
- a permanent establishment linked to any of the participants is established in a different jurisdiction and the arrangement forms part of the business of the permanent establishment;
- at least one of the participants in the arrangement carries on activities in another jurisdiction without being resident for tax purposes or creating a permanent establishment situated in that jurisdiction;
- at least one of the participants has dual residency for tax purposes;
- such an arrangement has a possible impact on the automatic exchange of information or the identification of beneficial ownership.

30 A Member State, see, for example, www.schengenvisainfo.com/eu-countries.

11.49 Cross-border tax planning arrangements may concern all taxpayers, including natural persons, legal persons (ie companies), and legal arrangements (ie trusts and foundations).

Examples 11.3

(1) Julian is UK resident in an arrangement that involves a BVI trust administered in Jersey by a Jersey licensed TSP. This would be a cross-border arrangement.

(2) Katherine's UK company establishes branches in Portugal and the Netherlands to take advantage of various tax breaks and treaty provisions. This would be a cross-border arrangement.

(3) A Puerto Rican export services company supplies services to the UK to take advantage of the tax breaks in Puerto Rico from Puerto Rico without a UK branch or agency or residence in the UK. This would be a cross-border arrangement.

(4) The Old Delaware Link was an arrangement whereby a US incorporated corporation was also UK resident under the centre of management and control test. It borrowed money at paid interest on the loan. At the time, the UK corporate tax rate was 52% and the US rate was 48%, deduction was claimed in both jurisdictions so that there was an effective 100% deduction. This was closed down by legislation in the UK etc. This would have been a cross-border arrangement.

(5) A series of Anstalts for the benefit of various discretionary trusts in the BVI, Cayman and St Kitts and Nevis as the beneficiaries with other Anstalts and discretionary trusts in Mauritius, Italy and the Seychelles as the beneficiaries with assets consisting of a series of companies with interlocking share rights which were discretionary are set up. This could have a possible impact on the automatic exchange of information or the identification of beneficial ownership. This would be a cross-border arrangement.

(6) Andrew sets up a series of UK trusts to own assets all of which had a UK situs. This would not be a cross-border arrangement as only one jurisdiction is involved.

Hallmarks set out in Annex IV

11.50 To be a 'reportable cross-border arrangement' not only does there need to be a cross-border arrangement, but that arrangement must contain at least one of the hallmarks set out in Annex IV. These are discussed at **11.216** below.

WHEN IS THE ARRANGEMENT AVAILABLE?

11.51 When an arrangement is available is, essentially, a matter of fact. A common-sense approach should be taken rather than a legalistic one to when an arrangement is available.

INTERMEDIARY, RELEVANT TAXPAYER AND WHO NEEDS TO REPORT?

11.52 The reporting obligation falls in the first place on the 'intermediary' and in some circumstances on 'the relevant taxpayer'. This raises the question of the meaning of 'intermediary' and 'the relevant taxpayer'. This is discussed below.

11.53 Under Council Directive 2018/822/EU, any person that designs, markets, organises or makes available for implementation or manages the implementation of a reportable cross-border arrangement is an intermediary.

11.54 An intermediary can be either an individual or a company (ie accountants, advisers, lawyers, banks, etc).

11.55 Intermediaries, who sell reportable cross-border tax arrangements to their clients, should report information on the arrangement to the tax authorities of their home Member State.

Example 11.4

Gio is based in Malta and sells cross-border arrangements throughout the EU that are within the Hallmarks. He needs to make his reports to the Maltese authorities.

11.56 An intermediary is also any person that provides, directly or by means of other persons, aid, assistance or advice with respect to designing, marketing, organising, making available for implementation or managing the implementation of a reportable cross-border arrangement.

Example 11.5

John is employed by TaxSchemesRUs to manage the implementation of tax schemes they have bought the right to sell in the EU from the designer.

TaxSchemesRUs and John could both fall within the definition of intermediary. However, *reg 13* of the Regulation may mean that John is not to be treated as an intermediary (see **11.63** et seq).

11.57 However, in the following situations, the obligation to report the arrangement shifts to the relevant taxpayer:

1. when an intermediary is a non-EU intermediary. An intermediary is considered non-EU when it is neither:
   - resident in a Member State; nor
   - maintains a permanent establishment in a Member State through which the services in:
     - respect of the arrangement are provided; nor
     - incorporated/governed by the laws of a Member State; nor
     - a member of a professional association in a Member State;
2. when there is no intermediary involved, ie an in-house arrangement;
3. when the taxpayer is notified that an intermediary has the right to a waiver due to legal professional privilege.

Examples 11.6

(1) Tax Avoidance Limited is a company incorporated in Panama from where it operates. It has no fixed place of business or agents in any EU Member State.

Tax Avoidance Limited is a non-EU intermediary. The reporting obligation then falls on others.

(2) The Rip Off group of companies decides to implement itself various transfer pricing arrangements involving EU member companies which it has designed itself such that there is no intermediary. It will usually have the reporting obligation.

MULTIPLE REPORTING

11.58 Where there is more than one Intermediary, the obligation to report lies with all intermediaries involved in the arrangement.

11.59 An Intermediary, however, is exempt from filing information to the extent that it has proof that this information has already been filed by another intermediary.

11.60 Where there is more than one relevant taxpayer, the Directive puts the primary obligation onto the relevant taxpayer who agreed the arrangement and then, on to the one who manages the implementation.

WHY ARE CROSS-BORDER TAX ARRANGEMENTS TO BE REPORTED?

11.61 The main aim of the Directive is to provide tax authorities with an early warning mechanism on new risks of tax avoidance and so allow them to deal with such matters more effectively. Before the DAC Directive, such cross-border arrangements did not need be reported under EU legislation.

WHO IS AN INTERMEDIARY?

11.62 It is necessary to know who an 'intermediary' is so it can be determined who has to make a report. This question is considered below.

11.63 The Regulation, *reg 2(1)* tells us 'intermediary', subject to *reg 13*, has the meaning given by Article 3(21) of the DAC. *Regulation 13* is an exception for employees (see **11.178** et seq).

11.64 Article 3(21) of the DAC states:

> '21. "intermediary" means any person that designs, markets, organises or makes available for implementation or manages the implementation of a reportable cross-border arrangement.
>
> It also means any person that, having regard to the relevant facts and circumstances and based on available information and the relevant expertise and understanding required to provide such services, knows or could be reasonably expected to know that they have undertaken to provide, directly or by means of other persons, aid, assistance or advice with respect to designing, marketing, organising, making available for implementation or managing the implementation of a reportable cross-border arrangement. Any person shall have the right to provide evidence that such person did not know and could not reasonably be expected to know that that person was involved in a reportable cross-border arrangement. For this purpose, that person may refer to all relevant facts and circumstances as well as available information and their relevant expertise and understanding.
>
> In order to be an intermediary, a person shall meet at least one of the following additional conditions:
>
> (a) be resident for tax purposes in a Member State;
>
> (b) have a permanent establishment in a Member State through which the services with respect to the arrangement are provided;
>
> (c) be incorporated in, or governed by the laws of, a Member State;
>
> (d) be registered with a professional association related to legal, taxation or consultancy services in a Member State.'

11.65 This is wide ranging and has been discussed at **11.53** et seq above.

THE REGULATIONS

Introductory

11.66 The government has exercised the powers under *FA 2019, s 84* through the *International Tax Enforcement (Disclosable Arrangements) Regulations 2020* (the 'Regulations') – see **11.22** above.

11.67 Many of the terms defined in DAC 6 have that meaning imported into the UK Regulations. This form of drafting tends to ensure compliance with EU requirements but does not always make for easy reading. Some of this has been discussed above.

Purpose of the Regulations?

11.68 The Explanatory Note to the Regulations says:

> 'These Regulations make provisions implementing Council Directive 2018/822 which amends Council Directive 2011/16/EU ("the DAC") on administrative cooperation in the field of taxation and repealing Directive 77/799/EEC and requires persons to report information in relation to certain types of arrangements known as reportable cross-border arrangements (defined in the DAC) to HMRC.'

Structure of the Regulations

11.69 The Regulations are divided into three parts[31]. These are:

---

31 The Explanatory Note reads: 'Part 1 contains introductory provisions. Regulation 1 provides for citation and commencement; authority for the limited retrospective effect is provided by section 84(2)(b) of the Finance Act 2019. Regulation 2 is an interpretation provision.

Part 2 sets out the reporting obligations and supplementary provisions. Regulation 3 concerns the reporting obligations of a UK intermediary, regulation 4 concerns the reporting obligations of a UK relevant taxpayer. "UK intermediary", "intermediary", "UK relevant taxpayer" and "relevant taxpayer" are defined in regulation 2 by reference to the DAC. Regulation 5 imposes an annual reporting requirement on UK relevant taxpayers. Regulation 6 specifies the information required to be reported in relation to a reportable cross-border arrangement. Regulation 7 disapplies the reporting obligation from intermediaries in relation to privileged information. Regulation 8 provides for an arrangement reference number. Regulation 9 makes provision for use of an electronic return system to make returns under these Regulations. Regulation 10 provides for the evidence to be given as proof of a return or filing of information. Regulation 11 permits an officer of Revenue and Customs to request information to determine whether the obligations under these Regulations have been satisfied. Regulation 12 contains provisions to be applied when applying the DAC in determining whether an arrangement is a reportable cross-border arrangement. Regulation 13 provides that employees are not subject to the reporting obligations.

Part 3 sets out the penalty provisions for breach of any obligation under the Regulations. Regulation 14 sets out the penalties. Regulations 15 and 17 provides for penalties to be determined by HMRC. Regulation 16 provides for penalties to be determined by the First-tier Tribunal. Regulation 18 sets out the time limits in which proceedings can be brought to determine a penalty by the First-tier Tribunal or a penalty determined by HMRC and

- Part 1 Introductory provisions (broadly citation and definitions);
- Part 2 Reporting obligations for intermediaries in relevant taxpayers and related matters;
- Part 3 Penalties for breach of obligations (to be determined by HMRC subject to appeal and 'reasonable excuse').

11.70 Some of the definitions have been discussed above to which discussion reference should be made as appropriate.

11.71 Some general matters are outlined in this section first before considering the detail.

These include:

- Reporting obligations.
- Reporting and the UK regulations.
- Who is an Intermediary?

REPORTING OBLIGATIONS

Introductory

11.72 The reporting obligations are dealt with in *Part 2* of the Regulations. They are considered in this below. For some of the definitions, see **11.30** et seq above.

Making a report in practice

11.73 Intermediaries and taxpayers, in essence, are to report reportable cross-border arrangement to the tax authority of the Member State in which they are resident. If they are not resident in the EU, there are further rules in DAC 6 to determine where they should make their report. For instance, if they have an EU permanent establishment that is connected with the arrangements or have other EU activities, they may have a reporting obligation.

11.74 A tax authority receiving a report under rules implementing DAC 6 must automatically exchange that information with tax authorities in other Member States, via the European Commission's central directory.

---

provides for the treatment of penalties as if tax charged in an assessment and due and payable. Regulation 19 provides for appeals against penalties determined by HMRC. Regulation 20 provides for cases where HMRC may reduce a penalty. Regulation 21 provides that no liability for a penalty arises where a person has a reasonable excuse for failing to comply with an obligation under the Regulations'.

WHEN MUST THE REPORT BE MADE?

11.75 The time within which the report must be made depends on the function and activity of the person in question and the type of arrangement.

11.76 Broadly, an intermediary must report within 30 days of the first of the following:

- the day after the arrangement is made available for implementation;
- the day after the arrangement is ready for implementation;
- the first step in implementing the arrangement is made.

11.77 If the intermediary meets the definition of an intermediary because they have provided aid, assistance or advice, they must report within 30 days of giving that aid, assistance or advice.

Example 11.7

Edwin makes a reportable cross-border arrangement available to implement on 15 June then Edwin must make a report within 30 days after the day after the date of availability (15th), ie 30 days from the 16th, ie 16 July.

11.78 If the reporting obligation relates to a marketable arrangement, meaning an arrangement that is designed, marketed, ready for implementation or made available for implementation without a need to be substantially customised, the intermediary must make an updated report every three months.

Example 11.8

Frances has a marketable scheme that merely requires names and addresses to be entered in the relevant forms, then there is a three-monthly update after the first report. If the first report is made as in Example 11.7 above, by 16 July, then the three-monthly update would need to be made before 16 October.

11.79 If the reporting obligation falls on the relevant taxpayer, they must make a report within 30 days of the first of the following:

- the day after the arrangement is made available for implementation to that taxpayer;
- the day after the arrangement is ready for implementation by that taxpayer;
- the first step in implementing the arrangement is made in relation to that taxpayer.

Example 11.9

Bryony buys a reportable cross-border arrangement from a non-EU intermediary and so is liable to report as the relevant taxpayer. The report is to be made by the earliest date of the following.

- If the arrangement was made available for implementation to Bryony on 1 March then Bryony must report with 30 days of the day after 1 March, ie 30 days from 2 March, ie 1 April.
- If the arrangement was ready for implementation by Bryony on 1 May then the report must be made by 30 days from 2 May, ie 1 June.
- If the first step in implementing the arrangement (eg signing the purchase contract which was the first step in the series) was made on 1 June then the report is to be made by 1 July.

11.80 Relevant taxpayers must file information about their use of the arrangement in each of the years for which they use it.

Reporting and the UK regulations

UK intermediaries and reporting

11.81 The first reporting obligation is on UK intermediaries and is imposed by *reg 3* of the Regulations.

The general rule in *reg 3(1)* is that:

> '... where a UK intermediary participates in a reportable cross-border arrangement, the UK intermediary must make a return within the specified period setting out the reportable information in relation to the reportable cross-border arrangement that is within the UK intermediary's knowledge, possession or control.'

This is subject to the exception in *subparagraph (2)* (report in other Member State or other intermediary has reported) and to the provisions in *reg 7* headed 'legal professional privilege'. These are discussed below at **11.109** et seq.

11.82 This raises the questions as to the meaning of:

- UK intermediary;
- return;
- specified period;
- reportable information;
- within the UK intermediary's knowledge, possession or control.

This has been discussed to some extent at **11.75** above.

What is a UK intermediary?

11.83 By *reg 2(1)* of the Regulations, 'UK intermediary' means an intermediary in relation to whom the UK is the Member State in any of paragraphs (a) to (d) of the list in Article 8ab(3) of the DAC. These read:

> '3. Where the intermediary is liable to file information on reportable cross-border arrangements with the competent authorities of more than one Member State, such information shall be filed only in the Member State that features first in the list below:
>
> (a) the Member State where the intermediary is resident for tax purposes;
>
> (b) the Member State where the intermediary has a permanent establishment through which the services with respect to the arrangement are provided;
>
> (c) the Member State which the intermediary is incorporated in or governed by the laws of;
>
> (d) the Member State where the intermediary is registered with a professional association related to legal, taxation or consultancy services.'

Examples 11.10

(1) Martin Ltd is a UK incorporated and resident intermediary. Accordingly, Martin Ltd is a UK intermediary as it falls with 3(a).

(2) Peter Ltd is a Channel Island company with an office in London through which reportable cross-border arrangements are sold. Peter Ltd is a UK Intermediary as it falls with 3(b).

(3) Richard Ltd is an Irish incorporated company whose centre of day-to-day business management, but not control, is in the UK but there is no UK permanent establishment. Richard Ltd is not a UK Intermediary under 3(c) as it is incorporated under, and governed by, Irish law.

(4) Susan Ltd is an Isle of Man company registered with the UK branch of the ACCA. Susan Ltd is a UK intermediary as it is registered with a professional association related to legal, taxation or consultancy services in the UK.

WHO IS AN INTERMEDIARY?

11.84 'An intermediary' is defined, very widely, as any person that designs, markets, organises or makes available for implementation or manages the implementation of a reportable cross-border arrangement. This would have caught some of the companies in the 1990s in the UK who developed and marketed tax strategies, eg Premier Strategies[32] now closed.

11.85 The definition is further extended to any person that knows, or could be reasonably expected to know, that they have undertaken to provide, directly or by means of other persons, aid, assistance or advice on designing, marketing, organising, making available for implementation or managing the implementation of a reportable cross-border arrangement.

Example 11.11

Steve sells membership of an international club that gives restaurant discounts but unknown to him, because he never asked or read the documents, tax breaks as well in EU countries. Steve could be reasonably expected to know he was marketing a reportable cross-border arrangement.

It is not unreasonable to expect him to have read the documents.

11.86 The definition also applies to tax advisers, accountants and lawyers, and could cover other types of professional adviser. Consequently, tax professionals must take DAC 6 very seriously. Failure to meet the requirements of the Regulations could lead to disciplinary proceedings as well as civil penalties.

11.87 A person is only an intermediary for these purposes if they:

- are resident in, incorporated in, or governed by the laws of, a Member State;
- have a permanent establishment (PE) in a Member State through which the relevant services are provided; or
- are registered with a professional association related to legal, taxation or consultancy services in a Member State.

See the discussion at **11.62** et seq and **11.84** above.

11.88 If there is more than one intermediary for an arrangement, the obligation to make a report falls on them all, unless they have proof that another intermediary has already made a report.

11.89 There is no obligation to report if to do so would breach national rules on legal professional privilege (LPP). In this case, the intermediary must notify another intermediary, or the relevant taxpayer, that they are obliged to make a report instead.

32 See www.thetimes.co.uk/article/tax-avoidance-no-longer-worth-the-risk-admits-tenon-nglwswtc9ts.

Return

11.90 'Return' is not specifically defined for these purposes. What information is to be reported is discussed below[33].

11.91 However, by virtue of *reg 9(1),* the return required under the Regulations must be made electronically to HMRC using an electronic return system:

> **'9 Electronic return system**
>
> (1) A return required under these Regulations must be made electronically to HMRC using an electronic return system.
>
> (2) The form and manner in which a return is made using an electronic return system is specified in specific or general directions given by the Commissioners for Her Majesty's Revenue and Customs.
>
> (3) A return which is made otherwise than in accordance with paragraphs (1) and (2) is treated as not having been made.
>
> (4) An electronic return system must incorporate an electronic validation process.
>
> (5) Unless the contrary is proved—
>
> (a) the use of an electronic return system is presumed to have resulted in the making of the return only if this has been successfully recorded as such by the relevant electronic validation process,
>
> (b) the time of making the return is presumed to be the time recorded as such by the relevant electronic validation process, and
>
> (c) the person delivering the return is presumed to be the person identified as such by any relevant feature of the electronic return system.'

11.92 By *reg 9(2)*, HMRC are to specify the form and manner in which a return is made using an electronic return system in specific or general directions[34].

Specified period

11.93 The return is to be made within the specified period. By *reg 3(3)* (as amended[35]):

33 See also www.gov.uk/guidance/report-a-cross-border-arrangement-to-hmrc.

34 See www.gov.uk/guidance/report-a-cross-border-arrangement-to-hmrc.

35 By the *International Tax Enforcement (Disclosable Arrangements) (Coronavirus) (Amendment) Regulations 2020, SI 2020/713.*

'The specified period is—

(a) in a case where the first step in the implementation of a reportable cross-border arrangement was made between 25 June 2018 and 1 July 2020, the period beginning on 1 January 2021 and ending on 28 February 2021,

(aa) in a case—

(i) where a reportable cross-border arrangement is made available for implementation, or is ready for implementation, or where the first step in its implementation has been made between 1 July 2020 and 31 December 2020, or

(ii) where a UK intermediary within the second paragraph of Article 3(21) of the DAC provided, directly or by means of other persons, aid, assistance or advice between 1 July 2020 and 31 December 2020,

the period beginning on 1 January 2021 and ending on 30 January 2021,

(b) in a case where the intermediary is notified of a reporting obligation in accordance with regulation 7, the period of 30 days beginning on the date that notification is received, and

(c) in any other case, a period of 30 days beginning on the earliest of—

(i) the day after the day the reportable cross-border arrangement is made available for implementation,

(ii) the day after the day the reportable cross-border arrangement is ready for implementation,

(iii) the day the first step in the implementation of the reportable cross-border arrangement is made, and

(iv) in relation to a UK intermediary within the second paragraph of Article 3(21) of the DAC, the day after the day the UK intermediary provided, directly or by means of other persons, aid, assistance or advice with respect to designing, marketing, organising, making available for implementation or managing the implementation of the reportable cross-border arrangement.

(4) If the reportable cross-border arrangement is a marketable arrangement, the UK intermediary must make a return at the end of every three month period beginning with the relevant date], setting out any new reportable information within Article 8ab(14)(a), (d), (g) or (h) of the DAC which has become available in respect of the reportable cross-border arrangement since that return or a previous return under this paragraph.

(5) In paragraph (4), "the relevant date" means the later of—

(a) 1 February 2021, and

(b) the date of the return under paragraph (1).'

11.94 Special provision was to be made in respect of the effect of COVID-19. This has to some extent become otiose because of the changes indicated in the Stop Press above.

Reportable information

11.95 By *reg 2(1)* of the Regulations 'reportable information' has the meaning given in *reg 6*.

11.96 *Regulation 6* is headed 'Reportable information'. It reads:

> '(1) The information required under regulation 3 or 4 to be reported in relation to a reportable cross-border arrangement is that set out in points (a) to (h) of Article 8ab (14) of the DAC.
>
> (2) In these Regulations, "reportable information", in relation to a reportable cross-border arrangement, means the information mentioned in paragraph (1).'

11.97 Article 8ab (14) of the DAC, so far as relevant, reads:

> '14. The information to be communicated by the competent authority of a Member State under paragraph 13 shall contain the following, as applicable:
>
> (a) the identification of intermediaries and relevant taxpayers, including their name, date and place of birth (in the case of an individual), residence for tax purposes, TIN and, where appropriate, the persons that are associated enterprises to the relevant taxpayer;
>
> (b) details of the hallmarks set out in Annex IV that make the cross-border arrangement reportable;
>
> (c) a summary of the content of the reportable cross-border arrangement, including a reference to the name by which it is commonly known, if any, and a description in abstract terms of the relevant business activities or arrangements, without leading to the disclosure of a commercial, industrial or professional secret or of a commercial process, or of information the disclosure of which would be contrary to public policy;
>
> (d) the date on which the first step in implementing the reportable cross-border arrangement has been made or will be made;
>
> (e) details of the national provisions that form the basis of the reportable cross-border arrangement;
>
> (f) the value of the reportable cross-border arrangement;

(g) the identification of the Member State of the relevant taxpayer(s) and any other Member States which are likely to be concerned by the reportable cross-border arrangement;

(h) the identification of any other person in a Member State likely to be affected by the reportable cross-border arrangement, indicating to which Member States such person is linked.'

11.98 DAC 6 does not itself specify the information that must be provided by intermediaries and taxpayers to the tax authority. Accordingly, this is a matter for the national implementing legislation. DAC 6 does, however, specify the information that the tax authorities should communicate to the central directory, and this must therefore provide the basis for the information that the authority will require from the intermediary or taxpayer. This seems to be the approach the UK has taken.

11.99 The information that must be communicated about a reportable cross-border arrangement is:

- identification details for the intermediaries and relevant taxpayers;
- the applicable hallmarks;
- a summary of the arrangement and the name by which it is commonly known, including 'a description in abstract terms of the relevant business activities or arrangements', without disclosing commercial, industrial or professional secrets or commercial processes, or information the disclosure of which would be contrary to public policy;
- the date of implementation of the first step of the arrangement;
- the national provision that forms the basis of the arrangement (this appears to be a reference to the tax rules that are potentially being avoided);
- the value of the arrangement;
- the Member States likely to be affected by the arrangement; and
- any other person in a Member State likely to be affected by the arrangement.

Under DAC 6, penalties for non-compliance with the reporting rules are to be established by the national implementing legislation which the UK has done in *Part 3* of the Regulations discussed at **11.183** et seq.

11.100 The information that reporting intermediaries need to provide to HMRC is aligned with the DAC 6 Directive, this includes the following information:

1. **Identification of intermediaries and relevant taxpayers**, including:

    (a) name;

    (b) date;

(c) place of birth (in the case of an individual);

(d) residence for tax purposes;

(e) TIN (Tax Identification Number);

(f) the persons that are associated enterprises to the relevant taxpayer (where appropriate).

2. **Details of the relevant hallmark(s)** that make the cross-border arrangement reportable.

3. **Summary of the content of the reportable cross-border arrangement**, including:

   (a) a reference to the name by which it is commonly known, if any;

   (b) description in abstract terms of the relevant business activities or arrangements (without disclosing commercial, industrial or professional secrets or information which would be contrary to public policy.

4. **Date** on which the first step in implementing the reportable cross-border arrangement has been made or will be made.

5. **Details of the national provisions** that form the basis of the reportable cross-border arrangement.

6. **Value** of the reportable cross-border arrangement.

7. **Identification of the Member State of the relevant taxpayer(s)** and any other Member States which are likely to be concerned by the reportable cross-border arrangement.

8. **Identification of any other person in a Member State likely to be affected by the reportable cross-border arrangement**, indicating to which Member States such person is linked.

Within the UK intermediary's knowledge, possession or control

11.101 This will essentially be a matter of fact. The issue will generally be related to possession or control. Possession usually involves control.

Civil Procedure Rules (CPR), Pt 31 sets out the rules about the disclosure and inspection of documents[36]. It would seem likely that the CPR approach would be used by a tribunal or court.

The Meaning of 'document' in this context is set out in CPR 31.4 which provides inter alia: '"document" means anything in which information of any description is recorded'.

36 See CPR 31.1(1).

The duty of disclosure limited to documents which are or have been in a party's control, CPR 31.8 provides:

(1) A party's duty to disclose documents is limited to documents which are or have been in his control.

(2) For this purpose, a party has or has had a document in his control if:

   (a) it is or was in his physical possession;

   (b) he has or has had a right to possession of it; or

   (c) he has or has had a right to inspect or take copies of it.

Exceptions to reporting

11.102 As noted above, *reg 3(1)* of the Regulations provides two exceptions: one for reports in other Member States and the other for legal professional privilege.

Report in another Member State?

11.103 This exception is set out in *reg 3(2)*, which provides:

> 'Paragraph (1) [the Reporting Obligation] does not apply to a UK intermediary ("I") in relation to a reportable cross-border arrangement if—
>
> (a) I is liable to file information in relation to the reportable cross-border arrangement with the competent authorities of another member State which when applying the list in Article 8ab(3) of the DAC features before, or in the same paragraph as, the United Kingdom, or
>
> (b) another intermediary who participates in the reportable cross-border arrangement has made a return setting out the reportable information required to be reported by I in relation to the reportable cross-border arrangement, and
>
> I has evidence that the reportable information required to be reported by I in relation to the reportable cross-border arrangement has been filed or returned.'

11.104 A UK intermediary (referred to in the legislation as 'I') does not have to report a cross-border arrangement if one or both of two sets of circumstances apply and I, the UK intermediary, has evidence that the filing abroad has taken place.

11.105 The first is where the UK intermediary, I, is to file with the fisc of another Member State where that state comes higher or equal with the UK when applying the list in Article 8ab (3) of the DAC.

11.106 The second is where another intermediary involved in the arrangement has made a report 'setting out the reportable information required to be reported by [the UK intermediary] in relation to the reportable cross-border arrangement'.

Examples 11.12

(1) Barry has a tax business which operates in Ireland and in the UK through a permanent establishment. Barry is resident in Ireland and the arrangement is for a hoped for Irish CAT advantage.

Barry's Irish residence is highest up the list in Article 8ab(3)(a). This is higher than the permanent establishment provision in Article 8ab(3)(b).

(2) Brian operates a tax business through a Cyprus company which provides a UK firm of accountants with ideas and arrangements for offshore planning and implementation. The accountants do enough that they could be UK intermediaries. Brian makes a report. The issue then is whether this report is one 'setting out the reportable information required to be reported by I [the UK intermediary] in relation to the reportable cross-border arrangement'.

Should the accountants ask for a copy the report Brian makes? It is considered it would be sensible to do so. Evidence of the report having been made is needed.

11.107 The question of evidence for this purpose is dealt with in *reg 10* of the Regulations. This reads:

> 'For the purposes of regulations 3(2) and 4(3), evidence that reportable information has been filed or returned must comprise the following—
>
> (a) the arrangement reference number or equivalent reference number issued by the competent authority of another member State, and
>
> (b) such other information which demonstrates to the satisfaction of an officer of Revenue and Customs that the intermediary or relevant taxpayer, as the case maybe, does not have knowledge, possession or control of any other reportable information in relation to the reportable cross-border arrangement.'

11.108 It puts a heavy burden as to evidence on I, the accountants in Example 11.12. It is for consideration as to whether a report in the UK should be filed at any rate? Possibly this is even more the case if the client objects.

'Legal professional privilege'

11.109 *Regulation 3(1)* of the Regulations is subject to *reg 7* (legal professional privilege). *Regulation 7(1)* provides 'Nothing in these Regulations requires a UK intermediary to disclose any privileged information'.

11.110 By virtue of *reg 7(3)*:

> 'In this regulation, "privileged information" means information with respect to which a claim to legal professional privilege, or, in Scotland, to confidentiality of communications, could be maintained in legal proceedings.'

Legal professional privilege is discussed in **Chapter 3**.

11.111 By *reg 7(2)*, subject to *para (1)*, a UK intermediary must notify any other intermediary, or, if none, the relevant taxpayer, as soon as reasonably practicable of the reporting obligations under *regs 3* or *4*, as the case may be, in relation to the reportable cross-border arrangement to which the privileged information relates.

Example 11.13

Solly, the solicitor who does not have to report by reason of LPP needs to inform Andy, the accountant also acting, of the reporting obligations 'as soon as reasonably practicable'. This gives some leeway on timing but there is much case law on this phrase and the particular circumstances could have a significant influence. It is clearly advisable to do this as quickly as possible. Could failure to do so give rise to disciplinary proceedings as well potential civil penalties[37]?

REPORTING OBLIGATIONS: UK RELEVANT TAXPAYERS

11.112 This is dealt with in *reg 4* (as amended) of the Regulations which provides:

> '4. (1) Subject to paragraph (3), where paragraph (2) applies, the UK relevant taxpayer must make a return within the specified period setting out the reportable information in relation to the reportable cross-border arrangement.
>
> (2) This paragraph applies where—
>
> (a) a UK relevant taxpayer participates in a reportable cross-border arrangement, and

37 *Regulation 14(2)(d).*

(b) no intermediary is required to file the reportable information in relation to the reportable cross-border arrangement under regulation 3 or with the competent authority of another member State.

(3) Paragraph (1) does not apply to a UK relevant taxpayer ("RT") in relation to a reportable cross-border arrangement if—

(a) RT is liable to file information in relation to the reportable cross-border arrangement with the competent authorities of another member State which when applying the list in Article 8ab (7) of the DAC features before the United Kingdom, or

(b) another relevant taxpayer—

(i) agreed the reportable cross-border arrangement with the intermediary, or

(ii) if there has been no such agreement, manages the implementation of the reportable cross-border arrangement, and

RT has evidence that the reportable information in relation to the reportable cross-border arrangement has been filed or returned.

(4) The specified period is—

(a) in a case where the first step in the implementation of a reportable cross-border arrangement was made between 25 June 2018 and 1 July 2020, the period beginning on 1 January 2021 and ending on 28 February 2021,

(aa) in a case where a reportable cross-border arrangement is made available for implementation, or is ready for implementation, or where the first step in its implementation has been made between 1 July 2020 and 31 December 2020, the period beginning on 1 January 2021 and ending on 30 January 2021,

(b) in a case where the relevant taxpayer is notified of a reporting obligation in accordance with regulation 7, the period of 30 days beginning on the date that notification is received, and

(c) in any other case, a period of 30 days beginning on the earliest of—

(i) the day after the day the reportable cross-border arrangement is made available for implementation to the relevant taxpayer,

(ii) the day after the day the reportable cross-border arrangement is ready for implementation by the relevant taxpayer, and

(iii) the day the first step in the implementation of the reportable cross-border arrangement is made in relation to the relevant taxpayer.'

11.113 *Regulation 10*, discussed above at **11.107**, deals with the question of evidence.

RELEVANT TAXPAYERS

11.114 If there is no intermediary, or LPP means that there is no intermediary that can make a report, the obligation to report falls instead on the relevant taxpayer.

11.115 The relevant taxpayer means any person:

- to whom a reportable cross-border arrangement is made available for implementation;
- who is ready to implement a reportable cross-border arrangement; or
- who has implemented the first step of such an arrangement.

11.116 See also the discussion at **11.57**.

WHAT TYPE OF ARRANGEMENTS ARE REPORTABLE?

General

11.117 DAC 6 applies to 'reportable cross-border arrangements'.

11.118 A cross-border arrangement means an arrangement concerning either more than one Member State, or a Member State and a third (non-EU) country, where at least one of the following conditions is met:

- not all the participants in the arrangement are tax resident in the same jurisdiction;
- a participant in the arrangement is tax resident in more than one jurisdiction (dual resident);
- a participant in the arrangement has a PE in another jurisdiction, and the arrangement forms part or the whole of the business of that PE;
- a participant in the arrangement carries on an activity in another jurisdiction without being tax resident or having a PE in that jurisdiction; or
- the arrangement has a possible impact on the automatic exchange of information or the identification of beneficial ownership.

11.119 A reportable cross-border arrangement is a cross-border arrangement that contains at least one of the hallmarks.

Hallmarks

11.120 The hallmarks are listed in an Annex to DAC 6 ('The Hallmarks'). The Annex is set out for the reader's convenience at **11.216** below.

11.121 The hallmarks are said to provide 'an indication of a potential risk of tax avoidance', However, there is no *mens rea* requirement of a tax avoidance motive or purpose.

11.122 The hallmarks have a very wide ambit. Potentially they catch a large number of transactions not normally thought to be tax avoidance.

11.123 For some of the hallmarks there is a 'main benefit test'. This is, broadly, that one of the main benefits which, having regard to all relevant facts and circumstances, a person may reasonably expect to derive from an arrangement is the obtaining of a tax advantage.

11.124 The Annex divides the hallmarks into 'generic' and 'specific' hallmarks.

Some, but not all, of these are subject to the 'main benefit test'. Accordingly, a tax advantage is not always needed for the reporting requirement to apply. This contrasts with the UK approach for DOTAS discussed in **Chapter 4**.

Part II of the Annex sets out the categories of hallmarks. These are as follows:

A. Generic hallmarks linked to the main benefit test:

   Broadly, arrangements that give rise to fees linked to the tax saving or involve mass-marketed schemes.

B. Specific hallmarks linked to the main benefit test:

   Broadly, this involves matters such as buying a loss-making company to exploit its losses in order to reduce tax liability or arrangements to convert income into capital to get a tax advantage.

C. Specific hallmarks related to cross-border transactions:

   This includes matters such as deductible cross-border payments between associated enterprises where the recipient is essentially subject to no tax, zero or almost zero tax.

   Some of these hallmarks are also subject to the main benefit test.

   Deductions for the same depreciation on an asset claimed in more than one jurisdiction.

   Some of these hallmarks (but not all) are subject to the main benefit test.

D. Specific hallmarks concerning automatic exchange of information and beneficial ownership:

   This Hallmark broadly applies to arrangements which have the effect of undermining the rules, or the absence thereof, on beneficial ownership or Directive 2014/107/EU or any other equivalent agreement on automatic exchange of financial account information.

E. Specific hallmarks concerning transfer pricing:

This hallmark applies to arrangements involving the use of unilateral safe harbours; the transfer of hard-to-value intangible assets when no reliable comparables exist and the projection of future cash flows or income are highly uncertain.

Accordingly, arrangements falling within hallmark categories A, B and certain parts of category C, are only reportable if they meet the 'Main Benefit' test, ie one of the main objectives of the arrangement is to obtain a tax advantage.

The main benefits test is considered at **11.161** et seq.

The hallmarks are discussed in detail at below.

HALLMARKS IN MORE DETAIL

Introduction

11.125 The hallmarks have been outlined above. They are now considered in detail in this section. Provision is made in *reg 12* of the Regulations for the 'Application of Annex IV of the DAC hallmarks':

> '**12**. In the application of Annex IV of the DAC for the purposes of these Regulations—
>
> (a) "tax advantage" has the meaning given in regulation 2(4);
>
> (b) in paragraph 4 of category C (specific hallmarks relating to transfer of assets in cross-border transactions), the amount treated as payable in consideration for the assets is the amount treated as payable for tax purposes in the jurisdictions involved;
>
> (c) category D (specific hallmarks concerning automatic exchange of information and beneficial ownership) must be interpreted in accordance with the Model Mandatory Disclosure Rules for CRS Avoidance Arrangements and Opaque Offshore Structures approved by the OECD on 8 March 2018 and its commentary published in OECD (2018), Model Mandatory Disclosure Rules for CRS Avoidance Arrangements and Opaque Offshore Structures, OECD, Paris;
>
> (d) category E (specific hallmarks concerning transfer pricing)—
>
> (i) does not apply to a cross-border arrangement if the relevant taxpayer and any associated enterprise in relation to the relevant taxpayer would be exempted from the basic transfer pricing rule by Chapter 3 of Part 4 to the Taxation (International and Other Provisions) Act 2010; and

(ii) must be interpreted in accordance with the Transfer Pricing Guidelines for Multinational Enterprises and Tax Administrations 2017 published by the OECD on 10 July 2017.'

A. Generic hallmarks linked to the main benefit test

11.126 For this group of hallmarks to apply:

- the main benefit test must be fulfilled; and
- one or more of three other conditions must be fulfilled.

The main benefit test is considered at **11.161** et seq.

Each of the three relevant conditions are considered next.

A.1 Condition of confidentiality

11.127 This part of the hallmark reads:

> 'An arrangement where the relevant taxpayer or a participant in the arrangement undertakes to comply with a condition of confidentiality which may require them not to disclose how the arrangement could secure a tax advantage vis-à-vis other intermediaries or the tax authorities.'

11.128 This is similar to the DOTAS provisions but apparently less wide.

'Undertakes to comply'

11.129 This undertaking does not on the wording need to be in writing. The undertaking could be oral or by conduct in theory.

11.130 Usually for practical reasons of enforcement it will be in writing. The person alleging a breach of confidence normally needs to prove that that is the case. A signed document is generally the easiest way to do that.

11.131 'Undertaking' is not defined in the legislation for these purposes. The *Shorter Oxford Dictionary* talks in its definition of a pledge or promise. The seems to be a word of potentially wide meaning in respect to which it would be hard to succeed on a technical close reading of the text.

11.132 A purposive or teleological interpretation would likely be taken by a court.

11.133 'Comply' is not defined specifically for these purposes. Its usual meaning would be along the lines of 'act in accordance with'.

'Condition of confidentiality'

11.134 This essentially means to keep confidential, ie not disclose to others.

11.135 This appears to be less wide than the DOTAS equivalent which 'may require them not to disclose how the arrangement could secure a tax advantage vis-à-vis other intermediaries or the tax authorities'.

11.136 This goes to what is to be kept confidential and is the information HMRC wants, ie how the arrangement purports to work.

A.2 Fee related to the tax advantage

11.137 This part of the hallmark reads:

> 'An arrangement where the intermediary is entitled to receive a fee (or interest, remuneration for finance costs and other charges) for the arrangement and that fee is fixed by reference to:
>
> (a) the amount of the tax advantage derived from the arrangement; or
>
> (b) whether or not a tax advantage is actually derived from the arrangement. This would include an obligation on the intermediary to partially or fully refund the fees where the intended tax advantage derived from the arrangement was not partially or fully achieved.'

11.138 The broad effect of this is that this part of the hallmark applies where the intermediary is entitled to a fee or other amount by reference to the amount of the tax advantage, or the fee is dependent on the tax advantage being obtained.

A.3 'substantially standardised documentation and/or structure'

11.139 This part of the hallmark reads:

> 'An arrangement that has substantially standardised documentation and/or structure and is available to more than one relevant taxpayer without a need to be substantially customised for implementation.'

11.140 This seems to be aimed at mass-marketed schemes but is potentially very wide. It seems to be aimed at arrangements where one just fills in and signs a standard form, but the wording seems to go wider.

11.141 This is similar to DOTAS. HMRC say in their Guidance on DOTAS at para 7.6.2:

> 'This hallmark only applies where there is a promoter of the arrangements (see paragraph 6.4) and, other than some exceptions, is intended to capture what are often referred to as "mass marketed schemes". The fundamental characteristic of such schemes is their ease of replication rather than the volume of take-up or how they are made available – the number of clients, or potential clients, can vary enormously, as can the way in which they are marketed.'

It would seem this is what this part of the Hallmark is aimed at.

B. Specific hallmarks linked to the main benefit test

11.142 As in category A, for this group of hallmarks in B to apply:

- the main benefit test must be fulfilled; and
- one or more of three other conditions fulfilled.

11.143 The main benefit test is considered at **11.161** et seq.

11.144 Each of the three relevant conditions are now considered.

This category of hallmarks seems to be aimed at classic means of tax avoidance by contriving steps to use losses, changing to capital where there is a lower tax rate and circular transactions.

B.1 'Contrived steps which consist in acquiring a loss-making company'

11.145 This part of the hallmark reads:

> 'An arrangement whereby a participant in the arrangement takes contrived steps which consist in acquiring a loss-making company, discontinuing the main activity of such company and using its losses in order to reduce its tax liability, including through a transfer of those losses to another jurisdiction or by the acceleration of the use of those losses.'

11.146 This provision seems aimed at the type of transactions in the *Corporation Tax Act 2010, s 673(2)* and *(4)*.

It is interesting to consider whether a profit-making company buying a loss-making company to use the losses would be caught here. On the wording it would seem not. Compare the *Corporation Tax Act 2010, s 730D*.

B.2 'Converting income into capital'

11.147 This part of the hallmark reads:

> 'An arrangement that has the effect of converting income into capital, gifts or other categories of revenue which are taxed at a lower level or exempt from tax.'

11.148 Tax rates on capital gains are often lower than on income. It can therefore be tax advantageous to have a capital gain or to fall within an exemption from capital gains taxation.

11.149 It may sometimes be difficult to determine whether the arrangement has the effect of converting income into capital. Would the sale of shares in a company which has retained profits have the effect of converting the income left in the company into capital? Technically, one would have thought not, but in some circumstances, it can have the same economic effect. Careful analysis will be needed.

B.3 'Circular transactions'

11.150 This part of the hallmark reads:

> 'An arrangement which includes circular transactions resulting in the round-tripping of funds, namely through involving interposed entities without other primary commercial function or transactions that offset or cancel each other or that have other similar features.'

An example of this might be the facts in the *Ramsey* case[38] which concerned a self-cancelling series of transactions intended to create artificial capital losses.

C. Specific hallmarks related to cross-border transactions

11.151

(1) An arrangement that involves deductible cross-border payments made between two or more associated enterprises where at least one of the following conditions occurs:

- (a) the recipient is not resident for tax purposes in any tax jurisdiction;
- (b) although the recipient is resident for tax purposes in a jurisdiction, that jurisdiction either:
  - (i) does not impose any corporate tax or imposes corporate tax at the rate of zero or almost zero;
  - (ii) is included in a list of third-country jurisdictions which have been assessed by Member States collectively or within the framework of the OECD as being non-cooperative;
- (c) the payment benefits from a full exemption from tax in the jurisdiction where the recipient is resident for tax purposes;
- (d) the payment benefits from a preferential tax regime in the jurisdiction where the recipient is resident for tax purposes.

(2) Deductions for the same depreciation on the asset are claimed in more than one jurisdiction.

(3) Relief from double taxation in respect of the same item of income or capital is claimed in more than one jurisdiction.

(4) There is an arrangement that includes transfers of assets and where there is a material difference in the amount being treated as payable in consideration for the assets in those jurisdictions involved.

38 *W T Ramsay Ltd v Inland Revenue Commissioners* [1982] AC 300.

11.152 This category of hallmark has the potential to catch transactions that are purely commercial, with no tax avoidance motive. Some have a main benefit test, and some do not, as set out below.

11.153 A cross-border arrangement is reportable if it involves deductible cross-border payments between associated enterprises and one of the following applies:

- the recipient is not tax resident in any jurisdiction;
- the recipient is tax resident in a jurisdiction with no corporation tax, or a corporation tax rate that is almost zero, and the main benefit test is met;
- the recipient is tax resident in a third (non-EU) jurisdiction that is assessed by Member States or the OECD as uncooperative;
- the payment is exempt from tax, or benefits from a preferential tax regime, in the recipient's home state, and the main benefit test is met.

There is a detailed definition of an associated enterprise that refers to ownership of 25% of the votes, capital or profits of another enterprise, or the ability to exercise significant influence over another enterprise.

11.154 A cross-border arrangement is also reportable if one of the following applies:

- deductions for the same depreciation on an asset are claimed in more than one jurisdiction;
- double tax relief for the same item of income or capital is claimed in more than one jurisdiction;
- the arrangement includes a transfer of assets and there is a material difference in the amount treated as consideration for the assets in the jurisdictions involved.

11.155 There is no main benefit test for these three types of arrangement.

Specific hallmarks concerning automatic exchange of information and beneficial ownership

11.156 A further category of reportable cross-border arrangements is designed to catch schemes that undermine, or exploit the absence of, international agreements on the automatic exchange of information on financial accounts. This applies to EU rules but also agreements with third countries, so covers both the DAC and the OECD's CRS.

11.157 For instance, cross-border arrangements would be reportable if they involve the use of an account that has similar features to those of the type of financial account that is subject to information exchange under the DAC or CRS, but that purports not to be such a financial account. The reclassification of income or capital into another product, or the conversion of a financial institution into a different type of financial institution, in a way that avoids the rules on automatic exchange of information, are further examples of arrangements that would be caught under this head.

11.158 Cross-border arrangements are also reportable if they involve a non-transparent legal or beneficial ownership chain and contain other features that circumvent the Fourth Money Laundering Directive 2015/849 (EU) (also known as DAC 5).

11.159 There is no main benefit test for these hallmarks, and although their primary focus is schemes that are intended to avoid reporting rules, there is no purpose test. They could, therefore, catch commercial arrangements that are not motivated by avoiding reporting requirements.

Specific hallmarks concerning transfer pricing

11.160 The final category of reportable cross-border arrangements, for which there is again no main benefit test, concerns transfer pricing and applies to arrangements involving:

- the use of unilateral safe harbour rules (for example, an exemption for small- and medium-sized enterprises);
- the transfer of hard-to-value intangibles;
- an intra-group cross-border transfer of functions, risks or assets, if as a result the transferor's profit-making capacity is reduced by more than 50%.

Main benefit test

11.161 All of the generic hallmarks, and some of the hallmarks only apply ('may only be taken into account') for these purposes of DAC 6 if they fulfil the main benefit test.

11.162 The main benefit test is satisfied if the main benefit or one of the main benefits which, having regard to all relevant facts and circumstances, a person may reasonably expect to derive from an arrangement is the obtaining of a tax advantage. In the context of hallmarks under paragraph 1 of category C, the presence of conditions set out in points (b)(i), (c) or (d) of paragraph 1 of category C cannot alone be a reason for concluding that an arrangement satisfies the main benefit test.

11.163 By *reg 2(1)* of the Regulations, 'tax' means any tax to which the DAC applies. This is not just UK tax.

11.164 *Regulation 2(4)* tells us what tax advantage includes. It provides:

'For the purposes of these Regulations, "tax advantage" includes—

(a) relief or increased relief from tax,

(b) repayment or increased repayment of tax,

(c) avoidance or reduction of a charge to tax or an assessment to tax,

(d) avoidance of a possible assessment to tax,

(e) deferral of a payment of tax or advancement of a repayment of tax, and

(f) avoidance of an obligation to deduct or account for tax,

where the obtaining of the tax advantage cannot reasonably be regarded as consistent with the principles on which the relevant provisions that are relevant to the cross-border arrangement are based and the policy objectives of those provisions.'

11.165 This is very similar, if not identical, to *section 208* of *FA 2013* – meaning of 'tax advantage' for the GAAR:

'A "tax advantage" includes—

(a) relief or increased relief from tax,

(b) repayment or increased repayment of tax,

(c) avoidance or reduction of a charge to tax or an assessment to tax,

(d) avoidance of a possible assessment to tax,

(e) deferral of a payment of tax or advancement of a repayment of tax, and

(f) avoidance of an obligation to deduct or account for tax.'

11.166 The GAAR Guidance is worth rereading on this bearing in mind here that tax is not limited to UK tax. Some of the relevant Guidance is set out below.

'C2 Tax advantage

C2.1 The expression 'tax advantage' is defined (in s208) to include any of the following:

- relief or increased relief from tax
- repayment or increased repayment of tax
- avoidance or a reduction of a charge to tax or an assessment to tax
- avoidance of a possible assessment to tax
- a deferral of a payment of tax or an advancement of a repayment of tax
- avoidance of an obligation to deduct or account for tax

C2.2 This definition of 'tax advantage' is inclusive (it is not necessarily exhaustive) and is intended to have a very wide meaning. It is intended to cover any form of tax benefit, for example:

- increasing deductions or losses
- decreasing income or gains
- obtaining timing advantages
- obtaining or increasing repayments of tax
- ensuring a potential tax charge does not arise (or is reduced)

C2.3 It is clear that 'tax' is limited to the taxes to which the GAAR applies.

C2.4 As well as being relevant to whether arrangements are tax arrangements (see paragraph C3 below) the concept of tax advantage also plays a part in counteraction. The GAAR provides that it is the tax advantages arising from abusive tax arrangements that are to be counteracted on a just and reasonable basis.

C2.5 The concept of a "tax advantage" is common in UK tax legislation. The language suggests that in deciding whether an advantage arises the actual tax position should be compared with another tax position.

The appropriate comparison or alternative tax position will depend on the facts but will usually derive from the arrangements that would have occurred without the abusive tax purpose (which may include no arrangement at all).

In situations where there is more than one alternative arrangement that might have been adopted if the taxpayer had not adopted an abusive arrangement, then the appropriate comparison would be the transaction that the taxpayer would most likely have carried out.

This might not be the arrangement that would give rise to the greatest tax liability.'

ANNUAL REPORTING REQUIREMENT

11.167 There is also an annual reporting requirement for a UK relevant taxpayer in the Regulations which applies in some circumstances.

11.168 This is found in *reg 5* which reads:

'(1) Where a UK relevant taxpayer participates in a reportable cross-border arrangement, the UK relevant taxpayer must make a return for—

(a) the tax year or accounting period, as the case may be, in which the first of the following occurs—

(i) the reportable cross-border arrangement is made available for implementation to the relevant taxpayer,

(ii) the reportable cross-border arrangement is ready for implementation by the UK relevant taxpayer, or

(iii) the first step in the implementation of the reportable cross-border arrangement is made in relation to the UK relevant taxpayer, and

(b) each subsequent tax year or accounting period, as the case may be, in which the UK relevant taxpayer's participation in the reportable cross-border arrangement has a tax advantage in relation to that UK relevant taxpayer.

(2) The return must set out—

(a) the arrangement reference number of the reportable cross-border arrangement, and

(b) the tax advantage of the reportable cross-border arrangement in relation to the UK relevant taxpayer for that tax year or accounting period.

(3) The return must be made—

(a) where the UK relevant taxpayer is a company, on or before the filing date for the company's tax return as set out in paragraph 14 of Schedule 18 to the Finance Act 1998 for the accounting period in which the first of the events in paragraph (1)(a) occurs or in which the reportable cross-border arrangement has a tax advantage in relation to that relevant taxpayer, or

(a) in any other case, on or before 31 January in the tax year following the tax year in which the first of the events in paragraph (1)(a) occurs or in which the reportable cross-border arrangement has a tax advantage in relation to that UK relevant taxpayer.'

11.169 This applies to a relevant taxpayer. The meaning of 'relevant taxpayer' is discussed at **11.115** et seq above.

ARRANGEMENT REFERENCE NUMBER

11.170 Where a person complies, or as the *Regulation* puts it, purports to comply with the reporting requirements in *regs 3(1)* or *4(1)*, HMRC is to allocate a reference number to the reportable cross-border arrangement.

11.171 This arrangement reference number (ARN) is to be notified to the person reporting.

11.172 The person receiving the arrangement reference number must within 30 days after 'the relevant date' notify the arrangement reference number to anyone who the UK intermediary or the UK relevant taxpayer knows, or should be reasonably expected to know, is an intermediary or relevant taxpayer in relation to that reportable cross-border arrangement.

11.173 'The relevant date', ie the date from after which the 30 days notification period runs, is the later of:

(a) the date on which the arrangement reference number was notified to the UK intermediary or UK relevant taxpayer; and

(b) the date on which the other intermediary or the other relevant taxpayer became an intermediary or relevant taxpayer in relation to that reportable cross-border arrangement.

Example 11.14

The ARN was notified to R E Porter on 1 June as the principal person required to report.

A N Other became the other person required to report on 1 October.

R E Porter must report by 1 July, ie 30 days of the date of notification of ARN (1 June).

A N Other must report by 31 October, ie 30 days of the date of becoming the other person required to report (1 October).

11.174 All of the above is dealt with in *reg 8* of the Regulations[39].

---

39 '**8.**—(1) Where a person complies, or purports to comply, with regulation 3(1) or 4(1) in relation to any reportable cross-border arrangement, HMRC must—

(a) allocate a reference number to the reportable cross-border arrangement, and

(b) notify that number to that person.

(2) A UK intermediary or UK relevant taxpayer who has been notified of an arrangement reference number must, within 30 days after the relevant date, notify that number to any person who the UK intermediary or UK relevant taxpayer knows or should reasonably be expected to know is an intermediary or relevant taxpayer in relation to that reportable cross-border arrangement.

(3) In paragraph (2), "the relevant date" means the later of—

(a) the date on which the arrangement reference number was notified to the UK intermediary or UK relevant taxpayer, and

(b) the date on which the other intermediary or the other relevant taxpayer became an intermediary or relevant taxpayer in relation to that reportable cross-border arrangement.

(4) In these Regulations, "arrangement reference number", in relation to a reportable cross-border arrangement, means the reference number allocated under paragraph (1).'

PROVISION OF INFORMATION – REG 11

11.175 HMRC are given power by notice to require a person reasonably suspected of being a UK intermediary or UK relevant taxpayer to provide such information or documents as is reasonably requires and as specified by written notice:

> '11.— (1) In order to determine whether or not the obligations arising under these Regulations have been complied with, an officer of Revenue and Customs may require a person who the officer reasonably suspects is a UK intermediary or UK relevant taxpayer to provide such information or documents as the officer reasonably requires as specified by written notice.
>
> (2) The information or documents required by notice under paragraph (1) must be provided—
>
> (a) within such period, being no less than 30 days, and
>
> (b) by such means and in such form,
>
> as is reasonably required by the officer of Revenue and Customs.'

11.176 Such information is to be provided by such means and in such form as HMRC reasonably require.

11.177 Penalty for breach is dealt with under *reg 11* as breach of a specified provision within *reg 14(2)(f)* – see **11.188**.

EMPLOYEES NOT INTERMEDIARIES – REG 13

11.178 Employees are excluded from being treated as an intermediary in relation to a reportable cross-border arrangement in certain circumstances[40].

11.179 These are where the person in question (referred to in the legislation as 'P'):

- is an employee of an employer ('E'); and
- E is an intermediary or relevant taxpayer in relation to the reportable cross-border arrangement.

---

40 '**13.**—(1) A person ("P") is not to be treated as an intermediary in relation to a reportable cross-border arrangement where—

(a) P is an employee of an employer ("E"), and

(b) E is an intermediary or relevant taxpayer in relation to the reportable cross-border arrangement.

(2) In this regulation, "employee" and "employer" have the meanings given by section 4 of the Income Tax (Earnings and Pensions) Act 2003 (as read with section 5(2) of that Act).

(3) For the purposes of this regulation, where E is connected to another person ("F"), P is to be treated as an employee of F as well as being an employee of E.

(4) In this regulation, E is connected with F where E is closely bound to F by financial, economic or organisational links.'

11.180 'Employees' for these purposes essentially has the meaning in the *Income Tax (Earnings and Pensions) Act 2003, s 4*).

11.181 Employees of an intermediary are not to be treated as an intermediary for the purposes of the Regulations.

11.182 This is also the case where the employer, E, is connected to another person by close financial, economic or organisational links.

PENALTIES AND THE REGULATIONS

Introductory

11.183 *Part 3* of the Regulations is headed 'Penalties for breach of obligations' and, unsurprisingly, this is what it deals with.

11.184 It is essentially a self-contained code unlike some other provisions that link to the general rules on penalties, eg residential property – see *FA 2019, Sch 2*.

General rule

11.185 The general provision about 'Penalties for failure to comply with Regulations' is found in *reg 14* of the Regulations.

11.186 By virtue of *reg 14(1)*:

> 'A person who fails to comply with any of the provisions of these Regulations specified in paragraph (2) is liable—
>
> (a) to a penalty not exceeding—
>
> (i) £5,000, or
>
> (ii) in the case of [certain specified provisions] if that amount appears to an officer of Revenue and Customs to be inappropriately low after taking into account all relevant considerations, £600 for each day during the initial period, and
>
> (c) if the failure continues after a penalty is imposed under sub-paragraph (a), to a further penalty or penalties not exceeding £600 for each day on which the failure continues after the day on which the penalty under sub-paragraph (a) was imposed (but excluding any day for which a penalty under this regulation has already been imposed).'

11.187 The above are civil penalties and they can soon rack up.

The specified provisions

11.188 The provisions specified in *reg 14(2)* are:

'(a) regulation 3(1) (UK intermediary's obligation to make a return of reportable information),

(b) regulation 3(4) (UK intermediary's obligation to make a return of new reportable information),

(c) regulation 4(1) (UK relevant taxpayer's obligation to make a return of reportable information),

(d) regulation 7(2) (UK intermediary's obligation to notify where legal professional privilege exclusion applies),

(e) regulation 8(2) (intermediary's obligation to notify arrangement reference number),

(f) regulation 11 (requirement to provide information).'

'Relevant considerations'

11.189 *Regulation 14* provides that:

'(3) For the purposes of this regulation and regulation 16[41], "relevant considerations" include—

  (a) the desirability of a penalty being set at a level which appears appropriate for deterring the person, or other persons, from similar failures to comply on future occasions having regard (in particular)—

    (i) in the case of a penalty for a UK intermediary's failure to comply with any obligation, to the amount of any fees received, or likely to have been received, by the UK intermediary in connection with the reportable cross-border arrangement, and

    (ii) in the case of a penalty for a UK relevant taxpayer's failure to comply with any obligation, to the amount of any advantage gained, or sought to be gained, by the UK relevant taxpayer in relation to any tax in relation to the reportable cross-border arrangement,

  (b) whether the failure giving rise to the penalty was deliberate,

  (c) any procedures maintained by the person liable to the penalty to secure the identification of reportable cross-border arrangements and compliance with obligations under these Regulations,

  (d) the reasonably foreseeable consequences of the failure.

(4) In this regulation, "the initial period" means the period—

41 Determination of penalty by First-tier Tribunal: daily penalty under *reg 14(1)(a)(ii)*.

(a) beginning with the relevant day, and

(b) ending on the earlier of—

(i) the day on which the penalty under paragraph (1)(a)(ii) is determined, and

(ii) the last day before the failure ceases.

(5) For the purpose of paragraph (4), "the relevant day" is the day specified in relation to the failure in the following table.

Failure	*Relevant day*
A failure to comply with regulation 3(1)	The first day after the end of the specified period prescribed in regulation 3(3)
A failure to comply with regulation 4(1)	The first day after the end of the specified period prescribed in regulation 4(4)
A failure to comply with regulation 7(2)	The day after the day the notification should have been made
A failure to comply with regulation 11	The first day after the latest time by which regulation 11 must be complied with as specified in the notice under that regulation

(6) A UK relevant taxpayer who fails to comply with regulation 5 (relevant taxpayer's obligation to make an annual report) is liable to a penalty not exceeding the relevant sum.

(7) In paragraph (6), "the relevant sum" means—

(a) in relation to a UK relevant taxpayer not falling within sub-paragraph (b) or (c), £5,000 in respect of each reportable cross-border arrangement to which the failure relates,

(b) in relation to a UK relevant taxpayer who has previously failed to comply with regulation 5 on one (and only one) occasion during the period of 36 months ending with the date on which the current failure to comply with that provision began, £7,500 in respect of each reportable cross-border arrangement to which the current failure relates (whether or not the same as the reportable cross-border arrangement to which the previous failure relates), or

(c) in relation to a UK relevant taxpayer who has previously failed to comply with regulation 5 on two or more occasions during the period of 36 months ending with the date on which the current failure to comply with that provision began, £10,000 in respect of each reportable cross-border arrangement to which the current failure relates (whether or not the same as the reportable cross-border arrangement to which any of the previous failures relates).'

DETERMINATION OF PENALTY BY HMRC UNDER REG 14(1)(A)(I) – REG 15

11.190 This provision applies to the £5,000 penalty under *reg 14(a)(i)*.

11.191 In the first instance, the penalty is to be determined by an officer of HMRC. The officer is to set the penalty at such amount as, in the opinion of that officer, is correct or appropriate.

11.192 Notice of a determination of a penalty under this regulation must be given to the person liable to the penalty.

11.193 After the notice of determination under this regulation has been given, the determination must not be altered except on appeal.

DETERMINATION OF PENALTY BY FIRST-TIER TRIBUNAL: DAILY PENALTY UNDER REG 14(1)(A)(II)

11.194 The specified provisions also need to be covered. This is dealt with by Reg 16, which provides:

'(1) An officer of Revenue and Customs may commence proceedings before the First-tier Tribunal for a penalty under regulation 14(1)(a)(ii).

(2) The person liable to the penalty must be a party to the proceedings.

(3) The First-tier Tribunal may determine a penalty in proceedings under this regulation.

(4) The amount of a penalty under regulation 14(1)(a)(ii) is to be arrived at after taking account of all relevant considerations.

(5) If the maximum penalty under regulation 14(1)(a)(ii) appears inappropriately low after taking account of those considerations, the penalty is to be of such amount not exceeding £1 million as appears appropriate having regard to those considerations.

(6) Where it appears to an officer of Revenue and Customs that a penalty under regulation 14(1)(a)(ii) has been determined on the basis that the initial period begins with a day later than that which the officer considers to be the relevant day, an officer of Revenue and Customs may commence proceedings for a re-determination of the penalty.

(7) In addition to any right of appeal on a point of law under section 11(2) of [the *Tribunals, Courts and Enforcement Act 2007*] TCEA 2007, the

person liable to the penalty may appeal to the Upper Tribunal against the determination of a penalty in proceedings under paragraph (1), but not against any decision which falls under section 11(5)(d) and (e) of that Act and was made in connection with the determination of the amount of the penalty.

(8) Section 11(3) and (4) of TCEA 2007 applies to the right of appeal under paragraph (7) as it applies to the right of appeal under section 11(2) of that Act.

(9) On any such appeal the Upper Tribunal may—

(a) if it appears that no penalty has been incurred, set the determination aside,

(b) if the amount determined appears to be appropriate, confirm the determination,

(c) if the amount determined appears to be excessive, reduce it to such other amount (including nil) as the Upper Tribunal considers appropriate, or

(d) if the amount determined appears to be insufficient, increase it to such amount not exceeding the permitted maximum as the Upper Tribunal considers appropriate.'

DETERMINATION OF PENALTY BY HMRC: FURTHER DAILY PENALTY UNDER REG 14(1)(B) AND PENALTY IN RELATION TO ANNUAL REPORT

11.195 Daily penalties can also arise. Provision for this is made in *reg 17* of the Regulations.

11.196 *Regulation 17* provides:

'(1) An officer of Revenue and Customs may make a determination imposing a penalty under regulation 14(1)(b) or (6) and setting it at such amount as, in the opinion of that officer, is correct or appropriate.

(2) Notice of a determination of a penalty under this regulation must be given to the person liable to the penalty and must state the date on which it is issued and the time within which an appeal against the determination may be made.

(3) After the notice of determination under this regulation has been given the determination must not be altered except in accordance with paragraph (4) or on appeal.

(4) If it is discovered by an officer of Revenue and Customs that the amount of a penalty determined under this regulation is or has become

insufficient, the officer may make a determination in a further amount so that the penalty is set at the amount which, in the opinion of that officer, is correct or appropriate.'

TIME LIMITS AND TREATMENT OF PENALTIES

11.197 *Regulation 18* deals with the time limits and treatment of penalties.

11.198 It sets out time limits within which proceedings in relation to a penalty must be dealt with by HMRC:

> '(1) Proceedings in relation to a penalty under regulation 14(1)(a)(ii) must be commenced, or a determination of a penalty under regulation 14(1)(a)(i) or (b) or (6) must be made, before the latest of the following dates—
>
> (a) the date 24 months after the date on which the inaccuracy or failure first came to the attention of an officer of Revenue and Customs,
>
> (b) the date six years after the date on which the person became liable to the penalty, and
>
> (c) in the case of a determination of a penalty under regulation 14(1)(b), the date three years after the date of determination of a penalty under regulation 14(1)(a).'

11.199 It also provides that the penalty is due and payable at the end of the period of 30 days beginning with the notice of determination or the determination by the FTT as the case may be (*reg 18(2)*).

11.200 The usual provision is made for a penalty to be treated as tax due and payable (*reg 18(3)*).

APPEALS AGAINST PENALTY DETERMINATIONS BY HMRC – REG 19

11.201 *Regulation 19(1)* makes provision for an appeal[42] to be brought against the determination of a penalty under *reg 15* or *17*:

> '(1) An appeal may be brought against the determination of a penalty under regulation 15 or 17 and, subject to the following provisions of this

42 *Regulation 19(3)–(5)* further states:
'(3) In addition to any right of appeal on a point of law under section 11(2) of TCEA 2007, the person liable to the penalty may appeal to the Upper Tribunal against the amount of the penalty which has been determined under paragraph (2), but not against any decision which falls under section 11(5)(d) and (e) of that Act and was made in connection with the determination of the amount of the penalty.
(4) Section 11(3) and (4) of TCEA 2007 applies to the right of appeal under paragraph (3) as it applies to the right of appeal under section 11(2) of that Act.
(5) On an appeal under this section the Upper Tribunal has the same powers as are conferred on the First-tier Tribunal by virtue of this regulation.'

regulation, the provisions of the Taxes Management Act 1970 relating to appeals have effect in relation to an appeal against such a determination as they have effect in relation to an appeal against an assessment to tax, except that references to the tribunal shall be taken to be references to the First-tier Tribunal.'

11.202 The *Taxes Management Act 1970* (*TMA 1970*) appeal provisions are, in general, to apply (*reg 19(2)*).

11.203 However, on an appeal under *reg 19*, *section 50(6)* to *(8)* of *TMA 1970* are not to apply.

11.204 It is further provided by *reg 19(2)*, however, that the First-tier Tribunal may:

'(a) if it appears that no penalty has been incurred, set the determination aside,

(b) if the amount determined appears to be appropriate, confirm the determination,

(c) if the amount determined appears to be excessive, reduce it to such other amount (including nil) as the First-tier Tribunal considers appropriate, or

(d) if the amount determined appears to be insufficient, increase it to such amount not exceeding the permitted maximum as the First-tier Tribunal considers appropriate.'

REASONABLE EXCUSE, SPECIAL REDUCTION, ETC

Introductory

11.205 As usual provision is made for reasonable excuse, as specially defined in the legislation, to negative a penalty and for a reduction of a penalty in special circumstances.

Reasonable excuse

11.206 Reasonable excuse is dealt with in *reg 21* of the Regulations headed 'Matters to be disregarded in relation to liability to penalties'[43].

11.207 There is no penalty if the person in question shows a 'reasonable excuse' within the special definition in the legislation.

43 *Regulation 21(1)* provides: 'Liability to a penalty under regulation 14 does not arise if the person satisfies an officer of Revenue and Customs or, on a determination by the First-tier Tribunal or an appeal notified to the tribunal, the tribunal that there is a reasonable excuse for a failure to do anything required to be done under these Regulations'.

11.208 As usual for penalties, 'reasonable excuse' does not have its plain and ordinary meaning but a special meaning for these purposes.

11.209 As is generally the case, an insufficiency of funds is not a reasonable excuse, but this has the words 'to do something' added to the usual provision. The words 'to do something' would presumably cover paying the tax.

11.210 Under *reg 21(2)*, reliance on legal advice is *not* a reasonable excuse if:

'(b) ... the person relies on legal advice if—

(i) the advice was given or procured by a person who is an intermediary within the first paragraph of Article 3(21) of the DAC in relation to the reportable cross-border arrangement to which the failure relates,

(ii) the advice was not based on a full and accurate description of the facts, or

(iii) the conclusions in the advice that the person relied upon were unreasonable.'

11.211 The client needs to take its own advice on a proper basis on which it can properly rely and act accordingly. Evidence needs to be retained that is admissible to show this is the case. The expense of the advice may save the cost of the penalty.

Examples 11.15

(1) The taxpayer fills in his return using wording for the white space given to him by the intermediary. This was not something the taxpayer can rely on as a reasonable excuse.

(2) The taxpayer relies on advice given on a set of assumed facts that are not a full and accurate description of the actual facts. He fills in his return using wording for the white space given to him by the intermediary. This was not something the taxpayer can rely on as a reasonable excuse.

(3) The advice sets out the law and inferences accurately but then states a conclusion to the contrary. The taxpayer fills in his return using wording for the white space given to him by the intermediary. This was not something the taxpayer can rely on as a reasonable excuse.

Consideration of reasonable excuse

11.212 Provision is made by *reg 21(3)* regarding maintaining reasonable procedures to identify cross-border reportable arrangements in respect of whether there is a reasonable excuse:

'(3) In considering whether a person had a reasonable excuse, the officer of Revenue and Customs or the tribunal must consider whether the person maintains such procedures as it is reasonable in all the circumstances to have in place to secure the identification of reportable cross-border arrangements and compliance with obligations under these Regulations.'

Effect of cesser of reasonable excuse

11.213 *Regulation 21(4)* provides that a reasonable excuse continues after a cesser so long as the failure is remedied without unreasonable delay.

Special reduction

11.214 *Regulation 20* provides that if an HMRC officer thinks it right because of special circumstances, the officer may reduce a penalty by staying it or agreeing a compromise:

> '**20.**—(1) If an officer of Revenue and Customs thinks it right because of special circumstances, the officer may reduce a penalty under this Part.
>
> (2) In paragraph (1), "special circumstances" does not include—
>
> (a) ability to pay, or
>
> (b) the fact that a potential loss of revenue from one taxpayer is balanced by a potential over-payment by another.
>
> (3) In paragraph (1), the reference to reducing a penalty includes a reference to—
>
> (a) staying a penalty, and
>
> (b) agreeing a compromise in relation to proceedings for a penalty.'

11.215 Special circumstances do not include ability to pay or that the loss of revenue from one taxpayer is balanced by potential over-payment by another.

Example 11.16

The taxpayer suffers the death of a close family member and is incapacitated by physical and mental illness for a number of months but recovers and deals with matters promptly. This might amount to special circumstances.

APPENDIX – ANNEX IV

11.216 The section below on Hallmarks is reproduced from Annex IV of Council Directive (EU) 2018/822 of 25 May 2018 amending Directive 2011/16/EU as regards mandatory automatic exchange of information in the field of taxation in relation to reportable cross-border arrangements (DAC 6) (at https://eur-lex.europa.eu/legal-content/EN/TXT/?uri=CELEX:32018L0822).

© European Commission

HALLMARKS

Part I. Main benefit test

Generic hallmarks under category A and specific hallmarks under category B and under points (b)(i), (c) and (d) of paragraph 1 of category C may only be taken into account where they fulfil the 'main benefit test'.

That test will be satisfied if it can be established that the main benefit or one of the main benefits which, having regard to all relevant facts and circumstances, a person may reasonably expect to derive from an arrangement is the obtaining of a tax advantage.

In the context of hallmark under paragraph 1 of category C, the presence of conditions set out in points (b)(i), (c) or (d) of paragraph 1 of category C can not alone be a reason for concluding that an arrangement satisfies the main benefit test.

Part II. Categories of hallmarks

A. Generic hallmarks linked to the main benefit test

1. An arrangement where the relevant taxpayer or a participant in the arrangement undertakes to comply with a condition of confidentiality which may require them not to disclose how the arrangement could secure a tax advantage vis-à-vis other intermediaries or the tax authorities.

2. An arrangement where the intermediary is entitled to receive a fee (or interest, remuneration for finance costs and other charges) for the arrangement and that fee is fixed by reference to:

   (a) the amount of the tax advantage derived from the arrangement; or

   (b) whether or not a tax advantage is actually derived from the arrangement. This would include an obligation on the intermediary to partially or fully refund the fees where the intended tax advantage derived from the arrangement was not partially or fully achieved.

3. An arrangement that has substantially standardised documentation and/ or structure and is available to more than one relevant taxpayer without a need to be substantially customised for implementation.

B. Specific hallmarks linked to the main benefit test

1. An arrangement whereby a participant in the arrangement takes contrived steps which consist in acquiring a loss-making company, discontinuing the main activity of such company and using its losses in order to reduce its tax liability, including through a transfer of those losses to another jurisdiction or by the acceleration of the use of those losses.

2. An arrangement that has the effect of converting income into capital, gifts or other categories of revenue which are taxed at a lower level or exempt from tax.

3. An arrangement which includes circular transactions resulting in the round-tripping of funds, namely through involving interposed entities without other primary commercial function or transactions that offset or cancel each other or that have other similar features.

C. Specific hallmarks related to cross-border transactions

1. An arrangement that involves deductible cross-border payments made between two or more associated enterprises where at least one of the following conditions occurs:

   (a) the recipient is not resident for tax purposes in any tax jurisdiction;

   (b) although the recipient is resident for tax purposes in a jurisdiction, that jurisdiction either:

      (i) does not impose any corporate tax or imposes corporate tax at the rate of zero or almost zero; or

      (ii) is included in a list of third-country jurisdictions which have been assessed by Member States collectively or within the framework of the OECD as being non-cooperative;

   (c) the payment benefits from a full exemption from tax in the jurisdiction where the recipient is resident for tax purposes;

   (d) the payment benefits from a preferential tax regime in the jurisdiction where the recipient is resident for tax purposes;

2. Deductions for the same depreciation on the asset are claimed in more than one jurisdiction.

3. Relief from double taxation in respect of the same item of income or capital is claimed in more than one jurisdiction.

4. There is an arrangement that includes transfers of assets and where there is a material difference in the amount being treated as payable in consideration for the assets in those jurisdictions involved.

D. Specific hallmarks concerning automatic exchange of information and beneficial ownership

1. An arrangement which may have the effect of undermining the reporting obligation under the laws implementing Union legislation or any equivalent agreements on the automatic exchange of Financial Account information, including agreements with third countries, or which takes advantage of the absence of such legislation or agreements. Such arrangements include at least the following:

   (a) the use of an account, product or investment that is not, or purports not to be, a Financial Account, but has features that are substantially similar to those of a Financial Account;

   (b) the transfer of Financial Accounts or assets to, or the use of jurisdictions that are not bound by the automatic exchange of Financial Account information with the State of residence of the relevant taxpayer;

   (c) the reclassification of income and capital into products or payments that are not subject to the automatic exchange of Financial Account information;

   (d) the transfer or conversion of a Financial Institution or a Financial Account or the assets therein into a Financial Institution or a Financial Account or assets not subject to reporting under the automatic exchange of Financial Account information;

   (e) the use of legal entities, arrangements or structures that eliminate or purport to eliminate reporting of one or more Account Holders or Controlling Persons under the automatic exchange of Financial Account information;

   (f) arrangements that undermine, or exploit weaknesses in, the due diligence procedures used by Financial Institutions to comply with their obligations to report Financial Account information, including the use of jurisdictions with inadequate or weak regimes of enforcement of anti-money-laundering legislation or with weak transparency requirements for legal persons or legal arrangements.

2. An arrangement involving a non-transparent legal or beneficial ownership chain with the use of persons, legal arrangements or structures:

   (a) that do not carry on a substantive economic activity supported by adequate staff, equipment, assets and premises; and

(b) that are incorporated, managed, resident, controlled or established in any jurisdiction other than the jurisdiction of residence of one or more of the beneficial owners of the assets held by such persons, legal arrangements or structures; and

(c) where the beneficial owners of such persons, legal arrangements or structures, as defined in Directive (EU) 2015/849, are made unidentifiable.

E. Specific hallmarks concerning transfer pricing

1. An arrangement which involves the use of unilateral safe harbour rules.

2. An arrangement involving the transfer of hard-to-value intangibles. The term 'hard-to-value intangibles' covers intangibles or rights in intangibles for which, at the time of their transfer between associated enterprises:

   (a) no reliable comparables exist; and

   (b) at the time the transaction was entered into, the projections of future cash flows or income expected to be derived from the transferred intangible, or the assumptions used in valuing the intangible are highly uncertain, making it difficult to predict the level of ultimate success of the intangible at the time of the transfer.

3. An arrangement involving an intragroup cross-border transfer of functions and/or risks and/or assets, if the projected annual earnings before interest and taxes (EBIT), during the three-year period after the transfer, of the transferor or transferors, are less than 50% of the projected annual EBIT of such transferor or transferors if the transfer had not been made.

Chapter 12

Miscellaneous forms of regulation

SIGNPOSTS

- Introduction: HMRC Standard for Agents and HMRC powers (see **12.1**).
- Fiduciary duties: the categories of a fiduciary relationship and solicitors' duties (see **12.3–12.14**).
- Restitution and remedies (see **12.15–12.19**).
- Misconduct in public office can lead to criminal and tortious liability (see **12.20–12.26**).
- Contempt of court happens when someone risks unfairly influencing a court case and can affect a trial's outcome (see **12.27–12.31**).
- Human rights (see **12.32–12.34**).
- Handling client money: rules of the relevant bodies (see **12.35–12.51**).
- Insurance: terms and requirements (see **12.52–12.57**).

INTRODUCTION

12.1 Tax professionals are subject to direct and indirect regulation as discussed in **Chapters 1** and **2**. The 'HMRC Standard for Agents' (see bit.ly/2LyuxDv), published in 2016 and updated in 2018 applies to all individuals and business involved in representing or advising taxpayers, located onshore or offshore (ie 'tax agents'). The essential point of distinction between tax agents and tax professionals is that the latter are members of, and regulated by, professional bodies (ie CIOT, ATT, TEP, ICAEW, SRA, BSB). The role of the PCRT in regulating professionals is discussed in **Chapter 3**. HMRC's Standard is discussed in **Chapters 1** and **3**, with the Standard fully set out in **Appendix 2**. While there is no single code regulating tax agents (whether professionals or non-professionals), as explained in this book there is an array of different forms of direct and indirect regulation which will apply to tax agents. Clearly, a small number of tax agents, who are not members of a professional body, are not subject to the ethical standards of the PCRT. HMRC has the ability to monitor tax agents and impose sanctions in the following ways[1]:

- HMRC powers 'Dishonest tax agent penalties' (*Finance Act 2012, Sch 38*).
- 'Public interest disclosures' (*Commissioners for Revenue and Customs Act 2005, s 20*)[2]. HMRC's ability to make disclosures relating to tax agents enables them to tackle examples of misconduct by agents who are members of professional bodies.
- Removal or suspension of the agent code, which allows access to HMRC online systems, where HMRC have engaged with advisers to improve standards and those standards do not improve.
- HMRC work with other parts of government and local authorities, for example making referrals to the Advertising Standards Authority where an adviser is suspected of false advertising.

12.2 There are various other matters that impact on a tax professional's behaviour, which include[3]:

- fiduciary duties;
- restitution;
- misfeasance in public office;
- contempt;
- human rights;
- handling client money.

Each of these will now be considered in turn.

FIDUCIARY DUTIES

General

12.3 Broadly, there are fiduciary duties where a person has to act in the best interests of someone else. This is sometimes called a 'duty of loyalty'.

1 See Jim Harra, 'The role of agents', *Tax Adviser* (June 2020) at www.taxadvisermagazine.com/article/role-agents.

2 See HMRC IDG60220 Information Disclosure Guide (published 2016 – last updated 3 December 2020) at www.gov.uk/hmrc-internal-manuals/information-disclosure-guide/idg60220. UK legislation available at www.legislation.gov.uk.

3 This is not an exhaustive list.

12.4 In *Bray v Ford* [1896] AC 44 Lord Halsbury LC in a well-known and oft quoted passage said:

> 'It is an inflexible rule of a Court of Equity that a person in a fiduciary position, … is not, unless otherwise expressly provided, entitled to make a profit; he is not allowed to put himself in a position where his interest and duty conflict. It does not appear to me that this rule is, as has been said, founded upon principles of morality. I regard it rather as based on the consideration that, human nature being what it is, there is danger, in such circumstances, of the person holding a fiduciary position being swayed by interest rather than by duty, and thus prejudicing those whom he was bound to protect. It has, therefore, been deemed expedient to lay down this positive rule.'

Who is a fiduciary?

12.5 In *Bristol and West Building Society v Mothew*, [1996] EWCA Civ 533 Millet LJ said:

> 'A fiduciary is someone who has undertaken to act for and on behalf of another in a particular matter in circumstances which give rise to a relationship of trust and confidence. The distinguishing obligation of a fiduciary is the obligation of loyalty. The principal is entitled to the single-minded loyalty of his fiduciary. This core liability has several facets. A fiduciary must act in good faith; he must not make a profit out of his trust; he must not place himself in a position where his duty and his interest may conflict; he may not act for his own benefit or the benefit of a third person without the informed consent of his principal.'

12.6 Typically, there are four categories of a fiduciary relationship. These are:

- trustee and beneficiary;
- business partners inter se;
- Company director and shareholder; and
- agent and principal.

12.7 Fiduciary duties include:

- a duty of confidentiality[4];
- a duty of no conflict[5]; and
- a duty not to profit from his position[6].

4 *Bolkiah v KPMG* [1999] 2 WLR 215; see also www.icaew.com/library/subject-gateways/law/legislation-and-cases/prince-jefri-bolkiah.

5 *Marks and Spencer plc v Freshfields Bruckhaus Deringer* [2004] EWCA Civ 741.

6 *Bristol and West Building Society v Mothew* [1996] EWCA Civ 533, [1996] 4 All ER 698.

Solicitors owe fiduciary duties

12.8 Solicitors owe duties to their client. These include fiduciary duties. The authority usually cited for this is *Nocton v Lord Ashburton* [1914] AC 932. This case involved negligent advice provided by a solicitor, Nocton, to Lord Ashburton. His Lordship purchased a house on Church Street, Kensington, London. The solicitor advised him to lease or sell part of the house. The house was security for a mortgage. As Nocton knew, this would make the security insufficient. This advanced the solicitor's own subsequent charge on the same property. Lord Ashburton alleged the advice was not given in good faith, but rather in Mr Nocton's self-interest and fraudulently. Fraud was not proved but the solicitor was held liable for negligence. This was before the emergence of a generalised tort of negligence[7].

12.9 Viscount Haldane LC, with whom Lord Atkinson concurred, said:

> 'There is a third form of procedure … and that is the old bill in Chancery to enforce compensation for breach of a fiduciary obligation. There appears to have been an impression that the necessity which recent authorities have established of proving moral fraud in order to succeed in an action of deceit has narrowed the scope of this remedy. For the reasons which I am about to offer to your Lordships, I do not think that this is so.
>
> … if moral fraud has not been established [as was the case here] the only question which remains is whether there has been such a breach of duty as gives rise to liability. Now such a duty might arise either at law or in equity … the Court of Chancery exercised an exclusive jurisdiction in cases which, although classified in that Court as cases of fraud, yet did not necessarily import the element of dolus malus.
>
> The Court took upon itself to prevent a man from acting against the dictates of conscience as defined by the Court, and to grant injunctions in anticipation of injury, as well as relief where injury had been done. Common instances of this exclusive jurisdiction are cases arising out of breach of duty by persons standing in a fiduciary relation, such as the solicitor to the client, illustrated by Lord Hardwicke's judgment in *Chesterfield v Janssen*. … My Lords, the solicitor contracts with his client to be skilful and careful. For failure to perform his obligation he may be made liable at law in contract or even in tort, for negligence in breach of a duty imposed on him. In the early history of the action of assumpsit this liability was indeed treated as one for tort.
>
> This, however, does not end the matter.
>
> When, as in the case before us, a solicitor has had financial transactions with his client, and has handled his money to the extent of using it to pay off a mortgage made to himself, or of getting the client to release from his mortgage a property over which the solicitor by such release has obtained

7 See *Donoghue v. Stevenson* [1932] AC 562.

further security for a mortgage of his own, a Court of Equity has always assumed jurisdiction to scrutinise his action. It did not matter that the client would have had a remedy in damages for breach of contract. Courts of Equity had jurisdiction to direct accounts to be taken, and in proper cases to order the solicitor to replace property improperly acquired from the client, or to make compensation if he had lost it by acting in breach of a duty which arose out of his confidential relationship to the man who had trusted him. This jurisdiction, which really belonged to the exclusive jurisdiction of the Court of Chancery.

My Lords, the conclusion at which I have arrived is that this action ought properly to have been treated as one in which the plaintiff had made out a claim for compensation either for loss arising from misrepresentation made in breach of fiduciary duty or for breach of contract to exercise due care and skill.

...

LORD DUNEDIN:

Viewing the matter as I must do, as under the rules of the law of England, the question that at once arises is, Was the remedy of the plaintiff at law or in equity, or had he a remedy in both?

Now, as I understand the matter, if the action had been brought at law, under the old system it could have been based either (i) on fraud, or (ii) on negligence, and the relief in either case would have been damages. But if based on fraud, then, in accordance with the decision in *Derry v Peek* (1), the fraud proved must be actual fraud; a mens rea, an intention to deceive. It is an action of deceit.

...

Turning now to equity, here again, as I understand the situation, there was a jurisdiction in equity to keep persons in a fiduciary capacity up to their duty. The matter has been exhaustively dealt with by my noble friend on the woolsack, and I do not propose to examine the cases. I will only make a few remarks. In the first place, it will be found that the word "fraud" in the older cases in Chancery is often used where the thing so characterised is a wrongful breach of duty, without a consideration of whether there is such a mens rea as would found an action for deceit. In the second place, all the cases are based upon the existence of a fiduciary relationship, and subsequently the breach of duty arising. Now, whenever we come to the idea of breach of duty we see how nearly the domains of law and equity approach, or perhaps, more strictly speaking, overlap.

...

If, then, we turn to the solicitor's position we may look at it in two aspects, which is not to look at two different things, but to look at the same thing from two different points of view. He has contracted to be diligent; he is negligent. Law will give a remedy … he may have put himself in a fiduciary position, and that fiduciary position imposes on him the duty of making a full and not a misleading disclosure of facts known to him when advising his client. He fails to do so. Equity will give a remedy to the client. This it does quite apart from the doctrine of *Derry v. Peek*, for in that case there was no fiduciary relationship, and the action had to be based on the representation alone.

But apart from that, for the reasons given by my noble friend the Lord Chancellor, I think there was here a remedy in equity for breach of duty.

LORD SHAW OF DUNFERMLINE: My Lords, I agree with the conclusion reached by the Lord Chancellor and with the judgment proposed.

Addressing myself to the merits of the case, I approach it, my Lords – in this respect differing to some extent from the line along which some of your Lordships have advanced – by suggesting that the first consideration in these cases ought always to be, What was the relation in which the parties stood to each other at the time of the transaction in respect of which the claim for damage, compensation, or restitution is made? In the answer to that question, in my judgment, may be found a solution of not a few of the difficulties which arise in such actions.

Once, my Lords, the relation of parties has been so placed, it becomes manifest that the liability of an adviser upon whom rests the duty of doing things or making statements by which the other is guided or upon which that other justly relies can and does arise irrespective of whether the information and advice given have been tendered innocently or with a fraudulent intent.

…

That once the relations of parties have been ascertained to be those in which a duty is laid upon one person of giving information or advice to another upon which that other is entitled to rely as the basis of a transaction, responsibility for error amounting to misrepresentation in any statement made will attach to the adviser or informer, although the information and advice have been given not fraudulently but in good faith.

It is admitted in the present case that misrepresentations were made; that they were material; that they were the cause of loss; that they were made by a solicitor to his client in a situation in which the client was entitled to rely, and did rely, upon the information received. I accordingly think that that situation is plainly open for the application of the principle of liability to which I have referred, namely, liability for the consequences of a failure of duty in circumstances in which it was a matter equivalent to contract between the parties that that duty should be fulfilled.'

12.10 Solicitors are also officers of the court.

12.11 The Solicitors Regulation Authority (SRA) document entitled 'Balancing duties in litigation' (November 2018) is a helpful starting point in considering this[8].

12.12 It is said there, 'Solicitors are officers of the court and their overriding duty is to the rule of law and the administration of justice. Nowhere is that more apparent than when conducting litigation'.

12.13 It is also said (at p 7):

> 'The solicitor's duties in litigation are clearly set out in the Legal Services Act 2007 (LSA), which makes clear that legal obligations extend beyond those owed to the client.
>
> Principles (a) and (d) emphasise the importance of the independence of lawyers, including their "duty to the court to act with independence in the interests of justice".
>
> Independence, in this context, clearly includes independence from the client. This has been set out clearly by the Solicitors Disciplinary Tribunal (SDT), as follows:
>
> > "A solicitor is independent of his client and having regard to his wider responsibilities and the need to maintain the profession's reputation, [they] must and should on occasion be prepared to say to [their] client 'What you seek to do may be legal but I am not prepared to help you do it'."[9]
>
> It is essential to the public interest in justice, in an adversarial legal system, that solicitors must be able to take cases forward fearlessly and effectively. There are limits to this, however, including that:
>
> - solicitors must bring and defend cases honestly
> - clients and sometimes solicitors have to sign statements of truth
> - it is improper to mislead the court or other parties
> - the prosecution must disclose documents that might damage a client's case if they are relevant to the case, unless these are privileged.
>
> If a solicitor knows that a client's case is not honestly brought, they must not act. Where there is suspicion or the context is high-risk, the solicitor's duty to the administration of justice, the court and the public interest demand proper checks of the instructions and evidence.'

8 See www.sra.org.uk/globalassets/documents/solicitors/freedom-in-practice/balancing-duties-in-litigation.pdf?version=49922b.

9 *In the matter of Paul Francis Simms*, Solicitors Disciplinary Tribunal, 2002

12.14 Reference should also be made to the section following that quoted above (at p 8). This reads:

> **'The Handbook and the solicitor's duties**
>
> These issues are reflected in the SRA Handbook. We are introducing new principles, codes and rules from 2019 onwards, however these will not change the core ethical duties of a solicitor. The discussion below covers the way those duties are set out in the Handbook at the time of this report's publication.
>
> The primary duties of the solicitor to various parties are clear and are set out in our principles. The outcomes that firms and regulated individuals must achieve reflect the importance of steering the course between these principles in particular:
>
> - Principle 1 requires solicitors to uphold the rule of law and the proper administration of justice.
> - Principle 2 sets out that solicitors must act with integrity.
> - Principle 3 requires solicitors not to allow their independence to be compromised.
> - Principle 4 sets out the obligation of solicitors to act in the best interests of the client.
> - Principle 7 requires solicitors to act in accordance with their legal and regulatory obligations.
>
> Outcome 1.2 of our Code of Conduct 2011 confirms that solicitors owe duties beyond those to their clients and that those duties can limit their right to pursue the client's case however the client wishes. It states, "you provide services to your clients in a manner which protects their interests in their matter, subject to the proper administration of justice". Outcome 1.3 clarifies this by requiring a solicitor to comply with the law and the Code of Conduct when deciding whether to act or to cease acting.
>
> **The solicitor and the court**
>
> The outcomes regarding duties to the court are as follows:
>
> - Outcome 5.1 bars solicitors from intentionally, knowingly or recklessly deceiving the court.
> - Outcome 5.2 requires that solicitors are not complicit with another's deception of the court.
>
> Indicative behaviour 5.5 describes the implication of this. If the solicitor knows that their client is committing perjury or otherwise misleading the court in any matter, then they should cease to act. The only exception is if the client agrees to inform the court of the deception.'

RESTITUTION

12.15 The Law of Restitution is a developing area of Law in England. It is often discussed in the context of 'unjust enrichment' and is often concerned with remedies.

12.16 The old remedy of *Quantum Meruit* (what is merited or derived) allowed recompense for work done as if there was a contract (*quasi ex contractu*).

12.17 Restitution can also cover payments made mistakenly.

12.18 It can apply as between the subject and the State and has a European Union equivalent.

12.19 It is a developing area of law that must be considered by any tax professional.

MISCONDUCT AND MISFEASANCE IN PUBLIC OFFICE

12.20 Misconduct in public office can lead to criminal and tortious liability in England.

12.21

> 'Briefly, misfeasance in public office is a tort remedy for harm caused by acts or omissions that amounted to:
>
> 1. an abuse of public power or authority;
> 2. by a public officer;
> 3. who either:
>   a. knew that he or she was abusing their public power or authority, or
>   b. was recklessly indifferent as to the limits to or restraints upon their public power or authority;
> 4. and who acted or omitted to act:
>   a. with either the intention of harming the claimant (so-called "targeted malice"), or
>   b. with the knowledge of the probability of harming the claimant, or
>   c. with a conscious and reckless indifference to the probability of harming the claimant.
>
> In short, misfeasance is an intentional tort, where the relevant intention is bad faith. Pleading bad faith is difficult, because the pleading rules require details, and professional conduct rules forbid practitioners supporting

obviously baseless allegations. Proving bad faith is even more difficult. Where they have a choice, the courts are strongly disposed to believing that bureaucratic error was caused by genuine mistake, even incompetence, rather than by bad faith. The result is that of the hundreds of misfeasance claims that are actually filed, very few make it to trial.

Most are filtered out for inadequate pleading of bad faith, or because an allegation of bad faith has no real prospect of success.

The courts often acknowledge that the tort of misfeasance in public office is not fully defined. According to Stratas JA in Canada's Federal Court of Appeal, misfeasance is "a notoriously complex tort whose precise elements have only been settled recently…". That turns out to be an understatement. Bad faith has attracted most of the attention so far, leaving the tort's other elements under-developed.'[10]

12.22 There are several ingredients that must be met before a court will conclude that there is misfeasance in public office:

- the defendant must be a public officer;
- the defendant must have been exercising his power as a public officer; and
- the defendant is either exercising targeted malice or exceeding his powers.

12.23 The Law Commission has a program of work on this topic, see 'Misconduct in public office' at www.lawcom.gov.uk/project/misconduct-in-public-office. The Law Commission published a report of their final recommendations on 4 December 2020.

12.24 The criminal offence of misconduct in public office dates back to the 13th century according to some. It is a common law offence which as yet is not subject to statute. The maximum penalty is life imprisonment.

12.25 The CPS guidance on this is illuminating, see www.cps.gov.uk/legal-guidance/misconduct-public-office, and the essence to be proved is that:

- a public officer acting as such;
- wilfully neglects to perform one's duty and/or wilfully misconducts himself.
- to such a degree as to amount to an abuse of the public's trust in the office holder;
- without reasonable excuse or justification[11].

10 See Mark Aronson, 'Misfeasance in Public Office' (Law Faculty, University of New South Wales): www.lawcom.gov.uk/app/uploads/2016/01/apb_tort.pdf.

11 CPS, 'Misconduct in Public Office' (16 July 2018), see www.cps.gov.uk/legal-guidance/misconduct-public-office.

12.26 This can apply to HMRC officers but can also apply to other tax professionals such as those who sit as fee paid judges.

CONTEMPT

12.27 A useful starting point is the government document, 'Contempt of court', available at www.gov.uk/contempt-of-court.

12.28 This manual includes the following:

> '"Contempt of court" happens when someone risks unfairly influencing a court case. It may stop somebody from getting a fair trial and can affect a trial's outcome.
>
> Contempt of court includes:
>
> - disobeying or ignoring a court order
> - taking photos or shouting out in court
> - refusing to answer the court's questions if you're called as a witness
> - publicly commenting on a court case, for example on social media or online news articles.'

12.29 Any person who gives a statement in proceedings must sign subject to a Statement of Truth which is in the following form[12]:

> 'I believe that the facts stated in this witness statement are true. I understand that proceedings for contempt of court may be brought against anyone who makes, or causes to be made, a false statement in a document verified by a statement of truth without an honest belief in its truth.'

12.30 The essence of the offence of contempt of court is conveniently set out in *Liverpool Victoria Insurance Company Ltd v Khan and Others* [2018] EWHC 2581, where Garnham J stated (at 6–11):

> '6. As has been observed on many occasions, the expression "contempt of court" is not an entirely happy one, suggesting as it does that what is in issue is the dignity of the court. It is not. The real nature of the offence is an interference with the administration of justice (see for example *AG v Newspaper Publishing PLC* [1988] Chancery 333 at 341).
>
> 7. In *Attorney General v Leveller Magazine Ltd* [1979] AC 440, Lord Diplock held [at page 449] that it is a contempt of court to engage in any conduct which involves an interference with the due administration of justice, either in a particular case or generally as a continuing process.

12 Civil Procedure Rules, Practice Direction 22: Statements of Truth, para 2.2: see www.justice.gov.uk/courts/procedure-rules/civil/rules/part22/pd_part22#2.1.

8. Contempt can be either civil or criminal. The distinction between the two was explained by Lord Toulson in *R. v O'Brien* [2014] UKSC 23:

> "The question whether a contempt is a criminal contempt does not depend on the nature of the court to which the contempt was displayed; it depends on nature of the conduct. To burst into a court room and disrupt a civil trial would be a criminal contempt just as much as if the court had been conducting a criminal trial. Conversely, disobedience to a procedural order of a court is not in itself a crime, just because the order was made in the course of criminal proceedings. To hold that a breach of a procedural order made in a criminal court is itself a crime would be to introduce an unjustified and anomalous extension of the criminal law. 'Civil contempt' is not confined to contempt of a civil court. It simply denotes a contempt which is not itself a crime."

9. There are a number of categories of civil contempt. One is provided for by CPR 32.14, which provides that "proceedings for contempt of court may be brought against a person if he makes, or causes to be made, a false statement in a document verified by a statement of truth without an honest belief in its truth." The majority, but not all, of the contempts in the present case fall into this category.

10. It was held in *Nield v Loveday* [2011] EWHC 2324 (Admin) that, in order for such an allegation of contempt to succeed, it must be shown that in addition "to knowing what you are saying is false, you have to have known that what you are saying is likely to interfere with the course of justice". A statement made by someone who does not care whether it is true or false is liable as if that person knew what was said was false (see *Berry Piling Systems Ltd v Sheer Projects Ltd* [2013] EWHC 347 (TCC)), but simple carelessness will not be sufficient (see paragraph 30(c) of the judgment in *Berry Piling*).

11. It is beyond argument that to forge the signature on a witness statement may also constitute an interference, or an attempted interference, with the administration of justice.'

12.31 In *Liverpool Victoria Insurance Company Ltd v Zafar* [2019] EWCA Civ 392, the Court of Appeal summarises the position on sentencing for contempt of court and relevant principles on sentencing. The principal penalties for contempt of court are a fine or committal to prison. *Section 14* of the *Contempt of Court Act 1981* provides, in material part:

'(1) In any cases where a court has power to commit a person to prison for contempt of court and (apart from this provision) no limitation applies to the period of committal, the committal shall (without prejudice to the power of the court to order his earlier discharge) be for a fixed term, and that term shall not on any occasion exceed two years in the case of committal by a superior court, or one month in the case of committal by an inferior court.

(2) In any case where an inferior court has power to fine a person for contempt of court and (apart from this provision) no limit applies to the amount of the fine, the fine shall not on any occasion exceed £2,500.'

This is a technical area where proper advice should be taken in any case of doubt.

HUMAN RIGHTS

12.32 The *Human Rights Act 1998* (*HRA 1998*) implemented the European Convention on Human Rights except for Article 13[13].

12.33 The rights and freedoms most frequently litigated in connection with Revenue matters include:

- Article 6 – right to a fair trial (see *Jussila v Finland* [2018] EWHC 2581).
- Article 8 – right to respect for private and family life.
- Article 14 – prohibition of discrimination.
- Article 1 of Protocol 1 – protection of property (see *Air Canada v United Kingdom* (App No 18465/91) [1995] ECHR 18465/91).

12.34 HMRC Manuals also make reference to *HRA 1998*. See CH300700 'The Human Rights Act and Penalties: when to tell the person about penalties and their rights'[14].

HANDLING CLIENT MONEY

Introductory

12.35 Where a client's funds are handled by a tax professional there is always a risk of the funds being misused by an errant professional.

12.36 This may be fraudulent, as in *Lipkin Gorman v Karpnale Ltd* [1991] 2 AC 548, where a conveyancing partner who was an authorised signatory on the firm's bank account took some £220,000 from the account. He used it to gamble at the Playboy Club.

12.37 Sometimes it may be that problems arise from a mixing of the professional's and the client's funds with tracing difficulties. This mixing

13 Article 13: Right to an effective remedy. Everyone whose rights and freedoms as set forth in this Convention are violated shall have an effective remedy before a national authority notwithstanding that the violation has been committed by persons acting in an official capacity.

14 March 2016 (updated November 2020), available at www.gov.uk/hmrc-internal-manuals/compliance-handbook/ch300700.

of funds was apparently common for solicitors to do and even to use funds unless earmarked for a particular purpose till the beginning of the 20th century. The Boer War and stock market falls caused a number of defalcations and accounting rules coming in.

12.38 There has been an increase in the regulation of how professionals hold and deal with client funds.

12.39 The American Bar Association (ABA) in 'A History of The Client Protection Rules'[15] states:

> 'Remedies for defalcation of clients' funds by lawyers were established in English Commonwealth countries at the beginning of the 20th century. Developments in the law regarding lawyers' responsibilities appear to be tied historically to depressed economic times during which lawyers misappropriated client funds.'

12.40 Each profession in England has its own provisions as to how clients' funds are to be dealt with. Breach of these rules can be a serious matter for many professionals. A solicitor can be struck off for breach of the accounts rules[16].

12.41 These rules generally predate AML and have a different function from AML. The function of these rules is mainly to protect the client.

12.42 These rules are considered below by reference to the relevant body.

The Bar Standards Board (BSB)

12.43 The position of barristers is relatively clear.

The BSB say the general rule is that a barrister must not receive, control or handle *client money* apart from what the client pays for the barrister's services. This is found in the BSB Handbook[17]. Client money is covered in Part 2 – C: The Conduct Rules at rules C73–C75[18].

15 See www.americanbar.org/groups/professional_responsibility/resources/client_protection/history.

16 Eg in 2015, former Law Society council member, Michael Webster, was jailed for eight months after being found guilty of making five fraudulent transactions from his law firm's client account to the value of £75,605.27. Webster, who was also struck off the Roll of Solicitors, was ordered to pay £48,000 to a Latvian-based indemnity insurer (see https://jglaw.co.uk/sra-accounts-rules-happens-breach).

17 Version 4.5 came into force on 1 September 2020: see www.barstandardsboard.org.uk/the-bsb-handbook.html.

18 At www.barstandardsboard.org.uk/the-bsb-handbook.html?part=E3FF76D3-9538-4B97-94C02111664E5709&audience=&q=client+money.

12.44 The relevant parts read:

'Rules C73–C75 – Client money Rules

rC73

Except where you are acting in your capacity as a *manager* or employee of an *authorised (non-BSB) body*, you must not receive, control or handle *client money* apart from what the client pays you for your services.

rC74

If you make use of a third party payment service for making payments to or from or on behalf of your *client* you must:

1. Ensure that the service you use will not result in your receiving, controlling or handling *client money*; and
2. Only use the service for payments to or from or on behalf of your *client* that are made in respect of legal services, such as fees, disbursements or settlement monies; and
3. Take reasonable steps to check that making use of the service is consistent with your duty to act competently and in your *client's* best interests.

rC75

The *Bar Standards Board* may give notice under this rule that (effective from the date of that notice) you may only use third party payment services approved by the *Bar Standards Board* or which satisfy criteria set by the *Bar Standards Board.*'

The Law Society

12.45 The Law Society has set out its guidance on Client Funds[19] and was last updated 21 April 2020.

12.46 The guidance reads as follows:

'The SRA Code of Conduct for Solicitors, RELs and RFLs requires solicitors to keep client money and assets safe. Your firm should have systems in place to do this.

The accounting systems and records that you should use are described in the SRA Accounts Rules, which came into force from November 2019.

Categories of money

Money held or received by your practice will be:

- client money held or received for a client

19 This can be found at www.lawsociety.org.uk/support-services/advice/articles/client-funds/#.

- money belonging to you or your firm, or
- money that does not relate to activities regulated by the SRA, which is not covered by the Accounts Rules

You must keep client money in a client account, separate from your firm's money. You must use each client's money only for that client's matters.

Client accounts

A client account is a practice's account used for holding client money. It must:

- be a bank or building society account
- be held at a branch or head office in England or Wales
- include the name of the relevant law firm or sole practitioner in the name of the account
- include the word "client" in the name of the account

A firm may have a separate designated account for a single client, or a general account that it uses for more than one client.

Protection for client accounts

The Financial Services Compensation Scheme protects deposits if a bank or building society fails. It covers:

- the first £85,000* deposited in a client account on behalf of a client
- "temporary high deposits" over £85,000, for up to six months, if they result from life events such as a property sale, an insurance payout, a compensation payment, a divorce settlement or an inheritance

*The £85,000 limit applies to the individual client, so if the client holds other money in the same bank or building society, this will also be counted towards the total.

It's unlikely that you'd be liable for client money that is lost through the collapse of a bank or building society, if you've followed the SRA Accounts Rules. However, if you've undertaken to pay money then you must meet this commitment.

See our practice note on protection for client accounts[20] and our guidance on cybersecurity[21].

Payments for your fees

Some of the money that you receive from a client will be intended to cover your fees.

---

20 At www.lawsociety.org.uk/topics/client-care/protection-for-client-accounts.

21 At www.lawsociety.org.uk/topics/cybersecurity.

Payments on account of costs are generally client money and must be held in a client account.

A payment from a client for a fixed agreed fee after you have delivered a bill is your firm's money and should be paid into an office account.

If you require payment of your fees from the money you hold for a client, you must first send them a bill of costs or other written notification of the specific amount. You may then transfer that amount from the client account to your office account, provided that there are sufficient funds held on behalf of the relevant client.

Accounting procedures

You must keep proper accounting records showing your dealings with:

- client money
- your firm's money relating to any client matter or trust matter

The accounting systems and records that you should use are described in the SRA Accounts Rules[22].

Under the Accounts Rules you're required to return client money promptly, which means you should return it as soon as there is no longer any proper reason to retain those funds.

Your obligation to return funds that rightfully belong to a client extends to all balances, regardless of how small the sum is.

Unclaimed client funds

There may be occasions when you have difficulty in returning money, such as where:

- your firm acquired the balance through a merger and you do not have the original details
- you sent a cheque to the client but they have not cashed it
- your client has not given instructions about what to do with the money
- your client has changed their contact details without telling you
- your client has died and you do not know who the executors are

You should take reasonable steps to find the client and return the money. The steps you should take will depend on how much money is involved.

If all efforts to return the money are unsuccessful, you should donate the money to charity.

You must follow the process in the SRA's Accounts Rules, and if the amount is over £500 you'll need to get approval from the SRA first.

22 At www.sra.org.uk/solicitors/standards-regulations/accounts-rules.

If you intend to withdraw the money but not pay it to a charity, you must apply to the SRA for authorisation, whatever the amount involved. This could arise for example if you have an outstanding bill to be paid, but you're unable to trace the client to deliver a bill of costs.

Breaches

If you discover a breach of the SRA Accounts Rules, it must be corrected promptly. This includes replacing any money that is improperly withheld or withdrawn from a client account.

The duty to correct breaches rests on the person who caused the breach and on all the principals in the firm.

Missing client money must be replaced from the principals' own resources, even if the money was misappropriated by an employee, and whether or not a claim is subsequently made on the firm's insurance or the SRA Compensation Fund.

Resources

SRA guidance:

SRA Code of Conduct for Solicitors, RELs and RFLs: www.sra.org.uk/solicitors/standards-regulations/code-conduct-solicitors

SRA Accounts Rules: www.sra.org.uk/solicitors/standards-regulations/accounts-rules

The prescribed circumstances in which you can withdraw client money from client account to pay it to a charity of your choice: www.sra.org.uk/solicitors/standards-regulations/withdraw-client-money

Practice notes:

Protection for client accounts: www.lawsociety.org.uk/topics/client-care/protection-for-client-accounts

Residual client balances: www.lawsociety.org.uk/topics/client-care/residual-client-balances

Helplines:

SRA Professional Ethics Helpline, for advice on the SRA Accounts Rules: www.sra.org.uk/home/contact-us; Tel: 0370 606 2577

Law Society Practice Advice Service, for advice and support on all aspects of legal practice: www.lawsociety.org.uk/contact-or-visit-us/helplines/practice-advice-service; Tel: 020 7320 5675.'

Institute of Chartered Accountants in England and Wales (ICAEW)

12.47 The ICAEW has published its guidance entitled 'Clients' Money Regulation 8a – Guidance' in 2017[23].

It reads:

> **'REGULATION 8A**
>
> A client bank account should only be used for receiving or making payments which relate to accountancy services which the Firm is performing, has performed or has been engaged to perform, for the client. The Firm must take steps to obtain and hold sufficient information to ensure that the client bank account is being used for a lawful and legitimate purpose and for bona fide transactions.
>
> **General principles**
>
> A firm's client bank account should not be used as a banking facility for clients. Deposits into and out of the account should have a connection to an accountancy service being performed by the firm and principals should at all times consider and understand the purpose for which payments are received and made. There should be a good reason why the firm's client bank account is being used rather than the client's own account.
>
> It is vital that principals remain vigilant to the risks posed by handling client money, and that they put in place systems to identify, assess and, if appropriate, document their response to risks. This is an ongoing obligation, both at the beginning and during the course of the engagement.
>
> Firms have existing obligations under the Code of Ethics to act with integrity and objectivity when handling client money. They must also assess and address risks in accordance with the Money Laundering Regulations 2007 and the Proceeds of Crime Act 2002, including the risk that firms' client bank accounts could be targeted as a means of legitimising fraudulent scams and other unlawful practices. This is why it is important for firms to have a good understanding of the source of the funds and the nature of the transactions passing through the account as part of their anti-money laundering checks and systems.
>
> **Clarification of terms**
>
> To assist principals in understanding their obligations we have clarified the following terms contained in the regulation:

23 Available at www.icaew.com/-/media/corporate/files/members/practice-centre/clients-money/icaew-clients-money-regulation-8a-guidance.ashx?la=en.

Accountancy services

Payments made into, and out of, the client bank account must relate either directly, or indirectly, to an accountancy service which the firm is performing for the client (or which it has performed for the client in the past or has been engaged to provide in the future). Such services would include, for example, outsourced payroll services and the drawing up of rental accounts.

To comply with clients' money regulation 8A there must be a clear and fixed intention (evidenced for example in an engagement letter or other correspondence) that the firm will be performing a service for the client at some point in the engagement or transaction.

Hold sufficient information

A firm should be able to demonstrate through contemporaneous, written records that it understands the nature of the engagement and the reason for, and source and destination of, particular transactions. It should also be able to demonstrate through written evidence the steps it took, and the conclusions it reached, in identifying, evaluating and responding to any threats both prior to, and during, the engagement. The records should be sufficient to enable an objective, reasonable and informed third party to accept the appropriateness of the firm's actions.

Lawful

The payment of client monies into and out of the client bank account must have a "lawful" purpose, i.e., the transaction(s) must not contravene the law or legal regulations in force at the time of the transaction or engagement.

Legitimate and bona fide

A transaction is likely to have a legitimate purpose if it is an expected course of action and not artificial or contrived. The following may constitute "red flags" which would require the firm to question and assess whether the client bank account is being used for a legitimate purpose and for bona fide transactions:

- unusual or unexpected transactions or instructions;
- large one-off transactions;
- funds deposited from an unknown source;
- instructions to transfer funds to an unknown payee;
- funds received from offshore and requests to make unusual payments offshore – particularly involving countries identified as high risk in HM Treasury's sanctions list;
- requests to use a client bank account from offshore clients or who have not been met;

- requests to transfer money which originated overseas to different individuals overseas;
- instructions from clients which do not fit with the firm's usual service provision;
- payments outside forecasts or budgets; or
- complaints from depositors regarding use of monies deposited into the client bank account.

Before receiving money or carrying out transactions on behalf of the client, members should understand the nature of, and reason for, each transaction in order to satisfy themselves that it is lawful and legitimate. This is in addition to the "know your client" checks and ongoing client due diligence obligations which are required to comply with anti-money laundering legislation. All steps carried out by the firm to assess risk should be appropriately documented.

It is essential that members consider whether there is a risk that either the main reason, or one of the main reasons, that the firm's involvement in the transactions is being procured is to lend credibility or assurance to depositors or third parties by establishing a UK location.

The obligation on the firm to satisfy itself that the client bank account is being used for a legitimate purpose, and for bona fide transactions, applies both prior to, and during, the course of the engagement. The ongoing nature of the duty requires firms to have systems and controls in place to identify and respond to risks on an ongoing basis. In cases where a risk is identified a firm may need to demonstrate that it has assessed and responded appropriately to the threat before proceeding.

The measures that a firm should have in place to evaluate and control risk will depend on factors such as whether the firm has worked with the client before, whether the client is based in the UK or offshore, and the nature and scope of the transaction or engagement.

It is not expected that a firm's principals would review and approve each transaction passing through the client bank account on an ongoing or daily basis. It would be sufficient for the principal with responsibility for the engagement to have a good understanding of the client and the nature of the expected transaction(s) at the beginning of the engagement. This knowledge would then need to be communicated to more junior members of staff with oversight of the day to day running of the client bank account. Staff would need to have sufficient training to identify risks and refer matters up to more senior members of staff for action as required.

In developing their controls and systems to respond to risk, it is recommended that firms refer to existing CCAB guidance on anti-money laundering and counter-terrorism financing obligations.

Offshore clients

There may be legitimate reasons why a firm may be requested to hold money on a temporary basis and/or to carry out transactions through its client bank account for an individual or corporate client, based offshore, who or which is experiencing delays in opening up a UK bank account. If the funds relate to services which the firm has performed, is performing currently or which it has been engaged to perform in the future, and the transaction is assessed as having a legitimate purpose, then this would not in itself contravene clients' money regulation 8A.

However, firms should exercise caution in these circumstances, particularly where the client is a new client and/or where there has been no prior meeting between one of the firm's principals and the client (if an individual) or a director of the client (if a corporate entity). In accordance with CCAB guidance, the firm will need to exercise enhanced due diligence in identifying the client at the beginning of the engagement. Further, the fact that the client has been (as yet) unable to open a bank account in the UK should be a key factor that the firm will need to take into account in determining whether to proceed with the engagement. If the client has been unable to open its own bank account to conduct its own transactions within 3 months then the firm should terminate the engagement and return the monies to the client unless the firm is provided with good reasons why there has been a delay in opening a bank account. If the firm elects to proceed, it will need to satisfy itself as to the reasons for the delay and ensure that it holds sufficient records of the investigation it has undertaken and the reasons for its decision.'

12.48 Additionally, case scenarios are set out which also link to AML.

12.49 There are also Help sheets published by the ICAEW which can be found on their website[24].

The Chartered Institute of Taxation (CIOT)

12.50 The CIOT sets out its guidance on this topic in its 'Professional Rules and Practice Guidelines'[25]:

'7.6 Clients' money

7.6.1 "Clients' money" means money of any currency which a member holds or receives for or from a client, and which is not immediately due and payable on demand to a member for their own account. Fees paid in advance for professional work agreed to be performed and clearly identifiable as such are excluded.

24 At www.icaew.com/%20technical/practice-resources/practice-helpsheets/clients-money-regulations-compliance-review?fromSearch=1.

25 Effective from 9 November 2018. Available at www.tax.org.uk/sites/default/files/181109%20 PRPG.pdf.

7.6.2 Due to the risks, controls and processes that need to be observed, a member should give very careful consideration before agreeing to hold client money.

7.6.3 A member is reminded to consider the money laundering legislation when allowing money to be passed though the client account.

7.6.4 A member who receives clients' money in connection with the carrying on by a member of investment business (as defined by the Financial Services and Markets Act 2000) must handle that money in accordance with the regulations of the regulatory authority with whom they are registered relating to the handling of such funds. The following guidance addresses only non-investment business clients' money.

7.6.5 Clients' money must be kept separate from money belonging to the firm and kept in a separate client account. A client account can be a current or deposit account at a bank or building society in the name of a member or their firm but it must also include the word 'client' in the title of the account. Clients' money can be kept either in a general client account, or in separate client accounts each designated with the name of a specific client, or in both.

7.6.6 The following conditions apply to client accounts:

- Written notice must be given to the bank concerned that all money standing to the credit of each client account is held by the firm as clients' money, and that the bank is not entitled to combine the account with any other account, or to exercise any right of set-off or counter-claim against money in that account in respect of any sum owed to it on any other account of the firm;
- Any interest payable in respect of sums credited to the account shall be credited to that account;
- The bank must describe the account in its records in such a manner to make it clear that the money in the account does not belong to a member;
- The bank should be required to acknowledge in writing that it accepts the terms of the notice.

7.6.7 Clients' money must only be used for the specific purposes agreed with the client. When received by the firm, it must be paid immediately into the appropriate client account or paid to the client direct or otherwise dealt with as the client instructs.

7.6.8 If a cheque, draft or electronic transfer includes both clients' money and non-clients' money, that cheque, draft or electronic transfer must be paid into the appropriate client account immediately and the non-clients' money must be withdrawn from the account as soon as practicable once the funds have cleared. Under no circumstances should clients' money be paid into the firm's own account.

7.6.9 Where money of any one client in excess of £10,000 is held or is expected to be held by the firm for more than 30 days, it is recommended that the money should be paid into a separate interest-bearing bank account designated as that of the client. In other cases, except where the amount of interest arising is likely to be immaterial (a matter for a member's judgement) clients' money must be deposited in an interest bearing account and the interest paid to the client.

7.6.10 Money held in a client account may be withdrawn only where properly authorised by a client in writing (including e-mail) or under the terms of the engagement letter.

7.6.11 A firm must at all times maintain records so as to show clearly the money it has received on account of its clients and the details of any other money dealt with by it through a client account, distinguishing the money of each client from the money of other clients and from firm money. Each client account must be reconciled against the balances shown in the client's ledger at least at six-monthly intervals (or more frequently if there are a high number of transactions), and the records of such reconciliation must be kept for at least six years from the date of the last transaction recorded therein.'

Financial Conduct Authority (FCA)

12.51 The FCA's handbook, 'Financial Conduct Authority's Handbook of rules and guidance', the section on client money can be helpful to consider on best practice[26].

INSURANCE

12.52 The terms of any relevant insurance policy can influence the way in which a tax professional operates and carries on business.

12.53 There may be a requirement to carry professional indemnity insurance a certain level[27]. There is a cost to this that may affect what business a tax professional can undertake.

---

26 Available at www.handbook.fca.org.uk/handbook/glossary/G160.html.

27 Eg, the BSB say 'If you hold a self-employed practising certificate, you must be a member of the Bar Mutual Indemnity Fund (BMIF)': www.barstandardsboard.org.uk/for-barristers/compliance-with-your-obligations/professional-indemnity-insurance.html. There is also a minimum level of cover: www.barstandardsboard.org.uk/uploads/assets/8a2304ca-241f-4a0f-bbd07501b766acd8/minimumtermsofcoverfortheself-employedbar.pdf. The ICAEW also have similar requirements, see Professional indemnity insurance (PII), which is compulsory for all ICAEW members who have a practising certificate and engage in public practice. PII is a requirement of a number of regulations.

12.54 The terms of the insurance may also restrict what can be done by a tax professional. For example, there may be an exclusion for US connected work. This is because the United States is perceived as a litigious society prone to high awards from juries which can restrict the insurer's appetite to engage even for a higher premium.

12.55 There may be an added premium for certain work such as advising on tax schemes.

12.56 The duty of *uberrimae fidei*, of utmost good faith, in insurance transactions requiring full disclosure of all relevant information can limit a professional's behaviour. Further, breach of this may render the insurance void as may breach of other terms. The terms of the policy need careful study.

12.57 The Law of Insurance is a complex area outside the scope of this book. In any case of doubt, appropriate professional advice must be sought.

Appendix 1

Checklist of some matters to consider in respect of any engagement

Note that the following list is not exhaustive and is provided merely for illustrative purposes[1].

1. What am I engaged to do?
2. What else could it include? Is it clear what is covered and what is not covered?
3. Who am I engaged by? Am I providing services to others? Could they reasonably think I am acting for them?
4. Who is the engagement with – Group companies etc?
5. How long is the engagement to last?
6. Has an engagement letter or terms of business been sent?
7. Has a duly signed copy of the engagement lateral terms of business been received back?
8. Does the letter clearly and accurately assess our services to be supplied? Does this fit in with questions 1 and 2 above?
9. Is it clear what the fee is? And how it is to be calculated? Is it VAT exclusive?
10. Basis of fees? Hourly rate? Hourly rate as default? What if rates change? Inflation link? Fixed fees? Basis? Additional work or services?
11. What is excluded? Is this sufficient?
12. Is there a cap on liability? Should there be? No responsibility for losses arising from the supply to the provider of incorrect or incomplete information, or to supply any appropriate information or to act on our advice provided or respond promptly to communications.

1 See, for example, the Chartered Institute of Taxation's Letters of Engagement at www.tax.org.uk/professional-standards/consultations-articles/engagement-letters.

13. Indemnify against any misrepresentation, whether intentional or unintentional, and supplied orally or in writing in connection with this agreement.
14. Does the insurance cover available match this? Are there any relevant exclusions, restrictions, etc in the insurance documentation?
15. Should there be restriction to liability only for advice in writing? Should the letter provide that only advice in writing can be relied on?
16. Does the letter limit the scope of the duty as well as restricting the amount that can be recovered?
17. Is there an exclusion for changes in the law? Should it cover retrospective changes and changes arising from case law and practice?
18. Exclude reliance on advice where there is a different scenario even if it is only because of a healthy lapse of time?
19. Does it spell out the client' obligations and responsibilities? Does it include obligation to notify changes of circumstances?
20. Are there provisions as to the commencement and termination of the engagement? Does it cover work done before the return of the engagement letter? Are they clear?
21. Does it deal with confidentiality and retention of information?
22. Is GDPR covered? What about similar matters, eg DPA? Privacy Notice needed or desirable?
23. FATCA, CRS, DAC 6, etc – other exchange of information and reporting?
24. Who owns copyright in letters, reports and similar matters?
25. Client documents– what is the position in respect to these? Should there be a provision that only copies are provided?
26. Lien over documents for non-payment of fees?
27. Retention of papers? Copies? How long? Storage?
28. Health and safety?
29. Professional obligations?
30. Right to access for others who might be perceived as having different interests and/or as competitors?
31. Variation?
32. Other services?
33. Commissions?
34. Client Monies?

35. Time limit to query invoices?

36. Interest for late payment?

37. Guarantee of payment by other persons, eg personal investment company?

38. Right to request payment up front?

39. Indemnity basis for all costs, expenses, etc?

40. No claims in respect of the engagement will be brought personally against any persons involved in performance of the engagement, whether actual or deemed servants or agents of the provider or not, including employees, office holders, consultants and third party contractors.

41. Liability in respect of breach of contract or breach of duty or fault or negligence or otherwise arising in connection with the engagement limited to the proportion ascribed to us by a court of competent jurisdiction and having regard to the contribution to the loss and damage in question of any other person (loss and damage having the same meaning as in the *Civil Liability (Contribution) Act 1978*). No application to any liability for death or personal injury or any other liability for which exclusion or restriction is prohibited by law or to liability arising as a result of fraud on the provider's part. No vicarious liability for fraud?

42. Any claim for breach of contract, breach of duty or fault or negligence or otherwise in connection with the engagement shall be brought within six years of the act or omission alleged to have caused the loss in question.

43. Quality control?

44. Complaints?

45. Conflicts of Interest?

46. Termination?

47. Non-solicitation?

48. Email and internet communication?

49. The *Contracts (Rights of Third Parties) Act 1999*, also indemnity from client against third party liabilities?

50. The *Proceeds of Crime Act 2002* and the *Money Laundering Regulations 2007.*

51. Confirmation nothing involved which could fall within the *Criminal Finances Act 2017.*

52. Force majeure?

53. Severance etc?

54. Working with third parties?
55. Professional Indemnity Insurance?
56. Disputes – mediation and arbitration?
57. Governing or applicable law and jurisdiction?
58. Is the client a 'consumer'? Does the *Consumers Rights Act 2015* apply? *Part 2* on Unfair Terms will be relevant if a consumer. Are the agreement terms fair, reasonable and appropriate? Include a checklist as to whether consumer? Should the individual sign a declaration or not regarding their status?
59. Note also the *Consumer Contracts (Information Cancellation and Additional Charges) Regulations 2013, SI 2013/3134.*
60. The *Provision of Services Regulations 2009, SI 2009/2999*? Is it (particularly *Part 2: Duties of Service Providers*) complied with?
61. Professional Rules?
62. AML etc? Need to meet client? Effect if do not?
63. What else?

Appendix 2

HMRC: the standard for agents

Updated 4 January 2018

www.gov.uk/government/publications/hmrc-the-standard-for-agents/hmrc-the-standard-for-agents

Reproduced with permission under the Open Government Licence for public sector information.

THE STANDARD FOR TAX AGENTS

1. OVERVIEW

HMRC recognises the value of having professional agents help taxpayers comply with their tax obligations.

The standard for agents is not new. HMRC first published a standard that sets out what it expects of agents in February 2016.

This updated standard includes requirements for providing advice on tax planning. It also makes clear that HMRC expects agents to comply fully with money laundering regulations.

1.1 Who the standard is for

These are HMRC's expectations of all individuals and businesses involved in professionally representing or advising taxpayers. The standard applies to all tax agents who transact with HMRC and to any professional who advises or acts on behalf of others in relation to their tax affairs.

HMRC's aim is to clarify what is expected of agents, particularly those who are not members of professional bodies.

1.2 What you can expect from us

If a customer wants an agent to deal with us on their behalf, we will deal with that agent courteously and professionally. We want to provide them with a service that is fair, accurate and based on mutual trust and respect. We also want to make it as easy as possible for agents to get things right. HMRC's Your Charter explains what all customers, including agents, can expect from us.

1.3 What we expect from you

We expect all agents who want to interact with HMRC to meet the HMRC standard set out on this page.

Most tax agents are members of professional bodies that set standards for behaviour such as Professional Conduct in Relation to Taxation (PCRT). HMRC has endorsed PCRT and encourages all agents to meet this standard. HMRC is working with the profession to agree a single common standard for all agents.

2. THE STANDARD

HMRC requires all tax agents to maintain high standards that promote tax compliance.

2.1 Integrity

We expect agents to be straightforward and honest with HMRC, for example, by:

- disclosing all relevant information
- not suggesting or implying that HMRC endorses or regulates their role as an agent

2.2 Professional competence and due care

We expect agents to:

- maintain correct and up-to-date knowledge of the areas of tax that they deal with
- work to prevent errors in their clients' tax calculations or claims, taking particular care not to include figures in returns or claims which are not sustainable

- advise their clients to take steps to set matters right where they find errors in their tax affairs (if the client is unwilling to correct matters, the agent should consider ceasing to act for them – if the agent continues to act for them, this could risk enabling tax evasion that may be subject to criminal investigation)
- comply fully with data protection law and regulations, including keeping online access credentials safe from unauthorised use at all times
- maintain the security of their systems and their HMRC account credentials against current threats

2.3 Professional behaviour

We expect agents to:

- comply fully with tax law and regulations relating to their professional activity, including registering under, and adhering to, the Money Laundering, Terrorist Financing and Transfer of Funds (Information on the Payer) Regulations 2017
- ensure that their own tax affairs are correct and up to date
- deal courteously and professionally with HMRC staff
- have clear terms of engagement with their clients

3. STANDARDS FOR TAX PLANNING

In addition to the above, HMRC expects agents to follow these principles when advising on tax planning.

3.1 Lawful

Agents must act lawfully and with integrity at all times, and expect the same from their clients.

Tax planning should be based on a realistic assessment of the facts and a credible view of the law.

Agents should advise their clients where there is a material uncertainty in the law, for example, if it is known that HMRC's view differs or is unknown. The risk and costs of challenge by HMRC, and any resultant court case, should be made clear to clients

3.2 Disclosure and transparency

HMRC expects any disclosure by agents to represent all relevant facts fairly.

3.3 Advising on tax planning arrangements

Agents must not create, encourage or promote tax planning arrangements or structures that:

- set out to achieve results that are contrary to the clear intention of Parliament in enacting relevant legislation
- are highly artificial or highly contrived and seek to exploit shortcomings in the relevant legislation

3.4 Professional judgement and appropriate documentation

HMRC expects agents to exercise professional judgement in applying these standards to particular client advisory situations.

Agents should keep timely notes of the rationale for judgements exercised in seeking to keep to these requirements.

4. MONITORING AND BREACHES

4.1 How HMRC monitors standards

HMRC collects evidence of any sub-standard agent behaviour in the course of its day-to-day compliance activity. The standard for agents will guide agent behaviour and make clearer the case for HMRC interventions relating to agents.

We are developing the way we work with agents as part of HMRC's Agents Strategy with the intention of better differentiating between agents according to the value they add or risks they present to compliance. As we use our data more effectively in this way, we will improve our ability to identify instances of poor tax agent standards.

4.2 What happens when the standard is breached

HMRC has several powers to address poor agent practice:

- we can disclose cases of suspected agent misconduct to professional bodies for them to investigate further and consider disciplinary action
- we can refuse to deal with a tax agent, pursue criminal cases, apply civil penalties where tax agents are found to have been dishonest, or suspend access to certain online services for tax agents
- HMRC's Agent Compliance Team regularly holds constructive conversations with agents where there are potential concerns about their practices

We expect all agents who interact with HMRC to keep to our standards, regardless of whether they are a member of a professional body, or which professional body they belong to.

5. STANDARDS ESTABLISHED BY PROFESSIONAL BODIES

HMRC does not regulate agents. The commercial tax services market is self-regulating.

It is estimated that around 70% of agents are members of professional bodies, many of which set out standards expected of their members.

5.1 Professional Conduct in Relation to Taxation

The largest accountancy and tax professional bodies share a standard known as 'Professional Conduct in Relation to Taxation' (PCRT).

If agents meet the PCRT standard, HMRC does not envisage that our, much briefer, summary of certain important principles will place further requirements on them.

HMRC will continue to work with professional bodies to agree a single common standard for all agents.

5.2 The PCRT's fundamental principles

Three of the five fundamental principles in PCRT are repeated in HMRC's standard. These are:

- integrity
- professional competence
- due care and professional behaviour

The maintenance of these is essential to the relationship between agents and HMRC.

The 2 principles not included are objectivity and confidentiality. These principles are fundamental to the agent-client relationship and it is the responsibility of the client to ensure they enter into contracts with agents covering these.

HMRC does not set expectations or regulate agent-client relationships – that is the domain of professional bodies.

Appendix 3

Warning notice

TAX AVOIDANCE YOUR DUTIES

© Solicitors Regulation Authority of The Cube, 199 Wharfside Street, Birmingham, B1 1RN

www.sra.org.uk/solicitors/guidance/tax-avoidance-duties/

Updated 25 November 2019 (Date first published: 21 September 2017)

STATUS

This document is to help you understand your obligations and how to comply with them. We may have regard to it when exercising our regulatory functions.

WHO IS THIS WARNING NOTICE RELEVANT TO?

All those we regulate involved either directly or indirectly advising clients about tax, handling client matters or transactions involving them in the design, implementation, organisation or management of tax affairs, schemes or arrangements.

THE SRA STANDARDS AND REGULATIONS

Principle 1: You act in a way that upholds the constitutional principle of the rule of law, and the proper administration of justice.

You have obligations not only to clients but also to the court and to third parties with whom you have dealings on your clients' behalf.

Principle 2: You act in a way that upholds public trust and confidence in the solicitors' profession and in legal services provided by authorised persons.

Members of the public should be able to place their trust in you. Any behaviour either within or outside your professional practice which undermines this trust damages not only you, but also the ability of the legal profession as a whole to serve society.

Principle 5: You act with integrity.

Integrity is central to your role as the client's trusted adviser and should characterise all your professional dealings with clients, the court, other lawyers and the public.

Principle 7: You act in the best interests of each client.

You should always act in good faith and do your best for each of your clients.

In addition to the above principles, relevant paragraphs in the code of conduct for solicitors, RELs and RFLs and code of conduct for firms will apply to your dealings with clients. In particular:

- Paragraphs 1.4 of the codes provide that you must not mislead or attempt to mislead others, either by your own acts or omissions or allowing or being complicit in the acts or omissions of others (including your client).
- Paragraph 3.2 of the code of conduct for solicitors, RELs and RFLs says you must ensure the service you provide to clients is competent and delivered in a timely manner.
- Paragraph 3.4 of the code for conduct of solicitors, RELs and RFLs and 4.2 of the code of conduct for firms says you must consider and take account of your client's attributes, needs and circumstances.
- Paragraph 8.6 of the code for solicitors, RELs and RFLs provides that you must give clients information in a way they can understand and you ensure they are in a position to make informed decisions about the services they need, how their matter will be handled and the options available to them.
- Paragraph 4.3 of the code for firms says you must make sure your managers and employees are competent to carry out their roles, and keep their professional knowledge and skills, as well as understanding of their legal, ethical and regulatory obligations, up to date. Similarly, paragraph 3.3 of the code for solicitors, RELs and RFLs provides that you must maintain your own competence to carry out your role and keep your professional knowledge and skills up to date.
- Paragraph 1.2 of both codes requires that you do not abuse your position by taking unfair advantage of clients or others.

OUR CONCERNS

We have concerns about anyone we regulate facilitating tax avoidance schemes that are aggressive in ways that go beyond the intentions of Parliament.

In SRA v Chan, Ali & Abode Solicitors Ltd [2015] EWHC 2659 (Admin) the High Court decided that the following allegation was proved in relation to a scheme to save Stamp Duty Land Tax (SDLT):

> "They involved themselves in transactions and/or facilitated, permitted or acquiesced in the promotion and/or implementation of schemes to avoid the payment of Stamp Duty Land Tax … in circumstances where the schemes were of a dubious nature and the respondents knew, or ought to have known concerns had been raised by both HMRC and counsel in relation to the nature of the transactions…"

The High Court also commented more widely in the case:

> "In my view, the evidence and the primary findings of fact of the tribunal – all eminently justified – compel a conclusion there was here a want of integrity and a failure to act with independence. They also compel a conclusion the respondents so acted as to diminish the trust the public would place in the respondents and the provision of legal services."

The tax system is a necessary part of our economic system, raising funds for public services and making for a healthy economy that serves society. You play an important role in helping taxpayers comply with their legal obligations.

You must also act with integrity in your own dealings with HMRC. In the case of SRA v Scott it was noted by the High Court that the solicitor: "…admitted there had been financial mismanagement of his firm in breach of Principle 8 of the SRA Principles 2011 (now paragraphs 2.1-2.5 of the Code for Firms), as evidenced by the firm's debt to HMRC of £232,317, which had led to the failure of the firm."

We have also seen a solicitor struck off the roll when allegations were found proven against him including that, "he declared to …HMRC… that he (together with his wife) had bought a property for a price lower than that which he paid …resulting in him paying too little in stamp duty land tax…, and being subjected to a penalty by HMRC."

OUR EXPECTATIONS

Acting with integrity

You are in a position of trust and not only owe duties to your client but also wider duties under the Principles. You have a duty to act in clients' interests by giving sound and competent advice while ensuring your advice does not go beyond the lawful arrangement of the clients' affairs.

We expect you to act with integrity at all times and for your dealings, and those on your clients' behalf, with HMRC are conducted on an open and honest basis and that you do not seek to rely on their lack of knowledge of your client's tax position.

When advising a client on avoidance of tax schemes you should make clear that any avoidance arrangements the client enters into might deliver tax outcomes that were never envisaged or intended by Parliament and may be challenged.

You should be clear as to the legal implications, the costs and penalties of non-compliance should the arrangement fail.

You should also consider your own position in facilitating such an arrangement. Should the arrangement be found to be abusive, your conduct may be called into question. To be involved in such arrangements is likely to reflect badly on you and to damage public confidence in those delivering legal services. You will leave yourself open to the risk of disciplinary proceedings as well as committing a criminal offence. Where you believe, as a consequence of your client's instructions, you are at risk then you should advise your client you cannot comply with their instructions and unless they change instructions you should terminate your retainer.

HMRC and the wider context

It is important that you are familiar with the underlying approach of HMRC which is changing rapidly. To make sure you are complying with your obligations above we expect you to familiar with the wider context of your work when dealing with tax affairs, schemes or arrangements.

HMRC will take action against what it refers to as "abusive tax avoidance schemes". This is explained by HMRC: "The General Anti Abuse Rule (GAAR) 2013 legislation comes into operation when the course of action taken by the taxpayer aims to achieve a favourable tax result that Parliament did not anticipate when it introduced the tax rules in question and, critically, where that course of action cannot reasonably be regarded as reasonable."

HMRC has also indicated it might challenge arrangements not caught by GAAR: "There may be tax avoidance arrangements that are challenged by HMRC using other parts of the tax code, but if they are not abusive, they are not within the scope of the GAAR."

The promotion or implementation of abusive arrangements (applying the definition set out in the GAAR, PCRT or otherwise) will lead both client and adviser into difficulties with HMRC and may leave you open to disciplinary action. The most common schemes we have seen in recent years have related to avoiding SDLT. We will continue to scrutinise any of these schemes carefully.

Legislation and the wider context

You might have clients who are using avoidance schemes. As a consequence of the Finance Act 2016, the Serial Tax Avoidance Regime came into force on 15 September 2016 and affected users of avoidance schemes from 6 April 2017. Under the regime sanctions and penalties are imposed on those using tax avoidance schemes. Anybody using an avoidance scheme is advised to provide information of the scheme to HMRC.

The Government has legislated for other anti-avoidance reform including "follower notices" and "accelerated payments" and intends to bring in a new penalty that can be applied to professionals who enable tax avoidance which HMRC later defeats. A penalty regime is already in force for those who enable offshore tax evasion or non-compliance, under s162 and Schedule 20 of the Finance Act 2016.

You must be fully familiar with all changes to ensure you comply with the Principles at all times, particularly the requirement to act with integrity.

Professional conduct in relation to taxation (PCRT)

Accountancy bodies have worked with HMRC to produce a statement of Professional Conduct in Relation to Taxation (PCRT). This is published on the websites of the accountancy bodies (and is liable to change). We welcome this statement and say that: "These standards reflect our own principles, particularly that solicitors must be honest and act with integrity, and uphold the rule of law."

We therefore expect you to be familiar with the PCRT and adhere to its standards.

Where you consider that a scheme is likely to be found to be abusive, you can advise a client to this effect. Where a scheme can reasonably be argued not to be abusive, you can advise a client to this effect, facilitate the scheme where so instructed by a client properly advised as to the risks, and litigate on behalf of a client as to the legality of the scheme where you can do so in a manner consistent with your duty to the Court.

It is for the relevant courts and tribunals to adjudicate on the legality of tax avoidance schemes. However, where schemes are found to be abusive, or where there is no finding but schemes contain indicators of abuse (such as, but not limited to, misleading conduct or the indicators set out in the GAAR or PCRT), and solicitors have facilitated such schemes, whether by providing supportive advice which advocates the use of such schemes, or does not sufficiently highlight the associated risks or otherwise, we will see this, on the face of things, as evidence of breach of the SRA Principles and are likely to investigate. If a solicitor gives advice to the effect that a scheme is likely to be found to be abusive and takes no steps to give effect to such a scheme, it is unlikely that enforcement action would be taken.

FURTHER HELP

If you require further assistance, please contact the Professional Ethics helpline

Appendix 4

The Law Society: Guidance for solicitors advising on tax

© The Law Society 2021. All rights reserved.

This page was printed on 06/01/2021 and the up-to-date version can be found online at https://www.lawsociety.org.uk/topics/tax/guidance-for-solicitors-advising-on-tax

GUIDANCE FOR SOLICITORS ADVISING ON TAX

This practical guidance for solicitors aims to assist you and help you make decisions when advising on tax. It summarises and explains how the high standards that you must uphold link to everyday professional practice.

Other important resources include the information on the SRA website, including the SRA Standards and Regulations and the SRA's related guidance and other resources.

HMRC's published internal guidance and other materials are useful on a wide variety of aspects of the state of the tax environment.

HMRC also publishes a Standard for Agents which sets out its expectations of individuals and businesses that professionally represent or advise taxpayers.

Seven other professional bodies, including the Chartered Institute of Taxation and the Society of Trust and Estate Practitioners, have developed another standard in this area called Professional Conduct in Relation to Taxation (PCRT). This was last substantively revised in 2017. Some solicitors are members of one of the seven bodies that have subscribed to the PCRT. For those members, our guidance explains the relation between the legal and regulatory obligations of solicitors and the PCRT rules.

We note finally that the government issued a call for evidence on raising standards in the tax advice market in March 2020. In that context, it is as important as ever that the high standards that apply to solicitors are well understood.

INTRODUCTION

Solicitors advise a wide range of clients on tax matters, including individuals, small businesses, charities, local authorities and major companies, including both UK companies and foreign companies seeking to invest in the UK. Solicitors represent clients on tax matters in all sectors of the economy, including agriculture, financial services, consumer goods, energy, engineering, construction and life sciences, and make an important contribution to the UK economy.

Tax advice often forms only a part of the advice provided by solicitors. This guidance (the 'Guidance') focuses on advice provided by solicitors in respect of tax, whatever the nature of the transaction or the context in which it occurs, including where the main focus of the advice is on a different aspect of law. It considers how a number of sets of rules and obligations that apply to solicitors apply to the giving of that advice.

The Law Society promotes high standards and aspirations for solicitors. This Guidance aims to support excellence in the profession for the public good by explaining and summarising, rather than extending, key aspects of the frameworks that apply to solicitors when they provide tax advice.

These frameworks include the contractual, tortious, fiduciary, statutory and regulatory rules that solicitors must respect and uphold when advising on tax, and they are backed up by an independent regulator (the Solicitors Regulation Authority) and an independent tribunal (the Solicitors Disciplinary Tribunal).

The frameworks promote the provision of high-quality legal advice from solicitors on taxation that upholds and promotes the rule of law and the integrity of the tax system.

Solicitors providing advice in respect of tax should therefore be aware of their roles and duties in law and regulation as they support people to navigate the application of tax law and practice in a complex environment.

KEY THEMES

While not a replacement for understanding the detailed rules and obligations discussed in this Guidance, some of the key themes are as follows:

1. Understand and agree the scope of your retainer

It is important that you and your client understand what is and is not within the scope of your advice. If you do not wish to advise generally on tax matters, you can agree a limited retainer, or agree to exclude tax matters from your advice.

2. Duty of care

Where your retainer includes tax matters, you are under a duty to exercise reasonable care and skill in providing tax advice.

3. Duties to advise within the scope of the retainer

You should address all relevant tax matters within the scope of the retainer that arise in relation to the transaction. This may include informing the client of ways to achieve their objectives in a way that does not give rise to particular tax costs.

4. Duty to warn of risks

Where your retainer includes tax, you should consider whether, in all the circumstances, you should warn your client of risks relating to the matter you are advising on. The warning of risks may be particularly important if the relevant tax rules are uncertain or unclear, or if there is an increased risk of HM Revenue & Customs (HMRC) challenge or of reputational risk to the client.

5. Regulatory duties

As well as the general legal requirements imposed on solicitors in the course of provision of legal services, you are subject to the rules and high ethical standards set by the Solicitors Regulation Authority (SRA), including the seven SRA principles discussed further below. These duties include:

- **duty to uphold the rule of law** – you are obliged to uphold the rule of law and the proper administration of justice. The courts have pointed out that the rule of law depends on the access of citizens to independent legal advice in respect of their rights and obligations – and that this is particularly significant in the area of tax law
- **duty to uphold service and competence levels** – you are obliged, both as a matter of law and under SRA rules, to provide a proper standard of service to your clients. This interacts with your duty of care (see (2) above) and the importance of agreeing an appropriate retainer for your advice (see (1) above). You may be entitled to rely on appropriate advice of a barrister but there are limitations to this
- **further duties** – there are other duties that may in some circumstances be relevant to tax advice, including:
  - you owe a duty of trust and confidence to your client
  - you may not obtain an advantage from transactions forming part of your retainer without full disclosure and client consent you should act in the best interests of each client
  - you should keep the affairs of current and former clients confidential unless disclosure is required or permitted by law or the client consents and you must act to maintain the client's legal professional privilege unless it is waived by the client

- you should uphold public trust and confidence in the solicitors' profession, including by seeking not to act unfairly in relation to a third party
- you must comply with the ethical standards of the solicitors' profession, and advise in respect of tax matters in an honest, accurate and even-handed manner

6. Tax evasion

You must not facilitate, or undertake or be knowingly concerned in, tax evasion. This is a criminal offence. A solicitor's firm is also under an obligation to have reasonable procedures in place to prevent its employees and other associated persons from criminally facilitating tax evasion by another (including by its client).

Guidance on conduct provided by other representative bodies and/or HMRC

The duties and obligations and regulatory framework to which solicitors are subject should be distinguished from the provisions of the document *Professional Conduct in Relation to Taxation* (pCRT) to which a number of professional advisory bodies are signatories. The pCRT sets out principles and standards which these bodies' members are expected to follow in giving tax advice.

The Law Society has not adopted the pCRT because the obligations of the solicitors' profession as a whole in this area are already set out by the law and the relevant regulatory rules governing solicitors. These rules have been formulated over centuries, and they comprehensively describe the relationship between solicitors and their clients. They draw the right balance for the solicitors' profession as a whole between protecting the interests of the client, the interests of the public and the rule of law, ensure that access to legal advice is preserved, and are backed up by an independent regulator.

However, solicitors advising on tax are recommended to be familiar with the content of the pCRT, which overlaps with many of the existing professional obligations on solicitors. For example, the five core principles of the pCRT (integrity; objectivity; professional competence and due care; confidentiality; and professional behaviour) are consistent with the legal and regulatory framework that applies to solicitors as described below.

The pCRT expressly provides that it is not to be interpreted so as to be in conflict with any professional duties of solicitors. Those solicitors that are subject to the pCRT because they are members of one of the signatory professional bodies should therefore comply with the obligations and duties required by the SRA and covered in this guidance in priority over the pCRT.

HMRC produces standards from time to time which set out its expectations of tax advisers. For example, HMRC publishes a Standard for Agents which sets out its expectations of individuals and businesses that professionally represent or advise taxpayers. Where relevant, solicitors may wish to consider the contents of this or any other HMRC standards, but those standards do not form part of a solicitor's professional obligations.

SCOPE OF THE RETAINER

If a client wishes to engage a solicitor who is willing to offer legal services then a retainer arises when that solicitor is instructed. This retainer will be governed by the terms upon which the solicitor agrees to act and by the duties imposed by law and regulation upon the solicitor.

A solicitor and client may, by agreement, limit the terms of the retainer which may in turn limit the solicitor's duties.

As a matter of good practice, the solicitor should confirm any such agreement in writing. If they do not do so, a court may not accept that any such restriction was agreed. (See *Sharon Minkin v Lesley Landsberg (Practising as Barnet Family Law)* [2015] EWCA Civ 1152, para 38.)

A solicitor who does not have the relevant specialist knowledge of tax should not advise on tax matters, and it would be advisable to exclude tax specifically from the retainer in those circumstances.

Solicitors who have specialist knowledge of certain tax areas, such as stamp duty land tax or inheritance tax, should make it clear in their retainer the limits to the areas on which they will advise. However in all cases, solicitors do have a duty to ensure their clients are in a position to make informed decisions about the advice they may need and the options available. The informed consent of the client should be obtained to any such limitations where there are or could be material tax issues beyond the competence of the relevant solicitor.

Even where a solicitor is willing to advise on tax, they may wish to include a provision in their client care letter reserving the right to instruct specialist tax counsel or to refer the client to tax advisers (along with the right to charge the client the fees incurred in doing so).

DUTY TO EXERCISE REASONABLE CARE AND SKILL

A retainer is a contract which will have both express and implied terms, which give rise to duties. One of the implied, if not express, duties on a solicitor under a retainer is the duty to exercise reasonable care and skill.

Solicitors also owe a duty of care in tort to their clients "to do that which a reasonably competent practitioner would do having regard to the standards normally adopted in his profession." (per Oliver J in *Midland Bank Trust Co Ltd v Hett Stubbs and Kemp* [1979] Ch 384 at 403.)

This means solicitors providing tax advice are under legal duties to maintain standards. These legal duties (under both contract and tort) are complemented by similar regulatory duties which are described under Regulatory duties below.

DUTY TO ADVISE WITHIN THE SCOPE OF THE RETAINER

To the extent that tax is not clearly excluded from the solicitor's retainer, a solicitor may be considered negligent if their advice does not address relevant tax matters that arise in relation to the transaction (see *Mason v Mills and Reeve* [2012] EWCA 498).

It is implicit in the solicitor's retainer that the solicitor will proffer advice which is reasonably incidental to the work being carried out. In determining what advice is reasonably incidental, it is necessary to have regard to all the circumstances of the case, including the character and experience of the client (*Minkin v Landsberg* [2015] WL 6966258 at [38]).

If a solicitor knows or ought to know about a way to achieve their client's tax objectives in a way that does not incur particular tax costs, they may be under a duty to advise the client about that. This may include, but is not limited to, claiming any available reliefs or exemptions.

For example, a conveyancing solicitor who was instructed to advise in relation to the purchase of a lease and the subsequent grant of a sub-lease by the purchaser was found to be negligent in failing to point out that this transaction exposed the client to a tax charge that would not have been incurred had the transaction been structured in a different way (*Hurlingham Estates v Wilde and Partners* [1997] 1 Lloyd's Rep 525).

Lightman J in the *Hurlingham Estates* case found that the solicitor should reasonably have appreciated that the client needed his advice and guidance about the tax liabilities arising from the transaction.

The courts have consistently found that professionals advising on tax are under an obligation to point out the "hidden" tax consequences of what the client proposes to do. This might involve informing the client about an alternative way of structuring a transaction to achieve the same economic result.

However, that obligation does not necessarily extend to more sophisticated tax planning (for example involving reformulation of the transaction in order to bring about particular tax consequences) as opposed to a mitigation of the tax liability which the transaction will otherwise produce.

This is particularly the case where solicitors have no reason to know that such planning opportunities are available. However, solicitors should consider their obligations, and whether to recommend that their client seeks specialist tax advice, on a case by case basis. (See generally *Hossein Mehjoo v Harben Barker and Harben Barker Ltd* [2014] EWCA Civ 358.)

Ultimately, this is a point that requires the solicitor to exercise careful judgement.

In giving any such specialist tax planning advice the solicitor should always consider all of their duties to their client and in the public interest, including the related need to warn appropriately of risk, discussed below.

DUTY TO WARN OF RISKS

Advising on tax often requires solicitors to make judgements on complex issues and uncertain outcomes. Even apparently straightforward situations can have complex, or uncertain, tax consequences.

Tax legislation changes regularly and can be difficult to interpret. Legislation may be introduced with a particular situation in mind, and may not cater adequately for other situations. Equally it may be drafted very broadly and apply to situations outside the stated policy intention of the legislation.

HMRC publishes guidance on many aspects of the tax legislation. However, HMRC's guidance is just its interpretation of the meaning of the law, and does not bind either HMRC or the courts. There are many instances where published guidance has had to be changed following a court decision. Furthermore, it is rarely possible for taxpayers to rely on HMRC guidance if there is a subsequent dispute with HMRC (see *The Queen (on the application of Aozora GMAX Investment) v HMRC* [2019] EWCA Civil 1643).

In this context, advice that is ultimately not upheld by the courts is not necessarily negligent or improperly given. However, solicitors do need to communicate risks to clients clearly, for example that the view they have taken as to the law may not be upheld, or that HMRC may take a different view.

Failure to give a specific warning that the solicitor's view may not be upheld may in itself constitute negligence if a reasonably competent practitioner in the relevant field with the expertise claimed by the solicitor would have given such a warning (*Barker v Baxendale Walker* [2017] EWCA Civ 2056; see also *Herrmann v Withers LLP* [2012] EWHC 1492 (Ch)).

Solicitors should consider the full range of legal interpretative rules and relevant case decisions in assessing risks and in determining which risks they need to bring to the client's attention.

The solicitor should also be aware of, and consider highlighting to the client, applicable legislation and principles of interpretation applied by the courts that might operate to counter the result that the client is seeking. For example, it may not be sufficient that a hoped-for tax result is justified on a literal reading of the words of a particular relevant statutory provision if a purposive reading of the legislation would suggest otherwise. See the Appendix: Aspects of the tax environment to consider.

Generally, when advising on tax, solicitors should consider and address all the risks that are appropriate in the circumstances. These may include:

- the risk that HMRC may challenge the analysis (which will depend on a number of factors but may generally be lower for a straightforward commercial transaction with limited or no tax benefit)
- any potential non-tax risks, including that the arrangements may alter the legal position of the parties (potentially in a detrimental way and regardless of whether the tax effects are as they were intended to be)
- reputational risks for the client (for example if what the client would like to do is likely to be perceived by HMRC as contrived or abusive, or as potentially giving rise to some sort of tax advantage that is not justified by the legislation)
- the possibility of interest and penalties, including enhanced penalties where applicable under the general anti-abuse rule (GAAR) or other rules, as well as the potential costs of any appeals or disagreements with HMRC

The character and experience of the client are among the relevant circumstances to be considered in determining the extent of a solicitor's duty to offer advice or information or warnings that are reasonably incidental to the work being carried out:

> "an experienced businessman will not wish to pay for being told that which he/she already knows. An impoverished client will not wish to pay for advice which he/she cannot afford. An inexperienced client will expect to be warned of risks which are (or should be) apparent to the solicitor but not to the client." (*Minkin v Landsberg* [2015] WL 6966258 at [38])

DUTY OF LOYALTY TO THE CLIENT

A solicitor owes fiduciary duties to a client. The relationship between solicitor and client is one of trust and confidence. This has been described as "one of the most important fiduciary relationships known to our law" (per Cozens-Hardy MR in *Re Van Laun* [1907] 2 KB 23 at 29). It means that a solicitor owes an obligation of loyalty to a client.

It follows that solicitors must not take any secret advantage whether or not any dishonesty is involved (*Boardman v Phipps* [1967] 2 AC 46). Solicitors should make full disclosure of any interest in a transaction for which they are retained and consider whether they can continue to act in such circumstances (*Spector v Ageda* [1973] Ch 30).

For example, it would not be appropriate for a solicitor to profit from tax arrangements in which their clients are involved without the informed consent of the clients.

A solicitor should also consider whether such arrangements are compatible with their regulatory duties (see Regulatory duties below). For example, when advising on a conveyancing transaction, a solicitor acting for a buyer should consider whether their client's lenders should be informed.

Solicitors must act in good faith, informing and consulting with the people they advise, and obtaining any necessary authority to act.

REGULATORY DUTIES

All solicitors must follow the rules and meet the high ethical standards set by the SRA, the profession's independent regulator. These rules, known as the SRA Standards and Regulations, exist for the benefit of the clients whom solicitors serve and in the public interest, and were updated with effect from 25 November 2019.

The SRA Standards and Regulations are supported by SRA guidance which indicates how the SRA may apply them and which is there to help solicitors in the judgments they make and comply with SRA regulations. Solicitors should be aware that the SRA has issued a warning notice on tax avoidance which should put them on alert as to the importance of regulatory compliance in a tax context.

Solicitors and law firms have a duty to co-operate openly and promptly with the SRA. If they fail to do so the SRA can require solicitors and firms to deliver documents or information, or to provide an explanation in person.

The SRA has further legal powers to take enforcement actions, including imposing sanctions such as fines. It can also refer a case to the Solicitors Disciplinary Tribunal (SDT) to adjudicate on alleged breaches of the rules and regulations.

The SDT, which is constituted as a Statutory Tribunal under section 46 of the Solicitors Act 1974, is independent of both the Law Society and the SRA, and has powers to prohibit a solicitor from practising or to impose substantial fines.

> The seven SRA Principles set out below are the fundamental tenets of ethical behaviour expected of solicitors. "You act:

- in a way that upholds the constitutional principle of the rule of law, and the proper administration of justice

- in a way that upholds public trust and confidence in the solicitors' profession and in legal services provided by authorised persons with independence
- with honesty
- with integrity
- in a way that encourages equality, diversity and inclusion
- in the best interests of each client"

These Principles are supplemented by the SRA Code of Conduct for Solicitors, RELs and RFLs (SCCS) and the Code of Conduct for Firms (SCCF) (the Codes), also introduced with effect from 25 November 2019.

Point 1 of the SCCS requires solicitors to maintain trust and act fairly. This includes: "You do not abuse your position by taking unfair advantage of clients or others." There is an equivalent provision for firms at point 1 of the SCCF.

Point 3 of the SCCS requires solicitors to uphold service and competence levels. Again, there is a similar requirement for firms at point 4 of the SCCF.

The regulatory duties above are also briefly discussed further below.

1. Duty to uphold the rule of law

As noted above, the first SRA Regulatory Principle requires solicitors to uphold the constitutional principle of the rule of law and the proper administration of justice.

In the tax context, the rule of law is reflected in the principle that no one is to be subject to taxation except as a result of legislation enacted for the purpose by Parliament. That legislation is interpreted by the courts. Tax is collected by HMRC, but HMRC is not the arbiter of whether or not tax is due. While the courts will give due weight to HMRC's views, ultimately they will interpret the laws as laid down by Parliament.

Equally, the making of filings and payment of tax imposed by such laws is a legal duty, and failure to make such filings and pay taxes lawfully due may attract penalties, interest, and, in some cases, prosecution.

The rule of law therefore "depends on the citizen being able without inhibition to find out what his legal position is. The complexity of the modern law and its progressive invasion of the interstices of daily life, have made this a public interest of greater importance than ever before. It is perhaps particularly significant in the area of tax law, where the citizen is brought up against the power of the state and the law is often technically complex." (*R (on the application of Prudential plc and another) v Special Commissioner of Income Tax and another* [2013] STC 376 at 405, per Lord Sumption).

The ability of citizens (and indeed the state) to have unfettered access to advice about their legal position is therefore a key pillar of the rule of law. Solicitors uphold the rule of law by advising on tax matters to ensure that the law is understood and realised in practice. Accessibility of legal advice is critical to the operation of the tax system in accordance with democratic principles. Solicitors who advise on tax therefore play a vital role in upholding both the rule of law and the integrity of the tax system.

Further, a key principle on which our liberal democracy depends is that every person is entitled to legal representation, no matter who they are (or, in the case of criminal defendants, what they are charged with).

This is reflected for barristers in the cab-rank rule under which a barrister is (with limited exceptions) generally required to accept instructions within their area of professional expertise regardless of the nature of the client or of the client's questions.

While this rule does not apply to solicitors (for good reasons, given the closer relationship that solicitors need to develop with their clients), many solicitors appropriately take the view that in order to uphold the rule of law, they will advise clients on matters within their competence (subject to all the other safeguards and principles summarised in this guidance), regardless of whether or not they (or others) agree with a particular tax or other outcome that the client is seeking to achieve.

2. Duty to maintain trust and act fairly

Solicitors are under a duty to act in a way that upholds public trust and confidence in the solicitors' profession and in legal services provided by authorised persons. They are also required by the Codes not to abuse their position by taking unfair advantage of clients or others. A solicitor who consciously takes unfair advantage of a third party would very likely breach this duty (see *SRA v Anderson Solicitors and others* [2013] EWHC 4021 (Admin) at [67]).

Applying this to advising on tax, a specific example of an area in which solicitors may need to take special care is if asked by a client to provide a generic opinion which the client will then provide to third parties. A solicitor should consider whether any such opinion adequately articulates the risks involved. What constitutes acting fairly in relation to a third party who is provided with such an opinion will depend on all the circumstances, including the nature of the third party by comparison with the client.

For example, where the client is in the business of marketing tax arrangements to individuals, a solicitor should consider carefully whether it is appropriate to issue an opinion in relation to a specific tax product with a view to that being provided to the client's potential customers where the solicitor has no relationship with those customers and knows nothing about their circumstances.

If the solicitor believes that something they are asked to do in the course of a retainer involves the solicitor taking unfair advantage of third parties, it may be necessary for the solicitor to consider ceasing to act for the client by terminating their retainer, assuming this can be done taking account of the terms of the retainer and the Codes.

The solicitor should provide reasonable notice of any decision to cease acting and explain the reason for that decision. The client should also be advised of any proper alternative options for obtaining legal advice and assistance to pursue their matter.

Finally, although this is unlikely given HMRC's resources and specialist knowledge, there might be circumstances where a solicitor is found to have taken unfair advantage of HMRC – for example if the solicitor intentionally made misleading statements to HMRC in the context of representing a client in a tax dispute.

3. Duty to act with integrity

Solicitors should always be careful to act with integrity in giving tax advice. The concept of integrity is wider than that of honesty. "Integrity connotes adherence to the ethical standards of one's own profession… Such a professional person is expected to be even more scrupulous about accuracy than a member of the public in daily discourse" (per Jackson LJ, *Wingate v The Solicitors Regulation Authority* [2018] EWCA Civ 366).

SRA guidance indicates cases where it is likely to take disciplinary action for lack of integrity, in certain circumstances including "where there has been a wilful or reckless disregard of standards, rules, legal requirements and obligations or ethics, including an indifference to what the applicable provisions are or to the impacts or consequences of a breach."

In a tax context, solicitors should act with integrity in the way they advise clients, such that they do not subordinate the interests of their clients to their own financial interests or allow personal interests to override the need to give appropriate and specific disclosures of context and warnings of risks (SRA v Chan [2015] EWHC 2659 (Admin)).

However, advising a client in relation to an arrangement that involves tax planning is not in itself a breach of this duty.

4. Duty to act in the best interests of the client

If a solicitor is approached to document or implement an arrangement designed by others, they should be careful to ensure it is in the best interests of the client. This may require them to carry out reasonable due diligence into the arrangements and the providers of the arrangements (para 32.56, *SRA v Mounteney*, SDT Case No. 12023-2019).

The solicitor may also need to consider whether the role their client plays in the arrangements exposes them to commercial and legal risks and advise appropriately.

5. Duty of confidentiality and maintenance of clients' privilege

You should keep the affairs of current and former clients confidential unless disclosure is required or permitted by law or the client consents. SRA guidance on this requirement states that:

> "Disclosure of information is only allowed where the client consents to it or it is permitted by law. Before approaching a client for consent, you should consider whether disclosure is necessary to proceed with a specific matter."

Solicitors should also consider the effect of legal professional privilege (LPP), including on whether disclosure to HMRC or other parties is permitted by law.

LPP is treated under English law as a fundamental common law right and a human right. It provides additional protections from disclosure in relation to certain confidential communications, and material evidencing such communications, that take place between clients and/or their lawyers and in some circumstances also between clients/lawyers and third parties. Read more in our practice note on legal professional privilege.

A solicitor who discloses confidential material relating to a client's affairs or waives privilege without the informed consent of their client would be in breach of their professional duties (see the SRA Standards and Regulations including paragraphs 6.3 and 6.4 of both the Code of Conduct for Solicitors and the Code of Conduct for Firms).

DUTY TO UPHOLD SERVICE AND COMPETENCE LEVELS

Both the law and the SRA Codes (see Regulatory duties above) provide that solicitors must ensure that they provide a proper standard of service to their clients. Solicitors should also refer to the SRA's statement of solicitor competence which defines the continuing competences that the SRA requires from all solicitors.

The statement of solicitor competence takes a broad definition of competence as being the ability to perform the roles and tasks required by one's job to the expected standard. It specifies a range of competencies around ethics, professionalism, judgement, technical legal practice, working with other people, and managing themselves and their work. This means, among other points, that solicitors should be able to:

- understand and apply the ethical concepts which govern their roles and behaviour as a lawyer
- maintain the level of competence and legal knowledge needed to practise effectively, taking into account changes in their role and/or practice context and developments in the law
- work within the limits of their competence and the supervision which they need, including disclosing when work is beyond their personal capacity and knowing when to seek expert advice
- apply understanding, critical thinking and analysis to solve problems
- develop and advise on relevant options, strategies and solutions, including identifying the consequences of different options
- establish and maintain effective and professional relations with clients, including providing information in a way clients can understand (taking into account their personal circumstances)
- inform clients in a timely way of key facts and issues, including risks

These obligations apply equally to tax matters where advising on tax is within the retainer.

THE GENERAL TAX ENVIRONMENT

Among other things, solicitors' duty to uphold service and competence levels (allied with the other solicitors' duties described above) will require them to consider, and advise their clients, how the following aspects apply to the particular facts and circumstances:

- the content of tax law
- the status of HMRC guidance
- the approach of the courts in interpreting tax
- legislation the GAAR
- the disclosure rules
- the requirements for tax return declarations

In addition, solicitors will need to understand the Enablers rules, and where applicable consider how they apply. These potentially impose penalties on a solicitor who advises in relation to an arrangement that is subsequently found to contravene the GAAR.

These aspects of the tax environment are summarised in the Appendix to this Guidance.

RELIANCE ON COUNSEL'S ADVICE

The duty to uphold service and competence levels arises where a solicitor instructs a barrister to provide an opinion on an issue. Although obtaining an opinion from counsel can be valuable in providing a proper standard of service to a client, solicitors should note that simply relying on counsel's opinion is not, by itself, sufficient to discharge their own duties.

Solicitors are generally entitled to rely on the advice of counsel properly instructed, but are not entitled to follow such advice blindly and are in the ordinary way obliged to apply their own expert professional minds to the substance of the advice received (*Davy-Chiesman v Davy-Chiesman* [1984] Fam 48).

However, where a solicitor is inexperienced or lacks the necessary expertise, it may be appropriate for them to rely on counsel. See *Swedac Ltd v Magnet Southern PLC* [1990] FSR 89 and *R v Luton Family Proceedings Court Justices ex parte R* (1998) 4 C.L. 51.

In some circumstances it may be necessary to withdraw instructions where the barrister's competence or reliability is in doubt (*re A (a minor)* [1988] Fam Law 339).

Solicitors should also consider carefully whether any counsel's opinion has been given on the basis of all the relevant facts.

For example, it is not uncommon for those marketing tax arrangements to provide potential users of those arrangements with an opinion from counsel that purports to cover those arrangements. Typically, however such opinions are given on the basis of a generic type of arrangement with a limited fact pattern. A solicitor who is subsequently asked by a client to assist with the implementation of an arrangement of that type should be aware that counsel's opinion might not necessarily apply to the facts of the client's case.

This may be a material issue in terms of the reliance that can be placed on the counsel's opinion because the precise way an arrangement is implemented can affect its tax treatment.

SOLICITORS AND THE PREVENTION OF TAX EVASION

Solicitors must not facilitate tax evasion by a client.

The law draws a clear distinction between tax evasion, which is a criminal offence involving dishonesty, and tax avoidance which is not. It is a criminal offence to undertake tax evasion, or to be knowingly concerned in tax evasion by another. A person can be knowingly concerned in tax evasion by providing any practical assistance with the necessary knowledge, and need not be directly involved in the provision of tax advice.

In addition, the Criminal Finances Act 2017 introduced a new strict liability corporate criminal offence which may apply to solicitors' firms if they fail to take reasonable steps to prevent the criminal facilitation by their employees or other persons acting for them or providing services to them of tax evasion by a third party.

Accordingly, if a member of a solicitors' firm's staff commits a criminal offence (with the necessary mental element) of facilitating tax evasion (including by a client), the firm could itself be criminally liable unless it can show that it has reasonable prevention procedures in place. For more information see our practice note on the Criminal Finances Act 2017.

CONCLUSION

As set out in the introduction to this guidance, solicitors providing tax advice should be aware of their roles and duties in law and regulation as they support people to navigate the application of tax law and practice in a complex environment.

We believe that, in doing so, solicitors contribute to an important public good by promoting the rule of law, which in turn supports the integrity and effectiveness of the tax system.

APPENDIX: ASPECTS OF THE TAX ENVIRONMENT TO CONSIDER

The facts

Tax advice should normally be specific to a client's facts and circumstances. Any assumptions of fact must be sound and verifiable.

Where relevant, solicitors should also consider any relevant interests of third parties (for example the lender in conveyancing transactions).

Solicitors asked to give generic opinions that do not take into account the position of specific taxpayers should consider whether a matter is too fact-sensitive for such an opinion properly to be given.

If a solicitor is comfortable that a generic opinion can be given, they should make the limitations of that opinion clear, including that the opinion is not given on the basis of the specific facts of those who may enter into the transaction.

Solicitors giving such an opinion should also consider and, where appropriate, warn about the potential risks for third parties who enter into transactions in reliance on the opinion (including a possible warning that the opinion may not be effective protection if HMRC argues that the taxpayer has failed to take reasonable care). It is advisable to give this warning in writing.

The content of tax law

Solicitors should advise based on the legal position, taking into account all rules of interpretation. Advice on the legal position involves considering all relevant anti-avoidance rules (whether targeted, general, or judicial).

Since 2010, over 100 measures have been introduced to tackle avoidance, evasion and non-compliance, which have significantly expanded the anti-avoidance laws. A list of those measures is included as Annex A to the government's policy paper of 13 March 2019, Tackling tax avoidance, evasion and other forms of non-compliance.

Solicitors should also be aware of advance payment notice and follower notices rules that mean those who use tax avoidance schemes may have to make a payment in advance to HMRC before the final tax has been agreed or determined and/or face enhanced penalties.

Understanding the status of HMRC guidance

Elected governments set tax policy, Parliament levies taxes by enacting laws for the purpose, and the courts interpret those laws.

HMRC is the body established by statute in the UK with the responsibility of administering the tax system. As part of its role, HMRC publishes internal guidance provided to tax inspectors which sets out HMRC's view on the meaning of legislation.

Solicitors should be aware that HMRC's views on the meaning of legislation in its guidance do not have legal force and they should advise clients accordingly. HMRC guidance can be valuable in providing insight into HMRC's view of particular provisions.

Taxpayers are free to challenge the views put forward by HMRC in its guidance, but equally they may face considerable hurdles in relying on statements made in guidance if HMRC decides not to apply it in a particular case (which could include where HMRC subsequently changes its view).

HMRC clearances

It is possible for taxpayers to apply to HMRC for clearances in some cases. Several tax statutes provide that taxpayers can apply for statutory clearance under them (for example on demergers and share exchanges).

Taxpayers may in some cases be able to apply for non-statutory clearance from HMRC where there is material uncertainty as to how tax law applies to a particular transaction.

A taxpayer's ability to rely on HMRC clearances depends on a number of factors including, importantly, the openness of the taxpayer in the application about all the relevant facts and issues.

The approach of the courts in interpreting tax legislation

The courts do not take a blinkered view of the law or the facts in coming to decisions on tax. Tax advice should be based on a realistic assessment of the facts and a credible view of the law.

There are many examples of the courts using purposive principles of construction – applying the legislation read purposively and taking a realistic view of the facts (*Barclays Mercantile Business Finance Ltd v Mawson* [2005] 1 AC 684). This has particularly been followed to defeat tax avoidance arrangements.

The General Anti-Abuse Rule (GAAR)

In the Finance Act 2013, Parliament enacted the GAAR, which was designed to counteract tax avoidance. An arrangement will be caught by the GAAR if it goes beyond anything which could "reasonably be regarded as a reasonable course of action" in relation to the relevant tax provisions.

A tax avoidance transaction that ultimately fails because of the GAAR is not illegal, provided that it does not involve dishonesty or concealment, but may result in a higher level of civil penalties for the taxpayer (for example additional penalties have been enacted for transactions that are counteracted under the GAAR).

Disclosure rules

The Disclosure of Tax Avoidance Schemes (DOTAS) rules (and equivalent rules for VAT, national insurance and SDLT) were introduced by the Finance Act 2004 and since then they have been successively expanded. These rules require disclosure of prescribed information to HMRC in relation to certain tax arrangements.

Special rules apply where legal professional privilege prevents solicitors from providing all or part of the prescribed information to HMRC. In these circumstances the solicitor's client (rather than the solicitor) is obliged to disclose the scheme.

In addition, EU Directive 2018/822 (DAC6) introduces new disclosure and reporting rules for intermediaries involved in designing and promoting certain cross-border arrangements that have certain features. Again, it is likely that a solicitor who is an intermediary will be precluded from making a disclosure because of legal professional privilege, but the solicitor is likely instead to need to notify either other intermediaries or the solicitor's client of their disclosure obligations under the rules.

The requirements for tax return declarations

When a taxpayer submits a tax return, it must contain a declaration that it is "to the best of his knowledge correct and complete".

Where the correct interpretation of the tax rules is unclear, the taxpayer is entitled to take a position that they believe to be correct in their return (and to add further disclosure to explain the uncertainty and the view taken). To avoid civil penalties, taxpayers must take "reasonable care" in arriving at that belief.

Legislation in Schedule 24 of the Finance Act 2007 makes it more difficult to rely on professional advice as a reasonable care defence in certain cases. See HMRC's Compliance Handbook CH81122.

A taxpayer who submits a return that they do not believe to be correct, and without adequate disclosure, may risk substantial additional civil penalties, and in the worst case may be committing a criminal offence.

A client may instruct a solicitor to act on their behalf in relation to dealings with HMRC (including tax returns). Solicitors who wish to deal with HMRC on a client's behalf must have formal authorisation to do so. They should also note HMRC's published Standard for Agents expectations as discussed in the Guidance.

The 'Enablers' rules

Schedule 16 of the Finance (No.2) Act 2017 introduced an enhanced penalties regime. In certain circumstances, this means that 'enablers' who design, market or facilitate abusive tax avoidance transactions that are defeated by HMRC may be exposed to penalties that relate to the fees earned for those services or may be publicly named. See the associated guidance produced by HMRC.

Appendix 5

Illustrative assumptions to incorporate into a tax professional's terms of engagement

The following assumptions are provided for illustrative purposes. The list of any assumptions will need to be considered by the tax professional on a case-by-case basis. Such assumptions must be brought to the specific attention of the client.

Terms and conditions: assumptions deemed to be incorporated by virtue of clause XX

Assumptions

The assumptions (subject to any explicit agreement the contrary or matter set out in the advice explicitly or implicitly) have been made (among other things) for the purposes of any advice provided under the terms of engagement, in addition to those made explicitly or implicitly made in any advice (whether in writing or otherwise):

1. All the transactions (as defined in the Taxation (International and Other Provisions) Act 2010, section 150) and associated transactions and/or steps are all carried out properly and legally and achieve their intended purpose.

2. There is power and capacity in the parties to do what is proposed, was done and associated matters and what is done is not void or voidable for any reason. There are no encumbrances or blocks to them doing what is contemplated.

3. The various transactions and/or steps are accepted as independent transactions and/or steps properly undertaken for proper ends and commercial purposes and not treated as anything else nor re-characterised or treated as undertaken for an unacceptable purpose but as genuine and/or bona fide transactions.

4. The transactions and/or steps are proper and acceptable transactions and/or steps and are treated as such and are not intended to confer any

gratuitous benefit or any bounty on any other person and are on proper and acceptable arm's length terms.

5. Any transfers are treated as transfers of the whole of the relevant asset and not, for example as a transfer of an income stream.
6. The statements made in the Instruction (whether in writing or otherwise) and any supplement to the Instruction as to residence and domicile are full and correct.
7. There is a strong commercial justification for what is proposed which has been clearly documented (eg in a business plan). Further the commercial reasons for this can be clearly demonstrated and that everything is properly implemented.
8. The relevant law and practice do not change.
9. What is done is proper, legal, and acceptable under any applicable law. The advice will not be used improperly or illegally and is not intended to be so used and nothing will be or has been done that could fall within the Financial Crimes Act 2017 or similar legislation whether in the UK or elsewhere nor within any common law matters that could give rise to similar liability.
10. All appropriate advice is taken before any implementation and acted upon.
11. All necessary and applicable matters including regulatory and similar matters (whether or not mentioned in the advice and notwithstanding the views expressed) are complied with and all requisite returns etc. made.
12. The transactions and/or steps contemplated are not unreasonable for the purposes of the GAAR and it is accepted that it is reasonable to implement them.
13. Unless otherwise stated in the Instruction or any supplement to the Instruction the shares in all the companies concerned (including any new companies) are held as investments and not as trading stock and the same is true of any assets and properties to be transferred within the group.
14. There has been no election to tax in respect of any relevant properties.
15. No relevant company with losses will have disposed of all its income producing assets [such that losses cannot be surrendered].
16. There is no group of companies.
17. Financing is accepted as only involving normal commercial loans as defined in the relevant legislation and there are no "equity holders" as defined so as to give rise to issues.
18. The ultimate parent and/or beneficial owners will be declared and are not such as to give rise to any legal and/or tax issues.

19. There are no related and/or connected parties involved.
20. All transactions take place on an acceptable and justifiable basis and that the SME limits are not exceeded before appropriate advice is taken.
21. All transactions are at market rates and terms and at arm's length and this can be proved by admissible irrefragable evidence.
22. Nothing is done so as to create a permanent establishment and/or constitute trading within the UK or any other relevant offshore entity.
23. Valuations are accepted as accurate and proper as are the forecasts and projections for matters such as capital allowances which are relied on for computations and for future profits etc.
24. What was/is done, and associated matters were/are not be events of default for any loan or banking purposes or give rise to any similar commercial difficulties. There are no loans or transfers so as to bring Schedule 4C to TCGA 1992 or similar matters into application.
25. The proposed transactions are completed before any adverse proposed changes to relevant legislation come in to force (including forestalling provisions).
26. Any relevant draft legislation is enacted and interpreted in the way assumed for the purposes of this advice.
27. There will be no diminution in the value of anyone's estate for IHT purposes.
28. The documents reflect what is proposed and intended in the advice and that the full documentation have not been seen.
29. The description of the position set out above is accurate and complete in all its aspects and deals with all relevant matters.
30. There are no unusual circumstances that have not been mentioned in writing or and/or otherwise and what is set out in this advice corresponds to what actually happens in practice.
31. Any person who is a participant in the transaction and/or tax planning steps will take appropriate relevant advice (including tax advice) and act on it before any implementation of the planning
32. Relevant local law advice will be taken by all relevant parties and acted upon before any implementation.
33. All these matters can be proved by cogent admissible evidence.

Index

[References are to paragraph number]